COMPUTER APPLICATIONS IN MUSIC
A Bibliography

THE COMPUTER MUSIC and DIGITAL AUDIO SERIES
Volume 4

COMPUTER APPLICATIONS IN MUSIC
A Bibliography

DETA S. DAVIS

A–R EDITIONS, INC.
Madison, Wisconsin

For Michael, Julia, and my parents

Library of Congress Cataloging in Publication Data

Davis, Deta S.
  Computer applications in music.

  (The Computer music and digital audio series ; 4)
  Includes index.
    1. Computer music—History and criticism—Bibliography.
  I. Title.   II. Series.
Ref ML128.C62D4   1988   016.781'028'5   88-70079
  ISBN 0-89579-225-7

A–R Editions, Inc.
315 West Gorham Street
Madison, Wisconsin 53703
(608) 251-2114

10   9   8   7   6   5   4   3   2   1

CONTENTS

A NOTE ABOUT THIS SERIES

The Computer Music and Digital Audio Series was established in 1985 to serve as a central source for books dealing with computer music, digital audio, and related subjects. During the past few decades, computer music and digital audio have developed as closely related fields that draw from a wide variety of disciplines: audio engineering, computer science, digital signal processing and hardware, psychology (especially perception), physics, and of course all aspects of music.

The series includes, but is not limited to, works in the following forms:

- textbooks at the undergraduate and graduate levels
- guides for audio engineers and studio musicians
- how-to books (such as collections of patches for synthesis)
- anthologies
- reference works and monographs
- books for home computer users and synthesizer players.

The series addresses audiences from a wide variety of disciplines and serves both beginners and practitioners in the field. By including material for all levels and all types of readers, it serves as a source of introductory material as well as a unified reference collection.

In 1986 the original publisher, William Kaufmann, decided to retire. After an extensive search for a suitable new publisher, the series moved to A–R Editions, Inc., from William Kaufmann, Inc. The present volume is the first to appear under the A–R Editions imprint. I am very grateful to William Kaufmann for his steadfast support of the series in its initial years, and I am now looking forward to developing the series in its new home.

This bibliography has been planned for the series since its very inception. Those of us working in the field have been frustrated by the lack of a comprehensive bibliography. It has been difficult and sometimes impossible to keep track of the extensive works of some people, or to find obscure but still interesting works that we all remember having seen but can't find in the library any more. The field is now so large that it is impossible to follow the many subareas in spite of one's best efforts.

A work of this size obviously does not arise overnight. The compiler has been part of the computer music community for many years and as such has had an insider's track on developments in the field that many bibliographers do not enjoy. A much smaller version of this bibliography appeared many years ago. Although it was extensive, it was difficult to use because the index contained only blind entries. It was experience with that index which led to the decision to include an author-title index here.

One does not normally read a bibliography from cover to cover. In doing so while editing this work, I was reminded of the breadth and depth of our field. One wonders at the multitude of languages represented here, the varied directions of research, and the unexpectedly large number of very early entries. Although any bibliography is by definition dated when it appears, this massive undertaking will serve as a welcome reference work for many years to come.

John Strawn
San Rafael, California

PREFACE

Purpose and Arrangement

This bibliography is a comprehensive listing of works regarding applications of the computer in music. The purpose of this bibliography is to record information on publications available in the field of computer music in a form that facilitates easy reference. It has been arranged alphabetically by author in twenty-five chapters, each on a specific subject area. This arrangement has been utilized to provide subject access more efficiently than a subject index, given the size of the bibliography. For example, with a subject index the heading "Computer-assisted Instruction" would have had nearly 300 blind citation numbers following it.

The arrangement also groups together those articles that tend to be of interest to the reader who is working in one area of computer music and is not primarily interested in other areas. For example, a researcher interested in sound generation can look in chapters such as "Sound Generation for Music—Synthesis Techniques" without having to sort through articles on education or musicology. Similarly, the music educator or musicologist has an aggregation of information available without having to sort through articles and books on digital hardware. The decision to place an article or book in one chapter rather than another has been based on the primary content of the item and my assessment of user needs. Although many other people were consulted in the placement of many items, I take full responsibility for the current arrangement.

This bibliography does not include software packages which contain discs and similar supporting material with musical applications. A catalog with descriptions of these music software packages, compiled by Barton K. Bartle and entitled *Computer Software in Music and Music Education: A Guide,* is being published by Scarecrow Press. Additionally, since software for commercial use is changing so rapidly, the best sources are the usual computer and music magazines or distributors such as Mix Bookshelf.

Content

Each citation lists all authors, full title, and a bibliographic description. Numbers, symbols, and wording on title pages of books and journals have been transcribed exactly when the primary source was available so that material can be located easily in library catalogs and computer databases. Otherwise, the format of the citations follows *The Chicago Manual of Style*. When guidelines have been lacking for unusual citations, I have incorporated parts of the International Standard Book Description (ISBD) for bibliographic description. Any title that is not in English, French, or German has an English translation following the original title. As is the usual practice, translations are not included for French and German because these languages are fairly commonly known. Review citations follow any item that has been reviewed. Abstract citations from the major abstracting services, when available, have also been included. These have been included so the user can readily obtain more information on items that may be hard to find. There is a list of abbreviations and acronyms in use in the field of computer music. A subject index was considered but then rejected, simply because the task was too large for human undertaking and would have doubled the size of an already thick book. The time involved to create this index also would have delayed publication significantly with little useable gain, since subject access is already provided by the format.

A brief description of each chapter follows. "Aesthetics" is about aesthetic and philosophical concerns related to the computer and its relationship to or effect on music. "Composition" concerns the use of the computer in the art of music composition. Here one finds stochastic algorithms for the creation of a piece of music, the use of the computer as an aid for determining tone rows, and other forms of computer-aided composition. "Compositions," on the other hand, is about specific pieces that were created using the computer. Concert reviews and descriptions of pieces by composers can be found here as well. "Conferences" contains reports and reviews of conferences on the computer in music and listings of conference proceedings. "Computers in Music Education" includes references on how to use the computer in the teaching of music and reports of specific applications.

"Digital Audio" includes the sampling theorem, analog/digital conversion theory, storing and editing sound on disk, the compact disk, and related fields. "Digital Signal Processing" covers the use of the computer to modify signals or sounds for many purposes including record restoration. "Electronic and Pipe Organs" includes the many ways the computer has been used to modify or control the performance of electronic and pipe organs. "Micro- and Mini-Computers" contains most articles on small computers. In cases where the small computer has been used in a specific application covered by another chapter in the bibliography, the article has generally been placed in the other chapter. "MIDI" (Musical Instrument Digital Interface) is about this specification and applications that have risen from its establishment. "Music Industry" covers the many areas in which the computer has been used in that industry, from concert ticketing to ASCAP performance tracking. "Music Printing and Transcription" includes articles from the first uses of the computer to print music to present uses for score and part creation and transcription. "Musical Instruments" contains items on the use of the computer to analyze and create specific instrumental sounds. "Musicological and Analytic Applications" includes items on musical analysis with the use of the computer and musicological and ethnomusicological studies. "Programming Languages and Software Systems" has articles and books on specific software languages and software descriptions for use in music (but not sound synthesis software, which is placed under "Sound Generation for Music—Software"). "Psychology and Psychoacoustics" covers psychological applications of the computer in music as well as how sound is heard and how specific sound synthesis techniques relate to human auditory perception. "Reference, Research, and Music Library Applications" contains books and articles on how the computer has been used in music research or as a reference tool. On-line searching and library applications such as music cataloging are covered.

Three chapters concern different aspects of music sound generation. "Sound Generation for Music—Hardware" has articles and books on hardware and computer systems for the generation of music. "Sound Generation for Music—Software" includes software applications specific to the generation of sound. "Sound Generation for Music—Synthesis Techniques" contains information on various techniques for the synthesis of sound such as frequency modulation (FM). "Sound Generation with Real-Time Applications" covers the use of the computer for real-time sound generation or the live performance of computer music. "Spatial Simulation and Room Acoustics" includes research on the use of the computer to model acoustics in actual or hypothetical spaces. "Speech" covers the use of speech in musical applications only. It does not include articles solely about the production of speech by computers. "Studios" includes descriptions and reports of various studios or computer music facilities.

"General" is the catch-all for articles and books that either do not fit into any of the above chapters or cover so many aspects of the field that they could not be placed in any one chapter. In particular, articles and books of the "How does the computer make music?" variety are here. It also includes items that could not be obtained for examination and titles that were not specific enough to determine placement in another chapter.

Research Methodology

Research for this bibliography covered many disciplines, from music and computer science to education and psychology. Secondary sources that I searched included *ACM Guide to Computing Literature, Applied Science and Technology Index, Business Index, Computer Abstracts* (CA), *Computer and Control Abstracts* (C&CA), *Computer and Information Systems* (C&IS), *Computing Reviews* (CR), *Current Index to Journals in Education* (CIJE), *Dissertation Abstracts* (DA), *Education Index, Electrical and Electronics Abstracts* (E&EA), *ERIC* (Resources in Education), *IEEE Publications Index, Magazine Index, Masters Abstracts, Music Index, Psychology Abstracts,* and *RILM.* Many of these items were found in engineering and other technical libraries rather than in music libraries. I also examined bibliographies of articles, books, and dissertations as well as items received at the Library of Congress. Additionally, relevant items from other bibliographies by Marc Battier (item 2743), Stefan M. Kostka (item 2812), and Sandra Tjepkema (item 2891) were examined and included.

Whenever possible, I examined each item included in this bibliography. In addition to utilizing the resources at the Library of Congress, I visited Sibley Music Library, Massachusetts Institute of Technology Libraries, Cornell University Libraries, University of Maryland Libraries, University of Rochester Libraries, Oxford University Libraries, IRCAM Library, the library at Centre Georges Pompidou, and the Bibliothèque Nationale. Some items listed here could not be examined because I was unable to find any library willing to provide interlibrary loan services. The cutoff date for compiling this bibliography was mid-1986.

Acknowledgments

I would like to thank first my husband, Michael A. Toman, who provided logistical and emotional support needed in compiling this bibliography. The following colleagues and friends were very helpful in providing citations and information: Donald Byrd, Otto Laske, Molly Macauley, Jean-Claude Risset, numerous colleagues at the Library of Congress, and especially Curtis Roads, who facilitated a two-day marathon scan of his private collection. Needed access to collections also was provided by Lenore Coral, Nina Millis-Davis, and David Wessel. A special thanks to Goffredo Haus for supplying many citations of Italian sources that I could not have obtained otherwise.

I appreciate greatly the help of John Strawn for his editing, William Kaufmann for his steadfastness in seeing the project through, and Andy Moorer for his support. For title translations that I was unable to do myself I would like to thank Louis Borea, James Dashow, and Sarah Pritchard for Italian, Cynthia Peyton for Spanish, Anna Della Porta and George Toth for Slavic languages, Margareta Jacobs for Scandinavian languages, and Judy Oroslan for Hungarian. Finally, I am very grateful to Resources for the Future and Charles Paulsen for providing word processing capability and computer assistance to preparing this volume.

LIST OF
ABBREVIATIONS

ACM	Association for Computing Machinery
AEDS	Association for Education Data Systems
AES	Audio Engineering Society
AFCET	Association Francaise pour la Cybernetique Economique et Technique
AFIPS	American Federation for Information Processing
AICA	Associazione Italiana per il Calcolo Automatico
ALMA	Alphanumeric Language for Musical Analysis
ASCAP	American Society of Composers, Authors, and Publishers
ASP	Automated Sound Program
ASP	Automated Synthesis Procedures
ASUC	American Society of University Composers
BARZREX	Bartok ARchives Z-symbol Rhythm EXtraction
BASIC	Beginner's All-purpose Symbolic Instruction Code
C&CA	Computer and Control Abstracts
C&IS	Computer and Information Systems
CA	Computer Abstracts
CAI	Computer Assisted Instruction
CARL	Computer Audio Research Laboratory (University of California, San Diego)
CASS	Computer Assisted Synthesizer System
CCRMA	Computer Center for Research in Music and Acoustics (Stanford University)
CEMAMu	Centre d'Etudes de Mathematique et d'Automatique Musicales
CHORDAL	Crane Heuristic ORgan DAta Language
CIJE	Current Index to Journals in Education
CIRPA	Canadian Independent Record Producers Association

CME	Center for Music Experiment (University of California, San Diego)
CNRS	Centre National de la Recherche Scientifique
CNUCE	Centro Nazionale Universitario di Calcolo Elettronico
CONHAN	CONtextual Harmonic ANalysis
COMMPUTE	Computer-Oriented Music Materials Processed for User Transformation of Exchange
CPEMC	Columbia-Princeton Electronic Music Center
CPU	Central Processing Unit
CR	Computing Reviews
CRT	Cathode Ray Tube
CSC	Centro di Sonologia Computazionale (University of Padova)
CSRG	Computer Systems Research Group (University of Toronto)
DA	Dissertation Abstracts
DARMS	Digital Alternative Representation of Music Scores
DCMP	Digital Computer Music Program
DECUS	Digital Equipment Computer Users Society
DOS	Disk Operating System
DUPACK	Darms Utility PACKage
E&EA	Electrical and Electronics Abstracts
ELMOL	Electronic Music Oriented Language
EMAMu	Equipe de Mathematique et Automatique Musicales
ERATTO	Equipe de Recherche sur l'Analyse et la Transcription des Textes par Ordinateur
GAIV	Groupe d'Art et d'Informatique de Vicennes
GAM	Groupe d'Acoustique Musicale
GMEB	Groupe de Musique Experimentale de Bourges
GRIPHOS	General Retrieval and Information Processor for Humanities-Oriented Studies
GRM	Groupe de Recherches Musicales
HMSL	Hierarchical Music Specification Language
ICA	Institute of Contemporary Arts
ICASSP	IEEE International Conference on Acoustics, Speech, and Signal Processing
ICMC	International Computer Music Conference
ICRH	Institute for Computer Research in the Humanities
IEEE	Institute of Electronic and Electrical Engineers
IERIV	Institut d'Etude et de Recherche en Information Visuelle
IETE	Institution of Electronics and Telecommunication Engineers (India)
IML	Intermediary Musical Language
IMS	Interactive Music System (University of Illinois)
I/O	Input/Output

IRCAM	Institute de Recherche et de Coordination Acoustique/Musique
IRE	Institute of Radio Engineers
IRMA	Information Retrieval for Multiple Musicological Applications
IRMA	Interactive, Real-Time Assembler
ISMUS	Iowa State computer MUsic System
K	Kilobyte(s) (1,024 bytes)
LENA	Laboratoire d'Electroacoustique Numerique-Analogique (University of Montreal)
LIMB	Laborattorio par l'Informatica Musicale (Biennale di Venezia)
LIME	Lippold's Interactive Music Editor
LMI	Linear Music Transcription
LSI	Large Scale Integration
MDI	Music Description Instruction
MEG	Music Editing and Graphics system
MIDI	Musical Instrument Digital Interface
MIR	Music Information Retrieval
MIT	Massachusetts Institute of Technology
MUSCOR	MUsic SCORing system
MUSICOL	MUSical Instruction Composition-Oriented Language
MUSICOMP	MUsic Simulator-Interpretor for COMpositional Procedures
MUSTRAN	MUSic TRANslator
NARM	National Association of Recording Merchandisers
PARC	Palo Alto Research Center
RAM	Random Access Memory
RILM	Repertoire International de Litterature Musicale
RMS	Root Mean Square
ROM	Read Only Memory
SAM	System for Analysis of Music
SEAMUS	Society for Electro-Acoustic Music in the United States
SIM	Societa per l'Informatica Musicale (Rome)
SMUT	System for MUsic Transcription
SMPTE	Society of Motion Picture and Television Engineers
SPL	Sound Pressure Level
SSSP	Structured Sound Synthesis Project (University of Toronto)
TEMPO	Transformational Electronic Music Process Organizer
VLMI	Very Large Musical Interval
VLSI	Very Large Scale Integration
WMN-code	White Mensural Notation code

AESTHETICS

1. "A propos de l'ordinateur dans la musique." *Le monde de la musique* 9,3 (1967): 10.

2. "A propos des mécanismes de création esthétique." *Extrait de cybernética no. 2.* Namur: Association internationale de cybernétique, 1967.

3. Appleton, Jon H. "Aesthetic Direction in Electronic Music." *Western Humanities Review* 18 (1964): 345-50.

4. Barbaud, Pierre. "Ars nova." *Automatisme* 15 (1970): 423-28.

5. ———. *La musique, discipline scientifique.* Paris: Dunod, 1968. 153 p.

6. Barraud, Jacques. "Musique et ordinateurs." *La revue musicale* 257 (1963): 9-12.

7. Bense, Max. "Kunst aus dem Computer." In *Methoden in Ergebnissen empirischer und experimenteller Ästhetik.* Stuttgart: Nadolski, 1957. (Exakte Ästhetik 5)

8. ———. "Projekter til en generativ aestetik." [Plans for a Generative Aesthetic] *Dansk musiktidsskrift* 41 (1966): 179-82. In Danish.

9. Branchi, Walter. "La communication musicale: 'pensee et moyen electronique'." In *Computer Music/Composition musicale par ordinateur; Report on an International Project Including a Workshop at Aarhus, Denmark in 1978,* ed. Marc Battier and Barry Truax. Ottawa: Canadian Commission for Unesco, 1980: 73-84.

10. Brün, Herbert. "Chaos and Organization." *ICA Bulletin* 166 (1967): 8-11.

11. ———. "Ersättning eller analogi: datamaskinmusikestetik." [Compensation or Analogy: Aesthetics of Computer Music] *Nutida musik* 9,7 (1965-66): 27-31. In Swedish.

12. ———. "From Musical Ideas to Computers and Back." In *The Computer and Music,* ed. Harry B. Lincoln. Ithaca: Cornell University Press, 1970: 23-36.

13.   ———. "Probleme der Verständigung." *Hi-Fi Stereophonie* 6 (1973): 587–98.

14.   ———. ". . .To Hold Discourse, at Least with a Computer." *Guildhall School of Music and Drama Review* (1973): 16–21.

15.   Carter, Jack. "The Music Thing." *Crescendo International* 14 (Feb. 1976): 18.

16.   Cohen, Joel E. "Information Theory and Music." *Behavioral Science* 7 (1962): 137–63.

17.   Degli Antoni, Giovanni, and Goffredo Haus. "Musica e causalità." [Music and Causality] *Bollettino LIMB* 3 (1983): 23–26.
       English version: "Music and Causality." In *Proceedings of the Venice 1982 International Computer Music Conference,* comp. Thom Blum and John Strawn. San Francisco, Calif.: Computer Music Association, 1985: 279–96.

18.   Foerster, Heinz von. "Sounds and Music." In *Music by Computers,* ed. Heinz von Foerster and James W. Beauchamp. New York: Wiley, 1969: 3–10.

19.   Gregory, Robin. "Music by Machine." *Musical Opinion* 82 (Oct. 1958): 21–23.

20.   Grossi, Pietro. "Computer and Music." *International Review of the Aesthetics and Sociology of Music* 4 (1973): 279–82.
       Summary in Croatian.

21.   Henahan, Donal J. "Future Mozart—Will He Be A.C. or D.C.?" *Chicago Daily News* (Mar. 7, 1964): Panorama 15.

22.   Higgins, D. "Does Avant-Garde Mean Anything?" *Arts in Society* 7,1 (1970): 28–31.

23.   Hijman, Julius. "Elektronische componeren?" [Electronic Composition?] *Mens en Melodie* 16 (1961): 141–45.
       In Dutch.

24.   Horn, Patrice. "Computer as Musician: Still a Long Way to Go." *Psychology Today* 8 (Nov. 1974): 145.

25.   Horwood, Wally. "Musical Musings: Living with Leisure." *Crescendo International* 21 (May 1983): 4.

26.   Howe, Hubert S. "Creativity in Computer Music." *BYTE* 4 (July 1979): 158–73.
       C&CA 14 (1979): 34788. *C&IS* 24 (1980): 232222C.

27.   Kaegi, Werner. "Die Musik unserer Zeit—ein Opfer der Technik?" *The World of Music* 13 (1971): 4–17.
       In German, English, and French.
       RILM 73 3956.

28.   Kayn, Roland. "Komponieren zwischen Computer und Kybernetik." *Melos/ Neue Zeitschrift für Musik* 3 (1977): 22–27.
       RILM 77 3745.

29. Keane, David. "Computer Music: Some Problems and Objectives in Applied Aesthetics." In *Proceedings of the 1980 International Computer Music Conference,* comp. Hubert S. Howe. San Francisco: Computer Music Association, 1982: 512–24.

30. Koenig, Gottfried Michael. "Integrazione estetica di partiture composte mediante elaboratore." [Aesthetical Integration of Scores Written Using a Computer] *Bollettino LIMB* 3 (1983): 27–34.

31. Kresánek, Josef. "Cit a vášen." [Sensitivity and Passion] *Slovenska hubda* 8 (1964): 104–08.
    In Slovak.

32. Laske, Otto E. "Toward a Definition of Computer Music." In *Proceedings, 1981 International Computer Music Conference, November 5–8,* comp. Larry Austin and Thomas Clark. Denton, Tex.: North Texas State University, 1983: 31–56.
    Reprinted in *Feedback Papers* 27–28 (März 1982): 9–24.

33. Lazzlo, Ervin. "Cybernetics of Musical Activity." *Journal of Aesthetics and Art Criticism* 31 (1973): 375–87.

34. Lesche, Carl. "Weltanschauung, science, technologie, et art." *La revue musicale* 268–69 (1971): 37–55.
    English version: "Weltanschauung, Science, Technology, and Art." In *Music and Technology.* Paris: La revue musicale, 1971: 39–55.

35. Minsky, Marvin. "Music, Mind, and Meaning." *Computer Music Journal* 5,3 (Fall 1981): 28–44.
    C&CA 17 (1982): 24517. *C&IS* 29 (1982): 82–01627C.

36. ———. "La musique, les structures mentales et le sens." In *Le compositeur et l'ordinateur.* Paris: IRCAM, 1981: 56–81.

37. Missal, Joshua. "The Fallacy of Mathematical Compositional Techniques." *American Music Teacher* 12 (Nov./Dec. 1962): 25, 33–35, 37.

38. "Die moderne Kunst, die Computer 'Kunst' und das Urheberrecht." *Archiv für Urheber-, Film-, Funk-, und Theaterrecht* 56 (1970): 117–48.
    In German, summaries in French and English.
    RILM 75 4710.

39. Mohring, Phillipp. "Können technische, insbesondere Computer-Erzeugnisse, Werke der Literatur, Musik, und Malerei sein?" *Archiv für Urheber-, Film-, Funk-, und Theaterrecht* 50 (1967): 835–43.

40. Moles, Abraham A. *Art et ordinateur.* Paris: Casterman, 1971: 190–222.

41. ———. "Art et ordinateur." *Communication et langages* 7 (Sept. 1970): 24–33.
    Excerpts of author's *Art et ordinateur.*

42. ———. *Kunst und Computer.* Cologne: DuMont Schauberg, 1973. 228 p.

43. ———. "The New Relationship Between Music and Mathematics." *Gravesaner Blätter* 23–24 (1962): 98–108.
Parallel English and German texts.

44. ———. "The Prospect of Electronic Instrumentation." *Gravesaner Blätter* 15–16 (1960): 21–44.
Parallel English and German texts.

45. Moore, F. Richard. "The Futures of Music." *Perspectives of New Music* 19 (Fall/Winter 1980–Spring/Summer 1981): 212–26.

46. Parkinson, G. H. R. "The Cybernetic Approach to Aesthetics." *Philosophy* 36 (Jan. 1961): 49–61.

47. Patrick, P. Howard. "Composer, Computer, and Audience." *Composer* 35 (Spring 1970): 1–3.

48. Philippot, Michel P. "Vingt ans de musique." *Revue d'esthétique* 20 (1967): 352–75.

49. Polaczek, Dietmar. "Konvergenzen? Neue Musik und die Kunst der Gegenwart." *Musica* [Kassel] 32,1 (1978): 29–33.
RILM 78 2004.

50. Portnoy, Julius. *Music in the Life of Man*. New York: Holt, Rinehart and Winston, 1963. 300 p.

51. Pousseur, Henri. *Fragments théoriques I sur la musique expérimentale*. Brussels: Editions de l'Institut de sociologie, Université libre de Bruxelles, 1970. 290 p.

52. Randall, J. K. "Three Lectures to Scientists." *Perspectives of New Music* 5 (Spring-Summer 1967): 124–40.

53. Reichardt, Jasia, ed. *Cybernetics, Art, and Ideas*. Greenwich, Conn.: New York Graphic Society, 1971. 156 p.
ERIC: ED 062 761. *RILM* 71 3189.

54. Richard, Albert. "Interrogatoire d'un musicien." *La revue musicale* 268–69 (1971): 31–35.
English version: "Interrogatory of a Musician." In *Music and Technology*. Paris: La revue musicale, 1971: 33–38.

55. Russcol, Herbert. *The Liberation of Sound*. Englewood Cliffs: Prentice-Hall, 1972.

56. Sandow, Gregory. "But is it Art?" *Village Voice* 26 (Mar. 4, 1981): 63.

57. Scat, Peter. "The Dream of Reason—the Reason of a Dream." *Keynotes: Musical Life in the Netherlands* 2 (1976): 39–47.

58. Schaeffer, Pierre. "De l'expérience musicale à l'expérience humaine." *La revue musicale* 274–75 (1971): 1–168.

59. ———. "La musique et les ordinateurs." *La revue musicale* 268–69 (1971): 57–88.
English version: "Music and Computers." In *Music and Technology.* Paris: La revue musicale, 1971: 57–92.
Czech translation: "Hudba a počítače." *Hudebni věda* (1972): 249–53.

60. Shapeiro, Harold. "Remarks." *Proceedings of the American Society of University Composers* 1 (1968): 54–55.

61. Shaw, Jane A. "Computers and the Humanities." *Electronic Age* 24 (Spring 1965): 26–29.

62. Strang, Gerald. "Ethics and Esthetics of Computer Composition." In *The Computer and Music,* ed. Harry B. Lincoln. Ithaca: Cornell University Press, 1970: 37–41.

63. Sychra, Antonin. "Die Anwendung der Kybernetik und der Informationstheorie in der marxistischen Ästhetik." *Beiträge zur Musikwissenschaft* 12 (1970): 83–108.

64. ———. "Möglichkeiten der Anwendung der Kybernetik und der Informationstheorie in der marxistischen Musikwissenschaft." *Beiträge zur Musikwissenschaft* 7 (1965): 402–7.

65. Walton, Ortiz M. "Some Implications for Afro-American Culture: Rationalism and Western Music." *Black World* 23 (Nov. 1973): 54–57.
CIJE 6 (1974): EJ 088 762.

66. Xenakis, Iannis. "In Search of a Stochastic Music." *Gravesaner Blätter* 4,11/12 (1958): 98–122.
Parallel German and English texts.

67. ———. "Wahrscheinlichkeitstheorie und Musik." *Gravesaner Blätter* 6 (Dec. 1956): 28–34.

68. ———; Olivier Messiaen; Michel Ragon; Olivier Revault d'Allones; Michel Serres; and Bernard Teyssèdre. *Arts/Sciences: Alloys.* New York, N.Y.: Pendragon Press, 1985. 133 p. (Aesthetics in Music no. 2)

69. Zaripov, Rudolph K. "Musik und Rechenautomat." *Ideen des exakten Wissens* 2 (1969): 71–77.

70. Zinovieff, Peter. "Don't Teach Mozart FORTRAN." In *Proceedings of the International Music and Technology Conference, August 24–28, 1981, University of Melbourne.* Parkville, Vic.: Computer Music Project, Dept. of Computer Science, University of Melbourne, 1981: 245–54.

COMPOSITION

71. Abbot, Alain. "Approche de composition d'une oeuvre electro-acoustique." In *Conférence des journées d'études, festival international du son*. Paris: Editions radio, 1973.

72. Abel, John F., and Paul S. Barth. "Computer Composition of Melodic Deep Structures." In *Proceedings, 1981 International Computer Music Conference, November 5-8*, comp. Larry Austin and Thomas Clark. Denton, Tex.: North Texas State University, 1983: 158-70.

73. Aho, Alan C.; Donald C. Lavoie; and James N. Paprocki. "MUSIM: Simulation of Music Composition Using GASP." In *Proceedings of the 1974 Winter Simulation Conference*. New York: ACM, 1974: 585-91.
C&IS 12: 93866C.

74. Altmayer, Nancy. "Music Composition: A Different Approach." *Creative Computing* 5 (Apr. 1979): 74-85.
C&CA 14 (1979): 31254.

75. Ames, Charles. "Applications of Linked Data Structures to Automated Composition." In *Proceedings of the International Computer Music Conference, 1985*, ed. Barry Truax. San Francisco, Calif.: Computer Music Association, 1985: 251-58.

76. Ananthanarayanan, K. R. "Computers and Music." *Journal of the Indian Musicological Society* 10 (Sept.-Dec. 1979): 23-30.
RILM 79 5225.

77. Anderson, David P. "A Forth Computer Music Programming Environment." In *1984 Rochester Forth Conference, Real Time Systems, Rochester, June 6-9, 1984, University of Rochester, Rochester, New York*. Rochester, NY: Institute for Applied Forth Research, 1984: 217-28.
C&CA 20 (1985): 35117.

78. Andriessen, Louis; Leo Geurts; and Lambert Meertens. "Componist en Computer." [Composer and Computer] *De Gids* 132 (1969): 304-11.
In Dutch.

79. Appleton, Jon H. "New Role for the Composer." *Music Journal* 27 (Mar. 1969): 28, 59–61.
Swedish version in *Nutida musik* 13,4 (1969–70): 38–41.
English, French, and German versions: "Electronic Music and the Composer's Future." *World of Music* 13,1 (1971): 29–40.

80. Arfib, Daniel. "Conception assistée par ordinateur en acoustique musicale." Thèse de docteur-ingenieur, Université d'Aix, Marseille II, 1977. 176 p.

81. Arveiller, Jacques. "Une approche informatique de situations d'improvisation." Communication au colloque "Creativité artificielle?", Sigma 9/Contact II, Bordeaux, Nov. 23, 1973. 8 p.

82. ———. "Comments on University Instruction in Computer Music Composition." *Computer Music Journal* 6,2 (Summer 1982): 72–78.
C&IS 29 (1982): 82–13614C.

83. ———. "SIMSIM: un programme qui simule l'improvisation." In *T-5, The Rational and Irrational in Visual Research Today, Match of Ideas, June 2, 1973.* Zagreb: Galerija Suvremene Umjetnosti, 1973: [28–30]

84. Attneave, Fred. "Stochastic Composition Processes." *Journal of Aesthetics and Art Criticism* 17 (1959): 503–10.

85. Attree, Richard. "Essays Before a System." In *Computer Music in Britain, 8th–11th April 1980.* London: Electro-Acoustic Music Association of Great Britain, 1980: 111–41.

86. Austin, Larry. "Computer-Assisted Composition." Paper presented at the 1983 International Computer Music Conference, Oct. 7–10, 1983, Rochester, N.Y.

87. Baecker, Ronald. "Towards an Effective Characterization of Graphical Interaction." Paper presented the IFIP W.G. 5.2 Workshop on Methodology of Interaction, Selliac, France.

88. ———; William Buxton; and William Reeves. "Towards Facilitating Graphical Interaction: Some Examples from Computer-Aided Musical Composition." In *Proceedings, 6th Man-Computer Communications Conference,* ed. M. Wein and E. Swail. Ottawa, Canada: National Research Council of Canada, 1979: 197–208.
Summary in French.

89. Baffioni, Claudio; Francesco Guerra; and Laura Tedeschini Lalli. "The Theory of Stochastic Processes and Dynamical Systems as a Basis for Models of Musical Structures." In *Musical Grammars and Computer Analysis,* ed. M. Baroni and L. Callegari. Florence: L. S. Olschki, 1984: 317–24. (Quaderni della rivista Italiana di musicologia 8)

90. Baker, Robert A. "MUSICOMP—Music Simulator-Interpreter for Compositional Procedures for the IBM 7090 Electronic Digital Computer." Urbana: University of Illinois Experimental Music Studio, July 1963. 44 p. (Technical Report no. 9)

91.   ———. "Preparation of Musicwriter Punched Paper Tapes for Use by the ILLIAC Electronic Digital Computer." Urbana: University of Illinois Experimental Music Studio, June 1961. 14 p. (Technical Report no. 2)

92.   Barbaud, Pierre. "Composing Music and Generating Sound by Computer." In *International Federation for Information Processing Congress 74. Vol. 4, Technological and Scientific Applications; Applications in the Social Sciences and the Humanities.* New York: American Elsevier Pub. Co., 1974: 872–74. Review by Jef Raskin in *Computing Reviews* 16 (1975): 28,212.

93.   ———. "Highlights of Some Magnificent Principles." *Page* 28 (Jan. 1973): 2.

94.   ———. "Musique algorithmique." *Esprit* 28 (Jan. 1960): 92–97. Also in *Bulletin technique de la Compaignie des machines bull* 2 (1961): 22.

95.   Baroni, Mario; Rosella Brunetti; and Carlo Jacoboni. "Progetto di grammatica generativa di melodie e di armonie." [Project for a Melody and Harmony-Generating Grammar] In *Atti del Quarto Colloquio di Informatica Musicale.* Pisa: CNUCE-CNR, 1981: 211–30.

96.   ———, and Carlo Jacoboni. "Computer Generation of Melodies: Further Proposals." *Computers and the Humanities* 17 (Mar. 1983): 1–18. *C&CA* 19 (1984): 10504. Review by D. M. Bowen in *Computing Reviews* 25 (1984): 8406–0502.

97.   Barrière, Jean-Baptiste; Yves Potard; and P. F. Basinée. "Models of Continuity Between Synthesis and Processing for the Elaboration and Control of Timbre Structures." In *Proceedings of the International Computer Music Conference, 1985,* ed. Barry Truax. San Francisco, Calif.: Computer Music Association, 1985: 193–98.

98.   Barton, D. E. "The Algorithmic Production of Tonal Chorales in an Early Nineteenth Century Harmonic Idiom." In *Tools for Improved Computing in the 80s, 17th Annual Technical Symposium: June 15, 1978, National Bureau of Standards, Gaithersburg, Md.,* ed. Paul A. Willis. New York: ACM, 1978: 238.

99.   Battier, Marc. "Modeles informatiques et pratique musicale." *Cahier musique* 3 (1983): 36–38.

100.   ———. "Re cosa materiale et le programme compositionnel ICOSA." *Artinfo/musinfo* 27 (1977): 21–45.

101.   Bauer-Mengelberg, Stefan, and Melvin Ferentz. "On Eleven-Interval Twelve-Tone Rows." *Perspectives of New Music* 3 (Spring-Summer 1965): 93–103.

102.   Beckwith, Sterling. "Is a Computer 'Composing Instrument' Possible?" In *Proceedings of the Second Annual Music Computation Conference, November 7-9, 1975, at the University of Illinois at Urbana-Champaign. Part 2, Composition with Computers,* comp. James Beauchamp and John Melby. Urbana, Ill.: University of Illinois: 1–6.

103.   Begley, Sharon. "The Creative Computers." *Newsweek* 100 (July 5, 1982): 58.

104. Belfiore, Alfonso. "ALGOMUSIC: An Algorithm for the Genesis of Musical Structures." In *Proceedings of the Venice 1982 International Computer Music Conference,* comp. Thom Blum and John Strawn. San Francisco, Calif.: Computer Music Association, 1985: 693–702a.

105. Berlind, Gary, and George W. Logemann. "An Algorithm for Musical Transposition." *Computer Studies in the Humanities and Verbal Behavior* 2 (1969): 102–8.

106. Bernardini, Nicola. "Semiotics and Computer Music Composition." In *Proceedings of the International Computer Music Conference, 1985,* ed. Barry Truax. San Francisco, Calif.: Computer Music Association, 1985: 169–84.

107. Blum, Thomas L. "Phthong: An Interactive System for Music Composition. In *Proceedings of the Venice 1982 International Computer Music Conference.* San Francisco, Calif.: Computer Music Association, 1985: 54–65.

108. Bolognesi, Tommaso. "Automatic Composition: Experiments with Self-Similar Music." *Computer Music Journal* 7,1 (Spring 1983): 25–36.
Revised version of a lecture presented at the Third Colloquium on Musical Informatics held at Padua University, Padua, Italy.
C&IS 32 (1984): 84–13319C.

109. ———. "Automazione di processi compositivi: criteri di utilizzo della sorgente stocastica." [Automation of Composing Processes: Using Criteria for the Stochastic Source] In *Aspetti teorici di Informatica Musicale.* Milan: CTU-Istituto di Cibernetica Università di Milano, 1977: 38–67.

110. ———. "Composizione automatica: dalla musica 1/f alla musica autosimile." [Automatic Composition: From 1/f Music to Automatic Music] In *Atti del Terzo Colloquio di Informatica Musicale,* ed. G. DePoli. Padua: Università di Padova, 1979: 129–60.

111. ———. "A Musical Game and Its Optimal Solution." In *Atti del Quarto Colloquio di Informatica Musicale.* Pisa: CNUCE-CNR, 1981: 26–36.

112. Borneman, Ernest. "One-Night Stand." *Melody Maker* 28 (29 Nov. 1952): 5.

113. Boulez, Pierre. "L'in(dé)fini et l'instant." In *Le compositeur et l'ordinateur.* Paris: IRCAM, 1981: 46–47.

114. Bowsher, J. M. "Calculator Program for Musical Notes." *Journal of the Audio Engineering Society* 28 (1980): 437–42.
Corrected in "Comments on 'Calculator Program for Musical Notes'," by B. Bernfeld in *Journal of the Audio Engineering Society* 28 (1980): 726.
C&CA 15 (1980): 30705.

115. Branchi, Walter. "Comporre nel suono." [Composing in Sounds] *Bollettino LIMB* 3 (1983): 21–22.

116. ———. "Composing within Sound (An Introduction)." In *Proceedings of the Venice 1982 International Computer Music Conference,* comp. Thom Blum and John Strawn. San Francisco, Calif.: Computer Music Association, 1985: 653–81.

117. Brediceanu, Mihai. "Topological Mappings Applied to Musical Sonorous Forms." In *Modern Trends in Cybernetics and Systems: Proceedings of the Third International Congress of Cybernetics and Systems, Bucharest, Romania, August 25-29, 1975,* ed. J. Rose and C. Bilciu. New York: Springer-Verlag, 1977: Vol. 3, 665-76.

118. Brooks, F. P.; A. L. Hopkins; P. G. Neumann; and W. V. Wright. "An Experiment in Musical Composition." *IRE Transactions on Electronic Computers* EC-6 (1957): 175-82.
      A correction appears in vol. EC-7 (1958): 60.

119. Brün, Herbert. "Composition with Computers." In *Cybernetic Serendipity,* ed. Jasia Reichardt. New York: Frederick A. Praeger, 1969: 20.

120. ———. "Mutatis Mutandis: Compositions for Interpreters." *Numus West* 4 (1973): 31-34.
      French version: "Mutatis Mutandis: compositions pour interpretes." *Les cahiers sesa* 5 (1973): 22-23.
      RILM 75 4418.

121. ———. "On the Conditions under which Computers Would Assist a Composer in Creating Music of Contemporary Relevance and Significance." *Proceedings of the American Society of University Composers* 1 (1968): 30-37.

122. ———. "La technologie et le compositeur." *La revue musicale* 268-69 (1971): 181-93.
      English version: "Technology and the Composer." In *Music and Technology.* Paris: La revue musicale, 1971: 181-92.

123. Buda, Patrick. "Jig." *Artinfo/musinfo* 29 (1978): 29-37.

124. Bukharaev, R. G., and J. S. Rytvinsskaya. "Simulating a Probabilistic Process Connected with Composing a Melody." *Kazan universitet uchenye zapiske* 122,4 (1962): 82-97.

125. Buxton, William. "Computers and the Composer: An Introductory Survey." *Faire* 4/5 (1977): 16-21.

126. ———. *Design Issues in the Foundation of a Computer-Based Tool for Music Composition.* Toronto: University of Toronto, 1978. (Technical Report CSRG-97)

127. ———; Sanand Patel; William Reeves; and Ronald Baecker. "On the Specification of Scope in Interactive Score Editors." Paper presented at the 1980 International Computer Music Conference, November 13-15, 1980, Queens College of the City University of New York.

128. ———; Sanand Patel; William Reeves; and Ronald Baecker. "Scope in Interactive Score Editors." *Computer Music Journal* 5,3 (Fall 1981): 50-56.
      Review by R. M. Mason in *Computing Reviews* 23 (Feb. 1982): 39,052.
      C&CA 17 (1982): 24519. *C&IS* 29 (1982): 82-01625C.

129. Caine, Hugh Le, and Gustav Ciamaga. "A Preliminary Report on the Serial Sound Structure Generator." *Perspectives of New Music* 6 (Fall-Winter 1967): 114–18.

130. "Un cas: la musique stochastique." *Musica Disques* 102 (Sept. 1962): 11.

131. Cena, D.; Pietro Grossi; and F. Lombardo. "Composizione fra informatica e programmazione." [Composition between Data Processing and Programming] In *Atti del convegno: Il comporre musicale nello spazio educativo e nella dimensione artistica,* 1982: 245–56.

132. ———; J. Martinez; and F. Michi. "Alcuni aspetti del rapporto composizione/modalità di fruizione dell'opera musicale alla luce delle possibilità offerte dall'informatica." [Changes in the Relationship Between Composing and Enjoying Music Owing to the Possibilities that Computer Science Offers] In *Atti del Quinto Colloquio di Informatica Musicale.* Ancona: Università di Ancona, 1983: 199–206.

133. Chadabe, Joel. "Interactive Composing: An Overview." *Computer Music Journal* 8,1 (Spring 1984): 22–27.
Also in *Proceedings of the 1983 Rochester International Computer Music Conference,* comp. Robert W. Gross. San Francisco, Calif.: Computer Music Association, 1984: 299–307.
C&CA 19 (1984): 36712. *C&IS* 32 (1984): 84–11766C.

134. ———. "Paths to a Point in a Musical Landscape." In *Proceedings of the International Music and Technology Conference, August 24–28, 1981, University of Melbourne, Australia.* Parkville, Vic.: Computer Music Project, Dept. of Computer Science, University of Melbourne, 1981: 2–12.
Also in *Proceedings, 1981 International Computer Music Conference, November 5–8,* comp. Larry Austin and Thomas Clark. Denton, Tex.: North Texas State University, 1983: 19–28.

135. ———. "System Composing." In *Proceedings of the Second Annual Music Computation Conference, November 7–9, 1975, at the University of Illinois at Urbana-Champaign. Part 2, Composing with Computers,* comp. James Beauchamp and John Melby. Urbana, Ill.: University of Illinois: 7–10.

136. Chernoff, Lionel. "The Determination of All Possible Hexachord-Generated, Twelve-Tone Rows Characterized by Bisymmetric Configurations of All the Simple Intervals." Ph. D. diss., Catholic University, 1968. 79 p.
DA 30:354A.

137. Christensen, C. "GRIN (Graphical Input) Language for the GRAPHIC-1 Console." Mimeographed. Murray Hill: Bell Telephone Laboratories.

138. Citron, Jack P. "Computer Music—With the Accent on Music." *Creative Computing* 6 (June 1980): 58–62.
C&CA 15 (1980): 36416.

139.   ———. "MUSPEC." In *The Computer and Music,* ed. Harry B. Lincoln. Ithaca: Cornell University Press, 1970: 97–111.

140.   Clough, John. "Computer Music and Group Theory." *Proceedings of the American Society of University Composers* 4 (1971): 10–19.

141.   Clynes, Manfred. "Secrets of Life in Music: Musicality Realised by Computer." In *Proceedings of the International Computer Music Conference, 1984,* ed. William Buxton. San Francisco, Calif.: Computer Music Association, 1985: 225–32.

142.   Cohen, Richard A. "An Intelligent Interface to the MUSIC-400 Real-Time Synthesis System." B.S. thesis, Massachusetts Institute of Technology, Dept. of Electrical Engineering and Computer Science, 1982. 53 p.

143.   Colquhon, Daryl G. "A Computer Application in Music Composition." Dept. of Computing Science, University of Adelaide, 1977. (Technical Report 77–07)
Also in *SIGLASH Newsletter* 13 (Mar. 1980): 21–28.
C&CA 15 (1980): 27760.

144.   "Composing by Computer at ISU." *Computers and Automation* 22 (Nov. 1973): 44.

145.   "Composing Computers." *Science Digest* 90 (Jan. 1982): 79.

146.   "Composing: Latest Creative Coup." *Science Digest* 92 (Apr. 1984): 34.

147.   "Computer als Komponisten-Helfer." *Funkschau* 51 (1979): 712–15.
C&CA 15 (1980): 25187.

148.   Corlett, P. N., and Charles Cain. "Anglican Chants by Computer." *Bulletin of the Institute of Mathematics and its Applications* 6 (Apr. 1970): 70–72.

149.   Dalla Vecchia, Wolfango. "Il programma EMUS nella didattica e nella prassi compositiva." [The EMUS Program in Teaching and Compositional Practice] In *Atti del Terzo Colloquio di Informatica Musicale,* ed. G. DePoli. Padua: Università di Padova, 1979: 36–40.

150.   Dalmasso, Gilbert. "Un programme compositionnel: 'Quartre etudes et variations'." *Artinfo/musinfo* 29 (1978): 56–68.

151.   ———, and Gilles Andrivet. "Deux programmes d'édition de musique." *Artinfo/musinfo* 12: 8–10.

152.   Dannenberg, Roger B., and Arthur H. Benade. "An Automated Approach to Tuning." In *Proceedings of the Rochester 1983 International Computer Music Conference,* comp. Robert W. Gross. San Francisco, Calif.: Computer Music Association, 1984: 81–90.

153.   Daudel, R., and N. Lemaire D'Agaggio. "Report on the International Colloquium on Relationships Between Science, Art, and Philosophy, Paris, November 1980." *Leonardo* 14 (1981): 297–98.

154. Davies, Gwenda. "Generation of Harmonised Melodies: A Student Project." *Computer Bulletin* Ser. 2, no. 25 (Sept. 1980): 11. *C&CA* 16 (1981): 3164.

155. Davis, Bob. "David Rosenboom: Recent Cybernetic Insights." *Synapse* 2 (Jan.-Feb. 1978): 18.

156. ———. "Gurella Electronics: More Monkey Business." *Synapse* 1 (Jan.-Feb. 1977): 26–29.

157. Dehn, Natalie Jane. "Computer Composition of Tonal Music." B.S. thesis, Massachusetts Institute of Technology, Dept. of Electrical Engineering and Computer Science, 1975. 75 p.

158. Dooley, Ann. "Researcher Uncovers Formula to Sweeten Generated Music." *Computerworld* 13 (Apr. 9, 1979): 57. *C&IS* 23 (1979): 223896C.

159. Doro, A. "Studi per una metodologia della composizione musicale." [Studies for a Methodology of Music Composition] In *Atti del Quinto Colloquio di Informatica Musicale.* Ancona: Università di Ancona, 1983: 207–12.

160. Dufourt, Hugues. "Les difficultés d'une prise de conscience théorique." In *Le compositeur et l'ordinateur.* Paris: IRCAM, 1981: 6–12.

161. Dworak, Paul E., and Philip Baczewski. "A Vector Field Model of Compositional Creativity." In *Proceedings of the 1980 International Computer Music Conference,* comp. Hubert S. Howe. San Francisco, Calif.: Computer Music Association, 1982: 443–56.

162. Dydo, J. Stephen. "Surface Control of Computer Music." In *Proceedings of the Venice 1982 International Computer Music Conference,* comp. Thom Blum and John Strawn. San Francisco, Calif.: Computer Music Association, 1985: 682–92.

163. Ebcioğlu, Kemal. "Computer Counterpoint." In *Proceedings of the 1980 International Computer Music Conference,* comp. Hubert S. Howe. San Francisco, Calif.: Computer Music Association, 1982: 534–43.

164. ———. "An Expert System for Schenkerian Synthesis of Chorales in the Style of J. S. Bach." In *Proceedings of the International Computer Music Conference, 1984,* ed. William Buxton. San Francisco, Calif.: Computer Music Association, 1985: 135–42.

165. Eimert, Herbert. "Die Reihe, das unbekannte Wesen." *Melos* 29 (1962): 219–22.

166. Englert, Giuseppe G. "Experiences Leading Towards Automated Composition." In *Computer Music / Composition musicale par ordinateur; Report on an International Project Including a Workshop at Aarhus, Denmark in 1978,* ed. Marc Battier and Barry Truax. Ottawa: Canadian Commission for Unesco, 1980: 95–104.

167.   ———. "Musique: composition automatique—automation composée."
        Informatique et sciences humaines 45 (Juin 1980): 37–50.
        Rev. and updated version: "Automated Composition and Composed Auto-
        mation." *Computer Music Journal* 5,4 (Winter 1981): 30–35.
        C&CA 17 (1982): 32046. *C&IS* 29 (1982): 82–1623C.

168.   ———. "Vers la composition automatique?" *Schweizerische Musikzeitung*
        118 (1978): 212–16.

169.   Farese, Silvio. *Sinform: un sistema per la gestione automatica dei dati.* [Sinform:
        A System for the Automatic Management of Data] Pisa: CNUCE, 1978. 29 p.

170.   Fencl, Zdeněk. "Komponující algorithmus a obsah informace." [Composi-
        tional Algorithms and General Information] *Kybernetika* 2 (1966): 243.
        In Polish.

171.   ———. "Počítač jako hudební nastroj." [Computing as a Musical Tool]
        Hudební věda 5 (1968): 101–16.
        Summaries in German (153–54), English (162), and Russian (168–69).
        In Czech.

172.   Ferentzy, E. N. "Computer Simulation of Human Behavior and Concept For-
        mation in Music Composition." *Computational Linguistics* 4 (1965): 93–106.

173.   ———, and M. Havass. "Human Movement Analysis by Computer: Elec-
        tronic Choreography and Music Composition." *Computational Linguistics* 3
        (1964): 129–88.

174.   Ferneyhough, Brian. "Compositeur-ordinateur-forme active." In *Le composi-
        teur et l'ordinateur.* Paris: IRCAM, 1981: 48–55.

175.   "The First Ballad to be Composed by an Electronic Computer." *International
        Musician* 55 (Aug. 1956): 21.

176.   Forys, Leonard J. "Music: Mood or Math." *Notre Dame Technical Review* 14
        (Jan. 1963): 26–27.

177.   Foxley, Eric. "The Harmonization of Melodies by Computer." *IUCC Bulletin*
        3 (Spring 1981): 31–34.
        C&CA 17 (1982): 5232.

178.   Fredlund, Lorne D., and Jeffrey R. Sampson. "An Interactive Graphics
        System for Computer-Assisted Musical Composition." *International Journal
        of Man-Machine Studies* 5 (1973): 585–605.
        C&IS 11: 75625C. *CIJE* 6 (1974): EJ 086 092; EJ 088 762.

179.   "From Handel and Haydn to the Headless Musician." *Science Dimension* 2
        (June 1970): 8–13.
        In English and French.

180. Fry, Christopher. "Computer Improvisation." *Computer Music Journal* 4,3 (Fall 1980): 48–58.
Also in *Proceedings of the 1980 International Computer Music Conference,* comp. Hubert S. Howe. San Francisco, Calif.: Computer Music Association, 1982: 457–75.
C&CA 16 (1981): 21867. *C&IS* 26 (1981): 81–00518C.

181. ———. "Flavors Band: A Language for Specifying Musical Style." *Computer Music Journal* 8,4 (Winter 1984): 20–34.
C&CA 20 (1985): 30998.

182. ———. "Flavors Band: An Environment for Processing Musical Scores." Paper presented at the 78th Convention of the Audio Engineering Society, May 3–6, 1985, Anaheim. Preprint 2224 (B-8).

183. ———. "Flavors Band: Beyond Computer Improvisation and/or a Meta-Composition Language." In *Proceedings of the Rochester 1983 International Computer Music Conference,* comp. Robert W. Gross. San Francisco, Calif.: Computer Music Association, 1984: 31–54.

184. Frykberg, Susan D. "Composer and Computer." *Man-Machine Studies* 13 (1978): 5–17.

185. Gagliardo, Emilio, and Mario Ghislandi. "Invito alla composizione enneade-cafonica." [An Invitation to Enneadecaphonic Composition] In *Atti del Quarto Colloquio di Informatica Musicale.* Pisa: CNUCE-CNR, 1981: 62–69.

186. Garcia, Antonio. "'Bemol': un juego musical." ['Bemol': A Musical Game] *Revista Española de electronica* 30 (Aug.-Sept. 1983): 72–77.
C&CA 19 (1984): 3479. *E&EA* 87 (1984): 2854.

187. Gardner, Martin. "Mathematical Games: The Arts as Combinatorial Mathematics, or, How to Compose Like Mozart with Dice." *Scientific American* 231 (Dec. 1974): 132–36.

188. ———. "Mathematical Games: White and Brown Music, Fractal Curves and One-Over-f Fluctuations." *Scientific American* 238 (Apr. 1978): 16–31.

189. Garr, Doug. "The Endless Scale." *Omni* 3 (Mar. 1981): 44–49, 102.

190. Gerrard, Graeme. "A Project in Computer Composition." In *Proceedings of the International Music and Technology Conference, August 24–28, 1981, University of Melbourne.* Parkville, Vic.: Computer Music Project, Dept. of Computer Science, University of Melbourne, 1981: 59–65.

191. Ghent, Emmanuel. "Further Studies in Compositional Algorithms." In *Proceedings of the 1978 International Computer Music Conference,* comp. Curtis Roads. Evanston, Ill.: Northwestern University Press, 1979: 185–91.

192. ———. "Further Studies in Interactive Computer Music Composition (II)." Paper presented at the 1977 International Computer Music Conference, University of California, San Diego, 26–30 October 1977.

193.   ———. "Programmed Signals to Performers: A New Compositional Resource." *Perspectives of New Music* 6 (Fall-Winter 1967): 96–106.

194.   ———. "Real-Time Interactive Compositional Procedure." *Proceedings of the American Society of University Composers* 11 (1978/1979): 94–101.

195.   ———. "Real-Time Interactive Compositional Procedures." Paper presented at the International Conference on Computer Music, October 28–31, 1976, Massachusetts Institute of Technology.

196.   Gill, Stanley. "A Technique for the Composition of Music in a Computer." *Computer Journal* 6 (1963–64): 129–33.

197.   Gleeson, Patrick. "Computer Performance & Composition." *Contemporary Keyboard* 5 (July 1979): 89.

198.   Goldberg, Theo. "The Prefiguration of a Musical Composition: Model of a Computer Graphics Program." In *Proceedings of the International Computer Music Conference, 1985,* ed. Barry Truax. San Francisco, Calif.: Computer Music Association, 1985: 233–36.

199.   ———, and Guenther F. Schrack. "Computer Graphic Aided Music Composition." *International Journal of Man-Machine Studies* 10 (1978): 263–71.
Also in *Proceedings of the Fifth Man-Computer Communications Conference.* Ottawa, Ont.: National Research Council Canada, 1977: 103–12.
C&CA 14 (1979): 19611. *C&IS* 22 (1978): 214140C; 18 (1978): 195363C.

200.   Good, Michael D. "SCOT: A Score Translator for Music II." B.S. thesis, Massachusetts Institute of Technology, Dept. of Electrical Engineering and Computer Science, 1979. 63 p.

201.   Green, Mark. "PROD: A Grammar Based Computer Composition Program." Paper presented at the 1980 International Computer Music Conference, November 13–15, 1980, Queens College of the City University of New York.

202.   Green, T. R. G. "Developing a Program to Write Four-Voice Rounds: An Example for the Non-Numerical." *Computer Education* 30 (Nov. 1978): 2–5.

203.   Greenhough, Michael. "A Computer Program for Melodic Improvisation." In *Computer Music in Britain, 8th–11th April 1980.* London: Electro-Acoustic Music Association of Great Britain, 1980: 67–71.

204.   Gressel, Joel W. "Rhythmic Applications of Geometric Series." Ph. D. diss., Princeton University, 1976. 165 p.
DA 37:1289A.

205.   ———. "Some Rhythmic Applications of Geometric Series." In *Proceedings of the Second Annual Music Computation Conference, November 7–9, 1975 at the University of Illinois at Urbana-Champaign. Part 2, Composition with Computers,* comp. James Beauchamp and John Melby. Urbana, Ill.: University of Illinois: 11–30.

206. Grossi, Pietro, and S. Michi. "Il calcolo combinatorio come strumento formale e di sviluppo nella composizione." [Combinatorial Calculus as a Formal Tool and for Development in Composition] In *Atti del Quarto Colloquio di Informatica Musicale*. Pisa: CNUCE-CNR, 1981: 70–75.

207. "Gulbransen Piano Used as Electronic Brain Writes 1,000 Popular Songs an Hour." *Piano Review* 115 (Sept. 1956): 21.

208. Hamlin, Peter, with Curtis Roads. "Interview with Herbert Brün." In *Composers and the Computer,* ed. Curtis Roads. Los Altos, Calif.: W. Kaufmann, 1985: 1–15.

209. Hansen, Victor E. "Pitch Sets and Their Relations to Melodies." B.S. thesis, Massachusetts Institute of Technology, Dept. of Electrical Engineering, 1972. 35 p.

210. Harris, R. P., and Barry E. Conyngham. "Towards a Computer System for Assisting Composers." In *Proceedings of the International Music and Technology Conference, August 24–28, 1981, University of Melbourne.* Parkville, Vic.: Computer Music Project, Dept. of Computer Science, University of Melbourne, 1981: 255–62.

211. Hatzis, Christos. "Towards an Endogenous Automated Music." *Interface* 9 (1980): 83–114.

212. Haus, Goffredo. "L'automazione electronica applicata alla elaborazione musicale." [Electronic Automation Applied to Musical Computing] *Automazione e strumentazione* 28 (Feb. 1980): 108–18.
    C&CA 15 (1980): 27745.

213. Havass, M. "A Simulation of Musical Composition: Synthetically Composed Folkmusic." *Computational Linguistics* 3 (1964): 107–27.

214. Haynes, Stanley. "15 Months of Musical Production Using a Real-Time Digital Sound Synthesis System." In *Proceedings, 1981 International Computer Music Conference, November 5–8,* comp. Larry Austin and Thomas Clark. Denton, Tex.: North Texas State University, 1983: 287–91.

215. Hiller, Lejaren A. "The Composer and the Computer." *Abacus* 1 (Summer 1984): 9–31.

216. ———. "Composition with Hierarchical Structures." Paper presented at the Second Annual Music Computation Conference, Nov. 7–9, 1975, Urbana, Ill.

217. ———. "Computer Generation of Sequential Musical Patterns." Paper presented at the 89th Meeting of the Acoustical Society of America, Austin, Tex. 1975.
    Abstract in *Journal of the Acoustical Society of America* 57, Suppl. 1 (Spring 1975): S10.

218. ———. "Computer Programs Used to Produce the Composition *Algorithms I.*" Buffalo, N.Y.: SUNY, Dept. of Music, 1983. 310 p. (Technical Report 13)

219.   ———. "Electronic and Computer Music." *St. Louis Post-Dispatch* (May 7, 1969): 5C.

220.   ———. "Jüngste Entwicklung auf dem Gebiet der Computer-Musik." In *Informationstheorie und Computermusik*. Mainz: Schott, 1964: 35–62. (Darmstädter Beiträge zur neuen Musik 8)

221.   ———. "Muzyczne zastosowanie elektronowych maszyn cyfrowych." [A Musical Application of Computers] *Ruch muzyczny* 6 (Apr. 15, 1962): 11–13.

222.   ———. "On the Use of a High-Speed Electronic Digital Computer for Musical Composition." M.M. thesis, University of Illinois, 1958. 174 p.

223.   ———. "Phrase Generation in Computer Music Composition." Buffalo, N.Y.: State University of New York, Buffalo, Oct. 1978. 163 p. (Technical Report no. 10)

224.   ———. "Phrase Structure in Computer Music." In *Proceedings of the 1978 International Computer Music Conference,* comp. Curtis Roads. Evanston, Ill.: Northwestern University Press, 1979: 192–213.

225.   ———. "Programming a Computer for Musical Composition." In *Papers from the West Virginia University Conference on Computer Applications in Music,* ed. Gerald Lefkoff. Morgantown: West Virginia University Library, 1967: 65–88.

226.   ———. "Programming the I-Ching Oracle." *Computer Studies in the Humanities and Verbal Behavior* 3 (1970–72): 140–53.
         Also appears in Lejaren A. Hiller, "Computer Programs Used to Produce the Composition HPSCHD." Buffalo: National Science Foundation Project No. GK–14191, Aug. 1972: 7–20. (Technical Report no. 4)

227.   ———. "Some Structural Principles of Computer Music." Abstract in *Journal of the American Musicological Society* 9 (1956): 247–48.

228.   ———. "Stochastic Generation of Note Parameters for Music Composition." In *Proceedings of the Venice 1982 International Computer Music Conference.* San Francisco, Calif.: Computer Music Association, 1985: 623–52.

229.   Holtzman, Steven R. "A Generative Grammar Definition Language for Music." *Interface* 9 (1980): 1–47.
         C&CA 16 (1981): 3174.

230.   ———. "Generative Grammars and the Computer-Aided Composition of Music." Doctoral thesis, University of Edinburgh, Dept. of Computer Science, 1980.

231.   ———. "The GGDL Computer-Aided Composition System." Paper presented at the 1980 International Computer Music Conference, November 13–15, 1980, Queens College of the City University of New York.

232.   ———. *GGDL Generative Grammar Definition Language.* Edinburgh: University of Edinburgh, Dept. of Computer Science, 1980.

233. ———. "GGDL Manual—Generative Grammar Definition Language." Edinburgh: University of Edinburgh, 1979. (Department of Computer Science Report)

234. ———. "Grammars and Computer Composition." In *Computer Music in Britain, 8th–11th April 1980.* London: Electro-Acoustic Music Association of Great Britain, 1980: 95–110.

235. ———. "Using Generative Grammars for Music Composition." *Computer Music Journal* 5,1 (Spring 1981): 51–64.
C&CA 16 (1981): 36852. *C&IS* 29 (1982): 82–4143C.

236. Howe, Hubert S. "Astrazioni: riflessioni sulla composizione mediante elaboratore." [Abstractions: Remarks on Computer-Based Composition] *Bollettino LIMB* 1 (1981): 74–81.

237. ———. "The Composer and Computer Music." In *The Liberation of Sound,* ed. Herbert Russcol. Englewood Cliffs, N.J.: Prentice-Hall, 1972: 276–87.

238. ———. "Composing by Computer." *Computers and the Humanities* 9 (1975): 281–90.
C&CA 11 (1976): 22469. *C&IS* 16: 158991C. *RILM* 76 15631.

239. ———. "Compositional Technique in Computer Sound Synthesis." *Proceedings of the American Society of University Composers* 7/8 (1972/1973): 25–30.

240. ———. "A General View of Compositional Procedure in Computer Sound Synthesis." *Proceedings of the American Society of University Composers* 3 (1970): 98–108.

241. Hunt, Michael F. "RANDHIND: A FORTRAN Program that Generates Two-Voiced Exercises According to the Rules Stated in Paul Hindemith's *The Craft of Music Composition* (Book II)." Ph. D. diss., Washington University, 1974. 134 p.
DA 35: 6182A. *RILM* 76 1649.

242. Inman, Kurt. "A Musical Number Guessing Game." *Creative Computing* 3 (Mar.-Apr. 1977): 110–11.

243. Jackson, Roland. "The Computer as a 'Student' of Harmony." In *Report of the Tenth Congress [of the International Musicological Society], Ljubljana 1967,* ed. Dragotin Cvetko. Kassel: Bärenreiter, 1970: 132–46.

244. Jaxitron. *Cybernetic Music.* Blue Ridge Summit, Pa.: Tab Books, 1985. 344 p.

245. Johnston, Ben. "Tonality Regained." *Proceedings of the American Society of University Composers* 6 (1971): 113–19.

246. Jones, Kevin J. "Compositional Applications of Stochastic Processes." *Computer Music Journal* 5,2 (Summer 1981): 45–61.
C&CA 17 (1982): 8912.

247. ———. "Computer Assisted Application of Stochastic Structuring Techniques in Musical Composition and Control of Digital Sound Synthesis Systems." Ph. D. thesis, The City University, London, 1980.

248. ———. "A Space Grammar for the Stochastic Generation of Multi-Dimensional Structures." In *Proceedings of the 1980 International Computer Music Conference*, comp. Hubert S. Howe. San Francisco, Calif.: Computer Music Association, 1982: 22–42.

249. ———. "Stochastic Music: Compositional Techniques and Applications." In *Atti del Quarto Colloquio di Informatica Musicale*. Pisa: CNUCE-CNR, 1981: 337–45.

250. ———. "Stochastic Processes in Computer Music." In *Computer Music in Britain, 8th–11th April 1980*. London: Electro-Acoustic Music Association of Great Britain, 1980: 73–93.

251. Jungheinrich, Hans-Klaus. "Erdenklang aus dem Foersterhaus; Bognermayr/Zuschraders 'computerakustische' Symphonie." *Hifi-Stereophonie* 21 (1982): 450–54.

252. Katz, Robert. "A Simpler Musical Calculator Program." *Journal of the Audio Engineering Society* 29 (Mar. 1981): 160–61.
      C&CA 16 (1981): 21877.

253. Keane, David. "The Quest for 'Musically Interesting' Structures in Computer Music." In *Proceedings, 1981 International Computer Music Conference, November 5–8*, comp. Larry Austin and Thomas Clark. Denton, Tex.: North Texas State University, 1983: 3–18.

254. Keith, Michael. "A Combinatorial Aspect of Computer Music Composition." In *Proceedings of the 1979 National Computer Conference on Personal Computing: New York, June 4–7, 1979*, ed. J. P. Lucas and R. E. Adams. Arlington, Va.: AFIPS Press, 1979: 313–17.

255. Kobrin, Edward G. "I Ching." *Source* 8 (July 1970): 1–7.

256. Koenig, Gottfried Michael. "Aesthetic Integration of Computer-Composed Scores." *Computer Music Journal* 7,4 (Winter 1983): 27–33.
      Also in *Proceedings of the Venice 1982 International Computer Music Conference*, comp. Thom Blum and John Strawn. San Francisco, Calif.: Computer Music Association, 1985: 613–22.
      C&CA 19 (1984): 19377. *C&IS* 32 (1984): 84–6920C. *E&EA* 87 (1984): 21933.

257. ———. "Composition Processes." In *Computer Music/Composition musicale par ordinateur; Report on an International Project Including a Workshop at Aarhus, Denmark in 1978*, ed. Marc Battier and Barry Truax. Ottawa: Canadian Commission for Unesco, 1980: 105–25.

258. ———. "Computer-Verwendung in Kompositionsprozessen." In *Music auf der Flucht vor sich selbst*. Munich: Hanser Verlag, 1969: 78–91. (Reihe Hanser 28)

259. ———. "Datorns användning i kompositoriska processer." [The Use of the Computer in Compositional Processes] *Nutida musik* 13,4 (1969–70): 26–31. In Swedish.

260. ———. *Electronic Music Course: Computer Composition.* Utrecht: Institute of Sonology at Utrecht State University, 1971.

261. ———. "Emploi des programmes d'ordinateur dans la creation musicale." *La revue musicale* 268–69 (1971): 89–112.
English version: "The Use of Computer Programmes in Creating Music." In *Music and Technology.* Paris: La revue musicale, 1971: 93–115.

262. ———. "My Experiences with Programmed Music." *Faire* 4/5 (1977): 26–30.

263. ———. "Notes on the Computer in Music." *The World of Music* 9,3 (1967): 3–13.
Parallel English, French, and German texts.

264. ———. "Processi compositivi." [Compositional Processes] In *Musica e elaboratore.* Venice: Biennale di Venezia, 1980: 37–49.

265. ———. "Project 1." *Electronic Music Reports* 2 (July 1970): 32–44.

266. ———. "PROJECT 2, A Programme for Musical Composition." *Electronic Music Reports* 3 (Dec. 1970): 1–161.
Reprinted by Amsterdam: Swets & Zeitlinger, 1977.

267. ———. "Projekt Eins—Modell und Wirklichkeit." *Musik und Bildung* 11 (Dec. 1979): 752–56.
Summary in English.
RILM 79 5666.

268. ———. *Protocol.* Utrecht: Institute of Sonology, 1979. 202 p. (Sonological Reports 4)
Review by Curtis Roads in *Computer Music Journal* 5,4 (Winter 1981): 76–77.

269. Konieczny, Jacek. "Zastosowanie maszyn cyfrowych do komponowania muzyki." [The Application of Computers in Composing Music] *Zeszyty naukowe państwowa wyzsza szkota muzyczna* 12 (1973): 121–42.
In Polish.
RILM 74 3957.

270. ———. "Zastosowanie maszyn cyfrowych w tworzeniu cantus firmus w kontrapunkcie w stylu ścisłym." [The Application of Computers to the Creation of Cantus Firmus Counterpoint in the Strict Style] *Zeszyty naukowe państwowej wyzszej szkoty muzyczej w gdansku* 14 (1975): 143–61.
In Polish.
RILM 76 4035.

271. Krellmann, Hanspeter. "Der Mathematiker unter den zeitgenössischen Komponisten." *Melos* 39 (1972): 322–24.

272. Kronland-Martinet, Richard. "An Educational System for Assisting Composition." Paper presented at the 1984 International Computer Music Conference, Oct. 19–23, Paris, France.

273. Kupper, Hubert. *Computer und musikalische Kompositionen.* Braunschweig: Vieweg, 1970. 41 p.

274.   ———. "Computer und musikalische Kompositionen." *Elektronische Daten-verarbeitung* 11 (1969): 492-97.

275.   ———. "GEASCOP—ein Kompositionsprogramm." *Informatik* 37 (1972): 629-55.
        RILM 76 1692.

276.   Kupper, Leo. "Elaboration de musique électronique à partir d'un ordinateur musical. Tendance à l'automatisation de la composition. Génération d'un monde sonore autonome par interstimulations d'automates sonores." *Faire* 2-3 (1975): 31-41.

277.   LaBarbara, Joan. "New Music." *High Fidelity/Musical America* 29 (June 1979): MA12-MA13.

278.   LaBrousse, F. "Sur la composition musicale automatique." Thèse de Docteur Ingénieur, Toulouse, 1968.

279.   Lachartre, Nicole. "Machinentum Firminiense: dernier-né de la musique algorithmique." *01-Informatique mensuel* 69 (Mai 1973): 47-50.

280.   Laske, Otto E. "Artificial Intelligence Topics in Computer-Aided Composition." Paper presented at the 1983 International Computer Music Conference, Oct. 7-10, 1983, Rochester, N.Y.

281.   ———. "Composition Theory: A New Discipline for Artificial Intelligence and Computer Music." In *Music and Mind.* Boston, Mass.: O. Laske, 1981: 157-95.

282.   ———. "Composition Theory in Koenig's Project One and Project Two." *Computer Music Journal* 5,4 (Winter 1981): 54-65.
        Review by R. M. Mason in *Computing Reviews* 23 (Oct. 1982): 39,833.
        C&CA 17 (1982): 32048. *C&IS* 29 (1982): 82-01629C.

283.   ———. "Toward a Theory of Interfaces for Computer Music Systems." *Computer Music Journal* 1,4 (Nov. 1977): 53-60.
        Adaption of Chapter 8 in the author's book *Music, Memory, and Thought.*
        Also in *Music and Mind.* Boston, Mass.: O. Laske, 1981: 123-30.
        C&IS 18 (1978): 197092; and 20 (1978): 207142C. *RILM* 77 5804. *RILM* 78 4044.

284.   Lay, J. E. "A Music Realization by Hybrid Computer." Paper presented at the 48th Convention of the Audio Engineering Society, May 7-10, 1974, Los Angeles.

285.   Layzer, Arthur. "The Digital Computer: Orchestra or Composer's Assistant?" *Creative Computing* 3 (Mar.-Apr. 1977): 90.

286.   Ledley, Robert S. *Programming and Utilizing Digital Computers.* New York: McGraw-Hill, 1962. 568 p.

287.   Lefkoff, Gerald. "Tuned Cyclic Tone Systems." In *Proceedings of the 1978 International Computer Music Conference,* comp. Curtis Roads. Evanston, Ill.: Northwestern University Press, 1979: 225-50.

288. Leitner, P. *Logische Programme für automatische Musik.* Vienna: Staatsprüfungsarbeit an der Technischen Hochschule, 1957.

289. Lerdahl, Fred, and Yves Potard. "L'aiuto del computer alla composizione." [Computer Aid to Composition] Paper presented at the 1982 International Computer Music Conference, Sept. 27–Oct. 1, Venice.

290. Levine, Steven. "Computer Music and the Human Interface: Imbedding Performance Knowledge at the Graphics Level." In *Proceedings, 4th Symposium on Small Computers in the Arts, October 25–28, 1984, Philadelphia, Pennsylvania.* Silver Spring, Md.: IEEE Computer Society Press, 1984: 103–13.
C&CA 20 (1985): 17291.

291. Levitt, David A. "A Melody Description System for Jazz Improvisation." M.S. thesis, Massachusetts Institute of Technology, Dept. of Electrical Engineering and Computer Science, 1981. 47 p.

292. Lewin, David. "An Interesting Global Rule for Species Counterpoint." *In Theory Only* 6 (Mar. 1983): 19–44.

293. Lidov, David, and A. James Gabura. "A Melody Writing Algorithm Using a Formal Language Model." *Computer Studies in the Humanities and Verbal Behavior* 4 (1973): 138–48.
C&CA 11 (1976): 9399. *CR* 17 (1976): 29,921.

294. Lima, Cândido. "Réflexions sur l'intuition et la rationalité en composition musicale: éléments pour une nouvelle pédagogie." Thèse pour le Doctorat de 3ème cycle, Université de Paris I, 1982. 359 p.

295. Lindblom, Björn, and Johan Sundberg. "Datorkomponerad musik." [Computer-Composed Music] *S71 Matematik och datorer i sprak- tal- och musik-forskning 1973/74.* Stockholm: Skriptor, 1973.

296. ———, and Johan Sundberg. "Music Composed by a Computer Program." *Speech Transmission Laboratory Quarterly Progress and Status Report* 4 (1972): 20–28.
RILM 72 2466.

297. Lorrain, Denis. *Une panoplie de canons stochastiques.* Paris: IRCAM, 1980. 74 p. (Rapports IRCAM 30/80)
English version: "A Panoply of Stochastic 'Canons'." *Computer Music Journal* 4,1 (Spring 1980): 53–81.
C&CA 16 (1981): 18377. *C&IS* 26 (1981): 263662C.

298. Loy, D. Gareth. "The Composer Seduced into Programming." *Perspectives of New Music* 19 (Fall-Winter 1980/Spring-Summer 1981): 184–98.

299. Lyon, Marjorie. "A Third Medium for the Music Composer: Computers." *Technology Review* 82 (Nov. 1979): 86–88.
Also in *Creative Computing* 6 (June 1980): 64–65.
C&CA 16 (1981): 3168.

300. MacDonald, Neil. "Music by Automatic Computers." *Computers and Automation* 7 (Mar. 1958): 8–9.

301.   Machover, Tod. "Le compositeur et l'ordinateur: quelques réflexions." In *Le compositeur et l'ordinateur.* Paris: IRCAM, 1981: 1–5.

302.   ———. "Thoughts on Computer Music Composition." In *Composers and the Computer,* ed. Curtis Roads. Los Altos, Calif.: W. Kaufmann, 1985: 90–111.

303.   ———; Stephen E. McAdams; Xavier Rodet; Marco Stroppa; and David L. Wessel. "Ideas about Timbre and Composition." In *Atti del Quinto Colloquio di Informatica Musicale.* Ancona: Università di Ancona, 1983: 146–55.

304.   Maconie, Robin, and Chris Cunningham. "Computers Unveil the Shape of Melody." *New Scientist* 94 (Apr. 22, 1982): 206–9.

305.   Mailliard, Bénédict. "Un studio numérique de travail sur le son." In *Le compositeur et l'ordinateur.* Paris: IRCAM, 1981: 38–45.

306.   Malherbe, Claudy; Gérard Assayag; and Michèle Castellegno. "Functional Integration of Complex Instrumental Sounds in Musical Writing." In *Proceedings of the International Computer Music Conference, 1985,* ed. Barry Truax. San Francisco, Calif.: Computer Music Association, 1985: 185–92.

307.   Malouf, Frederick L. "A System for Interactive Music Composition through Computer Graphics." D.A. diss., Ball State University, 1985.

308.   ———. "A System for Interactive Music Composition through Computer Graphics." In *Proceedings of the International Computer Music Conference, 1985,* ed. Barry Truax. San Francisco, Calif.: Computer Music Association, 1985: 225–32.
       A condensed version of the author's dissertation.

309.   Manning, Peter D. "Computers and Music Composition." *Proceedings of the Royal Musical Association* 107 (1980–1981): 119–31.

310.   Manoury, Philippe. "Natural and Artificial Compositional Processes." Paper presented at the 1984 International Computer Music Conference, Oct. 19–23, Paris, France.

311.   ———. "L'unificazione del pensiero sonologico e di quello organizzativo nella computer music." [The Unification of Sonic and Organizational Thought in Computer Music] Paper presented at the 1982 International Computer Music Conference, Sept. 27–Oct. 1, Venice.

312.   Mashayeki, Alireza, and Dary J. Mizelle. *Compositional Programming I: XPL Programming Techniques.* Hawthorne, N.Y.: Sonavera, 1979. 65 p.

313.   Mathews, Max V. "Computer Composers—Comments and Case Histories." *Page* 1 (Feb. 1970): 1.

314.   Matthews, Justus F. "Music 3150, A FORTRAN Program for Composing Music for Conventional Instruments." In *Proceedings of the 1978 International Computer Music Conference,* comp. Curtis Roads. Evanston, Ill.: Northwestern University Press, 1979: 251–71.

315. Matthews, Michael. "Algorithms for Harmonic Pitch Structure Generation." In *Proceedings, 1981 International Computer Music Conference, November 5–8*, comp. Larry Austin and Thomas Clark. Denton, Tex.: North Texas State University, 1983: 110–17.

316. McMorrow, Clyde H. "Concerning Music and Computer Composition in Computational Linguistics." *Communications of the Association for Computing Machinery* 16 (May 1973): 313.

317. Meinecke, Jon. "Stochastic Melody Writing Procedures: An Analysis Based Approach." In *Proceedings, 1981 International Computer Music Conference, November 5–8*, comp. Larry Austin and Thomas Clark. Denton, Tex.: North Texas State University, 1983: 118–32.

318. Melby, John. "Compositional Approaches to the Combination of Live Performers with Computer-Produced Tape." Paper presented at the International Conference on Computer Music, October 28–31, 1976, Massachusetts Institute of Technology.

319. ———. "Layers." *Bollettino LIMB* 2 (1982): 114–17.

320. Melzi, Giovanni, and Vito Ozzola. "Hardware e software per la composizione automatica in tempo reale." [Hardware and Software Oriented to Real Time Automatic Composition] In *Aspetti Teorici di Informatica Musicale*. Milan: CTU-Istituto di Cibernetica, Università di Milano, 1977: 72–79.

321. ———, and Vito Ozzola. "Una teoria neurale della musica e tecniche compositive derivate." [A Neural Theory of Music and Derived Composition Techniques] In *Proceedings of the Venice 1982 International Computer Music Conference*, comp. Thom Blum and John Strawn. San Francisco, Calif.: Computer Music Association, 1985: 719–21.

322. Metze, G., and J. Bauknight. "Magical Music Maker: A Four-Part Music-Making Program for the Illiac II." Mimeographed. Urbana: University of Illinois Digital Computer Laboratory File No. 609, 12 July 1964.

323. Mian, Gianantonio, and Graziano Tisato. "Composizione musicale e trattamento numerico della voce." [Musical Composition and Digital Voice Processing] *Bollettino LIMB* 4 (1984): 49–67.

324. Mikulska, Małgorzata. "Computer-Aided Composition: An Example." In *Proceedings, Symposium on Small Computers in the Arts, November 20–22, 1981, Philadelphia, Pennsylvania*. New York, N.Y.: IEEE, 1981: 15–18. *C&CA* 17 (1982): 19784.

325. ———. "Some Remarks on Computer-Assisted Composition." In *Proceedings, 1981 International Computer Music Conference, November 5–8*, comp. Thom Blum and John Strawn. Denton, Tex.: North Texas State University, 1983: 57–71.

326. Milani, Mario. *N-Tone Systems And Symmetrical Series*. Pisa: CNUCE, 1976. 23 p.

327. Minoli, Daniel. "A Stochastic Automata Approach to Computer Music." In *International Electrical, Electronics Conference & Exposition, Toronto, Canada, 5–7 Oct. 1981.* Don Mills, Ont.: IEEE, 1981: 180–81. *C&CA* 17 (1982): 32056.

328. Moles, Abraham A. "La musique algorithmique, première musique calculée." *Revue du son* 93 (Jan. 1961): 28–29.

329. Moog, Robert A. "On Synthesizers: Wendy Carlos on Computers." *Keyboard* 8 (Dec. 1982): 64.

330. ———. "Wendy Carlos: New Directions for a Synthesizer Pioneer." *Keyboard* 9 (Nov. 1982): 51–52, 58–63.
Reprinted in *The Art of Electronic Music,* comp. Tom Darter, ed. Greg Armbruster. New York: W. Morrow, 1984: 294–303.

331. Moorer, James A. "Music and Computer Composition." *Communications of the Association for Computing Machinery* 15 (1972): 104–13.
Comment by Stephen W. Smoliar: p. 1000–1001.
Reply by J. A. Moorer: p. 1001.
C&IS 11: 73477C.

332. Morton, Ian A., and John Lofstedt. "FORTRAN Music Programs Involving Numerically Related Tones." In *The Computer and Music,* ed. Harry B. Lincoln. Ithaca: Cornell University Press, 1970: 154–62.

333. Mullmann, Bernd. "Computer als Helfer in der Musik." *Neue Zeitschrift für Musik* 134 (1973): 232–33.

334. Myhill, Jim. "Controlled Indeterminacy: A First Step Towards a Semi-stochastic Music Language." *Computer Music Journal* 3,3 (Sept. 1979): 12–14.
Reprinted in *Foundations of Computer Music,* ed. Curtis Roads and John Strawn. Cambridge, Mass.: MIT Press, 1985: 581–87.
C&CA 15 (1980): 14087.

335. ———. "Some Simplifications and Improvements in the Stochastic Music Language." In *Proceedings of the 1978 International Computer Music Conference,* comp. Curtis Roads. Evanston, Ill.: Northwestern University Press, 1979: 272–317.

336. Nelson, Gary. "Reflections on my Use of Computers in Composition." In *Proceedings of the 1978 International Computer Music Conference,* comp. Curtis Roads. Evanston, Ill.: Northwestern University Press, 1979: 318–31.

337. Neumann, P. G., and H. Schappert. "Komponieren mit elektronischen Rechenautomaten." *Nachrichtentechnische Zeitschrift* 12 (1959): 403–7.
Abstract in *Annales des telecommunications* 14 (1959): 1364.

338. Newby, Kenneth. "A Low Cost Computer Music System for Realtime Composition." Paper presented at the 1984 International Computer Music Conference, Oct. 19–23, Paris, France.

339. Newcomb, B. "Arranging, Transposing with Computers." *The Songwriter's Review* 34,3 (1979): 6–7.

340. Olson, Harry F., and Herbert Belar. "Aid to Music Composition Employing a Random Probability System." *Journal of the Acoustical Society of America* 33 (1961): 1163–70. Comment by J. Murray Barbour: Vol. 34 (1962): 128–29.

341. Ozzola, Vito. "Software per composizioni seriali." [Software for Serial Compositions] In *Atti del Quarto Colloquio di Informatica Musicale*. Pisa: CNUCE-CNR, 1981: 76–85.

342. ———; Giovanni Melzi; and Azio Corghi. "Experiments in Stochastic Approximation of Musical Language." In *Musical Grammars and Computer Analysis,* ed. M. Baroni and L. Callegari. Florence: L. S. Olschki, 1984: 325–27. (Quaderni della rivista Italiana di musicologia 8)

343. Paccagnini, A. "Composizione elettronica: esperienze e spigolature didattiche." [Electronic Composition: Experiences and Teaching Gleanings] In *Musica ed elaboratore elettronico. Verso il musicale personale.* Milan: FAST, 1980.

344. Papadia, Loreto. "Analisi di una procedura per la realizzazione di una composizione mediante sintesi digitale." [Analysis of a Procedure for the Realisation of a Composition by Means of Digital Synthesis] In *Atti del Terzo Colloquio di Informatica Musicale,* ed. G. De Poli. Padua: Università di Padova, 1979: 261–70.

345. Parish, Brian. "A Practical Interactive Input Formatting Facility for MUSIC4BF." In *Proceedings of the International Music and Technology Conference, August 24–28, 1981, University of Melbourne.* Parkville, Vic.: Computer Music Project, Dept. of Computer Science, University of Melbourne, 1981: 120–33.

346. Pasquale, Joseph C. "A Musical Development and Performance System for Games." M.S. thesis, Massachusetts Institute of Technology, Dept. of Electrical Engineering and Computer Science, 1982. 490 p.

347. Petersen, Tracy L. "Interactive Digital Composition." In *Proceedings of the 1978 International Computer Music Conference,* comp. Curtis Roads. Evanston, Ill.: Northwestern University Press, 1979: 167–74.

348. Philippot, Michel P. "Musique et informatique." In *Révolutions informatiques.* Paris: Union Générale d'éditions, 1972: 373–86.

349. Poindron, Jacques. "Une fonction LISP qui fait des canons." *Artinfo/musinfo* 19 (1974): 31–34.

350. Polansky, Larry, and David Rosenboom. "HMSL (Hierarchical Music Specification Language): A Real-Time Environment for Formal, Perceptual, and Compositional Experimentation." In *Proceedings of the International Computer Music Conference, 1985,* ed. Barry Truax. San Francisco, Calif.: Computer Music Association, 1985: 243–50.

351. Potter, Gary M. "The Role of Chance in Contemporary Music." Ph. D. diss., Indiana University, 1971. 185 p.
DA 32:5273A.

352. "Les principes de composition de la musique algorithmique par des ensembles à traiter l'information." *Electro-calcul* 4 (Mar./Apr. 1962): 19–26.

353. Prusinkiewica, Przemyslaw. "Time Management in Interactive Score Editors." In *Proceedings of the International Computer Music Conference, 1984,* ed. William Buxton. San Francisco, Calif.: Computer Music Association, 1985: 275–80.

354. Pulfer, James K. "Computer Aid for Musical Composers." *Bulletin of the Radio and Electrical Engineering Division* [National Research Council of Canada] 20 (Apr. 1970): 44–48.

355. ———. "The Computer as an Aid to the Composition and Production of Commercial Music." Paper presented at the 42nd Convention of the Audio Engineering Society, May 2–5, 1972, Los Angeles.

356. ———. "Man-Machine Interaction in Creative Applications." *International Journal of Man-Machine Studies* 3 (1971): 1–11.

357. Radauer, Irmfried. "Computer-Komposition." *Melos/Neue Zeitschrift für Musik* 41 (1974): 278–86.

358. Rader, Gary M. "An Algorithm for the Automatic Composition of Simple Forms of Music Based on a Variation of Formal Grammars." Philadelphia: Moore School, University of Pennsylvania, 1973. 98 p. (Report no. 73–09)

359. ———. "The Formal Composition of Music." Ife, Nigeria: Dept. of Computer Science, University of Ife, 1977. (Technical Report no. 77–1)

360. ———. "A Method for Composing Simple Traditional Music by Computer." *Communications of the Association for Computing Machinery* 17 (1974): 631–38.
Review by Michael Kassler in *Computing Reviews* 16 (1975): 27,937.
CA 19 (1975): 293. *C&CA* 10 (1975): 7300.

361. Raeburn, Paul. "Vox Machina: The Music of the Machine." *Technology Review* 80 (May 1978): 10–11.
C&IS 19 (1978): 20185C.

362. Rampazzi, Teresa. "Mutamenti della concezione formale nel passaggio dai mezzi analogici a quelli digitali." [Changes in Formal Conception when Passing from Analog Electronic Instruments to Digital] In *Atti del Terzo Colloquio di Informatica Musicale,* ed. G. DePoli. Padua: Università di Padova, 1979: 44–49.

363. Randall, J. K. "Operations on Waveforms." In *Music by Computers,* ed. Heinz von Foerster and James W. Beauchamp. New York: Wiley, 1969: 122–28.
This is the third of the "Three Lectures" of item 52.

364. Renard, Jean. "Future Computing: Cinema Music by the Numbers." *Personal Computing* 1 (July/Aug. 1977): 122–27.

365. Riotte, André. "Un automate musical construit à partir d'une courte pièce de Bela Bartok." *Informatique et sciences humaines* 45 (Juin 1980): 25–36.

366. ———. "Génération des series équilibrées." Rapport interne EURATOM no. 353, Jan. 1963.

367. Risset, Jean-Claude. "Computer Synthesis of Sound Applied to Composition with Sonic Processes." In *Proceedings of the Venice 1982 International Computer Music Conference,* comp. Thom Blum and John Strawn. San Francisco, Calif.: Computer Music Association, 1985: 350–53.

368. ———. "Digital Techniques and Sound Structure in Music." In *Composers and the Computer,* ed. Curtis Roads. Los Altos, Calif.: W. Kaufmann, 1985: 114–38.

369. ———. "Stochastic Processes in Music and Art." In *Stochastic Processes in Quantum Theory and Statistical Physics,* ed. S. Albeverio, P. H. Combe, and M. Sirugue-Collin. Berlin: Springer-Verlag, 1982: 281–88. (Lecture Notes in Physics 173)

370. Roads, Curtis, ed. *Composers and the Computer.* Los Altos, Calif.: W. Kaufmann, 1985. 201 p. (The Computer Music and Digital Audio Series)
Contains items: 208, 302, 368, 372, 374, 376, 442, 496, 568.
Review by H. Wiley Hitchock in *Computer Music Journal* 10,1 (Spring 1986): 99–100.

371. ———. "Composing Grammars." Paper presented at the 1977 International Computer Music Conference, University of California, San Diego, 26–30 October 1977.

372. ———. "Improvisation with George Lewis." In *Composers and the Computer,* ed. Curtis Roads. Los Altos, Calif.: W. Kaufmann, 1985: 76–87.

373. ———. "Interactive Orchestration Based on Score Analysis." In *Proceedings of the Venice 1982 International Computer Music Conference,* comp. Thom Blum and John Strawn. San Francisco, Calif.: Computer Music Association, 1985: 703–17.

374. ———. "Interview with James Dashow." In *Composers and the Computer,* ed. Curtis Roads. Los Altos, Calif.: W. Kaufmann, 1985: 28–45.

375. ———. "IT: An Intelligent Composer's Assistant: A Proposal for a Knowledge-based System." Cambridge, Mass.: Massachusetts Institute of Technology, 1981. 104 p.

376. ———. "John Chowning on Composition." In *Composers and the Computer,* ed. Curtis Roads. Los Altos, Calif.: W. Kaufmann, 1985: 18–25.

377. ———. "Preliminary Report on the CME Composing Language Project." La Jolla, Calif.: Center for Music Experiment, University of California at San Diego, 1977. 59 p.

378. ———. "A Systems Approach to Composition." B.A. thesis, University of California, San Diego, 1976. 110 p.

379. ———. "Using Compositional Procedures." Toronto, Ont.: SSSP, Computer Systems Research Group, University of Toronto, 1979. 7 p.

380. Roberts, Seven K. "Music Composition: A New Technique." *Creative Computing* 5 (Feb. 1979): 42–43.
      C&CA 14 (1979): 25003. *C&IS* 23 (1979): 219782C.

381. ———. "Polyphony Made Easy." *BYTE* 4 (Jan. 1979): 104–109.
      Also in *The BYTE Book of Computer Music,* ed. Christopher P. Morgan. Peterborough, N.H.: BYTE Books, 1979: 117–20.
      C&IS 23 (1979): 219062C.

382. Rosler, Lawrence. "The Graphic–1 7094 Graphical Interaction System and the GRIN94 Language." Murray Hill, N.J.: Bell Telephone Laboratories.

383. Rothenberg, David. "A Language for Musical Composition and Analysis." Rutgers University, 1974.

384. ———. "A Nonprocedural Language for Music Composition." In *Proceedings of the Second Annual Music Computation Conference, November 7–9, 1975, at the University of Illinois at Urbana-Champaign. Part 2, Composition with Computers,* comp. James Beauchamp and John Melby. Urbana, Ill.: University of Illinois: 37–67.

385. Rothgeb, John E. "Harmonizing the Unfigured Bass: A Computational Study." Ph. D. diss., Yale University, 1968. 237 p.
      DA 30:1197A.

386. Rowe, Neil C. "Move Over Bach, Beethoven, and Brahms: Composing Music Through Computers." *Recreational Computing* 9 (Jan.-Feb. 1981): 49–51, 54–55.
      C&CA 16 (1981): 18382. *C&IS* 28 (1982): 81–10178C.

387. Saalfeld, Richard E. "An Interactive System for Computer-Aided Composition and Sound Synthesis." Ph. D. diss., Ohio State University, 1977. 373 p.
      DA 38:4442A-3A. *RILM* 78 1877.

388. Saariaho, Kaija. "Shaping a Compositional Network with Computer." In *Proceedings of the International Computer Music Conference, 1984,* ed. William Buxton. San Francisco, Calif.: Computer Music Association, 1985: 163–65.

389. Schaefer, Richard A. "Digital Generation of Equal Temperament." *IEEE Transactions on Acoustics, Speech, and Signal Processing,* Vol. ASSP-23 (1975): 329–33.

390. Schottstaedt, Bill. "Automatic Species Counterpoint." Stanford, Calif.: Center for Computer Research in Music and Acoustics, Stanford University, 1984. 35 p.

391. Schwartz, Elliott. *Electronic Music: A Listener's Guide.* New York: Praeger, 1973. 306 p.
Review by Fredrick Geissler in *Notes* 30 (1974): 531–32.
RILM 73 852.

392. Seay, Albert. "The Composer and the Computer." *Computers and Automation* 13 (Aug. 1964): 16–18.

393. Segre, A. M. "A System for the Generation of Four Voice Chorale Style Counterpoint Using Artificial Intelligence Techniques." In *Atti del Quarto Colloquio di Informatica.* Pisa: CNUCE-CNR, 1981: 231–52.

394. Seirup, John. "TR4P4, A FORTRAN Program Dealing with the Computer Simulation of Traditional Four-Part Harmony." Buffalo, N.Y.: State University of New York, Buffalo, July 1973. 25 p. (Technical Report no. 8)

395. Senn, Dan. "The White Side Program: The Application of Microcomputers to Music Composition Both as a Clerical Tool and as a Generative Device." In *Proceedings, 1981 International Computer Music Conference, November 5–8,* comp. Larry Austin and Thomas Clark. Denton, Tex.: North Texas State University, 1983: 215–24.

396. Severo, Richard. "Composers Program Sense of Humanity into Computer Music." *New York Times* (Mar. 23, 1982): 22(N); C3(LC)

397. Shakeshaft, L. "Composing Music Using a Nova 1210." *Computer Educator* 18 (Nov. 1974): 9–10.
C&CA 10 (1975): 3340.

398. Shmoys, David B. "The Transposition and Composition of Music by Computer." *Creative Computing* 3 (Mar.-Apr. 1977): 100.
C&CA 12 (1977): 23190.

399. Sica, G. "Cantata (ex machina)." [Cantata (ex machina)] In *Atti del Quinto Colloquio di Informatica Musicale.* Ancona: Università di Ancona, 1983: 195–96.

400. Siddall, J. C., and J. N. Siddall. "New Developments in Stochastic Music Composition." Paper presented at the 1977 International Computer Music Conference, University of California, San Diego, 26–30 October 1977.

401. Singer, Neil D. "Generating Improvised Music with Algorithms." B.S. thesis, Massachusetts Institute of Technology, Dept. of Electrical Engineering, 1973. 94 p.

402. Smith, Leland. "The 'SCORE' Program for Musical Input to Computers." In *Proceedings of the 1980 International Computer Music Conference,* comp. Hubert S. Howe. San Francisco, Calif.: Computer Music Association, 1982: 226–30.

403. Sowa, J. R. "A Machine to Compose Music." In *Geniac Manual.* New York: O. Eafield, 1964.

404.   Spiegel, Laurie. "Manipulations of Musical Patterns." In *Proceedings, Symposium on Small Computers in the Arts, November 20–22, 1981, Philadelphia, Pennsylvania.* New York, N.Y.: IEEE, 1981: 19–22.
        C&CA 17 (1982): 19785.

405.   Spurgeon, C. Paul. "Copyright and the Composer." *Canadian Composer* n176 (Dec. 1982): 8–11, 16–17.

406.   Stadlen, Peter. "When Computer Turns Composer." *Daily Telegraph* (Aug. 10, 1963): 11.

407.   Stockhausen, Karlheinz. "Elektronische Musik und Automatik." *Melos* 32 (1965): 337–44.

408.   Stoney, William. "Theoretical Possibilities for Equally Tempered Musical Systems." In *The Computer and Music,* ed. Harry B. Lincoln. Ithaca: Cornell University Press, 1970: 163–71.

409.   Strang, Gerald. "The Computer in Musical Composition." *Computers and Automation* 15 (Aug. 1966): 16–17.
        Also in *Cybernetic Serendipity,* ed. Jasia Reichardt. New York: Praeger, 1969: 26–28.

410.   Stroe, Aurel. "Compoziţii şi clase de compoziţii." [Composition and Classes of Composition] *Muzica* 21 (June 1971): 14–17.
        In Romanian.
        RILM 72 1097.

411.   Sundberg, Johan; Anders Askenfelt; and Lars Frydén. "Musical Performance: A Synthesis-by-Rule Approach." *Computer Music Journal* 7,1 (Spring 1983): 37–43.
        C&CA 18 (1983): 32104.

412.   Sutcliffe, Alan. "Examples of the Use of Computers in Music." In *Computers in the Creative Arts (A Studyguide),* ed. J. D. Lomax. Manchester: National Computing Centre, 1973: 37–44.

413.   "Syncopation by Automation." *Data from Electrodata* (Aug. 1956): 2–3.

414.   Tadeusiewicz, Ryszard, and Aleksander Sodo. "Kompozycje muzyczne z komputera." [Computer-Generated Musical Works] *Problemy* 12 (Dec. 1979): 25–30.
        In Polish.
        RILM 79 5669.

415.   Tamburini, Alessandro. "Le possibilita del computer nel procedimento musicale." [What Computers Can Do in Musical Processes] *Strumenti musicali* 49 (1984): 81–85.

416.   Tanner, Peter. *MUSICOMP, An Experimental Aid for the Composition and Production of Music.* Ottawa: National Research Council, Radio and Electrical Engineering Division, 1972. (ERB-869)

417. ———. *Some Programs for the Computer Generation of Polyphonic Music.* Ottawa: National Research Council, Electrical Engineering Division, 1972. (ERB-862)

418. Tänzer, Peter, and Erich Neumann. "Computer machen Musik." *Neue Zeitschrift für Musik* 130 (1969): 360–62.

419. Tarabella, Leonello. "A μ-Processor-Based System for Music Composition and Production." In *Proceedings of the Venice 1982 International Computer Music Conference,* comp. Thom Blum and John Strawn. San Francisco, Calif.: Computer Music Association, 1985: 154–61.

420. Tenney, James. "Musical Composition with the Computer." Abstract in *Journal of the Acoustical Society of America* 39 (1966): 1245.

421. Tew, M. L. "Interval Combinations, Predetermined by Computer, as the Harmonic Basis of Contemporary Music." *The Composer* [U.S.] 1 (1969–70): 157–64.

422. Thomas, Marilyn Taft. "Vivace: A Rule Based AI System for Composition." In *Proceedings of the International Computer Music Conference, 1985,* ed. Barry Truax. San Francisco, Calif.: Computer Music Association, 1985: 267–74.

423. Thostenson, Marvin S. "Scales." *Creative Computing* 3 (Mar-Apr 1977): 112. *C&CA* 12 (1977): 23192.

424. Tipei, Sever. "MP1: A Computer Program for Music Composition." In *Proceedings of the Second Annual Music Computation Conference, November 7–9, 1975, at the University of Illinois at Urbana-Champaign. Part 2, Composition with Computers,* comp. James Beauchamp and John Melby. Urbana, Ill.: University of Illinois: 68–82.

425. ———. "Solving Specific Compositional Problems with MP1." In *Proceedings, 1981 International Computer Music Conference, November 5–8.* Denton, Tex.: North Texas State University, 1983: 101–9.

426. Tramontini, A. "Il microelaboratore nella composizione musicale." [The Microcomputer in Musical Composition] *Bit* [Milan] 6 (1980): 103–10.

427. Treble, D. P. "Computers and Composition in Change Ringing." *Computer Journal* 13 (1970): 350–51.

428. Truax, Barry D. "The Compositional Organization of Timbre in a Binaural Space." In *Proceedings of the Rochester 1983 International Computer Music Conference,* comp. Robert W. Gross. San Francisco, Calif.: Computer Music Association, 1984: 262–69.

429. ———. "Models of Interactive Composition with the DMX-1000 Digital Signal Processor." In *Proceedings of the International Computer Music Conference, 1984,* ed. William Buxton. San Francisco, Calif.: Computer Music Association, 1985: 173–78.

430.   ———, and Jerry Barenholtz. "Models of Interactive Computer Composition." In *Computing in the Humanities: Proceedings of the Third International Conference on Computing in the Humanities,* ed. Serge Lusignan and John S. North. Waterloo, Ont.: The University of Waterloo Press, 1977: 209–19. *C&IS* 17 185337C.

431.   Ulrich, John Wade. "The Analysis and Synthesis of Jazz by Computer." In *5th International Joint Conference on Artificial Intelligence, 1977: Proceedings of the Conference.* Pittsburgh, Pa.: Dept. of Computer Science, Carnegie-Mellon University, 1977: 865–72.

432.   Vidolin, Alvise. "Alcune considerazione sulla formalizzazione dei processi compositivi." [Some Considerations on the Formalization of Compositional Procedures] In *Atti del Terzo Colloquio di Informatica Musicale,* ed. G. DePoli. Padua: Università di Padova, 1979: 211–23.

433.   ———. "Interazione fra i livelli di rappresentazione dell'informazione musicale nella composizione mediante elaboratore." [Interaction Among the Representation Levels of Musical Data in Computer Music Composition] *Automazione e strumentazione* 28 (Feb. 1980): 144–50. *C&CA* 15 (1980): 27744.

434.   Wesley-Smith, Martin. "Computer-Aided Audio-Visual Composition." In *Proceedings of the International Music and Technology Conference, August 24–28, 1981, University of Melbourne.* Parkville, Vic.: Computer Music Project, Dept. of Computer Science, University of Melbourne, 1981: 194–210.

435.   Whitney, John. "The Arts: Video." *Omni* 3 (Oct. 1980): 24, 154.

436.   "Will a Machine Compose a New Symphony?" *The School Musician* 31 (Jan. 1960): 59.

437.   Wilson, Don. "Will the Computer Replace the Composer?" *American Music Teacher* 33,2 (1983): 49.

438.   Wilson, Jack. "Music Composition by Analysis." *Creative Computing* 6 (Feb. 1980): 120–25.

439.   Wilson, Sven. "Kan datamaskinen vara tonsättare?" [Can the Computer Be a Composer?] *Nutida musik* 12 (1968–69): 48–49. In Swedish.

440.   Xenakis, Iannis. "Les chemins de la composition musicale." In *Le compositeur et l'ordinateur.* Paris: IRCAM, 1981: 13–32.

441.   ———. "Migrazioni nella composizione musicale." [Migrations in Music Composition] In *Musica e elaboratore.* Venice: Biennale di Venezia, 1980: 113–27.

442.   ———. "Music Composition Treks." In *Composers and the Computer,* ed. Curtis Roads. Los Altos, Calif.: W. Kaufmann, 1985: 172–92.

443.   ———. *Musiques formelles*. Paris: Editions Richard-Masse, 1963. 232 p. Published as *La revue musicale* 253–54 (1963).
English version, expanded: *Formalized Music*. Bloomington: Indiana University Press, 1971. 271 p.
One chapter, "Musique stochastic libre, a l'ordinateur," also appears in English and German in *Gravesaner Blätter* 26 (1965): 54–92, and in English, in *Cybernetics, Art, and Ideas,* ed. Jasia Reichardt. London: Studio Vista, 1971: 124–42.

444.   ———. *Musiques formelles: nouveaux principes formels de composition musicale.* Paris: Stock Musique, 1981. 260 p.

445.   ———. "Principali problemi riguardante la composizione musicale." [Peak Problems in Musical Composition and the Use of Computers] Paper presented at the 1982 International Computer Music Conference, Sept. 27–Oct. 1, Venice.

446.   Yunik, M., and G. W. Swift. "Tempered Music Scales for Sound Synthesis." *Computer Music Journal* 4,4 (Winter 1980): 60–65.
C&CA 16 (1981): 36848. *C&IS* 28 (1982): 81–16038C.

447.   Zaplitny, Michael. "Conversation with Iannis Xenakis." *Perspectives of New Music* 14 (Fall/Winter 1975): 86–103.

448.   Zaripov, Rudolf K. "Modelirovanie melodicheskikh variatsiĭ na ÉVM." [Computer Modeling of Melodic Variations] *Problemy Bioniki* 24 (1980): 8–15.
In Russian.
C&CA 16 (1981): 33990.

449.   ———. "Modelirovanie melodicheskikh variatsiĭ na tsifrovoĭ vychislitel'noĭ mashine." [Modeling Melodic Variations on a Digital Computer] *Problemy Kibernetiki* 40 (1983): 201–54.
In Russian.
C&CA 18 (1983): 43939.

450.   ———. "Modelirovanie transpozitsiĭ invariantnykh otnosheniĭ i muzykal'nykh variatsiĭ na vychislitel'noi mashine." [Computer Simulation of the Transposition of Invariant Relationships in Musical Variations] *Kybernetica* 9 (1973): 400–421.
In Russian.

451.   ———. *Musica con il calcolatore*. [Music with Computers] Padua: F. Muzzio, 1979.

452.   ———. "O programirovanyii processza szocsinyenyija." [About the Programmed Process of Composition] *Problemy Kibernetiki* 7 (1962): 151–60.
In Russian.

453.   ———. "On an Algorithmic Description of the Process Involved in the Composition of Music." *Automation Express* 3 (Nov. 1960): 17–19.
Russian version in *Doklady Akademiia Nauk SSSR* 132 (1960): 1283–86.

454. Zieliński, Gerard. *Komputer symulacja komponowania muzyki.* [Computer Simulation of Musical Composition] Warsaw: Centrum Obliczeniowe Polskiej Akademii Nauk, 1970. 18 p.
In Polish; summaries in English and Russian.
RILM 73 1386.

COMPOSITIONS

455. "256 Machines in Concert of Computer-Programmed Music." *Billboard* 81 (May 17, 1969): 63.

456. Ames, Charles. "About *Gradient.*" In *Proceedings of the Venice 1982 International Computer Music Conference,* comp. Thom Blum and John Strawn. San Francisco, Calif.: Computer Music Association, 1985: 722–49.

457. ———. "*Crystals:* Recursive Structures in Automated Composition." *Computer Music Journal* 6,3 (Fall 1982): 46–64.
C&CA 18 (1983): 7234. *C&IS* 31 (1983): 83–422C.

458. ———. "*Crystals:* Recursive Structures in Computer Music Composition." In *Proceedings of the 1980 International Computer Music Conference,* comp. Hubert S. Howe. San Francisco, Calif.: Computer Music Association, 1982: 614–43.

459. ———. "Notes on *Undulant.*" *Interface* 12 (1983): 505–23.
C&CA 19 (1984): 14745. *E&EA* 87 (1984): 16818.

460. ———. "*Protocol:* Motivation, Design, and Implementation of a Computer-Assisted Composition for Solo Piano." In *Proceedings, 1981 International Computer Music Conference, November 5–8,* comp. Larry Austin and Thomas Clark. Denton, Tex.: North Texas State University, 1983: 133–57.

461. ———. "*Protocol:* Motivation, Design, and Production of a Composition for Solo Piano." *Interface* 11 (1982): 213–38.
C&CA 18 (1983): 36172.

462. ———. "Stylistic Automata in *Gradient.*" *Computer Music Journal* 7,4 (Winter 1983): 45–56.
Italian version: "Automatismi stilistici di *Gradient.*" *Bollettino LIMB* 3 (1983): 11–19.
C&CA 19 (1984): 19379. *C&IS* 32 (1984): 84–6918C. *E&EA* 87 (1984): 21935.

463. ————. "*Undulant* for Seven Instruments." Ph. D. diss., State University of New York at Buffalo, 1984. 150 p.
DA 45:336A.

464. Armbruster, Greg. "*Ripples.*" *Computer Music Journal* 1,3 (June 1977): 40–47.
RILM 77 3705.

465. Austin, Larry. "*Caritas.*" *Source* 8,4 (1970): 42.

466. ————. "*HPSCHD.*" *Source* 4 (July 1968): 10–29.
Also appears in Lejaren A. Hiller. "Computer Programs Used to Produce the Composition *HPSCHD.*" Buffalo: National Science Foundation Project No. GK–14191, Aug. 1972: 205–13. (Technical Report no. 4)
Swedish version in *Nutida musik* 13,4 (1969–70): 16–25.

467. ————. "Phantasmagoria: A Chronicle of Computer-Assisted Composition/ Performance." In *Proceedings of the Venice 1982 International Computer Music Conference,* comp. Thom Blum and John Strawn. San Francisco, Calif.: Computer Music Association, 1985: 610–12.

468. Baggiani, Guido. "'Senza Voci': Between Analog and Digital Composition." In *Computer Music/Composition musicale par ordinateur; Report on an International Project Including a Workshop at Aarhus, Denmark in 1978,* ed. Marc Battier and Barry Truax. Ottawa: Canadian Commission for Unesco, 1980: 48–62.

469. Barbaud, Pierre. *Initiation à la composition musicale automatique.* Paris: Dunod, 1966. 106 p.

470. Barlow, Clarence. "Bus Journey to Parametron (All About *Coḡluotobüsisletmesi*)." *Feedback Papers* 21–23 (1980): 1–124.

471. ————. "The Making of *Coḡluotobüsisletmesi.*" Paper presented at the 1984 International Computer Music Conference, Oct. 19–23, Paris, France.

472. Barrière, Jean-Baptiste. "'Chréode': The Pathway to New Music with the Computer." *Contemporary Music Review* 1 (Oct. 1984): 181–201.
French version: "'Chréode I': Chemin vers une nouvelle musique avec l'ordinateur." *Musique de notre temps* 1 (Oct. 1984): 195–217.

473. ————. "A Piece for Computer Using CHANT and FORMES." Paper presented at the 1983 International Computer Music Conference, Oct. 7–10, 1983, Rochester, N.Y.

474. Belfiore, Alfonso. "Adattamento per elaboratore elettronico di una composizione per archi: un esperienza al terminale-audio TAU2." [Computer Adaptation of a Composition for Strings: An Experience with the TAU2 Audio-Terminal] In *Atti del Terzo Colloquio di Informatica Musicale,* ed. G. DePoli. Padua: Università di Padova, 1979: 15–35.

475. ————; Pietro Grossi; S. Michi. *Il calcolo combinatorio come strumento di lavoro nella composizione.* [Combinatorial Analysis as a Tool in Composition] Pisa: CNUCE, 1982. 17 p. (Rapporto interno C82-12)

476. Bennett, Gerald. "Journal of a Composition." *Informatique et sciences humaines* 45 (Juin 1980): 51-76.

477. Berg, Paul. "Concerning *I Never Knew You Cared.*" Utrecht, Dec. 1978.

478. ———. "*I Never Knew You Cared.*" *Computer Music Journal* 3,1 (Mar. 1979): 38-41.
Reprinted in *Foundations of Computer Music,* ed. Curtis Roads and John Strawn. Cambridge, Mass.: MIT Press, 1985: 173-79.
C&IS 24 (1980): 230387C.

479. ———. "Over *Locks and Dams.*" Utrecht, Dec. 1978. 4 p.

480. ———. "A Statement Concerning '*Six Loaves to Feed a Family of Five for a Week*'." Utrecht, May 1975. 36 p.

481. Berkeley, Edmund C. *The Computer Revolution.* Garden City: Doubleday, 1962: 170-71.

482. Blum, Thomas L. "*Dihedra.*" S.n.: S.l., 1974. 12 p.

483. ———. "*PHTHONG* for 10 Vocalists and Percussion." 1978. 14 p.

484. Boulanger, Richard. "Interview with Roger Reynolds, Joji Yuasa, and Charles Wuorinen." *Computer Music Journal* 8,4 (Winter 1984): 45-54.

485. Brün, Herbert. "Dust, More Dust, Destiny." In *Computer Music/ Composition musicale par ordinateur; Report on an International Project Including a Workshop at Aarhus, Denmark in 1978,* ed. Marc Battier and Barry Truax. Ottawa: Canadian Commission for Unesco, 1980: 85-86.

486. ———. "*Infraudibles.*" In *Music by Computers,* ed. Heinz von Foerster and James W. Beauchamp. New York: Wiley, 1969: 117-21.

487. ———. "*Sawdust.*" In *Lingua Press Collection Two Catalogue.* La Jolla, Calif.: Lingua Press, 1978.

488. Chadabe, Joel. "*Drum,* an Example of Interactive Composition." Paper presented at the 1982 International Computer Music Conference, Sept. 27–Oct. 1, Venice.

489. Chafe, Chris. "Realization of a Composition at CCRMA." Paper presented at the 1982 International Computer Music Conference, Sept. 27–Oct. 1, Venice.

490. Chailloux, Jerôme. "*KRWTH.*" *Artinfo/musinfo* 20: 1-16.

491. Clementi, Aldo. "Fantasia su roBErto FABbriCiAni." [Fantasia on roBErto FABriCiAni] *Bollettino LIMB* 3 (1983): 35-38.

492. ———. "Parafrasi." [Paraphrase] *Bollettino LIMB* 2 (1982): 78-79.

493. Dashow, James. "Note sul *Piccolo Principe.*" [Remarks on *Little Prince*] *Bollettino LIMB* 2 (1982): 118-28.

494. ———. "Presupposti teorici alla composizione di '*Conditional Assemblies*'." [Theoretical Assumptions to the Composition of '*Conditional Assemblies*'] *Bollettino LIMB* 1 (1981): 60-66.

495.   Dodge, Charles M. "The Composition of *Changes* and Its Computer Performance." D.M.A. diss., Columbia University, 1970. 98 p. *DA* 31:4816A. *RILM* 76 920.

496.   ———. "*In Celebration:* The Composition and Its Realization in Synthetic Speech." In *Composers and the Computer,* ed. Curtis Roads. Los Altos, Calif.: W. Kaufmann, 1985: 48–73.

497.   Dunn, David. "An Expository Journal of Extraction From Wilderness: Notes Toward an Environment Language." In *Proceedings of the International Music and Technology Conference, August 24–28, 1981, University of Melbourne.* Parkville, Vic.: Computer Music Project, Dept. of Computer Science, University of Melbourne, 1981: 16–25.

498.   Englert, Giuseppe G. "FRAGØLA: un instrument de musique et/øu une cømpøsitiøn." *Artinfo/musinfo* 22 (1977): 1–8 (1st group).

499.   Gaburo, Kenneth. "The Deterioration of an Ideal, Ideally Deteriorized: Reflections on Pietro Grossi's *Paganini al Computer.*" *Computer Music Journal* 9,1 (Spring 1985): 39–44.

500.   Gerbrich, Josef; Rudolf Ruzicka; and Jiri Stehlik. "The Computer Musical Compositions in Czechoslovakia." In *Proceedings of the International Computer Music Conference, 1984,* ed. William Buxton. San Francisco, Calif.: Computer Music Association, 1985: 303–9.

501.   Gerso, Andrew. "Reflections on *Répons.*" *Contemporary Music Review* 1 (Oct. 1984): 23–34.
French version: "Réflexions sur *Répons.*" *Musique de notre temps* 1 (Oct. 1984): 25–36.

502.   Gordon, John W. "A Different Drummer." M.A. project, Stanford University, 1974.

503.   Graziani, Mauro. "Esecuzione all'elaboratore di *Parafrasi.*" [Execution at the Computer of *Paraphrase*] *Bollettino LIMB* 2 (1982): 80–81.

504.   Griffiths, Paul. "Three Works by Jonathan Harvey: The Electronic Mirror." *Contemporary Music Review* 1 (Oct. 1984): 87–109.
French version: "Trois oeuvres de Jonathan Harvey: Le miroir électronique." *Musique de notre temps* 1 (Oct. 1984): 93–116.

505.   Grisey, G.; Jean-Baptiste Barrière; and P. F. Basinée. "*Les chants de l'amour,* a Piece for Computer Generated Tape and Mixed Choir." In *Proceedings of the International Computer Music Conference, 1985,* ed. Barry Truax. San Francisco, Calif.: Computer Music Association, 1985: 217–24.

506.   Guttman, N. "Notes on Computer Music Examples." *Gravesaner Blätter* 23–24 (1962): 126–31.
Parallel German and English texts.

507.   Hardy, Charles. "A Concert of Computer Music Reviewed." *Random Bits* 10 (Nov. 1974): 2–4.

508. Harvey, Jonathan. *"Mortuos Plango, Vivos Voco;* a Realization at IRCAM."
Computer Music Journal 5,4 (Winter 1981): 22–24.
C&CA 17 (1982): 32044. *C&IS* 28 (1982): 17303C.

509. ————; Denis Lorrain; Jean-Baptiste Barrière; and Stanley Haynes. "Notes
on the Realization of *Bhakti." Contemporary Music Review* 1 (Oct. 1984):
111–29.
French version: "Notes sur la realisation de *Bhakti." Musique de notre temps* 1
(Oct. 1984): 117–37.

510. Hatley, H. Jerome. *"Eclipse* for Orchestra and Microcomputer Synthesized
Tape." D.M.A. diss., University of Miami, 1984. 68 p.
DA 45:982A.

511. Haynes, Stanley. "Report on the Realization of York Höller's *Arcus." Con-
temporary Music Review* 1 (Oct. 1984): 41–66.
French version: "Rapport sur la réalisation d'*Arcus*, oeuvre de York Höller."
Musique de notre temps 1 (Oct. 1984): 43–68.

512. Henahan, Donald J. "Are We Ready for Computer Operas?" *New York
Times* (July 25, 1982): Sec. 2 pH 15 (N); pH 15–16 (L).

513. ————. "Comments on Classics." *Down Beat* 30 (Apr. 23, 1964): 33.

514. ————. "A Punchcard Cantata." *Chicago Daily News* (Mar. 3, 1964): 19.

515. Hiller, Lejaren A. "Composing the Second Movement of *Algorithms III."*
Buffalo, N.Y.: Experimental Music Studio, State University of New York,
Buffalo, Feb. 1980. 141 p. (Technical Report no. 12)

516. ————. "Composing with Computers: A Progress Report." *Computer Music
Journal* 5,4 (Winter 1981): 7–21.
C&CA 17 (1982): 32043. *C&IS* 28 (1982): 81–17302C.

517. ————. "Computer Programs Used to Produce the Composition
HPSCHD." Mimeographed. Buffalo: National Science Foundation Project
No. GK-14191, Aug. 1972. 236 p. (Technical Report no. 4)

518. ————. "Seven Electronic Studies for Two-Channel Tape Recorded (1963)."
Mimeographed. Urbana: University of Illinois Experimental Music Studio,
May 1963. 73 p. (Technical Report no. 6)

519. ————. "Some Compositional Techniques Involving the Use of Computers."
In *Music by Computers,* ed. Heinz von Foerster and James W. Beauchamp.
New York: Wiley, 1969: 71–83.

520. ————, and Ronald A. Baker. *"Computer Cantata:* A Study in Composition
Using the University of Illinois IBM 7090 and CSX-1 Electronic Digital Com-
puters." Urbana: University of Illinois School of Music Experimental Music
Studio, Oct. 1963. 22 p. (Technical Report no. 8)

521. ————, and Robert A. Baker. *"Computer Cantata:* A Study in Compositional
Method." *Perspectives of New Music* 3 (Fall-Winter 1964): 62–90.

522.   ———, and Robert A. Baker. "Computer Music." In *Computer Applications in the Behavioral Sciences,* ed. Harold Borko. Englewood Cliffs: Prentice-Hall, 1962: 424–51.

523.   ———, and Leonard M. Isaacson. *Experimental Music: Composition with an Electronic Computer.* New York: McGraw-Hill, 1959. 197 p.
Excerpts appear in *The Modeling of Mind,* ed. Kenneth M. Sayre and Frederick J. Crosson. Notre Dame: University of Notre Dame Press, 1963: 43–71.
Reprint published: Westport, Conn: Greenwood Press, 1979. 197 p.
Review by Werner Meyer-Eppler in *Archiv der elektrischen Übertragung* 14 (1960): 237.
Review by N. Gastinel in *Chiffres* 3 (1960): 125.
Review by Thomas H. O'Beirne in *The Computer Journal* 2 (1959/60): 205.
Review by Richard W. Hamming in *Computing Reviews* 1 (1960): 16.
Review by Peter Westergaard in *Journal of Music Theory* 3 (1959): 302–6.
Review by George F. McKay in *Journal of Research in Music Education* 7 (Fall 1959): 232.
Review by Robert L. Jacobs in *The Music Review* 22,4 (1961): 326–29.
Review by Peter A. Evans in *Music and Letters* 42 (1961): 369–71.
Review by Max V. Mathews in *Proceedings of IRE* 47 (1959): 1792.
Review by Miroslav Filip in *Slovenska hudba* 8 (1964): 128.
Review by Bernhard Hansen in *Neue Zeitschrift für Musik* 143 (1962): 147–48.

524.   ———, and Leonard M. Isaacson. "Musical Composition with a High-Speed Digital Computer." *Journal of the Audio Engineering Society* 6 (1958): 154–60.

525.   ———, and Raveesh Kumra. "Composing *Algorithms II* by Means of Change-Ringing." *Interface* 8 (1979): 129–68.

526.   Höller, York. "Composition of the Gestalt, or, the Making of the Organism." *Contemporary Music Review* 1 (Oct. 1984): 35–40.
French version: "Composition de la Gestalt, ou, la construction de l'organique." *Musique de notre temps* 1 (Oct. 1984): 37–42.

527.   ———. "'Resonance': Composition Today." *Contemporary Music Review* 1 (Oct. 1984): 67–76.
French version: "'Resonance': la composition aujourd'hui." *Musique de notre temps* 1 (Oct. 1984): 69–79.

528.   Howe, Hubert S. "Multi-Dimensional Arrays." Ph. D. diss., Princeton University, 1972. 162 p.
DA 33:2412A.

529.   "IFIP Congress 68 Computer-Composed Music Competition." *Musical Events* 23 (July 1968): 13.

530.   "Inside Stuff—Music." *Variety* 207 (July 11, 1962): 65.

531.   Johnson, Tom H. "New Music." *High Fidelity/Musical America* 25 (Oct. 1975): MA10–MA11.

532.   Kasemets, Udo. "Current Chronicle, United States, Ann Arbor." *Musical Quarterly* 50 (1964): 515–19.

533. Kaske, Stephan. "A Conversation with Clarence Barlow." *Computer Music Journal* 9,1 (Spring 1985): 19–28.

534. Keane, David. "Architecture and Aesthetics: The Construction and the Objectives of *Elektronikus Mozaïk*." In *Proceedings of the International Computer Music Conference, 1985,* ed. Barry Truax. San Francisco, Calif.: Computer Music Association, 1985: 199–206.

535. Kendall, Gary S. "Composing from a Geometric Model: *Five Leaf Rose.*" In *Proceedings of the 1980 International Computer Music Conference,* comp. Hubert S. Howe. San Francisco, Calif.: Computer Music Association, 1982: 382–403.
Also in *Computer Music Journal* 5,4 (Winter 1981): 66–73.
C&CA 17 (1982): 32049. *C&IS* 29 91982): 82–01624C.

536. Koblyakov, Lev. "Jean-Claude Risset—'Songes' (1979)(9')." *Contemporary Music Review* 1 (Oct. 1984): 171–73.
French version: "Jean-Claude Risset—'Songes' (1979)(9')." *Musique de notre temps* 1 (Oct. 1984): 183–85.

537. Kobrin, Edward G., and Theodore H. Ashford. "A Solution to the Problems of Vertical Serialization." *Perspectives of New Music* 6 (Spring-Summer 1968): 119–24.

538. Kuivila, Ronald. "*Untitled:* An Interactive Installation." In *Proceedings of the International Computer Music Conference, 1985,* ed. Barry Truax. San Francisco, Calif.: Computer Music Association, 1985: 337–39.

539. Lanza, Alcides. "Exploring Language." In *Proceedings of the International Computer Music Conference, 1985,* ed. Barry Truax. San Francisco, Calif.: Computer Music Association, 1985: 207–12.

540. Lorrain, Denis. *Inharmonique: analyse de la band magnetique de l'oeuvre de Jean Claude Risset.* Paris: IRCAM, 1980. 105 p. (Rapports IRCAM 26/80)

541. Loy, D. Gareth. "About AUDIUM—A Conversation with Stanley Shaff." *Computer Music Journal* 9,2 (Summer 1985): 41–48.

542. ———. "*Nekyia.*" D.M.A. diss., Stanford University, 1980. 129 p.
DA 40:5643A.

543. Lyon, Raymond. "*Algorithm I,* musique ecrit par une machine pour le film *Imprévisibles.*" *Guide du concert* 330 (Nov. 17, 1961): 385.

544. ———. "La musique algorithmique." *Guide du concert* 336 (Jan. 12, 1962): 610.

545. Machover, Tod. "Computer Music with and without Instruments." *Contemporary Music Review* 1 (Oct. 1984): 203–30.
French version: "Musique informatique avec et sans instruments." *Musique de notre temps* 1 (Oct. 1984): 219–46.

546. ———. "*Fusione Fugace*—testo esplicativo." [*Fusione Fugace*—Explanatory Notes] *Bollettino LIMB* 3 (1983): 39–55.

547. ———. "A Survey of Recent Compositional and Musical Research at IRCAM." Abstract in *Proceedings, 1981 International Computer Music Conference, November 5–8*. Denton, Tex.: North Texas State University, 1983: 29.

548. Marc, Joseph. "Computer Music Language Aids Interaction Between Composer and Choreographer." In *Proceedings of the Venice 1982 International Computer Music Conference*, comp. Thom Blum and John Strawn. San Francisco, Calif.: Computer Music Association, 1985: 606–9.

549. Mathews, Max V. "The Computer Music Record Supplement." *Gravesaner Blätter* 26 (1965): 116–17.
Parallel English and German texts.

550. Matthews, Justus F. "*HDORYUT:* Music Composed with Musical Instruction Composition Oriented Language, MUSICOL." Ph. D. diss., State University of New York at Buffalo, 1973. 185 p.
DA 34:810A.

551. Mattox, Janis R. "Digital Synthesis: A Composer's View." Paper presented at the 66th Convention of the Audio Engineering Society, May 6–9, 1980, Los Angeles, California.
Abstract in *Journal of the Audio Engineering Society* 28 (1980): 542.

552. McNabb, Michael. "*Dreamsong:* The Composition." *Computer Music Journal* 5,4 (Winter 1981): 36–53.
C&CA 17 (1982): 32047. *C&IS* 29 (1982): 82–016220.

553. Melby, John. "A Method of Controlling Local and Large-Scale Rhythmic Relationships in Twelve-Tone and Other Serial Compositions, *91 Plus 5*." Ph. D. diss., Princeton University, 1972. 160 p.
DA 34:811A. *RILM* 74 2869.

554. Milano, Dominic. "Wendy Carlos and the LSI Philharmonic Orchestra: Excerpts from *Ganymede* and *Io*." *Keyboard* 10 (Dec. 1984): 26–30. Sound sheet included.

555. Moog, Robert A. "Wendy Carlos & Michael Fremer Reveal the Secrets Behind the Soundtrack of *Tron*." *Keyboard* 8 (Nov. 1982): 53–57.

556. Motzkin, Elizabeth F. "Lightmusic." *Technology Review* 85 (Oct. 1982): 78–79.

557. Mumma, Gordon, and Alvin Lucier. "Electronic Music." *Proceedings of the American Society of University Composers* 5 (1970): 89–94.

558. Murail, Tristan. "Spectra and Pixies." *Contemporary Music Review* 1 (Oct. 1984): 157–70.
French version: "Spectres et lutins." *Musique de notre temps* 1 (Oct. 1984): 167–81.

559. Padberg, Mother Harriet Ann. "Computer-Composed Canon and Free-Fugue." Ph. D. diss., St. Louis University, 1964. 228 p.
DA 26:2240A.

560. Paresys, Gérard, and Jean-Francois Degremont. *"PLOINK." Artinfo/ musinfo* 26 (1977): 1-15.

561. Pasquotti, Corrado. *"Forma Magistra Ludi."* [*The Form of Magistra Ludi*] *Bollettino LIMB* 2 (1982): 102-9.

562. Patella, Giannantonio. "Note all'esecuzione tecnica di *Forma Magistra Ludi.*" [Remarks to the Technical Execution of *Forma Magistra Ludi*] *Bollettino LIMB* 2 (1982): 110-13.

563. Powley, Robert R. "Riposte: Musical Responsions to $F(X) = SIN(1.618X)-0.618(SIN(1.618X)-SIN(X))$." D.M.A. diss., University of Miami, 1980. 116 p. *DA* 41:2825A.

564. Ranta, Michael W. "The Avant-Garde Scene: *Piece for Jazz Set." Percussionist* 6 (1968-69): 13-20.

565. Razzi, Fausto. *"Progetto Secondo, 1980."* [*Progetto Secondo, 1980]* *Bollettino LIMB 1 (1981): 82-88.*

566. Risset, Jean-Claude. *"Passages* per flauto e nastro magnetico, sintetizzato mediante elaboratore." [*Passages* for Flute and Magnetic Tape, Synthesized Using a Computer] *Bollettino LIMB* 3 (1983): 69-82.

567. Roads, Curtis. "An Analysis of the Composition *ST/10* and the Computer Program *Free Stochastic Music* by I. Xenakis." Valencia, Calif.: California Institute of the Arts, 1973.

568. ————. "The Realization of *nscor.*" In *Composers and the Computer,* ed. Curtis Roads. Los Altos, Calif.: W. Kaufmann, 1985: 142-68.

569. Saariaho, Kaija. "Using the Computer in a Search for New Aspects of Timbre Organisation and Composition." In *Proceedings of the Rochester 1983 International Computer Music Conference,* comp. Robert W. Gross. San Francisco, Calif.: Computer Music Association, 1984: 270-74.

570. Sadie, S. "New Music." *Musical Times* 109 (Mar. 1968): 252.

571. Saucedo, Victor. *"Fluxions."* In *Sixth International Conference on Computers and the Humanities,* ed. S. K. Burton and D. D. Short. Rockville, Md.: Computer Science Press, 1983: 600-601. *C&CA* 19 (1984): 52065.

572. Savouret, Alain. "Sound Mutation and Musical Operation: Of the Expressive Power of Digital Processing." Paper presented at the 1984 International Computer Music Conference, Oct. 19-23, Paris, France.

573. Selleck, John. "An Insider's Guide to Computer Music Recordings." *Creative Computing* 3 (Mar.-Apr. 1977): 68-72. *C&CA* 12 (1977): 23185.

574. Singer, Malcolm J. "Micro-Compositional Techniques in Computer-Generated Music as Realized in *Sines of Our Time."* Paper presented at the 1982 International Computer Music Conference, Sept. 27-Oct. 1, Venice.

575.   Slonimsky, Nicolas. "New Music in Greece." *Musical Quarterly* 51 (1965): 225–35.

576.   Smalley, Denis. "Digital Transformations in *Tides.*" In *Proceedings of the International Computer Music Conference, 1985,* ed. Barry Truax. San Francisco, Calif.: Computer Music Association, 1985: 213–15.

577.   Smith, Patrick J. "Horizons '84: 'A Broader View' of New Romanticism is Very Broad Indeed." *High Fidelity/Musical America* 34 (Oct. 1984): MA24–MA25, MA40.

578.   ———. "Meet the Moderns." *High Fidelity/Musical America* 31 (June 1981): MA33–MA34.

579.   Stroppa, Marco. "Thoughts on *Traiettoria.*" Paper presented at the 1984 International Computer Music Conference, Oct. 19–23, Paris, France.

580.   Tamburini, Alessandro. "A proposito di *FRANGENTE B.*" [Regarding *FRANGENTE B*] In *Atti del Quinto Colloquio di Informatica Musicale.* Ancona: Università di Ancona, 1983: 84–85.

581.   Tenney, James. "Computer Music Experiments, 1961–64." *Electronic Music Reports* 1 (Sept. 1969): 23–60.
       Excerpts appear in *Cybernetic Serendipity,* ed. Jasia Reichardt. New York: Praeger, 1969: 21.
       German excerpts in *Musik und Bildung* 3 (1971): 355–58.

582.   ———. "*Noise Study.*" *Musik und Bildung* 3 (1971): 355–58.
       In German.
       RILM 71 2669.

583.   Tipei, Sever. "*Maiden Voyages*—A Score Produced with MP1." In *Proceedings of the International Computer Music Conference, 1985,* ed. Barry Truax. San Francisco, Calif.: Computer Music Association, 1985: 259–65.

584.   Torresan, Daniele. "Interpretazione ed esecuzione all'elaboratore della composizione *Cadenza Estesa e Coda.*" [Computer Interpretation and execution of the composition *Cadenza Estesa e Coda*] *Bollettino LIMB* 2 (1982): 94–100.

585.   ———. "La realizzazione di *A voi che lavorate sulla terra.*" [The Implementation of *A voi che lavorate sulla terra*] *Bollettino LIMB* 3 (1983): 67–68.

586.   Truax, Barry D. "Polyphonic Timbral Construction in *Androgyny.*" In *Proceedings of the 1978 International Computer Music Conference,* comp. Curtis Roads. Evanston, Ill.: Northwestern University Press, 1979: 355–77.

587.   ———. "Timbral Construction in *Arras* as a Stochastic Process." *Computer Music Journal* 6,3 (Fall 1982): 72–77.
       C&CA 18 (1983): 7236. *C&IS* 31 (1983): 83–1759C.

588.   Vaggione, Horacio. "The Making of *Octuor.*" *Computer Music Journal* 8,2 (Summer 1984): 48–54.
       Review by E. Gagliardo in *Computing Reviews* 26 (Feb. 1985): 8502–0151.

589. Vercoe, Barry. "*Digressions* for Voices, Instruments and Computer-Generated Sounds." Ph. D. diss., University of Michigan, 1969. 226 p.

590. Walsh, Michael. "Boulez ex Machina." *Time* 118 (Dec. 28, 1981): 66.

591. Wilson, Roy D. "*MCABC 0475:* An Original Composition." D.M.A. diss., North Texas State University, 1974. 252 p.
DA 36:4844A-5A.

592. Woodbury, Arthur. "*Velox.*" *Source* 7 (Jan. 1970): 49.

593. Xenakis, Iannis. "Trois pôles de condensation." In *Musique. Architecture.* Tournai: Casterman, 1971: 26–38.
Reprinted from Radio Varsovie, 1962.

COMPUTERS IN MUSIC EDUCATION

594. Abeles, Harold F. "Using an EXPER SIM (Experimental Simulation) Model in Teaching Graduate Research Courses in Music Education." *ERIC:* ED 175 463.
Also in *Indiana University Computing Network 6th Annual Conference on Academic Computing Applications.* Bloomington, Ind.: Wrubel Computing Center, 1969: 95.
ERIC: ED 180 441, p. 95.

595. Aikin, Jim. "Educational Software, 1984: An Overview." *Keyboard* 10 (June 1984): 35–40.

596. Allvin, Raynold L. "Automated Music Instruction: Devices & Strategies." Paper presented at the 46th Convention of the Audio Engineering Society, New York, Sept. 10–13, 1973.
Abstract in *Journal of the Audio Engineering Society* 21 (1973): 760.

597. ———. "Computer-Assisted Music Instruction: A Look at the Potential." *Journal of Research in Music Education* 19 (1971): 131–43.
Also, Los Gatos, Calif.: IBM Advanced Systems Development Laboratory, Sept. 23, 1968. (Report 16.164)

598. ———. "Computer-Assisted Music Instruction: Costs." *Educational Technology* 11 (Aug. 1971): 20–22.

599. ———. "The Development of a Computer-Assisted Music Instruction System to Teach Sight Singing and Ear Training." Ph. D. diss., Stanford University, 1967. 130 p.

600. ———. "Do Colleges and Universities Need an Automated Music Learning Center?" *Council for Research in Music Education Bulletin* 21 (Summer 1970): 32–46.

601. Alonso, Sydney. "A Computer Terminal for Music Instruction." Proceedings of the 85th Meeting of the Acoustical Society of America, 1973. 73 p.

602. ———; Jon H. Appleton; and Cameron Jones. "Description d'un systeme digital specifique pour l'enseignement, la composition, et l'execution de musique." *Faire* 2–3 (1975): 60–67.

603. ———; Jon H. Appleton; and Cameron Jones. "A Special Purpose Digital System for Musical Instruction, Composition, and Performance." *Computers and the Humanities* 10 (1976): 209–15.
C&CA 12 (1977): 5014. *RILM* 76 15659.

604. ———; Jon H. Appleton; and Cameron Jones. "A Special Purpose Digital System for the Instruction, Composition, and Performance of Music." In *Computers in Education: Proceedings of the IFIP 2nd World Conference,* ed. O. Leczrme and R. Lewis. Amsterdam: North Holland Press, 1975: 761–64. Also in *Proceedings of the 1975 Conference on Computers in the Undergraduate Curricula, CCUC/6, Hosted by Texas Christian University, Forth Worth, Texas June 16, 17, 18, 1976.* Fort Worth, Tex.: Dept. of Computer Science, Texas Christian University, 1975: 17–22.

605. Anshell, Pearl. "Music and Micros, Software Reviews: Practical Music Theory." *Music Educators Journal* 39 (Nov. 1984): 90–92.

606. Appell, Louise S., and Kathleen M. Hurley. "Individualized Instruction with Microcomputer Software." *Focus on Exceptional Children* 16 (Jan. 1984): 1–12.
CIJE 16 (1984): EJ 299 614.

607. Arenson, Michael A. "Computer-Based Ear Training Instruction for Non-Music Majors." In *Mission of the Future. Proceedings of the Annual Convention of the Association for the Development of Computer-Based Instructional Systems. Volume I, General Session Papers and Project Reports.* San Diego, Calif., Feb. 27 to Mar. 1, 1979: 949–57.
ERIC: ED 175 447.

608. ———. "The Effect of a Competency-Based Computer Program on the Learning of Fundamental Skills in a Music Theory Course for Non-Majors." *Journal of Computer-Based Instruction* 9 (1982): 55–58.
CIJE 15 (1983): EJ 279 797.

609. ———. "The Effect of a Computerized Competency-Based Education Program on Learning of Fundamental Skills in a Theory Course for Non-Majors." Paper presented at the Combined Annual Meetings of the American Musicological Society (Forty-Sixth Annual Meeting), College Music Society, and Society for Music Theory, November 6–9, 1980, Denver Hilton, Denver, Colorado.

610. ———. "An Examination of Computer-Based Educational Hardware at Twenty-eight NCCBMI Member Schools." *Journal of Computer-Based Instruction* 5 (Aug.-Nov. 1978): 38–40.
C&CA 14 (1979): 14063. *CIJE* 11 (1979): EJ 198 327.

611. ———. "Guidelines for the Development of Computer-Assisted Instruction Materials in Music Theory." In *New Directions in Educational Computing. Proceedings of the 1977 Winter Conference of the Association for the Development of Computer-Based Instructional Systems.* Wilmington, Del., Feb. 1977: 101–3.
ERIC: ED 148 297.

612. ———. "A Model for Systematic Revision of Computer-Based Instruction Materials in Music Theory." *Journal of Computer-Based Instruction* 7 (Feb. 1981): 78–83.
C&CA 16 (1981): 27627.

613. ———. "A Model for the First Steps in the Development of Computer-Assisted Instruction Materials in Music Theory." Ph. D. diss., Ohio State University, 1976. 339 p.
C&IS 17: 177145C. *DA* 37:6826A.

614. ———. "The Use of a Table Driver for Individualized Design of Computer-Based Instruction Materials in Music Theory." In *1982 Conference Proceedings of the Association for the Development of Computer-Based Instructional Systems, Vancouver, BC, Canada, 7 June 1982.* Bellingham, WA: ADCIS, 1982: 228–30.
C&CA 19 (1984): 10508.

615. ———, and Fred T. Hofstetter. "The GUIDO System and the PLATO Project." *Music Educators Journal* 69 (Jan. 1983): 46–51.
CIJE 15 (1983): EJ 275 323.

616. Ashley, Richard D. "Production Systems: Three Applications in Music." In *Proceedings of the Rochester 1983 International Computer Music Conference,* comp. Robert W. Gross. San Francisco, Calif.: Computer Music Association, 1984: 161–73.

617. Ashton, Alan C. "A Computer Stores, Composes, and Plays Music." *Computer and Automation* 20 (Dec. 1971): 43.

618. Ashton, David. "Teaching Music Fundamentals Using a Computer Controlled Organ and Display Scope." M.M. thesis, University of Utah, 1971.

619. Asselin, Maxine M. "Graphic Representation of Musical Concepts: A Computer-Assisted Instructional System." Ph. D. diss., University of Connecticut, 1972. 99 p.
C&IS 12: 91101C. *DA* 33:2966A. *RILM* 76 1702.

620. Bales, W. Kenton. "A Microcomputer-Based Table Driver for Learning Basic Serial Technique." *Journal of Computer-Based Instruction* 9, special issue (May 1983): 194–96.

621. ———. "A Model for Generative Harmonic Dictation." In *1980 Proceedings, Association for the Development of Computer-Based Instructional Systems.* Bellingham, Wash.: Western Washington University, 1980: 198–200.

622. ———, and Roger E. Foltz. "More for Less with Computers." *Clavier* 22,5 (1983): 46–47.

623. Bamberger, Jeanne. "Computer Music Teaching Machines." Paper presented at the 1980 International Computer Music Conference, November 13–15, 1980, Queens College of the City University of New York.

624. ———. "Learning to Think Musically: A Computer Approach to Music Study." *Music Educators Journal* 59 (Mar. 1973): 53–57.
CIJE 5 (1973): EJ 072 768.

625. ———. "Logo Music." *BYTE* 7 (Aug. 1982): 325, 328.

626. Bardige, Art. "The Problem-Solving Revolution." *Classroom Computer News* 3 (Mar. 1983): 44–46.
CIJE 15 (1983): EJ 277 048.

627. Beckwith, Sterling. "Composing Computers for Kids—A Progress Report." *The Canadian Music Book* 9 (1974): 148–54.

628. ———. "Reading, Writing, and Running: A Critique of Micro Musicianship." Paper presented at the 1980 International Computer Music Conference, November 13–15, 1980, Queens College of the City University of New York.

629. ———. "Talking Music with a Machine." *College Music Symposium* 15 (1975): 94–99.
RILM 75 4417.

630. ———. "The Well-Tempered Computer." *Music Educators Journal* 62 (Mar. 1976): 33–36.
CIJE 9 (1977): EJ 147 528.

631. Benward, Bruce C. "CAL in Music Designed for Use with a Companion Text." *Computers & Education* 8 (1984): 127–31.
C&CA 19 (1984): 19309. *C&IS* 32 (1984): 84–5262C.

632. Birchall, Steve. "Music Theory Software for the Apple." *SoftSide* 6,10 (1983): 78–81.
C&CA 19 (1984): 23715. *CIJE* 15 (1983): EJ 285 797.

633. Blais, F., and Martin Prével. "The Melocapteur: A Pitch Extractor Peripheral Design for Ear Training." In *Proceedings of the Fourth Canadian Symposium on Instructional Technology: Computer Technologies for Productive Learning: Winnipeg, Man., Canada, 19–21 Oct. 1983*. Ottawa, Ont.: National Research Council of Canada, 1983: 515–18.
C&CA 20 (1985): 7969.

634. Blank, George. "Computer-Based Training for Non-Computer Subjects." *Creative Computing* 10 (Aug. 1984): 54–57.
CIJE 16 (1984): EJ 303 361.

635. Blombach, Ann K. "OSU's GAMUT: Semi-Intelligent Computer-Assisted Music Ear Training." In *Sixth International Conference on Computers and the Humanities*. Rockville, Md.: Computer Science Press, 1983: 14–15.

636. Borry, Linda. "Meet the Music Teacher's New Assistant—A Microcomputer." *AEDS Monitor* 18 (Oct.-Dec. 1979): 21.
C&IS 25 (1980): 243455C.

637. Bridges, Nicholas. "The Development of Aural Perception of Selected Per-
      cepts of Musical Form Utilizing Programmed Instruction." Ed. D. diss.,
      Boston University, 1982. 199 p.
      DA 43:1073A.

638. Buehning, Walt, and Erv Schieman. "Simulation Can Teach Teachers."
      Music Educators Journal 69 (Jan. 1983): 54–55.
      CIJE 15 (1983): EJ 275 325.

639. Bukspan, Y. "MUSIMPLE: Computer-Based Learning of 7-Sign Music
      Notation System." In *General Survey of Systems Methodology: Proceedings of
      the Twenty-Sixth Annual Meeting of the Society for General Systems Research
      with the American Association for the Advancement of Science, Washington,
      D.C., 5–9 Jan. 1982,* ed. L. Troncale. Louisville, Ky.: Society for General Sys-
      tems Research, 1982: vol. 2, 765–78.
      C&CA 18 (1983): 7240.

640. Burrowes, Sharon, and Ted Burrowes. *Improving CAI in BASIC.* Eugene,
      Oreg.: International Council for Computers in Education, 1985. 91 p.
      ERIC: ED 257 414.

641. Cancelosi, Robert, and Richard B. Jones. "A Geometric Interpretation of
      Four-Part Harmony." *Proceedings of the American Society for Information
      Science* 18 (1981): 316–17.

642. Canelos, James J.; Barbara A. Murphy; Ann K. Blombach; and William C.
      Heck. "Evaluation of Three Types of Instructional Strategy for Learner
      Acquisition of Intervals." *Journal of Research in Music Education* 28 (1980):
      243–49.
      CIJE 13 (1981): EJ 239 739.

643. Ciamaga, Gustav. "Initiation du compositeur aux nouveaux procédés techno-
      logiques." *La revue musicale* 268–69 (1971): 139–47.
      English version: "The Training of the Composer in New Technological
      Means." In *Music and Technology.* Paris: La revue musicale, 1971: 143–50.

644. Clark, David B.; Colette T. Jousse–Wilkins; and D. T. Tuma. "Computer
      Aided Sight Reading." *Creative Computing* 6 (June 1980): 84–88.
      C&CA 16 (1981): 3137.

645. Clements, Peter J. "Design Considerations for Computer-Assisted Music
      Instruction." In *Proceedings of the Venice 1982 International Computer Music
      Conference,* comp. Thom Blum and John Strawn. San Francisco, Calif.: Com-
      puter Music Association, 1985: 511–33.

646. Cohen, D. "The Use of Microcomputers in Music Instruction." In *Microcom-
      puters in Education: Getting Started,* ed. N. A. Watson. Tempe, Ariz.: Arizona
      State University, Dept. of Elementary Education, 1981: CC 1.

647. "Computer Music Instruction: Challenges and Cautions." *Education Digest* 49
      (Oct. 1983): 55.

648. "Computerized Instruction." *Music Educators Journal* 56 (Oct. 1969): 100.

649. "Computers for Practicing." The *Instrumentalist* 37 (Mar. 1983): 94–95.

650. Cooper, Rose M. "The Efficacy of Computer Assisted Instruction Compared with Traditional Teacher-Taught and Self-Taught Methods of Teaching Beginning Music Theory." Ph. D. diss., University of North Carolina at Greensboro, 1975.
DA 36:5623A.

651. Dannenberg, Frances K.; Roger B. Dannenberg; and Philip L. Miller. "Teaching Programming to Musicians." In *Proceedings, 4th Symposium on Small Computers in the Arts, October 25–28, 1984, Philadelphia, Pennsylvania.* Silver Spring, Md.: IEEE Computer Society Press, 1984: 114–22.
C&CA 20 (1985): 17292.

652. "Databank: Experts on Educational Uses of Computers." *Music Educators Journal* 69 (Jan. 1983): 71–73.
CIJE 15 (1983): EJ 275 330.

653. Davidhazy, Andres. "Hopsichords in the Theory Class?" *Music Educators Journal* 58 (Sept. 1971): 44–47.

654. Deal, John J. "Computer-Assisted Programmed Instruction to Teach Pitch and Rhythm Error-Detection Skill to College Music Education Students." Ph. D. diss., University of Iowa, 1983. 156 p.
DA 44:3622A. *C&IS* 33 (1985): 85–461C.

655. "Decker Corp. to Unveil New Teaching Computer." *The Music Trades* 118 (Mar. 1970): 80.

656. "Decker: nach 39 Wochen Fertiger Musiker; Computer-Unterricht in USA über Fernsehen und Musikhandel." *Instrumentenbau Zeitschrift* 24 (Aug. 1970): 447.

657. Deihl, Ned C. "Computer-Assisted Instruction and Instrumental Music: Implications for Teaching and Research." *Journal of Research in Music Education* 19 (1971): 299–306.

658. ———. "Computers for Instrumental Music." *Music Journal* 28 (Apr. 1970): 57–61.

659. ———. *Development and Evaluation of Computer-Assisted Instruction in Instrumental Music. Final Report.* University Park: Pennsylvania State University, 1969.
ERIC: ED 035 314.

660. ———. "New Technology and Instrumental Music." *The Instrumentalist* 25 (Sept. 1970): 44–45.

661. ———, and Kenneth C. Partchey. "Status of Research: Educational Technology in Music Education." *Council for Research in Music Education Bulletin* 35 (Winter 1973): 18–29.

662. ———, and Rudolf E. Radocy. "Computer-Assisted Instruction: Potential for Instrumental Music Education." *Council for Research in Music Education Bulletin* 15 (Winter 1969): 1–7.

663. ———, and Rudolf E. Radocy. "Teaching Musicianship via Computer-Assisted Instruction." *Educational Technology* 11 (Aug. 1971): 23–24. *CIJE* 3 (1971): EJ 042 654.

664. ———, and Ray H. Ziegler. "Evaluation of a CAI Program in Articulation, Phrasing, and Rhythm for Intermediate Instrumentalists." *Council for Research in Music Education Bulletin* 31 (Winter 1973): 1–11.

665. Dillard, E. Margo, and Rosemary N. Killam. "The Effect of Technology in the Traditional Arts: Comparison and Contrast of Female and Male Music Students' Attitudes Toward Ear-Training Computer-Assisted Instruction (CAI)." In *Proceedings of NECC-82, National Educational Computing Conference 1982, Kansas City, Missouri, June 27–30, 1982,* ed. J. Smith and G. S. Moum. Columbia: University of Missouri, 1982: 141–54.

666. Dillingham, Larry M. "A Micro-Processor System as a Classroom Teaching Tool." *Technological Horizons in Education* 6 (Feb. 1979): 26–27. *CIJE* 11 (1979): EJ 200 169.

667. Dowling, W. J. "Musicians Learning Perceptual Skills Using a Computer-Based Teaching Machine." Abstract in *Journal of the Acoustical Society of America* 51 (1972): 138.

668. Duncan, Danny J. "Practices and Standards in the Teaching of Woodwind Technique Classes in the Music Education Curriculum in Selected Colleges and Universities in the United States." D.M.E. diss., Indiana University, 1978. 165 p. *DA* 39:7208A. *RILM* 78 1924.

669. Dworak, Paul E. "Computer-Assisted Instruction in Melodic Composition." In *Proceedings of NECC 1981, National Educational Computing Conference, Denton, TX, 17–19 June 1981,* D. Harris and L. Nelsonheern. Iowa City, Iowa: University of Iowa, 1981: 136–41. *C&CA* 17 (1982): 5210.

670. ———. "Employing a Dynamic Model of Creativity in Written Music Theory CAI." Paper presented at the National Society for Performance and Instruction, Eighteenth Annual Conference, Dallas, Texas, April 2, 1980.

671. ———. "Using Hierarchical Thinking Strategies in Creative Behavior." Abstract in *Proceedings, 1981 International Computer Music Conference, November 5–8,* comp. Larry Austin and Thom Blum. Denton, Tex.: North Texas State University, 1983: 213.

672. ———, and Jane Piper Clendinning. "Computer Pitch Recognition: A New Approach." In *Proceedings of the Rochester 1983 International Computer Music Conference,* comp. Robert W. Gross. San Francisco, Calif.: Computer Music Association, 1984: 174–93.

673. "Early Grade Ideas." *Classroom Computer Learning* 4 (Feb. 1984): 70–71.
      CIJE 16 (1984): EJ 293 865.

674. Eddins, John M. "Aural Perception of Differences in Musical Style: Strategies
      for Computer Assisted Instruction." Paper presented at the Combined Annual
      Meetings of the American Musicological Society (Forty-Sixth Annual
      Meeting), College Music Society, and Society for Music Theory, November 6–
      9, 1980, Denver Hilton, Denver, Colorado.

675. ———. "A Brief History of Computer-Assisted Instruction in Music." *Col-
      lege Music Symposium* 21 (Fall 1981): 7–14.

676. ———. "Random Access Audio in Computer-Assisted Music Instruction."
      Journal of Computer-Based Instruction 5 (Aug.-Nov. 1978): 22–29.
      C&CA 14 (1979): 14061. *CIJE* 11 (1979): EJ 198 325.

677. Edwards, John S.; Charles H. Douglas; and Robert W. John. "Developing a
      Music Education Thesaurus." *Journal of Research in Music Education* 21
      (1973): 20–29.
      CIJE 5 (1973): EJ 076 743. *RILM* 73 2608.

678. ———. "A Model Computer Assisted Information Retrieval System in Music
      Education." Ed. D. diss., University of Georgia, 1970. 206 p.
      DA 31:4198A.

679. ———, and Charles H. Douglas. "Model Computer-Assisted Information
      Retrieval System in Music Education." *Journal of Research in Music Education*
      20 (1972): 477–83.
      CIJE 5 (1973): EJ 073 597.

680. Ehle, Robert C. "Synthesizers, Anyone?" *Music Educators Journal* 57 (Jan.
      1971): 78–82.

681. Evans, James S. "Instructional Computing in the Liberal Arts: The Lawrence
      Experience." *Technological Horizons in Education* 11 (Feb. 1984): 98–103.
      CIJE 16 (1984): EJ 293 888.

682. "Experts on Educational Uses of Computers." *Music Educators Journal* 69
      (Jan. 1983): 71–73.

683. Favre, Jean-Michel. "Definition et implementation d'un langage pedagogique
      adapte à la programmation musicale." *Artinfo/musinfo* 28 (1978): 1–10.

684. Feldt, James R. von. "Computer Assisted Instruction in the Public School
      General Music Class: A Comparative Study." D.M.A. diss., University of
      Missouri-Kansas City, 1971. 107 p.
      RILM 73 4378. *DA* 33:2418A.

685. Ferentzy, E. N. "On Formal Music Analysis-Synthesis: Its Application in
      Music Education." *Computational Linguistics* 4 (1965): 107.

686. Foltz, Roger E. "Computer Instruction in Modal Counterpoint." Paper presented at the Combined Annual Meetings of the American Musicological Society (Forty-Sixth Annual Meeting), College Music Society, and Society for Music Theory, November 6–9, 1980, Denver Hilton, Denver, Colorado.

687. ———, and Dorothy S. Gross. "Integration of CAI into a Music Program." *Journal of Computer-Based Instruction* 6 (Feb. 1980): 72–76.
C&CA 15 (1980): 27752. *CIJE* 12 (1980): EJ 225 861.

688. Franklin, James L. "What's a Computer Doing in my Music Room?" *Music Educators Journal* 69 (Jan. 1983): 29–32.
CIJE 15 (1983): EJ 275 319.

689. Fujino, Masayuki, and Kohmei Hayama. "An Interactive Realtime Computer Music System." Paper presented at the 1980 International Computer Music Conference, November 13–15, 1980, Queens College of the City University of New York.

690. Gay, Leslie C. "A Study of the Compositional Applications of the AMUS System." Denton, Tex.: North Texas State University, Dec. 1977. 7 p.

691. ———. "A Study of the Effects of Frequency Variance on Duration Perception." M.A. thesis, North Texas State University, 1980.

692. Gena, Peter. "MUSICOL: Musical Instruction Composition Oriented Language." In *Computing in the Humanities: Proceedings of the Third International Conference on Computing in the Humanities,* ed. Serge Lusignan and John S. North. Waterloo, Ont.: The University of Waterloo Press, 1977: 165–73.
C&CA 13 (1978): 12161. *C&IS* 17: 185330C.

693. Goldberg, Adele, and Bonnie Tenenbaum. "Classroom Communication Media." *TOPICS in Instructional Technology* 1 (Jan. 1975): 61–68.
CIJE 8 (1975): EJ 114 535.

694. Gollnick, Doris J. "An Orchestra in Your Lap." *Music Educators Journal* 71 (Jan. 1985): 30–32.
CIJE 17 (1985): EJ 309 211.

695. Gooch, Sherwin. "PLATO Music Systems." In *New Directions in Educational Computing: Proceedings of the ADCIS 1978 Conference, Dallas, Texas, March 1978. ERIC:* ED 160 072, pp. 314–28. *ERIC:* ED 161 421.

696. Grigsby, B. "Report to the Chancellor: Project for Innovation in the Instruction Process Computer-Assisted-Instruction in Music." *Performing Arts Review* 8 (1978): 355–88b.

697. Gross, Dorothy S. "A Computer-Assisted Music Course and Its Implementation." In *Computing in the Humanities,* ed. Peter C. Patton, Renee A. Holoian. Lexington, Mass.: Lexington Books, 1981: 287–97.

698. ———. "An Intelligent Ear-Training Lesson." In *Proceedings of the International Computer Music Conference, 1984,* ed. William Buxton. San Francisco, Calif.: Computer Music Association, 1985: 179–83.

699.   ———, and Roger E. Foltz. "Ideas on Implementation and Evaluation of a Music CAI Project." *College Music Symposium* 21 (Fall 1981): 22–26.

700.   ———, and Wendy Griffin. "Implementation and Evaluation of a Computer-Assisted Course in Musical Aural Skills." *AEDS Journal* 15 (1982): 143–50.
C&CA 17 (1982): 44140. *C&IS* 31 (1983): 83–3034C. *CIJE* 14 (1982): EJ 267 348.

701.   Gross, Robert Wenzel. "A Comparison of Active Experience and Lecture-Discussion Methodology as Means for Developing Musical Knowledge, Musical Discrimination, and Musical Preference within an Electronic Music Course at the High School Level." D. Ed. diss., Pennsylvania State University, 1984. 160 p.
DA 45:3088A.

702.   Gruhn, Wilfried. "Elektronische Musik im Unterricht." *Musik und Bildung* 2 (June 1970): 6–10.

703.   "Gulbransen Market Tests MusiComputer Teaching System." *The Music Trades* 122 (Jan. 1974): 22.

704.   Hafner, Everett. "Computers, Synthesizers, and the Physics of Music." Paper presented at the Conference on Computers in the Undergraduate Curricula, Claremont, California, June 18, 19, 20, 1973.
ERIC: ED 081 206.

705.   Hair, Harriet I. "Music Terminology of Children, College Students, and Faculty Applications for Computer-Assisted Lessons." In *1982 Conference Proceedings of the Association for the Development of Computer-Based Instructional Systems, Vancouver, BC, Canada, 7 June 1982.* Bellingham, Wash.: ADCIS, 1982: 222–27.
C&CA 19 (1984): 10507.

706.   ———. "PLATO Said My Answer Was Terrific!" *Music Educators Journal* 63 (Jan. 1977): 55.
CIJE 9 (1977): EJ 159 756.

707.   Hamilton, Richard L., and Rosemary N. Killam. "Cost Effective Implementation of Music Notation on CRT Terminals." In *Mission of the Future. Proceedings of the Annual Convention of the Association for the Development of Computer-Based Instructional Systems. Volume I, General Session Papers and Project Reports.* San Diego, Calif., February 27 to March 1, 1979: 183–93.
ERIC: ED 175 447.

708.   ———, and Rosemary N. Killam. "An Integrated Data Management System for Computer-Assisted Instruction." In *1980 Proceedings, Association for the Development of Computer-Based Instructional Systems.* Bellingham, Wash.: Western Washington University, 1980: 51–54.

709.   Hayward, Stan. "Computer Aided Music." *Visual Education* (Jan. 1972): 21–22.

710.   Hegarty, A. "Teaching Music by Computer." *Music in Education* 34 (1970): 261.

711.   Heller, Jack J., et al. "Graphic Representation of Musical Concepts: A Computer Assisted Instructional System. Final Report." 41 p.
       ERIC: ED 058 745.

712.   Herrold, Rebecca M. "Computer-Assisted Instruction: A Study of Student Performance in the Stanford CAI Ear-Training Program." Paper presented at the Music Educators National Conference, Anaheim, California, 1974. 96 p.
       ERIC: ED 172 810.

713.   ————. "Computer Assisted Instruction in Music: A Study of Student Performance in the Stanford Ear-Training Program." Ph. D. diss., Stanford University, 1974.

714.   ————. "The Development and Trial of a Computer Managed Test of Music Fundamentals." Paper presented at the Oregon Council for Research in Teacher Education, Oregon State University, Nov. 16, 1977.
       ERIC: ED 171 312.

715.   Higgins, William R. "The Feasibility of Teaching Beginning Applied Clarinet with the Microcomputer." D. Ed. diss., Pennsylvania State University, 1981. 155 p.
       DA 42:126A–7A.

716.   Hillier, J. H. "A Musical Monologue." *Computer in the Schools* 5 (Oct. 1982): 19–20.
       C&CA 19 (1984): 3562.

717.   Hirsch, Hans-Ludwig, and Jürgen Weigmann. *Programmierte Einführung in die allgemeine Musiklehre.* Regensburg: Bosse, 1979. 206 p.
       Review by Manfred Wagner in *Österreichische Musikzeitschrift* 34 (Sept. 1979): 453.

718.   Hodges, D. "Microcomputers in University Instrumental Music Education Courses." *Dialogue in Instrumental Music Education* 7,1 (1983): 4–7.

719.   Hofstetter, Fred T. "Applications of the GUIDO System to Aural Skills Research, 1975–80." *College Music Symposium* 21 (Fall 1981): 46–53.

720.   ————. "Computer-Based Aural Training: The GUIDO System." *Journal of Computer-Based Instruction* 7 (Feb. 1981): 84–92.
       C&CA 16 (1981): 27628. *CIJE* 13 (1981): EJ 247 439.

721.   ————. "Computer-Based Recognition of Perceptual Patterns and Learning Styles in Rhythmic Dictation Exercises." *Journal of Research in Music Education* 29 (Winter 1981): 265–77.
       C&CA 17 (1982): 36191. *CIJE* 14 (1982): EJ 260 662.

722.   ———. "Computer-Based Recognition of Perceptual Patterns in Chord Quality Dictation Exercises." In *Computer-Based Instruction, A New Decade: 1980 Proceedings, Association for the Development of Computer-Based Instructional Systems.* Bellingham, Wash.: Western Washington Univeristy, 1980: 201–08.
C&CA 15 (1980): 33896.

723.   ———. "Computer-Based Recognition of Perceptual Patterns in Chord Quality Dictation Exercises." *Journal of Research in Music Education* 28 (Summer 1980): 83–91.
C&CA 16 (1981): 6255. *CIJE* 12 (1980): EJ 226 975.

724.   ———. "Computer-Based Recognition of Perceptual Patterns in Harmonic Dictation Exercises." In *New Directions in Educational Computing: Proceedings of the ADCIS 1978 Conference, Dallas, Texas, March 1978.*
Also in *Journal of Research in Music Education* 26 (1978): 111–19.
ERIC: ED 160 072, p. 192–201. *ERIC:* ED 161 411. *RILM* 78 4121.

725.   ———. "Controlled Evaluation of a Competency Based Approach to Teaching Aural Interval Identification." In *Mission of the Future. Proceedings of the Annual Convention of the Association for the Development of Computer-Based Instructional Systems. Volume I, General Session Papers and Project Reports.* San Diego, California, February 27 to March 1, 1979: 935–48.
ERIC: ED 175 447.

726.   ———. "The Design, Development, and Implementation of the University of Delaware Sound Synthesizer." *Journal of Computer-Based Instruction* 9 special issue (May 1983): 197–202.

727.   ———. "Foundation, Organization, and Purpose of the National Consortium for Computer-Based Musical Instruction." *Journal of Computer-Based Instruction* 3 (Aug. 1976): 21–33.
CIJE 9 (1977): EJ 159 153.

728.   ———. "GUIDO: An Interactive Computer-Based System for Improvement of Instruction and Research in Ear-Training." *Journal of Computer-Based Instruction* 1,4 (1978): 100–106.

729.   ———. "Instructional Design and Curricular Impact of Computer-Based Music Education." *Educational Technology* 18 (Apr. 1978): 50–53.
CIJE 11 (1979): EJ 189 175.

730.   ———. "Interactive Simulation/Games as an Aid to Musical Learning." In *New Directions in Educational Computing: Proceedings of the 1977 Winter Conference of the Association for the Development of Computer-Based Instructional Systems.* Wilmington, Del., February 1977: 104–17.

731.   ———. "Microelectronics and Music Education." *Music Educators Journal* 65 (Apr. 1979): 38–45.
CIJE 12 (1980): EJ 215 482.

732.   ———. "Music Dream Machines: New Realities for Computer-Based Musical Instruction." *Creative Computing* 3 (Mar.-Apr. 1977): 50–54.

733.   ———. "Musical Magic Squares." *Creative Computing* 3 (Mar.-Apr. 1977): 116.

734.   Horan, Catherine. "Music and Micros, Software Reviews: Elements of Music." *Music Educators Journal* 39 (Dec. 1984): 91–92.

735.   Hullfish, William R. "A Comparison of Response-Sensitive and Response-Insensitive Decision Rules in Presenting Learning Materials in Music Theory by Computer-Assisted Instruction." Ed. D. diss., State University of New York at Buffalo, 1969. 143 p.
DA 31:415A.

736.   ———. "A Comparison of Two Computer-Assisted Instructional Programs in Music Theory." *Journal of Research in Music Education* 20 (1972): 354–61.
CIJE 5 (1972): EJ 064 939.

737.   ———, and William Pottebaum. "Take on a Digital Assistant: The Computer as a Teaching Aid." *Music Educators Journal* 57 (Jan. 1971): 83–87.

738.   Hultberg, Mary Lou; Warren E. Hultberg; and Ted Tenney. "Project CLEF: CAI in Music Theory." In *Mission of the Future. Proceedings of the Annual Convention of the Association for the Development of Computer-Based Instructional Systems. Volume I, General Session Papers and Project Reports.* San Diego, California, February 27 to March 1, 1979: 928–34.
ERIC: ED 175 447.

739.   Hultberg, Warren E., and Mary Lou Hultberg. "CAI in Music Theory! Paradigms: Potential: Problems." In *Proceedings of a Fourth Conference on Computers in the Undergraduate Curricula: The Claremont Colleges, Claremont, California, June 18, 19, 20, 1973.* Claremont, Calif.: The Institute for Educational Computing, 1973: 222–25.
ERIC: ED 081 223.

740.   ———, and Mary Lou Hultberg. "Computer-Assisted Instructional Programs in Music Theory. Parts I and II." Santa Monica, Calif.: Rand Corporation, 1969/1970.

741.   Humphries, James A. "The Effects of Computer Assisted Aural Drill Time on Achievement in Musical Interval Identification." Ph. D. diss., Arizona State University, 1978. 105 p.
C&IS 22 (1978): 214530C. *DA* 39:1403A.

742.   ———. "The Effects of Computer-Assisted Aural Drill Time on Achievement in Musical Interval Identification." *Journal of Computer-Based Instruction* 6 (Feb. 1980): 91–98.
C&CA 15 (1980): 27756. *CIJE* 12 (1980): EJ 225 864.
Also in *Proceedings of the Third Canadian Symposium on Instructional Technology,* ed. E. I. Swail and G. Neal. Ottawa: National Research Council of Canada, 1980: 431–36.

743.   John, Robert W. "New Tools for Research in Music Education." *Music Educators Journal* 55 (Apr. 1969): 87–88.

744. Jones, Dorothy Stewart. "Now is the Hour." *School Musician* 54 (Nov. 1982): 8–9.

745. Jones, Morgan J. "Computer-Assisted Instruction in Music: A Survey with Attendant Recommendations." Ph. D. diss., Northwestern University, 1975. 154 p.
DA 36:7264A-5A.

746. Jones, Richard B.; M. Fronhofer; J. Schettine; and Robert Cancelosi. "Pedagogical Methods in Four Part Harmony Theory Using Micro-Computers." In *Computers in Education,* ed. B. Lewis and D. Tagg. Amsterdam: North-Holland, 1981: 215–22.

747. Jousse-Wilkins, Colette. "Report on Initial Development of Microcomputer Programs in Reading and Aural Training for Music Students." In *Computer-Based Instruction: A New Decade: 1980 Proceedings, Association for the Development of Computer-Based Instructional Systems.* Bellingham, Wash.: Western Washington University, 1980: 20–23.
C&CA 15 (1980): 30711.

748. ———. "Solfege with Interactive Microcomputer Programs." In *Informatique et musique, Second Symposium International,* ed. Hélène Charnassé. Ivry-sur-Seine: ELMERATTO, CNRS, 1983: 71–78.

749. Kalipolites, Marcus. "A Programmed Course in Acoustics in Music for Junior High School." D.M.A. diss., University of Missouri-Kansas City, 1972. 213 p. Abstract in *Missouri Journal of Research in Music Education* 3 (1972): 112–13.
DA 34:1313A. *RILM* 73 4388.

750. Kellner, Charlie; Ellen V. B. Lapham; and Laurie Spiegel. "The Alphasyntauri: A Keyboard Based Digital Playing and Recording System with a Microcomputer Interface." In *Microcomputers in Education: Getting Started,* ed. N.A. Watson. Tempe, Ariz.: Arizona State University, Dept. of Elementary Education, 1981: BB 1.

751. Kent, William P. "Helping You Understand Music in the Electronic Age." *Instructor* 79 (May 1970): 62–63.

752. ———. "Keyboard Computer-Assisted Music Instruction: Summary of the Project Plan." *Council for Research in Music Education Bulletin* 19 (Winter 1970): 20–21.

753. Kieren, Thomas E. *LOGO in Education: What, How, Where, Why, and Consequences.* Edmonton: Alberta Dept. of Education, Planning Services Branch, Dec. 1984. 53 p.
ERIC: ED 258 536.

754. Killam, Rosemary N.; Philip Baczewski; Antoinette Corbett; Paul E. Dworak; Jana Kubitza; Michael Morgan; and Lawrence Woodruff. "Research Applications in Music CAI." *College Music Symposium* 21 (Fall 1981): 37–44.

755. ———; Philip Baczewski; Antoinette Corbett; J. McCachren; and Michael Morgan. "Computer-Assisted Instruction in Music." *Pipeline* 6 (Fall 1981): 3–4.
CIJE 14 (1982): EJ 255 506.

756. ———, and W. Kenton Bales. "Music CAI: A Model for Epistemological Research Applications." In *Proceedings of the Third Canadian Symposium on Instructional Technology,* ed. E. I. Swail and G. Neal. Ottawa: National Research Council of Canada, 1980: 417–30.

757. ———, and Paul V. Lorton. "Computer Assisted Instruction in Music: Ear-Training Drill and Practice." In *Proceedings of Conference on Computers in the Undergraduate Curricula, Washington State University, Pullman, Washington, June 24, 25, 26, 1974.* Pullman, Wash.: Dept. of Computer Science, Washington State University, 1974: 263–73.

758. ———; Paul V. Lorton; and Earl D. Schubert. "Interval Recognition: Identification of Harmonic and Melodic Intervals." *Journal of Music Theory* 19 (1975): 212–34.

759. Kitagaki, Ikuo; Y. Shimizu; and Kunihiro Suetake. "A Trial on Musical Tone Recognition Utilizing a Computer." *Journal of the Acoustical Society of Japan* 33 (1977): 464–69.
In Japanese.
C&CA 13 (1978): 10172.

760. ———, and Kunihiro Suetake. "Piano Training System on the Use of a Micro-Computer of the Characteristic Extraction of the Learners' Playing a Fundamental Etude." Abstract in *Proceedings, 1981 International Computer Music Conference, November 5–8,* comp. Larry Austin and Thomas Clark. Denton, Tex.: North Texas State University, 1983: 214.

761. Klára, S. Horváth. "Alkotó, Kísérletezö Munka az Ország Zeneiskoláiban." [Creative and Experimental Work in the Music Schools of Hungary] *Parlando* 20/1–5 (Jan.-May 1978): 1–4; 15–19; 7–12; 9–14; 13–16.
RILM 78 1907.

762. "Der Klavierlehrer ist ein Computer mit Bildschirm." *Instrumentenbau-Zeitschrift* 25 (1971): 338–39.

763. Knezevic, B. "Kompjuterizacija nastave muzickog vaspitanja." [The Computerization of Teaching Music Students] *Zvuk* 2 (Summer 1975): 60–62.
In Serbo-Croatian.

764. Kolb, Randall M. "A Real-Time Microcomputer-Assisted System for Translating Aural, Monophonic Tones into Music Notation as an Aid in Sightsinging." Ph. D. diss., Louisiana State University and Agricultural and Mechanical College, 1984. 364 p.
DA 45:2297A.

765. Kuhn, Wolfgang E. "Computer-Assisted Instruction in Music: Drill and Practice in Dictation." *College Music Symposium* 14 (Fall 1974): 89–101.
RILM 74 4012.

766. ——, and Raynold L. Allvin. "Computer-Assisted Teaching: A New Approach to Research in Music." *Journal of Research in Music Education* 15 (1967): 305-15.

767. ——, and Paul V. Lorton. "CAI in Basic Musicianship." In *1981 Western Educational Computing Conference and Trade Show, San Francisco, CA, 19-20 Nov. 1981.* California: California Educational Computing Consortium, 1981: 1-6.
C&CA 18 (1983): 36156.

768. ——, and Paul V. Lorton. "Computer-Assisted Instruction in Music: Analysis of Student Performance, 1973-80." In *Proceedings of NECC 1981, National Educational Computing Conference, Denton, TX, 17-19 June 1981,* ed. D. Harris and L. Nelsonheern. Iowa City, Iowa: University of Iowa, 1981: 142-48.
C&CA 17 (1982): 5211.

769. ——, and Paul V. Lorton. "Computer Assisted Instruction in Music: Ten Years of Evolution." In *Computers in Education,* ed. B. Lewis and D. Tagg. Amsterdam: North-Holland, 1981: 207-14.

770. ——, and Paul V. Lorton. "Learning Music at the Computer." In *The Best of the Computer Faires: Conference Proceedings of the 8th West Coast Computer Faire,* ed. Jim C. Warren. Woodside, Calif.: Computer Faire, 1983: 51-56.

771. ——, and Paul V. Lorton. "Personal Computer Assisted Instruction in Music." In *The Best of the Computer Faires: Conference Proceedings of the 6th West Coast Computer Faire,* ed. Jim C. Warren. Woodside, Calif.: Computer Faire, 1981: 181-87.

772. Kuyper, J. Quentin. "MISTI: A Computer-Assisted Instruction System in Music Theory and Fundamentals." Ph. D. diss., University of Iowa, 1981. 262 p.
DA 42:4641A.

773. ——. "Music More Music." *Creative Computing* 3 (Mar.-Apr. 1977): 109.
C&CA 12 (1977): 23191.

774. ——. "Sharps and Flats." *Creative Computing* 3 (Mar.-Apr. 1977): 114.
C&CA 12 (1977): 23193.

775. Kuzmich, John. "Computers Today: An Economical Way To Start." *Music Educators Journal* 39 (Nov. 1984): 36-39, 98-104.

776. ——. "Computers Today: How to Choose What's Right for Your Program. Part I." *The Instrumentalist* 39 (Sept. 1984): 14-18.

777. ——. "Computers Today: Looking at a 'Real-Time' System. Part II." *The Instrumentalist* 39 (Oct. 1984): 26-34.

778. ——. "Computers Today: Upgrading your Apple." *Music Educators Journal* 39 (Mar. 1985): 60-65.

779.   Lamb, Martin R. "Andre Tchaikovsky Meets the Computer: A Concert Pianist's Impromptu Encounter with a Musicianship Teaching Aid." *International Journal of Man-Machine Studies* 10 (1978): 593–602.
C&CA 14 (1979): 19613. *C&IS* 23 (1979): 221794C.

780.   ———. "The Computer as a Musicianship Teaching Aid." Ph. D. thesis, University of Canterbury, Christchurch, New Zealand, 1979.

781.   ———. "Computer Games for Developing Musical Skills." In *Proceedings, 1981 International Computer Music Conference, November 5–8,* comp. Larry Austin and Thomas Clark. Denton, Tex.: North Texas State University, 1983: 397–413.

782.   ———. "An Interactive Graphical Modeling Game for Teaching Musical Concepts." *Journal of Computer-Based Instruction* 9 (1982): 59–63.
CIJE 15 (1983): EJ 279 798.

783.   ———. "New Techniques for Teaching Musical-Instrument Performance." In *Proceedings, Graphics Interface '82,* ed. K. B. Evans and E. M. Kidd. Ottawa: National Research Council of Canada, 1982: 103–6.
C&CA 18 (1983): 7244. *C&CA* 31 (1983): 83–6572C.

784.   ———. "Two Heuristics for Computer-Aided Musical Instruction." *Proceedings of the American Society for Information Science* 18 (1981): 317.

785.   ———, and R. H. T. Bates. "Computerized Aural Training: An Interactive System Designed to Help Both Teachers and Students." *Journal of Computer-Based Instruction* 5 (Aug.-Nov. 1978): 30–37.
CIJE 11 (1979): EJ 198 326.

786.   ———, and V. Buckley. "A User-Interface for Teaching Piano Keyboard Techniques." In *INTERACT '84, First IFIP Conference on Human-Computer Interaction, London, England, 4–7 Sept. 1984.* Amsterdam: Elsevier, 1984: 201–8.
C&CA 20 (1985): 4090.

787.   Largent, Edward J. "Music CAI Programs and Youngstown State University." In *Sixth International Conference on Computers and the Humanities,* ed. S. K. Burton and D. D. Short. Rockville, Md.: Computer Science Press, 1983: 339–43.
C&CA 19 (1984): 52035.

788.   Laske, Otto E. "Toward a Theory of Musical Instruction." In *Theory Only: Journal of the Michigan Music Theory Society* 2 (June-July 1976): 43–66.
Also in *Interface* 5 (Nov. 1976): 125–48.
Also in *Music and Mind.* Boston, Mass: O. Laske, 1981: 219–42.

789.   Lawrence, Joy E., and Anne Marie Allison. "Plug into a Computer to Plan Your Repertory." *Music Educators Journal* 65 (Dec. 1978): 38–43.
CIJE 11 (1979): EJ 204 082.

790. Lee, James L. "The Effectiveness of a Computer-Assisted Program Designed to Teach Verbal-Descriptive Skills Upon an Aural Sensation of Music." Ed. D. diss., East Texas State University, 1975. 237 p.
DA 36:1363A-4A.
Review by Joseph Youngblood in *Bulletin of the Council for Research in Music Education* 62 (Spring 1980): 42–44.

791. Lees, Heath. "Computerized Aural Training—a Personal View." *The Australian Journal of Music Education* 27 (Oct. 1980): 33–35.

792. Lemons, Robert M. "The Development and Trial of Microcomputer-Assisted Techniques to Supplement Traditional Training in Musical Sightreading." D.M.A. diss., University of Colorado at Boulder, 1984. 138 p.
DA 45:2023A.

793. Lindeman, Carolynn A. "Computer-Assisted Instruction in Music: A Program in Rhythm for Preservice Elementary Teachers." D.M.A. diss., Stanford University, 1979. 188 p.
C&IS 25 (1980): 243461C. *DA* 40:731A.

794. Lorton, Paul V.; Michael A. Arenson; Bruce C. Benward; and Roger E. Foltz. "New Directions in Computer-Assisted Instruction." Panel discussion at the 1983 International Computer Music Conference, Oct. 7–10, 1983, Rochester, N.Y.

795. ———, and Rosemary N. Killam. "Data Analysis and Retention: Experience and Recommendations." In *Proceedings of the 1977 Winter Conference of the Association for the Development of Computer-Based Instructional Systems.* Wilmington, Del., February, 1977: 298–307.

796. ———, and Rosemary N. Killam. "Modeling the Student and the Discipline in CAI Drill and Practice." In *The Papers of the ACM SIGCSE-SIGCUE Technical Symposium, Computer Science and Education,* ed. Ron Colman, Paul Lorton. New York, N.Y.: ACM, 1976: 223–35. (SIGCSE Bulletin vol. 8, no. 1) (SIGCUE Topics vol. 2)

797. ———; Rosemary N. Killam; and Wolfgang E. Kuhn. "A Computerized System for Research and Instruction in Music." In *Computers in Education: Proceedings of the IFIP 2nd World Conference,* ed. O. Lecarme and R. Lewis. Amsterdam: North-Holland Press, 1975: 765–69.

798. ———; Rosemary N. Killam; and Wolfgang E. Kuhn. "Research on Computer-Assisted Instruction in Music." In *University-Level Computer-Assisted Instruction at Stanford: 1968–1980,* ed. P. Suppes. Stanford, Calif.: Institute for Mathematical Studies in the Social Sciences, 1981: 877–93.

799. ———, and Wolfgang E. Kuhn. "A Microcomputer Application for Instruction in Music." In *Involving Micros in Education: Proceedings of the IFIP TC 3 and University of Lancaster Joint Working Conference on Involving Micros in Education, Lancaster, England, 24–26 March 1982,* ed. R. Lewis and E. D. Tagg. Amsterdam; New York: North-Holland, 1982: 63–67.

800.   ———, and Wolfgang E. Kuhn. "A Microcomputer Based Curriculum System for Basic Musicianship." In *Ninth Australian Computer Conference Schools Symposium 1982, Hobart, Tasmania, Australia, 26–28 Aug. 1982.* Sandy Bay, Tasmania, Australia: Australian Computer Society, 1982: 127–35.

801.   Matthews, William. "Computers, Music, and the Arts: A Liberal Arts College Course." In *Proceedings, 3rd Symposium on Small Computers in the Arts, October 14–16, 1983, Philadelphia, Pa.* Los Angeles, Calif.: IEEE Computer Society, 1983: 86–88.
        C&CA 19 (1984): 28110.

802.   Mayer, Alfred. "Does the Physical Aspect of Music-Making Cause Negative Experiences?" *Music Educators Journal* 61 (Mar. 1975): 57–60, 109–12.
        CIJE 8 (1975): EJ 113 535.

803.   McCauley, Carol S. *Computers and Creativity.* New York: Praeger, 1974. 160 p.
        Review by Paul Berry in *Computers and the Humanities* 9 (1975): 257–58.

804.   McGinty, Tony, and Fran Reinhold, eds. "The Big Sift." *Electronic Learning* 4 (May-June 1985): 15–32, 37, 42–43.
        CIJE 17 (1985): EJ 318 668.

805.   Medsker, Larry. "A Course in Computers and Music." *Collegiate Microcomputer* 1 (1983): 133–40.
        CIJE 17 (1985): EJ 308 665.

806.   "Middle Grade Ideas." *Classroom Computer Learning* 4 (Feb. 1984): 74–75.
        CIJE 16 (1984): EJ 293 866.

807.   Minetree, R. "Music Software for Micro-Computers." *Dialogue in Instrumental Music Education* 7,1 (1983): 12–18.

808.   *Mission of the Future: Proceedings of the Annual Convention of the Association for the Development of Computer-Based Instructional Systems. Volume I, General Session Papers and Project Reports.* San Diego, Calif., Feb. 27 to Mar. 1, 1979. *ERIC:* ED 175 447.
        Contains items: 607, 707, 725, 738, 831.

809.   Moore, B. "A CAI Music Lab in the Middle School." *Dialogue in Instrumental Music Education* 7,1 (1983): 19–23.

810.   Moore, Herb. "What Shape Does Music Have?" *Classroom Computer Learning* 5 (Mar. 1985): 38–41.
        CIJE 17 (1985): EJ 315 868.

811.   Morrill, Dexter G. "An Undergraduate Course for an Interactive Computer Music System." In *Proceedings of Conference on Computers in the Undergraduate Curricula, Washington State University, Pullman, Washington, June 24, 25, 26, 1974.* Pullman, Wash.: Dept. of Computer Science, Washington State University, 1974: 79–85.

812. Mortenson, Glenn R. "Development and Use of Computerized Procedures for Scoring Sight Reading of Rhythms to Compare the Effectiveness of Metric and Representational Notation with Conventional Notation." Ph. D. diss., Northwestern University, 1970. 207 p.
Abstract in *Computers and the Humanities* 8 (1974): 123–24.
DA 31:4205A. *RILM* 76 1745.

813. Muro, Don. "The Musician and the Electronic Medium: Computer Music Systems." *International Musician* 81 (Feb. 1983): 1, 12.

814. Murphy, Brian J. "Educational Programs for the Very Young." *Creative Computing* 9 (Oct. 1983): 107–18.
CIJE 15 (1983): EJ 285 885.

815. Newcomb, Steven R. "LASSO: A Computer-Based Tutorial in Sixteenth-Century Counterpoint." Ph. D. diss., Florida State University, 1983. 1382 p.
DA 44:3201A.

816. ———; Bradley K. Weage; and Peter Spencer. "MEDICI: Tutorial in Melodic Dictation." *Journal of Computer-Based Instruction* 7 (Feb. 1981): 63–69.
C&CA 16 (1981): 27625.

817. Ottman, Robert W.; Rosemary N. Killam; R. M. Adams; W. Kenton Bales; S. Bertsche; Leslie C. Gay; D. B. Marshall; D. A. Peak; and D. Ray. "Development of a Concept-Centered Ear-Training CAI System." *Journal of Computer-Based Instruction* 6 (Feb. 1980): 79–86.
C&CA 15 (1980): 22754. *CIJE* 12 (1980): EJ 225 862.

818. "Over 8,000 Attend First Roger Williams Opening." *The Music Trades* 118 (June 1970): 50.

819. Papert, Seymour, and Cynthia Solomon. *Twenty Things to Do With a Computer.* Cambridge: Massachusetts Institute of Technology, Artificial Intelligence Lab, 1971. (Artificial Intelligence Memo no. 248)
ERIC: ED 077 240.

820. Parrish, James W. "Computer Research as a Course of Study in Music Education: Development of an Exemplary Sequence of Teacher-Guided and Self-Instructional Learning Modules for College Music Majors." Ph. D. diss., Florida State University, 1977. 113 p.
C&IS 23 (1979): 217665C. *DA* 39:3216A.

821. Pea, Roy D. *Prospects and Challenges for Using Microcomputers in School.* New York, N.Y.: Bank Street College of Education, Center for Children and Technology, 1984. 23 p. (Technical Report no. 27)
ERIC: ED 249 927.

822. Peelle, Howard A. "Computer Metaphors: Approaches to Computer Literacy for Educators." *Weaver of Information and Perspectives on Technological Literacy* 1 (Spring 1983): 10–11.
CIJE 15 (1983): EJ 281 769.

823.   ———, and Stuart Smith. "Instructional Applications of Computer Music."
        In *Proceedings of the 1980 International Computer Music Conference,* comp.
        Hubert S. Howe. San Francisco, Calif.: Computer Music Association, 1982:
        61–73.

824.   Persson, L. N. "Computer-Aided Instruction for the Guitar." *Soundboard* 6,3
        (1979): 96–98.

825.   Peters, G. David. "Audio Interfacing of the PLATO Computer-Assisted
        Instructional System for Music Performance Judging." In *Proceedings of the
        Second Annual Music Computational Conference, November 7–9, 1975 at the
        University of Illinois at Urbana-Champaign. Part 4, Information Processing Sys-
        tems,* comp. James Beauchamp and John Melby. Urbana, Ill.: University of
        Illinois: 79–94.

826.   ———. "The Complete Computer-Based Music System: A Teaching
        System—A Musician's Tool." In *New Directions in Educational Computing:
        Proceedings of the 1977 Winter Conference of the Association for the Develop-
        ment of Computer-Based Instructional Systems.* Wilmington, Del., February,
        1977: 93–100.
        ERIC: ED 148 297.

827.   ———. "Computer-Assisted Instruction Applications to Standardized Music
        Achievement Testing." In *New Directions in Educational Computing: Proceed-
        ings of ADCIS 1978 Conference, Dallas, Texas, March, 1978:* 184–91.
        ERIC: ED 160 088. *ERIC:* ED 160 072, p. 184–91.

828.   ———. "Computer-Assisted Instruction of Instrumental Music." *The Instru-
        mentalist* 30 (Sept. 1975): 46–47.

829.   ———. "Computer-Based Education in Music: Courseware Selection and
        Evaluation." Paper presented at the Combined Annual Meetings of the Amer-
        ican Musicological Society (Forty-Sixth Annual Meeting), College Music
        Society, and Society for Music Theory, November 6–9, 1980, Denver Hilton,
        Denver, Colorado.

830.   ———. "Computer Technology in Instrumental Music Instruction." *The
        Instrumentalist* 37 (Feb. 1983): 35–37.

831.   ———. "Courseware Development for Micro-Computer Based Education in
        Music." In *Mission of the Future: Proceedings of the Annual Convention of the
        Association for the Development of Computer-Based Instructional Systems.
        Volume I, General Session Papers and Project Reports.* San Diego, Calif., Feb.
        27 to Mar. 1, 1979: 922–27.
        ERIC: ED 175 447.

832.   ———. "Feasibility of Computer-Assisted Instruction for Instrumental Music
        Education." Ed. D. diss., University of Illinois at Urbana-Champaign, 1974.
        191 p.
        DA 35:1478A-9A. *RILM* 75 2744.
        Review by Joseph Youngblood in *Bulletin of the Council for Research in Music
        Education* 46 (Spring 1976): 47–51.

833. ———. "Hardware Development for Computer-Based Instruction." *College Music Symposium* 21 (Fall 1981): 15–21.

834. ———. "Percussion Instruction Methods by Computer." *The Instrumentalist* 32 (Jan. 1978): 41–43.

835. ———. "Teacher Training and High Technology." *Music Educators Journal* 70 (Jan. 1984): 35–39.
CIJE 16 (1984): EJ 292 281.

836. Phelps, Roger P. "Seminar in State Music Supervision." *Council for Research in Music Education Bulletin* 15 (Winter 1969): 8–13.

837. Placek, Robert W. "Choosing the Best Software for Your Class." *Music Educators Journal* 72 (Sept. 1985): 49–53.
CIJE 17 (1985): EJ 321 710.

838. ———. "Consortium Services for the Acquisition of Instructional Computing Materials." *Journal of Computer-Based Instruction* 9, special issue (May 1983): 203–5.

839. ———. "Design and Trial of a Computer-Assisted Lesson in Rhythm." Ed. D. diss., University of Illinois at Urbana-Champaign, 1972. 320 p.
Review by David Swanzy in *Bulletin of the Council for Research in Music Education* 47 (Summer 1976): 29–34.
DA 34:813A. *RILM* 74 1203.

840. ———. "Design and Trial of a Computer-Assisted Lesson in Rhythm." *Journal of Research in Music Education* 22 (1974): 13–23.
RILM 74 3995.

841. ———. "Design and Trial of Computer-Assisted Lessons in Rhythm." Paper presented at the Combined Annual Meetings of the American Musicological Society (Forty-Sixth Annual Meeting), College Music Society, and Society for Music Theory, November 6–9, 1980, Denver Hilton, Denver, Colorado.

842. ———. "A Model for Integrating Computer-Assisted Instruction Materials into the Music Curriculum." *Journal of Computer-Based Instruction* 6 (1980): 99–105.
CIJE 12 (1980): EJ 225 865.

843. Platte, Jay D. "The Effects of a Microcomputer-Assisted Instructional Program on the Ability of College Choral Ensemble Members to Sing Melodic Configurations at Sight." D.A. diss., Ball State University, 1981. 85 p.
DA 42:1368A-9A.

844. Ploeger, Floyd D. *The Effectiveness of Microcomputers in Education.* Austin, Tex.: Southwest Educational Development Lab., 1983. 105 p.
ERIC: ED 246 876.

845. ———. The Effectiveness of Microcomputers in Education: A Quick Guide to the Research. Austin, Tex.: Southwest Educational Development Lab., 1983. 50 p.
ERIC: ED 246 838.

846.   Prével, Martin. "Computer-Assisted Ear Training: From Research to Practical Applications: Essential Elements of a Minimal Student Terminal." In *Proceedings of the Third Canadian Symposium on Instructional Technology,* ed. E. I. Swail and G. Neal. Ottawa: National Research Council of Canada, 1980: 407–16.

847.   ———. "The Development of Open Drills in the Context of Computer-Based Ear Training." *Journal of Computer-Based Instruction* 9 (Autumn 1982): 74–77.
         C&CA 18 (1983): 25651. *CIJE* 15 (1983): EJ 279 799.

848.   ———. "Low-Cost, Computer-Assisted Ear Training." *Journal of Computer-Based Instruction* 6 (Feb. 1980): 77–78.
         C&CA 15 (1980): 27753.

849.   Radocy, Rudolf E. "Computerized Criterion-Referenced Testing of Certain Nonperformance Musical Behaviors." *Council for Research in Music Education Bulletin* 28 (Spring 1972): 1–6.

850.   ———. "Development and Refinement of a Computerized Criterion-Referenced Test of Certain Nonperformance Musical Behaviors." *Journal of Research in Music Education* 20 (Summer 1972): 225.

851.   ———. "Development of a Computerized Criterion-Referenced Test for Certain Nonperformance Musical Behaviors Requisite to Teaching Music." Ed. D. diss., Pennsylvania State University, 1971. 147 p.
         DA 32:2556A.

852.   Ramsey, Darhyl S. "Programmed Instruction Using Band Literature to Teach Pitch and Rhythm Error Detection to Music Education Students." *Journal of Research in Music Education* 27 (Fall 1979): 149–62.
         C&CA 15 (1980): 14093.

853.   ———. "Programmed Instruction Using Full-Score Band Literature to Teach Pitch and Rhythm Error Detection Skill to College Music Education Students." Ph. D. diss., University of Iowa, 1978. 653 p.
         DA 39:4798A-9A.
         Review by Donald W. Roach in *Council for Research in Music Education Bulletin* 65 (Winter 1981): 87–92.

854.   Reich, Nancy B. "The Subject is Computers." *Music Educators Journal* 55 (Feb. 1969): 47–49, 115–18.

855.   "Reports of Chapter Meetings." *College Music Symposium* 20 (Fall 1980): 174–77.

856.   Robinson, Russell L. "The Development and Evaluation of Microcomputer-Assisted Music Instruction Program for the Improvement of Tonal Memory." Ph. D. diss., University of Miami, 1984. 138 p.
         C&IS 33 (1985): 85–3821C. *DA* 45:1065A.

857. Rosenthal, Roseanne K. "A Data-Based Approach to Elementary General Music Teacher Preparation." Ed. D. diss., Syracuse University, 1982. 167 p.
DA 43:2920A.

858. Rumery, Kenneth R. "Bringing Your Classroom On-Line." *Music Educators Journal* 71 (Jan. 1985): 21–24.
CIJE 17 (1985): EJ 309 210.

859. Sanders, William H. "The Effect of Computer-Based Instructional Materials in a Program for Visual Diagnostic Skills Training of Instrumental Music Education Students." Ph. D. diss., University of Illinois at Urbana-Champaign, 1980. 129 p.
C&IS 26 (1981): 267407C. *DA* 41:2492A.

860. Saul, Thomas N. "Three Applications of the Computer in the Education of Music Teachers." Ph. D. diss., University of Rochester, Eastman School of Music, 1976.
Review by C. Boody in *Bulletin of the Council of Research in Music Education* 56 (Fall 1978): 39–43.
C&IS 16: 163571C. *DA* 37:1867A-8A.

861. Schrader, David L. "Microcomputer-Based Teaching." *College Music Symposium* 21 (Fall 1981): 27–36.

862. ———. "Microcomputers Come to Music." *The Instrumentalist* 35 (Feb. 1981): 24–25.

863. ———, and David B. Williams. "Microcomputers and Music Learning: The Development of the Illinois State University Fine Arts Instruction Center, 1977–1981." In *Proceedings of the 57th Annual Meeting, National Association of Schools of Music, Dallas, Texas, 1981*. Reston, Va.: National Association of Schools of Music, 1982: 40–47.

864. Schwaegler, David G. "A Computer-Based Trainer for Music Conducting: The Effects of Four Feedback Modes." Ph. D. diss., University of Iowa, 1984. 157 p.
DA 45:2794A.

865. Schwartz, Richard. "Roll Over, Schoenberg: A Computer-Generated Tone Row." *Music Educators Journal* 70 (Apr. 1984): 46–47.
CIJE 16 (1984): EJ 295 994.

866. Smith, Irwin S. "Design and Simulation of an Experimental Microcomputer-Based Instructional System for Music." Ed. D. diss., University of Massachusetts, 1980. 201 p.
C&IS 26 (1981): 259777C. *DA* 40:6183A.

867. Smith, William M. "Technological Instruction in Higher Education: The Dartmouth Experience." *Technological Horizons in Education* 6 (Nov. 1979): 36–39, 46.
CIJE 12 (1980): EJ 213 384.

868. Steele, Douglas J., and Barry L. Wills. "Microcomputer-Assisted Instruction for Musical Performance Skills." In *Computers in Education,* ed. B. Lewis and D. Tagg. Amsterdam: North-Holland, 1981: 199–206.

869. ———, and Barry L. Wills. "Microcomputer-Assisted Instruction for Musical Performance Skills." *Technological Horizons in Education* 9 (Jan. 1982): 58–60, 64.
CIJE 14 (1982): EJ 258 495.

870. Stefani, Gino. "La competenza musicale comune: un progetto di ricerca." [Basic Musical Competence: A Research Project] *Ricerche di psicologia* 12 (1979): 31–44.
RILM 79 2025.

871. Stevens, Robin. "Computers in Music Education: Future Directions and Opportunities for Australia." *Australian Journal of Music Education* n31 (Oct. 1982): 5–15.

872. Steward, L. R. "Here's What Classroom Computers Can Do." *American School Board Journal* 169 (Mar. 1982): 32, 45.
CIJE 14 (1982): EJ 259 504.

873. Švaboda, Zdenka. "Programmierter Unterricht auf dem Gebiet der Musikerziehung in der ČSSR." *Programmiertes Lernen. Unterrichtstechnologie und Unterrichtsforschung* 9 (1972): 215–25.
RILM 76 4148.

874. Swanzy, David. "Computer-Assisted Management of Schools of Music." In *Proceedings of the 15th Annual Convention, Association for Educational Data Systems, Fort Worth, Texas, U.S.A. 25–29 April 1977.* Washington, D.C.: Association for Educational Data Systems, 1978: 272–75.
C&CA 13 (1978): 18645.

875. ———. "The Computer in Music Education: Present and Future." *Educational Technology* 11 (Aug. 1971): 25–26.

876. ———. "Setting Technology to Music." *Educational Technology* 11 (Aug. 1971): 9.

877. ———. "The Versatile Computer; Moving Toward an Efficient, Functional Computer Laboratory to Assist in Music Learning." *Music Educators Journal* 62 (Mar. 1976): 37–41.
CIJE 9 (1977): EJ 147 529.

878. Taylor, Jack A. "Computers as Music Teachers." *Music Educators Journal* 69 (Jan. 1983): 43–45.
CIJE 15 (1983): EJ 275 322.

879. ———. *Introduction to Computers and Computer Based Instruction in Music.* Tallahassee, Fla.: Center for Music Research Press, 1981. (CMR Report X–4)

880. ———. "The MEDICI Melodic Dictation Computer Program: Its Design, Management, and Effectiveness as Compared to Classroom Melodic Dictation." *Journal of Computer-Based Instruction* 9 (Autumn 1982): 64–73. *C&CA* 18 (1983): 25650.

881. ———. "Professional Report: CBI Research and Development Centers— Center for Music Research, Florida State University." *Journal of Computer-Based Instruction* 9 (Spring 1983): 171–72. *C&CA* 18 (1983): 40649.

882. ———, and James W. Parrish. "A National Survey on the Uses of, and Attitudes Toward, Programmed Instruction and Computers in Public School and College Music Education." *Journal of Computer-Based Instruction* 5 (Aug.– Nov. 1978): 11–21. *C&CA* 14 (1979): 14060. *CIJE* 11 (1979): EJ 198 324.

883. Thieme, Darius M. "The Applicability of Computer Assisted Instruction in College Music Theory." *American Music Teacher* 25 (Feb.-Mar. 1976): 18–19.

884. Thompson, Edgar J. "Sight-Singing Constant Rhythm Pitch Phrases: A Computer-Assisted Instructional System." Ph. D. diss., University of Utah, 1973. 115 p. *DA* 34:4319A. *RILM* 76 1778.

885. Thornburg, David D., and Pam Beane. "Early Grade Ideas." *Classroom Computer Learning* 4 (Nov.-Dec. 1983): 62–63. *CIJE* 16 (1984): EJ 290 399.

886. ———, and Pam Beane. "Upper Grade Ideas." *Classroom Computer Learning* 4 (Nov.-Dec. 1983): 68–69. *CIJE* 16 (1984): EJ 290 401.

887. Thostenson, Marvin S. "A Project in Aural Interval Identification, Phase One." Paper presented at the Annual Meeting of the Association for the Development of Computer Based Instructional Systems, Dallas, Texas, 1–4 March 1978. *ERIC*: ED 160 087.

888. ———. "Two Important Principles for Constructing Computer-Based Music Instruction Programs—The Circle of Fifths and Key Transposition." In *New Directions in Educational Computing: Proceedings of the 1977 Winter Conference of the Association for the Development of Computer-Based Instructional Systems.* Wilmington, Del., Feb., 1977: 89–92. *ERIC*: ED 148 297.

889. Trimble, G., and S. Frye. "Microcomputers: A New Tune for an Old Song." In *Microcomputers in Education: Getting Started,* ed. N. A. Watson. Tempe, Ariz.: Arizona State University, Dept. of Elementary Education, 1981: AA 1.

890. Turk, Gayla C. "Development of the Music Listening Strategy—TEMPO: Computer Assisted Instruction in Music Listening." Ph. D. diss., University of Kansas, 1984. 171 p. *DA* 45:2436A.

891. Turrietta, A. A., and Cheryl R. Turrietta. "Computer Music Applications in Education: The Soundchaser Computer Music System." In *AEDS 21st Annual Convention Proceedings: Frontiers in Educational Computing, Portland, Or., 9–13 May 1983.* Washington, D.C.: Association for Educational Data Systems, 1983: 346–49.
C&CA 19 (1984): 3551. *C&IS* 32 (1984): 84–8507C.

892. Tutaj, Duane. "Music and Micros, Software Reviews: M.E.C.C. Music Theory." *Music Educators Journal* 39 (Feb. 1985): 95–97.

893. Ulbrich, M. *Tabellen zur Notenschrift; ein Programm für angehende Berufsmusiker.* Stuttgart: Hochschul-Verlag, 1978. 130 p.
Review by Clemens Kuhn in *Musica* 33 (1979): 286.

894. Upitis, Rena. "A Computer-Assisted Instruction Approach to Music for Junior-Age Children: Using ALF for Teaching Music Composition." In *Proceedings of the Venice 1982 International Computer Music Conference,* comp. Thom Blum and John Strawn. San Francisco, Calif.: Computer Music Association, 1985: 479–510.
ERIC: ED 225 650.

895. ———. "Milestones in Computer Music Instruction." *Music Educators Journal* 69 (Jan. 1983): 40–42.
CIJE 15 (1983): EJ 275 321.
Also in *The Education Digest* 49 (Oct. 1983): 55–57.

896. Vaughan, Arthur C. "A Study of the Contrast between Instruction and the Traditional Teacher/Learner Method of Instruction in Basic Musicianship." Ph. D. diss., Oregon State University, 1978. 152 p.
DA 38:3357A.
Review by Ned C. Deihl in *Council for Research in Music Education Bulletin* n64 (Fall 1980): 80–82.

897. Wagner, Christoph; Ernst Piontek; and Ludwig Teckhaus. "Piano Learning and Programmed Instruction." *Journal of Research in Music Education* 21 (1973): 106–22.
RILM 73 4223. *CIJE* 5 (1973): EJ 081 466.

898. Wallace, Robert L. "Your Sort of Computer Program!" *Music Educators Journal* 71 (Jan. 1985): 33–36.
CIJE 17 (1985): 309 212.

899. Watanabe, Nan T. "Computer-Assisted Music Instruction Utilizing Compatible Audio Hardware in Computer-Assisted Aural Drill." Ph. D. diss., University of Illinois at Urbana-Champaign, 1981. 191 p.
DA 42:3900A.

900. ———. "Review of Audio Interfacing Literature for Computer-Assisted Music Instruction." *Journal of Computer-Based Instruction* 6 (Feb. 1980): 87–90.
C&CA 15 (1980): 27755. *CIJE* 12 (1980): EJ 225 863.

901.   Wells, Colin. "Harmonic Duo: Music & Computers." *The Times Educational Supplement* 3531 (Mar. 2, 1984): 48–50.

902.   Wille, Lee. "Computer-Assisted Music Instruction." *The Instrumentalist* 36 (Feb. 1982): 30–33.

903.   Williams, David B. "Microcomputers Interface with the Arts." *Music Educators Journal* 69 (Jan. 1983): 39.

904.   Wilson, Mary L. P. "The Development of CAI Programs for Teaching Music Fundamentals to Undergraduate Elementary Education Music Methods Classes." Ph. D. diss., Louisiana State University and Agricultural and Mechanical College, 1981. 203 p.
        DA 42:1044A.

905.   Wittlich, Gary E. "Computers and Music Education." *School Musician* 55 (Nov. 1983): 38–39.

906.   ———. "Computers and Music Instruction: Prospects and Problems." In *Third Annual Conference on Instructional Computing Applications, South Bend, Indiana, 5 March 1976.* Bloomington, Ind.: Indiana University, 1976: 116–20.
        C&CA 11 (1976): 17146.

907.   ———. "Developments in Computer Based Music Instruction and Research at Indiana University." *Journal of Computer-Based Instruction* 6 (Feb. 1980): 62–71.
        C&CA 15 (1980): 27740. *CIJE* 12 (1980): EJ 225 860.

908.   ———. "Evaluating Microcomputers for the Delivery of Music Instruction." *School Musician* 55 (Jan. 1984): 38–39.

909.   ———. "Evaluating Microcomputers for the Delivery of Music Instruction. Part II." *School Musician* 55 (Mar. 1984): 18–19.

910.   ———. "Microcomputers, Music, and Instruction." *School Musician* 54 (Nov. 1982): 4–7.

911.   ———. "Music Rudiments Programs." *School Musician* 55 (May 1984): 14–15.

912.   ———. "TRIPLE P: A Comprehensive Computer-Based Program in Pitch Pattern Perception." In *Computer-Based Instruction: A New Decade: 1980 Proceedings, Association for the Development of Computer-Based Instructional Systems.* Bellingham, Wash.: Western Washington University, 1980: 213–19.
        C&CA 16 (1980): 33898.

913.   Wolfe, George. "Creative Computers: Do They 'Think'?" *Music Educators Journal* 69 (Jan. 1983): 59–62.
        CIJE 1983: EJ 275 328.

914.   Woodruff, Earl; Carl Bereiter; and Marlene Scardamalia. "On the Road to Computer Assisted Compositions." *Journal of Educational Technology Systems* 10,2 (1981–82): 133–48.
      C&CA 17 (1982): 24464.

915.   Yukoo, Yoshinori, and Keizo Nagaoka. "Computerized Methods for Evaluating Musical Performances and for Providing Instruction Techniques for Keyboard Instruments." *Computers & Education* 9 (1985): 111–26.
      C&CA 20 (1985): 30928.

916.   Zinn, Karl, and David Zinn. "Atari Music Composer." *Creative Computing* 7 (Apr. 1981): 28–29.
      C&CA 16 (1981): 36843.

917.   Zuckerman, Faye. "Apple Software Offers Course in Music Theory." *Billboard* 95 (Dec. 24, 1983): 41.

CONFERENCES

918. *8. Tonmeistertagung 19.–22. November 1969 Hamburg. Durchgeführt vom Verband deutscher Tonmeister und Toningenieure e.V.* Cologne: Westdeutscher Rundfunk, 1969. *RILM* 73 1599.

919. "Abstracts from the Third Colloquium on Musical Informatics, Padua University, Italy." *Computer Music Journal* 3,3 (Sept. 1979): 38–41.

920. Ager, Klaus. "2. Internationale Computermusik-Konferenz." *Melos/Neue Zeitschrift für Musik* 4 (1978): 136–38.

921. Appleton, Jon H. "Report from Yale: Festival of Contemporary American Music." *Current Musicology* 3 (Spring 1966): 65–68.

922. ———. "Report on the Stockholm Electronic Music Festival VII and the ICEM Conference on Electroacoustic." *Computer Music Journal* 10,1 (Spring 1986): 95–96.

923. *Atti del Quarto Colloquio di Informatica Musicale.* [Proceedings of the Fourth Colloquium on Computer Music] Pisa: CNUCE-CNR, 1981. 352 p. Contains items: 95, 111, 185, 206, 249, 341, 393, 1159, 1262, 2167, 2796, 2974, 3213, 3521, 3543, 3637, 4048, 4129, 4208, 4285, 4337.

924. *Atti del Quinto Colloquio di Informatica Musicale.* [Proceedings of the Fifth Colloquium on Computer Music] Ancona: Università di Ancona, 1983. 212 p. Contains items: 132, 159, 303, 399, 580, 1070, 1135, 2129, 2203, 2639, 2640, 2954, 3005, 3197, 3271, 3335, 3389, 3399, 3604, 3636, 3644, 3843, 3877, 3882, 3950, 4336.

925. *Atti del Terzo Colloquio di Informatica Musicale.* [Proceedings of the Third Colloquium on Computer Music] Padua: Università di Padova, 1979. 260 p. Contains items: 110, 149, 344, 362, 432, 474, 1178, 1831, 2048, 2070, 2254, 3071, 3387, 3409, 3541, 3631, 3634, 3819, 3846, 4057, 4088.

926. Austin, Larry, and Thomas Clark, comp. *Proceedings, 1981 International Computer Music Conference, November 5–8.* Denton, Tex.: School of Music, North Texas State University, 1983. 422 p. Contains items: 32, 72, 134, 214, 253, 315, 317, 325, 395, 425, 461, 547, 671, 760, 781, 1846, 1896, 2016, 2032, 2095, 2134, 2323, 2334, 2392, 2685, 2696, 3008, 3141, 3183, 3216, 3218, 3235, 3262, 3317, 3339, 3341, 3359, 3492, 3584, 3587, 3610, 3708, 3797, 3821, 3834, 3856, 3957, 3973, 3983, 3988.

927. Baroni, Mario, and Laura Callegari, eds. *Musical Grammars and Computer Analysis: Atti del Convegno (Modena, 4–6 Ottobre 1982).* Florence: L. S. Olschki, 1984. 374 p. Contains items: 89, 342, 2043, 2069, 2170, 2171, 2242, 2274, 2352, 2419, 2426, 2427, 2455, 2461, 2481, 2485.

928. Battier, Marc, and Barry D. Truax, eds. *Computer Music/Composition musicale par ordinateur; Report on an International Project Including a Workshop at Aarhus, Denmark in 1978.* Ottawa: Canadian Commission for Unesco, 1980. 205 p.
Review by D. Laszlo in *Computer Music Journal* 5,4 (Winter 1981): 75–76. Contains items: 9, 166, 257, 468, 485, 1010, 2933, 3557, 3580, 3723, 3748, 3781, 4043, 4066, 4552.

929. Beauchamp, James W., and John Melby, comps. *Composition with Computers: Proceedings of the Second Annual Music Computation Conference, Nov. 7–9, 1975. Part 2.* Urbana: University of Illinois, 1975. 83 p. Contains items: 102, 205, 384, 424, 4265.

930. ———, and John Melby, comps. *Hardware for Computer-Controlled Sound Synthesis: Proceedings of the Second Annual Music Computation Conference, Nov. 7–9, 1975. Part 3.* Urbana: University of Illinois, 1975. 59 p. Contains items: 1062, 2943, 3062, 3223.

931. ———, and John Melby, comps. *Information Processing Systems, Proceedings of the Second Annual Music Computation Conference, Nov. 7–9, 1975. Part 4.* Urbana: University of Illinois, 1975. 96 p. Contains items: 825, 1903, 2142, 2713, 3861.

932. ———, and John Melby, comps. *Software Synthesis Techniques, Proceedings of the Second Annual Music Computation Conference, Nov. 7–9, 1975. Part 1.* Urbana: University of Illinois, 1975. 75 p. Contains items: 1124, 3648, 3679, 3714, 3737, 3760, 3941.

933. Bernard, Jonathan W., and Martin Brody. "Report on the National Meeting of the Society for Music Theory." *Computer Music Journal* 6,2 (Summer 1982): 65–71.

934. Blesser, Barry A.; B. Locanthi; and Thomas G. Stockham, eds. *Digital Audio.* New York, N.Y.: Audio Engineering Society, 1983. 268 p.
Review by K. Tanawa in *Computer Music Journal* 9,1 (Spring 1985): 61.

935. Blum, Thomas L.; Curtis Abbott; Larry Austin; Marc Battier; James W. Beauchamp; James Dashow; Wesley Fuller; Dorothy S. Gross; E. Hargs; Gary S. Kendall; Otto E. Laske; D. Gareth Loy; Joseph Marc; Alan Marr; Bruce Pennycook; Stephen T. Pope; and John Strawn. "Report on the 1982 International Computer Music Conference." *Computer Music Journal* 7,2 (Summer 1983): 8–35.

936. ———, and John Strawn, comps. *Proceedings of the Venice 1982 International Computer Music Conference.* San Francisco, Calif.: Computer Music Association, 1985. 749 p. Contains items: 17, 104, 107, 116, 162, 228, 256, 321, 367, 373, 419, 456, 467, 548, 645, 894, 1174, 1451, 1560, 1607, 1638, 1803, 1834, 1858, 2028, 2031, 2133, 2222, 2243, 2727, 2918, 2937, 2941, 2972, 2999, 3081, 3127, 3165, 3330, 3451, 3460, 3487, 3508, 3586, 3641, 3729, 3761, 3777, 3832, 3884, 3955, 3965, 3972, 3974, 3999, 4000, 4224.

937. Bolognesi, Tommaso; Giovanni De Poli; and Goffredo Haus. "The Fourth Colloquium on Musical Informatics." *Interface* 10 (1981): 245–50.

938. ———; Giovanni De Poli; and Goffredo Haus. "Quarto Colloquio di Informatica Musicale." [Fourth Colloquium on Computer Music] *Strumenti musicali* 20/21 (1981): 146–49.

939. Borry, Linda. "Musical Match and Binary Bach." *AEDS Monitor* 11 (Dec. 1972): 12–13.

940. Brickle, Frank. "Music Computation Conference II." *Contemporary Music Newsletter* 9,5 (1975): 1–2.

941. Buxton, William, ed. *Proceedings of the International Computer Music Conference, 1984: IRCAM, Paris, France, October 19–23, 1984.* San Francisco, Calif.: Computer Music Association, 1985. 318 p. Contains items: 141, 353, 388, 429, 500, 698, 1076, 1100, 1165, 1569, 1900, 1983, 2113, 2683, 2723, 3021, 3272, 3287, 3337, 3356, 3380, 3383, 3393, 3395, 3428, 3430, 3491, 3507, 3603, 3635, 3652, 3694, 3718, 3783, 3808, 3811, 3820, 3853, 3883, 3904, 3907, 3908.

942. Charnassé, Hélène, ed. *Informatique et musique, Second Symposium International: Organisé par L'Equipe ERATTO, Orsay, 6–9 Juillet 1981.* Ivry: ELMERATTO, C.N.R.S., 1983. 260 p. Contains items: 748, 1904, 1967, 2066, 2137, 2185, 2211, 2291, 2338, 2339, 2369, 2407, 2408, 2444, 2462, 2514, 2565, 2784, 2832, 2836, 4036.

943. Clough, John. "The First International Conference on Computer Music." *In Theory Only* 2 (Nov. 1976): 34–35.
RILM 76 7039.

944. "College Music Society: Report of the Eighth Annual Meeting, Second Session." *College Music Symposium* 6 (Fall 1966): 124–33.

945. "Computer Music Conference Held at Northwestern." *School Musician* 50 (Dec. 1978): 39.

946. *Computer Music In Britain, 8th–11th April 1980.* London: Electro-Acoustic Music Association of Great Britain, 1980. Contains items: 85, 203, 234, 250, 1434, 2607, 3289, 3368, 3417, 3921, 3992.

947. *Conférence des journées d'études, festival international du son.* Paris: Ed. Radio, 1973.
RILM 74 1077.

948. Cvetko, Dragotin, ed. *Report of the Tenth Congress [of the International Musicological Society], Ljubljana 1967.* Kassel: Bärenreiter, 1970. 506 p. Contains items: 243, 2082, 2161, 2256, 2321, 2342, 2376, 2401, 2476, 2761.

949. "Digicon Revisited." *Keyboard* 11 (July 1985): 20.

950. Ducasse, Henri. "Compte-rendu des journées d'études d'informatique musicale." *Informatique et sciences humaines* 19 (Dec. 1973): 67–70.

951. ——, ed. *Informatique musicale 1977. Textes des conférences. Equipe Eratto.* Paris: Centre de documentation sciences humaines, 1978. 222 p.
RILM 78 2401.

952. Elschek, Oskár. "Ludová pieseň a samočinný počítač 2: druhý seminár o využití samočinných počítačov pri štúdiu l'udových piesni, Bratislava 16.–17. Október 1973." [Folksongs and the Computer 2: Seminar in Bratislava, 16–17 October 1973] *Musicologica Slovaca* 6 (1978): 163–65.
In Slovak.

953. Evarts, John. "Stockholm." *World of Music* 12,3 (1970): 52–56.
In English, French, and German.

954. Gamarekian, Edward. "Music Composed by Computer Among Wonders Heard at Parley." *Washington Post and Times Herald* (Dec. 31, 1958): A6.

955. Glahn, Henrk; Søren Sørensen; and Peter Ryom, eds. *IMS Report 1972.* Copenhagen: W. Hansen, 1974.
In English, German, and French.
RILM 76 179.

956. Greenhough, Michael. "Sound and Music Synthesis Using Combined Mainframe/Microcomputer and Analogue Synthesizer Systems." *Electro Acoustic Music* 1 (1985): 12–13.

957. Gross, Robert, W., comp. *Proceedings of the Rochester 1983 International Computer Music Conference.* San Francisco, Calif.: Computer Music Association, 1984. 307 p. Contains items: 152, 183, 428, 569, 616, 672, 1098, 1168, 2056, 2114, 2635, 2728, 3194, 3263, 3311, 3429, 3448, 3483, 3540, 3643, 3650, 3674.

958. ——; with Conrad Cummings; Deta S. Davis; Ruth Dreier; Craig Harris; Mark Kahrs; Stephan Kaske; Dexter G. Morrill; Bruce Pennycook; Stephen T. Pope; and John Strawn. "Report on the 1983 International Computer Music Conference." *Computer Music Journal* 8,2 (Summer 1984): 7–23.

959. Gryč, Stephen M. "Music Computation Conference II." *In Theory Only* 1 (Feb.-Mar. 1976): 3–5.
RILM 76 3940.

960. Harris, R. P., ed. *Proceedings of the International Music and Technology Conference, August 24–28, 1981, University of Melbourne, Australia.* Parkville, Vic.: Computer Music Project, Dept. of Computer Science, University of Melbourne, 1981. 262 p. Contains items: 70, 134, 190, 210, 345, 434, 497, 1172, 1424, 1670, 1962, 3265, 3397, 3478, 3624, 3721, 3752, 4127.

961. Haus, Goffredo. "Digital audio alla AES Convention." [Digital Audio at the AES Convention] *Strumenti musicali* 29 (1982): 56–62.

962. ———. "Matematica e musica (Cronaca di una ricerca: i Colloqui di Informatica Musicale)." [Mathematics and Music (News from Research: The Colloquia on Computer Music)] *Strumenti musicali* 1 (1979): 95–99.

963. ———. "Numero e Suono: International Computer Music Conference 1982 (I)." [Digit and Sound: International Computer Music Conference 1982 (I)] *Strumenti musicali* 35 (1982): 70–77.

964. ———. "Numero e Suono: International Computer Music Conference 1982 (II)." [Digit and Sound: International Computer Music Conference 1982 (II)] *Strumenti musicali* 36 (1982): 68–74.

965. ———. "Quinto Colloquio di Informatica Musicale." [The Fifth Colloquium on Computer Music] *Strumenti musicali* 48 (1983): 75–78.

966. ———. "Summing up the Situation of Computer Music in Italy at the Conference of Milan." *Interface* 9 (1980): 115–21.

967. ———; with Nicola Bernardini; James Dashow; Giovanni De Poli; Eugenio Giordani; Mauro Graziani; Richard Karpen; Andrea Libretti; Curtis Roads; Maurizio Rubbazzer; Nicola Sani; Sylviane Sapir; Daniele Torresan; Barry D. Truax; and Elio Verdi. "Report from the 1984 International Computer Music Conference." *Computer Music Journal* 9,2 (Summer 1985): 20–40.

968. Heckmann, Harald. "Computer Aids in Music Libraries and Archives." *Fontes Artis Musicae* 26 (1979): 100–101.
RILM 79 2106.

969. Helm, Everett. "Rapport de l'Unesco sur la reunion de Stockholm." *La revue musicale* 268–69 (1971): 195–208.
English version: "Unesco Report on the Stockholm Meeting." In *Music and Technology*. Paris: La revue musicale, 1971: 193–206.

970. Hertlein, Grace C. "Report on the 2nd International Conference on Computers and the Humanities, Los Angeles, Calif., U.S.A." *Leonardo* 9 (Winter 1976): 43–45.

971. Holý, Dušan. "2. seminař o využiti samočinného počítače při studiu lidové pisně." [2nd Seminar in the Use of Computers for the Study of Folk Songs] *Národopisné aktuality* 11 (1974): 240–42.
In Czech.

972.   ———; Karel Pala; and Miloš Štědroň, eds. *Lidová píseň a samočinný počítač 3. Sborník materiáluze 3. semináře o využití samočinného počítače při studiu lidové písně* (Brno 15.-16.10.1974). [Folk Music and the Computer 3. A Collected Volume of Materials from the Third Seminar on the Application of Computers in the Study of Folk Song] Prague: Státni pedagogické nakladatelství, 1976. 411 p.
In Czech and Slovak; summaries in English and German.
RILM 76 182.
Review by Bohuslav Benes in *Jahrbuch für Volksliedforschung* 18 (1973): 157–58.
Contains items: 2060, 2190, 2225, 2279, 2330, 2415, 2525, 2558.

973.   Howe, Hubert S. "Music and Electronics: A Report." *Perspectives of New Music* 4 (Spring-Summer 1966): 68–75.

974.   ———. "Report on the International Music and Technology Conference." *Computer Music Journal* 6,2 (Summer 1982): 45–51.

975.   Kassler, Jamie C. "Report from London: Cybernetic Serendipity." *Current Musicology* 7 (1968): 47–59.

976.   Keane, David. "The Bourges International Festival of Experimental Music: A Retrospective." *Computer Music Journal* 8,3 (Fall 1984): 51–59.

977.   Laske, Otto E. "Notes on the International Conference on Music, Reason, and Emotion." *Computer Music Journal* 8,4 (Winter 1984): 55.

978.   Lefkoff, Gerald, ed. *Papers from the West Virginia University Conference on Computer Applications in Music.* Morgantown: West Virginia University Library, 1967. 105 p.
Review by Harry B. Lincoln in *Notes* 25 (1968): 39–40.
Review by James W. Pruett in *Computer Studies in the Humanities and Verbal Behavior* 1 (Oct. 1968): 155.
Review by Donald J. Shetler in *Music Educators Journal* 55 (Jan. 1969): 77–79.
Review by A. Wayne Slawson in *Journal of Music Theory* 12 (1968): 105–11.
Contains items: 225, 2208, 2355, 2754.

979.   Lincoln, Harry B. "The Computer Seminar at Binghamton: A Report." *Notes* 23 (1967–68): 236–40.

980.   Lubar, David. "Sights and Sounds at PCAF." *Creative Computing* 7 (Jan. 1981): 40–42.
C&CA 16 (1981): 27619.

981.   Maltese, Accorto. "Il Terzo Colloquio di Informatica Musicale, 2-3 April, University of Padova." *Interface* 8 (1979): 91–101.

982.   McConkey, Jim. "Report from the Sixth Annual West Coast Computer Faire." *Computer Music Journal* 5,3 (Fall 1981): 60–61.
C&IS 29 (1982): 82–01628C.

983.   ———. "Report from the Synthesizer Explosion." *Computer Music Journal* 8,2 (Summer 1984): 59–60.

984.   ———. "Report on the Fourth Annual Symposium on Small Computers in the Arts." *Computer Music Journal* 9,2 (Summer 1985): 53–59.

985.   ———. "Report on the Symposium on Small Computers in the Arts." *Computer Music Journal* 6,2 (Summer 1982): 61–64.

986.   ———. "Report on the Third Annual Symposium on Small Computers in the Arts." *Computer Music Journal* 8,2 (Summer 1984): 41–47.

987.   ———. "The Second Annual Symposium on Small Computers in the Arts." *Computer Music Journal* 7,3 (Fall 1983): 25–30.

988.   McDonough, J. "See Big Turnout for US Festival; Expect 25,000 at Combination Music-Computer Fair." *Billboard* 94 (Aug. 28, 1982): 26.

989.   McLean, Priscilla. "At North Texas State: Computer Music." *Hi Fidelity/ Musical America* 32 (Mar. 1982): MA34, MA40.

990.   Michaud-Pradeilles, Catherine. "Informatique musicale." *Revue de musicologie* 59 (1973): 308–11.

991.   Milano, Dominic. "DIGICON '85 International Arts Conference on Computers and Creativity." *Keyboard* 11 (1985): 20, 118.

992.   Miller, Fred. "The 58th AES Convention: Digital Is Here." *High Fidelity/ Musical America* 28 (Feb. 1978): 112–14.

993.   Moberg, Dick. "Philadelphia Computer Music Festival." *Creative Computing* 5 (Oct. 1979): 107.

994.   Morehen, John. "Orsai Conference." *The Musical Times* 122 (Sept. 1981): 623.

995.   *Music and Technology, Stockholm Meeting June 8–12, 1970.* Paris: La revue musicale, 1971. 208 p.
        RILM 74 1673.
        Review by Fritz Winckel in *Die Musikforschung* 27 (1974): 480–81.

996.   *Musica ed elaboratore elettronico. Verso il laboratorio musicale personale.* [Proceedings of the Conference Music and Computers: Towards the Personal Music Laboratory] Milan: FAST, 1980. 160 p. Contains items: 343, 2067, 2102, 2935, 3642, 3906, 3925, 3931, 4004, 4171.

997.   *Numero e Suono.* [Digit and Sound] Venezia: Biennale di Venezia, 1982. 296 p.

998.   Päch, Susanne. "Report on the Ars Electronica 80 Symposium Held at Linz, Austria, in September 1980." *Leonardo* 14 (1981): 206–07.

999.   Page, Tim. "Computers and Composers." *New York Times* (Oct. 10, 1983): p. 20(N); p. C14(L).

1000.   Pascall, Robert D. "Music Analysis by Computer: A Conference Report." *Computers and the Humanities* 14 (1980): 79.

1001.   ———. "Nottingham." *The Musical Times* 120 (1979): 851.

1002.   Pellegrino, Ronald. "ASUC's Fourth Annual Conference (1969)." *Perspectives of New Music* 8 (Fall-Winter 1969): 155–56.

1003. Pruett, James W. "The Harpur College Music-Computer Seminar: A Report." *Computer and the Humanities* 1 (1966–67): 34–48.

1004. Roads, Curtis. "A Personal Assessment." In *Computer Music/Composition musicale par ordinateur; Report on an International Project at Aarhus, Denmark in 1978*. Ottawa: Canadian Commission for Unesco, 1980: xxvii–xxxiii. In English and French.

1005. ———, comp. *Proceedings of the 1978 International Computer Music Conference*. Evanston, Ill.: Northwestern University Press, 1979. Contains items: 191, 224, 287, 314, 335, 336, 347, 586, 1103, 1153, 1251, 1261, 1272, 1274, 1804, 1872, 1922, 1935, 1961, 1985, 2112, 2132, 2221, 2250, 2286, 2421, 2456, 2551, 2655, 2682, 2911, 2962, 3284, 3358, 3365, 3479, 3503, 3504, 3577, 3616, 3862, 3881, 3905, 3987, 4572.

1006. ———. "Report on the 1978 International Computer Music Conference." *Computer Music Journal* 2,4 (late Dec. 1978): 21–27.

1007. ———. "Report on the International Conference on Musical Grammars and Computer Analysis." *Computer Music Journal* 7,2 (Summer 1983): 36–42.

1008. ———. "Report on the IRCAM Conference: The Composer and the Computer." *Computer Music Journal* 5,3 (Fall 1981): 7–27.
Review by P. J. Drummond in *Computing Reviews* 25 (Aug. 1984): 8408–0683.

1009. ———. "Symposium on Computer Music Composition." *Computer Music Journal* 10,1 (Spring 1986): 40–63.

1010. ———. "The Unesco Workshop on Computer Music at Aarhus, Denmark." *Computer Music Journal* 2,3 (Dec. 1978): 30–32.
Reprinted in *Computer Music/Composition musicale par ordinateur; Report on an International Project Including a Workshop at Aarhus, Denmark in 1978*, ed. Marc Battier and Barry Truax. Ottawa: Canadian Commission for Unesco, 1980: xi–xxv.
In English and French.

1011. Rothstein, Edward. "Computers Face the Music at Texas Conference." *New York Times* (Nov. 5, 1981): p. C21(LC), col. 2.

1012. Sani, Nicola. "A proposito di un convegno sull'informatica musicale: Tirrenia, Settembre 1982. Inserimento della computer music nell'organizzazione del lavoro musicale." [Regarding a Conference on Computer Music: Tirrenia, Sept. 1982. Integration of Computer Music into the Organization of Musical Endeavors] *Quaderni di Informatica Musicale* 10/11 (1983).

1013. ———. *Informatica, Musica/Industria: Pensiero compositivo, ricerca, didattica, sviluppo industrial.* [Information Processing, Music Industry: Compositional Thought, Research, Pedagogy, Industrial Development] Milan: Edizioni Unicopli, 1984. 328 p.
Review by Curtis Roads in *Computer Music Journal* 9,4 (Winter 1985): 66.

1014. Silverman, Faye-Ellen. "Report from New York City: Computer Conference, June 1973." *Current Musicology* 17 (1974): 77–80. *RILM* 74 844.

1015. Stearns, David Patrick. "Eastman Computer Conference." *High Fidelity/ Musical America* 34 (Feb. 1984): MA30–MA32.

1016. Stewart, David N. "Circuit: A Report." *Perspectives of New Music* 11 (Spring-Summer 1973): 265–68. *RILM* 73 4536.

1017. Stockmann, Erich, ed. *Studia Instrumentorum Musicae Popularis II. Bericht über die 3. Internationale Arbeitstagung der Study Group on Folk Musical Instruments des International Folk Music Council in Stockholm 1969.* Stockholm: Musikhistoriska museet, 1972. 196 p. In German and English. *RILM* 73 143.

1018. Strapac, Susan. "MUSICOMP 76." *Computers and the Humanities* 10 (1976): 343–45.

1019. Strawn, John. "Report from the 1980 Audio Engineering Society Convention in Los Angeles." *Computer Music Journal* 4,3 (Fall 1980): 66–73.

1020. ———; Curtis Abbott; Philip Baczewski; James W. Beauchamp; Thomas Blum; William Buxton; Peter J. Clements; G. Dietrich; Charles M. Dodge; Wesley Fuller; Dorothy S. Gross; Robert W. Gross; David Jaffe; Gary S. Kendall; Dexter G. Morrill; Bruce Pennycook; Amy Quate; and James Stiles. "Report on the 1981 International Computer Music Conference." *Computer Music Journal* 6,2 (Summer 1982): 11–31.

1021. ———; Curtis Abbott; Thomas Blum; Nan Earle; Dorothy S. Gross; Laurie Hollander; and Leland Smith. "Report on the International Computer Music Conference, Queens College, November 1980." *Computer Music Journal* 5,2 (Summer 1981): 36–44.

1022. Stroppa, Marco. "Biennale Musica di Venezia: i nuovi spazi sonori dell'informatica musicale." [Biennale Musica di Venezia: The New Realms of Sound in Computer Music] *Bit* [Milan] 23 (1981): 18–21.

1023. Suchoff, Benjamin. "A National Science Computer Network: A Report on the First Working Seminar." *Computers and the Humanities* 7 (1972): 96–97. *RILM* 72 2750.

1024. Šuster, Mojca. "Broj i zvuk." [Number and Sound] *Zvuk* n4 (Winter 1982): 92–94. In Croatian.

1025. Taubman, Howard. "Play it Again, I.B.M." *The New York Times* (Nov. 14, 1966): 54:1.

1026.   Truax, Barry D., ed. *Proceedings of the International Computer Music Conference, 1985: Centre for the Arts, Simon Fraser University, Burnaby, B.C., Canada, August 19-22, 1985.* San Francisco, Calif.: Computer Music Association, 1985. 429 p. Contains items: 75, 97, 106, 198, 306, 308, 350, 422, 505, 534, 538, 539, 576, 583, 1050, 1099, 1183, 1472, 1541, 1561, 1690, 1747, 1752, 1826, 1906, 1982, 2035, 2050, 2054, 2673, 2684, 2985, 2997, 3051, 3098, 3108, 3115, 3132, 3177, 3206, 3221, 3226, 3394, 3446, 3506, 3607, 3660, 3742, 3753, 3756, 3758, 3763, 3769, 3779, 3788, 3789, 3809, 3831, 3849, 3867, 3922, 3981, 4020, 4102, 4330, 4488.

1027.   Ungvary, Tamas. "2. International Computer Music Conference; San Diego, USA." *Nutida Musik* 21 (1977-1978): 65-66.

1028.   Valinsky, Eric. "Performances at the International Computer Music Conference." *Synapse* 2 (Jan-Feb. 1978): 12-14.

1029.   Vercoe, Barry. "Music Computation Conference: A Report and Commentary." *Perspectives of New Music* 13 (Fall-Winter 1974): 234-38. *RILM* 74 3961.

1030.   White, Julie. "Digicon '83." *Computer Music Journal* 8,1 (Spring 1984): 43-47.

1031.   White, Kathleen J. "Report on the 74th Audio Engineering Society Convention." *Computer Music Journal* 8,2 (Summer 1984): 55-58.

1032.   Wishart, Trevor. "1984 International Computer Music Conference." *Electro Acoustic Music* 1 (1985): 13-17.

DIGITAL AUDIO

1033. Abbott, Curtis. "Efficient Editing of Digital Sound on Disk." *Journal of the Audio Engineering Society* 32 (1984): 394–402.

1034. Anderton, Craig. "Digital Audio Basics." In *Synthesizers and Computers.* Milwaukee, Wis.: H. Leonard Pub. Corp., 1985: 14–18.

1035. Barbeau, Louis C., and M. J. Corinthios. "A Tutorial on the Construction and Operation of a High-Quality Audio Conversion System." *Computer Music Journal* 8,2 (Summer 1984): 24–40.
Review by H. P. Avey in *Computing Reviews* 26 (Mar. 1985): 8503–0175. *C&IS* 32 (1984): 84–16425C. *E&EA* 87 (1984): 53449.

1036. Berkovitz, Robert. "Audio's Digital Future." *Stereo Review* 39 (July 1977): 81–84.

1037. Blesser, Barry A. "Digital Processing of Audio Signals." Paper presented at the Midwest Acoustics Conference, Apr. 5, 1975, Evanston, Ill.

1038. ———. "An Investigation of Quantization Noise." *Journal of the Audio Engineering Society* 22 (1974): 20–22.

1039. ———; Karlo Baeder; and Ralph Zaorski. "A Real-Time Digital Computer for Simulating Audio Systems." *Journal of the Audio Engineering Society* 23 (1975): 618.

1040. "Computer music e produzione di programmi radiotelevisivi." [Computer Music and the Production of Radio and Television Broadcasts] In *Aspetti teorici di Informatica Musicale.* Milan: CTU-Istituto di Cibernetica, Università di Milano, 1977: 94–95.

1041. Doi, Toshitada; Yoshikazu Tsuchiya; and Akira Iga. "On Several Standards for Converting PCM Signals into Video Signals." *Journal of the Audio Engineering Society* 26 (1978): 641–49.

1042. Freeman, Dennis M. "Slewing Distortion in Digital-to-Analog Conversion." *Journal of the Audio Engineering Society* 25 (1977): 178–83.

1043. Greenspun, Philip. "Audio Analysis I: Phase Correction for Digital Systems." *Computer Music Journal* 8,4 (Winter 1984): 13–19.

1044. Gussow, Seth J. "A Wide-Range Analog to Digital Converter." B.S. thesis, Massachusetts Institute of Technology, Dept. of Mechanical Engineering, 1980. 22 p.

1045. Haus, Goffredo. "Registrazione digitale del suono (I): elementi introduttivi." [Digital Sound Recording. Part 1, Introductory Elements] *Strumenti musicali* 27 (1982): 94–100.

1046. ———. "Registrazione digitale del suono (II): cosa offre il mercato." [Digital Sound Recording. Part 2, What the Marketplace Offers] *Strumenti musicali* 28 (1982): 78–84.

1047. ———. "Registrazione digitale del suono (III): i registratori audio PCM della AEG Telefunken." [Digital Sound Recording. Part 3, The PCM Audio Recorders at AEG Telefunken] *Strumenti musicali* 30–31 (1982): 89–91.

1048. Hausler, Wolf Detlef. "Der 'Digitalregler' als Weg zum automatischen Studio." In *Tonmeistertagung (10.) 19.–22. November 1975, Köln Bericht.* Cologne: Welzel and Hardt, 1976.

1049. Hayashi, S.; M. Honda; and N. Kitawaki. "Adaptive Predictive Coding Scheme and Its Real Time Processing at 64Kb/s for Wide-Band Speech and Music Signals." *Electrical Communication Laboratories Technical Journal* 32 (1983): 2327–38.
In Japanese.
C&CA 19 (1984): 20071. *E&EA* 87 (1984): 26018.

1050. Hebel, Kurt J. "A Machine-Independent Sound Conversion/Storage System." In *Proceedings of the International Computer Music Conference, 1985,* ed. Barry Truax. San Francisco, Calif.: Computer Music Association, 1985: 125–27.

1051. Hillen, Peter. "Analog to Digital Conversion." *Synapse* 2 (July/Aug. 1977): 36–37.

1052. ———. "S/H and A/D Conversion." *Synapse* 2 (Jan./Feb. 1978): 54–55.

1053. ———. "Using an A/D Converter." *Synapse* 2 (Nov./Dec. 1977): 49.

1054. Hutchins, Bernard. "The Effect of Effective Sample-and-Hold with Digital Signals." *Electronotes* 14, special issue A (Dec. 1982): 29–34.

1055. Ingebretsen, Robert B.; Thomas G. Stockham; and Richard B. Warnock. "A Portable Off-Line Tape Recorder for Recording, Archiving and Duplicating Digitized Music." Paper presented at the International Conference on Computer Music, October 28–31, 1976, Massachusetts Institute of Technology.

1056. Jones, Peter. "London Studio 1st with Mix Computer; NECAM Unique." *Billboard* 89 (Feb. 19, 1977): 36.

1057. Karwoski, Rick. "Predictive Coding for Greater Accuracy in Successive Approximation A/D Converters." Paper presented at the 57th Convention of the Audio Engineering Society, May 10–13, 1977, Los Angeles. Preprint no. 1228 A-6.
Abstract in the *Journal of the Audio Engineering Society* 25 (1977): 514.

1058. Kountz, John C. "Functional Specifications for Digital Computer-Assisted Post-Production Mix-Down." Paper presented at the 54th Convention of the Audio Engineering Society, May 4–7, 1976. AES Preprint no. 1097.

1059. Kowalski, Michael J., and Andrew S. Glassner. "The N.Y.I.T. Digital Sound Editor." *Computer Music Journal* 6,2 (Spring 1982): 66–73. Review by L. R. Medsker in *Computing Reviews* 23 (1982): 39,960. *C&IS* 29 (1982): 82–6394C.

1060. Kriz, J. Stanley. "An Audio Analog-Digital-Analog Conversion System." Paper presented at the 55th Convention of the Audio Engineering Society, Oct. 29–Nov. 3, 1976, New York, N.Y. Preprint No. 1142. Abstract in the *Journal of the Audio Engineering Society* 24 (1976): 859.

1061. ———. "A 16-Bit A–D–A Conversion System for High Fidelity Audio Research." *IEEE Symposium on Speech Recognition, Carnegie-Mellon University, April 15–19, 1974, Contributed Papers.* New York: IEEE, 1974: 278–79. Also in *IEEE Transactions on Acoustics, Speech, and Signal Processing* 23 (1975): 146–49.

1062. ———. "The Specification of Digital-to-Analog Converters for Audio." In *Proceedings of the Second Annual Music Computation Conference, November 7–9, 1975 at the University of Illinois at Urbana-Champaign. Part 3, Hardware for Computer-Controlled Sound Synthesis,* comp. James Beauchamp and John Melby. Urbana, Ill.: University of Illinois: 43–48.

1063. Lee, Francis F., and David Lipschutz. "Floating Point Encoding for Transcription of High Fidelity Audio Signals." Paper presented at the International Conference on Computer Music, October 28–31, 1976, Massachusetts Institute of Technology.

1064. Leunig, Peter H. "Möglichkeiten der Automatisierung im Studio betrieb." In *Tonmeistertagun (10.) 19.–22. November 1975, Köln Bericht.* Cologne: Welzel and Hardt, 1976.

1065. McGill, James F. "An Introduction to Digital Recording and Reproduction." In *Digital Audio Engineering,* ed. John Strawn. Los Altos: W. Kaufmann, 1985: 1–28. (The Computer Music and Digital Audio Series)

1066. Minoli, Daniel. "Digital Techniques in Sound Reproduction. Part 1." *Audio* 64 (Apr. 1980): 54–61.

1067. ———. "Digital Techniques in Sound Reproduction. Part 2." *Audio* 64 (May 1980): 34–42.

1068. Moorer, James A. "The Digital Coding of High-Quality Musical Sound." *Journal of the Audio Engineering Society* 27 (1979): 657–66. *E&EA* 83 (1980): 5736.

1069. Pascoe, Robert D. "The How's and Why's of D/A and A/D Converters." *Popular Electronics* 11 (Apr. 1977): 53–56.

1070. Rubbazzer, Maurizio. "Convertitori D/A a 16 bit per audio professionale." [Professional Audio 16-bit D/A Converters] In *Atti del Quinto Colloquio di Informatica Musicale.* Ancona: Università di Ancona, 1983: 51–55.

1071. Rush, Loren; James A. Moorer; and D. Gareth Loy. "All-Digital Sound Recording and Processing." Paper presented at the International Conference on Computer Music, October 28–31, 1976, Massachusetts Institute of Technology.
       Also presented at the 57th Convention of the Audio Engineering Society, October 29, 1976.
       Abstract in the *Journal of the Audio Engineering Society* 24 (1976): 854.

1072. Sadashige, K., and H. Matsushima. "Recent Advances in Digital Audio Technology." Paper presented at the 66th Convention of the Audio Engineering Society, May 6–9, 1980, Los Angeles, Calif.

1073. Sanchez, Al. "A New Ultralinear 16-Bit Digital-to-Analog Conversion System for Professional Audio." Paper presented at the 66th Convention of the Audio Engineering Society, May 6–9, 1980, Los Angeles, Calif.

1074. Sasaki, Lawrence H., and Kenneth C. Smith. "Digital to Analogue Converter Systems for Audio." Unpublished manuscript. Toronto: Dept. of Electrical Engineering, University of Toronto, 1978.

1075. Serafine, Frank. "The Sound with the Image." *db Sound Engineering Magazine* 15 (May 1981): 46–52.
       C&IS 28 (1982): 81–14976C.

1076. Stautner, John P. "Musical Recording, Editing, and Production Using the Compusonics DSP-2000." In *Proceedings of the International Computer Music Conference, 1984,* ed. William Buxton. San Francisco, Calif.: Computer Music Association, 1985: 131–33.

1077. Steiger, Richard. "Very Wide Dynamic Range Digital-to-Audio Converters for Computer Music Synthesis." Paper presented at the 52nd Convention of the Audio Engineering Society, Oct. 31-Nov. 3, 1975, New York.
       Abstract in *Journal of the Audio Engineering Society* 23 (1975): 834.

1078. Stockham, Thomas G. "A/D and D/A Converters: Their Effect on Digital Audio Fidelity." Paper presented at the 41st Convention of the Audio Engineering Society, Oct. 5–8, 1971, New York. Preprint no. 834.
       Abstract in the *Journal of the Audio Engineering Society* 19 (1971): 880.

1079. Strawn, John. *Digital Audio Engineering: An Anthology.* Los Altos, Calif.: W. Kaufmann, 1985. 144 p. (The Computer Music and Digital Audio Series) Contains items: 1065, 1083, 3179, 3228, 3967.

1080. ———. "Digital Recording. Part One." *Contemporary Keyboard* 7 (Mar. 1981): 16–18, 20.

1081. ———. "Digital Recording. Part Two." *Contemporary Keyboard* 7 (June 1981): 18–22.

1082. Talambiras, Robert P. "Digital-to-Analog Converters: Some Problems in Producing High Fidelity Signals." *Computer Design* 15 (Jan. 1976): 63–69.

1083. ———. "Limitations on the Dynamic Range of Digitized Audio." In *Digital Audio Engineering,* ed. John Strawn. Los Altos: W. Kaufmann, 1985: 29–60.

1084. ———. "Some Considerations in the Design of Wide Dynamic Range Audio Digitizing Systems." Paper presented at the 57th Convention of the Audio Engineering Society, May 10–13, 1977, Los Angeles. AES Preprint no. 1226. Abstract in the *Journal of the Audio Engineering Society* 25 (1977): 514.

DIGITAL SIGNAL
PROCESSING

1085. Adams, G. J. "Measuring Speaker Motion with a Laser." *Audio* 65 (Sept. 1981): 40–49.

1086. Bariaux, D.; G. Cornelissen; J. DePrins; J. L. Guisset; and J. Willems. "Method for Spectral Analysis of Musical Sounds, Description and Performances." *Acustica* 32 (May 1975): 307–13.
Abstract in *The Engineering Index Annual* 74 (1975): 049363.

1087. Beauchamp, James W. "A Computer System for Time-Variant Harmonic Analysis and Synthesis of Musical Tones." Urbana: University of Illinois Experimental Music Studio, Aug. 1967. 63 p. (Technical Report no. 15)
Also in *Music by Computers,* ed. Heinz von Foerster and James W. Beauchamp. New York: Wiley, 1969: 19–62.

1088. ———, and James P. Fornango. "Transient Analysis of Musical Tones with Digital Filters." Paper presented at the 31st Convention of the Audio Engineering Society, Oct. 10–14, 1966, New York City.
Abstract in *Journal of the Audio Engineering Society* 15 (1967): 96.

1089. Bersano, James R. "Formalized Aspect Analysis of Sound Texture." Ph. D. diss., Indiana University, 1979. 347 p.
RILM 79 1673. *DA* 41:11A.

1090. Cahn, Frederick. "Pitch Translation of Trumpet Tones." In *ICASSP 83 Proceedings, IEEE International Conference on Acoustics, Speech, and Signal Processing, Boston, Massachusetts, 14–16 April 1983.* New York: IEEE, 1983: 1380–83.
E&EA 86 (1983): 40007.

1091. Chabrel, Stephane, and Gerard Charbonneau. "Sound Analysis by Mini-Computer in Conversational Mode." *Onde Electronique* 56 (Aug.-Sept. 1976): 356–66.
C&CA 11 (1976): 31331.

1092. Chowning, John M.; John M. Grey; Loren Rush; and James A. Moorer. *Computer Simulation of Music Instrument Tones in Reverberant Environments.* Stanford University, Dept. of Music, Center for Computer Research in Music and Acoustics, June 1974. (Report no. STAN-M-1)

1093. Clendinning, Jane Piper. "Computer Recognition of Pitch for Musical Applications." M.M. thesis, North Texas State University, 1983. 82 p. *Masters Abstracts* 22 (1984): 170.

1094. Cogan, Robert. *New Images of Musical Sound.* Cambridge, Mass.: Harvard University Press, 1984. 177 p. Review by John Strawn in *Computer Music Journal* 10,1 (Spring 1986): 97–98.

1095. Crochiere, R. E., and P. Penfield. "On the Efficient Design of Bandpass Digital Filter Structures." *IEEE Transactions on Acoustics, Speech, and Signal Processing,* Vol. ASSP-23 (1975): 380–83.

1096. DeCrescent, Ron. "A Computer-Based Research Laboratory for Sound-Processing and Analysis." Paper presented at the 45th Convention of the Audio Engineering Society, May 15–18, 1973, Los Angeles.

1097. Depalle, Philippe. *Analyse numérique des sons: codage par prédiction linéaire, estraction de formants.* Université du Maine, Sept. 1984. (Memoire de D.E.A.)

1098. Dolson, Mark B. "Musical Applications of the Phase Vocoder." In *Proceedings of the Rochester 1983 International Computer Music Conference,* comp. Robert W. Gross. San Francisco, Calif.: Computer Music Association, 1984: 100–103.

1099. ———. "Recent Advances in Musique concrète at CARL." In *Proceedings of the International Computer Music Conference, 1985,* ed. Barry Truax. San Francisco, Calif.: Computer Music Association, 1985: 55–60.

1100. ———. "Refinements in Phase-Vocoder-Based Modification of Music." In *Proceedings of the International Computer Music Conference, 1984,* ed. William Buxton. San Francisco, Calif.: Computer Music Association, 1985: 65–66.

1101. ———. "A Tracking Phase Vocoder and Its Use in the Analysis of Ensemble Sounds." Ph. D. diss., California Institute of Technology, 1982. 134 p. *C&IS* 32 (1984): 84–536C. *DA* 44:255B.

1102. Favreau, Emmanuel. "Elaborazione numerica di segnali nel processore in tempo reale 4X." [Digital Signal Processing of the Real Time Processor 4X] Paper presented at the 1982 International Computer Music Conference, Sept. 27–Oct. 1, Venice.

1103. Ferretti, Ercolino. "Nuance Blending for the Synthesis of a Brass Choir." In *Proceedings of the 1978 International Computer Music Conference,* comp. Curtis Roads. Evanston, Ill.: Northwestern University Press, 1979: 142–50.

1104. ———. "Nuances in the Synthesis of 'Live' Sounds." Paper presented at the 1977 International Computer Music Conference, University of California, San Diego, 26–30 October 1977.

1105.   ———. "Some Research Notes on Music with the Computer." *Proceedings of the American Society of University Composers* 1 (1968): 38–41.

1106.   Foster, Scott, and A. Joseph Rockmore. "Signal-Processing for the Analysis of Musical Sound." In *ICASSP 82 Proceedings: IEEE International Conference on Acoustics, Speech, and Signal Processing, Paris, France, 3–5 May 1982.* New York: IEEE, 1982: 89–92.
E&EA 86 (1983): 3794.

1107.   Freedman, M. David. "Technique for the Analysis of Musical-Instrument Tones." Abstract in *Journal of the Acoustical Society of America* 38 (1965): 912.

1108.   ———. "A Technique for the Analysis of Musical Instrument Tones." Ph. D. diss., University of Illinois, 1965. 146 p.
DA 26 :7216.
Also, Urbana, Ill.: University of Illinois Biological Computer Laboratory, 1965. 146 p. (Technical Report no. 6 [10718])

1109.   Frigo, Luciano, and Tiziano Sinigaglia. "Procedure per l'analisi e la sintesi del segnale vocale." [Procedures for Analysis and Synthesis of Voice Signals] *Bollettino LIMB* 4 (1984): 107–14.

1110.   Gish, Walter C. "Analysis and Synthesis of Musical Instrument Tones." Paper presented at the 61st Meeting of the Audio Engineering Society, Nov. 3–6, 1978, New York. AES Preprint no. 1410 (J-3).
Abstract in the *Journal of the Audio Engineering Society* 26 (1978): 998.

1111.   Gordon, John W., and John Strawn. "An Introduction to the Phase Vocoder." In *Digital Audio Signal Processing: An Anthology,* ed. John Strawn. Los Altos, Calif.: W. Kaufmann, 1985: 221–70. (The Computer Music and Digital Audio Series)

1112.   Hamm, Russell O. "Fast Pitch Detection." Paper presented at the 58th Convention of the Audio Engineering Society, Nov. 4–7, 1977, New York. Preprint no. 1265.
Abstract in the *Journal of the Audio Engineering Society* 25 (1977): 1067.

1113.   Hiller, Lejaren A. *Analysis and Synthesis of Musical Sounds by Analog and Digital Techniques: An Interim Progress Report to the National Science Foundation.* Urbana: University of Illinois Press, 1967.

1114.   ———, and James W. Beauchamp. "Review of Completed and Proposed Research on Analysis and Synthesis of Musical Sounds by Analog and Digital Techniques." Mimeographed. Urbana: University of Illinois Experimental Music Studio, July 1967. 90 p. (Technical Report no. 19)

1115.   Hirsch, Julian D. "Computerized Speaker Measurement." *Stereo Review* 43 (Aug. 1979): 33–34.

1116.   Hutchins, Bernard A. "Digital Envelope Generator Design Based on Digital Filter Structures." *Electronotes* 14, special issue A (Dec. 1982): 2–10.

1117. ———. "Guide to Digital Filter Network Design." *Electronotes* Chapter 1, 14 (Nov. 1982): 3–8; Chapter 2, 14, special issue A (Dec. 1983): 11–28; Chapter 3, 14, special issue B (Mar. 1983): 3–12; Chapter 4, 14, special issue B (Mar. 1983): 13–28; Chapter 5, 15, special issue C (July 1983): 3–23.

1118. ———. "An Introduction to Hilbert Transform Theory and Applications." *Electronotes* 14 (Feb. 1982): 7–17.

1119. ———. "Methods of Digital Oscillator Design Based on Digital Filter Structures." *Electronotes* 14 (July 1982)

1120. Janssons, E. V., and Johan Sundberg. "Long-Time-Average-Spectra Applied to Analysis of Music. Part I, Method and General Applications." *Acustica* 34 (1975): 15–19.

1121. Justice, James H. "Analytic Signal Processing in Music Computation." *IEEE Transactions on Acoustics, Speech, and Signal Processing,* Vol. ASSP-27 (1979): 670–84.
C&CA 15 (1980): 19699. *C&IS* 25 (1980): 243462C.

1122. ———. "Frequency Domain Design of Recursive Digital Filters Using Pade Approximation Techniques." Tulsa, Okla.: University of Tulsa, 1975. (Technical Report)

1123. ———. "Frequency Domain Design of Two-Dimensional Recursive Filters." Tulsa, Okla.: University of Tulsa, 1975. (Technical Report)

1124. ———. "Recursive Digital Filtering in Music Computation." In *Proceedings of the Second Annual Music Computation Conference, November 7–9, 1975 at the University of Illinois at Urbana-Champaign. Part 1, Software Synthesis Techniques,* comp. James Beauchamp and John Melby. Urbana, Ill.: University of Illinois: 22–32.

1125. ———. "A Technique for Calculating Time-Variant Filters." Paper presented at the 1977 International Computer Music Conference, University of California, San Diego, 26–30 October 1977.

1126. ———, and J. L. Shanks. "Stability Criterion for N-Dimensional Digital Filters." *IEEE Transactions on Automated Control* AC–18: 284–86.

1127. Kashima, Kyle. "The Bounded-Q Frequency Transform." Stanford, Calif.: Dept. of Music, Stanford University, 1985. (Technical Report STAN–M–28)

1128. ———, and A. Joseph Rockmore. "Acoustic Processing Methods for Musical Sounds Based on a Recursive Constant-Q Transform." Paper presented at the 1984 International Computer Music Conference, Oct. 19–23, Paris, France.

1129. Katz, Robert. "Converting Pitch to Frequency." *BYTE* 6 (Feb. 1981): 92–94.

1130. Keene, Sherman. "The Soundstream Digital Music Computer: Recording, Editing, and Beyond." *db Sound Engineering Magazine* 16 (Sept. 1982): 34–38.
C&CA 18 (1983): 36168.

1131.   Kendall, Gary S. "Theory and Application of Digital Filtering in Computer-Generated Music." Ph. D. diss., University of Texas at Austin, 1982. 387 p. *DA* 43:581A.

1132.   Klapholz, Jesse. "Digital Sampling and FFT Analysis of Acoustic Sources: A Micro-Computer Implementation." In *Proceedings, 4th Symposium on Small Computers in the Arts, October 25-28, 1984, Philadelphia, Pennsylvania.* Silver Spring, MD: IEEE Computer Society Press, 1984: 89-97. *C&CA* 20 (1985): 17289.

1133.   Larsson, Bjorn. "Pitch Tracking in Music Signals." *Speech Transmission Laboratory Quarterly Progress and Status Report* 4 (1977): 1-8. *RILM* 77 4017.

1134.   Martissa, E. "Estratto dalla tesi di laurea: 'Analisi e sintesi di processi pseudo-musicali'." [Analysis and Synthesis of Pseudo-Musical Processes: Abstract from the Graduation Thesis] In *Aspetti teorici di Informatica Musicale.* Milan: CTU-Istituto di Cibernetica, Università di Milano, 1977: 80-93.

1135.   Mian, Gianantonio, and Graziano Tisato. "Applicazioni musicali di un sistema per l'analisi e la sintesi della voce." [Applications to Music of a System for Voice Analysis and Synthesis] In *Atti del Quinto Colloquio di Informatica Musicale.* Ancona: Università di Ancona, 1983: 114-28.

1136.   Miller, N. J. "Pitch Detection by Data Reduction." *IEEE Transactions on Acoustics, Speech, and Signal Processing,* Vol. ASSP-23 (1975): 72-79.

1137.   Moore, F. Richard. "An Introduction to the Mathematics of Digital Signal Processing." In *Digital Audio Signal Processing: An Anthology,* ed. John Strawn. Los Altos, Calif.: W. Kaufmann, 1985: 1-67. Reprinted from the *Computer Music Journal.*

1138.   ————. "An Introduction to the Mathematics of Digital Signal Processing. Part I, Algebra, Trigonometry, and the Most Beautiful Formula in Mathematics." *Computer Music Journal* 2,1 (July 1978): 38-47.

1139.   ————. "An Introduction to the Mathematics of Digital Signal Processing. Part II, Sampling, Transforms, and Digital Filtering." *Computer Music Journal* 2,2 (Sept. 1978): 38-60.

1140.   Moore, Michael. "The Seeger Melograph Model C." In *Selected Reports in Ethnomusicology,* Volume II, No. 1, ed. Mantle Hood. Los Angeles: University of California, 1974: 2-13.

1141.   Moorer, James A. "L'elaborazione dei segnali nella computer music." [Signal Processing in Computer Music] In *Musica e elaboratore.* Venice: Biennale di Venezia, 1980: 51-94.

1142.   ————. "The Hetrodyne Filter as a Tool for Analysis of Transient Waveforms." Stanford, Calif.: Computer Science Dept., Stanford University, 1973. (Stanford Artifical Intelligence Laboratory Memo AIM-208)

1143.   ———. "The Optimum Comb Method of Pitch Period Analysis of Contin-
uous Digitized Speech." Stanford Calif.: Computer Science Dept., Stanford
University, 1973. (Stanford Artifical Intelligence Laboratory Memo ALM-207)
Reprinted in *IEEE Transactions on Acoustics, Speech and Signal Processing,*
Vol. ASSP-22 (1974): 330–38.

1144.   ———. "Signal Processing Aspects of Computer Music: A Survey." *Proceed-
ings of the IEEE* 65 (1977): 1108–37.
C&IS 17: 185336C.
Reprinted in the *Computer Music Journal* 1,1 (Feb. 1977): 4–37.
C&IS 18 (1978): 189695C. *RILM* 77 4020.
Also in *Digital Audio Signal Processing: An Anthology,* ed. John Strawn. Los
Altos, Calif.: W. Kaufmann, 1985: 149–220.

1145.   ———. "The Use of the Phase Vocoder in Computer Music Applications."
Journal of the Audio Engineering Society 26 (1978): 42–45.
C&CA 13 (1978): 13020. *E&EA* 81 (1978): 25573.

1146.   ———, and Mark Berger. "Linear-Phase Bandsplitting: Theory and Applica-
tions." Paper presented at the 76th Convention of the Audio Engineering
Society, Oct. 8–11, 1984, New York. AES Preprint no. 2132.
Abstract in *Journal of the Audio Engineering Society* 32 (1984): 1000.

1147.   Otis, Alton B. "Low-Pass Digital Filtration." In "Four Sound Processing Programs for the Illiac II Computer and D/A Converter," ed. James W. Beauchamp. Urbana: University of Illinois Experimental Music Studio, Sept. 1968:
1–15. (Technical Report no. 14)

1148.   ———. "Time Rate Changing." In "Four Sound Processing Programs for
the Illiac II Computer and D/A Converter," ed. James W. Beauchamp.
Urbana: University of Illinois Experimental Music Studio, Sept. 1968: 38–49.
(Technical Report no. 14)

1149.   Peled, Abraham, and Bede Liu. *Digital Signal Processing: Theory, Design, and
Implementation.* Malabar, Fla.: R.E. Krieger, 1985. 304 p.

1150.   Petersen, Tracy L. "Acoustic Signal Processing the the Context of a Perceptual
Model." Ph. D. diss., University of Utah, 1980.

1151.   ———. "The Composer as Surgeon: Performing Phase Transplants." Paper
presented at the 1977 International Computer Music Conference, University of
California, San Diego, 26–30 Oct. 1977.

1152.   ———. "Theory and Implementation of the Critical Band Transform."
Paper presented at the 1980 International Computer Music Conference,
November 13–15, 1980, Queens College of the City University of New York.

1153.   ———. "Time-Frequency Analysis in the Context of a Perceptual Model." In
Proceedings of the 1978 International Computer Music Conference, comp.
Curtis Roads. Evanston, Ill.: Northwestern University Press, 1979: 582–84.

1154.   Pikler, Andrew G. "Musical Transfer Functions and Processed Music." *IRE
Transactions on Audio* AU-10 (1962): 47–52.

1155.   Piszczalski, Martin B., and Bernard A. Galler. "Predicting Musical Pitch from Component Frequency Ratios." *Journal of the Acoustical Society of America* 66 (1979): 710–20.
C&CA 14 (1979): 34800.

1156.   Potter, Charles. "Sonic Transliteration Applied to Descriptive Music Notation." Paper presented at the 1980 International Computer Music Conference, November 13–15, 1980, Queens College of the City University of New York.

1157.   *Programs for Digital Signal Processing.* New York: IEEE Press, 1979.
Review by Julius O. Smith in *Computer Music Journal* 5,2 (Summer 1981): 62–66.

1158.   Reinecke, Hans-Peter, and Dagmar Droysen. "Methoden zur Untersuchung nichtstationärer Schallvorgänge dargestellt an der Analyse eines Hammerflügels." In *Elektronische Datenverarbeitung in der Musikwissenschaft,* ed. Harald Heckmann. Regensburg: G. Bosse, 1967: 175–85.

1159.   Reinhard, P. "Distorsione non lineare della somma di due cosinusoidi: analisi dello spettro tramite matrici." [Non-Linear Distortion of the Sum of Two Cosine Waves: Spectrum Analysis Using Matrices] In *Atti del Quarto Colloquio di Informatica Musicale.* Pisa: CNUCE-CNR, 1981: 160–83.

1160.   Risberg, Jeffrey S. "Process Model Formulation for Analysis of Timbre and Articulation." Paper presented at the 1980 International Computer Music Conference, November 13–15, 1980, Queens College of the City University of New York.

1161.   Rush, Loren. "The Tuning of Performed Music." Paper presented at the 1982 International Computer Music Conference, Sept. 27–Oct. 1, Venice.

1162.   ———, and James A. Moorer. "Editing, Mixing, and Processing Digitized Audio Waveforms." Paper presented at the 57th Convention of the Audio Engineering Society, May 10–13, 1977, Los Angeles.
Abstract in *Journal of the Audio Engineering Society* 25 (1977): 514.

1163.   Schloss, W. Andrew. "Goal-Directed Signal Processing." Paper presented at the 1983 International Computer Music Conference, Oct. 7–10, 1983, Rochester, N.Y.

1164.   Scott, Samuel T., and Harold A. Stromberg. "Simple Hybrid Systems for Accurate Synthesis and Analysis of Harmonic Spectra." *Conference Record of the IEEE International Conference on Acoustics, Speech and Signal Processing, 12–14 April 1976, Philadelphia, Pa.* New York: IEEE, 1976: 630–32.

1165.   Smith, Julius O. "An Allpass Approach to Digital Phasing and Flanging." In *Proceedings of the International Computer Music Conference, 1984,* ed. William Buxton. San Francisco, Calif.: Computer Music Association, 1985: 103–9.

1166.   ———. "Fundamentals of Digital Filter Theory." *Computer Music Journal* 9,3 (Fall 1985): 13–23.

1167. ———. "An Introduction to Digital Filter Theory." In *Digital Audio Signal Processing: An Anthology,* ed. John Strawn. Los Altos, Calif.: W. Kaufmann, 1985: 69–135.

1168. ———. "Spectral Pre-Processing for Audio Digital Filter Design." In *Proceedings of the Rochester 1983 International Computer Music Conference,* comp. Robert W. Gross. San Francisco, Calif.: Computer Music Association, 1984: 58–80.

1169. ———. "Techniques for Digital Filter Design and System Identification with Application to the Violin." Ph. D. diss., Stanford University, 1983. 260 p.

1170. ———. "Waveguide Digital Filters." Stanford, Calif.: Center for Computer Research in Music and Acoustics, Dept. of Music, Stanford University, Mar. 1985.

1171. ———, and James B. Angell. "A Constant-Gain Digital Resonator Tuned by a Single Coefficient." *Computer Music Journal* 6,4 (Winter 1982): 36–40.

1172. Sosnin, Jim. "Digital Sound Processing: Studio Effects by Computer." In *Proceedings of the International Music and Technology Conference, August 24–28, 1981, University of Melbourne.* Parkville, Vic.: Computer Music Project, Dept. of Computer Science, University of Melbourne, 1981: 134–49.

1173. Stanley, Gerald. "TDS Computing." *Audio* 67 (Nov. 1983): 38–42.

1174. Stautner, John P. "Analysis and Synthesis of Music Using a Model of the Auditory Transform." In *Proceedings of the Venice 1982 International Computer Music Conference.* San Francisco, Calif.: Computer Music Association, 1985: 466–78.

1175. ———. "Listening and Performing: Control of Computer Music Using the Auditory Transform." Paper presented at the 1983 International Computer Music Conference, Oct. 7-10, 1983, Rochester, N.Y.

1176. Strawn, John, ed. *Digital Audio Signal Processing: An Anthology.* Los Altos, Calif.: W. Kaufmann, 1981. 283 p.
Contains items: 1111, 1137, 1144, 1167, 3713.

1177. Tisato, Graziano. "Analisi dei suoni multipli mediante elaboratore elettronico." [Computer Analysis of Multiple Sounds] *Il fagotto* (1982): 131–37.

1178. ———. "Analisi digitale dei suoni multifonici." [Digital Analysis of Multiphonic Sounds] In *Atti del Terzo Colloquio di Informatica Musicale,* ed. G. De Poli. Padua: Università di Padova, 1979: 107–28.

1179. ———. "Analisi digitale dei suoni musicali." [Digital Analysis of Musical Sounds] *Bollettino LIMB* 1 (1981): 46–58.

1180. Titchener, Paul F. "Adaptive Spectral Analysis and Signal Modeling with Applications to Music and Speech." Ph. D. diss., Stanford University, 1984. 240 p.
DA 45:306B.

1181.   Tjernlund, Per. "Eine statistische Methode für Grundfrequenzmessungen mit einem Computer." In *Studia Instrumentorum musicae popularis II,* ed. Erich Stockmann. Stockholm: Musikhistoriska museet, 1972: 77–81.

1182.   Tucker, Warren H., and R. H. T. Bates. "A Pitch Estimation Algorithm for Speech and Music." *IEEE Transactions on Acoustics, Speech, and Signal Processing,* Vol. ASSP-26 (1978): 597–604.
C&IS 22 (1978): 214183C. *E&EA* 82 (1979): 9273.

1183.   Voelkel, Andrew. "A Cost Effective Input Processor-Pitch Detector for Electronic Violin." In *Proceedings of the International Computer Music Conference, 1985,* ed. Barry Truax. San Francisco, Calif.: Computer Music Association, 1985: 15–17.

1184.   Wagner, Byron B. "Audio Snapshots: Using an Inexpensive Real-Time Spectrum Analyzer with Still-Frame and Slow-Motion Capabilities for Electronic Music Synthesis and Speech Recognition." Paper presented at the 60th Convention of the Audio Engineering Society, May 2–5, 1978, Los Angeles. Abstract in *Journal of the Audio Engineering Society* 26 (1978): 574.

1185.   Wallraff, Dean. "Digital Signal Processing for Musicians." Paper presented at the 1983 International Computer Music Conference, Oct. 7–10, 1983, Rochester, N.Y.

1186.   Williams, Christopher J. "A Harmonic Extraction System for Musical Tone Analysis." B.S. thesis, Massachusetts Institute of Technology, Dept. of Electrical Engineering and Computer Science, 1979. 55 p.

1187.   Wogram, Klaus. "Ein Echtzeit-Stimmungsmessgerät für musikalische Klänge. Parts I–III." *Das Musikinstrument* 28 (1979): 529–31, 704–06, 809–11.
RILM 79 5959.

1188.   ———, and G. Ramm. "Ein digitales Messgerät zur schnellen und genauen Ermittlung von stimmungsfehlern musikalischer Klänge." *Acustica* 34 (1976): 162–72.
RILM 76 1967.

1189.   Zimmerman, Mark. "A Beginner's Guide to Spectral Analysis. Part 1, Tiny Timesharing Music." *BYTE* 6 (Feb. 1981): 68–90.
C&CA 16 (1981): 15678.

RECORD RESTORATION

1190.   Berger, Ivan. "Caruso by Computer." *The Saturday Review* 3 (Oct. 4, 1975): 47–48.

1191.   Brand, David. "Latest Computers See, Hear, Speak, and Sing—and May Outthink Man." *Computers and Automation* 22 (Oct. 1973): 11–13.

1192. Deutsch, W. A., and A. Noll. "The Restoration of Historical Recordings by Means of Digital Signal Processing." Paper presented at the 75th Annual Convention of the Audio Engineering Society, Mar. 27–30, 1984, Paris. AES Preprint 2091.
Abstract in *Journal of the Audio Engineering Society* 32 (1984): 468.

1193. Goodfriend, James. "Computers, Ghosts, and Other Talents." *Stereo Review* 37 (Nov. 1976): 60.

1194. Klein, Larry. "Two Hundred Years of Recording." *Stereo Review* 39 (July 1977): 72–74.

1195. Morehouse, Ward. "Caruso Sings Again." *Christian Science Monitor* 67 (Jan. 9, 1975): 1, 5.

1196. Newcomb, Steven R., and Sherwin Gooch. "Rise Up, Rachmaninoff." *Creative Computing* 6 (June 1980): 66–71.
C&CA 16 (1981): 3169.

1197. Pease, Edward. "Computer Restoration of Caruso and McCormack Recordings: A Critical Report and the Soundstream Process." *The NATS Bulletin* 35 (Nov.-Dec. 1978): 8–14.

1198. Penchansky, Alan. "Sound Restoration Improves." *Billboard* 89 (Dec. 3, 1977): 68.

1199. Stockham, Thomas G. "Caruso Lives Again." *Creative Computing* 6 (June 1980): 72.
C&CA 16 (1981): 3170.

ELECTRONIC AND PIPE ORGANS

1200. Ashton, Alan C. "A High Level Minicomputer Controlled Organ System for Music Education." Paper presented at the ACM Computer Science Conference, Washington, D.C., 18–20 February 1975. *C&CA* 11 (1976): 12101. *C&IS* 14: 133218.

1201. Bartholomew, Paul. "Auto-Bell Digital Player." *The American Organist* 14 (Oct. 1980): 21.

1202. Challis, David. "A Microprocessor Organ Design." *IEEE Student Papers* (1978): 247–57.

1203. Clarke, Shiela. "Computerizing the Pipe Organ: Meet Programmer Prentiss Knowlton." *Contemporary Keyboard* 4 (Oct. 1978): 9–11.

1204. "Computer Composes and Plays Music." *Woodwind World* 11 (Apr. 1972): 5, 9.

1205. "Computer Makes Organ Self-Correcting." *The Music Trades* 128 (July 1980): 104–7.

1206. "Der Computer merkt sich die Klangfarben." *Musik International-Instrumentenbau-Zeitschrift* 34 (Sept. 1980): 632–33.

1207. "Computer Now Makes Organ A Player-Organ Like Pianos." *The School Musician* 44 (Aug.-Sep. 1972): 61–63.

1208. "Der Computer ruft die Töne auf." *Instrumentenbau-Zeitschrift* 30 (1976): 98.

1209. Curran, Lawrence. "Pipe Organ Goes Digital." *Electronics* 44 (May 1971): 79–82.
RILM 71 4336.

1210. Deforeit, Charles. "Un microprocesseur pour construire un orgue." *Electronique et applications industrielles* 255 (15 June 1978): 61–63. *C&CA* 14 (1979): 8107.

1211. Deutsch, Ralph. "Digital System for a Realistic Organ Tone Generator." Paper presented at the 41st Convention of the Audio Engineering Society, Oct. 5–8, 1971, New York.

1212. "Digital Electronics on the Pipe Organ." *Musik International-Instrumentenbau-Zeitschrift* 35 (Aug. 1981): 584.

1213. Dittmar, Lohmeier. "Neuer Bausatz für Digitalorgel: Bits machen Musik." *Funkschau* 25 (Dec. 9, 1983): 39–41. *E&EA* 87 (1984): 16813.

1214. Easson, R. D. "Microcomputer Organ Interface and Music Editor." *Wireless World* 89 (June 1983): 63–66. *E&EA* 86 (1983): 45747.

1215. ———. "Organ Interface for Microcomputer." *Wireless World* 89 (July 1983): 39–41, 53. *C&CA* 18 (1983): 36175. *E&EA* 86 (1983): 51513.

1216. Emerson, Phillip L.; Elizabeth Camus; and Chris Richards. "Two-Voice Music Programming System: The PDP-9 as an Automatic Electronic Organ." *Behavioral Research Methods and Instrumentation* 3 (1971): 164–66. *RILM* 72 2392.

1217. Falconi, Roberto. "L'avvento dei microprocessori nell'organo elettronico." [The Introduction of Microprocessors in Electronic Organs] *Automazione e strumentazione* 28 (Feb. 1980): 151–52.

1218. Giaimo, Richard J. "Design for Pipe Organ Emulation by Computer." B.S. thesis, Massachusetts Institute of Technology, Dept. of Electrical Engineering and Computer Science, 1981. 443 p.

1219. Henschen, Lawrence J., and S. H. Yau. "A Microcomputer Unit Organ Relay." In *MIMI 76, Proceedings of the International Symposium on Mini and Micro Computers, November 8–11, 1976, Toronto,* ed. M. H. Hamza. Long Beach, Calif.: IEEE Computer Society, 1977: 206–12.

1220. Hermosa, Antonio. "Estructura y circuiteria del organo electronico. Unidad de ritmos y automatismos. Secuenciador con CI-MOS." [Structure and Circuitry of Electronic Organs. Rhythm and Automatic Stages and Rhythm Sequencer Using MOS IC's] *Mundo Electron* 85 (May 1979): 85–95. In Spanish, summary in English. *C&CA* 14 (1979): 34801.

1221. Irons, B. M. "Correspondence: The Better-Tempered Clavier?" *International Journal of Mini and Microcomputers* 1 (1978): 35–36. *C&CA* 14 (1979): 28228.

1222. Knowlton, Prentiss H. "Computer Meets Keyboard, or, Look Ma, no Hands." *Synapse* 1 (Jan.-Feb. 1977): 10–11.

1223. Lederer, Jeffrey H. "A Computer Driven Pipe Organ." In *Proceedings of the ACM Computer Science Conference,* Anaheim, California, February 1976.

1224.   ———. "An Inexpensive Computer-Driven Organ Playing System." Paper presented at the International Conference on Computer Music, October 28–31, 1976, Massachusetts Institute of Technology.

1225.   ———. "Organ Music Language Manual." Pittsburgh: Dept. of Computer Science, University of Pittsburgh, Nov. 1976.

1226.   Lottermoser, W. "Computer-Orgel von Eivind Groven in Reinstimmung." *Instrumentenbau-Zeitschrift* 28 (1974): 526–27.

1227.   Miller, Richard S., and Martin B. Berry. "A Merged Pipe Organ Binary-Analog Correlator." *IEEE Journal of Solid State Circuits* SC-17 (1982): 20–27. *C&IS* 29 (1982): 82–494C.

1228.   "Music by Computer." *Dr. Dobbs Journal of Computer Calisthenics and Orthodontia* 1,9 (1976): 280. *C&IS* 18 (1978): 189702C.

1229.   "Musizieren Elektronisch Prüfen oder Anregen." *Instrumentenbau-Zeitschrift* 26 (1972): 339.

1230.   "Organ Linked to Computer Composes and Plays Music." *The Music Trades* 119 (Nov. 1971): 54–57.

1231.   Phelps, Lawrence. "The Third-Kind of Organ: Its Evolution and Promise." *The Diapaison* 74 (Mar. 1983): 14–18.

1232.   Pontzious, Richard. "Full Organ Sound from a Computer." *San Francisco Examiner* (Apr. 28, 1985): scene 4.

1233.   Raskin, Jef. "The Microcomputer and the Pipe Organ." *BYTE* 3 (Mar. 1978): 56–68. Also in *The BYTE Book of Computer Music,* ed. Christopher P. Morgan. Peterborough, N.H.: BYTE Books, 1979: 19–26.

1234.   ———. "A Pipe Organ/Micro Computer System." In *First West Coast Computer Faire Conference Proceedings,* ed. Jim C. Warren, Jr. Palo Alto, Calif.: Computer Faire, 1977: 131–33.

1235.   Ravaglia, Giuseppe. "New LSI Single-Chip Organ with Solo and Accompaniment." *IEEE Transactions on Consumer Electronics* CE-25 (1979): 504–14.

1236.   Rieländer, Michael. "Wo liegt die Zukunft der elektronischen Orgel?: Neue Wege elektronischer Klangbildung durch Anwendung der Schumann'schen Klangfarbengesetze." *Das Musikinstrument* 25 (1976): 1295–97. *RILM* 77 1470.

1237.   Schreier, Paul G. "Microcomputer Plays Organ Pieces Humans Find Highly Difficult." *EDN* 23 (May 20, 1978): 19–22. *C&CA* 13 (1978): 32032.

1238.   "Sounds of Great Pipe Organs Produced by Musical Computer." *Machine Design* 43 (June 24, 1971): 10.

1239.   Streuli, F. "Ton-König." *Radio-TV-Electronic* 38 (Aug. 1978): 197–207. *C&CA* 14 (1979): 16927. *E&EA* 82 (1979): 23841.

1240. Suding, Robert. "The Pipe Organ and the Microcomputer." In *Proceedings, Symposium on Small Computers in the Arts, November 20–22, 1981, Philadelphia, Pennsylvania.* New York, N.Y.: IEEE, 1981: 5–7.
C&CA 17 (1982): 19781.

1241. "Verkauf mit Computerhilfe." *Instrumentenbau-Musik International* 33 (1979): 366.

MICRO- AND
MINI-COMPUTERS

1242.   "The 64 Sounds Off." *Commodore Computing International* 3 (Oct. 1984):
        7–10.
        C&CA 20 (1985): 25714.

1243.   Abram, Michael. "A Minicomputer-Controlled Music Synthesizer." *Elec-tronotes* 7 (Sept. 1975): 4–7.

1244.   Actor, L. "Advanced Music System." *SoftSide* 6 (Oct. 1982): 78–82.
        E&EA 86 (1983): 15076.

1245.   Adelson, R. M. "Music Keys for the BBC Microcomputer." *Electronics &
        Wireless World* 90 (July 1984): 22–23, 29.
        C&CA 20 (1985): 12356. *E&EA* 87 (1984): 55101.

1246.   ———. "Music Keys for the BBC Microcomputer. Part II." *Electronics &
        Wireless World* 90 (Dec. 1984): 17–20, 34.
        E&EA 88 (1985): 14561.

1247.   Ahl, David H. "Micro Composer from Micro Music, Inc." *Creative Com-puting* 6 (Feb. 1980): 30–31.
        C&CA 15 (1980): 25185.

1248.   Aikin, Jim. "Keyboard Report: Hybrid Arts Miditrack II Sequencer for Atari
        Computers." *Keyboard* 11 (Dec. 1985): 112–13.

1249.   Akagiri, Y.; A. Takubo; Minao Shibata; H. Emura; and S. Watabe. "The
        MULTI 8 Personal Computer." *Mitsubishi Denki Giho* 57,12 (1983): 58–63.
        In Japanese.
        E&EA 87 (1984): 33043.

1250.   Aker, Sharon Zardetto. "Speculations on Spectra Video." *Microcomputing* 7
        (Dec. 1983): 83–88.

1251. Allouis, Jean-Francois. "Use of High Speed Micro-processors for Digital Synthesis." In *Proceedings of the 1978 International Computer Music Conference,* comp. Curtis Roads. Evanston, Ill.: Northwestern University Press, 1979: 26–28.
Also in *Computer Music Journal* 3,1 (Mar. 1979): 14–17, 56.
Revised and updated version in *Foundations of Computer Music,* ed. Curtis Roads and John Strawn. Cambridge, Mass.: MIT Press, 1985: 281–88.
C&CA 14 (1979): 34789.

1252. "Ample Etudes." *Home Computer Advanced Course* 55 (1985): 1090–91.
C&CA 20 (1985): 28759. *E&EA* 88 (1985): 37380.

1253. Anderson, John J. *Commodore 64 Sight and Sound.* Morris Plains, N.J.: Creative Computing Press, 1984. 136 p.

1254. Antonovich, Michael P. "Apple Sounds." *Compute! The Journal for Progressive Computing* 4 (Nov. 1982): 185.
C&CA 18 (1983): 7295.

1255. Arfib, Daniel. "Will the Small Fry Swallow the Big Fish?" Paper presented at the 1984 International Computer Music Conference, Oct. 19–23, Paris, France.

1256. Artikoglu, Ethem. "Musikprogramm für den TM 990." *Funkschau* 52 (18 July 1980): 71–72.
C&CA 15 (1980): 30702.

1257. Asuar, José V. "Un sistema para hacer música con un microcomputador." [A System to Make Music on a Microcomputer] *Revista musical chilena* 34 (Jul.–Sept. 1980): 5–28.
In Spanish.

1258. Aughton, J. "March to a Different Drummer." *Personal Computer World* 5 (Jan. 1982): 90–99, 189.
C&CA 17 (1982): 40427.

1259. Baker, A. "Music Player." *Interface Age* 6 (Mar. 1981): 22–24.
C&IS 27 (1981): 81–13403C.

1260. Barbour, G. "Musik 64." *Your Computer* 4 (Sept. 1984): 80–82.
C&CA 20 (1985): 17299.

1261. Bartlett, Martin. "A Microcomputer-Controlled Synthesis System for Live Performance." *Computer Music Journal* 3,1 (Mar. 1979): 25–29.
Also in *Proceedings of the 1978 International Computer Music Conference,* comp. Curtis Roads. Evanston, Ill.: Northwestern University Press, 1979: 29–33.
Revised version with title "Software for a Microcomputer-Controlled Synthesizer for Live Performance." *In Foundations of Computer Music,* ed. Curtis Roads and John Strawn. Cambridge, Mass.: MIT Press, 1985: 539–50.
C&CA 14 (1979): 34790. *C&IS* 24 (1980): 230385C.

1262. Bartolini, M., and G. Berardo. "Musica e personal computer." [Music and Personal Computers] In *Atti del Quarto Colloquio di Informatica Musicale.* Pisa: CNUCE-CNR, 1981: 253–57.

1263. Bass, Steven C., and Thomas W. Goeddel. "The Efficient Digital Implementation of Subtractive Music Synthesis." *IEEE Micro* 1 (Aug. 1981): 24–37. Review by J. F. Raskin in *Computing Reviews* 22 (Nov. 1981): 38,668. *C&CA* 17 (1982): 2725. *C&IS* 28 (1982): 81–10177C.

1264. Baudouin, C. "Sinclair Sound Board." *Hobby Electronics* 5 (June 1983): 20–23. *E&EA* 86 (1983): 40709.

1265. Behrendt, Bill. *Music and Sound for the Commodore 64.* Englewood Cliffs, N.J.: Micro Text Publications, 1983. 185 p.

1266. Belian, Barry. "The Atari Musician." *Compute! The Journal for Progressive Computing* 5 (May 1983): 214–16. *C&CA* 18 (1983): 28880.

1267. Bell, Raymond J. "Soulful Software Sounds." *Kilobaud Microcomputing* 5 (May 1981): 195–98. *C&CA* 16 (1981): 30812.

1268. Berger, Myron. "High C's from IC's." *High Fidelity/Musical America* 33 (June 1983): 48–49.

1269. Beverley, P. "The BBC Micro and Fourier Synthesis." *Electronics & Computing Monthly* 3 (May 1983): 78–80. *C&CA* 18 (1983): 28895.

1270. Birchall, Steve. "Apple Music: Two New Systems, Soundchaser & Alpha Syntauri." *SoftSide* 6 (Oct. 1982): 102–6. *C&CA* 18 (1983): 11131. *E&EA* 86 (1983): 15077.

1271. Bland, G. "Give Us a Tune." *Practical Computing* 7 (Nov. 1984): 70–71. *C&CA* 20 (1985): 7992.

1272. Blum, Richard D. "A Low-Cost, Inexpensive, Real-Time, Frequency-Modulation Hardware Module for Mini-and Micro-Computers." In *Proceedings of the 1978 International Computer Music Conference,* comp. Curtis Roads. Evanston, Ill.: Northwestern University Press, 1979: 34–45.

1273. Bobe, W. "Minimal Microcomputer System Generates Melodies." *Radio Fernsehen Elektronik* 34 (Jan. 1985): 55. In German. *C&CA* 20 (1985): 31015. *E&EA* 88 (1985): 37381.

1274. Boody, Charles G. "The Micro-Computer as an Input Device for Musical Analysis or Composition by Computer." In *Proceedings of the 1978 International Computer Music Conference,* comp. Curtis Roads. Evanston, Ill.: Northwestern University Press, 1979: 637–44.

1275. Bouchard, Richard. "You Can Have Sound on Your Computer!!!" *SoftSide* 2 (Aug. 1980): 66–69.

1276. Bowen, J., and Greg Armbruster. "Professional Music Perspectives." *Apple Orchard* 5 (Mar. 1984): 44–46.
C&CA 20 (1985): 4085.

1277. Bowers, Phillip. "Musical Notes for the Apple." *Micro* [Chelmsford, Mass.] 72 (June 1984): 20–22.

1278. Boyde-Shaw, B. "Speech and Music." *Electronics & Computing Monthly* 3 (June 1983): 64–65.
C&CA 18 (1983): 32107.

1279. Brendle, F., and M. Brendle. "Musical Apple: Versatile Tone and Sound Generator for the Apple." *Chip* 5 (May 1984): 256–58.
In German.
E&EA 87 (1984): 44312.

1280. Burden, D. "Electronic Drum Sequencer: Software for BBC Micro." *Electronics & Music Maker* 4 (Nov. 1984): 96–98.
C&CA 20 (1985): 21603. *E&EA* 88 (1985): 26152.

1281. Butterfield, Jim. "Commodore 64 Music." *Commodore User* 1 (Oct. 1983): 8–9.

1282. ———. "Commodore 64 Music: Happy Birthday." *Compute! The Journal for Progressive Computing* 6 (Oct. 1984): 177–78.
C&CA 20 (1985): 4094.

1283. Buxton, William; William Reeves; Guy Fedorkow; Kenneth C. Smith; and Ronald Baecker. "A Microcomputer-Based Conducting System." *Computer Music Journal* 4,1 (Spring 1980): 8–21.
C&CA 16 (1981): 15680. *C&IS* 26 (1981): 265458C.

1284. Cage, Gary. "Melody Dice." *SoftSide* 5 (Nov. 1981): 31–46.

1285. Callery, Michael. *Commodore Magic: Create Astonishing Graphics and Sound Effects for Your Commodore 64!* New York: E. P. Dutton, 1984. 231 p.

1286. Campbell, T., and Larry McClain. "Musicalc." *Popular Computing* 4 (Nov. 1984): 158–62.
C&CA 20 (1985): 17257.

1287. Carpenter, Paul, and Roger Clark. "Playing Music on the RML 380Z." *Computer Education* no. 38 (June 1981): 7.
C&CA 16 (1981): 30809.

1288. Carter, Robert T. "μC Helps Tune Musical Instruments." *EDN* 26 (May 13, 1981): 154.
C&CA 16 (1981): 33984.

1289. Cassel, Don. *Graphics, Sound & Music for the Commodore 64.* Dubuque, Iowa: W. C. Brown, 1985. 166 p.

1290. Chamberlain, Craig. "Pokey Player II." *SoftSide* 6 (Dec. 1982): 49–51.
C&CA 18 (1983): 15324.

1291.   ———, and Harry Bratt. "Pokey Player." *SoftSide* 6 (Oct. 1982): 58–70.
E&EA 86 (1983): 15075.

1292.   ———, and Harry Bratt. "Pokey Player III." *SoftSide* 6 (Feb. 1983): 89–90.
C&CA 18 (1983): 22573.

1293.   Chamberlin, Hal. "Advanced Real-Time Music Synthesis Techniques."
BYTE 5 (Apr. 1980): 70–94, 180–96.
Review by Michael Kassler in *Computing Reviews* 21 (Aug. 1980): 36,622.
C&CA 15 (1980): 25182. *C&IS* 25 (1980): 247699C.

1294.   ———. "Delayed Playback Music Synthesis Using Small Computers." In *The Best of the Computer Faires. Volume VII, Conference Proceedings of the 7th West Coast Computer Faire,* ed. Jim C. Warren, Jr. Woodside, Calif.: Computer Faire, 1982: 133–39.
Also In *Proceedings, Symposium on Small Computers in the Arts, November 20–22, 1981, Philadelphia, Pennsylvania.* New York, N.Y.: IEEE, 1981: 27–32.
C&CA 17 (1982): 19787.

1295.   ———. "Digital Music Synthesis. Part 2." *Creative Computing* 7 (July 1981): 140–56.
C&CA 17 (1982): 28469.

1296.   ———. "High Quality Direct Music Synthesis Using Microprocessors." In *The Best of the Computer Faires. Volume 3, Conference Proceedings of the 3rd West Coast Computer Faire,* ed. Jim C. Warren, Jr. Los Angeles: Computer Faire, 1978: 44.

1297.   ———. *Musical Applications of Microprocessors.* New Rochelle, N.J.: Hayden Book Co., 1980. 661 p. (The Hayden Microcomputer Series)
Review by Thom Blum in *Computer Music Journal* 6,2 (Summer 1982): 79–83.
Review by David B. Williams and David C. Braught in *Music Educators Journal* 68 (Nov. 1981): 66–68.
C&IS 26 (1981): 26995C.

1298.   ———. *Musical Applications of Microprocessors.* 2nd ed. Hasbrouck Heights, N.J.: Hayden Book Co., 1985. 802 p.

1299.   ———. "A Professional Quality Digital Audio Peripheral for Small Computers." In *Proceedings, 3rd Symposium on Small Computers in the Arts, October 14–16, 1983, Philadelphlia, Pa.* Los Angeles, Calif.: IEEE Computer Society, 1983: 74–80.
C&CA 19 (1984): 31882. *E&EA* 87 (1984): 38963.

1300.   ———. "A Sampling of Techniques for Computer Performance of Music."
BYTE 2 (Sept. 1977): 62–83.
Also in *The BYTE Book of Computer Music,* ed. Christopher P. Morgan. Peterborough, N.H.: BYTE Books, 1979: 47–64.
C&CA 13 (1978): 2571. *C&IS* 17: 181346C.

1301.   ———. "Simulation of Musical Instruments. Part 1." *Kilobaud Microcomputing* 5 (Jan. 1981): 53–58.
C&CA 16 (1981): 15689.

1302. ———. "Simulation of Musical Instruments. Part 2." *Kilobaud Microcomputing* 5 (Feb. 1981): 142–48.
C&CA 16 (1981): 18378.

1303. ———. "Software Techniques of Digital Music Synthesis. Part 1." *Creative Computing* 7 (June 1981): 88–98.
C&CA 17 (1982): 8908.

1304. ———. "Techniques for the Computer Performance of Music." Paper presented at the Music Symposium, Sheridan College, Oakville, Ontario, June 1980.

1305. Chapman, J. "BeeBMIDI. Part I." *Electronics & Music Maker* 4 (June 1984): 52.
C&CA 19 (1984): 47422. *E&EA* 87 (1984): 48638.

1306. ———. "BeeBMIDI. Part III." *Electronics & Music Maker* 4 (Aug. 1984): 68–72.
E&EA 87 (1984): 61125.

1307. ———. "BeeBMIDI. Part IV." *Electronics & Music Maker* 4 (Nov. 1984): 90.
C&CA 20 (1985): 21601. *E&EA* 88 (1985): 26150.

1308. ———. "BeeBMIDI. Part V." *Electronics & Music Maker* 4 (Dec. 1984): 106–8.
C&CA 20 (1985): 25711. *E&EA* 88 (1985): 31264.

1309. ———. "BeeBMIDI. Part VI." *Electronics & Music Maker* 4 (Jan. 1985): 92–96.
C&CA 20 (1985): 25713. *E&EA* 88 (1985): 31276.

1310. ———. "BeeBMIDI. Part VII." *Electronics & Music Maker* 5 (Mar. 1985): 92–93.

1311. ———, and D. Eagle. "BeeBMIDI. Part II." *Electronics & Music Maker* 4 (July 1984): 60–64.
C&CA 19 (1984): 47429. *E&EA* 87 (1984): 55094.

1312. "Chimes with Conviction: Musicalc for the C64." *Chip* 2 (Feb. 1985): 206–7. In German.
C&CA 20 (1985): 25708.

1313. Ciarcia, Steve. *Ask BYTE*. Berkeley, Calif.: Osborne McGraw-Hill, 1986. 323 p.

1314. ———. "Sound Off." *BYTE* 4 (July 1979): 34–51.

1315. ———. "The Toy Store Begins at Home." *BYTE* 4 (Apr. 1979): 10–18.

1316. Coates, R. F. "Assembly Language Programming." *Electronics & Wireless World* 89 (Nov. 1983): 39–41.
E&EA 87 (1984): 39–41.

1317.   Coenraads, J., and H. T. Mouftah. "Microprocessor Controlled Music Per-
        formance in the Home-of-the-Future Network." In *Canadian Communica-
        tions & Power Conference, Montreal, 15–17 Oct. 1980.* New York: IEEE, 1980:
        402–5.
        C&CA 16 (1981): 12982.

1318.   ————, and H. T. Mouftah. "A Music Subscriber Interface for the Home-of-
        the Future Network." In *International Conference on Communications,
        Denver, CO, 14–18 June 1981: Conference Record.* New York, N.Y.: IEEE,
        1981: v. 2, p. 24.2/1–5.
        C&CA 17 (1982): 7525.

1319.   Colbert, Paul. "Then There Were Three." *Melody Maker* 57 (Dec. 18, 1982):
        60, 63.

1320.   ————. "The Write One." *Melody Maker* 58 (May 28, 1983): 37.

1321.   Colosimo, Frank. "VIC Music Maker." *Compute! The Journal for Progressive
        Computing* 6 (Dec. 1984): 130–34.
        C&CA 20 (1985): 12353.

1322.   Colsher, William L. "Make Music with the Atari." *Microcomputing* 6 (June
        1982): 80–81.
        C&CA 17 (1982): 36186.

1323.   Comerford, P. J. "Bradford Musical Instrument Simulator." *IEE Proceedings
        A, Physical Science, Measurement and Instrumentation, Management and Edu-
        cation Reviews* 128 (July 1981): 364–72.
        C&CA 16 (1981): 30507.

1324.   *Compute!'s First Book of Commodore 64 Sound and Graphics.* Greensboro,
        N.C.: Compute! Publications, 1983. 275 p.
        Contains items: 1333, 1514, 1578.

1325.   "Computer Music." *Microcomputer Printout* 4 (Apr. 1983): 51–59.
        C&CA 18 (1983): 25690.

1326.   "Connect a Keyboard to a Commodore 64." *Commodore Computing Interna-
        tional* 2 (Dec. 1983): 16–25.
        C&CA 19 (1984): 23723.

1327.   Cook, M. "Tune in to a Digital Frequency Meter." *Micro User* 2 (Sept. 1984):
        137–40.

1328.   Cooper, Elizabeth, and Yvon Kolya. "Orchestra-80." *BYTE* 6 (Nov. 1981):
        264–72.
        C&CA 17 (1982): 8924.

1329.   Cooper, James. "Modifications & Maintenance: Computers, Love 'em or
        Leave 'em Alone." *Keyboard* 11 (July 1985): 80–81.

1330.   Cowart, Robert. "Keyboard Report: Atari 520ST Computer." *Keyboard* 12
        (Feb. 1986): 116–19.

1331. Cowie, B. "Editing on the Model 64." *Electronics & Music Maker* 4 (June 1984): 35–36.
E&EA 87 (1984): 48635.

1332. ———. "Step-Time Composition on the Model 64." *Electronics & Music Maker* 4 (Sept. 1984): 90–92.
C&CA 20 (1985): 4083. *E&EA* 88 (1985): 3785.

1333. Crowley, W. J. "Songster." In *Compute!'s First Book of Commodore 64 Sound and Graphics.* Greensboro, N.C.: Compute! Publications, 1983: 231–37.

1334. Cummings, Steve. "Keyboard Report: Octave Plateau Sequencer Plus Software for the IBM PC." *Keyboard* 11 (Nov. 1985): 98–102.

1335. ———. "Keyboard Report: Southworth Total Music Macintosh Software." *Keyboard* 11 (Dec. 1985): 114–120.

1336. Daley, P., and B. Tripp. "VIC Player." *Micro-6502/6809 Journal* no. 61 (June 1983): 72–80.
C&CA 18 (1983): 36187.

1337. Daley, R. F. "C–64 Sounds Off!" *Microcomputing* 7 (July 1983): 38.

1338. Dally, William J. "Faster Audio Processing with a Microprocessor." *BYTE* 4 (Dec. 1979): 54–76.

1339. Davids, Cary N. "JazZ-80." *Kilobaud Microcomputing* 4 (May 1980): 148–54.

1340. ———. "Name that Tune." *Kilobaud Microcomputing* 5 (May 1981): 148–53.
C&CA 16 (1981): 29505.

1341. Day, Jim. "The Forte Music Programming Language." *Recreational Computing* 8 (July/Aug. 1979): 28–29.

1342. Dechelle, F., and C. D'Alessandro. *Synthèse en temps réel sur un microprocesseur. TMS 320.* Paris: Université Paris 6, Sept. 1984. (Rapports de D.E.A.)

1343. DeFord, R. "The Mountain Music System." *Interface Age* 7 (Mar. 1982): 90–93.
C&CA 17 (1982): 24522.

1344. Devlin, Joe. "Graphics and Music for the Color Computer." *Creative Computing* 9 (Dec. 1983): 97–101.

1345. Dimond, Stuart D. "Microprocessor-Based Control and Generation Techniques for Electronic Music." Paper presented at the 54th Convention of the Audio Engineering Society, May 4–7, 1976, Los Angeles.

1346. Doerschuk, Bob. "Dave Smith, the Designer of the Prophet Discusses Microprocessors and Programmability." *Contemporary Keyboard* 5 (Nov. 1979): 60–68.

1347. Doone, Tenny. "Quartet of SC/MP's Plays Music for Trios." *EDN* 23 (Sept. 20, 1978): 57–60.

1348.   Doren, G. Kevin. "Controlling the Digital Synthesis Process." In *Proceedings, Symposium on Small Computers in the Arts, November 20–22, 1981, Philadelphia, Pennsylvania.* New York, N.Y.: IEEE, 1981: 23–26.
        C&CA 17 (1982): 19786.

1349.   Dorner, J. "The Sound of Music." *Personal Computer World* 8 (Jan. 1985): 192–94.

1350.   Dotto, L. "Small Computers Carve out New Market." *ComputerData* 5 (Nov. 1980): 33–34.

1351.   Dunn, Howard. "Using the Micro-Computer to Select Music." *The Instrumentalist* 35 (Nov. 1980): 22–23.

1352.   Eddington, Donald J. "The Mozart Machine." *Compute! The Journal for Progressive Computing* 6 (Jan. 1984): 160–70.

1353.   Edwards, John S. "Composing Music on a Personal Computer: A Digitized Blend of Sharps and Flats." *onComputing* 3 (Fall 1981): 67–69.
        C&CA 17 (1982): 13200.

1354.   ———. "Highly Personal Music: Software for Apple, Atari, and Radio Shack Computers." *Popular Computing* 2 (June 1983): 104–10.
        C&CA 18 (1983): 28826.

1355.   Elkins, John Rush. "Music Programmer." *SoftSide* 5 (Nov. 1981): 67–75.

1356.   Ellis, David. "Acorn Music 500: Synthesizer Hardware and Software for the BBC Micro." *Electronics & Music Maker* 4 (Dec. 1984): 102–04.
        C&CA 20 (1985): 25710. *E&EA* 88 (1985): 31263.

1357.   ———. "ATPL Symphony Keyboard: Add-on for BBC Micro." *Electronics & Music Maker* 5 (Mar. 1985): 88–89.
        C&CA 20 (1985): 35108.

1358.   ———. "The CX5M Revisited. Part 1." *Electronics & Music Maker* 5 (Mar. 1985): 82–84.
        C&CA 20 (1985): 35106.

1359.   ———. "Greengate DS 3 Sound Sampling System for Apple II/IIe." *Electronics & Music Maker* 4 (Oct. 1984): 92–94.
        C&CA 20 (1985): 7988. *E&EA* 88 (1985): 8644.

1360.   ———. "The Jen Musipack 1.0." *Electronics & Music Maker* 4 (June 1984): 20–22.
        C&CA 19 (1984): 47418. *E&EA* 87 (1984): 48631.

1361.   ———. "SCI Model 64 Sequencer." *Electronics & Music Maker* 4 (June 1984): 33–34.
        C&CA 19 (1984): 47419. *E&EA* 87 (1984): 48634.

1362.   ———. "Soundchaser." *Practical Computing* 5 (Oct. 1982): 54–56.
        C&CA 18 (1983): 204.

1363. ———. "Yamaha CX5M Music Computer and Software." *Electronics & Music Maker* 4 (Oct. 1984): 82–84. *C&CA* 20 (1985): 7985. *E&EA* 88 (1985): 8641.

1364. Erb, J. "MusiCalc, the Program for Music Fans." *HC Mein Home Computer* 11 (Nov. 1984): 98–100. In German. *C&CA* 20 (1985): 17264.

1365. "Erfolg mit Kleincomputern." *Instrumentenbau-Zeitschrift* 26 (1972): 28.

1366. Ericson, O. "Computers as Music Machines." *Elteknik med aktuell elektronik* 26 (Sept. 1983): 72–76. In Swedish. *C&CA* 19 (1984): 8633. *E&EA* 87 (1984): 72–76.

1367. Fabbri, Tony. *Animation, Games, and Sound for the Commodore 64.* Englewood Cliffs, N.J.: Prentice-Hall, 1984. 222 p.

1368. ———. *Animation, Games, and Sound for the IBM PC.* Englewood Cliffs, N.J.: Prentice-Hall, 1983. 189 p.

1369. ———. *Animation, Games, and Sound for the TI 99/4A.* Englewood Cliffs, N.J.: Prentice-Hall, 1984. 247 p.

1370. ———. *Animation, Games, and Sound for the VIC-10.* Englewood Cliffs, N.J.: Prentice-Hall, 1984. 217 p.

1371. Fell, D. A. "Music While You Work." *BEEBUG* 3 (June 1984): 10–13.

1372. Fink, Michael. "The Well-Tempered Apple." *Creative Computing* 9 (July 1983): 196–98. *C&CA* 18 (1983): 40670.

1373. Finlay, D. "Micro Music Making." *Personal Computer World* 4 (Mar. 1981): 85–89, 146. *C&CA* 16 (1981): 21891.

1374. ———, and Kevin J. Jones. "Apple Arpeggio." *Personal Computer World* 4 (May 1981): 116–21. *C&CA* 16 (1981): 30848.

1375. Fischer, C. "Data to Music Conversion: A Low Cost Peripheral Circuit for Your Computer." *Polyphony* 3,2 (1977): 5.

1376. Forson, Henry. "VIC Harmony." *Compute! The Journal for Progressive Computing* 4 (Nov. 1982): 74–78. *C&CA* 18 (1983): 7284.

1377. Garcia, Antonio. "Generación de sonidos musicales mediante microprocessador. Pt. I." [Using a Microprocessor to Produce Musical Notes. Part I] *Revista española de electronica* 30 (June 1983): 52–54. In Spanish.

1378.   ———. "Generación de sonidos musicales mediante microprocessador. Pt. II." [Using a Microprocessor to Produce Musical Notes. Part II] *Revista española de electronica* 30 (July 1983): 52–56.
In Spanish.
C&CA 18 (1983): 44017. *E&EA* 86 (1983): 62960.

1379.   Gehman, Walt, and Lee E. Sumner. *Advanced Applesoft Techniques with Sound and Graphics*. Blue Ridge Summit, Pa.: Tab Books, 1985. 162 p.

1380.   Gietmann, Willi, and Willi Billen. "PET macht Musik." *Funkschau* 52 (July 18, 1980): 75.
C&CA 15 (1980): 30703.

1381.   Gold, Richard. "A Terrain Reader." In *The BYTE Book of Computer Music*, ed. Christopher P. Morgan. Peterborough, N.H.: BYTE Books, 1979: 129–35.

1382.   Goldstein, Shelby. "Making Music with your Vic." *Creative Computing* 9 (July 1983): 43–44, 47.
C&CA 18 (1983): 40709.

1383.   Gorgens, A. "Formula 1." *HC Mein Home Computer* 9 (Sept. 1984): 112–24.
In German.
C&CA 20 (1985): 25716.

1384.   Grant, J., and D. Burden. "OMDAC Update. Part I." *Electronics & Music Maker* 4 (Sept. 1984): 80.

1385.   ———, and D. Burden. "OMDAC Update. Part II." *Electronics & Music Maker* 4 (Oct. 1984): 89–90.
C&CA 20 (1985): 7987. *E&EA* 88 (1985): 8643.

1386.   Gray, Stephen B. "Electronic Music in Small Packages." *Creative Computing* 7 (Sept. 1981): 294–96.
C&CA 17 (1982): 13211.

1387.   ———. "TRS-80 Strings." *Creative Computing* 8 (Feb. 1982): 208–13.

1388.   ———. "TRS-80 Strings." *Creative Computing* 8 (July 1982): 216–23.

1389.   ———. "TRS-80 Strings." *Creative Computing* 9 (July 1983): 288–92.

1390.   Green, D. "Musicomp, a Music-Synthesizing Program for Apple." *InfoWorld* 4 (Apr. 12, 1982): 30–33.
C&CA 17 (1982): 36176.

1391.   Griffin, Ray. "Chips that Chirp, Whistle, and Buzz: Getting Sound from ICs." *Machine Design* 51 (Nov. 22, 1979): 108–12.

1392.   Grokett, Russell A. "PET's Built-in Synthesizer." *Polyphony* 5 (May-June 1979): 10–12.

1393.   Gygli, W. "BASIC Conducts, Apple Performs." *Mikro- und Kleincomputer* 4 (Feb. 1982): 71–74.
In German.
C&CA 17 (1982): 36182.

1394. Hagerty, Roger. "Random Music." *Compute! The Journal for Progressive Computing* 6 (Mar. 1984): 176–78.
C&CA 19 (1984): 27976.

1395. Halfhill, Tom R. "Sound Synthesis." *Compute! The Journal for Progressive Computing* 5 (Jan. 1983): 26–34.
C&CA 18 (1983): 15282.

1396. Hammond, Ray. *The Musician and the Micro.* Poole: Blandford Press, 1983. 192 p.

1397. Hansen, Finn E. "TI960A Minicomputeren pa Musikvidenskabeligt Institut." [The TI960A Minicomputers at the Institute of Musicology] In "3 Foredrag Over Emnet: Autonome Computere Herunder Minicomputere og Deres Anvendelse i Forbindelse med Regionale Edbcentre." Aarhus: University of Aarhus, 1974. (Technical Report RECAU-74-39)

1398. Hart, Glenn. "The Musicraft Development System." *Creative Computing* 6 (Oct. 1980): 49–51.
C&CA 16 (1981): 18386.

1399. Haus, Goffredo. "JEN Music Computer: un personal musicale italiano." [JEN Music Computer: An Italian Music-oriented Personal Computer] *Strumenti musicali* 52 (1984): 105–06.

1400. ———. "Il personal computer al servizio della musica: verso il laboratorio musicale personale." [Personal Computers at Music's Disposal: Towards the Personal Music Laboratory] *Strumenti musicali* 3 (1980): 69–73.

1401. Havey, Paul M. "Musical Atari Keyboard." *Compute! The Journal for Progressive Computing* 5 (Aug. 1983): 204–7.
C&CA 18 (1983): 43960.

1402. Heilborn, John. *Compute!'s Beginner's Guide to Commodore 64 Sound.* Greensboro, N.C.: Compute! Publications, 1984. 219 p.

1403. ———. "Making Sound with Blips." In *Compute!'s Second Book of VIC: VIC 2.* Greensboro, N.C.: Compute! Publications, 1983: 92–100.

1404. Helmers, Carl. "Add a Kluge Harp to Your Computer." *BYTE* 1 (Oct. 1975): 14–18.
Reprinted in *Creative Computing* 3 (Mar.-Apr. 1977): 46–49.

1405. ———. "The Kludgehorn: An Experiment in Homebrew Computer Music." In *First West Coast Computer Faire Conference Proceedings,* ed. Jim C. Warren, Jr. Palo Alto, Calif.: Computer Faire, 1977: 118–27.

1406. ———. "Microprocessor Control of a Communications Process: Implementing a Symphony." *IEEE Transactions on Aerospace and Electronic Systems,* Vol. AES-12 (1976): 662.

1407. Hemingway, Bruce, and David K. Barton. "Microprocessors: A Multiprocessing Approach to Real-Time Digital Sound Synthesis." Paper presented at the International Conference on Computer Music, October 28–31, 1976, Massachusetts Institute of Technology.

1408. Hemsath, Bill. "Microprocessors in Electronic Music. Part 1." *Electronotes* 7 (Nov. 1975): 11–13.

1409. ———. "Microprocessors in Electronic Music. Part 2." *Electronotes* 7 (Dec. 1975): 16–19.

1410. Herman, G. "Musical Micros. Part I." *Which Micro and Software Review* (Aug. 1984): 51–55.
    C&CA 19 (1984): 47433. *E&EA* 87 (1984): 55098.

1411. ———; P. Penfold; and M. Jenkins. "Musical Micros. Part II." *Which Micro and Software Review* (Nov. 1984): 16–24.
    C&CA 20 (1985): 7989. *E&EA* 88 (1985): 8666.

1412. Hermosa, Antonio. "Introduction to Microcomputerized Music, Application Using the MC6801 Microcomputer." *Mundo Electronico* 94 (Mar. 1980): 103–12.
    C&CA 15 (1980): 25189.

1413. Herold, Raymond J. *Compute!'s Guide to TI-99/4A Sound and Graphics.* Greensboro, N.C.: Compute! Publications, 1984. 210 p.

1414. Hickman, I. "Making Music." *Computing Today* 5 (June 1983): 26–29.
    C&CA 18 (1983): 26–29.

1415. Higgins, R. J.; R. K. Goodall; and R. Vedanayagam. "The Performing Musician and the Personal Computer." In *The Best of the Computer Faires. Volume V, Conference Proceedings of the 5th West Coast Computer Faire,* ed. Jim C. Warren. Woodside, CA: Computer Faire, 1980: 127–34.

1416. Hill, J. "Step-Time Sequencing for Wasp Synthesizer and Commodore 64." *Electronics & Music Maker* 4 (Nov. 1984): 100–102.
    C&CA 20 (1985): 21604. *E&EA* 88 (1985): 26153.

1417. Hine, R. "Keyboard for Your BBC." *Your Computer* 4 (Sept. 1984): 70–72.
    E&EA 88 (1985): 20427.

1418. Hiney, Barny, and Lars Rogers. "SC/MP—A Very Musical Processor." *Compute* 3 (Nov.-Dec. 1977): 2–7.
    C&CA 13 (1978): 15787.

1419. Hobson, Jack. "Neelco's Music Box for PET." *Creative Computing* 6 (June 1980): 52.
    C&CA 16 (1981): 3167.

1420. Hopkins, R. "Mozart Lives." *Your Computer* 3 (Mar. 1983): 54–61.
    C&CA 18 (1983): 22616.

1421. Hopton, J. "Programming the Microprocessor—A Music Program for the D2 Microprocessor." *Electronic Technology* 12 (Nov.-Dec. 1978): 237.
    C&CA 14 (1979): 12607.

1422. Horlacher, Wes; Leslie Horlacher; and Susan Kenny. "Cultivating Creativity: How Computers Can Help." *SoftSide* 6 (Sept. 1983): 34–35.
    CIJE 15 (1983): EJ 285 795.

1423.   Howe, Hubert S. "Electronic Music and Microcomputers." *Interface* 7 (1978): 57–68.
Also in *Perspectives of New Music* 16 (Fall/Winter 1977): 70–84.
C&CA 13 (1978): 32033. *RILM* 77 6044. *RILM* 78 3863.

1424.   ———. "Some Applications of Microcomputers in Electronic Music Synthesis." In *Proceedings of the International Music and Technology Conference, August 24–28, 1981, University of Melbourne.* Parkville, Vic.: Computer Music Project, Dept. of Computer Science, University of Melbourne, 1981: 66–84.

1425.   Howell, S. "Siel 16-Track Live Sequencer." *Electronics & Music Maker* 4 (Feb. 1985): 82–83.
C&CA 20 (1985): 35105.

1426.   Hunkins, Arthur B. "Player ZX81, a Tune-Playing Program for the Sinclair/ Timex." *Compute! The Journal for Progressive Computing* 5 (Jan. 1983): 142–43.
C&CA 18 (1983): 15382.

1427.   Inggs, Michael. "Johann Sebastian Byte." *Personal Computer World* 1 (July 1978): 34–36.
C&CA 13 (1978): 29124.

1428.   Jaco, Jerry M. "Working with SID." *Compute! The Journal for Progressive Computing* 5 (Oct. 1983): 277–88.
C&CA 19 (1984): 6800.

1429.   James, M. "BBC Programming." *Computing Today* 4 (Dec. 1982): 20–22.
C&CA 18 (1983): 11149.

1430.   ———. "The Musical Oric." *Electronics & Computing Monthly* 3 (Aug. 1983): 57–59.
C&CA 18 (1983): 42946.

1431.   Jenkins, Susan E. "Sound Systems on Micros." In *Proceedings, 3rd Symposium on Small Computers in the Arts, October 14–16, 1983, Philadelphia, Pa.* Los Angeles, Calif.: IEEE Computer Society, 1983: 36–40.
C&CA 19 (1984): 31878. *E&EA* 87 (1984): 38962.

1432.   Jessop, Paul M. "Play On: Computer Music—Some Thoughts on Data Storage." *Personal Computer World* 1 (Jan. 1979): 21–23.
C&CA 14 (1979): 14088.

1433.   Jigour, Robin J.; Charlie Kellner; and Ellen V. B. Lapham. "The AlphaSyntauri Instrument: A Modular and Software Programmable Digital Synthesizer System." In *Proceedings, Symposium on Small Computers in the Arts, November 20–22, 1981, Philadelphia, Pennsylvania.* New York, N.Y.: IEEE, 1981: 51–55.
C&CA 17 (1982): 19789.

1434.   Jones, Kevin J. "Sound Generating Techniques on the ITT2020 and Apple II Computers." In *Computer Music in Britain, 8th–11th April 1980.* London: Electro-Acoustic Music Association of Great Britain, 1980: 13–16.

1435. Jones, M. "Autographics Microsound 64 Keyboard." *Electronics & Music Maker* 4 (July 1984): 16–18.
C&CA 19 (1984): 47427. *E&EA* 87 (1984): 55092.

1436. ————. "The Musical Oric." *Electronics & Computing Monthly* 3 (Aug. 1983): 57–59.
C&CA 18 (1983): 42946.

1437. Jones, P. "Computer/Synth Keyboard Interface." *Electronics Today International* 11 (Dec. 1982): 93.
E&EA 86 (1983): 62945.

1438. Kahn, Donald, and Nevin B. Scrimshaw. *Discover Your VIC-20: A Beginner's Guide to Real Programming.* Cambridge, Mass.: Birkhauser Boston, 1983. 94 p.
C&IS 33 (1985): 85–4735C.

1439. Kaufman, Richard. "Computer-Aided Filter Design." *Audio* 67 (Nov. 1983): 28–31.

1440. Keith, Michael. "Automatic Computer Composition of Bluegrass Tunes." In *Proceedings, 2nd Symposium on Small Computers in the Arts, October 15–17, 1982, Philadelphia, Pa.* Los Angeles, Calif.: IEEE Computer Society, 1982: 29–33.
C&CA 18 (1983): 28835.

1441. ————. "BACH." *Creative Computing* 7 (Feb. 1981): 70–73.
C&CA 17 (1982): 5228.

1442. ————. "BACH: A System for Music Composition and Display on a Microcomputer." In *Personal Computing Digest, National Computer Conference, Personal Computing Festival, May 20–22, 1980, Anaheim, California.* Arlington, Va.: AFIPS, 1980: 129–34.

1443. ————. "NCC: A Program that Composes Canons." In *Proceedings, Symposium on Small Computers in the Arts, November 20–22, 1981, Philadelphia, Pennsylvania.* New York, N.Y.: IEEE, 1981: 11–14.
C&CA 17 (1982): 19783.

1444. Kelling, S. "Music Software." *Your Computer* 4 (Sept. 1984): 77–79.
C&CA 20 (1985): 17298.

1445. Kennewell, John. "How to Make Music with Your Mini Scamp." *Electronics Australia* 39 (Sept. 1977): 91, 93.

1446. Kerber, R. J. Bob. "Programmable Microprocessor Can Play a Tune." *Electronics* 55 (Nov. 30, 1982): 116–19.
C&CA 18 (1983): 11089.

1447. "Key Notes." *Home Computer Advanced Course* 49 (1985): 961–62.
C&CA 20 (1985): 25717.

1448. Kitching, Lucy K. "Microprocessor-Controlled Music Machine." *Computer Education* no. 42 (Nov. 1982): 6.
C&CA 18 (1983): 3339.

1449. Kitsz, Dennis B. "Build a TRS-80-to-Synthesizer Interface." *Kilobaud Microcomputing* no. 12 (Dec. 1980): 32–38.

1450. ———. "A Simple Voltage-Controlled Synthesizer." *Microcomputing* 47 (Dec. 1980): 66–70.

1451. Kleen, Leslie D. "A Generalized Orchestra Compiler for the Z80 Microprocessor." In *Proceedings of the Venice 1982 International Computer Music Conference*. San Francisco, Calif.: Computer Music Association, 1985: 92–99.

1452. Knight, Timothy Orr. *Commodore 64 Graphics and Sounds*. Indianapolis, Ind.: H. W. Sams, 1984. 128 p.

1453. ———. *Graphics and Sounds on the IBM PC*. Indianapolis, Ind.: H. W. Sams, 1984. 94 p.

1454. ———. *TI-99/4A Graphics and Sounds*. Adapted for the TI-99/4A by Gregory L. Guntle. Indianapolis, Ind.: H. W. Sams, 1984. 101 p.

1455. Knott, B. "BEEBUG Plays Bach." *BEEBUG* 3 (July 1984): 4–6.

1456. Kriwaczek, P. "Micro Music." *Computing Today* 4 (Nov. 1982): 45–48. *C&CA* 18 (1983): 11084.

1457. ———. "Micro Music. Part II." *Computing Today* 4 (Dec. 1982): 37–40. *C&CA* 18 (1983): 9794.

1458. Kuegler, H. "With Ease to the Triple Sound: Definition and Generation of Tones." *Chip* 1 (Jan. 1985): 169–76. In German.

1459. Kupke, D. "Super Sound with Your Superboard II." *Microcomputing* 47 (Dec. 1980): 130–31.

1460. Landsberg, B. "Some Notes on the Apple. Part II." *Computing Today* 5 (Feb. 1984): 51–53. *C&CA* 19 (1984): 36715.

1461. ———. "The Sound of Music on the BBC Micro." *Educational Computing* 3 (Sept. 1982): 39. *C&CA* 18 (1983): 7237.

1462. Lane, B. "A Microcomputer Controls Audio Equipment." *Elektronica* [Netherlands] 31 (Nov. 4, 1983): 21–31. In Dutch. *E&EA* 87 (1984): 16797.

1463. Lane, John Michael. "Programming 64 Sound. Part 1." *Compute! The Journal for Progressive Computing* 6 (June 1984): 134–39. *C&CA* 19 (1984): 36742.

1464. ———. "Programming 64 Sound. Part 2." *Compute! The Journal for Progressive Computing* 6 (July 1984): 124–29.

1465.   Lawler, Brian H. "Musical Scales on the VIC." *Compute! The Journal for Progressive Computing* 5 (Mar. 1983): 147.
         C&CA 18 (1983): 19410.

1466.   LeBrun, Marc. "Notes on Microcomputer Music." In *First West Coast Computer Faire Conference Proceedings,* ed. Jim C. Warren, Jr. Palo Alto, Calif.: Computer Faire, 1977: 128–30.
         Also in *Computer Music Journal* 1,2 (Apr. 1977): 30–35.
         C&IS 18 (1978): 189692C. *RILM* 77 4018.

1467.   Lederer, Jeffrey H.; Tom Dwyer; and Margot Critchfield. "A Two Computer Music System." *BYTE* 3 (Mar. 1978): 8–12, 48–54.
         Also in *The BYTE Book of Computer Music,* ed. Christopher P. Morgan. Peterborough, N.H.: BYTE Books, 1979: 9–18.
         C&CA 13 (1978): 29109. *C&IS* 18 (1978): 195364C.

1468.   Lee, Robert. "Sound Generator." In *Compute!'s Second Book of VIC: VIC 2.* Greensboro, N.C.: Compute! Publications, 1983: 88–91.

1469.   Lehrman, Paul D. "The Alpha and the Apple: A Musical Team." *High Fidelity/Musical America* 33 (Sept. 1983): 51–54.

1470.   ———. "Say Hello to SID." *High Fidelity/Musical America* 33 (Dec. 1983): 69–72.

1471.   Leibson, Steve. "The Ackerman Digital System Noisemaker." *Microcomputing* 47 (Dec. 1980): 124–27.

1472.   Lentczner, Mark G. "Sound Kit: A Sound Manipulator." In *Proceedings of the International Computer Music Conference, 1985,* ed. Barry Truax. San Francisco, Calif.: Computer Music Association, 1985: 141–44.

1473.   Leonard, Steve. "Computers for Keyboardists: Computer Peripheral Enhancements (or, Getting More Bytes from Your Apple)." *Keyboard* 11 (Dec. 1985): 98.

1474.   ———. "Computers for Keyboardists: Computers, How They Do What They Do for Keyboard Players." *Keyboard* 12 (Feb. 1986): 98.

1475.   ———. "Computers for Keyboardists: Computerus Interruptus, or, Why that Software May Not Run on an Enhanced Apple IIe." *Keyboard* 11 (July 1985): 82–83.

1476.   ———. "Computers for Keyboardists: Data Transmission, Data Storage & Input/Output Devices." *Keyboard* 11 (Oct. 1985): 95.

1477.   ———. "Computers for Keyboardists: Some Computer Basics: Bits, Bytes, Buses & Turning Little Numbers into Big Ones." *Keyboard* 11 (Sept. 1985): 78, 91.

1478.   Lesh, Richard, and Alan J. Zett. "Music Editor." *SoftSide* 5 (Nov. 1981): 55–59.

1479. Levine, Steven, and Bill Mauchly. "AlphaSyntauri Music Synthesizer." *BYTE* 6 (Dec. 1981): 108–28.
C&CA 17 (1982): 13202.

1480. Lewis, Tony. "Build a Digital VCO!" *Polyphony* 6 (July/Aug. 1980): 8–15.

1481. ———. "Microcomputers in Real Time Audio. Part 1, Hardware." *Polyphony* 5 (Mar./Apr. 1980): 10–12.

1482. ———. "Microcomputers in Real Time Audio. Part 2, Software." *Polyphony* 6 (May/June 1980): 12–13, 18.

1483. Libbey, Robert L. "The Ideal Combo—A Microprocessor and a Music Synthesizer." *Polyphony* 3 (Feb. 1978): 7–10.

1484. Linderholm, Owen. "TI 99/4 Music Maker Module." *Creative Computing* 7 (Aug. 1981): 26.
C&CA 17 (1982): 5230.

1485. Longton, Michael. "SAM: Priorities in the Design of a Microprocessor-Based Music Program." *Interface* 10 (Mar. 1981): 83–95.
C&CA 16 (1981): 33985.

1486. Lord, Richard H. "Fast Fourier for the 6800." *BYTE* 4 (Feb. 1979): 108–19.

1487. ———. "Fast Fourier Transformations for the 6800." In *The BYTE Book of Computer Music,* ed. Christopher P. Morgan. Peterborough, N.H.: BYTE Books, 1979: 105–16.

1488. ———. "The Microcomputer as a Musical Instrument." In *Proceedings, 2nd Symposium on Small Computers in the Arts, October 15–17, 1982, Philadelphia, Pa.* Los Angeles, Calif.: IEEE Computer Society, 1982: 1–3.
C&CA 18 (1983): 28831.

1489. Lorton, Paul V., and Wolfgang E. Kuhn. "Micro-Based Melodies." *Educational Computing* 3 (Apr. 1982): 31–32.
C&CA 17 (1982): 32051.

1490. Lubar, David. "Passport to Great Sound." *Creative Computing* 7 (Nov. 1981): 20–22.
C&CA 17 (1982): 24515.

1491. Macielinski, A. "Play that Boogie." *Your Computer* 3 (Mar. 1983): 68–69.
C&CA 18 (1983): 22619.

1492. Makosinski, Art. "Tuning up the 1802: A Simple Music Composition Trainer." *BYTE* 7 (July 1982): 442–47.

1493. Mancini, Joseph. "Computer Music Pioneer Turns His Attention to Micros." *InfoWorld* 5 (June 27, 1983): 29–30.

1494. Mansfield, R. "Sequential Circuits Music Sequencer for Commodore 64." *Compute! The Journal for Progressive Computing* 7 (Jan. 1985): 104–08.
C&CA 20 (1985): 17262. *E&EA* 88 (1985): 20426.

1495. Margolin, Jed. "A Musical Synthesizer for the KIM-1." *Interface Age* 4 (Mar. 1979): 64–67.
C&CA 14 (1979): 34799. *C&IS* 23 (1979): 221798C.

1496. Marquis, Dave. "Machine Language Programming of Computer Music." In *Proceedings of the 9th West Coast Computer Faire, 1984.* Reston, Va.: Reston Pub. Co., 1984: 364–70.

1497. Marshall, Tom. "Atari Music Player." *Micro* [Chelmsford, Mass.] no. 68 (Jan. 1984): 49–56.
C&CA 19 (1984): 23722.

1498. Martin, Steven L. "Micro Mixdown: There's a 65K Helper in the Recording Studio." *Interface Age* 5 (Jan. 1980): 62–64.

1499. Marum, Steve. "Computer Music the Easy Way. Part 1." *Kilobaud Microcomputing* no. 12 (Dec. 1980): 72–82.
C&CA 16 (1981): 15687.

1500. ———. "Computer Music the Easy Way. Part 2." *Kilobaud Microcomputing* 5 (Jan. 1981): 60–75.
C&CA 16 (1981): 15690.

1501. Mason, Gerard. *Advanced Programming for the Oric.* London: McGraw-Hill, 1984: 78–105.

1502. Mathieu, Blaine. "Apple Sounds: From Beeps to Music. Part 1." *Compute! The Journal for Progressive Computing* 5 (Oct. 1983): 258–60.
C&CA 19 (1984): 6798.

1503. ———. "Apple Sounds: From Beeps to Music. Part 2." *Compute! The Journal for Progressive Computing* 5 (Nov. 1983): 201–06.
C&CA 19 (1984): 10531.

1504. "Mattel Electronics Offers Video Game/Keyboard Computer." *Music Trades* 131 (Apr. 1983): 27–28.

1505. Mauchly, J. William. "Merging Event Lists in Real-Time." In *Proceedings, 2nd Symposium on Small Computers in the Arts, October 15–17, 1982, Philadelphia, Pa.* Los Angeles, Calif.: IEEE Computer Society, 1982: 23–28.
C&CA 18 (1983): 28834.

1506. McKay, Blair D., and Barry L. Wills. "Microprocessor-Supervised Digital Synthesizers." In *Proceedings of the 1980 International Computer Music Conference,* comp. Hubert S. Howe. San Francisco, Calif.: Computer Music Association, 1982: 324–36.

1507. McMahan, Mike. *Graphics and Sound for Your Personal Computer.* Dallas: Wordware Pub., 1985. 192 p.

1508. Mecchia, W., and V. Monaci. "PET pratico: sintesi sonora." [Practical PET: Sound Synthesis] *Bit* [Milan] 24 (1982): 149–51.

1509. Mechtler, Peter. "Der Heimcomputer als neues Musikinstrument?" *Österreichische Musikzeitschrift* 38 (1983): 443.

1510. Megill, D., and H. Ganz. "Combined Art and Music Performances on Micro-computers." In *1982 Western Educational Computing Conference and Trade Show, San Diego, CA, 18–19 Nov. 1982*. Calif.: California Educational Computing Consortium, 1982: 115–17.
C&CA 18 (1983): 40676.

1511. Menchinelli, Sergio. "A Microcomputer Approach to the Polyphonic Music Synthesizer." Paper presented at the 56th Convention of the Audio Engineering Society, March 1–4, 1977, Paris. Preprint no. 1211.

1512. Mercuri, Rebecca T. "Music Editors for Small Computers—A Comparative Study." *Creative Computing* 7 (Feb. 1981): 18–24.
C&CA 17 (1982): 5227.

1513. Merker, Oskar. "ZX81 à la carte. (3), Software voller Klang." *Funkschau* 24 (Nov. 25, 1983): 74–77.
C&CA 19 (1984): 14744.

1514. Metcalf, Chris, and Marc Sugiyama. "MusicMaster." In *Compute!'s First Book of Commodore 64 Sound and Graphics*. Greensboro, N.C.: Compute! Publications, 1983: 238–49.

1515. ———, and Marc Sugiyama. "MusicMaster for the Commodore 64." *Compute! The Journal for Progressive Computing* 5 (June 1983): 122–33.
C&CA 18 (1983): 32106.

1516. "Micro Chip Off the Block." *Melody Maker* 58 (Feb. 5, 1983): 28.

1517. Milano, Dominic. "Keyboard Report: Commodore Amiga Computer." *Keyboard* 12 (Feb. 1986): 112–15.

1518. ———. "Roland DG Compu-Music/CMU-800." *Apple Orchard* 5 (Mar. 1984): 42–43.
C&CA 20 (1985): 4084. *E&EA* 88 (1985): 3789.

1519. Miller, Jim. "Personal Composer." *Computer Music Journal* 9,4 (Winter 1985): 27–37.

1520. Mizelle, Dary J. "Software Development for a Micro-Computer-Controlled Digital Synthesizer." Paper presented at the 1980 International Computer Music Conference, November 13–15, 1980, Queens College of the City University of New York.

1521. Moog, Robert A. "Musical Uses of Home Computers: Pack up Your Computer in Your Ol' Gig Bag." In *Synthesizers and Computers*. Milwaukee, Wis.: H. Leonard Pub. Corp., 1985: 52–56. From *Keyboard* May 81-July 81.

1522. ———. "On Synthesizers: Breadboarding Interface Circuits." *Keyboard* 8 (Apr. 1982): 57.

1523. ———. "On Synthesizers: Computer-Synthesizer Interface." *Keyboard* 8 (Jan. 1982): 70, 72.

1524. ———. "On Synthesizers: Computer/Synthesizer Interfaces." *Keyboard* 8 (May 1982): 52.

1525.   ———. "On Synthesizers: More on Computer-Based Sequencers." *Keyboard* 7 (July 1981): 72.

1526.   ———. "On Synthesizers: More on Computer Control." *Keyboard* 8 (June 1982): 64.

1527.   ———. "On Synthesizers: Musical Uses of Personal Computers." *Contemporary Keyboard* 7 (June 1981): 63.

1528.   ———. "On Synthesizers: Programmable Resistor and Attenuator." *Keyboard* 8 (Mar. 1982): 54, 66.

1529.   ———. "On Synthesizers: Simple Circuits for Computer Control. Part 1." *Keyboard* 8 (Feb. 1982): 67.

1530.   ———. "On Synthesizers: The AlphaSyntauri." *Keyboard* 7 (Nov. 1981): 76–77.

1531.   Moore, Herb. "See What You Hear & Hear What You See." *Recreational Computing* 8 (Nov.-Dec. 1979): 8–10.
         C&IS 24 (1980): 241144C.

1532.   ———. *Sound and Graphics for the Commodore 64.* New York: Wiley, 1985. 240 p.

1533.   ———. "Sounds of the Atari in BASIC." *Interface Age* 6 (Mar. 1981): 56–60.
         C&CA 16 (1981): 21876. *C&IS* 28 (1982): 13402C.

1534.   ———. "Sounds of the Atari in BASIC. Part II, Color Graphics." *Interface Age* 6 (Apr. 1981): 50–54.

1535.   ———. "Sounds of the Atari in BASIC. Part III, Entering Note Values." *Interface Age* 6 (May 1981): 50–52.
         C&CA 16 (1981): 30811. *C&IS* 28 (1982): 81–14408C.

1536.   ———. "Sounds of the Atari in BASIC. Part IV, Allowing Data Input." *Interface Age* 6 (June 1981): 50–54.
         C&CA 16 (1981): 33986.

1537.   ———. "Sounds of the Atari in BASIC. Part V, Random Generation of Sound." *Interface Age* 6 (July 1981): 48–50.
         C&CA 16 (1981): 33987.

1538.   ———. "Sounds of the Atari in BASIC. Part VI, Creation of Sound Effects." *Interface Age* 6 (Aug. 1981): 54–55.

1539.   ———; Judy Lower; and Bob Albrecht. *Atari Sound and Graphics: A Self-Teaching Guide.* New York: Wiley, 1982. 234 p.

1540.   Moore, M. P. "ZX81 Music Board. Part II." *Electronics Today International* 12 (May 1983): 54–59.
         C&CA 19 (1984): 31866.

1541.   Morris, Stephen. "A Personal Computer, Musical Knowledge-Based System Using Active Objects." In *Proceedings of the International Computer Music Conference, 1985,* ed. Barry Truax. San Francisco, Calif.: Computer Music Association, 1985: 237–42.

1542.   Morris, William. "Fugue." *SoftSide* 3 (Jan. 1981): 74–76.

1543.   ———, and John Cope. "Apple Fugue." *SoftSide* 6 (Oct. 1982): 83–86.
        C&CA 18 (1983): 11078.

1544.   ———, and John Cope. "Flight of the Bumble Bee." *SoftSide* 5 (Nov. 1981):
        23–30.

1545.   ———, and John Cope. "Messiah." *Softside* 3 (Apr. 1981): 20–21.

1546.   ———, and John Cope. "Tunein!" *SoftSide* 5 (July 1982): 58–61.
        C&CA 17 (1982): 44222.

1547.   Morriss, Jeff C. "Music Synthesis in the FORTH Programming Environ-
        ment." In *1982 Rochester FORTH Conference on Data Bases and Process Con-
        trol, May 18–21, 1982*. Rochester, N.Y.: Institute for Applied Forth Research,
        1982: 79–96.
        C&CA 19 (1984): 27959. *E&EA* 87 (1984): 33047.

1548.   Moshell, J. M., and C. E. Hughes. *Imagination: Music*. New York, N.Y.:
        J. Wiley, 1983.
        C&IS 32 (1984): 84–3807C.

1549.   Multer, K. A. "Compleat Artarist." *Microcomputing* 7 (Mar. 1983): 122.

1550.   Murray, R. "Orchestra 85 Composer's Edition & Orchestra 90." *SoftSide* 6
        (Oct. 1982): 50–52.
        E&EA 86 (1983): 15073.

1551.   "Music Micro, Please." *Practical Computing* 2 (May 1979): 46–49.
        C&CA 14 (1979): 25006.

1552.   "Music on the BBC Micro." *Electronics & Wireless World* 91 (Mar. 1985):
        78–79.

1553.   "Music Programming for the CBM 'PET' Computer." *CBM/PET News* 2
        (1981): 20–22.
        In German.
        C&CA 17 (1982): 24613.

1554.   Myers, Peter H. "Teach KIM to Sing." In *The BYTE Book of Computer
        Music,* ed. Christopher P. Morgan. Peterborough, N.H.: BYTE Books, 1979:
        125–28.

1555.   Nasman, Leonard. "Atari Music Composer Cartridge." *Creative Computing* 7
        (Jan. 1981): 26.
        C&CA 16 (1981): 27617.

1556.   Nelson, P. I. "Advanced Sound Effects on the 64." *Compute! The Journal for
        Progressive Computing* 7 (Feb. 1985): 129–33.
        C&CA 20 (1985): 31078.

1557.   "A New Breed of Microprocessor." *Computer Music Journal* 2,2 (Sept. 1978):
        62–64.

1558. "New Musical Expressions." *Home Computer Advanced Course* 26 (1984): 82–84.
E&EA 87 (1984): 61137.

1559. Newman, R. "Music Maker." *Your Computer* 4 (Feb. 1984): 130–35.
C&CA 19 (1984): 27991.

1560. Noetzel, Andrew S. "A Multimicrocomputer System for Real-Time Music Synthesis: Design and Implementation." In *Proceedings of the Venice 1982 International Computer Music Conference,* comp. Thom Blum and John Strawn. San Francisco, Calif.: Computer Music Association, 1985: 217–24.

1561. ———. "The Use of Interpolating Memories for Music Processing by Microcomputer." In *Proceedings of the International Computer Music Conference, 1985,* ed. Barry Truax. San Francisco, Calif.: Computer Music Association, 1985: 129–34.

1562. North, Steve. "ALF/Apple Music Synthesizer." *Creative Computing* 5 (June 1979): 102–3.
C&CA 15 (1980): 6879.

1563. ———. "Four Systems, Plus a Music Program." *Creative Computing* 4 (Mar.-Apr. 1978): 28–37.
C&CA 13 (1978): 21467.

1564. Norton, Peter. "Sound Abilities: The PCjr." *PC Magazine* 3 (Jan. 1984): 137–41.

1565. O'Beirne, T. H. "From Mozart to the Bagpipe, with a Small Computer." *Bulletin of the Institute of Mathematics and Its Applications* 7 (Jan. 1971): 11–16.

1566. O'Haver, T. C. "Audio Processing with a Microprocessor." *BYTE* 3 (June 1978): 166–73.

1567. ———. "More Music for the 6502." *BYTE* 3 (June 1978): 140–41.
C&CA 13 (1978): 29113. *C&IS* 19 (1978): 23621C.

1568. Oppenheim, David. "Microcomputer to Synthesizer Interface for a Low Cost System." *Computer Music Journal* 2,1 (July 1978): 6–11.

1569. Orlarey, Yann. "MLOGO: un langage de programmation orienté composition musicale." In *Proceedings of the International Computer Music Conference, 1984,* ed. William Buxton. San Francisco, Calif.: Computer Music Association, 1985: 273–74.

1570. Orlofsky, Thomas P. "Computer Music: A Design Tutorial." *BYTE* 6 (Mar. 1981): 317–32.
C&CA 16 (1981): 18373.

1571. Oura, Toshio; Tomoaki Isozaki; Sachiyuki Toufuku; and Hatsuhide Igarashi. "A Single-Chip Sound Synthesis Microcomputer." In *1982 IEEE International Solid-State Circuits Conference, Digest of Technical Papers, San Francisco, CA, 10–12 Feb. 1982.* New York: IEEE, 1982: 270–71.
C&CA 17 (1982): 32055.

1572. Owens, Peter. "Four Short Programs for the Timex/Sinclair." *Popular Computing* 3 (Jan. 1984): 190–92.
C&CA 19 (1984): 19394.

1573. Ozzola, Vito. *Musica con il Commodore 64.* [Music with the Commodore 64] Milan: Mondadori, 1984. 142 p.

1574. Paturzo, Bonaventura Antony. *Making Music with Microprocessors.* Blue Ridge Summit, Pa.: TAB Books, 1984. 286 p.
Review by S.W. Cooper in *Computer Music Journal* 9,4 (Winter 1985): 66–67.

1575. Pearce, C. F., and R. T. Atherton. "Minicomputer Music." *Computer Education* 16 (Feb. 1974): 7–8.

1576. Peckett, D. S. "Enveloped by BBC Sounds." *Practical Computing* 6 (Mar. 1983): 126–29.
C&CA 18 (1983): 22627.

1577. ———. "Making Music." *Computing Today* 3 (Dec. 1981): 61–64.
C&CA 17 (1982): 13263.

1578. Peele, George. "Understanding Sound." In *Compute!'s First Book of Commodore 64 Sound and Graphics.* Greensboro, N.C.: Compute! Publications, 1983: 211–27.

1579. Perkins, Bob. "Modification of Celestial Music." *Creative Computing* 9 (July 1983): 202–4.
C&CA 18 (1983): 40672.
Related to the article by L. Christopherson in vol. 8 (Mar. 1982): 134–42.

1580. "Personal Computing '77: A Look Around." *Polyphony* 3,2 (1977): 8–10.

1581. Pesticcio, G., and David Bristow. "Sounds Inviting." *Acorn User* 25 (Aug. 1984): 47.
C&CA 20 (1985): 12330.

1582. Pfenninger, E. "Music for OSI." *Mikro- und Kleincomputer* 3 (Feb. 1981): 56–58.
In German.
C&CA 16 (1981): 33978.

1583. Pfister, Henry L. "Developing a Personal Computer Music System." In *Personal Computing Digest, National Computer Conference, Personal Computing Festival, May 20–22, 1980, Anaheim, California.* Arlington, Va.: AFIPS, 1980: 119–24.

1584. ———. "A Microcomputer Music Synthesizer." In *The Best of the Computer Faires. Volume 3, Conference Proceedings of the 3rd West Coast Computer Faire,* ed. Jim C. Warren, Jr. Los Angeles: Computer Faire, 1978: 36–41.

1585. Plumber, Doc. "The Joy of Sound from SOUNDWARE." *Recreational Computing* 8 (Nov.-Dec. 1979): 16–20.

1586. Powell, Roger. "Home Computer Sequencer: Flow Chart." *Keyboard Magazine* 7 (Sept. 1981): 50.

1587.   ———. "Practical Synthesis: Home Computer Sequencer." *Contemporary Keyboard* 7 (Feb. 1981): 67.
Reprinted as "Home Computers as Sequencers: Design Your Own Control Program." In *Synthesizers and Computers*. Milwaukee, Wis.: H. Leonard Pub. Corp., 1985: 37–38.

1588.   ———. "Practical Synthesis: Home Computer Sequencer. Part II." *Contemporary Keyboard* (June 1981)
Reprinted as "Home Computers as Sequencers: Home Computer Software and Hardware." In *Synthesizers and Computers*. Milwaukee, Wis.: H. Leonard Pub. Corp., 1985: 39–40.

1589.   ———. "Practical Synthesis: Home Computer Sequencer, Flow Chart." *Keyboard* 7 (Sept. 1981): 50.
Reprinted as "Designing Your Sequencer Software." In *Synthesizers and Computers*. Milwaukee, Wis.: H. Leonard Pub. Corp., 1985: 43–44.

1590.   ———. "Using the Microcomputer as a Multichannel Compositionally Oriented Controlled-Voltage Sequencer for Synthesizers." Paper presented at the 60th convention of the Audio Engineering Society, May 2–5, 1978, Los Angeles.

1591.   Pytlik, William F. "PET I/O Port Expander." *Kilobaud Microcomputing* 9 (Sept. 1980): 56–57.
C&CA 16 (1981): 3177.

1592.   Rafuse, R. A. "The Layman's Guide to Digital Logic Gates." *Polyphony* 3,2 (1977): 11–15.

1593.   Regena, C. "Programming the TI: The Singing Computer." *Compute! The Journal for Progressive Computing* 6 (Aug. 1984): 115–18.

1594.   Reifsnider, Randal J. "Musical TI Keyboard." *Compute! The Journal for Progressive Computing* 6 (Sept. 1984): 148–49.

1595.   Rinder, Robert. *Cookbook of Creative Programs for the Commodore 64*. New York: New American Library, 1984: 51–86.

1596.   ———. *Cookbook of Creative Programs for the IBM PC and PCjr: Projects for Music, Animation, and Telecommunications*. New York: New American Library, 1985. 243 p.

1597.   Roberts, M. "Digital Duet." *Your Commodore* 1 (Dec. 1984): 74–76.
C&CA 20 (1985): 31112.

1598.   Rosenstein, Larry S. "A Microcomputer-based MUSE." B.S. thesis, Massachusetts Institute of Technology, Dept. of Electrical Engineering and Computer Science, 1979. 58 p.

1599.   Rosmini, Dick. "The MC-8 Micro Composer." *High Fidelity/Musical America* 28 (May 1978): 130.

1600.   Rossum, David P. "Some Thoughts on Microprocessors in Electronic Music." *Computer Music Journal* 1,2 (Apr. 1977): 62–63.
RILM 77 4022.

1601. Rotberg, E. "The Rotberg Synthesizer." *SoftSide* 6 (Oct. 1982): 54–56.
E&EA 86 (1983): 15074.

1602. Rozenberg, Maurice. "Microcomputer-Controlled Sound Processing Using Walsh Functions." *Computer Music Journal* 3,1 (Mar. 1979): 42–47.
C&CA 14 (1979): 34791. *C&IS* 24 (1980): 230388C.

1603. Ryan, Joel. "Constraints on a Real Microcomputer Based Music Performance System." Paper presented at the 1982 International Computer Music Conference, Sept. 27-Oct. 1, Venice.

1604. Sandberg-Diment, Erik. "Commodore Finds Its Voice." *New York Times* (Apr. 24, 1984): p. 14 (N); p. C4(L).

1605. ———. "Mastering Melodies." *Science Digest* 92 (July 1984): 82–83.

1606. Santoiemma, Maurizio. "Introduzione all'uso del PDP 11/34 e al colloquio con l'IBM 370/158." [Introduction to the Use of the PDP 11/34 and to Communications with the IBM 370/158] *Bollettino LIMB* 4 (1984): 103–6.

1607. Sapir, Sylviane, and Richard Kronland-Martinet. "Use of Microprocessors in Real Time Synthesis of Sounds: An Example of a Small System." In *Proceedings of the Venice 1982 International Computer Music Conference,* comp. Thom Blum and John Strawn. San Francisco, Calif.: Computer Music Association, 1985: 66–72.

1608. Scagnoli, Joseph R. "Music and Micros, Software Reviews: Pyware." *Music Educators Journal* 39 (Sept. 1984): 25–28.

1609. Scarborough, John. "Atari's Sound System." *Compute! The Journal for Progressive Computing* 5 (Jan. 1983): 48–50.
C&CA 18 (1983): 15372.

1610. Schreiber, Linda M. "Music from A to G." *Personal Computing* 2 (May 1978): 68–69.

1611. Schroder-Limmer, W. "Music with Microcomputers: Analogue and Digital Synthesizers." *Chip* 5 (May 1984): 264–67.
In German.
C&CA 19 (1984): 36714. *E&EA* 87 (1984): 44313.

1612. Scott, Robert F. "Play a Tune with these new IC's." *Radio-Electronics* 53 (Mar. 1982): 78–79.

1613. Scrimshaw, Nevin B., and James Vogel. *Introduction to the Commodore 64: Adventures in Programming.* Cambridge, MA: Birkhaeuser Boston, 1983. 124 p.
Also published by Softext, Inc., Cambridge, Mass., 1983.
C&IS 33 (1985): 85–1556C.

1614. Sedacca, B. "Add-On Synthesizers." *Practical Computing* 6 (June 1983): 118–21.
E&EA 86 (1983): 40726.

1615. Seif, Joseph B. "The Production of Multi-Voiced Music on a Microcomputer Without the Use of Synthesizers." In *Modeling and Simulation. Volume 12, Proceedings of the Twelfth Annual Pittsburgh Conference*, ed. W. G. Vogt and M. H. Mickle. Research Triangle Park, N.C.: Instrument Society of America, 1981: 1435–38.

1616. "Setting the Tone." *Home Computer Advanced Course* 38 (1984): 746–48. *E&EA* 88 (1985): 14562.

1617. Shapiro, Gerald M. "A Touch-Sensitive Keyboard for Electronic Music." *Journal of the Audio Engineering Society* 30 (Oct. 1982): 732–34. *E&EA* 86 (1983): 9595.

1618. Sherbon, James W. "Chips and Diodes of Microcomputers." *Music Educators Journal* 69 (Jan. 1983): 32–38. *CIJE* 15 (1983): EJ 275 320.

1619. Sierad, Ted B. "Tune in with Some Chips." *BYTE* 2 (Sept. 1977): 84–94. Also in *The BYTE Book of Computer Music*, ed. Christopher P. Morgan. Peterborough, N.H.: BYTE Books, 1979: 27–32. *C&CA* 13 (1978): 2572. *C&IS* 17: 181357C. *E&EA* 81 (1978): 5367.

1620. Silver, Howard. "Get Set to Tune Up Your TRS-80." *Creative Computing* 7 (Dec. 1981): 176–82. *C&CA* 17 (1982): 24516.

1621. Silverman, Lida A. "Music-Synthesis Software: A Beginner's Guide." *High Fidelity/Musical America* 33 (Dec. 1983): 66–67.

1622. Simonton, John S. "In Pursuit of the Wild QuASH." *Polyphony* 3 (1977): 19–22.

1623. ———. "Pink Tunes." *Polyphony* 4 (July/Aug. 1978): 22–26.

1624. ———. "Potpourri and the Apple Connection." *Polyphony* 3,2 (1977): 28–31.

1625. ———. "What the Computer Does: An Introduction." *Polyphony* 3,1 (1977): 5–7.

1626. Smith, Gary E. "Music and Micros, Software Reviews: 'Halftime' Computerized Charting System." *Music Educators Journal* 39 (Sept. 1984): 19–25.

1627. "Sounding out the Micro." *Which Micro and Software Review* (Apr. 1984): 20–23. *C&CA* 19 (1984): 36778.

1628. Spiegel, A. "The Little One is not Mute: Music with the Sinclair ZX81." *Chip* 2 (Feb. 1985): 167–68. In German. *C&CA* 20 (1985): 25707.

1629. Spiegel, Laurie. "Macromusic from Micros." *Creative Computing* 7 (May 1981): 68–74. *C&CA* 16 (1981): 36842.

1630.   Stanger, M. "Singalong." *A&B Computing* 1 (Oct. 1984): 104–7.
C&CA 20 (1985): 21606.

1631.   Stanley, William D., and Steven J. Peterson. "Fast Fourier Transforms on your Home Computers." In *The BYTE Book of Computer Music,* ed. Christopher P. Morgan. Peterborough, N.H.: BYTE Books, 1979: 97–104.

1632.   Steed, Mike. "SYSound." *Compute! The Journal for Progressive Computing* 6 (Sept. 1984): 146–48.

1633.   Strien, J. J. A. van. "Microcomputer for Use as a Tuning Aid." *Radio Elektronica* 29 (Feb. 25, 1981): 11–15.
In Dutch.
C&CA 16 (1981): 21896.

1634.   Struve, Bill. "A $19 Music Interface." *BYTE* 2 (Dec. 1977): 48–50, 60–69, 170–71.
Also in *The BYTE Book of Computer Music,* ed. Christopher P. Morgan. Peterborough, N.H.: BYTE Publications, 1979: 33–46.
C&CA 13 (1978): 13016. *C&IS* 18 (1978): 189689C.

1635.   Suchoff, Michael. "Digital Recording of Melodies Played on a Keyboard by Microprocessor Control." *Electronotes* 7 (Oct. 1975): 5–13.

1636.   Sutcliffe, Alan. "Patterns." *Personal Computer World* 4 (Aug. 1981): 110–12.
C&CA 17 (1982): 2763.

1637.   Sutton, James. *Power Programming the Commodore 64: Assembly Language, Graphics, and Sound.* Englewood Cliffs, N.J.: Prentice-Hall, 1985. 337 p.

1638.   Swift, G. W., and M. Yunik. "A Microprocessor Based Keyboard Instrument for Microtonal Music." In *Proceedings of the Venice 1982 International Computer Music Conference,* comp. Thom Blum and John Strawn. San Francisco, Calif.: Computer Music Association, 1985: 588–600.

1639.   Swift, M. D. "Microprocessor-Based Polyphonic Keyboard for Music Synthesizer." In *IREECON International Digest of Papers, Melbourne, 1977.* Sidney: IREE, 1977: 352–54.
C&IS 18 (1978): 192018C; 23 (1979): 217670C.

1640.   Swirsky, Robert. "Electric Duet." *Popular Computing* 2 (Mar. 1983): 164–66.
C&CA 18 (1983): 22580. *C&IS* 31 (1983): 83–4374C.

1641.   Szepesi, Z. "Run this Program and Jog Your Memory." *Microcomputing* 7 (Jan. 1983): 86–89.

1642.   Tait, S. "Music Micro, Please. Part II, Digital Synthesis." *Personal Computer World* 7 (Jan. 1984): 188–90.
C&CA 19 (1984): 31870.

1643.   Tarabella, Leonello. *Il linguaggio PRIMULA per la programmazione musicale su micro calcolatori.* [The PRIMULA Language for Music Programming on Micro Computers] Pisa: CNUCE, 1981. 32 p.

1644. Taylor, Robert P. "Bottom-Up Bizet: Reflections of Implementing Release 234.5 of the Pearl Fishers." *Creative Computing* 3 (Mar.-Apr. 1977): 91–95.

1645. Tedsen, Fred. "16-Bit Atari Music." *Compute! The Journal for Progressive Computing* 5 (Mar. 1983): 214–20.
C&CA 18 (1983): 19428.

1646. Theis, Bill, and Tim Theis. "Music and Micros, Software Review: 'Marching Band Computer Show Design Software'." *Music Educators Journal* 39 (Oct. 1984): 92–96.

1647. Therkell, G. J. "Use of a Microcomputer for Acoustic Analysis of Studios and Control Rooms." *Australian Sound Recording* 1/8–9 (1979): 23–24.
RILM 79 5946.

1648. Thornburg, David D. "Computer-Assisted Explorations with Music." *Compute! The Journal for Progressive Computing* 6 (Aug. 1984): 24–26.

1649. Tomlinson, R. "Play It Again, Beeb." *Personal Computer World* 7 (Dec. 1984): 172–75.
E&EA 88 (1985): 20430.

1650. Traister, Robert J. *Music & Speech Programs for the IBM PC.* Blue Ridge Summit, Pa.: Tab Books, 1983. 178 p.

1651. Tubb, Philip. "Apple Music Synthesizer." *Creative Computing* 6 (June 1980): 74–83.
C&CA 15 (1980): 36417.

1652. ———. "Musical Subroutines." *Creative Computing* 8 (Mar. 1982): 124–32.
C&CA 17 (1982): 28470. *CIJE* 14 (1982): EJ 260 328.

1653. "Tuning Up." *Home Computer Advanced Course* 52 (1985): 1029–31.
C&CA 20 (1985): 28521.

1654. Turrier, C. "Initiation: A Microorgan." *Micro systemes* 35 (Oct. 1983): 205–9. In French.
C&CA 19 (1984): 6763.

1655. Turrietta, Cheryl R. "Building a Music System." *Music Educators Journal* 69 (Jan. 1983): 52–53.
CIJE 15 (1983): EJ 275 324.

1656. Tyler, Tommy N. "Make Beautiful Music on an 8085." *EDN* 26 (Apr. 29, 1981): 181–84.
C&CA 16 (1981): 36856.

1657. Urschel, Robert. "The GI Programmable Sound Generator." *Microcomputing* 47 (Dec. 1980): 134–40.
Also in *Kilobaud Microcomputing* 12 (Dec. 1980): 134–40.
C&CA 16 (1981): 15688.

1658. Valentine, R. *Timex Sinclair 2068: What Can You Do with It?* New York, N.Y.: J. Wiley, 1983. 118 p.
C&IS 32 (1984): 84–4736C.

1659. Van Buskirk, Trudy. "Music with the Apple Alf." Paper presented at the Music Symposium, Sheridan College, Oakville, Ontario, June 1980.

1660. Vernon, P. "Make Music with Your Computer." *Electronics Australia* 45 (Aug. 1983): 90–99, 141.
C&CA 19 (1984): 3565. *E&EA* 86 (1983): 62943.

1661. Vogel, James, and Nevin B. Scrimshaw. *The Commodore 64 Music Book: A Guide to Programming Music and Sound.* Cambridge, Mass.: Softext, Inc., 1983. 130 p.
Review by Michael Nicita and Ronald Petrusha in *The Reader's Guide to Microcomputer Books.* Brooklyn, N.Y.: Golden-Lee, 1984: 371.
C&IS 33 (1985): 85–473C.

1662. Voskuil, Jon. "Electric Duet." *SoftSide* 5 (May 1982): 53–54.
C&CA 17 (1982): 40422.

1663. ———. "Music Machine." *SoftSide* 5 (Nov. 1981): 61–65.

1664. Waite, Mitch. *Microsoft Macinations: An Introduction to Microsoft BASIC for the Apple Macintosh.* Bellevue, Wash.: Microsoft Press, 1985. 497 p.

1665. Watt, Dan. "Musical Microworlds." *Popular Computing* 3 (Aug. 1984): 91–94.
CIJE 16 (1984): EJ 304 491.

1666. Waugh, I. "Making Music on the Beeb. Part I." *BEEBUG* 3 (Jan.-Feb. 1985): 15–20.

1667. West, Marcus. "Sequemuse: A Hybrid Computer-Music System." *Interface* 11 (1982): 47–60.

1668. Westbrook, D. J. "A Screen Driven Music Synthesizer." *BEEBUG* 3 (Aug.-Sept. 1984): 24–28.

1669. White, Loring C. "Music from the Altair 8800 Computer." In *The BYTE Book of Computer Music,* ed. Christopher P. Morgan. Peterborough, N.H.: BYTE Books, 1979: 121–24.

1670. Whittle, Robin. "The Casiotone M-10, MT-30, and VL-1: The Smallest Computer Musical Instruments." In *Proceedings of the International Music and Technology Conference, August 24–28, 1981, University of Melbourne.* Parkville, Vic.: Computer Music Project, Dept. of Computer Science, University of Melbourne, 1981: 211–18.

1671. Wills, Barry L.; Douglas J. Steele; and Blair D. McKay. "Microcomputers and Music: Lowcost Systems with Multiple Applications." *Proceedings of the American Society for Information Science* 18 (1981): 317–18.

1672. Willson, M. Joseph. "A Microprocessor Architecture for Musical Signal Synthesis." Paper presented at the ACM Computer Science Conference, Washington, D.C., 18–20 February 1975.
C&CA 11 (1976): 12104 *C&IS* 14: 133220C.

1673. Wilson, Blake. "VIC Musician." *Compute! The Journal for Progressive Computing* 5 (July 1983): 212–14.

1674. Wilson, Stephen. *Using Computers to Create Art.* Englewood Cliffs, N.J.: Prentice-Hall, 1986. 380 p.

1675. Winter, Frank. "Music and the Personal Computer." *Compute* 1 (Nov./Dec. 1980): 18–21.

1676. Winter, M. J. "Major & Minor: VIC Music Theory." *Compute! The Journal for Progressive Computing* 5 (Apr. 1983): 252–54.
       C&CA 18 (1983): 25644.

1677. "Wired for Sound." *Home Computer Advanced Course* 28 (1984): 553–55.
       C&CA 19 (1984): 52000. *E&EA* 87 (1984): 61139.

1678. Wittlich, Gary E; John W. Schaffer; and Larry R. Babb. *Microcomputers and Music.* Englewood Cliffs, N.J.: Prentice-Hall, 1986. 321 p.

1679. Wohlhart, D. "Apple by Notes: Transcription Program for the Apple II." *Chip* 4 (Apr. 1985): 292–4.
       C&CA 20 (1985): 31002.

1680. Wright, Jim. "Micro Music for the TRS-80." *Creative Computing* 6 (Jan. 1980): 34.

1681. Wright, Maurice. "New Horizons for Microcomputer Music." *Creative Computing* 3 (Mar.-Apr. 1977): 75.

1682. Wrightson, K. "Music Hardware." *Your Computer* 4 (Sept.1984): 65–68.
       C&CA 20 (1985): 17297.

1683. Yannes, Bob. "Keyboard Matrix Interface for EK-3." *Polyphony* 3,2 (1977): 20.

1684. Yantis, Michael A. "A Microprocessor Based Live-Performance Instrument." Paper presented at the 1977 International Computer Music Conference, University of California, San Diego, 26–30 October 1977.

1685. Yavelow, Christopher. "Music Software for the Apple Macintosh." *Computer Music Journal* 9,3 (Fall 1985): 52–67.

1686. Youngblood, Joseph. "Plot It Yourself: Display FM Waveforms on Your Apple or IBM with these BASIC Programs." *Keyboard* 11 (Nov. 1985): 42–43.

1687. Zett, Alan J. "Commanding BASIC." *SoftSide* 5 (Nov. 1981): 52–53.

1688. ———, and Fred J. Condo. "IBM-PC." *SoftSide* 6 (Nov. 1982): 51–61.
       C&CA 18 (1983): 15303.

MIDI

1689. Anderton, Craig. *MIDI for Musicians*. New York: Amsco Publications, 1986. 105 p.

1690. Arfib, Daniel. "Man-Machine Dialog Using MIDI Files." In *Proceedings of the International Computer Music Conference, 1985,* ed. Barry Truax. San Francisco, Calif.: Computer Music Association, 1985: 325–28.

1691. Bernardini, Nicola. "L'interfaccia MIDI." [The MIDI Interface] *AudioReview* 30 (1984): 84–88.

1692. ———. "L'interfaccia MIDI: ultimo bollettino di guerra." [The MIDI Interface: The Last Communique] *AudioReview* 33 (1984): 106–09.

1693. Bortone, G. "Interfaccia digitale MIDI (I)." [The MIDI Interface (I)] *Strumenti musicali* 51 (1984): 17–20.

1694. ———. "Interfaccia digitale MIDI (II)." [The MIDI Interface (II)] *Strumenti musicali* 52 (1984): 21–35.

1695. ———. "Interfaccia digitale MIDI (III)." [The MIDI Interface (III)] *Strumenti musicali* 53 (1984): 17–24.

1696. ———. "Interfaccia digitale MIDI (IV)." [The MIDI Interface (IV)] *Strumenti musicali* 54/55 (1984): 15–20.

1697. Colbert, Paul. "MIDI." *Melody Maker* 58 (June 4, 1983): 39.

1698. Cooper, James. "MIDI Specs & Switching Project." *Keyboard* 11 (Jan. 1985): 57, 78.

1699. ———. "Mind over MIDI: Circuit Checkers, Code Cracking & Continuous Clocks." *Keyboard* 12 (May 1986): 100–104.

1700. ———. "Mind over MIDI: Data Transmission, Mixing & Filtering." *Keyboard* 11 (Dec. 1985): 104–7.

1701. ———. "Mind over MIDI: Is There Life after the NAMM Show." *Keyboard* 12 (Apr. 1986): 100–101.

1702. ———. "Mind over MIDI: Puttin' on the Bits." *Keyboard* 12 (Feb. 1986): 100–101.

1703.   ———. "Modifications & Maintenance: Radio MIDI, Disk Care & Feeding, & Techno Miscellany." *Keyboard* 11 (Oct. 1985): 91, 93.

1704.   ———. "What MIDI Isn't and Why." *Keyboard* 11(Apr. 1985): 72, 98.

1705.   Cummings, Steve. "Keyboard Report: Fairlight Voicetracker & Cherry Lane Pitchrider Pitch-to-MIDI Converters." *Keyboard* 11 (Dec. 1985): 124–27, 135.

1706.   ———. "Keyboard Report: Mark of the Unicorn Performer, Sequencer for the Macintosh." *Keyboard* 12 (May 1986): 124–28.

1707.   ———. "Keyboard Report: Opcode Systems Midimac Sequencer for the Macintosh." *Keyboard* 11 (Nov. 1985): 92–96.

1708.   ———. "Keyboard Report: Syntech MIDI Sequencer Software." *Keyboard* 11 (Dec. 1985): 122–23.

1709.   Droman, David C. *Exploring MIDI—The Musical Instrument Digital Interface.* North Hollywood, Calif.: International MIDI Association Publications, 1985. 78 p.
Review by Curtis Roads in *Computer Music Journal* 9,2 (Summer 1985): 60.

1710.   Ellis, David. "Amstrad CPC464 Home Computer." *Electronics & Music Maker* 4 (Nov. 1984): 84–86.
C&CA 20 (1985): 21600. *E&EA* 88 (1985): 26149.

1711.   ———. "Electromusic Research MIDI Software and Hardware for the BBC Micro." *Electronics & Music Maker* 4 (Aug. 1984): 82–84.
E&EA 87 (1984): 61127.

1712.   ———. "Inside MIDI." *Electronics & Music Maker* 4 (June 1984): 39–45.
E&EA 87 (1984): 48636.

1713.   ———. "Jellinghaus Music Systems: MIDI Computer Interface and Software." *Electronics & Music Maker* 4 (July 1984): 82–84.
C&CA 19 (1984): 47431. *E&EA* 87 (1984): 55096.

1714.   ———. "LEMI Future Shock and AMP83: MIDI Hardware and Software for Apple II Micro." *Electronics & Music Maker* 4 (Jan. 1985): 84–86.
C&CA 20 (1985): 25712. *E&EA* 88 (1985): 31275.

1715.   ———. "The MIDI and the Micro." *Electronics & Music Maker* 4 (June 1984): 46–48.
C&CA 19 (1984): 47421. *E&EA* 87 (1984): 48637.

1716.   ———. "Passport Designs MIDI/4 Software and Interface." *Electronics & Music Maker* 4 (Sept. 1984): 82–83.
C&CA 20 (1985): 4081. *E&EA* 88 (1985): 3783.

1717.   "Expanding MIDI: Two New Developments from Sycologic." *Electronics & Music Maker* 4 (Sept. 1984): 34.
C&CA 20 (1985): 4079. *E&EA* 88 (1985): 3780.

1718.   Frederick, Dave. "Keyboard Report: Forte Music, MIDI Mod for Pianos." *Keyboard* 12 (Feb. 1986): 108–11.

1719. ———. "Keyboard Report: MIDI Data Processing Software & Hardware." *Keyboard* 12 (Apr. 1986): 120–23, 136.

1720. ———. "Keyboard Report: MIDI Merge Devices." *Keyboard* 12 (May 1986): 118, 144.

1721. Goldstein, D. "Roland Mother Keyboard MIDI System." *Electronics & Music Maker* 4 (Oct. 1984): 40–42.
E&EA 88 (1985): 8636.

1722. Grant, J., and S. Parr. "Spectrum MIDI." *Electronics & Music Maker* 4 (July 1984): 30–36.
E&EA 87 (1984): 55093.

1723. Greenwald, Ted. "Keyboard Report: Master Tracks for Apple II from Passport." *Keyboard* 12 (May 1986): 112–17.

1724. ———. "Keyboard Report: Nady Wireless Link MIDI Transmitter." *Keyboard* 12 (Apr. 1986): 115, 136.

1725. ———. "Keyboard Report: Sight & Sound, MIDI Ensemble Software." *Keyboard* 12 (Feb. 1986): 128–35.

1726. ———. "MIDI Sequencer Software: Ten Leading Programmers Tell Why Computer Magic Won't Solve All Your Musical Problems (Yet)." *Keyboard* 12 (May 1986): 34–45.

1727. Joe, Radcliffe. "Roland Bows Interface System: First of Its Kind for Music Industry, Firm Claims." *Billboard* 95 (Feb. 19, 1983): 45.

1728. Leonard, Steve. "Computers for Keyboardists: Getting MIDI Bytes Out of Your Computer." *Keyboard* 12 (Apr. 1986): 104–05.

1729. ———. "Computers for Keyboardists: What Do You Say to a Naked Interface Card?" *Keyboard* 12 (May 1986): 98.

1730. Loy, D. Gareth. "Musicians Make a Standard: The MIDI Phenomenon." *Computer Music Journal* 9,4 (Winter 1985): 8–26.

1731. "The Melody Makers." *Home Computer Advanced Course* no. 25 (May 1984): 481–83.
E&EA 87 (1984): 55104.

1732. Meyer, Chris. "Computer Control Using MIDI: A Few Suggestions." In *Synthesizers and Computers*. Milwaukee, Wis.: H. Leonard Pub. Corp., 1985: 100–101.

1733. "MIDI 1.0 Specification." In *Synthesizers and Computers*. Milwaukee, Wis.: H. Leonard Pub. Corp., 1985: 114–26.

1734. *MIDI, Musical Instrument Digital Interface Specification 1.0.* Sun Valley, Calif.: IMA, International MIDI Association, 1983. 14 p.

1735. Milano, Dominic. "Keyboard Report: MIDI Switchers by Cooper, Kamlet & Zaphod." *Keyboard* 12 (Feb. 1986): 120–21.

1736. ———. "Keyboard Report: Texture MIDI Sequencer Software." *Keyboard* 11 (July 1985): 90–94.

1737. ———. "Mind over MIDI: Mixing & Merging, Local On/Off & Compatability." *Keyboard* 11 (Oct. 1985): 101.

1738. ———. "Mind over MIDI: Note Numbers, Delay & Apple IIc Interfaces." *Keyboard* 11 (Nov. 1985): 87.

1739. ———. "Mind over MIDI: Spec Addendum, Software Channelizing & DX7 ROM Updates." *Keyboard* 11 (Aug. 1985): 68.

1740. ———. "Mind over MIDI: Switching Nightmares & a Rundown of MIDI Modes." *Keyboard* 11 (July 1985): 76.

1741. ———. "Mind over MIDI: Tuning into Channels & Chaining." *Keyboard* 11 (Sept. 1985): 75.

1742. ———. "Turmoil in MIDI-Land: The Fast-Growing Synthesizer Industry Struggles to Implement a Standard Digital Interface." *Keyboard* 10 (June 1984): 42–63, 106.
Reprinted in *Synthesizers and Computers*. Milwaukee, Wis.: H. Leonard Pub. Corp., 1985: 81–99.

1743. Moog, Robert A. "M.I.D.I. (Musical Instrument Digital Interface): What It Is, What It Means to You." *Keyboard* 9 (July 1983): 19–25.
Reprinted as: "MIDI (Musical Instrument Digital Interface): What It Is, What It Does." In *Synthesizers and Computers*. Milwaukee, Wis.: H. Leonard Pub. Corp., 1985: 73–80.

1744. ———. "Using MIDI with Position-Sensing Musical Control Devices." Paper presented at the 1984 International Computer Music Conference, Oct. 19–23, Paris, France.

1745. *MUSE, MIDI Users Sequencer/Editor Owner's Guide*. Los Angeles: Roland Corp., 1985. 103 p. (Roland Music Software Series)

1746. Pearce, S. "Sound: Musical Connections." *Commodore Computing International* 3 (Oct. 1984): 15–19.
C&CA 20 (1985): 24153.

1747. Prusinkiewicz, Przemyslaw. "Graphics Interfaces for MIDI-Equipped Synthesizers." In *Proceedings of the International Computer Music Conference, 1985*, ed. Barry Truax. San Francisco, Calif.: Computer Music Association, 1985: 319–24.

1748. Queen, G. "Elka Project Series X30." *Electronics & Music Maker* 4 (Jan. 1985): 22.

1749. Robinson, K. "Roland MPU401 MIDI Processing Unit and MRC Real-Time Recorder Program." *Electronics & Music Maker* 4 (Sept. 1984): 32.
C&CA 20 (1985): 4078. *E&EA* 88 (1985): 3779.

1750. "Sounds in Sequence." *Home Computer Advanced Course* 27 (1984): 534–36.
E&EA 87 (1984): 61138.

1751. Tobenfeld, Emile. "A General-Purpose Sequencer for MIDI Synthesizers." *Computer Music Journal* 8,4 (Winter 1984): 43–44. *C&CA* 20 (1985): 31000. *E&EA* 88 (1985): 37375.

1752. Waisvisz, Michel. "The Hands, A Set of Remote MIDI-Controllers." In *Proceedings of the International Computer Music Conference, 1985,* ed. Barry Truax. San Francisco, Calif.: Computer Music Association, 1985: 313–18.

1753. White, P. "Yamaha D1500, MIDI Digital Delay." *Electronics & Music Maker* 4 (Nov. 1984): 32. *E&EA* 88 (1985): 26144.

1754. ———. "Zypher Electronics Digi-Atom 4800 Analogue-to-MIDI Converter." *Electronics & Music Maker* 4 (Sept. 1984): 22. *C&CA* 20 (1985): 4076. *E&EA* 88 (1985): 3776.

1755. Wilson-Smith, M. "Synthetic Fibre." *Home Computer Advanced Course* 29 (1984): 561–63. *E&EA* 87 (1984): 61140.

MUSIC INDUSTRY

1756. "Bar Coding Favored by 83% of Members Surveyed by NARM." *Variety* 298 (Apr. 2, 1980): 75.

1757. Beckmen, Tom. "Technology's Role in Market Expansion: Harnessing Computers to Interest a Larger Population Segment in Music Making." *Music Trades* 130 (Dec. 1982): 61–62.

1758. "Bilingual Canadian Disk Catalog, a Videotex System, Unveiled at Midem in CIRPA-ADISQ Show." *Variety* 305 (Jan. 27 1982): 73, 80.

1759. "*Billboard* Launching BIN, Radio Playlist Service." *Billboard* 93 (Apr. 18, 1981): 3, 31.

1760. Blaine, David B. "Commentary: Going 'On-line' to Oblivion." *Billboard* 93 (Nov. 21, 1981): 16.

1761. Burlingame, M. "Concert Production's New Ally: A Computer Learns the Score." *Symphony Magazine* 34,1 (1983): 11–13.

1762. "CAM Computer Given Complete Musical Access." *Variety* 294 (Apr. 18, 1979): 99.

1763. "Canadian Computer Disk Catalog Given a New Synthesized Voice." *Variety* 309 (Jan. 26, 1983): 67, 70.

1764. "CAPAC's New Computer System: The Univac 90/30, How it Works." *The Canadian Composer* 124 (Oct. 1977): 16–17, 42–43.
Also in French.

1765. "The Computer is Launched." *Performing Right* 45 (Oct. 1966): 10–11.

1766. "Computer Progress Report." *Performing Right* 43 (Oct. 1965): 12; 44 (Apr. 1966): 27.

1767. Costlow, T. "Curing the Music Business Blues." *Interface Age* 4 (Mar. 1979): 50–53.
C&IS 23 (1979): 222392C.

1768. David, Hal. "ASCAP Plans Predicated on Technological Change." *Variety* 301 (Jan. 14, 1981): 273, 276.

1769. Diamond, Israel. "Data Processing: The Music Scene." *Billboard* 82 (Jan. 17, 1970): M5-M6.

1770. "Electronics in the Service of Music." *Performing Right* 42 (May 1965): 8–9.

1771. "Electronische Datenverarbeiter für die Musikindustrie." *Instrumentenbau-Zeitschrift* 27 (1973): 708–11.

1772. Farrell, David. "National Catalog Due to Compile, Computerize." *Billboard* 93 (Sept. 5, 1981): 59.

1773. "From Box Office to BOCS Office." *Symphony Magazine* 32 (Dec. 1981): 49–50.

1774. Hall, Claude. "Canadians to Computer Programming." *Billboard* 87 (Oct. 25, 1975): 1.

1775. ———. "Computer Targets Market." *Billboard* 89 (Sept. 17, 1977): 22.

1776. Harrison, Mike. "The Electronic Magazine is Here." *Billboard* 93 (Apr. 25, 1981): 29.

1777. "Increasing Home Computer Use Seen Spurring Legit B.O. Sales." *Variety* 307 (June 23, 1982): 83, 90.

1778. Leise, Fred, and William K. Holstein. "The Computer: A New Member for Your Symphony Planning Committee?" *Symphony News* 29 (Feb. 1978): 9–11.

1779. Lichtman, Irv. "PolyGram Develops Royalty, Copyright Computer System." *Billboard* 92 (May 31, 1980): 12.

1780. Mandel, Howard. "Never Fear the Computer Here." *Billboard* 93 (Aug. 29, 1981): 27, 48.

1781. McCullaugh, Jim. "1st Computer in U.S. Studio." *Billboard* 89 (June 11, 1977): 5, 45.

1782. Meyer, Frank. "ABC Computers Make Decisions, But People Still Input Music Info." *Variety* 288 (Sept. 14, 1977): 93, 96.

1783. ———. "Clive Davis Raps Computerized Bigness for Taking 'Art' Out of Biz." *Variety* 290 (Mar. 22, 1978): 109, 111.

1784. Moberg, Dick. "Music Medium of the Future." *Interface Age* 4 (Mar. 1979): 54–55.
      C&CA 14 (1979): 34797. *C&IS* 23 (1979): 221796C.

1785. "Modern Equipment, Methods are Useless Without Accuracy on the Part of Music Creators." *The Music Scene* 288 (Mar.-Apr. 1976): 2.

1786. Morner, C.-G. Stellan. *Samarbetet mellan FOA index och Sveriges Radios Musikavdelning.* [The Collaboration Between FOA Index and the Music Department of the Swedish Broadcasting Corporation] Stockholm: Forsvarets Forskningsanstalt, 1973. (FOA P Rapport C 8348-M6)
      In Swedish.
      RILM 74 4.

1787. "New Computer System Aids BMI in Tracking Biz Around the World." *Variety* 290 (Feb. 19, 1978): 68.

1788. Nusser, Dick. "CBS Unveils New Discomputer—Ultimate Disk Cutter." *Billboard* 89 (Nov. 5, 1977): 87.

1789. Olmsted, B. "Computerization: Another Side to Orchestra Programming." *Symphony Magazine* 34,1 (1983): 31–33.

1790. Penchansky, Alan. "Jukebox Makers Take to Electronic Microprocessors." *Billboard* 90 (Nov. 25, 1978): 3, 98.

1791. Porter, Martin, and Cristina D'Angeles. "IBM PC Rocks and Rolls." *PC Magazine* 3 (Jan. 1984): 252–58.

1792. Price, Joe X. "Wonder Purchases British Vocoder Speech 'Machine'." *Billboard* 89 (Mar. 19, 1977): 43.

1793. Reed, John A. "A Study of the Use of System Simulation for Symphony Orchestra Trend Analysis and Forecasting." Ed.D. diss., University of Kansas, 1980. 110 p.
C&IS 26 (1981): 265457C. *DA* 41:1880A.

1794. "San Antonio Symph Tuning up Public's Musical Tastes with Computer Test." *Variety* 240 (Nov. 3, 1965): 49.

1795. Schultz, Brad. "On-line System Tracks Music Use for Royalties." *Computerworld* 12 (Mar. 6, 1978): 12.
C&IS 18 (1978): 195368C.

1796. Shore, Michael, and Larry McClain. "Computers Rock the Music Business." *Popular Computing* 2 (June 1983): 96–102.
C&CA 18 (1983): 28825.

1797. Sippel, John. "Computer Technology Grows, Publishers Hear." *Billboard* 91 (Oct. 20, 1979): 35.

1798. "TCG Surveys Computerization in Performing Arts Organizations." *Symphony News* 30 (Dec. 1979): 7.

1799. Terry, Kenneth. "Labels Look at Potential Savings of Internal Use of Bar Coding; CBS Records Leads the Pack." *Variety* 313 (Nov. 23, 1983): 107, 110.

1800. "Ticketron Increases Range of Services as Technology Booms." *Variety* 310 (Apr. 6, 1983): 75.

1801. *Videotex, a Thousand and One Applications. Videotex in General.* Ottawa, Ont.: Dept. of External Affairs, 1983. 53 p.
ERIC: ED 255 204.

1802. Winn, Merle. "Computerized Bank Envisioned for Orchestras." *Symphony News* 28 (Dec. 1977): 25.

MUSIC PRINTING AND TRANSCRIPTION

1803. Andronico, Alfio, and Alberto Ciampa. "On Automatic Pattern Recognition and Acquisition of Printed Music." In *Proceedings of the Venice 1982 International Computer Music Conference,* comp. Thom Blum and John Strawn. San Francisco, Calif.: Computer Music Association, 1985: 245-78.

1804. Aperghis-Tramoni, Christian. "Coding and Drawing Musical Scores." In *Proceedings of the 1978 International Computer Music Conference,* comp. Curtis Roads. Evanston, Ill.: Northwestern University Press, 1979: 619-36.

1805. Askenfelt, Anders. "Automatic Notation of Played Music." *Speech Transmission Laboratory Quarterly Progress and Status Report* 1 (1976): 1-11.
RILM 76 1597.

1806. ———. "Automatic Notation of Played Music: The VISA Project." *Fontes Artis Musicae* 26 (1979): 109-20.
RILM 79 4061.

1807. Bauer-Mengelberg, Stefan. "Impromptu Remarks on New Methods of Music Printing." *Proceedings of the American Society of University Composers* 1 (1968): 23-26.

1808. BeaDaniel, Matt. "Automated Transcription of Music." B.S. thesis, Massachusetts Institute of Technology, Dept. of Electrical Engineering and Computer Science, 1983. 19 p.

1809. "Beim Musikverlag kommen Druckfertige Partituren an." *Musik International-Instrumentenbau Zeitschrift* 34 (Aug. 1980): 573-74.

1810. Bendix, Peter. "Music Transcriber." *Kilobaud Microcomputing* no. 12 (Dec. 1980): 43-63.
C&CA 16 (1981): 15685.

1811. Bengtsson, Ingmar; Alf Gabrielsson; and Barbro Gabrielsson. "RHYTHMSYVARD—a Computer Program for Analysis of Rhythmic Performance." *Svensk tidskrift för musikforskning* 60 (1978): 15-24.
RILM 78 1757.

1812.   ———; Per-Arne Tove; and Stig-Magnus Thorsen. "Sound Analysis and Rhythm Research Ideas at the Institute of Musicology in Uppsala." In *Studia Instrumentorum Musicae Popularis II. Bericht über die 3. Internationale Arbeitstagung der Study Group on Folk Musical Instruments des International Folk Music Council in Stockholm 1969,* ed. Erich Stockmann. Stockholm: Musikhistorska museet, 1972: 53–76. *RILM* 73 1382.

1813.   Böker-Heil, Norbert. "Plotting Conventional Music Notation." *Journal of Music Theory* 16 (1972): 72–101.

1814.   ———. "Weisse Mensuralnotation als Computer-Input und -Output." *Acta Musicologica* 43 (1971): 21–33.

1815.   Brender, Maurita, and Ronald F. Brender. "Computer Transcription and Analysis of Mid-Thirteenth Century Musical Notation." *Journal of Music Theory* 11 (1967): 198–221.

1816.   Buxton, William. "Tutorial Introduction to *Scriva.*" In *Music Software User's Manual,* ed. W. Buxton. 2nd ed. Toronto: Computer Systems Research Group, University of Toronto, 1981.

1817.   ———, and Kenneth C. Smith. "The Evolution of the SSSP Score Editing Tools." Toronto: C.S.R.G., University of Toronto, 1979.

1818.   ———; Richard Sniderman; William Reeves; Sanand Patel; and Ronald Baecker. "The Evolution of the SSSP Score Editing Tools." *Computer Music Journal* 3,4 (Dec. 1979): 14–25, 60.
          Reprinted in *Foundations of Computer Music,* ed. Curtis Roads and John Strawn. Cambridge, Mass.: MIT Press, 1985: 376–402.
          C&CA 15 (1980): 22349. *C&IS* 25 (1980): 243464C.

1819.   Byrd, Donald. "Human Engineering in a Portable Music Notation System." In *Proceedings of the 1980 International Computer Music Conference,* comp. Hubert S. Howe. San Francisco, Calif.: Computer Music Association, l982: 306–23.

1820.   ———. "Music Notation by Computer." Ph. D. diss., Indiana University, 1984. 240 p.

1821.   ———. "A System for Music Printing by Computer." *Computers and the Humanities* 8 (1974): 161–72.
          CA 19 (1975): 859. *C&CA* 10 (1975): 7308. *RILM* 75 3165.

1822.   ———. "Transcription by Plotter." *Random Bits* 5 (May 1970): 1, 6–8.

1823.   "The Calcomp Plotter." *Random Bits* 4 (Dec. 1968): 2–3.

1824.   Campbell, Warren C. "Computer Analysis of Musical Performance." Ph. D. diss., University of Connecticut, 1970. 84 p.
          DA 31:6396A. *RILM* 76 1893.

1825.   Cantor, Don. "A Computer Program that Accepts Common Musical Notation." *Computers and the Humanities* 6 (1971–72): 103–09.

1826. Chafe, Chris; David A. Jaffe; Kyle Kashima; Bernard Mont-Reynard; and Julius O. Smith. "Techniques for Note Identification in Polyphonic Music." In *Proceedings of the International Computer Music Conference, 1985,* ed. Barry Truax. San Francisco, Calif.: Computer Music Association, 1985: 399–405.

1827. ———; Bernard Mont-Reynaud; and Loren Rush. "Toward an Intelligent Editor of Digital Audio: Recognition of Musical Constructs." *Computer Music Journal* 6,1 (Spring 1982): 30–41.
Review by Harry B. Lincoln in *Computing Reviews* 24 (Mar. 1983): 40,203.
C&IS 29 (1982): 82–6397C.

1828. Champernowne, D. G. "Music from EDSAC." Cambridge, England: University of Cambridge Technical Report, 1961.

1829. Chang, Jih-Jie, and Max V. Mathews. "Program for Automatically Plotting the Scores of Computer Sound Sequences." Mimeographed. Murray Hill: Bell Telephone Laboratories, [n.d.]

1830. ———, and Max V. Mathews. "Score-Drawing Program." *Journal of the Audio Engineering Society* 15 (1967): 279–81.

1831. Charnassé, Hélène. "Automatic Transcription of German Lute Tablatures: From Abstract to Polyphonic Notation." *In Atti del Terzo Colloquio di Informatica Musicale,* ed. G. DePoli. Padua: Università di Padova, 1979: 65–77.

1832. ———. "A French Experience in the Field of Music Information: The ERATTO System." Paper presented at the Symposium on Computer Studies in Music, 6–9 July 1979, Nottingham University, U.K.

1833. ———. "Les instruments a cordes pincées (luth, vihuela, cistre, guitare) et la transcription automatique des tablatures." *University of Ottawa Quarterly* 51 (1981): 281–95.

1834. ———. "La transcription automatique des tablatures de luth allemandes: recherche de l'algorithme de la structure polyphonique." In *Proceedings of the Venice 1982 International Computer Music Conference,* comp. Thom Blum and John Strawn. San Francisco, Calif.: Computer Music Association, 1985: 577–87.

1835. ———. "La transcription automatique des tablatures; un aspect de la recherche méthodologique, l'identification des notes altérées." In *Informatique musicale 1977. Textes des conferences, Equipe ERATTO.* Paris: Centre de documentation sciences humaines, 1978: 83–99.
Abstracts in English, French, and German.
RILM 78 3922.

1836. ———, and Henri Ducasse. "De l'emploi de l'ordinateur pour la transcription des tablatures." *Revue de musicologie* 57 (1971): 107–33.

1837. ———, and Henri Ducasse. "Des presses de Pierre Ballard à l'ordinateur." *Revue de musicologie* 54 (1968): 233–44.

1838.   Cheek, S. C. "Common Music Notation, Computers and Graphics." *Computers & Graphics* 5, 2–4 (1980): 87–91.
C&CA 16 (1981): 9812. C&IS 26 (1981): 267408C.

1839.   Clements, Peter J. "Computers and Musical Notation." *Studies in Music* 5 (1980): 145–72.

1840.   ————. "Elaboratori e notazione musicale." [Computers and Musical Notation] In *Musica e elaboratore*. Venice: Biennale di Venezia, 1980: 153–70.

1841.   "The Coming Revolution in Music Publishing." *Selmer Bandwagon* 10 (1962): 16–19.

1842.   "Computer Scoring—A Boon for the Composer." *The Music Trades* 125 (Jan. 1977): 34.

1843.   "Computer Transcription." *Music Educators Journal* 65 (Apr. 1979): 94.

1844.   "The Computerized Musical Notation." *The Instrumentalist* 34 (Aug. 1979): 88.

1845.   Craig, John. "The Music Men and Their Incredible Printing Machine." *Creative Computing* 5 (June 1979): 48–49.
C&CA 15 (1980): 6857.

1846.   Crawford, David. "Gregory's Scribe: Interactive Graphics for Music Notation before 1600." In *Proceedings, 1981 International Computer Music Conference, November 5–8*, comp. Larry Austin and Thomas Clark. Denton, Tex.: North Texas State University, 1983: 417–421.

1847.   ————, and Jon Zeeff. "Gregory's Scribe: Inexpensive Graphics for Pre-1600 Music Notation." *Computer Music Journal* 7,1 (Spring 1983): 21–24.
C&CA 18 (1983): 32102.

1848.   Cummings, Steve. "Keyboard Report: Notation/Sequencing Software for IBM PC, Apple IIe & Macintosh Computers." *Keyboard* 11 (Aug. 1986): 82–88.

1849.   De Poli, Giovanni. *Musica, programme de codage de la musique: manuel d'utilisation*. Paris: IRCAM, 1978. (Rapports IRCAM 7/78)

1850.   Debiasi, Giovanni B., and Giovanni De Poli. "MUSICA: A Language for the Transcription of Musical Texts for Computers." Paper presented at the International Conference on Computer Music, October 28–31, 1976, Massachusetts Institute of Technology.

1851.   ————, and Giovanni De Poli. "MUSICA (Musicae Usitata Scriptura Idonee Calculatoribus Aptata): A Language for the Transcription of Musical Texts for Computers." *Interface* 11 (1982): 1–27.

1852.   Ducasse, Henri. "Vers une démarche générale de transcription et d'édition par ordinateur de musique instrumentale ancienne: réalités- applications-perspectives." Thèse de 3ème cycle, Université Paris V, 1977.

1853. Eremenko, Konstantin. *O perspektivah razvitija simfoničeskogo orkestra.* [On the Prospects for Development of the Symphony Orchestra] Kiev: Muzyčna Ukraina, 1974. 270 p.
In Russian.
RILM 75 2674.

1854. Ermedahl, Gunnar. "Notskrift och inspelning som underlag för musikalisk analys." [Notation and Sound Recordings as a Basis for Musical Analysis] *Svensk tidskrift för musikforskning* 57,2 (1975): 65–66.
In Swedish.
RILM 75 2586.

1855. Fantino, Yves; Jean Marmet; and Denis Jaeger. "Un périphérique d'ordinateur à l'usage des musiciens: composants technologiques du peripheriques et programmes d'utilisation." In *Informatique musicale. Journées d'études 1973. Textes des conférences, E.R.A.T.T.O.* Paris: C.N.R.S., 1973: 204–18.
RILM 74 3844.

1856. Filip, Miroslav. "Proznámky k transkripčnému kódu." In *Lidová píseň a samočinný počítač I,* ed. Dušan Holý and Oldřich Sirovátka. Brno: Klub ūzivatelů MSP, 1972: 189–93.
In Czech; summary in English.

1857. Foster, Scott; W. Andrew Schloss; and A. Joseph Rockmore. "Toward an Intelligent Editor of Digital Audio: Signal Processing Methods." *Computer Music Journal* 6,1 (Spring 1982): 42–51.
Review by E. Gagliardo *Computing Reviews* 24 (May 1983): 40,360.
C&IS 29 (1982): 82–6396C.

1858. Frydén, Lars; Johan Sundberg; and Anders Askenfeld. "From Music Score to Sound: A Rule System for Musical Performance of Melodies." In *Proceedings of the Venice 1982 International Computer Music Conference,* comp. Thom Blum and John Strawn. San Francisco, Calif.: Computer Music Association, 1985: 426–36.

1859. Galler, Bernard A., and Martin B. Piszczalski. "Automatic Music Notation Translation from Sound via 3-Dimensional Harmonic Analysis." Ann Arbor, Mich., 1978. 17 p.

1860. Gerle, Hans. *Tabulatur auff die Laudten, Nuremberg, 1533, Transcription Automatique, par le Groupe E.R.A.T.T.O.* Fascicule I, Préludes. Fascicule II, Chansons et pièces Allemande. Paris: Société francaise de musicologie, 1975.
Review by Ian Harwood in *Lute Society Journal* 18 (1976): 66–69.

1861. Gold, M.; John P. Stautner; and Steven Haflich. "An Introduction to Scot." Cambridge, Mass.: Massachusetts Institute of Technology Experimental Music Studio, 1980.

1862. Gomberg, David A. "A Computer-Oriented System for Music Printing." D.Sc. diss., Washington University, 1975. 126 p.
DA 36:4584B.

1863.   ———. "A Computer-Oriented System for Music Printing." *Computers and the Humanities* 11 (1977): 63–80.
CA 22 (1978): 3545. C&CA 13 (1978): 29117. C&IS 19 (1978): 203624C.

1864.   Hanzelin, Fred L. "The Software for Computer-Assisted Graphical Representation of Single Instrument Melodic Lines and Harmonic Spectra Using DARMS Encoding and Acoustical Data." D.M.A. diss., University of Illinois at Urbana-Champaign, 1978.
C&IS 21 (1978): 210984C. DA 39:14A. RILM 78 1833.

1865.   Haus, Goffredo. "EMPS: A System for Graphic Transcription of Electronic Music Scores." *Computer Music Journal* 7,3 (Fall 1983): 31–36.
C&CA 19 (1984): 6765. C&IS 32 (1984): 84–2131C.

1866.   ———, and E. Rossi. "EMPS: un sistema per la trascrizione grafica di partiture elettroniche." [EMPS: A System for Graphic Transcription of Electronic Scores] *Strumenti musicali* 44/45 (1983): 77–82.

1867.   Heller, Jack J., and Warren C. Campbell. "Music Performance Analysis." *Council for Research in Music Education Bulletin* 24 (Spring 1971): 1–9.

1868.   Henke, W. L. "Two-Dimensional Notations for the Specification of Sound and Music Synthesis." Abstract in *Journal of the Acoustical Society of America* 50 (1971): 128.

1869.   Hiller, Lejaren A., and Robert A. Baker. "Automated Music Printing." *Journal of Music Theory* 9 (1965): 129–52.
Letter to the editor by Stefan Bauer-Mengelberg, vol. 9 (1965): 340–41.

1870.   Hogg, J., and Richard Sniderman. "Score Input Tools Project Report." Toronto: SSSP/CSRG, University of Toronto, 1979.

1871.   Horowitz, David. "A Model of Timing Information from Analyzed Musical Performances." Paper presented at the 1983 International Computer Music Conference, Oct. 7–10, 1983, Rochester, N.Y.

1872.   Hultberg, Warren E. "Computer-Based Processes for Tablature Transcription: Input Language Applications and Development; Analytical Aspects." In *Proceedings of the 1978 International Computer Music Conference,* comp. Curtis Roads. Evanston, Ill.: Northwestern University Press, 1979: 689–719.

1873.   Jaeger, Denis. "Entrée accelerée avec édition instantanée de partitions musicales à l'aide d'un calculateur." Rapport presenté au Séminaire de l'E.m.a.mu. le 17 Mars 1972 à la Maison des sciences de l'homme. Mars 1972. 15 p.

1874.   ———. "Un périphérique d'ordinateur à l'usage des musiciens: problèmes d'interprétation de la musique et d'édition de partitions." Thèse de 3ème cycle, Grenoble I, 1974. 158 p.
Abstract in *French in French Language Dissertations in Music.* New York: Pendragon Press, 1979.

1875.   Janssens, Hans, and Walter G. Landrieu. "Melowriter, a Digital Music Coding Machine." *Interface* 5 (1976): 225–47.
C&CA 12 (1977): 20681.

1876. Kassler, Michael. "A Critical-Edition Problem Resolved." *Musicol* 5 (1979): 155–58.
RILM 79 5599.

1877. ———. "An Essay Toward Specification of a Music-Reading Machine." Mimeographed. Princeton: Princeton University Music Dept., Nov. 1963. 30 p.
Also in *Musicology and the Computer,* ed. Barry S. Brook. New York: City University of New York Press, 1970: 151–75.

1878. ———. "A System for the Automatic Reduction of Musical Scores." Paper presented at the Seminar in Mathematical Linguistics, Harvard University, Cambridge, 1960.

1879. Knowlton, Prentiss H. "Capture and Display of Keyboard Music." *Datamation* 18 (May 1972): 56–60.
CIJE 4 (1972): EJ 061 818.

1880. ———. "Interactive Communication and Display of Keyboard Music." Ph. D. diss., University of Utah, 1971. 101 p.
DA 32:2649B.

1881. Kornfeld, William A. "Everything You Always Wanted to Know About MUZACS but Were Afraid to Grovel Through the Code to Find Out." Cambridge, Mass.: Massachusetts Institute of Technology Artifical Intelligence Laboratory, 1981.

1882. Lederer, Jeffrey H. "Music Language Graphics Editor User's Manual." Dept. of Computer Science, University of Pittsburgh, June 1976.

1883. LeLouche, Ruddy. "Un système conversationnel d'édition de musique (S.C.E.M.)." In *Informatique musicale 1977, Textes des conférences, Equipe ERATTO*. Paris: Centre de documentation sciences humaines, 1978: 101–54. Abstracts in English, French, and German.
RILM 78 3929.

1884. LePage, W. R. "APL Simulation of Musical Staff Notation." In *APL Congress 73,* ed. P. Gjerlov, H. J. Helms, and J. Nielsen. Copenhagen: North-Holland Pub. Co., 1973: 281–88.
CA 18 (1974): 1378.

1885. Lincoln, Harry B. "A Special Computer Typography for Thematic Indexing of Music." In *Informatique musicale 1977, Textes des conférences, Equipe ERATTO*. Paris: Centre de documentation sciences humaines, 1978: 27–35. Abstracts in English, French, and German.
RILM 78 2282.

1886. ———. "Toward a Computer Typography for Music Research: A Progress Report." In *Information Processing 71: Proceedings of the IFIP Congress 1971*. Amsterdam: North Holland, 1972: 1427–30.
Review by Benjamin Suchoff in *Computing Reviews* 14 (1973): 224–25.

1887. Lindgren, Richard K. "Chord: A Program for Computer-Aided Music Transcription." *Creative Computing* 6 (July 1980): 138–39.
C&CA 16 (1981): 9813.

1888. Longuet-Higgins, H. Christophe, and Mark J. Steedman. "On Interpreting Bach." In *Machine Intelligence 6,* ed. Bernard Meltzer and Donald Mitchie. New York: American Elsevier, 1971: 221–42.

1889. "The Magic Music Box." *The Music Trades* 127 (June 1979): 42–48.

1890. Mars, P., and J. M. Cattanach. "Automatic Transcription of Keyboard Music." *Proceedings of the Institute of Electrical Engineering* 124 (May 1977): 436–40.
C&CA 12 (1977): 16797. *C&IS* 17: 175203C.

1891. ———, and J. A. Cattanach. "Keyboard Music Transcription by Computer." *Electronics and Power* 23 (1977): 651–53.

1892. Mathews, Max V., and Lawrence Rosler. "Graphical Language for the Scores of Computer Generated Sounds." *Perspectives of New Music* 6 (Spring-Summer 1968): 92–118.
Reprinted in *Music by Computers,* ed. Heinz von Foerster and James W. Beauchamp. New York: J. Wiley, 1969: 84–114.
Reprinted in *Perspectives on Notation and Performance,* ed. Benjamin Boretz and Edward T. Cone. New York: Norton, 1976: 153–79.
Abstract in *Journal of the Acoustical Society of America* 40 (1966): 1252.

1893. Maxwell, John Turner. "Mockingbird: An Interactive Composer's Aid." M.S. thesis, Massachusetts Institute of Technology, Dept. of Electrical Engineering and Computer Science, 1981. 122 p.

1894. ———, and Severo M. Ornstein. *Mockingbird: A Composer's Amanuensis.* Palo Alto, Calif.: Xerox Corp., 1983. 20 p. (CSL-83-2)

1895. ———, and Severo M. Ornstein. "Mockingbird: A Composer's Amanuensis." *BYTE* 9 (Jan. 1984): 384–401.
C&CA 19 (1984): 23712. *C&IS* 32 (1984): 84–5281C.

1896. ———, and Severo M. Ornstein. "Mockingbird: A Composer's Amanuensis." Abstract in *Proceedings, 1981 International Computer Music Conference, November 5–8,* comp. Larry Austin and Thomas Clark. Denton, Tex.: North Texas State University, 1983: 422.
Abstract also in *Digest of Papers, Spring COMPCON 83: Intellectual Leverage for the Information Society, San Francisco, CA, 28 Feb-3 March 1983.* New York: IEEE, 1983: 114.

1897. Melanson, Jim. "Computers Vital Link to Publishing Future." *Billboard* 87 (Mar. 29, 1975): 6.

1898. Mercuri, Rebecca T. "MANUSCRIPT: Music Notation for the Apple II." In *Proceedings, Symposium on Small Computers in the Arts, November 20–22, 1981, Philadelphia, Pennsylvania.* New York, N.Y.: IEEE, 1981: 8–10.
C&CA 17 (1982): 19782.

1899. Miller, Fred. "The McLeyvier Speaks English, Writes Music, Remembers Everything." *High Fidelity/Musical America* 32 (Feb. 1982): 74, 82.

1900. Minciacchi, Marco, and Diego Minciacchi. "Music Editing and Graphics (MEG 1.00): A Personal Computer Based Operative System for Editing and Printing Musical Scores." In *Proceedings of the International Computer Music Conference, 1984,* ed. William Buxton. San Francisco, Calif.: Computer Music Association, 1985: 257-72.

1901. Molin, Armando Dal. "Second Generation Music Input Terminals: The PCS-300 Music CRT." Paper presented at the International Conference on Computer Music, October 28-31, 1976, Massachusetts Institute of Technology.

1902. ———. "A Terminal for Music Manuscript Input." *Computers and the Humanities* 12 (1978): 287-89.
C&CA 14 (1979): 22208. C&IS 23 (1979): 226105C.

1903. ———. "The X-Y Typewriters and Their Application as Music Input Terminals for the Computer." In *Proceedings of the Second Annual Music Computation Conference, November 7-9, 1975 at the University of Illinois at Urbana-Champaign. Part 4, Information Processing Systems,* comp. James Beauchamp and John Melby. Urbana, Ill.: University of Illinois: 28-53.

1904. Monfils, Michel. "L'analyse et la transcription des tablatures: vers une nouvelle orientation des travaux." In *Informatique et musique, Second Symposium International,* ed. Hélène Charnassé. Ivry: ELMERATTO, CNRS, 1983: 207-25.

1905. ———. "Trascrizione mediante elaboratore di intavolature per liuto: programmazione delle regole interpretative in relazione al contesto." [Computer Transcription of Lute Tablatures: Programming the Interpretation Rules Related to the Context] Paper presented at the 1982 International Computer Music Conference, Sept. 27-Oct. 1, Venice.

1906. Mont-Reynaud, Bernard, and Mark Goldstein. "On Finding Rhythmic Patterns in Musical Lines." In *Proceedings of the International Computer Music Conference, 1985,* ed. Barry Truax. San Francisco, Calif.: Computer Music Association, 1985: 391-97.

1907. Moorer, James A. "On the Segmentation and Analysis of Continuous Musical Sound by Digital Computer." Ph. D. diss., Stanford University, 1975. 226 p. Reprinted: Stanford, Calif.: Center for Computer Research in Music and Acoustics, Dept. of Music, Stanford University, 1975. (Report no. STAN-M-3)
DA 36:4585B.

1908. ———. "On the Transcription of Musical Sound by Computer." *Computer Music Journal* 1,4 (Nov. 1977): 32–38.
Also in *Proceedings of the Second USA-Japan Computer Conference, Tokyo, Japan, 26–28 August 1975.* Montvale, N.J.: American Federation of Information Processing Societies, 1975: 312–17.
C&CA 11 (1976): 14780. *C&IS* 18 (1978): 197091C; and 20 (1978); 207140C.
RILM 77 5651.

1909. "Music Automatically Transcribed into Manuscript." *Instrumentenbau Musik International* 30 (1976): 738.

1910. *Music Printing Option for the Synclavier.* White River Junction, Vt.: New England Digital Corp., 1984. 119 p.

1911. "Music Transposition by Computer." *Computing News* 5 (Sept. 1, 1957): 108/3–108/7.

1912. "Musical Notation by Electronic Data Processing." *Instrumentenbau Musik International* 32 (1978): 443.

1913. "Musical Plotter Knows the Score at University of Toronto." *Calcomp Newsletter* (May/June 1967)

1914. "Musiknotendruck der Computer." *Musica* 25 (1971): 54.

1915. Nelson, Gary. "Computerized Music Printing." West Lafayette, Ind.: Dept. of Creative Arts, Purdue University, n.d.
C&IS 13: 107885C.

1916. Nelson, Randolph. "A Graphics Text Editor for Music. Part 1, Structure of the Editor." *BYTE* 5 (Apr. 1980): 124–38.
C&CA 15 (1980): 25183. *C&IS* 25 (1980): 247254C.

1917. Niihara, T.; M. Imai; and S. Inokuchi. "Transcription of Sung Song." *Transactions of the Society of Instrument and Control Engineers* 20 (Oct. 1984): 940–45.
In Japanese.
C&CA 20 (1985): 17948.

1918. "Notenschrift aus dem elektronischen Datenverarbeiter." *Instrumentenbau Musik International* 31 (1977): 514.

1919. Orodenken, Maurie. "Computer Used in Doctoring Sheet Music: Charge." *Billboard* 89 (June 25, 1977): 5.

1920. Orsted, Knuo. "New Danish Computer Prints Music Scores." *Billboard* 88 (Mar. 20, 1976): 3.

1921. Patel, Sanand. "Score Editor Design: The Foundations of Scriva." Toronto: SSSP/CSRG, University of Toronto, 1979.

1922. Piszczalski, Martin B., and Bernard A. Galler. "The Analysis and Transcription of Musical Sound." In *Proceedings of the 1978 International Computer Music Conference,* comp. Curtis Roads. Evanston, Ill.: Northwestern University Press, 1979: 585–618.

1923. ———, and Bernard A. Galler. "Automatic Music Transcription." *Computer Music Journal* 1,4 (Nov. 1977): 24–31.
C&IS 18 (1978): 197090C; and 20 (1978): 207139C. *RILM* 77 5686.

1924. ———, and Bernard A. Galler. "Computer Analysis and Transcription of Musical Sound." In *Proceedings of the Research Symposium on the Psychology and Acoustics of Music,* ed. Edward P. Asmus, Jr. Lawrence, Kan.: University of Kansas, 1978.

1925. ———, and Bernard A. Galler. "Computer Analysis and Transcription of Performed Music: A Project Report." *Computers and the Humanities* 13 (1979): 195–206.
C&CA 15 (1980): 14082.

1926. ———; Bernard A. Galler; Robert W. Bossemeyer; Mehdi Hatamian; and Fred J. Looft. "Performed Music: Analysis, Synthesis, and Display by Computer." *Journal of the Audio Engineering Society* 29 (1981): 38–46.
C&CA 16 (1981): 15682.

1927. Prerau, David S. "Computer Pattern Recognition of Printed Music." *AFIPS Conference Proceedings* 39 (1971): 153–62.

1928. ———. "Computer Pattern Recognition of Standard Engraved Music Notation." Ph. D. diss., Massachusetts Institute of Technology, 1970.
Review by Michael Kassler in *Perspectives of New Music* 11 (Fall-Winter 1972): 250–54.

1929. ———. "DO-RE-MI: A Program that Recognizes Music Notation." *Computers and the Humanities* 9 (1975): 25–29.
CA 20 (1976): 57. C&CA 10 (1975): 25615. C&IS 14: 133226C. *RILM* 76 1605.

1930. Price, Joe X. "$18,000 Musecom II: A Magical Computer Aids Music Publishing." *Billboard* 89 (Mar. 26, 1977): 6.
Reprinted in *Educator* 9,4 (1977): 32–33.

1931. Prusinkiewicz, Przemyslaw. "INTERSCORE, An Interactive Score Editor for Microcomputers." In *Proceedings, 4th Symposium on Small Computers in the Arts, October 25–28, 1984, Philadelphia, Pennsylvania.* Silver Spring, Md.: IEEE Computer Society Press, 1984: 58–64.
C&CA 20 (1985): 17285.

1932. Pruslin, Dennis H. "Automatic Recognition of Sheet Music." Sc. D. diss., Massachusetts Institute of Technology, 1966. 94 p.
Review by Michael Kassler in *Perspectives of New Music* 11 (Fall-Winter 1972): 250–54.

1933. Raskin, Jef. "Using the Computer as a Musician's Amanuensis. Part 1, Fundamental Problems." *BYTE* 5 (Apr. 1980): 18–28.
C&CA 15 (1980): 25181.

1934. ———. "Using the Computer as a Musician's Amanuensis. Part 2, Going from Keyboard to Printed Score." *BYTE* 5 (May 1980): 120–28.

1935.   Reeves, William; William Buxton; Robert Pike; and Ronald Baecker. "Ludwig: An Example of Interactive Computer Graphics in a Score Editor." In *Proceedings of the 1978 International Computer Music Conference,* comp. Curtis Roads. Evanston, Ill.: Northwestern University Press, 1979: 392–409.

1936.   Regener, Eric. "A Linear Music Transcription for Computer Input." Mimeographed. Princeton: Princeton University Music Dept., 23 Mar. 1964. 100 p.

1937.   Render, Charles R. "Development of a Computer Program to Arrange and Print Traditional Music Notation." Ed. D. diss., University of Illinois, 1981. 181 p.
C&IS 31 (1983): 83–4373C. *DA* 42:3752B

1938.   Reynolds, Kentyn. "Scoring Music Directly from Keyboard Playing." In *The Best of the Computer Faires: Conference Proceedings of the 8th West Coast Computer Faire,* ed. Jim C. Warren, Jr. Woodside, Ca.: Computer Faire, 1983: 57–64.

1939.   Risset, Jean-Claude. "Ordinateurs et graphisme musical." *Musique en jeu* 13 (Nov. 1973): 87–93.

1940.   Roads, Curtis. "A Note on Music Printing by Computer." *Computer Music Journal* 5,3 (Fall 1981): 57–59.
C&CA 17 (1982): 24520.

1941.   Rowe, Neil. "Machine Perception of Musical Rhythms." B.S. thesis, Massachusetts Institute of Technology, 1975. 48 p.

1942.   Rumery, Leonard R. "NEWNOTE: Printing Choral Music by Computer." *Journal of Computer-Based Instruction* 7 (Feb. 1981): 58–62.
C&CA 16 (1981): 27624.

1943.   Rush, Loren; Chris Chafe; Bernard Mont-Reynaud; and W. Andrew Schloss. "An Intelligent System for the Knowledge-Driven Analysis of Performed Music." Paper presented at the 1982 International Computer Music Conference, Sept. 27-Oct. 1, Venice.

1944.   Sapir, Sylviane. "Libreria GRAFIZ per la stampa di grafici al terminale video." [The GRAFIX Library for Plotting on Video Terminals] *Bollettino LIMB* 4 (1984): 131.

1945.   Schloss, W. Andrew. "On the Automatic Transcription of Percussive Music: From Acoustic Signal to High-Level Analysis." Ph. D. diss., Stanford University, 1985.
Also published: Stanford, Calif.: Stanford University, Dept. of Music, 1985. (Technical Report STAN-M-27)

1946.   ———. "On the Automatic Transcription of Percussive Music: Recent Progress." Paper presented at the 1984 International Computer Music Conference, Oct. 19–23, Paris, France.

1947.   Smith, Leland. "Editing and Printing Music by Computer." *Journal of Music Theory* 17 (1973): 292–309.
RILM 74 1111.

1948. ———. "Letter to the Editor." *Journal of Music Theory* 17 (1973): 175–76.

1949. ———. "Printing Music by Computer." Film presented at the 1980 International Computer Music Conference, November 13–15, 1980, Queens College of the City University of New York.
Abstract in *Proceedings of the 1980 International Computer Music Conference,* comp. Hubert S. Howe. San Francisco, Calif.: Computer Music Association, 1982: 305.

1950. *Specimen de transcription automatique: Hans Gerle, tabulatur auff die Laudten, Nuremberg, 1533.* Prepared by Equipe ERATTO. Paris: C.N.R.S., Mars 1974. 25 p.
RILM 74 3857.
Review by Hans Radke in *Die Musikforschung* 31 (1978): 235–36.

1951. Spyridis, H.; E. Roumeliotis; and H. Papadimitraki-Chlichlia. "A Computer Approach to the Construction and Analysis of a Pitch-Curve in Music." *Acustica* 51 (1982): 180–82.
C&CA 18 (1983): 7217.

1952. "Stanford Unveils Computer Transcriber." *Keyboard* 11 (Apr. 1985): 12.

1953. Summers, I. "Computer-Assisted Music Typography." *Professional Printer* 19 (July 1974): 22.
C&CA 11 91976): 9406.

1954. Sundberg, Johan, and Per Tjernlung. "A Computer Program for the Notation of Played Music." *Speech Transmission Laboratory, Quarterly Progress and Status Report* 2–3 (1970): 46–49.

1955. "Taped Music Converted into Musical Notation." *Instrumentenbau Musik International* 32 (1978): 442.

1956. Teranishi, Toshiharu; Yasuhiko Watanabe; Yosai Araki; and Yoshio Sugimori. "A Method of Music Score Description on Computer." *Transactions of the Institute of Electronics and Communication Engineers of Japan,* Part A J67A (Oct. 1984): 990–91.
In Japanese.
C&CA 20 (1985): 17272.

1957. Tojo, Akio, and Hiroshi Aoyama. "Automatic Recognition of Music Score." In *Proceedings, 6th International Conference on Pattern Recognition,* ed. M. Lang. Los Alamitos, Calif.: Computer Society Press, 1982: 1223.
C&CA 18 (1983): 11092.

1958. "Tonbandmusik elektronisch ins Notenbild Übertragen." *Instrumentenbau-Musik International* 31 (1977): 514.

1959. "Transcribe Your Music While You Play." *The Instrumentalist* 31 (Feb. 1977): 47.

1960. "UM Computer Can Transcribe Music." *School Musician* 50 (Mar. 1979): 22–23.

1961.   Wallraff, Dean. "NEDIT—A Graphic Editor for Musical Scores." In *Proceedings of the 1978 International Computer Music Conference,* comp. Curtis Roads. Evanston, Ill.: Northwestern University Press, 1979: 410–29.

1962.   Watson, Charles R. "A Computer System for the Analysis of Music." In *Proceedings of the International Music and Technology Conference, August 24–28, 1981, University of Melbourne.* Parkville, Vic.: Computer Music Project, Dept. of Computer Science, University of Melbourne, 1981: 175–93.

1963.   Wedgewood, Mary. "Avant-Garde Music: Some Publication Problems." *Library Quarterly* 45 (Apr. 1976): 137–52.
        RILM 76 4500.

1964.   Wittlich, Gary E.; Donald Byrd; and Rosalee J. Nerheim. "A System for Interactive Encoding of Music Scores Under Computer Control." *Computers and the Humanities* 12 (1978): 309–19.
        C&CA 14 (1979): 22209. *C&IS* 23 (1979): 223894C.

1965.   "Yamaha's New Music Printing Marvel: Portable Keyboard Prints Music Instantly." *Music Trades* 130 (Aug. 1982): 54.

1966.   Yurchenkov, Vadim. "Explains A-R Computer Printing." *Billboard* 93 (Sept. 12, 1981): 48.

BRAILLE PRINTING

1967.   Bauge, Micheline. "Transcription par micro-ordinateur des partitions musicales en braille." In *Informatique et musique, Second Symposium International,* ed. Hélène Charnassé. Ivry: ELMERATTO, CNRS, 1983: 199–205.

1968.   "Computer Will Be Used to Translate Music Braille." *School Musician* 48 (Nov. 1976): 58.

1969.   "First Year's Work on Computer-Assisted Braille Music Ended." *Library of Congress Information Bulletin* 31 (1972): 406.
        RILM 73 2809.

1970.   Geant, Micheline, and Christophe Meneau. "Des partitions musicales au langage braille: reproduction automatique par ordinateur." In *Informatique musicale 1977. Textes des conférences. Equipe ERATTO.* Paris: Centre de documentation sciences humaines, 1978: 155–90.
        Abstracts in English, French, and German.

1971.   Humphreys, John. "A Computer-based System for Production of Braille Music." Ph. D. thesis, University of Warwick, 1979.
        C&CA 16 (1981): 3180.

1972.   ———. "A Computer-based System for the Production of Braille Music." In *Computerized Braille Production, Today and Tomorrow,* ed. D. W. Croisdale, H. Kamp, and H. Werner. Berlin: Sprinter-Verlag, 1983: 241–54.

1973. "Library of Congress Has Received a $25,000 Grand From the Kulas Foundation to Begin Work on a Set of Computer Programs Translating Music Notation into Braille." *Library of Congress Information Bulletin* 30 (1971): 22–23.
RILM 71 3384.

1974. "Library of Congress to Translate Music into Braille." *Woodwind World* 11 (Apr. 1972): 28.

1975. McLean, Bruce. "Translating DARMS into Musical Braille." *Braille Automation Newsletter* 2 (Aug. 1976): 65–67.

1976. McLuen, Roy E. "A Comprehensive Performance Project in Saxophone Literature with an Essay Consisting of a New Embossed-Dot Music Notation System for the Blind Based on Braille Principles and Computer Music Notation Systems." D.M.A. thesis, University of Iowa, 1973. 357 p.
DA 35:501A. *RILM* 74 1106.

1977. Patrick, P. Howard, and Patricia Friedman. "Computer Printing of Braille Music Using the IML-MIR System." *Computers and the Humanities* 9 (1975): 115–21.
CA 20 (1976): 2568. *C&CA* 11 (1976): 9392. *C&IS* 15: 140517. *RILM* 75 3175.

1978. ———, and Rosalind E. Patrick. "Computers and Music Braille." *Braille Automation Newsletter* 2 (Aug. 1976): 52–61.

1979. Watking, William, and John Siems. "SAMBA and RUMBA: Systems for Computer Assisted Translation of Braille Music." *Braille Automation Newsletter* 2 (Aug. 1976): 47–51.

1980. Wilkinson, Sally. "Computer-Assisted Transcription of Braille Music." *Braille Automation Newsletter* 2 (1976): 68–71.

1981. ———. "Investigation into the Feasibility of Computer-Assisted Transcription of Music into Braille Notation." M.Sc. Project Report, School of Information Sciences, The Hatfield Polytechnic, Sept. 1975.

MUSICAL
INSTRUMENTS

1982. Adrien, Jean-Marie, and Xavier Rodet. "Physical Models of Instruments: A Modular Approach, Applications to Strings." In *Proceedings of the International Computer Music Conference, 1985,* ed. Barry Truax. San Francisco, Calif.: Computer Music Association, 1985: 85–89.

1983. Angeloni, Gabrielle, and Danti Giordani. "Research on Morphological Similarities in Sound Signals Originated from Instrumental Sounds." In *Proceedings of the International Computer Music Conference, 1984,* ed. William Buxton. San Francisco, Calif.: Computer Music Association, 1985: 87–90.

1984. Beauchamp, James W. "Analysis and Synthesis of Cornet Tones Using Nonlinear Interharmonic Relationships." *Journal of the Audio Engineering Society* 23 (1975): 778–95.

1985. ———. "Brass Tone Synthesis by Spectrum Evolution Matching with Nonlinear Functions." *Computer Music Journal* 3,2 (June 1979): 35–43.
Also in *Proceedings of the 1978 International Computer Music Conference,* comp. Curtis Roads. Evanston, Ill.: Northwestern University Press, 1979: 85–107.
Reprinted in *Foundations of Computer Music,* ed. Curtis Roads and John Strawn. Cambridge, Mass.: MIT Press, 1985: 95–113.

1986. ———. "Time Variant Spectra of Violin Tones." *Journal of the Acoustical Society of America* 56 (1974): 995–1004.
C&CA 10 (1975): 7310.
Abstract in *The Engineering Index Annual* 74 (1975): 049353.

1987. Castellengo, Michèle. *Sons multiphoniques aux instruments à vent.* Paris: IRCAM, 1982. (Rapports IRCAM 34/82)

1988. Chafe, Chris. "A Comparison of Timbres Inherent in Traditional Violoncello Playing." *Catgut Acoustical Society Newsletter* 29 (1978): 19–22.

1989. Chowning, John M. "Conceptual Model for the Generation of String Tones." Paper presented at the IRCAM Symposium on Musical- and Psycho-acoustics, Paris, 1977.

1990. "Computer Makes Music of Trumpet Sounds." *Science News Letter* 88 (Dec. 11, 1965): 375.

1991. "Computer Produces Trumpet Sounds." *Journal of the Acoustical Society of America* 39 (1966): 760.

1992. Dausell, Tinne. "Samspilformen, traditionelle instrumenter/elektronisk lyd." [The Harmony, Traditional Instruments/Electronic Sound] Dissertation, University of Aarhus, 1974.
In Danish.

1993. El-Hassan Ben Mohammed, Mohammed, and Shyam L. Srivastava. "Fourier Spectra of the Notes of Oboe and Violin on Computer Controlled Spectrum Analyzer." *National Academy Science Letters* 5 (1982): 165–68.
C&CA 18 (1983): 12955.

1994. Ferretti, Ercolino. "Intensity Characteristics of a Synthesis Model for Producing Brass Sounds." Paper presented at the International Conference on Computer Music, October 28–31, 1976, Massachusetts Institute of Technology.

1995. Firth, Ian M. "The Wolf Tone in the Cello: Acoustic and Holographic Studies." *Speech Transmission Laboratory Quarterly Progress and Status Report* 4 (1974): 42–56.
RILM 76 3109.

1996. Freedman, M. David. "Analysis of Musical Instrument Tones." *Journal of the Acoustical Society of America* 41 (1967): 793–806.

1997. Gabrielsson, Alf, and E. V. Jansson. "An Analysis of Long-Time-Average-Spectra of Twenty-Two Quality-Rated Violins." *Speech Transmission Laboratory Quarterly Progress and Status Report* 2–3 (1976): 20–34.

1998. Graziani, Mauro. "Strutture armonica dei suoni della chitarra." [Harmonic Structures of Guitar Sounds] *Laboratorio musica* 26/27 (1981): 31–32.

1999. ———. "Struttura armonica dei suoni del clarinetto." [Harmonic Structures of Clarinet Sounds] *Laboratorio musica* 22 (1981): 30–32.

2000. ———. "Struttura armonica dei suoni del flauto." [Harmonic Structures of Flute Sounds] *Laboratorio musica* 24 (1981): 33–34.

2001. ———. "Struttura armonica dei suoni del pianoforte." [Harmonic Structures of Piano Sounds] *Laboratorio musica* 29/30 (1981): 32–33.

2002. Hech, T. E. "Computerized Guitar Research: A Report." *Soundboard* 5,4 (1978): 104–7.

2003. Hiller, Lejaren A. and Pierre Ruiz. "Synthesizing Musical Sounds by Solving the Wave Equation for Vibrating Objects." *Journal of the Audio Engineering Society* 19 (1971): 462–70, 542–51.
Also appears in: Robert F. Brainerd. "Two Musical Applications of Computer Programming." Buffalo: National Science Foundation Project No. GK14191, Sept. 1972: 63–71. (Technical Report no. 3)

2004.   Kurfürst, Pavel. "Hudební nastroje jako akustické zdroje a možnosti jejich třídení pomocí samočinného počítače." [Musical Instruments as Acoustical Sources and Possibilities for their Classification with the Aid of the Computer] *Opus Musicum* 8,8 (1975): 234–37.
In Slovak.

2005.   LaCornerie, Pierre, and Claude Cadoz. "An Instrument-Simulation Based System for Sound Synthesis in Real Time." Paper presented at the 1984 International Computer Music Conference, Oct. 19–23, Paris, France.

2006.   Lee, R. M. "An Investigation of Two Violins Using a Computer Graphic Display." *Acustica* 32 (Feb. 1975): 78–88.
C&CA 10 (1975): 12086. *RILM* 76 4425.

2007.   Leuenberger, Gary. "Patch of the Month: Solo Trumpet for the DX7." *Keyboard* 11 (Dec. 1985): 95.

2008.   Luce, David A. "Dynamic Spectrum Changes of Orchestral Instruments." *Journal of the Audio Engineering Society* 23 (1975): 565–68.

2009.   ———. "Physical Correlates of Nonpercussive Musical Instrument Tones." Ph. D. diss., Massachusetts Institute of Technology, 1963. 362 p.

2010.   Mathews, Max V.; Joan E. Miller; and John R. Pierce. "Computer Study of Trumpet Tones." Abstract in *Journal of the Acoustical Society of America* 38 (1965): 912–13.

2011.   Moorer, James A., and John M. Grey. "Lexicon of Analyzed Tones. Part 1, A Violin Tone." *Computer Music Journal* 1,2 (Apr. 1977): 39–45. Editorial notes by John Snell.
C&IS 18 (1978): 189694C. *RILM* 77 1959.

2012.   ———, and John M. Grey. "Lexicon of Analyzed Tones. Part 2, Clarinet and Oboe Tones." *Computer Music Journal* 1,3 (June 1977): 12–29. Editorial notes by John Strawn.
RILM 77 4034.

2013.   ———, and John M. Grey. "Lexicon of Analyzed Tones. Part 3, The Trumpet." *Computer Music Journal* 2,2 (Sept. 1978): 23–31. Editorial notes by John Strawn.
C&IS 21 (1978): 210982C.

2014.   Morgan, Christopher P. "Notes on Anatomy: The Piano's Reproductive System." *BYTE* 2 (Sept. 1977): 122–25.
Also in the author's *The BYTE Book of Computer Music*. Peterborough, N.H.: BYTE Books, 1979: 81–84.

2015.   Morrill, Dexter G. *The Dynamic Aspects of Trumpet Phrases*. Paris: IRCAM, 1981. (Rapports IRCAM 33/81)
In English and French.

2016. ———. "The Dynamic Aspects of Trumpet Phrases." Abstract in *Proceedings, 1981 International Computer Music Conference, November 5–8,* comp. Larry Austin and Thomas Clark. Denton, Tex.: North Texas State University, 1983: 315.

2017. ———. "Trumpet Algorithms for Computer Composition." *Computer Music Journal* 1,1 (Feb. 1977): 46–52.
Reprinted in *Foundations of Computer Music,* ed. Curtis Roads and John Strawn. Cambridge, Mass.: MIT Press, 1985: 30–44.
C&IS 18 (1978): 189696C. *RILM* 77 4021.

2018. Mulhern, Tom. "Guitars of Tomorrow?" *Guitar Player* 16 (Oct. 1982): 58–70, 132.

2019. Piszczalski, Martin B. "Spectral Surfaces from Performed Music. Part 1." *Computer Music Journal* 3,1 (Mar. 1979): 18–24.
Reprinted in *Feedback Papers* 19 (Feb. 1980): 18–24.
Review by M. Kassler in *Computing Reviews* 22 (1981): 37,868.
C&IS 24 (1980): 230389C. *RILM* 79 5957.

2020. ———. "Spectral Surfaces from Performed Music. Part 2." *Computer Music Journal* 3,3 (Sept. 1979): 25–27.
Reprinted in *Feedback Papers* 19 (Feb. 1980): 25–27.
C&IS 24 (1980): 238879C.

2021. Plitnik, G., and William Strong. "Digital Filter Techniques for Synthesis of Bassoon Tones." Abstract in *Journal of the Acoustical Society of America* 47 (1970): 131.

2022. Pratt, R. L.; S. J. Elliott; and J. M. Bowsher. "The Measurement of the Acoustic Impedance of Brass Instruments." *Acustica* 38 (1977): 236–46.
Summaries in English, German, and French.
RILM 77 6067.

2023. Ramasubramaniam, N., and R. B. Thosar. "Computer Simulation of Instrumental Music." New Delhi: T.I.F.R. Computer Section, 1969. (Technical Report no. 59)
Also published: *Journal of the Computer Society of India* 1 (Dec. 1970)

2024. Risset, Jean-Claude. "Analyse de sons de trompette à l'aide d'un calculateur électronique." *Comptes rendus hebdomadaires des seances de l'Academie des Sciences* t. 262, Série B (27 Juin 1966): 1650–53.

2025. ———. "Computer Study of Trumpet Tones." Murray Hill: Bell Telephone Laboratories, 1966. 40 p. (Internal Report)
Abstract in *Journal of the Acoustical Society of America* 38 (1965): 912.

2026. ———. "Synthèse de sons à l'aide de calculateurs électroniques appliquée à l'étude de sons de trompette." *Comptes rendus hebdomadaires des seances de l'Academie des sciences,* t. 263, série B (Juil. 11, 1966): 111–14.

2027. ———, and Max V. Mathews. "Analysis of Musical-Instrument Tones." *Physics Today* 22 (Feb. 1969): 23–30.

2028. Rogers, John E., and Robert Carrier. "Piano Simulations." In *Proceedings of the Venice 1982 International Computer Music Conference,* comp. Thom Blum and John Strawn. San Francisco, Calif.: Computer Music Association, 1985: 358–66.

2029. Ruiz, Pierre. "Technique for Simulating the Vibrations of Strings with a Digital Computer." M.M. thesis, University of Illinois, 1970.

2030. Silvian, L. J.; Howard Dunn; and S. D. White. "Absolute Amplitude and Spectra of Certain Musical Instruments and Orchestra." Bell Telephone System Monograph no. 3181, 1959.

2031. Smith, Julius O. "Synthesis of Bowed Strings." In *Proceedings of the Venice 1982 International Computer Music Conference,* comp. Thom Blum and John Strawn. San Francisco, Calif.: Computer Music Association, 1985: 308–40.

2032. Stewart, David N. "Innovative Programming Method for Sound Waveform Production: A Plucked String Sound." In *Proceedings, 1981 International Computer Music Conference, November 5–8,* comp. Larry Austin and Thomas Clark. Denton, Tex.: North Texas State University, 1983: 309–314.

2033. Stewart, Stephen E. "Functional Model of a Simplified Clarinet." Ph. D. diss., Brigham Young University, 1979. 51 p.
C&IS 24 (1980): 238885C. *DA* 40:2235B.

2034. Strawn, John. "Modeling Musical Transitions." Ph. D. diss., Stanford University, 1985. 243 p.
Also issued as: Report no. STAN-M-26. Stanford, Calif.: Center for Computer Research in Music and Acoustics, Dept. of Music, Stanford University, 1985.

2035. ———. "Orchestral Instruments: Analysis of Performed Transitions." In *Proceedings of the International Computer Music Conference, 1985,* ed. Barry Truax. San Francisco, Calif.: Computer Music Association, 1985: 347–53.
Also presented at the 78th Convention of the Audio Engineering Society, May 3–6, 1985, Anaheim. AES Preprint 2229.

2036. Strong, William, and Melville Clark. "Perturbations of Synthetic Orchestral Wind-Instrument Tones." *Journal of the Acoustical Society of America* 41 (1967): 39–52.

2037. ———, and Melville Clark. "Synthesis of Wind-Instrument Tones." *Journal of the Acoustical Society of America* 41 (1967): 39–52.

2038. Tjernlund, Per; Johan Sundberg; and Frans Fransson. "Grundfrequenzmessungen an Schwedischen Kernsplatfloten." In *Studia Instrumentorum Musicae Popularis II. Bericht über die 3. Internationale Arbeitstagung der Study Group on Folk Musical Instruments des International Folk Music Council in Stockholm 1969,* ed. Erich Stockmann. Stockholm: Musikhistoriska museet, 1972: 77–96. *RILM* 73 1385.

2039. Tomek-Schumann, Sabine. "Akustische Untersuchungen an Hammerflügeln." *Jahrbuch des Staatlichen Instituts für Musikforschung* 1974 (1975): 127–72.
RILM 76 195.

2040. Woodson, Craig. "The Effect of a Snare on the Tone of a Singleheaded Frame Drum, the Moroccan *Bendir*." In *Selected Reports in Ethnomusicology,* Volume II, No. 1, ed. Mantle Hood. Los Angeles: University of Calfornia, 1974: 102–17.

2041. Young, Frederick J. "Open Tones of Musical Horns." Abstract in *Journal of the Acoustical Society of America* 40 (1966): 1252.

2042. Yunik, M.; M. Borys; and G. W. Swift. "A Digital Flute." *Computer Music Journal* 9,2 (Summer 1985): 49–52.

MUSICOLOGICAL
AND ANALYTIC
APPLICATIONS

2043. Adamo, Giorgio. "Towards a Grammar of Musical Performance: A Study of a Vocal Style." In *Musical Grammars and Computer Analysis,* ed. M. Baroni and L. Callegari. Florence: L. S. Olschki, 1984: 245–54. (Quaderni della rivista Italiana di musicologia 8)

2044. Addison, Don. "Elements of Style in Performing the Chinese *P'i-p'a.*" In *Selected Reports in Ethnomusicology,* Volume II, No. 1, ed. Mantle Hood. Los Angeles: University of California, 1974: 118–39.

2045. Alphonce, Bo H. "The Invariance Matrix." Ph. D. diss., Yale University, 1974. 495 p.
DA 36:16A.

2046. ———. "Music Analysis by Computer—A Field for Theory Formation." *Computer Music Journal* 4,2 (Summer 1980): 26–35.
C&CA 16 (1981): 21869. *C&IS* 29 (1982): 82–00493C.

2047. Ambrosini, Claudio. "Cadenza estesa e coda." [The Cadenza Prolongs the Coda] *Bollettino LIMB* 2 (1982): 82–92.

2048. ———. "Formalizzazione dei processi esecutivi della musica rinascimentale veneziana." [Formalization of Performance Processes in Venetian Rennaissance Music] In *Atti del Terzo Colloquio di Informatica Musicale,* ed. G. DePoli. Padua: Università di Padova, 1979: 224–35.

2049. Aperghis-Tramoni, Christian. "Une structure d'acquisition automatique d'information musicale." In *Informatique musicale 1977. Textes des conferences. Equipe ERATTO,* ed. Henri Ducasse. Paris: Centre de documentation sciences humaines, 1978: 63–81.
Abstracts in English, French, and German.

2050. Ashley, Richard D. "KSM: An Essay in Knowledge Representation in Music." In *Proceedings of the International Computer Music Conference, 1985,* ed. Barry Truax. San Francisco, Calif.: Computer Music Association, 1985: 383–90.

2051. Ashton, Alan C., and Robert F. Bennion. "Interpretation of a Linear Music Notation for Automatic Playing and Graphing of Classical Music Scores." Film presented at the International Conference on Computer Music, October 28–31, 1976, Massachusetts Institute of Technology.

2052. Babbitt, Milton. "The Use of Computers in Musicological Research." *Perspectives of New Music* 3 (Spring-Summer 1965): 74–83.

2053. Baggi, Denis L. "Realization of the Unfigured Bass by Digital Computer." Ph. D. diss., University of California, Berkeley, 1974.
C&CA 10 (1975): 17423. *DA* 35:256B.

2054. Balaban, Mira. "Foundations for Artificial Intelligence Research of Western Tonal Music." In *Proceedings of the International Computer Music Conference, 1985,* ed. Barry Truax. San Francisco, Calif.: Computer Music Association, 1985: 375–82.

2055. ———. "Toward a Computerized Analytical Research of Tonal Music." Ph. D. diss., Rehovat, Israel, Weizmann Institute of Science, 1981. 386 p.

2056. ———. "Towards a Computer Research of Tonal Music." In *Proceedings of the Rochester 1983 International Computer Music Conference,* comp. Robert W. Gross. San Francisco, Calif.: Computer Music Association, 1984: 138–60.

2057. Bales, W. Kenton, and Joan C. Groom-Thornton. "AMUS: A Score Language for Computer-Assisted Applications in Music." In *AEDS Proceedings of the 17th Annual Convention, Detroit, Michigan, May 14–18, 1979.* Washington, D.C.: AEDS, 1979: 47–50.
C&IS 24 (1980): 230313C.

2058. Ballo, Igor. "FIS, metóda triedenia melódií z hl'adiska podobnosti." [FIS, a Method of Melody Classification Based on Aspects of Similarity] *Musicologica Slovaca* 6 (1978): 175–82.
In Slovak.
RILM 78 1773.

2059. Ballová, Lúba. "Algoritmizácia vyhodnocovania podobnosti melódií." [An Algorithmic Method for Evaluating Melodic Similarities] *Musicologica Slovaca* 6 (1978): 167–74.
In Slovak.
RILM 78 1774.

2060.   ———. "Štruktúra testovaćich súorov pre výskum podobnosti." [The Structure of Test Sets in the Investigation of Similarities] In *Lidová píseň a samočinný počítač 3. Sborník materiáluze 3. semináře o využití samočinného počítače pri studiu lidové písně* (Brno 15.-16.10.1974), ed. Dušan Holý, Karel Pala, and Miloš Štědroň. Prague: Státní pedagogické nakladatelství, 1976: 211–28.
In Slovak; summary in English.
RILM 76 1260.

2061.   ———, and Igor Ballo. "Paralely v problematike strojového spracovania lúdovej hudby a hudobnohistorických prameňov." [Parallels in the Problems of Machine Conduction of Folk Music and Musical/Historical Sources] In *Lidová píseň a samočinný počítač I,* ed. Dušan Holý and Oldřich Sirovátka. Brno: Klub uživatelů MSP, 1972: 195–202.
In Slovak; summary in English.

2062.   Balzano, Gerald J. "The Group-Theoretic Description of 12-Fold and Microtonal Pitch Systems." *Computer Music Journal* 4,4 (Winter 1980): 66–84.
C&CA 16 (1981): 36849. *C&IS* 28 (1982): 81–16041C.

2063.   Barbaud, Pierre. "Méthodes d'analyse de textes harmoniques." In *Informatique musicale. Journées d'études Oct. 1973. Textes des conférences. E.R.A.T.T.O.* Paris: C.N.R.S., 1973: 165–76.
RILM 74 3906.

2064.   ———. "Structure et simulation de l'harmonie classique et de son évolution." *Science de l'art* numéro spécial (1966).

2065.   Baron, John H. "First Report on the Use of Computer Programming to Study the Secular Solo Songs in France from 1600 to 1660." In *Bericht über den internationalen musikwissenschaftlichen Kongress, Bonn 1970,* ed. Carl Dahlhaus, Hans-Joachim Marx, Magda Marx-Weber, and Günther Massenkeil. Kassel: Bärenreiter, 1971: 333–36.
RILM 73 4269.

2066.   Baroni, Mario. "A Project of a Grammar of Melody." *In Informatique et musique, Second Symposium International,* ed. Hélène Charnassé. Ivry: ELMERATTO, CNRS, 1983: 55–69.

2067.   ———. "Studi di una grammatica musicale." [Studies on a Musical Grammar] In *Musica ed elaboratore elettronico.* Milan: FAST, 1980: 81–94.

2068.   ———. "Sulla nozione di grammatica musicale." [On the Notion of Musical Grammar] *Rivista Italiana di musicologia* 16,2 (1981): 240–79.

2069.   ———; Rossella Brunetti; Laura Callegari; and Carlo Jacoboni. "A Grammar for Melody: Relationships Between Melody and Harmony." In *Musical Grammars and Computer Analysis,* ed. M. Baroni and L. Callegari. Florence: L. S. Olschki, 1984: 201–218. (Quaderni della rivista Italiana di musicologia 8)

2070. ———, and Carlo Jacoboni. "Analogie formali in frasi diverse di una composizione monodica." [Formal Analogies in Different Phrases of a Monodic Composition] In *Atti del Terzo Colloquio di Informatica Musicale,* ed. G. DePoli. Padua: Università di Padova, 1979: 54–64.

2071. ———, and Carlo Jacoboni. "Analysis and Generation of Bach's Choral Melodies." In *Proceedings of the First International Congress of Semiotics of Music, Beograd, 17-21, October 1973.* Pesaro: Centro di Iniziativa Culturale, 1975: 125–34.

2072. ———, and Carlo Jacoboni. *Verso una grammatica della melodia.* [Toward a Grammar of Melody] Bologna: Università di Bologna, 1976. 154 p. (Antiquae Musicae Italicae Studiosi)
RILM 76 15383.
English translation: *Proposal for a Grammar of Melody: The Bach Chorales.* Montreal: University of Montreal Press, 1978. 155 p. (Semiologie et analyse musicales)
RILM 78 1804.

2073. ———, and Carlo Jacoboni. "Verso una grammatica della melodia." [Toward a Grammar of Melody] In *Aspetti teorici di Informatica Musicale.* Milan: CTU—Istituto di Cibernetica, Università di Milano, 1977: 4–8.

2074. Barth-Wehrenalp, Renate. "Studien zu Adam de la Hale." Ph. D. diss., University of Vienna, 1974. 190 p.
RILM 76 2386.

2075. Bartiminski, Jerzy. "Komputery w badaniach nad pieśnia ludowa." [Computers and Research on Folk Songs] *Literature ludowa* 19 (Jan.-Feb. 1975): 54–56.
In Polish.

2076. Bauer-Mengelberg, Stefan. "Computer-Implemented Music Analysis and the Copyright Law." *Computer and the Humanities* 14 (1980): 1–19.
C&CA 15 (1980): 30695.

2077. ———. "The Ford-Columbia Input Language." In *Musicology and the Computer,* ed. Barry S. Brook. New York: City University of New York Press, 1970: 48–52.

2078. Bazelow, Alexander R. "Integer Matrices with Fixed Row and Column Sums." In *Second International Conference on Combinatorial Mathematics.* New York: New York Academy of Science, 1979: 593–94. (Annals of the New York Academy of Sciences v. 319)

2079. Bebbington, Brian. "Folkmusic and Computers." *African Music* 4,2 (1968): 56–58.

2080. Bengtsson, Ingmar. "Numericode—a Code System for Thematic Incipits." *Svensk tidskrift för musikforskning* 49 (1967): 5–40.

2081.   ———. "On Melody Registration and 'Mona'." In *Elektronische Datenverarbeitung in der Musikwissenschaft,* ed. Harald Heckmann. Regensburg: G. Bosse, 1967: 136–74.

2082.   ———. "Studies with the Aid of Computers of 'Music as Performed'." In *Report of the Tenth Congress [of the International Musicological Society], Ljubljana, 1967,* ed. Dragotin Cvetko. Kassel: Bärenreiter, 1970: 443–44.

2083.   ———; Alf Gabrielsson; and Stig-Magnus Thorsén. "Empirisk rytm-forskning. En orientering om musikvetenskaplig bakgrund, utveckling och några aktuella projekt." [Empirical Rhythm Research: An Orientation in the Musical Background, Development, and Some Current Projects] *Svensk tidskrift för musikforskning* 51 (1969): 49–118.
          In Swedish, summary in English.

2084.   Bent, Ian, and John Morehen. "Computers in the Analysis of Music." *Proceedings of the Royal Musical Association* 104 (1977–78): 30–46.
          RILM 78 1807.

2085.   Berlind, Gary. "GRIPHOS: An Interim Report." *Current Musicology* 5 (1967): 149–52.

2086.   ———, and George W. Logemann. "TPOSE: A Program for Musical Transposition." *Institute for Computer Research in the Humanities Newsletter* (1967)

2087.   Bernard, Jean J. "Sciences exactes et musicologie." In *Informatique musicale. Journées d'études 1973. Textes des conférences. E.R.A.T.T.O.* Paris: C.N.R.S., 1973: 115–24.

2088.   Bernard, Jonathan W. "A Theory of Pitch and Register for the Music of Edgard Varèse." Ph. D. diss., Yale University, 1977. 455 p.
          DA 38:3125A-6A. *RILM* 77 1591.

2089.   Bernstein, Lawrence F. "Data Processing and the Thematic Index." *Fontes Artis Musicae* 11 (1964): 159–65.

2090.   ———. "Problems in the Stylistic Analysis of the 16th-Century Chanson." Report of the Annual Meeting of the American Musicological Society, New Orleans, Dec. 1966.

2091.   ———, and Joseph P. Olive. "Computers and the 16th-Century Chanson: A Pilot Project at the University of Chicago." *Computers and the Humanities* 3 (1968–69): 153–60.

2092.   Bernzott, Philip. "Musical Analysis with Computer: Some Programs and Descriptions." M.M. thesis, Chicago Musical College, 1968. 45 p.

2093.   Bertoni, A.; Goffredo Haus; G. Mauri; and M. Torelli. "Analysis and Compacting of Musical Texts." In *Aspetti teorici di Informatica Musicale.* Milan: CTU—Istituto di Cibernetica, Università di Milano, 1977: 9–25.
          Also in *Journal of Cybernetics* 8 (1978): 257–72.
          C&IS 23 (1979): 217668C.

2094. Binkley, Thomas E. "Electronic Processing of Musical Materials." In *Elektronische Datenverarbeitung in der Musikwissenschaft,* ed. Harald Heckmann. Regensburg: G. Bosse, 1967: 1–20.

2095. Blair, William F. "A Selection Method for Organization of Proportions and Musical Intervals for Composition and Analytic Purpose." In *Proceedings, 1981 International Computer Music Conference, November 5–8,* comp. Larry Austin and Thomas Clark. Denton, Tex.: North Texas State University, 1983: 332–47.

2096. Blombach, Ann K. "A Conceptual Framework for the Use of the Computer in Music Analysis." Ph. D. diss., Ohio State University, 1976. 347 p. *DA* 37:4682A. *C&IS* 16: 172954C.

2097. ———. "An Introductory Course in Computer-Assisted Music Analysis: The Computer and the Bach Chorales." *Journal of Computer-Based Instruction* 7 (Feb. 1981): 70–77. *C&CA* 16 (1981): 27626.

2098. Böker-Heil, Norbert. "Ein algebraisches Modell des Dur-Moll-Tonallen Systems." In *Bericht über den 1. internationalen Kongress für Musiktheorie, Stuttgart 1971,* ed. Peter Rummenholler, Friedrich Reininghaus, and Jurgen H. Traber. Stuttgart: Ichthys, 1972: 64–107. *RILM* 75 4465.

2099. ———. "Musikalische Stilanalyse und Computer. Einige Grundsätzliche Erwägungen." In *IMS Report 1972, Report of the Eleventh Congress, Copenhagen 1972,* ed. Henrik Glahn, Søren Sørensen, and Peter Ryom. Copenhagen: W. Hansen, 1974: 45–50.

2100. ———. "Pattern-Matching and Musical Similarity." Paper presented at the Symposium on Computer Studies in Music, 6–9 July 1979, Nottingham University, UK.

2101. ———. "Statistical Analysis of Music." Paper presented at the International Symposium on Computers and Musicology, Music Dept., University of Nottingham, 1979.

2102. Bolognesi, Tommaso; A. Casini; G. Castellini; Silvio Farese; and L. Lelli. "Reparto Musicologia del CNUCE-C.N.R. di Pisa—Attivitá e linee di ricerca." [The Musicology Department of CNUCE-C.N.R. (National Research Council) at Pisa—Activity and Trends] In *Musica ed elaboratore elettronico.* Milan: FAST, 1980: 7–25.

2103. Boody, Charles G., and J. Riedel. "A Computer Aided Study of Ecuadorean Urban Music." *Computers and the Humanities* 15 (Aug. 1981): 61–74. *C&CA* 17 (1982): 16860.

2104. Bowles, Edmund A. "Computers in Musicology." In *Computers for the Humanities?* New Haven: Yale University Press, 1965: 104–06.

2105. ———. "Musicke's Handmaiden: Or Technology in the Service of the Arts." In *The Computer and Music,* ed. Harry B. Lincoln. Ithaca: Cornell University Press, 1970: 3–20.

2106. ———, and Arthur Mendel. "Musicology and the Computer: Discussion." In *Musicology and the Computer,* ed. Barry S. Brook. New York: City University of New York Press, 1970: 37–45.

2107. Brantley, Daniel L. "Disputed Authorship of Musical Works: A Quantitative Approach to the Attribution of the Quartets Published as Haydn's Opus 3." Ph. D. diss., University of Iowa, 1977. 92 p. *DA* 38:1723–4A. *RILM* 77 516.

2108. Bridgman, Nanie. "Catalogue par incipit musicaux." *Informatique et sciences humaines* 19 (Dec. 1973): 33–38. *RILM* 74 1502.

2109. Brincker, Jens. "Kvantitative musikanalyse." [Quantitative Music Analysis] *Dansk musiktidsskrift* 41 (1966): 175–78. In Danish.

2110. Brinkman, Alexander R. "Another Look at the Melodic Process in Johann Sebastian Bach's 'Orgelbüchlein'." Paper presented at the Forty-fifth Annual Meeting of the American Musicological Society meeting jointly with the Society for Music Theory, November 1–4, 1979, The Biltmore, New York.

2111. ———. "A Binomial Representation of the Pitch Parameter for Computer Processing of Musical Data." Abstract in *Proceedings of the 1980 International Computer Music Conference,* comp. Hubert S. Howe. San Francisco, Calif.: Computer Music Association, 1982: 245.

2112. ———. "A Computer-Assisted Analysis of Melodic Borrowing from the Cantus Firmus in the Chorale Preludes in Bach's 'Orgelbüchlein'." In *Proceedings of the 1978 International Computer Music Conference,* comp. Curtis Roads. Evanston, Ill.: Northwestern University Press, 1979: 732–60.

2113. ———. "A Data Structure for Computer Analysis of Musical Scores." In *Proceedings of the International Computer Music Conference, 1984,* ed. William Buxton. San Francisco, Calif.: Computer Music Association, 1985: 233–42.

2114. ———. "A Design for a Single Pass Scanner for the DARMS Music Coding Language." In *Proceedings of the Rochester 1983 International Computer Music Conference,* comp. Robert W. Gross. San Francisco, Calif.: Computer Music Association, 1984: 7–30.

2115. ———. "Johann Sebastian Bach's 'Orgelbüchlein': A Computer-Assisted Analysis of the Influence of the Cantus Firmus on the Contrapuntal Voices." Ph. D. diss., University of Rochester, Eastman School of Music, 1978. 857 p. *DA* 39:1913A–4A. *C&IS* 22 (1978): 214529C. *RILM* 78 1775.

2116. ———. "The Melodic Process in Johann Sebastian Bach's 'Orgelbüchlein'." *Music Theory Spectrum* 2 (1980): 46–73.

2117.   ———. "Toward a Library of Utility Computer Programs for the Music Theorist." Rochester, N.Y., Sept. 1975. Computer printout.

2118.   Broeckx, Jan L., and Walter G. Landrieu. "Comparative Computer Study of Style, Based on Five Liedmelodies." *Interface* 1 (Apr. 1972): 29–92.

2119.   Bronson, Bertrand H. "Mechanical Help in the Study of Folk Song." *Journal of American Folklore* 62 (Apr./June 1949): 81–86.

2120.   ———. "Toward the Comparative Analysis of British-American Folk Tunes." *Journal of American Folklore* 74 (Apr./June 1959): 165–91.

2121.   Brook, Barry S., ed. *Musicology and the Computer. Musicology 1966–2000: A Practical Program. Three Symposia.* New York: City University of New York Press, 1970. 275 p.
          Review by Francois Lesure in *Revue de musicologie* 57 (1971): 239.
          Review by John E. Rothgeb in *Computers and the Humanities 6* (1971–72): 56–58.
          Review by Barry Vercoe in *Perspectives of New Music* 9/10 (Fall-Winter 1971): 323–30.
          Review in *Yearbook of the International Folk Music Council* 3 (1971): 164–65.
          Abstract in *Data Processing Digest* 19 (July 1973): 26.
          ERIC: ED 081 187.
          Contains items: 1877, 2077, 2106, 2122, 2210, 2231, 2297, 2310, 2343, 2377, 2473, 2574, 2744, 2755.

2122.   ———. "The Plaine and Easie Code." In *Musicology and the Computer,* ed. Barry S. Brook. New York: City University of New York Press, 1970: 53–56.

2123.   ———. "The Simplified 'Plaine and Easie Code System' for Notating Music: A Proposal for International Adoption." *Fontes Artis Musicae* 12 (1965): 156–60.

2124.   ———. "Style and Content Analysis in Music: The Simplified 'Plaine and Easie Code'." In *The Analysis of Communication Content,* ed. George Gerbner, et al. New York: J. Wiley, 1969: 287–96.

2125.   ———, and Murray Gould. "Notating Music with Ordinary Typewriter Characters (A Plaine and Easie Code System for Musicke)." *Fontes Artis Musicae* 11 (1964): 142–55.
          Commentaries follow the article.
          Also published (without commentaries) by Queens College of the City University of New York, 1964. 13 p.

2126.   Bryden, John R. "Chant Index—Incipit Title, Thematic, and Selected Melodic Pattern Index of the Chant in Contemporary Liturgical Books of the Roman Catholic Church." Ph. D. diss., Wayne State University, 1962.

2127.   Burkhart, Charles. "Schoenberg's *Farben:* An Analysis of Op. 16, No. 3." *Perspectives of New Music* 12 (Fall-Winter 1973/Spring-Summer 1974): 141–72.

2128.   Burns, Betty Beryl Remy. "An Electronic Data Processing System for the Organization and Documentation of the 16th-Century Motet." Ph. D. diss., University of Cincinnati, 1972. 243 p.
DA 33:3691A. RILM 73 4532.

2129.   Camilleri, L. "Aspetti di grammaticalità a musicalità nella melodia." [Aspects of Grammaticality and Musicality in Melody] In Atti del Quinto Colloquio di Informatica Musicale. Ancona: Università di Ancona, 1983: 179–85.

2130.   Castman, Bernt; L. E. Larsson; and Ingmar Bentsson. "Ett dataprogram (RHYTHMSYVARD) för bearbetning av rytmiska durationsvärden." [A Computer Program for Analysing Rhythmic Durations] Mimeographed. Uppsala: Institutionen för musikvetenskap, 1974.
In Swedish.

2131.   Caton, Margaret. "The Vocal Ornament Takīyah in Persian Music." In Selected Reports in Ethnomusicology, Volume II, No. 1, ed. Mantle Hood. Los Angeles: University of California, 1974: 42–53.

2132.   Celona, John A. "Command-String Notation—A New Music Notation System." In Proceedings of the 1978 International Computer Music Conference, comp. Curtis Roads. Evanston, Ill.: Northwestern University Press, 1979: 645–88.

2133.   Chalmers, John H. "Construction and Harmonization of Microtonal Scales in Non-12-Tone Equal Temperaments." In Proceedings of the Venice 1982 International Computer Music Conference, comp. Thom Blum and John Strawn. San Francisco, Calif.: Computer Music Association, 1985: 534–55.

2134.   ———, and Ervin M. Wilson. "Combination Product Sets and Other Harmonic and Melodic Structures." In Proceedings, 1981 International Computer Music Conference, November 5–8, comp. Larry Austin and Thomas Clark. Denton, Tex.: North Texas State University, 1973: 348–62.

2135.   Chalupka, Ľubomír, and Viera Chalupková. "Spracovanie súboru ľudových piesní na SP MSP 2A." [Processing a Series of Folk Songs by the MSP 2A Computer] Musicologica Slovaca 6 (1978): 203–8.
In Slovak.
RILM 78 1760.

2136.   Chalupková, Viera. "Tonálna analýza súboru piesní a jej vyhodnotenie." [Tonal Analysis of a Series of Songs and Its Evaluation] Musicologica Slovaca 6 (1978): 209–15.
In Slovak.
RILM 78 1780.

2137.   Charnassé, Hélène. "Informatique et musicologie en 1981—Musicology and Data Processing in 1981." In Informatique et musique, Second Symposium International, ed. Hélène Charnassé. Ivry: ELMERATTO, CNRS, 1983: 7–20.

2138.   ———. "Musicologie et informatique: les grands axes de recherche." Informatique et sciences humaines 19 (Dec. 1973): 19–31.
RILM 74 1732.

2139.   ———. "Une tentative d'introduction de l'informatique en musicologie." In *Aspects de la recherche musicologique au Centre national de la recherche scientifique.* Paris: Editions du Centre national de la recherche scientifique, 1984: 179–92.

2140.   ———. "Towards a Data Base in Musicology: The Computer Processing of the Bridgman File." In *Proceedings of the 1980 International Computer Music Conference,* comp. Hubert S. Howe. San Francisco, Calif.: Computer Music Association, 1982: 644–52.

2141.   ———. "Transcription automatique de tablatures: intérêts, limities." In *Informatique musicale. Journées d'études 1973. Textes des conférences. E.R.A.T.T.O.* Paris: C.N.R.S., 1973: 25–47.
        RILM 74 3840.

2142.   ———. "La transcription automatique des tablatures: le language d'entree." In *Proceedings of the Second Annual Music Computation Conference, November 7–9, 1975 at the University of Illinois at Urbana-Champaign. Part 4, Information Processing Systems,* comp. James Beauchamp and John Melby. Urbana, Ill.: University of Illinois: 13–27.

2143.   ———, and Henri Ducasse. "Data Processing Makes Old Instrumental Music Accessible." *CNRS Research* 3 (1976): 40–48.
        RILM 76 3988.

2144.   ———, and Henri Ducasse. "Une nouvelle application de l'informatique aux sciences humaines: la transcription de musique ancienne." *Le Courrier du CNRS* 8 (Apr. 1973): 25–29.
        RILM 74 3839.

2145.   ———, and Raymond Meylan, eds. *Ein newes sehr Künstlichs Lautenbuch, Hans Gerle, (1552), Books I, II, Preludes.* Ivry: ELMERATTO. v. 1, 63 p.; v. 2, 74 p.
        Review by Harry B. Lincoln in *Computers and the Humanities* 12 (1978): 369.

2146.   ———, and Raymond Meylan. *Tablature pour les luths, Hans Gerle, Nuremberg Formschneider, 1533; transcription automatique par le groupe ERATTO du CNRS.* Paris: Heugel, 1975. 2 v., 85 p.
        Review by Ian Harwood in *Lute Society Journal* 18 (1976): 66–69.
        Review by Harry B. Lincoln in *Computers and the Humanities* 12 (1978): 369.
        Review by Hans Radke in *Die Musikforschung* 31 (1978): 235–36.

2147.   Chmúrny, Rudolf. "DIS, metóda vyhodnocovania podobnosti melódií." [DIS, a Method for Evaluating Melodic Similarities] *Musicologica Slovaca* 6 (1978): 183–86.
        In Slovak.
        RILM 78 1776.

2148.   Cobin, Marian W. "Musicology and the Computer in New Orleans." *Computers and the Humanities* 1 (1966–67): 131–33.

2149.   Cohen, Dalia, and Ruth Katz. *The Israeli Folk Song: A Methodological Example of Computer Analysis of Monophonic Music.* Jerusalem: Magnes, 1977. 96 p. (Yuval Monograph Series 6) *RILM* 77 3206.

2150.   ———, and Ruth Katz. "Quantitative Analysis of Monophonic Music: Towards A More Precise Definition of Style." *Orbis Musicae* 2 (1973–74): 83–96.

2151.   Cohen, Norman. "Computerized Hillbilly Discography: The Gennett Project." *Western Folklore* 30 (1971): 182–93.

2152.   Collins, Walter S. "A New Tool for Musicology." *Music and Letters* 46 (1965): 122–25.

2153.   "The Computer Goes Musical at University of Texas-Austin." *The School Musician* 45 (Feb. 1974): 42.

2154.   "Computer Helps Research." *African Music* 4,1 (1966/1967): 78.

2155.   Crane, Frederick, and Judith Fiehler. "Numerical Methods of Comparing Musical Styles." In *The Computer and Music,* ed. Harry B. Lincoln. Ithaca: Cornell University Press, 1970: 209–22.

2156.   "Crescendos and Computers." *National Music Council Bulletin* 26 (Fall 1965): 35.

2157.   Csébfalvy, K., and M. Havass. "A Direct Computer Processing of Folk Tunes." *Computational Linguistics* 4 (1965): 125–29.

2158.   ———; M. Havass; P. Járdányi; and L. Vargyas. "Systematization of Tunes by Computers." *Studia Musicologica* 7 (1965): 253–57.

2159.   Curry, James L. "A Computer-Aided Analytical Study of Kyries in Selected Masses of Johannes Ockeghem." Ph. D. diss., University of Iowa, 1969. 232 p. *DA* 30:3969A.

2160.   Czekanowska-Kuklińska, Anna. "Comparative and Quantitative Methods in International Research Project on Folk Music." *Ethnologia Slavica* 8–9 (1976–77): 307–18. *RILM* 78 1125.

2161.   ———. "Polish Mathematical Methods in Classification of Slavic Folk Songs." In *Report of the Tenth Congress [of the International Musicological Society], Ljubljana 1967,* ed. Dragotin Cvetko. Kassel: Bärenreiter, 1970: 440–43 + illus.

2162.   ———. "Zastosowanie polskich metod statystycznych do klasifikacji melodii ludowych." [The Application of Polish Statistical Methods in the Classification of Folk Melodies] *Muzyka* 14,1 (1969): 3–18. In Polish.

2163. Davis, Stephen A., and Alan D. Levit. "Apparatus for Processing Music as Data." In *System Design—A Discipline in Transition*. *Digest of Papers from the 14th IEEE Computer Society International Conference, 28 February-3 March 1977, San Francisco, California*. New York: IEEE, 1977: 122-23. *C&CA* 13 (1980): 2580. *C&IS* 16: 170851C.

2164. De Berardinis, P. T. "Analisi strutturale della musica atonale (II)." [Analysis of Structures of Atonal Music. Part II] *Quaderni di Informatica Musicale* 4 (1984): 19-30.

2165. ———. "Analisi strutturale della musica atonale (III)." [Analysis of Structures of Atonal Music. Part III] *Quaderni di Informatica Musicale* 5 (1984): 31-40.

2166. ———. "Il microcomputer nell'analisi strutturale della musica atonale." [The Microcomputer in Analysing the Structure of Atonal Music] *Quaderni di Informatica Musicale* 1 (1983): 7-26.

2167. De Stefano, S.; Goffredo Haus; and A. Stigliz. "Descrizione di processi musicali per mezzo di operatori geometrici: un esempio applicativo." [Describing Musical Processes by Geometric Operators: An Application] In *Atti del Quarto Colloquio di Informatica Musicale*. Pisa: CNUCE-CNR, 1981: 37-61.

2168. Debiasi, Giovanni B. "Principio di funzionamento degli elaboratori elettronici numerici: applicazioni degli elaborati elettronici numerici in musicologia." [Operating Principles of Computers: Computer Applications in Musicology] In *Atti del Primo Seminario di studi e ricerche sul linguaggio musicale*. Venice: Instituto Musicale F. Canneti, 1977.

2169. ———, and Giovanni De Poli. "Linguaggio di trascrizione di testi musicali per elaboratori elettronici." [Transcription Languages for Works of Computer Music] In *Atti del Quarto Seminario di studi e ricerche sul linguaggio musicale*. Venice: Instituto Musicale F. Canneti, 1984: suppl. n. 1.

2170. Deliège, Célestin. "Some Unsolved Problems in Schenkerian Theory." In *Musical Grammars and Computer Analysis,* ed. M. Baroni and L. Callegari. Florence: L. S. Olschki, 1984: 71-82. (Quaderni della rivista Italiana di musicologia 8)

2171. Delli Pizzi, Fulvio. "Analisi e psicanalisi nello studio della 'poietica'?" [Analysis and Psychoanalysis of the Study of Poiesis] In *Musical Grammars and Computer Analysis,* ed. M. Baroni and L. Callegari. Florence: L. S. Olschki, 1984: 353-62. (Quaderni della rivista Italiana di musicologia 8)

2172. Detlovs, V., and Bonis Šidiškis. "Universal'nyj algoritm moduljacij." [The Universal Algorithm of Modulations] *Latvijskij matematičeskij ežegodnik* 13 (1973): 185-226. In Russian. *RILM* 76 1645.

2173.   Dillon, Martin, and Michael Hunter. "Automated Identification of Melodic Variants in Folk Music." *Computers and the Humanities* 16 (Oct. 1982): 107–17.
C&CA 18 (1983): 15279.

2174.   Donohue, Joseph. "The London Stage 1800–1900: A Data Base for a Calendar of Performances on the 19th Century London Stage." *Computers and the Humanities* 9 (1975): 179–85.
C&CA 11 (1976): 9395.

2175.   Downs, Philip G. "The Development of the Great Repertoire in the Ninteenth Century." Ph. D. diss., University of Toronto, 1964. 346 p.
DA 28:1093A.

2176.   Drummond, Philip J. "Computational Musicology and the New Quadrivium." *Musicology* 4 (1974): 45–56.

2177.   Ducasse, Henri. "Introduction." *Informatique et sciences humaines* 19 (Dec. 1973): 7–15.

2178.   ———. "Une méthode de traitement automatique de la musique ancienne." *Journal de la Societé de statistique de Paris* 3 (1974): 216–21.

2179.   ———. "Un problème de saisie de l'information: le traitement des tablatures." *Informatique musicale. Journées d'études 1973. Textes des conférences.* *E.R.A.T.T.O.* Paris: C.N.R.S., 1973: 48–65.
RILM 74 3843.

2180.   ———, and Denys Pages. "La saisie et la reproduction automatique des notations vocales des XVe et XVIe siècles, application: automatisation d'un fichier d'incipit musicaux." In *Informatique musicale 1977. Textes des conférences, Equipe ERATTO.* Paris: Centre de documentation sciences humaines, 1978: 37–62.
Abstracts in English, French, and German.
RILM 78 1757.

2181.   ———, and Denys Pages. "Un systeme de constitution et d'exploitation de donnees pour l'identification et l'analyse de textes musicaux." *Revue de musicologie* 62 (1976): 292–93.
RILM 76 2105.

2182.   Duisberg, Robert. "A Digital Representation of Musical Samples and a Calculation Thereon of Autocorrelation as a Function of Frequency and Two Musical Compositions." D.M.A. diss., University of Washington, 1980. 149 p.
C&IS 26 (1981): 265459C. *DA* 41:1826A.

2183.   Dürrenmatt, Hans-Rudolf; Murray Gould; and Jan LaRue. "Die Notierung thematischer Incipits auf 'Mark-Sense-Cards'." *Fontes Artis Musicae* 17 (1970): 15–23.

2184. Eisenstein, Judith K. "Medieval Elements in the Liturgical Music of the Jews of Southern France and Northern Spain." *Musica Judaica* 1 (1975-76): 33-53. *RILM* 75 3189.

2185. Ellis, Mark R. "Are Traditional Statistical Models Valid for Quantitative Musical Analysis?" In *Informatique et musique, Second Symposium International,* ed. Hélène Charnassé. Ivry: ELMERATTO, CNRS, 1983: 185-95.

2186. ———. "Linear Aspects of J. S. Bach's the Well-Tempered Clavier: A Quantitative Survey." Diss., University of Nottingham, 1980.

2187. Elschek, Oskár. "Hudobná notácia a samočinné počítace." [Musical Notation and Computers] In *Lidová písen a samočinný počítač I,* ed. Dušan Holý and Oldřich Sirovátka. Brno: Klub uživatelů MSP, 1972: 163-88.
Summary in English.

2188. ———, ed. *Musikklassifikation und EDV.* [Music Classification and Electronic Data Processing] Bratislava: Slovenská akadémia vied, 1976. 101 p. (Seminarium Ethnomusicologicum. Abstracts 6)
In Slovak, German, and English.
RILM 76 1263.

2189. Elscheková, Alica. "General Considerations on the Classification of Folk Tunes." *Studia Musicologica* 7 (1965): 259-62.

2190. ———. "Klasifikácie krátkych motivických úsekov nestrofických i strofických piesní tradičnými i netradičnými technikami." [Classification of Short Motivic Parts of Strophic and Non-Strophic Songs by Traditional and Nontraditional Techniques] In *Lidová píseň a samočinný počítač 3. Sborník materiálůze 3. semináře o využití samočinného počítače při studiu lidové písně* (Brno 15.-16.10.1974), ed. Dušan Holý, Karel Pala, and Miloš Štědroň. Prague: Státní pedagogické nakladatelství, 1976: 219-43.
In Slovak, summary in German.
RILM 76 1690.

2191. ———. "Methods of Classification of Folk Tunes." *Journal of the International Folk Music Council* 18 (1966): 56-76.

2192. ———. "Metóda vyhodnocovania melodických podobností pomocou klasifikačných tabuliek." [A Method for Evaluating Melodic Similarities with the Aid of Classification Tables] *Musicologica Slovaca* 6 (1978): 187-98.
RILM 78 1777.

2193. ———. "Vynášanie zimy a prinášanie leta v Gemeri: funkcia, tematika a hudobná charakteristika." [Taking Away the Winter and Bringing in the Summer in Gemer: Function, Themes, and Musical Characteristics] *Gemer, národopisné stúdie 2; Martin* 2 (1976): 235-331.
In Slovak, summaries in German and Hungarian.
RILM 76 1340.

2194. Entwisle, Jeffrey L. "Visual Perception and Analysis of Musical Scores." B.S. thesis, Dept. of Humanities, Massachusetts Institute of Technology, 1973. 41 p.

2195.   Erickson, Raymond F. *DARMS: A Reference Manual.* New York: DARMS Project, Dept. of Music, Queens College, CUNY, 1976.
RILM 76 15274.

2196.   ———. "'The DARMS Project:' A Status Report." *Computers and the Humanities* 9 (1975): 291–98.
C&CA 11 (1976): 22470. *C&IS* 16: 157990C.

2197.   ———. "The Ford-Columbia Music Representation (DARMS)." Mimeographed. New York, 1971. 50 p.

2198.   ———. "A General-Purpose System for Computer Aided Musical Studies." *Journal of Music Theory* 13 (1969): 276–94.

2199.   ———. "Musical Analysis and the Computer: A Report on Some Current Approaches and the Outlook for the Future." *Computers and the Humanities* 3 (1968–69): 87–104.
Slightly revised version in *Journal of Music Theory* 12 (1968): 240–63.

2200.   ———. "Musicomp 76 and the State of DARMS." *College Music Symposium* 17 (1977): 90–101.
RILM 77 1528.

2201.   ———. "Rhythmic Problems and Melodic Structure in Organum Purum: A Computer-Assisted Study." Ph. D. diss., Yale University, 1970. 430 p.
Abstract and brief notes in *Computers and the Humanities* 6 (1972): 254.
DA 31:6645A.

2202.   Erickson, Robert. *Sound Structure in Music.* Berkeley: University of California Press, 1975. 205 p.

2203.   Escot, P. "The Hidden Geometry of Music." In *Atti del Quinto Colloquio di Informatica Musicale.* Ancona: Università di Ancona, 1983: 186–94.

2204.   Ferentzy, E. N. "Progress Report on the Project 'Analysis of Musical Styles by an Electronic Computer Sponsored by Washington State University'." Pullman: Washington State University, 1966.

2205.   Fiore, Mary E. "Webern's Use of Motive in the *Piano Variations.*" In *The Computer and Music,* ed. Harry B. Lincoln. Ithaca: Cornell University Press, 1970: 115–22.

2206.   Flora, Reis. "The Acoustic Behavior of the *Piri* and the *Hichiriki.*" In *Selected Reports in Ethnomusicology,* Volume II, No. 1, ed. Mantle Hood. Los Angeles: University of California, 1974: 140–57.

2207.   Fornůsek, Jaroslav. "Aplikace zkuseností z projektování úloh na samocinném pocítaci pro oblast lidové písne." [Application of Experience in Designing Computer Programs in the Field of Folk Songs] In *Lidová písen a samočinný počítač I,* ed. Dušan Holý and Oldřich Sirovátka. Brno: Klub uživatelů MSP, 1972: 11–18.
In Czech; summary in English.

2208. Forte, Allen. "Computer-Implemented Analysis of Musical Structure." In *Papers from the West Virginia University Conference on Computer Applications in Music,* ed. Gerald Lefkoff. Morgantown: West Virginia University Library, 1967: 31–42.

2209. ———. "A Program for the Analytic Reading of Scores." *Journal of Music Theory* 10 (1966): 330–64.
Also published as "Syntax-Based Analytic Reading of Musical Scores." Massachusetts Institute of Technology Project MAC Technical Report no. 39, Apr. 1967. 36 p.

2210. ———. "The Structure of Atonal Music: Practical Aspects of a Computer-Oriented Research Project." In *Musicology and the Computer,* ed. Barry S. Brook. New York: City University of New York Press, 1970: 10–18.

2211. Foxley, Eric. "The Harmonisation of Melodies for the Measurement of Melodic Variations." In *Informatique et musique, Second Symposium International,* ed. Hélène Charnassé. Ivry: ELMERATTO, CNRS, 1983: 93–114.

2212. Frankel, Robert E.; Stanley J. Rosenschein; and Stephen W. Smoliar. "A LISP-Based System for the Study of Schenkerian Analysis." *Computers and the Humanities* 10 (1976): 21–32.
CA 21 (1977): 2245. *C&CA* 12 (1977): 5010. *RILM* 76 15526.

2213. ———; Stanley J. Rosenschein; and Stephen W. Smoliar. "Schenker's Theory of Tonal Music—Its Explication Through Computational Processes." *International Journal of Man-Machine Studies* 10 (1978): 121–38.
Abstract in *Computers and the Humanities* 13 (1979): 90.
C&CA 14 (1979): 2502. *C&IS* 20 (1978): 207147C. *CR* 19 (1978): 33,517. *RILM* 78 1824.

2214. Fraser, Robert. "Computer Implementation of Musical Linguistics." Durham, England, n.d.
C&IS 13: 107878C.

2215. ———. "Rhythmic Structure and the Computer." Paper presented at the Symposium on Computer Studies in Music, 6–9 July 1979, Nottingham University, U.K.

2216. Fuller, David. "Mechanical Musical Instruments as a Source for the Study of 'notes inégales'." *Bulletin of the Musical Box Society International* 20 (1974): 281–93.
RILM 75 2568.

2217. Fuller, Ramon C. "Toward a Theory of Webernian Harmony, via Analysis with a Digital Computer." In *The Computer and Music,* ed. Harry B. Lincoln. Ithaca: Cornell University Press, 1970: 123–31.

2218. Gabura, A. James. "Computer Analysis of Musical Style." In *Association for Computing Machinery Proceedings of the 20th National Conference.* New York: Association for Computing Machinery, 1965: 303–14.

2219. ———. "Music Style Analysis by Computer." M.S. thesis, University of Toronto, 1967.

2220. ———, and C. C. Gotlieb. "A System for Keypunching Music." *Bulletin of the Computer Society of Canada* 8 (Winter 1967/1968): 14–22.

2221. Gadviev, Shamil Allgedar. "Statistic Analysis of Structure of Azerbaijan Folk Songs." In *Proceedings of the 1978 International Computer Music Conference,* comp. Curtis Roads. Evanston, Ill.: Northwestern University Press, 1979: 761–74.
In English and Russian.

2222. Gagliardo, Emilio, and Mario Ghislandi. "Did Beethoven Use the Enneadecaphonic Algorithm?" In *Proceedings of the Venice 1982 International Computer Music Conference,* comp. Thom Blum and John Strawn. San Francisco, Calif.: Computer Music Association, 1985: 556–62.

2223. Garbutt, Terry. "The Visible Music System." Paper presented at the Music Symposium, Sheridan College, Oakville, Ontario, June 1980.

2224. Garvin, Paul C. "Computer Processing and Cultural Data: Problems of Method." In *The Use of Computers In Anthropology.* The Hague: Mouton & Co., 1965: 134–35.

2225. Gelnár, Jaromír, and Lubomír Šváb. "Analýza rytmického průběho va folklórnich nápěvech pomocí matematický ch metod." [The Analysis of the Rhythmic Course of Folk Airs by Mathematical Methods] In *Lidová píseň a samočinný počítac 3. Sborník materiáluze 3. semináře o využití samočinného počítače při studiu lidové písně* (Brno 15.–16.10.1974), ed. Dušan Holý, Karel Pala, and Miloš Štědroň. Prague: Státní pedagogické nakladatelství, 1976: 245–52.
In Czech; summary in German.
RILM 76 1265.

2226. Gena, Peter. "The Programming and Synthesis of Balbastre's 'Romance'." *Bulletin of the Musical Box Society International* 20 (1974): 278–79.

2227. Gilbert, Steven E. "The Trichord: An Analytic Outlook for Twentieth-Century Music." Ph. D. diss., Yale University, 1970. 204 p.
DA 31:2956A.

2228. Giles, Ray. "*Ombak* in the Style of the Javanese Gong." In *Selected Reports in Ethnomusicology,* Volume II, No. 1, ed. Mantle Hood. Los Angeles: University of California, 1974: 158–65.

2229. Goller, Gottfried. "Zur Bezeichnung der Neumen in der germanischen Choralnotation." In *Gesellschaft für Musikforschung. Bericht über den Internationalen Musikwissenschaftlichen Kongress, Leipzig 1966,* ed. Carl Dahlhaus, Reiner Kluge, Ernst H. Meyer, and Walter Wiora. Kassel: Bärenreiter; Leipzig: VEB Deutscher Verlag für Musik, 1970: 173–75.
RILM 72 1058.

2230. Gould, Murray. "A Keypunchable Notation for the Liber Usualis." *Elektronische Datenverarbeitung in der Musikwissenschaft,* ed. Harald Heckmann. Regensburg: G. Bosse, 1967: 25–40.

2231. ———, and George W. Logemann. "ALMA: Alphanumeric Language for Music Analysis." In *Musicology and the Computer,* ed. Barry S. Brook. New York: City University of New York Press, 1970: 57–90.

2232. Grauer, Victor A. "Some Song-Style Clusters—A Preliminary Study." *Ethnomusicology* 9 (1965): 265–71.

2233. Greussay, Patrick. "Un modèle informatique de description de structures musicales." *Recherches linguistiques* 1 (1972): 89–128.

2234. ———. "Modèles de descriptions symboliques en analyse musicale." Thèse de 3ème cycle, UER Linguistique-Informatique, Université Paris VIII, Juin 1973. 270 p.
Abstract in French in *French Language Dissertations in Music.* New York: Pendragon Press, 1979.

2235. ———. "Procedures LISP d'analyse de relations harmoniques." *Artinfo/ musinfo* 13: 1–7.

2236. ———. "Structures de controle en description symbolique d'analyses musicales." In *Informatique musicale. Journées d'études 1973. Textes des conférences. E.R.A.T.T.O.* Paris: C.N.R.S., 1973: 177–203.

2237. Gross, Dorothy S. "Computer Applications to Music Theory: A Retrospective." *Computer Music Journal* 8,4 (Winter 1984): 35–42.
C&CA 20 (1985): 30999.

2238. ———. "A Computer Package for Music Analysis." In *2nd Indiana University Computer Network Conference on Instructional Computer Applications, Kokomo, Indiana, March 7, 1975.* Bloomington, Ind.: Indiana University, 1975: 6–10.
C&CA 11 (1976): 14781.

2239. ———. "A Computer Project in Harmonic Analysis." In *Proceedings of the 1980 International Computer Music Conference,* comp. Hubert S. Howe. San Francisco, Calif.: Computer Music Association, l982: 525–32.

2240. ———. "A Computer Project in Music Analysis." In *Computing in the Humanities,* ed. Peter C. Patton, Renee A. Holoian. Lexington, Mass.: Lexington Books, 1981: 299–313.

2241. ———. "A Set of Computer Programs to Aid in Music Analysis." Ph. D. diss., Indiana University, 1975. 358 p.
Abstract in *Computational Musicology Newsletter* 2 (Mar. 1975): 16.
DA 36:2478A-9A. *RILM* 75 2685.

2242. ———. "A Study in Rhythmic Complexity of Selected Twentieth-Century Works." In *Musical Grammars and Computer Analysis,* ed. M. Baroni and L. Callegari. Florence: L. S. Olschki, 1984: 337–44. (Quaderni della rivista Italiana di musicologia 8)

2243. Grossi, Pietro, and Graziano Bertini. "A Program for Tomographic Analysis of Musical Texts." In *Proceedings of the Venice 1982 International Computer Music Conference,* comp. Thom Blum and John Strawn. San Francisco, Calif.: Computer Music Association, 1985: 563–76.

2244. Gutknecht, Dieter. "Untersuchungen zur Melodik des Hugenottenpsalters." Ph. D. diss., University of Cologne, 1972. 207 p. *RILM* 72 259.

2245. Haefer, John R. "Selected Cantatas of Alan Hovhaness: A Linear Analysis." M.M. diss., University of Arizona, 1971. *RILM* 71 893.

2246. Hall, Donald E. "Objective Measurement of Goodness-of-Fit for Tunings and Temperaments." *Journal of Music Theory* 17 (Fall 1973): 274–91. *RILM* 74 1024.

2247. ———. "Quantitative Evaluation of Musical Scale Tunings." *American Journal of Physics* 42 (1974): 543–52. *C&IS* 13: 117078C. *RILM* 75 2613.

2248. Hall, Thomas B. "Some Computer Aids for the Preparation of Critical Editions of Renaissance Music." *Tijschrift van de Vereniging voor Nederlandse Muziekgeschiedenis* 25 (1975): 38–53. *RILM* 76 3990.

2249. Halmos, Istvàn; M. Havass; and György Köszegi. "Experiments in Automation of Analysis, Systematization, and Listing of Monodic Folk Tunes." Budapest: Institute for Musicology, Hungarian Academy of Sciences, 1975. 15 p. French version: "Recherches en automatisation d'analyses, de systematisation, et de listing de melodies populaires monodiques." *Artinfo/musinfo* 27 (1977): 1–20. Translated from Hungarian to French by Marc Battier. Review by Carolyn Rabson in *Computer and the Humanities* 13 (1979): 240–41.

2250. ———; György Köszegi; and György Mandler. "Computational Ethnomusicology in Hungary in 1978." In *Proceedings of the 1978 International Computer Music Conference,* comp. Curtis Roads. Evanston, Ill.: Northwestern University Press, 1979: 775–83.

2251. "'Hanschen Klein' im Computer." *Musikalische Jugend* 16,5 (1967): 11.

2252. Hansen, Finn E. "Det Gregorianske repertoire i Codex H159 Montpellier." [The Gregorian Repertory in the Montpellier Codex H159] *Dansk aarbog for musikforskning* 5 (1966–67): 181–82. In Danish. *RILM* 75 490.

2253. Hanson, Jens L. "An Operational Approach to Theory of Rhythm." Ph. D. diss., Yale University, 1969. 234 p. *DA* 30:3972A.

2254. Haus, Goffredo. "Trasformazione di testi musicali per mezzo di operatori." [Transformation of Musical Texts by Means of Operators] In *Atti del Terzo Colloquio di Informatica Musicale,* ed. G. DePoli. Padua: Università di Padova, 1979: 178–93.

2255. Heckmann, Harald, ed. *Elektronische Datenverarbeitung in der Musikwissenschaft.* Regensburg: G. Bosse, 1967. 237 p.
Review by Norbert Böker-Heil in *Die Musikforschung* 25 (1972): 106–8.
Review by Oskár Elschek in *Slovenska Hubda* 13,9–10 (1969): 379–81.
Review by Fritz Winckel in *Musica* 22 (Mai-Juni 1968): 188–89.
Abstract in *Mens en melodie* 23 (Dec. 1968): 381–82.
Contains items: 1158, 2081, 2094, 2230, 2257, 2347, 2370, 2378, 2400, 2469, 2474, 2487, 2500.

2256. ———. "Elektronische Datenverarbeitung in der Musikwissenschaft." In *Report of the Tenth Congress [of the International Musicological Society], Ljubljana 1967,* ed. Dragotin Cvetko. Kassel: Bärenreiter, 1970: 424–27.

2257. ———. "Elektronische Datenverarbeitung in Musikdokumentation und Musikwissenschaft. Eine Einleitung." In *Elektronische Datenverarbeitung in der Musikwissenschaft,* ed. Harald Heckmann. Regensburg: G. Bosse, 1967: vii–xvii.

2258. ———. "Musikwissenschaft, Dokumentation, Information." In *Festschrift Karl Gustav Fellerer zum 70. Geburtstag am 7. Juli 1972 Überreicht von Kollegen, Schülern und Freunden,* ed. Heinrich Huschen. Cologne: Volk, 1973: 219–24. (Musicae Scientiae Collectanea 12)
RILM 74 1739.

2259. ———. "Musikwissenschaft und Computer." *Nova Acta Leopoldina* 37 (1972): 619–27.
RILM 72 2935.

2260. ———. "Neue Methoden der Verarbeitung musikalischer Daten." *Die Musikforschung* 17 (1964): 381–83.

2261. ———. "Zur Dokumentation musikalischer Quellen des 16. und 17. Jahrhunderts." In *Bericht über den Internationalen Musikwissenschaftlichen Kongress [der Gesellschaft für Musikforschung], Kassel 1962,* ed. Georg Reichert and Martin Just. Kassel: Bärenreiter, 1963: 342–45.

2262. Heike, Georg. "Informationstheorie und musikalische Komposition." *Melos* 28 (1961): 269–72.

2263. Heinemann, William W. "The DARMS Plotter: A New Automated Music Output Program." In *Sixth International Conference on Computers and the Humanities,* ed. S. K. Burton and D. D. Short. Rockville, Md.: Computer Science Press, 1983: 253–59.
C&CA 19 (1984): 52024.

2264. Helmer, Axel, and Wolfram Uhlmann. "Retrieval of Historical Data: Towards a Computerized Concert Index at the Swedish Archives of Music History." *Fontes Artis Musicae* 16 (1969): 48–56.

2265. Helmers, Carl. "Experiments with Score Input from a Digitizer." In *Personal Computing Digest, National Computer Conference, Personal Computing Festival, May 20–22, 1980, Anaheim, California*. Arlington, Va.: AFIPS, 1980: 135–38.

2266. Henriksen, Jon P. "Satsteknisk analyse ved hjelp av datamaskin. En musikologisk vinning?" [Musical Analysis by Means of a Computer: A Musicological Gain?] M.A. diss., University of Oslo, 1976. 135 p.
In Norwegian.
RILM 76 4001.

2267. Hessert, Norman D. "The Use of Information Theory in Musical Analysis."
Ph. D. diss., Indiana University, 1971. 94 p.
DA 32:4650A. *RILM* 71 1536.

2268. Hewlett, Walter B., and Eleanor Selfridge-Field. *Directory of Computer Assisted Research in Musicology, 1985*. Menlo Park, Calif.: Center for Computer Assisted Research in the Humanities, 1985. 56 p.

2269. Hickey, P. J.; Luigi Logrippo; R. Pelinski; and E. C. Strong. "Internal and External Representation of Musical Notation for an Ethnomusicological Project." In *Proceedings of the Tenth Ontario Universities Computing Conference*. Ottawa: University of Ottawa, 1979.

2270. Hill, George R. "The Thematic Index to the Köchel Catalog." *Institute for Computer Research in the Humanities Newsletter* 4,7 (1968): 8sq.

2271. Hiller, Lejaren A. "Information Theory and Musical Analysis." Urbana: University of Illinois Experimental Music Studio, July 1962. 40 p. (Technical Report no. 5)

2272. ———. *Informationstheorie und Computermusik*. Mainz: B. Schott's Söhne, 1964. 62 p. (Darmstadter Beiträge zur neuen Musik 8)

2273. ———, and C. Bean. "Information Theory Analysis of Four Sonata Expositions." *Journal of Music Theory* 10 (Spring 1966): 96–137.

2274. ———, and Burt Levy. "General System Theory as Applied to Music Analysis. Part 1." In *Musical Grammars and Computer Analysis*, ed. M. Baroni and L. Callegari. Florence: L. S. Olschki, 1984: 295–316. (Quaderni della rivista Italiana di musicologia 8)

2275. Hofstetter, Fred T. "Computer Applications to Music at the Ohio State University: Summer 1971 through Winter 1973." Paper presented at the International Conference on Computers in the Humanities, Minneapolis, Minnesota, July 22, 1973.
ERIC: ED 082 511.

2276. ———. "The Nationalistic Fingerprint in Nineteenth Century Romantic Chamber Music." *Computers and the Humanities* 13 (1979): 105–19.
C&CA 15 (1980): 10059.
Review by J. Wenker in *Computing Reviews* 21 (1979): 36,046.

2277. ————. "A Quantitative Method for the Study of Musical Style Applied to National Differences and Similarities in the Use of Melodic Intervals During the Mid-Nineteenth to Early Twentieth Centuries." Ph. D. diss., Ohio State University, 1974. 226 p.
DA 35:5445A.

2278. Holtzman, Steven R. "A Program for Key Determination." *Interface* 6 (1977): 29–56.
RILM 77 3641.

2279. Holý, Dušan. "Dosavadní postupy a výsledky studia lidové písně pomocí samočinného počítače na půde ČSSR." [Progress and Results to Date in the Study of Folk Song in the ČSSR with the Application of Computer Technology] In *Lidová píseň a samočinný počítač 3. Sborník materiálůze 3. semináře o využití samočinného počítače pri studiu lidové písně* (Brno 15.–16.10.1974), ed. Dušan Holý, Karel Pala, and Miloš Štědroň. Prague: Státní pedagogické nakladatelství, 1976: 25–35.
In Czech; summary in English.
RILM 76 1266.

2280. ————. "Nový návrh dokumentačního záznamu lidové písně pro samočinný počítač." [A New Proposal for Computerized Documentation of Folk Songs] *Musicologica Slovaca* 6 (1978): 235–42.
In Czech; summary in German.
RILM 78 1135.

2281. ————; Antonín Bartošík; and Stanislav Zabadal. "Cil-ukoly-postupy-perspktivy." [Aim-Mission-Progress-Perspectives] In *Lidová píseň a samočinný počítač I,* ed. Dušan Holý and Oldřich Sirovátka. Brno: Klub uživatelů MSP, 1972: 19–43.
In Czech; summary in English.

2282. ————; Antonín Bartošik; and Stanislav Zabadal. "Samočinný počítač—pomocník při analýze a klasifikaci lidových písní." [Analysis and Classification of Folk Songs by Computer] *Opus Musicum* 2 (1970): 155–64.
In Czech.
RILM 71 1210.

2283. ————, and Karel Pala. "Navrh 'dokumentacniho zaznamu' lidove pisne pro samočinný počítač." [Proposal for "Documentation Records" for Folk Songs in an Automated System] *Slovensky narodopis* 21 (1973): 51–60.
In Czech.

2284. ————, and Oldřich Sirovátka, eds. *Lidová píseň a samočinný počítač I.* [Folk Songs and Computers] Brno: Klub uzivatelu MSP, 1972. 258 p.
In Czech.
Contains items: 1856, 2061, 2187, 2207, 2281, 2358, 2423, 2434, 2550, 2588, 2809, 2877.

2285. Hosovsky, Vladimir. "The Experiment of Systematizing and Cataloguing Folk Tunes Following the Principles of Musical Dialectology and Cybernetics." *Studia Musicologica* 7 (1965): 273–86.

2286.   ———; Igor Mkrtoumian; and Edward Hakopian. "Armenian Universal Structural-Analytical Catalogue of Musical Texts-UNSACAT." In *Proceedings of the 1978 International Computer Music Conference,* comp. Curtis Roads. Evanston, Ill.: Northwestern University Press, 1979: 784–89.

2287.   ———; Igor Mkrtoumian; and Edward Hakopian. "Armjanskij universal'nyj katalog musykal'nyh tekstov." [The Armenian Comprehensive Catalogue of Musical Texts] *Vestnik obscestvennyh nauk* 5 (1979): 88–91.
In Russian; summary in Armenian.
RILM 79 2172.

2288.   Howe, Hubert S. "Some Combinatorial Properties of Pitch Structures." *Perspectives of New Music* 4 (Fall-Winter 1965): 45–61.

2289.   Hudson, Barton. "Toward a Comprehensive French Chanson Catalog." In *The Computer and Music,* ed. Harry B. Lincoln. Ithaca: Cornell University Press, 1970: 277–87.

2290.   Huglo, Michel. "Le classement par ordinateur des listes de repons liturgiques: les problèmes musicologiques." In *Informatique musicale. Journées d'études 1973. Textes des conférences. E.R.A.T.T.O.* Paris: C.N.R.S., 1973: 125–34.
RILM 74 4227.

2291.   ———. "Musicologie medievale et informatique." In *Informatique et musique, Second Symposium International,* ed. Hélène Charnassé. Ivry: ELMERATTO, CNRS, 1983: 135–45.

2292.   Hultberg, Warren E. "Transcription of Tablature to Standard Notation." In *The Computer and Music,* ed. Harry B. Lincoln. Ithaca: Cornell University Press, 1970: 288–92.

2293.   Imai, M.; T. Niihara; and S. Inokuchi. "Transcription of Japanese Folk-Song." In *Seventh International Conference on Pattern Recognition, Montreal, Quebec, Canada, 30 July-2 Aug. 1984.* Silver Spring, Md.: IEEE Computer Society Press, 1984: vol. 2, 905–7.
C&CA 20 (1985): 31019.

2294.   Inokuchi, S. "Musical Database." *Journal of the Institute of Electronics and Communication Engineers of Japan* 64 (May 1981): 466–68.
In Japanese.
C&CA 17 (1982): 28471.

2295.   Jackson, David L. "Horizontal and Vertical Analysis Data Extraction Using a Computer Program." Ph. D. diss., University of Cincinnati, 1981. 423 p.
DA 42:4196A.

2296.   Jackson, Roland. "Harmony Before and After 1910: A Computer Comparison." In *The Computer and Music,* ed. Harry B. Lincoln. Ithaca: Cornell University Press, 1970: 132–46.

2297.   ———. "A Musical Input Language and a Sample Program for Musical Analysis." In *Musicology and the Computer,* ed. Barry S. Brook. New York: City University of New York Press, 1970: 130–50.

2298. ———, and Philip Bernzott. "Harmonic Analysis with Computer: A Progress Report." *Institute for Computer Research in the Humanities Newsletter* 1 (May 1966): 3–4.

2299. Jacquot, Jean. "Problèmes d'édition des tablatures de luth." In *Informatique musicale. Journées d'études 1973. Textes des conférences. E.R.A.T.T.O.* Paris: C.N.R.S., 1973: 10–24. *RILM* 74 3863.

2300. Jammers, Ewald; M. Bielitz; I. Bender; and W. Ebenhöh. *Das Heidelberger Programm für die elektronische Datenverarbeitung in der musikwissenschaftlichen Byzantinistik.* Berlin: Springer, 1970. 23 p. (Heidelberger Akademie der Wissenschaften. Mathematisch-Naturwissenschaftliche Klasse. Sitzungsberichte; Jahrg. 1969/70, Abh. 2)

2301. Jansen, Paule. "Dépouillement des périodiques du XVIIe et du XVIIIe siècle." In *Informatique musicale. Journées d'études 1973. Textes des conférences. E.R.A.T.T.O.* Paris: C.N.R.S., 1973: 93–103. *RILM* 74 1741.

2302. Joiner, Richard E. "Gregorian Chant." *Computer Studies in the Humanities and Verbal Behavior* 2 (1969): 213–19.

2303. Jones, Alexander M., and Hubert S. Howe. "IML, An Intermediary Musical Language." Mimeographed. Princeton: Princeton University Music Dept., Feb. 1964. 15 p.

2304. Kaegi, Werner. "A Minimum Description of the Linguistic Sign Repertoire." *Interface* 2 (1973): 141–56; and 3 (1974): 137–57.

2305. Karp, Theodore. "A Computer Program to Test for the Presence of Melodic Formulae within the Repertoire of Notre Dame *Organa Dupla.*" Davis, Calif.: University of California at Davis, 1967. (Research Report)

2306. ———. "A Test for Melodic Borrowing among Notre Dame *Organa Dupla.*" In *The Computer and Music,* ed. Harry B. Lincoln. Ithaca: Cornell University Press, 1970: 293–95.

2307. Kassler, Michael. "Decision of a Musical System." *Communications of the Association for Computing Machinery* 5 (1962): 223. Also published: Princeton: Princeton University Music Dept., Dec. 1961.

2308. ———. "The Decision of Arnold Schoenberg's Twelve-Note-Class System and Related Systems." Mimeographed. Princeton: Princeton University Music Dept., 1961.

2309. ———. "Explication of the Middleground of Schenker's Theory of Tonality." *Miscellanea Musicologica* 9 (1977): 72–81.

2310. ———. "IML-MIR." In *Musicology and the Computer,* ed. Barry S. Brook. New York: City University of New York Press, 1970: 178–81.

2311.   ———. "MIR, A Simple Programming Language for Musical Information Retrieval." Mimeographed. Princeton: Princeton University Music Dept., Mar. 1964. 22 p.
Updated version in *The Computer and Music,* ed. Harry B. Lincoln. Ithaca: Cornell University Press, 1970: 299–327.

2312.   ———. *Proving Musical Theorems I: The Middleground of Heinrich Schenker's Theory of Tonality.* Sydney: Basser Dept. of Computer Science, University of Sydney, 1975. (Technical Report no. 103)

2313.   ———. "A Report of Work, Directed Toward Explication of Schenker's Theory of Tonality, Done in Summer 1962 as the First Phase of a Project Concerned with the Applications of High-Speed Automatic Digital Computers to Music and Musicology." Mimeographed. Princeton: Princeton University Music Dept., 1964.

2314.   ———. "A Representation of Current, Common Musical Notation; Manual for Keypunchers." Mimeographed. Princeton: Princeton University Music Dept., 1963.

2315.   ———. "A Sketch of the Use of Formalized Languages for the Assertion of Music." *Perspectives of New Music* 1 (Spring 1963): 83–94.

2316.   Kirschenbaum, Howard. "Music Analysis by Computer." *Music Educators Journal* 53 (Feb. 1967): 94–97.

2317.   Kjellberg, Erik. "En tematisk katalog med numericode. Ett projekt vid SMA." [A Thematic Catalog with Numeric Codes: A Project with EDP] *Svensk tidskrift för musikforskning* 50 (1968): 125–32.
In Swedish; summary in English.

2318.   Kluge, Reiner. *Faktorenanalytische Typenbestimmung an Volksliedmelodien. Versuch einer typologischen Ordnung Altmärkischer Melodien—Sammlung Parisius, Stockmann, u.a.—mit Hilfe eines Rechenautomaten ZRA1.* Leipzig: VEB Deutscher Verlag für Musik, 1974.
Review by Wolfram Steinbeck in *Jahrbuch für Volksliedforschung* 21 (1976): 217–28.
RILM 76 6482.

2319.   ———. "Versuch einer typologischen Systematik Altmärkischer Volkslieder durch Faktorenanalyse mit Hilfe eines Elektronischen Rechenautomaten ZRA I." Thèse de doctorat, Musikwissenschaftliches Institut der Humboldt-Universität, Berlin.

2320.   ———. "Volksliedanalyse und -systematisierung mit Hilfe eines Rechenautomaten." In *Bericht über den Internationalen Kongress [der Gesellschaft für Musikforschung], Leipzig 1966,* ed. Carl Dahlhaus, Reiner Kluge, Ernst H. Meyer, and Walter Wiora. Kassel: Bärenreiter; Leipzig: VEB Deutscher Verlag für Musik, 1970: 458–65.

2321. ———. "Zur automatischen quantitativen Bestimmung musikalischer Ähnlichkeit." In *Report of the Tenth Congress [of the Interntional Musicological Society], Ljubljana 1967,* ed. Dragotin Cvetko. Kassel: Bärenreiter, 1970: 450–57.

2322. Kolosick, J. Timothy. "A Computer-Assisted, Set-Theoretic Investigation of Vertical Simultaneities in Selected Piano Compositions by Charles Ives." Ph. D. diss., University of Wisconsin-Madison, 1981. 174 p.
DA 42:2925A.

2323. ———. "Microcomputers and Future Work in Computer-Assisted Music Analysis." In *Proceedings, 1981 International Computer Music Conference, November 5–8,* comp. Larry Austin and Thomas Clark. Denton, Tex.: North Texas State University, 1983: 325–31.

2324. ———. "SETS, a Program for Set-Theoretic Music Analysis." In *Computer-Based Instruction: A New Decade: 1980 Proceedings, Association for the Development of Computer-Based Instructional Systems.* Bellingham, Wash.: Western Washington University, 1980: 209–12.
C&CA 15 (1980): 33897.

2325. Kostka, Stefan M. "The Hindemith String Quartets: A Computer-Assisted Study of Selected Aspects of Style." Ph. D. diss., University of Wisconsin, 1969. 349 p.
DA 31:786A.

2326. ———. "Recent Developments in Computer-Assisted Musical Scholarship." *Computers and the Humanities* 6 (1971–72): 15–21.
Letter to the editor by Stefan Bauer-Mengelberg *Computers and the Humanities* 6 (1971–72): 110.

2327. Kuksa, Emanuel. "Duvaj na generátoru." [Duvaj by a Computer] *Opus musicum* 5,1 (1973): 4–9.
In Czech.
RILM 73 2322.

2328. Kupper, Hubert. "Computer und Musikwissenschaft." *IBM Nachrichten* 180 (1966): 297–303.

2329. ———. "Statistische Untersuchungen zur Modusstruktur der Gregorianik." Ph. D., Cologne, 1970.
Also published: Regensburg: G. Bosse, 1970. 70 p. (Kölner Beiträge zur Musikforschung 56)
Abstract in *Die Musikforschung* 24 (1971): 451.

2330. Kurfürst, Pavel. "Uplatnění matematických metod při zkoumání lidových hudebních nástrojů." [The Application of Mathematical Methods in the Investigation of Folk Instruments] In *Lidová píseň a samočinný počítač 3. Sborník materiáluze 3. semináře o využití samočinného počítače při studiu lidové písně* (Brno 15.–16.10.1974), ed. Dušan Holý, Karel Pala, and Miloš Štědroň.

Prague: Státní pedagogické nakladatelství, 1976: 311–32.
In Czech; summary in English.
RILM 76 1438.

2331.   Kuttner, Fritz A. "Musicologist Reveals His Affair with Susie." *HiFi/Stereo Review* 15 (Sept. 1965): 54–57.

2332.   Labussiere, Annie. "Codage des structures rythmo-mélodiques à partir de créations vocales." In *Informatique musicale. Journées d'études 1973. Textes des conférences. E.R.A.T.T.O.* Paris: C.N.R.S., 1973: 66–92.

2333.   Ladner, Robert. "Computer Analysis of Music Forms." *Music Journal* 26 (Oct. 1968): 33, 58.

2334.   Lagassé, Denise A. "A Model Computer Program for the Parametral Analysis of Atonal Music." In *Proceedings, 1981 International Computer Music Conference, November 5–8,* comp. Larry Austin and Thomas Clark. Denton, Tex.: North Texas State University, 1983: 363–94.

2335.   Lande, Tor Sverre. "Music Analysis with SIMULA 67." Paper presented at the 7th SIMULA Users' Conference, Lake Como, Italy, Sept. 12–14, 1979. *C&IS* 24 (1980): 241143C.

2336.   ———. "Musikkanalyse med datamaskin." [Music Analysis with Computers] *Studia Musicologica Norvegica* 4 (1978): 47–60.
In Norwegian, summary in English.

2337.   ———, and Arvid O. Vollsnes. "MUSIKUS: A System for Musical Analysis by Computer." Paper presented at the Forty-fifth Annual Meeting of the American Musicological Society, meeting jointly with the Society for Music Theory, November 1–4, 1979, The Biltmore, New York City.

2338.   Landy, Leigh. "Arabic Taqsim Improvisation: A Methodological Musical Study Using Computers." In *Informatique et musique, Second Symposium International,* ed. Hélène Charnassé. Ivry: ELMERATTO, CNRS 1983: 21–30.

2339.   ———. "Computer Musicology and Politics: Why Are They Never Associated?" In *Informatique et musique, Second Symposium International,* ed. Hélène Charnassé. Ivry: ELMERATTO, CNRS, 1983: 243–53.

2340.   ———. "Digital Alternative Representation for Music Systems." In *Informatique musicale 1977, Textes des conférences, Equipe ERATTO,* ed. Henri Ducasse. Paris: Centre de documentation sciences humaines, 1978: 15–26.
Abstracts in English, French, and German.
RILM 78 3911.

2341.   LaRue, Jan. "ALMA: Alphanumeric Language for Music Analysis." New York: Institute for Computer Research in the Humanities, New York University, Jan. 1966.

2342.   ———. "Future Technological Directions." In *Report of the Tenth Congress [of the International Musicological Society], Ljubljana 1967,* ed. Dragotin Cvetko. Kassel: Bärenreiter, 1970: 457–60.

2343. ———. "New Directions for Style Analysis." In *Musicology and the Computer,* ed. Barry S. Brook. New York: City University of New York Press, 1970: 194–97.

2344. ———. "Some Computer Aids to Musicology." In *Bericht über den Internationalen Musikwissenschaftlichen Kongress [der Gesellschaft für Musikforschung], Leipzig 1966,* ed. Carl Dalhaus, Reiner Kluge, Ernst H. Meyer, and Walter Wiora. Kassel: Bärenreiter; Leipzig: VEB Deutscher Verlag für Musik, 1970: 466–69.

2345. ———. "Two Options for Input of Thematic Incipits." *Institute for Computer Research in the Humanities Newsletter* 4 (Nov. 1968): 3–6.

2346. ———. "Two Problems in Musical Analysis: The Computer Lends a Hand." In *Computers in Humanistic Research,* ed. Edmund A. Bowles. Englewood Cliffs: Prentice-Hall, 1967: 194–203.

2347. ———, and Marian W. Cobin. "The Ruge-Seignelay Catalogue: An Exercise in Automated Entries." In *Elektronische Datenverarbeitung in der Musikwissenschaft,* ed. Harald Heckmann. Regensburg: G. Bosse, 1976: 41–56.

2348. ———, and George W. Logemann. "EDP for Thematic Catalogues." *Notes* 22 (1965–66): 1179–86.

2349. ———, and Mary Rasmussen. "Numerical Incipits for Thematic Catalogues." *Fontes Artis Musicae* 9 (1965): 72–75.

2350. Laske, Otto E. "In Search of a Generative Grammar for Music." *Perspectives of New Music* 12 (Fall-Winter 1973/Spring-Summer 1974): 351–78.
Reprinted from "Introduction to a Generative Theory of Music." *Sonological Reports,* No. 1, Institute of Sonology, Utrecht (Jan. 1973).
Also in *Music and Mind.* Boston, Mass.: O. Laske, 1981: 31–45.

2351. ———. "Introduction to a Generative Theory of Music." *Sonological Reports* 1 (1975): 1–103 (2nd group).

2352. ———. "KEITH: A Rule-System for Making Music-Analytical Discoveries." In *Musical Grammars and Computer Analysis,* ed. M. Baroni and L. Callegari. Florence: L. S. Olschki, 1984: 165–99. (Quaderni della rivista Italiana di musicologia 8)

2353. ———. "On Problems of a Performance Model for Music." *Sonological Reports* 1 (1975): 1–136 (1st group).

2354. Lefkoff, Gerald. "Automated Discovery of Similar Segments in the Forty-Eight Permutations of a Twelve-Tone Row." In *The Computer and Music,* ed. Harry B. Lincoln. Ithaca: Cornell University Press, 1970: 147–53.

2355. ———. "Computers and the Study of Musical Style." In *Papers from the West Virginia University Conference on Computer Applications in Music,* ed. Gerald Lefkoff. Morgantown: West Virginia University Library, 1967: 45–61.

2356.   Leipp, Emile. "Une methode d'étude des echelles musicales et ethniques—apports de l'acoustique musicale à l'étude digitale des musiques ethniques." In *Informatique musicale. Journées d'études 1973. Textes des conférences. E.R.A.T.T.O.* Paris: C.N.R.S., 1973: 144–57.
         RILM 74 3244.

2357.   ———, and Moncef Mlouka. "L'apport de l'acoustique musicale dans l'étude des musiques ethniques." *Conférences des journées d'études. Festival du son* (1974): 80–95.
         RILM 74 3244.

2358.   Leng, Ladislav. "O niektorých možnostiach využitia SP pri klasifikácii ozdibovaných ludových inštrumentálnych melódií." [On a Few Possibilities in the Use of Computers in the Classification of Instrumental Folk Melodies] In *Lidová píseň a samočinný počítač I,* ed. Dušan Holý and Oldřich Sirovátka. Brno: Klub uživatelů MSP, 1972: 207–13.
         Summary in English.

2359.   Lewis, David S. "Two Parameters of Melodic Line as Stylistic Discriminants." Ph. D. diss., West Virginia University, 1968. 128 p.
         DA 29:1243A.
         Review by Hubert S. Howe in *Perspectives of New Music* 9/10 (Fall-Winter 1971): 350–55.

2360.   Lieberman, Fredric. "The Chinese Long Zither Ch'in: A Study Based on the *Mei-an Ch'in-p'u.*" Ph. D. diss., University of California, Los Angeles, 1977. 850 p.
         DA 38:538A. *RILM* 77 1157.

2361.   ———. "Computer-Aided Analysis of Javanese Music." In *The Computer and Music,* ed. Harry B. Lincoln. Ithaca: Cornell University Press, 1970: 181–92.

2362.   Lincoln, Harry B., ed. *The Computer and Music.* Ithaca, N.Y.: Cornell University Press, 1970. 354 p.
         Review by K. Attenborough in *International Journal of Man-Machine Studies* 4 (1972): 489–91.
         Review by Paul Earls in *Yearbook for Inter-American Musical Research* 7 (1971): 178–83.
         Reviews by Raymond F. Erickson in *Computing Reviews* 11 (1970): 650–52; and *Journal of the American Musicological Society* 25 (1972): 102–07.
         Review by Pierre Gaillard in *Revue de musicologie* 57 (1971): 85–86.
         Review by David C. Handscomb in *Music and Letters* 52 (1971): 86–88.
         Review by Marcia Herndon in *Ethnomusicology* 16 (1972): 290–92.
         Review by Max V. Mathews in *Computer Studies in the Humanities and Verbal Behavior* 3 (1970–71): 224–25.
         Review by Peter J. Pirie in *The Music Review* 32 (1971): 184–88.
         Review by John E. Rothgeb in *Computers and the Humanities* 5 (1970–71): 178–82.
         Review by Tito Tonietti in *Nuova rivista musicale Italiana* 5 (1971): 1092–96.

Review by Barry Vercoe in *Perspectives of New Music* 9/10 (Fall-Winter 1971): 323–30.
Review by Thomas Walker in *Notes* 27 (1970): 272–73.
Review in *Numus-West* 4 (1973): 60.
Review in *Zvuk* 1 (1973): 114–15.
Contains items: 12, 62, 139, 332, 408, 2105, 2205, 2217, 2219, 2289, 2292, 2296, 2306, 2311, 2354, 2361, 2541, 2586, 2890, 4254.

2363. ———. "A Computer Application in Musicology: The Thematic Index." In *Information Processing 68: Proceedings of IFIP Congress 1968,* ed. A. J. H. Morrell. Amsterdam: North Holland, 1969: 957–61.
RILM 75 117.

2364. ———. *Development of Computerized Techniques in Music Research with Emphasis on the Thematic Index.* Washington: Office of Education, U.S. Dept. of Health, Education, and Welfare, 1968. 39 p.
ERIC: ED 027 609.

2365. ———. *Development of Computerized Techniques in Music Research with Emphasis on the Thematic Index.* Washington: Office of Education, U.S. Dept. of Health, Education, and Welfare, 1969. 15 p.
ERIC: ED 041 031.

2366. ———. "Encoding, Decoding, and Storing Melodies for a Data Base of Renaissance Polyphony: A Progress Report." In *Proceedings on Very Large Data Bases, Tokyo, Japan, 6–8 October 1977.* New York: IEEE, 1977: 277–82.
C&CA 13 (1978): 6822.

2367. ———. *Kompyûtâ to Ongaku.* Translated by Minao Shibata and Tokumaru Yoshihiko, et al. Tokyo: Kawai-gakufu, 1972. 357 p.
Japanese translation of *The Computer and Music.*
RILM 73 1627.

2368. ———. "Musicology and the Computer: The Thematic Index." In *Computers in Humanistic Research,* ed. Edmund A. Bowles. Englewood Cliffs: Prentice-Hall, 1967: 184–93.

2369. ———. "Preliminary Studies of Melody as Wave Form." In *Informatique et musique, Second Symposium International,* ed. Hélène Charnassé. Ivry: ELMERATTO, CNRS 1983: 43–54.

2370. ———. "Some Criteria and Techniques for Developing Computerized Thematic Indices." In *Elektronische Datenverarbeitung in der Musikwissenschaft,* ed. Harald Heckmann. Regensburg: G. Bosse, 1967: 57–62.

2371. ———. *A Study of Computer Techniques for Music Research.* Washington: Office of Education, U.S. Dept. of Health, Education, and Welfare, 1970. 13 p.
ERIC: ED 043 650.

2372. ———. "Teaching Computer Applications in Musicology." In *IBM Symposium on Introducing the Computer into the Humanities,* 1969: 67–71. (Document G320-1044-0)

2373. ———. "The Thematic Index: A Computer Application to Musicology."
       Computers and the Humanities 2 (1967–68): 215–20.

2374. Liu, Marjory. "The Influence of Tonal Speech on *K'unch'ü* Opera Style." In
       Selected Reports in Ethnomusicology, Volume II, No. 1, ed. Mantle Hood. Los
       Angeles: University of California, 1974: 62–86.

2375. Locke, Eleanor G. "!G !K2- !M3:4 (2E.U(O)): Folk Song Research and Com-
       puter Science." *Kodály envoy* 3 (Dec. 1976): 2–4.

2376. Lockwood, Lewis. "Computer Assistance in the Investigation of Accidentals
       in Renaissance Music." In *Report of the Tenth Congress [of the International
       Musicological Society], Ljubljana 1967,* ed. Dragotin Cvetko. Kassel:
       Bärenreiter, 1970: 444–49.

2377. ———. "A Stylistic Investigation of the Masses of Josquin Desprez with the
       Aid of the Computer: A Progress Report." In *Musicology and the Computer,*
       ed. Barry S. Brook. New York: City University of New York Press, 1970:
       19–27.

2378. Logemann, George W. "The Canon in the Musical Offering of J. S. Bach: An
       Example of Computational Musicology." In *Elektronische Datenverarbeitung
       in der Musikwissenschaft,* ed. Harald Heckmann. Regensburg: G. Bosse, 1967:
       63–87.

2379. ———, and Gary Berlind. "The MUSE System for Music Analysis." Mimeo-
       graphed. New York: New York University Institute for Computer Research in
       the Humanities, 1966.

2380. Logrippo, Luigi, and Bernard Stepien. "Statistical Software Tools for
       Computer-Assisted Analysis of Music." In *Applied Systems and Cybernetics:
       Proceedings of the International Congress on Applied Systems Research and
       Cybernetics. Volume V, Systems Approaches in Computer Science and Mathe-
       matics,* ed. G. E. Lasker. New York: Pergamon Press: 2553–63.

2381. Lomax, Alan. "Africanisms in New World Negro Music." In *The Haitian
       Potential: Research and Resources of Haiti,* ed. Vera Rubin and Richard
       P. Schaedel. New York: Teachers College Press, 1975: 38–53.

2382. Lönn, Anders. "Trends and Tendencies in Recent Swedish Musicology." *Acta
       Musicologica* 44 (1972): 11–25.

2383. Lospinuso, Margaret F., and Martin Dillon. "American Shape-Note Tunes."
       *Perspectives in Computing: Applications in the Academic and Scientific Com-
       munity* 1 (1981): 40–48.
       Review by J. L. Dawson in *Computing Reviews* 22 (Dec. 1981): 38,794.

2384. Ludvova, Jitka. "The Application of Analytical Methods of Information
       Theory to Tonal Music." In *De Musica Disputationes Pragenses,* 2., ed. Robert
       Smetana. Kassel: Bärenreiter, 1974: 72–85.

2385. Malá, Hana. "Statistická srovnávací sborů Leoše Janáčka a moravských lidových písní." [A Statistical Comparison of the Work of Leos Janacek and Moravian Folk Songs] *Hudební věda* 4 (1967): 602–27.
In Czech; English summary: p. 706–7.

2386. Marillier, Cecil G. "Computer Assisted Analysis of Tonal Structure in the Classical Symphony." In *Proceedings of the 1980 International Computer Music Conference,* comp. Hubert S. Howe. San Francisco, Calif.: Computer Music Association, l982: 544–64.

2387. ———. "Tonal Structure in the Symphonies of F. J. Haydn." M.A. diss., University of Otago, 1971. 1509 p.
RILM 73 3495.

2388. Mason, Robert M. "An Encoding Algorithm and Tables for the Digital Analysis of Harmony." *Journal of Research in Music Education* 17 (1969): 286–300, 369–87.

2389. ———. *Modern Methods of Music Analysis Using Computers.* Peterborough, N.H.: Schoolhouse Press, 1985. 299 p.

2390. Maultsby, Portia K. "Afro-American Religious Music: 1619–1861: Historical Development; Computer Analysis of One Hundred Spirituals." Ph. D. diss., University of Wisconsin-Madison, 1974. 460 p.
DA 35:7343A. *C&IS* 14: 135748C.

2391. ———. "Seeks Computer Derivation of Musical Roots." *MAAC Newsletter* 5,6 (1972)

2392. McLean, Bruce. "Current Problems in Score Input Methods." Abstract in *Proceedings, 1981 International Computer Music Conference, November 5–8,* comp. Larry Austin and Thomas Clark. Denton, Tex.: North Texas State University, 1983: 171.

2393. ———. "The Design of a Portable Translator for DARMS." In Proceedings of the 1980 International Computer Music Conference, comp. Hubert S. Howe. San Francisco, Calif.: Computer Music Association, 1982: 246–64.

2394. Meehan, James R. "An Artificial Intelligence Approach to Tonal Music Theory." In *Proceedings of the ACM National Conference.* New York: ACM, 1979: 116–20.
Revised version in *Computer Music Journal* 4,2 (Summer 1980): 60–65.
C&CA 16 (1981): 21872.

2395. Mendel, Arthur. "Some Preliminary Attempts at Computer-Assisted Style Analysis in Music." *Computers and the Humanities* 4 (1969–70): 41–52.

2396. ———. "Towards Objective Criteria for Establishing Chronology and Authenticity: What Help Can the Computer Give?" In *Josquin des Prez, Proceedings of the International Josquin Festival-Conference Held at the Juilliard School at Lincoln Center in New York City, 21–25 June 1971,* ed. Edward E. Lowinsky. London: Oxford University Press, 1976: 297–308.

2397.   Meylan, Raymond. "L'énigme de la musique des basses danses du quinzième siècle." Doctorate of Lettres, University of Zürich, 1968.
Also published: Berne-Stuttgart: P. Haupt, 1968. (Publications de la Societé suisse de musicologie. Série II, 17)
Abstract in French in *French Language Dissertations in Music*. New York: Pendragon Press, 1979: 37.

2398.   ———. "Limites de l'objectivité dans les écritures instrumentales de la Renaissance." In *Informatique musicale. Journées d'études 1973. Textes des conférences*. *E.R.A.T.T.O.* Paris: C.N.R.S., 1973: 1–9.
RILM 74 3849.

2399.   ———. "Recherche de parentés parmi les basses danses du quinzième siècle." *Acta Musicologica* 38 (1966): 46–66.

2400.   ———. "Symbolisierung einer Melodie auf Lochkarten." In *Elektronische Datenverarbeitung in der Musikwissenschaft*, ed. Harald Heckmann. Regensburg: G. Bosse, 1967: 21–24.

2401.   ———. "Théorie de la centonisation." In *Report of the Tenth Congress [of the International Musicological Society], Ljubljana 1967*, ed. Dragotin Cvetko. Kassel: Bärenreiter, 1967: 427–30.

2402.   ———. "Utilisation des calculatrices electroniques pour la comparaison interne du repertoire des basses danses du quinzième siècle." *Fontes Artis Musicae* 12 (1965): 128–34.

2403.   Mlouka, Moncef. "Traitement numerique des musiques ethniques—apports de l'acoustique musicale à l'étude digitale des musiques ethniques." In *Informatique musicale. Journées d'études 1973. Textes des conférences*. *E.R.A.T.T.O.* Paris: C.N.R.S., 1973: 158–64.
RILM 74 3244.

2404.   Moomaw, Charles J. "A PL-1 Program for the Harmonic Analysis of Music by the Theories of Paul Hindemith and Howard Hanson." M.M. thesis, University of Cincinnati, 1973. 436 p.
RILM 74 1121. *Masters Abstracts* 12 (1974): 48.

2405.   Morehen, John. "Adrian Willaert's *Musica Nova* (1559): A Computer Assisted Study in Text Underlay." Paper presented at the Symposium on Computer Studies in Music, 6–9 July 1979, Nottingham University, U.K.

2406.   ———. "A Neglected Tool in Musical Analysis." *Music Teacher and Piano Student* 57 (Apr. 1978): 11–12.

2407.   ———. "Statistics in the Analysis of Musical Style." In *Informatique et musique, Second Symposium International*, ed. Hélène Charnassé. Ivry: ELMERATTO, CNRS, 1983: 169–83.

2408.   ———. "Thematic Indexing by Plotter from DARMS Input." In *Informatique et musique, Second Symposium International*, ed. Hélène Charnassé. Ivry: ELMERATTO, CNRS, 1983: 31–42.

2409. ———, and Ian Bent. "Computer Applications in Musicology." *Musical Times* 120 (1979): 563–66.
RILM 79 4444.

2410. Morris, Robert, and Daniel Starr. "The Structure of All-Interval Series." *Journal of Music Theory* 18 (1974): 364–89.

2411. Morse, Margaret B. "A Quantitative Stylistic Analysis of the Agnus Dei Mass Movements of Guillaume Dufay Supporting the Doubtful Authenticity of the *Missa Caput*." M.M. diss., Hartt College of Massachusetts, 1974.
RILM 74 1972.

2412. Morton, David. "Vocal Tones in Traditional Thai Music." In *Selected Reports in Ethnomusicology,* Volume II, No. 1, ed. Mantle Hood. Los Angeles: University of Calfornia, 1974: 88–99.

2413. Morton, Ian A. "Judgmental Factors in the Perception of Tonal Music." St. Paul, Minn., n.d.
C&IS 13: 107855C.

2414. Moyle, Alice M. "Pitch and Loudness Ambits in Some North Australian Songs." In *Selected Reports in Ethnomusicology,* Volume II, No. 1, ed. Mantle Hood. Los Angeles: University of California, 1974: 16–30.

2415. Móži, Alexander. "Pokus o harmonickú analýzu inštrumentálnej hudby pomocou numerického kódového systému." [An Experiment in Harmonic Analysis of Instrumental Music by Means of the Numeric Code System] In *Lidová píseň a samočinný počítac 3. Sborník materiáľuze 3. semináře o využití samočinného počítače při studiu lidové písně* (Brno 15.–16.10.1974), ed. Dušan Holý, Karel Pala, and Miloš Štědroň. Prague: Státní pedagogické nakladatelství, 1976: 287–309.
In Slovak; summary in English.
RILM 76 1651.

2416. ———. "Príspevok k triedeniu ľudových piesní na základe číselného kódového systému." [The Classification of Folk Songs on the Basis of a Numerical Code System] *Musicologica Slovaca* 6 (1978): 285–96.
In Slovak; summary in German.
RILM 78 1139.

2417. Murken, Hinrich. "Translingo." *Creative Computing* 9 (July 1983): 117, 121.

2418. "Music in Machine-Readable Form." *Computers and the Humanities* 6 (Jan. 1972): 176–78.

2419. Narmour, Eugene. "Toward an Analytical Symbology: The Melodic, Harmonic, and Durational Functions of Implication and Realization." In *Musical Grammars and Computer Analysis,* ed. M. Baroni and L. Callegari. Florence: L. S. Olschki, 1984: 83–114. (Quaderni della rivista Italiana di musicologia 8)

2420.   Nelson, Gary. "Anton Webern's *Five Canons,* Opus 16: A Test Case for Computer-Aided Analysis and Synthesis of Musical Style." Ph. D. diss., Washington University, 1974. 237 p.
DA 35:2324A-5A. *C&IS* 14:128618C.
Abstract in *Missouri Journal of Research in Music Education* 3 (1975): 93.

2421.   Nerheim, Rosalee J. "Design and Applications of an Alphanumeric Representation of Music." In *Proceedings of the 1978 International Computer Music Conference,* comp. Curtis Roads. Evanston, Ill.: Northwestern University Press, 1979: 720–31.

2422.   ———. "MIST: A Music Information System." In *Indiana University Computing Network, 6th Annual Conference on Academic Computer Applications,* ed. M. Stentz and L. Motsinger. Bloomington, Ind.: Wrubel Computing Center, 1979: 90–94.
ERIC: ED 180 441, p. 90–94. *ERIC:* ED 180 444.

2423.   Neufeld, Ludvik. "Spracovanie piesňových nápevov na samočinných počítačoch v Maďarsku." [The Conducting of Choral Tunes in Computers in Hungary] In *Lidová píseň a samočinný počítač I,* ed. Dušan Holý and Oldřich Sirovátka. Brno: Klub uživatelů MSP, 1972: 203–6.
In Czech; summary in English.

2424.   Newcomb, Steven R. "LASSO: An Intelligent Computer-based Tutorial in Sixteenth-Century Counterpoint." *Computer Music Journal* 9,4 (Winter 1985): 49–61.

2425.   Nunez, Inaki. "Analisis del cancionero popular vasco." [Analysis of popular Basque songs] Doctoral thesis, Mondragon, 1972. 298 p.

2426.   O'Maidin, Donncha. "Computer Analysis of Irish and Scottish Jigs." In *Musical Grammars and Computer Analysis,* ed. M. Baroni and L. Callegari. Florence: L. S. Olschki, 1984: 329–36. (Quaderni della rivista Italiana di musicologia 8)

2427.   Oppo, Franco. "Per una teoria generale del linguaggio musicale." [For a General Theory for Musical Linguistics] In *Musical Grammars and Computer Analysis,* ed. M. Baroni and L. Callegari. Florence: L. S. Olschki, 1984: 115–30. (Quaderni della rivista Italiana di musicologia 8)

2428.   Ottosen, Knud. "Le traitement des donnes—le classement par ordinateur des listes de repons liturgiques." In *Informatique musicale. Journées d'études 1973. Textes des conférences. E.R.A.T.T.O.* Paris: C.N.R.S., 1973: 135–43.

2429.   Oudal, Robert D. "The 1968 Introductory Seminar in the Use of Computers in Musical Projects." *Student Musicologists at Minnesota* 3 (1968–69): 66–109.

2430.   Owen, Jonathan. "Computer Implementation of Harmonic Analysis of Music." *IUCC Bulletin* 1 (Winter 1979): 119–21.
C&CA 15 (1980): 22355.

2431. Pacholczyk, Józef M. "Vibrato as a Function of Model Practice in the Qur'an Chant of Shaikh 'Abdu'l-Basit' Adbus-Samad." In *Selected Reports in Ethnomusicology*, Volume II, No. 1, ed. Mantle Hood. Los Angeles: University of California, 1974: 32–41.

2432. Packer, Leo S. "Technology for the Music Scholar." Paper presented at the Joint Annual Meeting of the American Musicological Society and the Contemporary Music Society, Dec. 29, 1965, Ann Arbor, Mich.

2433. Paisley, William J. "Identifying the Unknown Communicator in Painting, Literature, and Music: The Significance of Minor Encoding Habits." *Journal of Communication* 14 (1964): 219–37.

2434. Pala, Karel. "Možnosti popisu sémantiky lidové písne." [The Possibilities of Description of the Semantics of Folk Songs] In *Lidová písen a samočinný počítač I*, ed. Dusan Holý and Oldřich Sirovátka. Brno: Klub uživatelů MSP, 1972: 63–77.
In Czech; summary in English.

2435. Pao, Miranda Lee. "Bibliometrics and Computational Musicology." *Collection Management* 3 (Spring 1979): 97–109.

2436. ———. "Collaboration in Computational Musicology." *Journal of the American Society for Information Science* 33 (Jan. 1982): 38–43.
C&IS 29 (1982): 82–5110C.

2437. Pape, U. "Ein Verfahren zur Verschlüsselung und Symbolisierung von Kompositionen in Hinblick auf eine Musikanalyse mit EDV-Anlagen." *Elektronische Datenverarbeitung* 11 (July 1969): 342–45.

2438. Papworth, D. G. "Computers and Change-Ringing." *Computer Journal* 3 (1960–61): 47–50.

2439. Pascall, Robert. "Computer and Process: A Response to the Symposium." Paper presented at the Symposium on Computer Studies in Music, 6–9 July 1979, Nottingham University, U.K.

2440. Patrick, P. Howard. "A Computer-Study of a Suspension-Formation in the Masses of Josquin Desprez." Ph. D. diss., Princeton University, 1973. 218 p.
DA 34:7269A-70A.

2441. ———. "A Computer Study of a Suspension Formation in the Masses of Josquin Desprez." *Computers and the Humanities* 8 (1974): 321–31.
CA 19 (1975): 2004. *C&CA* 10 (1975): 28487. *C&IS* 13: 105723C.

2442. ———, and Karen Strickler. "A Computer Assisted Study of Dissonance in the Masses of Josquin Desprez." *Computers and the Humanities* 12 (1978): 341–64.
C&CA 14 (1979): 22212. *C&IS* 23 (1979): 228075C.

2443. Patrick, Robert L. "A Computer-Based Thematic Index to the Works of Heinrich Schütz." D.M.A. diss., University of Kentucky, 1971. 367 p.
DA 33:778A. *RILM* 76 65.

2444.   Pearce, Alastair. "Troubadours and Transposition: A Computer-Aided Study." *Computers and the Humanities* 16 (1982): 11–18.
Abstract in *Informatique et musique, Second Symposium International,* ed. Hélène Charnassé. Ivry: ELMERATTO, CNRS, 1982: 167.
C&CA 18 (1983): 11080.

2445.   Pederson, Donald M. "Some Techniques for Computer-Aided Analysis of Musical Scores." Ph. D. diss., University of Iowa, 1968. 543 p.
Review by Hubert S. Howe in *Perspectives of New Music* 9/10 (Fall-Winter 1971): 350–55.
DA 29:1919A. *RILM* 76 1683.

2446.   Pennycook, Bruce. "Computer-Music Interfaces: A Survey." *ACM Computing Surveys* 17 (1985): 267–89.

2447.   Pepper, William. "University of Iowa: Music Research and the Computer." *Current Musicology* 9 (1969): 19–20.

2448.   Peterson, Don L. "Tonal Characteristics in the Kyrie and Sanctus Sections of Twelve *L'Homme armé* Masses: A Computer Assisted Study." Ph. D. diss., University of Wisconsin-Madison, 1975. 216 p.
DA 36: 4842A-3A.

2449.   Peterson, Richard A., and David G. Berger. "Cycles in Symbol Production: The Case of Popular Music." *American Sociological Review* 40 (1975): 158–73.

2450.   Pierce, John R. "Attaining Consonance in Arbitrary Scales." *Journal of the Acoustical Society of America* 40 (1966): 249.

2451.   ———. *Symbols, Signals, and Noise.* New York: Harper, 1961. 305 p.

2452.   Pikler, Andrew G. "History and Theory of the Tonal Spiral." Abstract in *Journal of the Acoustical Society of America* 40 (1966): 1253.

2453.   Pinkerton, Richard C. "Information Theory and Melody." *Scientific American* 194 (Feb. 1956): 77–86.

2454.   Piotrowski, Zbigniew. "O zastosowaniu komputerów w muzyce mówi Lejaren Hiller." [Lejaren Hiller Speaks about the Use of Computers in Music] *Ruch muzyczny* 4 (Feb. 1974): 3–4.
In Polish.
RILM 74 3157.

2455.   Plenckers, Leo J. "A Pattern Recognition System in the Study of the 'Cantigas de Santa Maria'." In *Musical Grammars and Computer Analysis,* ed. M. Baroni and L. Callegari. Florence: L. S. Olschki, 1984: 59–64. (Quaderni della rivista Italiana di musicologia 8)

2456.   Polansky, Larry. "A Hierarchical Gestalt Analysis of Ruggles' *Portals.*" In *Proceedings of the 1978 International Computer Music Conference,* comp. Curtis Roads. Evanston, Ill.: Northwestern University Press, 1979: 790–852.

2457. Prével, Martin. "Proposal for a Notation to be Used in Encoding Musical Texts for Computer Programming." *Journal of Computer-Based Instruction* 5 (Aug.-Nov. 1978): 1–10.
C&CA 14 (1979): 14059. *CIJE* 11 (1979): EJ 198 323.

2458. Price, James D. "Music Analysis by Computer." Philadelphia: Franklin Institute Research Laboratories, 1967. (Technical Report)

2459. Rabson, Gustave, and Carolyn Rabson. "The National Tune Index: A Systems Overview." *Computers and the Humanities* 15 (1981): 129–37.
C&CA 17 (1982): 19772.

2460. Rahn, John. "On Some Computational Models of Music Theory." *Computer Music Journal* 4,2 (Summer 1980): 66–72.
C&CA 16 (1981): 21873.

2461. ———. "Teorie su alcuni mottetti del'*Ars Antiqua,* con relative considerazzioni metodologiche." [Theories on Some Motets of the *Ars Antiqua* with Methodological Considerations] In *Musical Grammars and Computer Analysis,* ed. M. Baroni and L. Callegari. Florence: L. S. Olschki, 1984: 38–58. (Quaderni della rivista Italiana di musicologia 8)

2462. ———. "Toward a Theory for Chord Progression." In *Informatique et musique, Second Symposium International,* ed. Hélène Charnassé. Ivry: ELMERATTO, CNRS, 1983: 79–92.

2463. Rakowski, Andrzej. "O zastosowaniu cyfrowych maszyn matematycznych do muzyki." [About the Application of Cyphering Machines in Music] *Muzyka kwartalnik* 7,3 (1962): 83–95.
In Polish.

2464. Ramey, Michael J. "A Classification of Musical Instruments for Comparative Study." Ph. D. diss., University of California, Los Angeles, 1974. 329 p.
DA 35:6754A-5A.

2465. ———. "Comparative Studies of Musical Instruments." *Computers and the Humanities* 10 (1976): 93–100.
C&CA 12 (1977): 5012. *C&IS* 16: 163572C. *RILM* 76 1440.

2466. Ramsten, Märta. "Samarbetsformer inom nordisk folkmusikforskning. Rapport från NIF-seminariet vid 7: e nordiska musikforskarkongresseni Trondheim." [Inter-Nordic Cooperation in Folk Music Research. Report of the NIF Seminar at the 7th Congress of Nordic Musicologists, Trondheim] *Svensk tidskrift för musikforskning* 57,2 (1975): 61–63.
In Swedish.
RILM 75 319.

2467. Rao, Paladugu V., and Padma Rangachari. "The Use of the Computer in Indian Music." *Music Bulletin, University Music Centre* [India] 22,23,24 (1972)

2468. Ravnikar, Bruno. "Nekaj rezultatov proučevanja glasbene folklore z meto-dami matematične štatistike." [Some Results of Studying Folk Music by Means of Mathematical-Statistical Methods] *Rad XVII Kongressa Saveza Udruženja folklorista Jugoslavije* (1972): 271–86.
In Slovenian; summary in English.
RILM 72 2201.

2469. Reckziegel, Walter. "Musikanalyse: eine exakte Wissenschaft." In *Elektronische Datenverarbeitung in der Musikwissenschaft,* ed. Harald Heck-mann. Regensburg: G. Bosse, 1967: 203–24.

2470. ———. "Die Notenschrift im Computer dargestellt." *Studia Musicologica* 9 (1967): 395–406.

2471. ———. "Theorien zur Formalanalyse mehrstimmiger Musik." In *Forschungsberichte des Landes Nordrhein-Westfalen Nr. 1768.* Cologne: Westdeutscher Verlag, 1967: 5–37.

2472. Regener, Eric. "Layered Music—Theoretic Systems." *Perspectives of New Music* 6 (Fall-Winter 1967): 52–62.

2473. ———. "A Multi-Pass Linear Music Transcription." In *Musicology and the Computer,* ed. Barry S. Brook. New York: City University of New York Press, 1970: 181–84.

2474. ———. "A Multiple-Pass Transcription and a System for Music Analysis by Computer." In *Elektronische Datenverarbeitung in der Musikwissenschaft,* ed. Harald Heckmann. Regensburg: G. Bosse, 1967: 89–102.

2475. Reid, John W. "The Treatment of Dissonance in the Works of Guillaume Dufay: A Computer Aided Study." Ph. D. diss., University of Colorado at Boulder, 1981. 331 p.
DA 42:1369A.

2476. Reinecke, Hans-Peter. "Anwendung informationstheoretischer und korrela-tionsstatistischer Verfahren für die Analyse musikalischer Strukturen." In *Report of the Tenth Congress [of the International Musicological Society], Ljubljana 1967,* ed. Dragotin Cvetko. Kassel: Bärenreiter, 1970: 430–34.

2477. ———. "Erläuterungen zur modernen Dokumentations-Technik." In *Bericht über den Internationalen Musikwissenschaftlichen Kongress [der Gesellschaft für Musikforschung], Kassel 1962,* ed. Georg Reichert and Martin Just. Kassel: Bärenreiter, 1963: 336–37.

2478. ———. "Über den Zusammenhang zwischen Stereotypen und Klangbeis-pielen verschiedener musikalischer Epochen." In *Bericht über den Internationalen Musikwissenschaftlichen Kongress [der Gesellschaft für Musikforschung], Leipzig 1966,* ed. Carl Dahlhaus, Reiner Kluge, Ernst H. Meyer, and Walter Wiora. Kassel: Bärenreiter; Leipzig: VEB Deutscher Verlag für Musik, 1970: 499–509.

2479. Rhodes, Willard. "The Use of the Computer in the Classification of Folk Tunes." *Studia Musicologica* 7 (1965): 339–43.

2480. Rijavec, Andrej. "Primena moderne tehnologije u muzikologiji i muzičkoj teoriji u jugoslaviji." [Applications of Modern Technology in Musicology and Music Theory in Yugoslavia] *Zvuk* 87–88 (1968): 464–467.
Summary in English.

2481. Riotte, André. "From Traditional to Formalized Analysis: In Memoriam Jean Barraqué, Some Examples Drawn from his Unpublished Analysis of Anton Webern's *Piano Variations,* op. 27." In *Musical Grammars and Computer Analysis,* ed. M. Baroni and L. Callegari. Florence: L. S. Olschki, 1984: 131–153. (Quaderni della revista Italiana di musicologia 8)

2482. ———. "Informatique musicale: jonction nouvelle entre art et science." *Euro-Spectra* 13 (Mar. 1974): 2–15.
In French, German, Italian, and English.
RILM 74 1750.

2483. ———. "Un modèle informatique d'une pièce de Stravinsky." *Artinfo/ musinfo* 29 (1978): 1–27.

2484. Roads, Curtis. "Grammars as Representations for Music." *Computer Music Journal* 3,1 (Mar. 1979): 48–55.
Expanded and rev. version in *Foundations of Computer Music,* ed. Curtis Roads and John Strawn. Cambridge, Mass.: MIT Press, 1985: 403–42.
Italian version: "Le grammatiche comme rappresentazioni della musica" in *Musica e elaboratore,* ed. A. Vidolin. Venice: Biennale di Venezia, 1980: 139–51.
Review by M. Kassler in *Computing Reviews* 21 (Dec. 1980): 37,170.
C&CA 14 (1979): 34792. *C&IS* 24 (1980): 231505C.

2485. ———. "An Overview of Music Representations." In *Musical Grammars and Computer Analysis,* ed. M. Baroni and L. Callegari. Florence: L. S. Olschki, 1984: 7–37. (Quaderni della rivista Italiana di musicologia 8)

2486. Roark, Raleigh M. "A Low-Cost Micro-Processor Based Data-Acquisition System for Ethnomusicological Transcription." M.A. diss., University of Washington, 1977. 56 p.
RILM 78 3286.

2487. Robinson, Tobias D. "IML-MIR: A Data-Processing System for the Analysis of Music." In *Elektronische Datenverarbeitung in der Musikwissenschaft,* ed. Harald Heckmann. Regensburg: G. Bosse, 1967: 103–35.

2488. Rogers, John E. "Some Properties of Non-Duplicating Rotational Arrays." *Perspectives of New Music* 7 (Fall-Winter 1968): 80–102.

2489. ———. "Toward a System of Rotational Arrays." *Proceedings of the American Society of University Composers* 2 (1969): 61–74.

2490. Rohrer, Hermann G. "Musikalische Stilanalyse auf der Grundlage eines Modelles für Lernprozesse." Ph. D. diss., Erlangen, 1970. Published in Berlin by Siemens Aktiengesellschaft, 1970. 152 p.

2491. Roller, Gilbert H. "Development of a Method for Analysis of Musical Compositions Using an Electronic Digital Computer." *Journal of Research in Music Education* 13 (1965): 249–52.

2492. ———. "The Development of the Methods for Analysis of Musical Composition and for the Formation of a Symmetrical Twelve-Tone Row Using the Electronic Digital Computer." Ph. D. diss., Michigan State University, 1964. 487 p.
DA 25:2555.

2493. Rothgeb, John E. "Simulating Musical Skills by Digital Computer." In *Proceedings of the ACM National Conference.* New York: ACM, 1979: 121–25. Revised version in *Computer Music Journal* 4,2 (Summer 1980): 36–40.
C&CA 16 (1981): 21870. *C&IS* 29 (1982): 82–01632C.

2494. ———. "Some Uses of Mathematical Concepts in Theories of Music." *Journal of Music Theory* 10 (1966): 200–215.

2495. Rubenstein, Nancy O. "A FORTRAN Computer Program for Transcribing Franconian Rhythm." Ph. D. diss., Washington University, 1969. 147 p.
Review by Harry B. Lincoln in *Council for Research in Music Education Bulletin* 29 (Summer 1972): 39–41.
Abstract in *Computers and the Humanities* 8 (1974): 124–25.
DA 30:5474A. *RILM* 76 1608.

2496. Russell, Roberta C. "A Set of Microcomputer Programs to Aid in the Analysis of Atonal Music." D.M.A. diss., University of Oregon, 1983. 168 p.
DA 45:14A.

2497. Scherrer, Deborah K., and Philip K. Scherrer. "An Experiment in the Computer Measurement of Melodic Variation in Folksong." *Journal of American Folklore* 84 (1971): 230–41.

2498. Schiødt, Nanna. "A Computer-Aided Analysis of Thirty-Five Byzantine Hymns." In *Studies in Eastern Chant II,* ed. Milos Velimirovic. London: Oxford University Press, 1971.
RILM 71 3527.

2499. ———. "Data Processing Applied to Byzantine Chant." *Fontes Artis Musicae* 12 (1965): 122–23.

2500. ———, and Bjarner Svejgaard. "Application of Computer Techniques to the Analysis of Byzantine Sticherarion Melodies." In *Elektronische Datenverarbeitung in der Musikwissenschaft,* ed. Harald Heckmann. Regensburg: G. Bosse, 1967: 187–201.

2501. Schnell, Christoph. *Die Eingabe musikalischer Information als Teil eines Arbeitsintrumentes: ein Beitrag zur Computeranwendung in der Musikwissenschaft.* Bern; New York: P. Lang, 1985. 490 p. (Europäische Hochschulschriften. Reihe XXXVI, Musikwissenschaft Bd. 13)
Originally the author's thesis, Philosophische Fakultät, Universität Zürich, 1985.

2502. Selleck, John. "Computer Partitioning." *Proceedings of the American Society of University Composers* 7/8 (1972/1973): 90–110.

2503. ———, and Roger Bakeman. "Procedures for the Analysis of Form: Two Computer Applications." *Journal of Music Theory* 9 (1965): 281–93.

2504. Sentieri, Alfred R. "A Method for the Specification of Style Change in Music: A Computer-Aided Study of Selected Venetian Sacred Compositions from the Time of Gabrieli to the Time of Vivaldi." Ph. D. diss., Ohio State University, 1978. 244 p.
DA 39:2612A. *RILM* 78 4002.

2505. Simoni, Mary H. "The Computer Analysis of Atonal Music: An Application Program Using Set Theory." Ph. D. diss., Michigan State University, 1983. 125 p.
DA 45:14A.

2506. Simonton, Dean Keith. "Thematic Fame and Melodic Originality in Classical Music: A Multivariate Computer-Content Analysis." *Journal of Personality* 48 (1980): 206–19.

2507. Smith, Arthur T. "Charles Butler's *The Principles of Music in Singing and Setting, with the Twofold Use Thereof, Ecclesiastical and Civil* (1636): A Computer Assisted Transliteration of Book I and the First Chapter of Book II with Introduction, Supplementary Notes, Commentary, and Appendices." Ph. D. diss., Ohio State University, 1974. 558 p.
DA 35:5453A.

2508. Smoliar, Stephen W. "A Computer Aid for Schenkerian Analysis." In *Proceedings of the ACM National Conference*. New York: ACM, 1979: 110–59.
C&CA 16 (1981): 21871. *C&IS* 29 (1982): 82-00492C.

2509. ———. "Music Programs: An Approach to Music Theory Through Computational Linguistics." *Journal of Music Theory* 20 (1976): 105–31.
RILM 76 1628.

2510. ———. "Music Theory—A Programming Linguistic Approach." *Proceedings of the ACM Annual Conference, August 1972, Boston*. New York: ACM, 1972: 1001–14.
Review by Benjamin Suchoff in *Computing Reviews* 14 (1973): 25,015.
RILM 74 3885.

2511. ———. "Process Structuring and Music Theory." *Journal of Music Theory* 18 (1974): 308–36.
Also issued as University of Pennsylvania, Moore School of Electrical Engineering Technical Report, Philadelphia, May 1974.
RILM 74 3960.

2512. ———. "SCHENKER: A Computer Aid for Analysing Tonal Music." *SIGLASH Newsletter* 10 (Dec. 1976-Mar. 1977): 30–61.

2513.   ———. "Systematic Aspects of Musical Activity." *Gesellschaft für Informatik e. V. 3. Jahrestagung* (1973): 246–50.
Also issued as Israel Institute of Technology Computer Science Dept. Technical Report no. 28, Haifa, Israel, June 1973.
RILM 74 3951.

2514.   Snell, James L. "Computerized Hierarchical Generation of Tonal Compositions." Abstract in *Informatique et musique, Second Symposium International,* ed. Hélène Charnassé. Ivry: ELMERATTO, CNRS, 1983: 197.

2515.   ———. "Design for a Formal System for Deriving Tonal Music." M.A. thesis, State University of New York, Binghamton, 1979.

2516.   ———. "Design for a Formal System for Deriving Tonal Music." Paper presented at the Forty-fifth Annual Meeting of the American Musicological Society, meeting jointly with the Society for Music Theory, November 1–4, 1979, The Biltmore, New York City.

2517.   ———. "Design for a Formal System that Generates Tonal Music." Paper presented at the Symposium on Computer Studies in Music, 6–9 July 1979, Nottingham University, U.K.

2518.   Sorensen, Olve. "Metoder og metodeproblemer ved harmonisk analyse med EDB." [Methods and Problems of Methods in Harmonic Analysis with Electronic Data Processing] *Studia musicologica norvegica* 4 (1978): 201–16.
In Norwegian, summary in English.

2519.   Spiegel, Laurie. "Sonic Set Theory: A Tonal Music Theory for Computers." In *Proceedings, 2nd Symposium on Small Computers in the Arts, October 15–17, 1982, Philadelphia, Pa.* Los Angeles, Calif.: IEEE Computer Society, 1982: 15–21.
C&CA 18 (1983): 28833.

2520.   Spivacke, Harold. "A New Journal of Abstracts for Musicologists." *Computers and the Humanities* 2 (1967–68): 120–24.

2521.   Spyridis, H., and E. Roumeliotis. "Fourier Analysis and Information Theory on a Musical Composition." *Acustica* 52 (Mar. 1983): 255–62.
C&CA 18 (1983): 25668.

2522.   Stech, David A. "A Computer-Assisted Approach to Microanalysis of Melodic Lines." Ph. D. diss., Michigan State University, 1976. 840 p.
DA 37:3261A. *C&IS* 16:166008C.

2523.   ———. "A Computer-Assisted Approach to Microanalysis of Melodic Lines." *Computers and the Humanities* 15 (1981): 211–21.

2524.   Štědroň, Miloš. "K analyze vokalni melodiky Janáčekovy opěry *Věc Makropulos* s využitim samočinneho počitače." [Towards the Analysis of the Vocal Melodies in Janacek's Opera *Věc Makropulos* with the Use of Computers] *Hudebni Veda* 21,1 (1975): 46–64.
In Czech; summary in German.

2525. ———. "K intervalovým charakteristi kám jednot livých rolí v Janáčekově opěre *Věc Makropulos,* úvahy nad výsledky počítačové analýzy vokalní melodiky." [On the Interval Characteristics of the Individual Roles in Janácek's Opera *Věc Makropulos,* Reflections on the Results of a Computer Analysis] In *Lidová píseň a samočinný počítač 3. Sborník materiálůze 3. semináře o využití samočinného počítače při studiu lidové písně* (Brno 15.-16.10.1974), ed. Dušan Holý, Karel Pala, and Miloš Štědroň. Prague: Státní pedagogické nakladatelství, 1976: 263-85.
In Czech; summary in English.
RILM 76 1694.

2526. ———. "Možnosti interavlové a melodické analýsy." [The Possibility of Intervals and Melodic Analysis] *Opus musicum* 3 (1971): 202-8.
In Czech.

2527. ———. "Zjišt'ování typičnosti některých melodických struktur ve vokální melodice Janáčkovy opěry *Věc Makropulos* zapomoci SP." [Determination by Computer of Melodic Characteristics on the Vocal Music of Janácek's opera *Věc Makropulos*] *Musicologica Slovaca* 6 (1978): 187-98.
In Czech.
RILM 78 781.

2528. Steinbeck, Wolfram. *Struktur und Ähnlichkeit: Methoden automatisierter Melodieanalyse.* Kassel: Bärenreiter, 1982. 417 p.
Review in *Musikhandel* 34 (1983): 258.

2529. ———. "The Use of the Computer in the Analysis of German Folk Songs." *Computers and the Humanities* 10 (1976): 287-96.
C&CA 12 (1977): 19088. *C&IS* 16: 168934C. *RILM* 76 13472.

2530. ———. "Zur Methodik der Analyse deutscher volkstümlicher Lieder mit Hilfe elektronischer Rechenanlagen." In *Beiträge zur Musikgeschichte Nordeuropas: Kurt Gudewell zum 65. Geburtstag,* ed. Uwe Haensel. Wolfenbüttel: Möseler Verlag, 1978: 323-41.

2531. Stiles, G. S. "Spectral Music." *Interface Age* 4 (Mar. 1979): 56-63.
C&CA 14 (1979): 34798. *C&IS* 23 (1979): 221797C.

2532. Strange, Allen. "Toward an Isometric Pitch System." *Asterisk* 1 (May 1975): 13-22.

2533. Stroppa, Marco. "The Analysis of Electronic Music." *Contemporary Music Review* 1 (Oct. 1984): 175-80.
French version: "Sur l'analyse de la musique électronique." *Musique de notre temps* 1 (Oct. 1984): 187-93.

2534. ———. "Sull'analisi della musica elettronica." [On Electronic Musis Analysis] *Bollettino LIMB* 4 (1984): 69-70.

2535. Struble, William T. "Talking in Music Language with a Computer." *Computers and People* 25 (Jan. 1976): 33.

2536.   Styles, B. C. "Describing Music to a Computer." *International Journal of Man-Machine Studies* 6 (Jan. 1974): 125–34.
C&IS 12: 96369C. *CIJE* 6 (1974): EJ 096 629.

2537.   Suchoff, Benjamin. "Bartók, Ethnomusicology, and the Computer." *Institute for Computer Research in the Humanities Newsletter* 4 (Dec. 1968): 3–6.

2538.   ———. "A Bartóki népzenekutatás és as elektronikus számítógépek." [Folk Music Research According to Bartók and Computers] *Muzsica* 13 (July 1970): 6–8; 13 (Aug. 1970): 4–6.
In Hungarian.
Romanian version: "Aplicarea calculatoarelor electronice la etnomuzicologia bartokiană." [The Use of the Computer in the Ethnomusicological Method of Bartok] *Muzica* 20 (Nov. 1970): 10–14.
RILM 71 1306.

2539.   ———. "The Computer and Bartok Research in America." In *Magya zenetörteneti tanulmanyok mosonyi mihaly és Bartók Bela emlékére,* ed. Ferenc Bonis. Budapest: Zenemükiado, 1973: 313–27.
Also in *Journal of Research in Music Education* 19 (1971): 3–16.

2540.   ———. "Computer Applications to Bartók's Serbo-Croatian Material." *Tempo* 80 (Spring 1967): 15–19 + illus.

2541.   ———. "Computer-Oriented Comparative Musicology." In *The Computer and Music,* ed. Harry B. Lincoln. Ithaca: Cornell University Press, 1970: 193–206.

2542.   ———. "Computerized Folk Song Research and the Problem of Variants." *Computers and the Humanities* 2 (1967–68): 155–58.

2543.   ———. *GRIPHOS Application of Bartok's Turkish Folk Music Material.* Stony Brook: Center for Contemporary Arts and Letters, State University of New York at Stony Brook, 1975. 14 p. (Spectra Publication no. 1)
C&IS 16: 166004C. *ERIC:* ED 122 743.

2544.   ———. "Lexicographical Index of Maramures Vocal Melodies." In *Rumanian Folk Music,* Volume 5, by Bela Bartok. The Hague: Martinus Nijhoff, 1975: 270–94.
Review by Harry B. Lincoln in *Computers and the Humanities* 11 (1977): 319.

2545.   ———. "Lexicographical Index of Melodies." In *Rumanian Folk Music,* Volume 4, by Bela Bartok. The Hague: Martinus Nijhoff, 1975: 550–601.
Review by Harry B. Lincoln in *Computers and the Humanities* 11 (1977): 319.

2546.   ———. "Lexicographical Index of Turkish Vocal Melodies." In *Turkish Folk Music From Asia Minor,* by Bela Bartok. Princeton: Princeton University Press, 1976: 271–79.

2547.   ———. "Some Problems in Computer-Oriented Bartókian Ethnomusicology." *Ethnomusicology* 13 (1969): 489–97.
Romanian version, with French summary, in *Revista de etnografie si folclor* 14 (1969): 343–52.

2548. ———. *Yugoslav Folk Music.* New York: State University of New York Press, 1978. 4 v.
Review by Bernard Lortat-Jacob in *Fontes Artis Musicae* 27 (1980): 118–19.

2549. Sukho, Lee, and Young Kyung Ahn. "A Music Information Processing System." *Journal of the Korea Information Science Society* 9 (Nov. 1982): 1–12. *C&CA* 20 (1985): 30993.

2550. Sulitka, Andrej. "K problematike informácií a základnych údajov o lúdovej piesni pri spracování na SP." [Towards the Problem of Information and the Fundamental Description of Folk Songs by Working in Data Processing] In *Lidová píseň a samočinný počítač I,* ed. Dušan Holý and Oldřich Sirovátka. Brno: Klub uživatelů MSP, 1972: 103–10.
In Czech; summary in English.

2551. Sward, Rosalie L. "The Computer Assists in Attempting to Solve a Problem of Twentieth Century Music." In *Proceedings of the 1978 International Computer Music Conference,* comp. Curtis Roads. Evanston, Ill.: Northwestern University Press, 1979: 853–72.

2552. ———. "An Examination of the Mathematical Systems Used in Selected Compositions of Milton Babbitt and Iannis Xenakis." Ph. D. diss., Northwestern University, 1981. 609 p.
DA 42:1848A.

2553. Tabachnik, N. F. "Combinatorial Cantatas." *Yale Scientific Magazine* 48,3 (1974): 4–6.
C&IS 12: 98569C.

2554. Tänzer, Peter. "Der Computer als Lektor." *Musik und Bildung* 4 (1972): 461–65.
RILM 72 3964.
Review in *Computers and the Humanities* 9 (Mar. 1975): 88.

2555. Taranu, C. "Aspecte ale evolutiei conceptului despre ritm în muzica secolului nostru." [Aspects of the Evolution of the Concept Concerning Rhythm in the Music of Our Century] *Lucrari de muzicologie* 1 (1965): 81–82.
In Romanian; summaries in English, French, Italian, and Russian.

2556. Teitelbaum, Richard. "Intervallic Relations in Atonal Music." *Journal of Music Theory* 9 (1965): 72–127.

2557. Tenney, James. "The Chronological Development of Carl Ruggles' Melodic Style." *Perspectives of New Music* 16 (Fall 1977): 36–69.
RILM 77 5766.

2558. Tesar, Stanislav. "K možnostem využití SP v hymnologii." [On the Possibilities of Applying the Computer in Hymnology] In *Lidová píseň a samočinný počítač 3. Sborník materiálůze 3. semináře o využití samočinného počítače při studiu lidové písně* (Brno 15.–16.10.1974), ed. Dušan Holý, Karel Pala, and Miloš Štědroň. Prague: Státní pedagogické nakladatelství, 1976: 253–61.
In Czech; summary in English.
RILM 76 2014.

2559.   Trowbridge, Lynn M. "A Computer Programming System for Renaissance Music." Paper presented at the Annual Meeting of the American Musicological Society, Toronto, Nov. 1970.

2560.   ———. "The Fifteenth-Century French Chanson: A Computer-Aided Study of Styles and Style Change." Ph. D. diss., University of Illinois at Urbana-Champaign, 1982. 454 p.
        DA 42:4643A.

2561.   Tsuboi, K., and M. Ishizuka. "Melody Analysis of Japanese Folk Song Based on a Production System." In *Seventh International Conference on Pattern Recognition, Montreal, Quebec, Canada, 30 July-2 August 1984*. Silver Spring, Md.: IEEE Computer Society Press, 1984: v. 2, 714–16.
        C&CA 20 (1985): 25720.

2562.   Urup, Henning. "Danske folkedanse. En beskrivelse og undersøgelse af det Danske folkelige melodistof med hertil hørende danse beskrivelser." [Danish Folk Dances: A Description and Examination of the Danish Folk Music with Dance Descriptions] M.A. diss., University of Copenhagen, 1972. 167 p.
        In Danish.
        RILM 75 2196.

2563.   ———. "Registrering af spillemands musik med henblik pa databehanding." [Registration of Folk-Dance Tunes for Data-Processing] *Dansk aarbog for musikforskning* 6 (1968–72): 236–39.
        In Danish.
        RILM 75 2197.

2564.   Vaglio, Anthony J. "The Compositional Significance of Joseph Schillinger's *System of Musical Composition* as Reflected in the Works of Edwin Gerschefski." Ph. D. diss., University of Rochester, Eastman School of Music, 1977. 413 p.
        DA 38:5119A. *RILM* 77 1641.

2565.   Vendome, Richard. "The Calculation and Evaluation of Keyboard Temperaments by Computer." In *Informatique et musique, Second Symposium International*, ed. Hélène Charnassé. Ivry: ELMERATTO, CNRS, 1983: 227–42.

2566.   Vikis-Freibergs, Vaira, and Imants F. Freibergs. "The Sun-Songs of Latvian Folklore: A Computer-Accessible Corpus." *Journal of Baltic Studies* 9 (Spring 1978): 20–31.
        RILM 78 3536.

2567.   Vogel, Martin. *Die Lehre von den Tonbeziehungen. Orpheus Schriftenreihe zu Grundfragen der Musik 16*. Bonn: Verlag für Systematische Musikwissenschaft, 1975. 480 p.
        RILM 76 4448.

2568. Waeltner, Ernst. "Plan und Durchführung des 'Lexicon Musicum Latinum' II: Archivaufbau mit Hilfe maschineller Datenverarbeitung." In *Bericht über den Internationalen Musikwissenschaftlichen Kongress [der Gesellschaft für Musikforschung], Kassel 1962,* ed. Georg Reichert and Martin Just. Kassel: Bärenreiter, 1963: 351–52.

2569. Wagner, Christoph. "Experimentelle Untersuchungen über das Tempo." *Österreichische Musikzeitschrift* 12 (1974): 589–604.
RILM 76 4026.

2570. Wedgewood, Richard B. "The Music Theories of Camille Durutte: A Contribution to the Study of Nineteenth Century French Music Theory." Ph. D. diss., University of Wisconsin, 1976. 254 p.
DA 37:2490A. *RILM* 76 4045.

2571. Wenker, Jerome R. "A Computational Method for the Analysis of Anglo-American Folksongs." M.A. thesis, Indiana University, 1964.

2572. ———. "Computer-Aided Analysis of Anglo-Canadian Folktunes." Ph. D. diss., Indiana University, 1978. 706 p.
CR 21 (1980): 36,337. *C&IS* 25 (1980): 243460C. *DA* 40:1001A. *RILM* 78 1386.

2573. ———. "A Computer-Aided Analysis of Canadian Folksongs." In *Computing in the Humanities: Proceedings of the Third International Conference on Computing in the Humanities Sponsored by the University of Montreal and the University of Waterloo, August 2–6, 1977 at Waterloo, Ontario,* ed. Serge Lusignan and John S. North. Waterloo, Ont.: The University of Waterloo Press, 1977: 221–31.
Review by G. Logan in *Computing Reviews* 19 (1978): 33105.
C&CA 13 (1978): 13039. *C&IS* 17: 185324C.

2574. ———. "A Computer Oriented Music Notation Including Ethnomusicological Symbols." In *Musicology and the Computer,* ed. Barry S. Brook. New York: City University of New York Press, 1970: 91–129.

2575. ———. "A Method of Preparing Music for Computer Analysis." Mimeographed. Bloomington: Indiana University, 1962.

2576. ———. "MUSTRAN II: A Foundation for Computational Musicology." In *Computers in the Humanities,* ed. J. L. Mitchell. Minneapolis: University of Minnesota Press, 1974: 267–80.

2577. ———, and Portia K. Maultsby. "An Overview of Some Analysis Programs." Mimeographed. Bloomington, Ind.: Indiana University. n.d. 19 p.

2578. Whitby-Strevens, C. "The Harmonic Movement of Bach Chorales." *Bulletin of the Institute of Mathematics and Its Applications* 6 (Apr. 1970): 73–76.

2579. Whitney, T. G. "Music Analysis: SLAM Simplified, or, How the Computer Compares 16th Century Bourgeois with Eighteenth Century Bach." *Creative Computing* 3 (Mar.-Apr. 1977): 88–90.
C&CA 12 (1977): 23189.

2580. Willis, Thomas C. "Music in Orchestra Hall: A Pilot Study in the Use of Computers and other Data Processing Equipment for Research in the History of Musical Performance." Ph. D. diss., Northwestern University, 1966. 286 p. *DA* 27:2172A.

2581. Winckel, Fritz. "Das Werkgefüge von Musikstrukturen in der Analyse durch Computer und Kybernetik." In *Festschrift Kurt Blaukopf*, ed. Irmgard Bontinck and Otto Brusatti. Vienna: Universal Edition, 1975: 156–63. *RILM* 76 1923.

2582. Winograd, Terry. "Linguistics and the Computer Analysis of Tonal Harmony." *Journal of Music Theory* 12 (1968): 2–49.

2583. Wittlich, Gary E. "Programming a Computer for Music Analysis." *Your Musical Cue* 5 (Apr. 1969): 3–13.

2584. Wolff, Anthony B. "Problems of Representation in Musical Computing." *Computers and the Humanities* 11 (1977): 3–12. *CA* 22 (1978): 3549. *C&CA* 13 (1978): 29115. *C&IS* 19 (1978): 201786C. *RILM* 77 1538.

2585. Wright, Maurice. "Alpha-Numeric Music System." *Dr. Dobb's Journal of Computer Calisthenics and Orthodontia* 1,5 (1976): 148–54. *C&IS* 18 (1978): 189703C.

2586. Youngblood, Joseph E. "Root Progression and Composer Identification." In *The Computer and Music,* ed. Harry B. Lincoln. Ithaca: Cornell University Press, 1970: 172–78.

2587. Zemanek, Heinz H. "Aspekte der Informationsverarbeitung und Computeranwendung in der Musik." In *Experimentelle Music. Raum-Music, Visuelle Music, Medien Musik, Wort Musik, Elektronik Musik, Computer Music. Internationale Woche für Experimentelle Music 1968,* ed. Fritz Winckel. Berlin: Mann, 1970: 59–72.

2588. Zilynskyj, Orest. "Text lidové písně jako předmět strojového rozboru." [Text of Folksongs as a Subject of Machine Analysis] In *Lidová píseň a samočinný počítač I,* ed. Dušan Holý and Oldřich Sirovátka. Brno: Klub uživatelů MSP, 1972: 97–102. In Czech; summary in English.

2589. Zimmerly, John D. "A Computer-Assisted Study of Selected Kyries from the Parody Masses of Clemens Non Papa." M.A. thesis, Michigan State University, 1978. 96 p. *Masters Abstracts* 17 (1979): 150.

PROGRAMMING LANGUAGES AND SOFTWARE SYSTEMS

2590. Abbott, Curtis. "Machine Tongues I." *Computer Music Journal* 2,1 (July 1978): 4–8, 18.

2591. ———. "Machine Tongues II." *Computer Music Journal* 2,2 (Sept. 1978): 4–6.

2592. ———. "Machine Tongues III." *Computer Music Journal* 2,3 (Dec. 1978): 7–9.
C&IS 22 (1978): 214533C.

2593. ———. "Machine Tongues V." *Computer Music Journal* 3,2 (June 1979): 6–11, 28.

2594. Balaban, Mira, and Neil V. Murray. "Machine Tongues X: Prolog." *Computer Music Journal* 9,3 (Fall 1985): 7–12.

2595. Berg, Paul. "A User's Manual for SSP." Utrecht: Institute of Sonology, 1978.

2596. Brainerd, Robert F. "Two Musical Applications of Computer Programming." Buffalo: National Science Foundation Project No. GK- 14191, Sept. 1972. 125 p. (Technical Report no. 3)

2597. Brown, Frank. "The Language Scriptu." *Interface* 6 (1977): 9–28.
RILM 77 3741.

2598. Byrd, Donald. "An Integrated Computer Music Software System." *Computer Music Journal* 1,2 (Apr. 1977): 55–60.
C&IS 18 (1978): 189691. *RILM* 77 5646.

2599. ———. "JANUS 2.1 User's Guide." Bloomington: Indiana University, Dec. 6, 1974. 5 p.

2600. Durham, T. "If Music Be the Food of Love, Program On." *Computer Magazine* (Nov. 8, 1984): 26–27.
C&CA 20 (1985): 11172.

2601.   Forte, Allen. *SNOBOL 3 Primer: An Introduction to the Computer Program-*
        ming Language. Cambridge: MIT Press, 1967.
        Review in *Computers and the Humanities* 2 (1968): 256–62.

2602.   Gena, Peter. "MUSICOL Manual, Version I." Buffalo, N.Y.: National Sci-
        ence Foundation Project No. GK–14191, May 1973. (Technical Report no. 7)

2603.   Greussay, Patrick. *Initiation à la programmation en LISP 510.* Paris: Institut
        d'intelligence artificielle, UER linguistique-informatique, Université Paris
        VIII, Fev. 1974. 74 p.

2604.   ———. "MUSIQUE: descriptions de procedures de lecture, procedures de
        description de lectures, procedures de lecture de procedures." *Artinfo/musinfo*
        19 (1974): 1–30.

2605.   ———. "S-Expressions." In *T-5, The Rational and Irrational in Visual*
        Research Today, Match of Ideas [Symposium], June 2, 1973. Zagreb: Galerija
        suvremene umjetnosti, 1973: 151–56.

2606.   Hofstetter, Fred T. "A Computer System for Musical Description." *Journal of*
        the Graduate Music Students at the Ohio State University 3 (Spring 1972): 4–42.

2607.   Holtzman, Steven R. "The Edinburgh GGDL Composition/Synthesis
        System." In *Computer Music in Britain, 8th–11th April 1980.* London: Electro-
        Acoustic Music Association of Great Britain, 1980: 17–20.

2608.   Kemeny, John G., and Thomas E. Kurtz. *Basic Programming.* 3rd ed. New
        York: J. Wiley, 1980: 314–23.

2609.   Kornfeld, William. "Machine Tongues VII: LISP." *Computer Music Journal*
        4,2 (Summer 1980): 6–12.

2610.   Levitt, David A. "Machine Tongues X. Constraint Languages." *Computer*
        Music Journal 8,1 (Spring 1984): 9–21.
        C&CA 19 (1984): 35007.

2611.   Lieberman, Henry. "Machine Tongues IX: Object-Oriented Programming."
        Computer Music Journal 6,3 (Fall 1982): 8–21.
        C&CA 18 (1983): 5957.

2612.   Powell, Roger. "Introduction to Assembly Language." *Keyboard* 7 (July
        1981): 74.
        Reprinted as "Home Computers as Sequencers: Introduction to Assembly
        Language." In *Synthesizers and Computers.* Milwaukee, Wis.: H. Leonard
        Pub. Corp., 1985: 41–42.

2613.   Reitman, Walter R. "Information Processing Languages and Heuristic Pro-
        grams: A New Stage in the Bead Game." In *Bionics Symposium: Living*
        Prototypes—The Key to New Technology, 13-14-15 September 1960. Wright-
        Patterson Air Force Base, Ohio: Directorate of Advanced Systems Tech-
        nology, Wright Air Development Division, Air Research and Development
        Command, U.S. Air Force, 1960: 409–17. (WADD Technical Report 60–600)

2614. Roads, Curtis. "Machine Tongues IV." *Computer Music Journal* 3,1 (Mar. 1979): 8–13.
C&CA 14 (1979): 33897. *C&IS* 24 (1980): 230390C.

2615. ———. "Machine Tongues VI." *Computer Music Journal* 3,4 (Dec. 1979): 6–8.

2616. Robinson, Tobias D. "A Short Description of the MIR Compiler." Mimeographed. Princeton: Princeton University Music Dept.

PSYCHOLOGY AND PSYCHOACOUSTICS

2617. Bamberger, Jeanne. "Capturing Intuitive Knowledge in Procedural Descriptions." Paper presented at the International Conference on Computer Music, October 28–31, 1976, Massachusetts Institute of Technology.

2618. ———. "Developing a Musical Ear: A New Experiment." Cambridge, Mass.: M.I.T. Artificial Intelligence Laboratory, July 1972. 17 p. (Memo no. 264)

2619. ———. "Logo Music Projects: Experiments in Musical Perception and Design." Cambridge, Mass.: M.I.T. Artificial Intelligence Laboratory, May 1979. (Memo no. 523)

2620. ———. "The Luxury of Necessity." Cambridge, Mass.: M.I.T. Artificial Intelligence Laboratory, Dec. 1974. 23 p. (Memo no. 312)

2621. ———. "What's in a Tune." Cambridge, Mass.: M.I.T. Artificial Intelligence Laboratory, Nov. 1974. 51 p. (Memo no. 314)

2622. Batel, Günther. "Über die Komponenten der Musik: Eine Statistische Untersuchung in der Musik-psychologie." *R.E.L.O. revue* 4 (1976): 13–35.

2623. Beauchamp, James W. "Discrimination of Small but Significant Differences in Synthetic Tone Quality: A Pilot Study." Paper presented at the Iowa Acoustics Colloquium, University of Iowa, 1985.

2624. Bianchini, L. "Struttura, formalizzazione, percezione estetica nella musica per elaboratore." [Structure, Formalization, and Aesthetic Perceptions in Computer Music] *Quaderni di informatica musicale* 5 (1984): 51–59.

2625. Biock, Hans-Reinhard. "Zur Intonationsbeurteilung Kontextbezogener Sukzessiver Intervalle." Ph.D. diss., University of Cologne, 1975. Published by Regensburg: Bosse, 1975. 190 p. (Kölner Beitrage zur Musikforschung 82) *RILM* 76 7620.

2626. Bird, R. "Computer-Controlled System for Recording Modification and Presentation of Two-Channel Musical Stimuli." *Behavior Research Methods and Instrumentation* 8 (1976): 24–28.

2627.   Blesser, Barry A. "Perceptual Issues in Digital Processing of Music." In *ICASSP 81 Proceedings: IEEE International Conference on Acoustics, Speech, and Signal Processing, March 30, 31, April 1, 1981, Atlanta, Georgia.* New York: IEEE, 1981: vol. 2, 583–86.
C&CA 16 (1981): 30818.

2628.   Bly, Sara Ann. "Sound and Computer Information Presentation." Ph.D. diss., University of California, Davis, 1982. 116 p.

2629.   Bolognesi, Tommaso; Mario Milani; and Leonello Tarabella. *Tre esperienze di psico-acustica musicale.* [Three Experiences in Psychoacoustic Music] Pisa: CNUCE, 1977. 34 p.

2630.   Bregman, Albert S., and Alexander I. Rudnicky. "Auditory Segregation: Stream or Streams?" *Journal of Experimental Psychology: Human Perception and Performance* 1 (1975): 263–67.

2631.   Campbell, Warren C. "A Computer Simulation of Musical Performance Adjudication." *Experimental Research in the Psychology of Music* 7 (1971): 1–40.
RILM 73 4496.

2632.   Charbonneau, Gérard. "Timbre and the Perceptual Effects of Three Types of Data Reduction." *Computer Music Journal* 5,2 (Summer 1981): 10–19.
C&CA 17 (1982): 8909.

2633.   ———, and Jean-Claude Risset. "Acoustique: circularité de jugements de hauteur sonore." *Comptes rendus hebdomadaires des séances de l'Académie des sciences,* Série B 277 (Nov. 26, 1973): 623–26.

2634.   Charles, Daniel. "L'eterno ritorno del timbro." [The Eternal Return of Timbre] In *Musica e elaboratore.* Venice: Biennale di Venezia, 1980: 95–99.

2635.   Clynes, Manfred. "The Code of Musicality—Incorporated into Real Time Computer Performance." In *Proceedings of the Rochester 1983 International Computer Music Conference,* comp. Robert W. Gross. San Francisco, Calif.: Computer Music Association, 1984: 91–99.

2636.   Cohen, Annabel J.; Paul Isaacs; Sam Flores; David Harrison; and J. Bradley. "The Computer as Interdisciplinary Catalyst: Music and Psychology." In *Computing in the Humanities: Proceedings of the Third International Conference of Computing in the Humanities Sponsored by the University of Montreal and the University of Waterloo, August 2–6, 1977 at Waterloo, Ontario,* ed. Serge Lusignan and John S. North. Waterloo, Ont.: The University of Waterloo Press, 1977: 197–207.
C&CA 13 (1978): 13037. *C&IS* 17: 185328C.

2637.   Dannenbring, Gary L., and Albert S. Bregman. "The Effect of Silence on Auditory Stream Segregation." *Journal of the Acoustical Society of America* 59 (1976): 987–89.

2638.   ———, and Albert S. Bregman. "Stream Segregation and the Illusion of Overlap." *Journal of Experimental Psychology: Human Perception and Performance* 2 (1976): 544–55.

2639.   De Berardinis, P. T.; C. Costantini; and M. Piccinino. "Audioterapia: utilizzazione del suono a sintesi digitale a fini terapeutici." [Audiotherapy: Using Digital Synthesis Sounds for Therapeutic Purposes] In *Atti del Quinto Colloquio di Informatica Musicale*. Ancona: Università di Ancona, 1983: 159–75.

2640.   Doati, R. "Un'applicazione musicale della teoria gestaltica sulla percezione di strutture temporali." [An Application in Music of Gestalt Theory on Perception of Time Structures] In *Atti del Quinto Colloquio di Informatica Musicale*. Pisa: CNUCE-CNR, 1981: 313–316.

2641.   Ehresman, David E., and David L. Wessel. *Perception of Timbral Analogies*. Paris: IRCAM, 1978. 29 p. (Rapports IRCAM 13/78)
RILM 78 4274.

2642.   Evans, Stanford. "The Aural Perception of Mathematical Structures." *Proceedings of the American Society of University Composers* 6 (1971): 46–48.

2643.   Forsythe, Rosemary. "The Development and Implementation of a Computerized Preschool Measure of Musical Audiation." Ph.D. diss., Case Western Reserve University, 1984. 348 p.
DA 45:2433A.

2644.   Goguen, Joseph A. "Complexity of Hierarchically Organized Systems and the Structure of Musical Experiences." *International Journal of General Systems* 3 (1976): 233–51.

2645.   Gordon, John W. "Perception of Attack Transients in Musical Tones." Stanford, Calif.: CCRMA, Dept. of Music, Stanford University, 1984. 138 p. (Report no. STAN-M-17)

2646.   ———. "Perceptual Attack Time of Orchestral Instrument Tones." Paper presented at the 1982 International Computer Music Conference, Sept. 27–Oct. 1, Venice.

2647.   ———, and John M. Grey. "Perception of Spectral Modifications on Orchestral Instrument Tones." *Computer Music Journal* 2,1 (July 1978): 24–31.
C&IS 20 (1978): 207145C.

2648.   Grey, John M. "Exploration of Musical Timbre Using Computer-Based Techniques for Analysis, Synthesis and Perceptual Scaling." Ph.D. diss., Stanford University, 1975. 159 p.
Reprinted as *An Exploration of Musical Timbre*. Stanford, Calif.: Center for Computer Research in Music and Acoustics, Dept. of Music, Stanford University, 1975. (Report no. STAN-M-2)
C&IS 15: 140513C. *DA* 36:1945B.

2649.   ———. "Multidimensional Perceptual Scaling of Musical Timbre." *Journal of the Acoustical Society of America* 61 (May 1977): 1270–77.

2650.   ———. "Timbre Discrimination in Musical Patterns." *Journal of the Acoustical Society of America* 64 (1978): 467–72.

2651.   ———, and John W. Gordon. "Perception of Spectral Modifications on Orchestral Instrument Timbres." *Journal of the Acoustical Society of America* 63 (May 1978): 1493–1500.

2652.   ———, and James A. Moorer. "Perceptual Evaluations of Synthesized Musical Instrument Tones." *Journal of the Acoustical Society of America* 62 (Aug. 1977): 454–62.

2653.   Heller, Jack J., and Warren C. Campbell. *Computer Analysis of the Auditory Characteristics of Musical Performance.* Washington: U.S. Dept. of H.E.W., Office of Education, 1972. 124 p.
ERIC: ED 065 442. *RILM, 73* 2761.

2654.   Henning, Margherita M. "An Experiment Designed to Investigate the Use of Music as a Diagnostic Tool in Psychopathology." Ph.D. diss., University of New Mexico, 1966. 143 p.
DA 28:3505A.

2655.   Howe, Hubert S. "Timbral Structures for Computer Music." In *Proceedings of the 1978 International Computer Music Conference,* comp. Curtis Roads. Evanston, Ill.: Northwestern University Press, 1979: 214–24.

2656.   Kawano, Hiroshi. "The Informational Analysis of Musical Communication." *Journal of the Japanese Musicological Society* 15, 3–4: 1–21.
In Japanese.

2657.   Konecni, Valdimir J., and Dianne Sargent-Pollock. "Choice Between Melodies Differing in Complexity under Divided-Attention Conditions." *Journal of Experimental Psychology: Human Perception and Performance* 2 (Aug. 1976): 347–56.
CIJE 9 (1977): EJ 152 876.

2658.   Laske, Otto E. "Essays on Psychomusicology." In *Music and Mind.* Boston, Mass.: O. Laske, 1981: 254–304.

2659.   ———. "The Information-Processing Approach to Musical Cognition." *Interface* 3 (Dec. 1974): 108–36.
Also in *Music and Mind.* Boston, Mass.: O. Laske, 1981: 63–78.
C&CA 10 (1975): 17421.
Originally appeared as "Information-Processing Psychology Today: Its Problems and Methods." Subfaculteit Psychologie, State University of Utrecht, The Netherlands, May 1974. (Onderzoeks-memorandum AMS-3)

2660.   ———. *Music, Memory, and Thought: Explorations in Cognitive Musicology.* Ann Arbor, Mich.: University Microfilms International, 1977. 342 p.
RILM 77 3984.

2661.   ———. "Musical Acoustics (Sonology): A Questionable Science Reconsidered." *Numus-West* 6 (1974): 35–40.

2662.   ———. "Musical Semantics, a Procedural Point of View." *Proceedings of the 1st International Congress on Semiotics of Music, Beograd, 17–21 Oct. 1973.* Pesaro: Centro di Iniziativa Culturale, 1975: 214–24.

2663.   ———. "On Psychomusicology." *International Review of the Aesthetics and Sociology of Music* 6 (Winter 1975): 21–40. Also in *Music and Mind.* Boston, Mass.: O. Laske, 1981: 245–53.

2664.   ———. "Toward a Theory of Musical Cognition." *Interface* 4 (Dec. 1975): 147–208. Also appears as Onderzoeksmemorandum AMS-10, Subfaculteit Psychologie, Afdeling Methodolgie en Statistiek, State University of Utrecht, The Netherlands, May 1975. 87 p.

2665.   ———. "Toward a Theory of User Interfaces for Computer Music System." Paper presented at the International Conference on Computer Music, October 28–31, 1976, Massachusetts Institute of Technology.

2666.   ———. "Toward an Explicit Cognitive Theory of Musical Listening." *Computer Music Journal* 4,2 (Summer 1980): 73–83. Also in *Music and Mind.* Boston, Mass.: O. Laske, 1981: 111–22. *C&CA* 16 (1981): 21874. *C&IS* 29 (1982): 82–01630C.

2667.   ———. "Understanding the Behavior of Users of Interactive Computer Music Systems." *Interface* 7 (1978): 159–68. Also in *Music, Memory, and Thought,* Chapter 4. Ann Arbor, Mich.: University Microfilms International. Also in *Music and Mind.* Boston, Mass.: O. Laske, 1981: 139–48. *C&CA* 14 (1979): 14057.

2668.   Letowski, T. "Difference Limen for Nonlinear Distortion in Sine Signals and Musical Sounds." *Acustica* 34 (1975): 106–10.

2669.   Longuet-Higgins, H. Christopher. "Perception of Melodies." *Nature* 263 (1976): 646–53. *C&CA* 12 (1977): 2412.

2670.   ———. "The Perception of Music." *Interdisciplinary Science Reviews* 3 (June 1978): 148–56. *C&CA* 14 (1979): 5271.

2671.   Manoury, Philippe. "La flèche du temps." *Cahier musique* 3 (1983): 22–33. English version: "The Arrow of Time." *Contemporary Music Review* 1 (Oct. 1984): 131–45. Reprinted in *Music de notre temps* 1 (Oct. 1984): 139–55.

2672.   ———. "The Role of the Conscious." *Contemporary Music Review* 1 (Oct. 1984): 147–56. French version: "La part consciente." *Musique de notre temps* 1 (Oct. 1984): 157–66.

2673. Martens, William L. "Palette: An Environment for Developing an Individualized Set of Psychophysically Scaled Timbres." In *Proceedings of the International Computer Music Conference, 1985,* ed. Barry Truax. San Francisco, Calif.: Computer Music Association, 1985: 355–65.

2674. ———. "Psychophysical Scaling of Synthetic Timbres: An Essential Step in Interfacing the User and Synthesis Software." Paper presented at the 1984 International Computer Music Conference, Oct. 19–23, Paris, France.

2675. Mathews, Max V. "Analysis and Synthesis of Timbres." In *Music Room and Acoustics.* Stockholm: Royal Swedish Academy of Music, 1977: 4–18.

2676. ———, and Joan E. Miller. "Pitch Quantizing for Computer Music." Abstract in *Journal of the Acoustical Society of America* 38 (1965): 913.

2677. ———, and John R. Pierce. *Harmony and Nonharmonic Partials.* Paris: IRCAM, 1980. (Rapports IRCAM 28/80)

2678. McAdams, Stephen E. "The Auditory Image: A Metaphor for Musical and Psychological Research on Auditory Organization." In *Cognitive Processes in the Perception of Art,* ed. W. Ray Crozier and Anthony J. Chapman. Amsterdam: North-Holland, 1984: 289–323. (Advances in Psychology 19)

2679. ———. "Fusione spettrale e la creazione di immagini uditive." [Spectral Fusion and the Creation of Auditory Images] *Bollettino LIMB* 2 (1982): 36–51.

2680. ———. "Spectral Fusion and the Creation of One or More Voices with the Same Spectrum." Paper presented at the 1980 International Computer Music Conference, November 13–15, 1980, Queens College of the City University of New York.

2681. ———, and Albert S. Bregman. "Hearing Musical Streams." *Computer Music Journal* 3,4 (Dec. 1979): 26–43, 60, 63.
Reprinted in *Foundations of Computer Music,* ed. Curtis Roads and John Strawn. Cambridge, Mass.: MIT Press 1985: 658–98.
C&CA 15 (1980): 22350. *C&IS* 25 (1980): 243456C. *CR* 21 (Sept. 1980): 36,764.

2682. ———, and Albert S. Bregman. "The Perceptual Factoring of Acoustic Sequences into Musical Streams." In *Proceedings of the 1978 International Computer Music Conference,* comp. Curtis Roads. Evanston, Ill.: Northwestern University Press, 1979: 501–81.

2683. ———; Serge Gladkoff; and Jean-Pierre Keller. "AISE: A Prototype Laboratory for Musical Research and the Development of Conceptual Tools." In *Proceedings of the International Computer Music Conference, 1984,* ed. William Buxton. San Francisco, Calif.: Computer Music Association, 1985: 143–61.

2684. ———, and Kaija Saariaho. "Qualities and Functions of Musical Timbre." In *Proceedings of the International Computer Music Conference, 1985,* ed. Barry Truax. San Francisco, Calif.: Computer Music Association, 1985: 367–74.

2685. ———, and David L. Wessel. "A General Synthesis Package Based on Princi-
ples of Auditory Perception." Abstract in *Proceedings, 1981 International
Computer Music Conference, November 5–8,* comp. Larry Austin and Thomas
Clark. Denton, Tex.: North Texas State University, 1983: 308.

2686. McCarthy, James F. "The Pitch Test." *Creative Computing* 10 (Mar. 1984):
211–12, 216–17.
C&CA 19 (1984): 31865.

2687. Millar, Jana Kubitza. "The Aural Perception of Pitch-Class Set Relations: A
Computer-Assisted Investigation." Ph.D. diss., North Texas State University,
1984. 237 p.
DA 45:679A.

2688. Moorer, James A. *On the Loudness of Complex, Time-Variant Tones.* Stanford, Calif.: Center for Computer Research in Music and Acoustics, Dept. of
Music, Stanford University, 1975. (Report no. STAN-M-4)

2689. Morton, Ian A. "Analysis of Tonal Music at the Level of Perception." In
Computers in the Humanities, ed. J. L. Mitchell. Minneapolis: University of
Minnesota Press, 1974: 261–66.

2690. Nosselt, Volker. "The Problem of 'Klingen' in the Context of Acoustical Theories." Paper presented at the 2nd Central Europe Section, Convention of the
Audio Engineering Society, Mar. 14–16, 1972, Munich.

2691. Pedersen, Paul. "The Mel Scale." *Journal of Music Theory* 9 (1965): 295–308.

2692. "People, Places, Programs." *Behavioral Science* 4 (1959): 170–72.

2693. Pierce, John R., and Max V. Mathews. "Control of Consonance and Dissonance with Nonharmonic Overtones." In *Music by Computers,* ed. Heinz von
Foerster and James W. Beauchamp. New York: Wiley, 1969: 129–32.

2694. Piszczalski, Martin B., and Bernard A. Galler. "A Computational Model of
Music Listening." In *Proceedings, Graphics Interface '82,* ed. K. B. Evans and
E. M. Kidd. Ottawa: National Research Council of Canada, 1982: 89–96.
C&CA 18 (1983): 7243. *C&IS* 31 (1983): 83–3046C.

2695. ———, and Bernard A. Galler. "A Computer Model of Music Recognition."
In *Music, Mind, and the Brain,* ed. Manfred Clynes. New York: Plenum Press,
1982: 399–416.

2696. ———, and Bernard A. Galler. "Perceptual Organization in Music Lis-
tening." In *Proceedings, 1981 International Computer Music Conference,
November 5–8,* comp. Larry Austin and Thomas Clark. Denton, Tex.: North
Texas State University, 1983: 299–307.

2697. Randall, J. K. "Theories of Musical Structure as a Source for Problems in
Psychoacoustical Research." Abstract in *Journal of the Acoustical Society of
America* 39 (1966): 1245.

2698. Rasch, Rudi. "Muziekwaarnemingsonderzoek en de computer." [Music Perception Research and the Computer] *Mens en melodie* 33 (1978): 289–94.

2699. Reitman, Walter R. "Creative Problem Solving: Notes from the Autobiography of a Fugue." In the author's *Cognition and Thought, An Information-Processing Approach.* New York: J. Wiley, 1965: 166–80.

2700. Risset, Jean-Claude. *Hauteur et timbre des sons.* Paris: IRCAM, 1978. 18 p. (Rapports IRCAM 11/78)
Also in *Bulletin d'audiophonologie* 8,3 (1978): 7–26.
RILM 78 4355.

2701. ———. "Musical Acoustics." In *Handbook of Perception,* Vol. IV. ed. Edward C. Carterette and Morton P. Friedman. New York: Academic Press, 1978: 521–64.

2702. ———. *Musical Acoustics.* Paris: IRCAM, 1978. 56 p. (Rapports IRCAM 8/78)
RILM 78 4289.

2703. ———. *Paradoxes de hauteur.* Paris: IRCAM, 1978. 10 p. (Rapports IRCAM 10/78)
RILM 78 4356.

2704. ———. "Paradoxes de hauteur: le concept de hauteur n'est pas le meme pour tout le monde." In *Proceedings of the 7th International Conference on Acoustics.* Budapest: Akademiai Krado, 1971: vol. 3, 613–16.

2705. ———. "Pitch Control and Pitch Paradoxes Demonstrated with Computer-Synthesized Sounds." Abstract in *Journal of the Acoustical Society of America* 46 (1969): 88.

2706. ———. "Pitch Paradoxes Demonstrated with Computer-Synthesized Sounds." Murray Hill: Bell Telephone Laboratories, 1970.

2707. ———. "Some Recent Developments in Computer-Generated Tone Qualities." Paper presented at the 36th Convention of the Audio Engineering Society, Apr. 1969, Los Angeles.
Abstract in *Journal of the Audio Engineering Society* 17 (1969): 348.

2708. ———. "Sur l'analyse, la synthèse, et la perception des sons etudiées à l'aide de calculateurs électroniques." Thèse de doctorat, Paris-Orsay, 1967. 128 p. Abstract in French in *French Language Dissertations in Music.* New York: Pendragon Press, 1979.

2709. ———, and Max V. Mathews. "Computer-Synthesized Sounds and Tone Quality Studies." In *Proceedings of the 7th International Congress on Acoustics.* Budapest: Akadémiai Kiado, 1971: v. 1, 261–64.

2710. ———, and David L. Wessel. "Exploration of Timbre by Analysis and Synthesis." In *The Psychology of Music,* ed. D. Deutsch. New York: Academic Press, 1982: 25–58.

2711. ———, and David L. Wessel. "Indagine sul timbre mediante analisi e sintesi." [Research on Timbre Using Analysis and Synthesis] *Bollettino LIMB* 2 (1982): 12–35.

2712.   Rogers, John E.; John Rockstroh; and Philip Batstone. "Music-Time and Clock-Time Similarities Under Tempo Change." Paper presented at the 1980 International Computer Music Conference, November 13–15, 1980, Queens College of the City University of New York.

2713.   Rosenboom, David. "A Model for Detection and Analysis of Information Processing Modalities in the Nervous System Through an Adaptive, Interactive, Computerized, Electronic Music Instrument." In *Proceedings of the Second Annual Music Computation Conference, November 7–9, 1975 at the University of Illinois at Urbana-Champaign. Part 4, Information Processing Systems,* comp. James Beauchamp and John Melby. Urbana, Ill.: University of Illinois: 54–78.

2714.   Rosenstein, Milton. "Computer-Generated Pure Tones and Noise and Its Application to Psychoacoustics." *Journal of the Audio Engineering Society* 21 (1973): 121–26.

2715.   Rothenberg, David. "A Mathematical Model for Measurement and Classification of Context Embedded Stimuli." New York: New York University Data Processing and Computation Laboratory, 1964. Air Force Office of Scientific Research Grant No. AF-AFOSR 484–64.

2716.   ———. "The Measurement of Vocalic and Tonal Contexts." New York: New York University Data Processing and Computation Laboratory, 1964. Air Force Office of Scientific Research Grant No. AF-AFOSR 484–64.

2717.   ———. "A Topological Model for the Perception of Context-Embedded Timbres." Paper presented at the International Conference on Computer Music, October 28–31, 1976, Massachusetts Institute of Technology.

2718.   Searle, Campbell L. "Analysis of Music from an Auditory Perspective." *The Humanities Association Review* 30 (Winter-Spring 1979): 93–103.

2719.   Shaffer, L. H. "Performances of Chopin, Bach, and Bartok: Studies in Motor Programming." *Cognitive Psychology* 13 (July 1981): 326–76. *C&CA* 16 (1981): 36841.

2720.   Shepard, Roger N. "Circularity of Judgements of Relative Pitch." *Journal of the Acoustical Society of America* 36 (1964): 2346–53.

2721.   Šidiškis, Bonis T. "O podsoznatel'nom postroenii sistem otcheta chastot tonov v protsessakh vospriiatiia muzyki." [On Subconscious Construction of Reference Systems of Tonal Frequencies in Music Perception Processes] *Avtomatika* 13 (Sept.-Oct. 1980): 83–85.
In Russian.
English translation in *Soviet Automatic Control* 13 (Sept.-Oct. 1980): 73–76. *C&CA* 16 (1981): 34719. *C&IS* 28 (1982): 81–11798C.

2722.   ———. "Ob informacionnom aspekte vos prijutiju intervalov i sozvucij muzyki." [On the Informational Aspect of Interval and Chord Perception in Music] *Matematices kie metody v social'nyh naukah* 4 (1974): 68–97.
In Russian; summaries in Lithuanian and English.
RILM 74 4159.

2723. Slawson, A. Wayne. "Operations on Timbre: Perspectives and Problems." In *Proceedings of the International Computer Music Conference, 1984,* ed. William Buxton. San Francisco, Calif.: Computer Music Association, 1985: 167–71.

2724. ———. "Vowel Quality and Musical Timbre as Functions of Spectrum Envelope and Fundamental Frequency." *Journal of the Acoustical Society of America* 43 (1968): 87–101.

2725. Slaymaker, Frank H. "Chords from Tones Having Stretched Partials." *Journal of the Acoustical Society of America* 47 (June 1970): 1569–71.

2726. Steedman, Mark J. "The Formal Description of Musical Perception." Ph.D. diss., Edinburgh University, 1972.

2727. Strawn, John. "Research on Timbre and Musical Contexts at CCRMA." In *Proceedings of the Venice 1982 International Computer Music Conference,* comp. Thom Blum and John Strawn. San Francisco, Calif.: Computer Music Association, 1985: 437–65.

2728. ———. "Spectra and Timbre." Abstract in *Proceedings of the Rochester 1983 International Computer Music Conference,* comp. Robert W. Gross. San Francisco, Calif.: Computer Music Association, 1984: 57.

2729. Tenney, James. *Hierarchical Temporal Gestalt Perception in Music: A 'Metric Space' Model.* Toronto: York University, 1978.

2730. ———. "A Metric Space Model of Temporal Gestalt Perception." Paper presented at the 1977 International Computer Music Conference, University of California, San Diego, 26–30 October 1977.

2731. ———. "The Physical Correlates of Timbre." *Gravesaner Blätter* 26 (1965): 103–9.

2732. Thome, Diane D. "Toward Structural Characterization of the Timbral Domain." Ph.D. diss., Princeton University, 1973. 75 p. *DA* 34:5236A-7A.

2733. Wessel, David L. "Psychoacoustics and Music: Report from Michigan State University." *Page* 30, n.d.

2734. ———. "Lo spazio timbrico come strutture di controllo musicale." [Timbric Space as a Control Structure in Music] In *Musica e elaboratore.* Venice: Biennale di Venezia, 1980: 101–12.

2735. ———. "Timbre Space as a Musical Control Structure." *Computer Music Journal* 3,2 (June 1979): 45–52.
Also, Paris: IRCAM, 1978. 8 p. (Rapports IRCAM 12/78)
Originally entitled: "Low Dimensional Control of Musical Timbre."
Reprinted in *Foundations of Computer Music,* ed. Curtis Roads and John Strawn. Cambridge, Mass.: MIT Press, 1985: 640–57.

2736. ———, and John M. Grey. *Conceptual Structures for the Representation of Musical Material.* Paris: IRCAM, 1978. (Rapports IRCAM no. 14)

2737.   ———, and Bennett K. Smith. "Psychoacoustic Aids for the Musician's Exploration of New Material." Paper presented at the 1977 International Computer Music Conference, University of California, San Diego, 26–30 October 1977.

2738.   ———; Bennett K. Smith; and David E. Ehresman. "Psychoacoustic Experimentation as a Prelude to Musical Composition." Paper presented at the 96th Convention of the Acoustical Society of America, Honolulu, Hawaii, December 1978.
Abstract in *The Journal of the Acoustical Society of America* 64 (1978): S170.

2739.   White, Benjamin W. "Recognition of Distorted Melodies." *American Psychologist* 13 (1958): 384.
Abstract of paper presented at the 66th Annual Convention of the American Psychological Association, July 1958.

REFERENCE, RESEARCH, AND MUSIC LIBRARY APPLICATIONS

2740. Allison, Anne Marie, and Joy E. Lawrence. "Choralist—A Computerized Index to Choral Octavo Scores." *Collection Management* 3 (Spring 1979): 79–96.

2741. Bahler, Peter B. "Electronic and Computer Music: An Annotated Bibliography of Writings in English." M.A. thesis, University of Rochester, 1966. 128 p.

2742. Bartlitz, Eveline. "Computerwunder sind Mythen—10 Jahre RILM: 5-Jahres-Index 1967–1971." *Beiträge zur Musikwissenschaft* 19,3 (1977): 216–19. *RILM* 77 4220.

2743. Battier, Marc. *Musique et informatique, une bibliographie indexée.* In collaboration with Jacques Arveiller. Ivry-sur-Seine: Editions ELMERATTO, CNRS, 1978. 176 p.
RILM 76 4699.
Review by Howard Accurso in *Notes* 36 (1979): 376–77.

2744. Berlind, Gary, comp. "Writings on the Use of Computers in Music." *College Music Symposium* 6 (Fall 1966): 143–57.
Later version in: *Musicology and the Computer,* ed. Barry S. Brook. New York: City University of New York Press, 1970: 229–70.

2745. Blombach, Ann K. "Making Computer Capabilities Accessible to Musicians." Summary in *SIGSOC Bulletin* 12–13 (Aug. 1981): 63.
C&CA 17 (1982): 13215.

2746. Böker-Heil, Norbert. "Computer-Einsatz bei der Serie A/II RISM: Möglichkeiten, Bedingungen, Vorschläge." *Fontes Artis Musicae* 22 (1975): 86–89.

2747.   ———; Harald Heckmann; and Ilse Kindermann. *Das Tenorlied. Mehrstim-mige Lieder in deutschen Quellen 1450–1580.* Band I: Drucke. Kassel: Bärenreiter, 1979. (Catalogus Musicus IX)

2748.   Boody, Charles G. "Non-Compositional Applications of the Computer to Music: An Evaluative Study of Materials Published in America Through June 1972." Ph.D. diss., University of Minnesota, 1975. 186 p.
DA 36:3196A-7A. *RILM* 75 361.
Reviewed by W. Kuhn in *Council for Research in Music Education Bulletin* 53 (Winter 1977): 45–47.
Rebuttal by C. G. Boody in *Council for Research in Music Education Bulletin* 53 (Winter 1977): 47–48.

2749.   Bowles, Edmund A., comp. "Computerized Research in the Humanities: A Survey." *ACLS Newsletter* special supplement (June 1966)

2750.   Bowles, Garrett H. "Automated Bibliographic Control of Music." *Proceedings of the American Society for Information Science* 18 (1981): 318.

2751.   ———. "Computer-Produced Thematic Catalog: An Index to the *Pièces de violes* of Marin Marais, Volume 1." Ph.D. diss., Stanford University, 1978. 185 p.
C&IS 23 (1979): 217664C. *DA* 39:3204A. *RILM* 78 2270.

2752.   ———. "A Computer-Produced Thematic Catalog: The 'Pièces de violes' of Marin Marais." *Fontes Artis Musicae* 26 (1979): 102–7.

2753.   ———, comp. *Directory of Music Library Automation Projects.* Philadelphia: Music Library Association, 1979. 23 p.

2754.   Brook, Barry S. "Music Bibliography and the Computer." In *Papers from the West Virginia University Conference on Computer Applications in Music,* ed. Gerald Lefkoff. Morgantown: West Virginia University Library, 1967: 11–27.

2755.   ———. "Music Documentation of the Future." In *Musicology and the Computer,* ed. Barry S. Brook. New York: City University of New York Press, 1970: 28–36.

2756.   ———. "Music Literature and Modern Communication: Revolutionary Potentials of the ACLS/CUNY/RILM Project." *College Music Symposium* 9 (Fall 1969): 48–59.
Also in *Acta Musicologica* 42 (1970): 205–17.
German version in *Beiträge zur Musikwissenschaft* 13 (1971): 18–30.

2757.   ———. "*Repertoire international de litterature musicale (RILM)* Report No. 5: Leipzig, June 1970." *Fontes Artis Musicae* 18 (1971): 73–77.
RILM 71 1.

2758.   ———. "*RILM.*" *Computers and the Humanities* 1 (1966–67): 103–8.

2759.   ———. "*RILM*—eine neuartige internationale Fachbibliographie der Musikwissenschaft." *Die Musikforschung* 21 (1968): 423–26.

2760.   ———. "*RILM* Inaugural Report: January 1967." *Notes* 23 (1966–67): 462–67.

2761. ———. *"RILM* Report No. 2: September 1967." *Notes* 24 (1967–68): 457–58. Also in *Fontes Artis Musicae* 15 (1968): 2–3. Also in *Report of the Tenth Congress [of the International Musicological Society], Ljubljana 1967,* ed. Dragotin Cvetko. Kassel: Bärenreiter, 1970: 463–65.

2762. ———. *"RILM*: Report No. 10: Montreal, August 1975." *Fontes Artis Musicae* 23 (1976): 82–84.

2763. ———. "Some New Paths for Music Bibliography." In *Computers in Humanistic Research,* ed. Edmund A. Bowles. Englewood Cliffs: Prentice-Hall, 1967: 204–11.

2764. ———. "A Tale of Thematic Catalogues." *Notes* 29 (1972–73): 407–15.

2765. ———. "Utilization of Data Processing Techniques in Music Documentation." *Fontes Artis Musicae* 12 (1965): 112–22.

2766. ———. "World Music Documentation System: A Phantasy." In *Challenges in Music Education,* ed. Frank Callaway. Perth: University of Western Australia, 1976: 302–12. *RILM* 76 2304.

2767. ———, and Richard D. Leppert. "The Research Center for Musical Iconography of the City University of New York." *College Music Symposium* 13 (Fall 1973): 106–13. *RILM* 73 2968.

2768. ———; Anders Lönn; and Carol Neuls-Bates. *"RILM*: Report No. 9: Jerusalem, August 18–24, 1974." *Fontes Artis Musicae* 22 (1975): 56–58.

2769. ———, and Catherine Massip. *"RILM* Report No. 14: Salzburg, 1979." *Fontes Artis Musicae* 27 (1980): 111–12.

2770. ———, and Nanna Schiødt. *"RILM* Report No. 3: September 1968." *Fontes Artis Musicae* 16 (1969): 24–27.

2771. ———, and Nanna Schiødt. *"RILM* Report No. 6: St. Gall, August 1971." *Fontes Artis Musicae* 19 (1972): 192–95.

2772. ———, and Nanna Schiødt. *"RILM*: Report No. 7: Bologna and Copenhagen, September-August 1972." *Fontes Artis Musicae* 20 (1973): 15–18.

2773. ———, and Nanna Schiødt. *"RILM*: Report No. 8: London, August 26–31, 1973." *Fontes Artis Musicae* 21 (1974): 19–22.

2774. ———, and Nanna Schiødt. *"RILM*: Report No. 11: Bergen, August 1976." *Fontes Artis Musicae* 24 (1977): 35–38.

2775. ———, and Nanna Schiødt. *"RILM*: Report No. 12: Mainz, September 11–16, 1977." *Fontes Artis Musicae* 25 (1978): 100–101.

2776. ———, and Nanna Schiødt. *"RILM*: Report No. 13: Lisbon, 27 July 1978." *Fontes Artis Musicae* 26 (1979): 124–25.

2777.   Carter, Nancy F. "Sheet Music Index on a Microcomputer." *Information Technology and Libraries* 2 (Mar. 1983): 52–55. *CIJE* 15 (1983): EJ 279 822.

2778.   "CIRPA/ADISQ Requests Coin for Disk Catalog Development; On-Line Service Bows this Fall." *Variety* 308 (Sept. 1, 1982): 77.

2779.   "Computerized Hillbilly Discography Project: Final Report Summary." *The John Edwards Memorial Foundation Quarterly* 7,1 (1971): 35–36.

2780.   Coover, James B. "Computers, Cataloguing, and Cooperation." *Notes* 25 (1968–69): 437–46.

2781.   Corsi, Patrick. *Définition d'un code pour partition musicale proche du compositeur et interface avec le programme de synthèse de sons musicaux MUSICV. Bibliographie en informatique musicale.* Grenoble: Institut national polytechnique de Grenoble, Ecole nationale superieur d'informatique et de mathematiques appliquées de Grenoble, 1977.

2782.   "Cumulative Music Index Promoted." *Journal of Research in Music Education* 14,3 (1966): 225.

2783.   Davis, Deta S. "Computer Applications in Music: A Bibliography." In *Proceedings of the 1980 International Computer Music Conference,* comp. Hubert S. Howe. San Francisco, Calif.: Computer Music Association, 1982: 653–824.

2784.   Drummond, Philip J. "The Choice Between Custom and Package Software for Music Bibliography." In *Informatique et musique, Second Symposium International,* ed. Hélène Charnassé. Ivry: ELMERATTO, CNRS, 1983: 147–59.

2785.   ———. "Computer Applications to Music: An Historical Introduction and Critical Bibliography, 1949–1983." M.S. thesis, University of New South Wales, 1984.

2786.   Eagle, Charles T., and Sidney A. Prewitt. "A Computer-Assisted Information Retrieval System in Music Therapy: A Word-and-Author Index of Published Studies." *Journal of Music Therapy* 11 (Winter 1974): 181.

2787.   Eddins, John M., and S. A. Floyd. "A Computerized Bibliographical Index of Musical Scores by Black American Composers Prior to 1910." In *New Directions in Educational Computing: Proceedings of the ADCIS 1978 Conference, Dallas, Texas, March 1978:* 275.

2788.   Erickson, Raymond F. "The Uses of Computers in Music: A State of the Art Report." In *Proceedings of the First USA-Japan Computer Conference.* Montvale, N.J.: American Federation of Information Processing Societies, Inc.; Tokyo: Information Processing Society of Japan, 1972: 124–29. *RILM* 73 179.

2789.   Field, Connie. "What Can Be Accomplished at the Terminal?" In *Retrospective Conversion of Music Materials,* ed. Dorothy Gregor. Washington, D.C.: Bibliographic Service Development Program, Council on Library Resources, 1984: 43–52.

2790. Garland, Catherine R. "Music: Online at Last." In *Automation at the Library of Congress: Inside Views,* ed. Suzanne E. Thorin. Washington, D.C.: Library of Congress Professional Association, 1986: 11–14.

2791. ———. "Retrospective Conversion of Subject Headings and Series." In *Retrospective Conversion of Music Materials,* ed. Dorothy Gregor. Washington, D.C.: Bibliographic Service Development Program, Council on Library Resources, 1984: 23–32.

2792. Glazier, Ed. "Post-Input Authority Work for Retrospective Conversion of Bibliographic Items for Music: What are the Possibilities?" In *Retrospective Conversion of Music Materials,* ed. Dorothy Gregor. Washington, D.C.: Bibliographic Service Development Program, Council on Library Resources, 1984: 53–74.

2793. Goudy, Allie Wise. "Music Coverage in Online Databases." *Database* 5 (Dec. 1982): 39–57.
C&CA 18 (1983): 14662. *CIJE* 15 (1983): EJ 272 991.

2794. Gregor, Dorothy, ed. *Retrospective Conversion of Music Materials: Report of a Meeting Sponsored by the Council on Library Resources, July 18–19, 1984, Wayzata, Minnesota.* Washington, D.C.: Bibliographic Service Development Program, Council on Library Resources, 1984. 118 p.
ERIC: ED 253 232.

2795. Griffin, Marie P. "The IJS Jazz Register and Indexes: Jazz Discography in the Computer Era." *Annual Review of Jazz Studies* 1 (1982): 110–27.

2796. Haus, Goffredo. "Il sistema informativo del Laboratorio di Informatica Musicale dell'Istituto di Cibernetica di Milano." [The Information System of the Laboratorio di Informatica Musicale (Computer Music Laboratory) at Istituto di Cibernetica at Milan] In *Atti del Quarto Colloquio di Informatica Musicale.* Pisa: CNUCE-CNR, 1981: 258–76.

2797. Heck, Thomas F. "Computerized Bibliographic Retrieval in Music: A State-of-the-Art Critique." In *Sixth International Conference on Computers and the Humanities,* ed. S. K. Burton and D. D. Short. Rockville, Md.: Computer Science Press, 1983: 249–262.
Review by H. B. Lincoln in *Computing Reviews* 25 (June 1984): 8406–0501.

2798. Heckmann, Harald. "Musik—Dokumentation; Musik—Information: Elektronische Datenverarbeitung und Musik." *Neue Zeitschrift für Musik* 134 (1973): 479–82.
RILM 74 3877.

2799. Helmer, Axel. "Fran källorna till forskarna. Om dokumentationsarbetet vid Svenskt musikhistoriskt arkiv." [From the Sources to the Scholars. The Documentation Activities of the Swedish Music History Archive] In *Svenska musikperspektiv. Minnesskrift vid kungl. Musikaliska akademiens 200-Arsjubileum 1971,* ed. Gustav Hillstrom. Stockholm: Nordiska musikförlaget,

1971.
In Swedish, summary in English.
RILM 71 3402.

2800.   ———. "KONSINF: Konsertinformation. Försök med ADB-behandling av musikhistoriska data." [Concert Information: An Experiment in Computer Processing of Historical Data] *Svenskt musikhistoriskt arkiv bulletins* 11 (1974): 1–13.
In Swedish.
RILM 74 1.

2801.   Hickerson, Joseph C. "Computer Machine-Readable Cataloging at the Archive of Folk Song, Library of Congress." *Association for Recorded Sound Collections Journal* 1 (Summer 1969): 8–9.

2802.   Hodges, Anthony. "Music Conservatory Libraries in the U.K.: Recent Developments." *Fontes Artis Musicae* 24 (1977): 138–41.
Summaries in French and German.
RILM 77 4138.

2803.   Horner, John. *Special Cataloguing, with Particular Reference to Music, Films, Maps, Serials, and Multi-Media Computerised Catalogue.* Hamden, Conn.: Linnet Books; London: C. Bingley, 1973. 327 p.
Review by Sanford Berman in *Library Journal* 99 (1974): 2455.
Review by Jean Lunn in *Canadian Library Journal* 31 (Aug. 1974): 361.
Review by William C. Petru in *Special Libraries 66 (1975): 405.*

2804.   John, Robert W. "Information Storage and Retrieval: Computers Take the Search Out of Research." *Music Educators Journal* 57 (Mar. 1971): 88–89.

2805.   Jones, P. M. "Printed Music and the MARC Format." *Program* 10 (Oct. 1976): 119–22.
C&CA 12 (1977): 5019.

2806.   Kassler, Michael. "Toward Musical Information Retrieval." *Perspectives of New Music* 4 (Spring-Summer 1966): 59–67.

2807.   ———. "A Trinity of Essays." Ph.D. diss., Princeton University, 1967. 269 p.
DA 28:3702A.

2808.   Kirstein, Finn, and Claus Smith-Nielsen. "Musicat: A Technical Description of the Danish Music Cataloguing Project." *Fontes Artis Musicae* 24 (1977): 69–71.
RILM 77 5.

2809.   Klímová, Dagmar. "Styčné body katalogizace lidová písně a lidové prózy." [Points of Concurrence in the Cataloging of Folk Songs and Folk Prose] In *Lidová píseň a samočinný počítač I,* ed. Dušan Holý and Oldřich Sirovátka. Brno: Klub uživatelů MSP, 1972: 125–39.
Summary in English.

2810.   Kline, Lanaii. *Song File Match.* Los Alamitos, Calif.: Southwest Regional Laboratory for Educational Research and Development, 1972. *C&IS* 15: 143446C. *ERIC*: ED 108 645.

2811.   Kondracki, Miroslaw; Marta Stankiewicz; and Frits C. Weiland. *Internationale Diskographie elektronischer Musik.* Mainz: Schott, 1979. 174 p.

2812.   Kostka, Stefan M. *A Bibliography of Computer Applications in Music.* Hackensack, N.J.: J. Boonin, 1974. 58 p.
        Review by John E. Druesedow in *Computers and the Humanities* 9 (1975): 147–48.
        Review by Sharon P. Ferris in *American Reference Books Annual* 4 (1975): 490.
        Review by Michael Kassler in *Computing Reviews* 15 (1974): 27, 134.
        C&IS 14: 130923C. *RILM* 74 1577.

2813.   Kraus, Egon. "Bibliographie: Die mathematischen und physikalischen Grundlagen der Musik. Informationstheorie—Kybernetik—Computer und Musik." *Musik und Bildung* 4 (1972): 475–77.

2814.   Kucianová, Anna. "Spracovanie hudobnín v rámci automatizovaného systému SNB." [Processing of Music in the Framework of the Automatized System of National Bibliography] *Knižnice a vedecké informácie* 13,1 (1981): 7–11.
        In Slovak.
        C&CA 16 (1981): 24031.

2815.   Lane, William S. "The Application of Information Science Technology to a Select Body of Music Education Materials." Ed.D. diss., University of Georgia, 1974. 308 p.
        DA 35:5447A.

2816.   ———. "The Application of Information Science Technology to Music Education Materials." *Journal of Research in Music Education* 22 (1974): 251–57.

2817.   *LASER Manual for Cataloguing Monographs and Music.* London: London South Eastern Library Region L.A.S.E.R., 1975. 27 p.

2818.   "LC Implements Music Online." *MLA Newsletter* 57 (Sept.-Oct. 1984): 3, 5.

2819.   Lillehaug, Leland A. "The Computer, a New Assistant in Your Music Library." *School Musician* 54 (Nov. 1982): 10–12.

2820.   Lincoln, Harry B. "The Computer and Music Research: Prospects and Problems." *Council for Research in Music Education Bulletin* 18 (Fall 1969): 1–9.

2821.   ———. "The Current State of Music Research and the Computer." *Computers and the Humanities* 5 (1970–71): 29–36.

2822.   ———. "A Large Data Base for Music Research: A Progress Report." *SIGLASH Newsletter* 10–11 (1977–78): 43–51.
        C&CA 14 (1979): 25007.

2823.   ————. "Progress Report on a Computer-Assisted Thematic Catalogue of 16th Century Italian Secular Repertoire." Paper presented at the meeting of the New York State Chapter of the American Musicological Society, October 4–5, 1980, Rochester, New York.

2824.   ————. "Toward a 'Nuovo Vogel' with Computer-Generated Incipits in Staff Notation." Paper presented at the Symposium on Computer Studies in Music, 6–9 July 1979, Nottingham University, U.K.

2825.   ————. "Use of the Computer in Music Research: A Short Report on Accomplishments, Limitations, and Future Needs." *Computers and the Humanities* 8 (1974): 285–89.
CA 19 (1975): 2013. C&CA 11 (1976): 25612. RILM 75 373.

2826.   ————. "Uses of the Computer in Music Composition and Research." In *Advances in Computers 12,* ed. Morris Rubinoff. New York: Academic Press, 1972: 73–114.
Review by Raymond F. Erickson in *Computing Reviews* 14 (1973): 26,072.

2827.   Lindberg, Folke. "Gramophone Record Catalogues Based on EDP Routines." *Fontes Artis Musicae* 21 (1974): 28–32.
RILM 74 1598.

2828.   Lindner, Richard J. "A Cataloging Technique and a Computer-Aide System for Retrieving Information About Brass Music." Ph.D. diss., University of Iowa, 1971. 462 p.
Review by Joseph Youngblood in *Bulletin of the Council for Research in Music Education* 44 (1975): 18–22.
DA 32:5270A. RILM 76 8.

2829.   Lönn, Anders. "Svenskt musikhistoriskt arkiv." [Swedish Music History Archive] *Fontes Artis Musicae* 21 (1974): 9–10.
RILM 74 1420.

2830.   Malm, William P. "A Computer Aid in Musical Instrument Research." In *Studia instrumentorum musicae popularis. III Festschrift to Ernst Emsheimer on the Occasion of his 70th Birthday, January 15th, 1974,* ed. Gustaf Hillstrom. Stockholm: Nordiska musikförlaget, 1974: 119–22.
RILM 74 3570.

2831.   Maruyama, Leonore S., and Henriette D. Avram. "Commissions de travail: Cataloguing and the Computer." *Fontes Artis Musicae* 19 (Sept./Dec. 1972/ 73): 164–71.

2832.   Massip, Catherine. "Quelques applications pratiques de l'informatique au catalogage des manuscrits." In *Informatique et musique, Second Symposium International,* ed. Hélène Charnassé. Ivry: ELMERATTO, CNRS, 1983: 127–33.

2833.   Mayson, William A. "Organizing the Instrumental Music Ensemble Library with the Aid of a Machine-Assisted System." D.M.A. diss., Ohio State University, 1982. 106 p.
DA 43:13A.

2834. McRae, Lynn T. *Computer Catalog of Ninteenth-Century American-Imprint Sheet Music.* Charlottesville, Va.: University of Virginia Library, 1977. Review by James W. Pruett in *Notes* 33 (June 1977): 815–16.

2835. Melby, Carol, comp. *Computer Music Compositions of the United States 1976.* Cambridge, Mass.: Massachusetts Institute of Technology; Beverly Hills, Calif.: Distributed by Theodore Front Musical Literature, 1976. 28 p. *RILM* 76 8359.

2836. Meneau, Christophe. "Gestion d'une bibliotheque par micro-ordinateur." In *Informatique et musique, Second Symposium International,* ed. Hélène Charnassé. Ivry: ELMERATTO, CNRS, 1983: 161–66.

2837. Miller, Karen. "Syncopation Automation: An Online Thematic Index." *Information Technologies and Libraries* 1 (Sept. 1982): 270–74. *C&CA* 18 (1983): 15281.

2838. Miller, Miriam. "Computer Cataloging and the Broadcasting Library." *Fontes Artis Musicae* 24 (1977): 74–75. *RILM* 77 8.

2839. Mills, Patrick. "Cataloguing Commission: Working Group on Computer Cataloguing." *Fontes Artis Musicae* 29 (1982): 46.

2840. Mörner, C.-G. Stellan. *Klassificationssystem för grammofonskivor och ljudband samt musikalier, baserat på ADB-rutiner enligt CORSAIR:s programsystem, FOA.* [Classification System for Sound Recordings and Music Scores Based on EDP Routines According to the CORSAIR Program System, FOA] Stockholm: Försvarets Forskningsanstalt, 1972. (FOA P Rapport C 8348-M6) In Swedish. *RILM* 74 3.

2841. Nagosky, John P. "Computerized Opera." *Your Musical Cue* 1 (Jan. 1973): 4–10. *RILM* 73 1476.

2842. O'Keeffe, Vincent. "Mathematical-Musical Relationships: A Bibliography." *Mathematics Teacher* 65 (1972): 315–24. *CIJE* 4 (1972): EJ 057 940.

2843. "Opera Brain at Indiana University." *Central Opera Service Bulletin* 15 (Summer 1973): 9.

2844. Ottosen, Knud. "Le classement par ordinateur des listes de repons liturgiques: le traitement des donnees." In *Informatique musicale. Journées d'étude 1973. Textes des conférences, E.R.A.T.T.O.* Paris: CNRS, 1973. *RILM* 74 1506.

2845. Papakhian, Arsen Ralph. "Uniquely Musical Access Points (Coded)." In *Retrospective Conversion of Music Materials,* ed. Dorothy Gregor. Washington, D.C.: Bibliographic Service Development Program, Council on Library Resources, 1984: 33–41.

2846. Parker, Olin G., and Richard M. Graham. "An Information Retrieval System for Music Therapy." *Journal of Music Therapy* 9,3 (1972): 147–55.

2847. Parker, Roger. "Let Order Prevail." *High Fidelity/Musical America* 33 (June 1983): 44–46.

2848. Parrish, James W. "The DOMI Project: A Feasibility Study to Identify, Structure, and Computerize Databases of Music Information." In *Sixth International Conference on Computers and the Humanities,* ed. S. K. Burton and D. D. Short. Rockville, Md.: Computer Science Press, 1983: 479–83.
C&CA 19 (1984): 52051.

2849. Pennycook, Bruce. "Towards a Standard Audio Format: Preliminary Literature Search." Kingston, Ont.: Queens University, 1981?

2850. Peters, G. David, and John M. Eddins. "Applications of Computers to Music Pedagogy, Analysis, and Research: A Selected Bibliography." *Journal of Computer-Based Instruction* 5 (Aug.-Nov. 1978): 41–44.
C&CA 14 (1979): 14064. *CIJE* 11 (1979): EJ 198 328.

2851. Phillips, Linda N. "Piano Music by Black Composers: A Computer-Based Bibliography." D.M.A. diss., Ohio State University, 1977. 305 p.
DA 38:4441A. *RILM* 78 98.

2852. Philp, Geraint J. "An International Bibliography for Printed Music: A Feasibility Study." *Fontes Artis Musicae* 29 (1982): 83–84.

2853. Pollin, Burton R. *Music for Shelley's Poetry.* New York: Da Capo Press, 1974.

2854. Preston, Michael J. *A Complete Concordance to the Songs of the Early Tudor Court. Compendia; Computer-Generated Aids to Literary and Linquistic Research.* Leeds, Great Britain: Maney, 1972. 433 p.
RILM 75 102.

2855. Pruett, James W. "Notes for Notes." *Notes* 31 (Dec. 1974): 281–85.
RILM 74 1423.

2856. Rao, Paladugu V. "Music Information Services System (MISS)." Manuscript, Eastern Illinois University, Charleston, June 1975.
ERIC: ED 108 706.

2857. Ravizza, Victor. "Zu einem internationalen Repertorium der Musikikonographie." *Acta Musicologica* 44 (Jan.-June 1972): 101–8.
RILM 72 2876.

2858. Reckziegel, Walter. "Musikbibliographie und Datenspeicher." *Fontes Artis Musicae* 12 (1965): 123–28.

2859. "Register of Voice Research." *Music Educators Journal* 65 (Nov. 1978): 75.

2860. Régnier, Francis. "La nouvelle situation de la recherche musicale, face à l'ordinateur, instrument de synthèse." In *Conférence des journées d'études du festival international du son.* Paris: Editions Chiron, 1971: 126–40.

2861. ———. "Situation de la recherche musicale face à la revolution informatique." *Electronic Music Reports* 4 (Sept. 1971): 8–29.

2862. Reich, Nancy B., comp. *A Catalog of the Works of William Sydeman: A Machine-Readable Pilot Project in Information Retrieval.* New York: New York University, Division of Music Education, 1968. 17 p.

2863. "Research by Computer." *The Instrumentalist* 32 (Feb. 1978): 38.

2864. Richer-Lortie, Lyse. "Muscadet; ou, le traitement electronique de la documentation concernant la musique au Canada." *The Canadian Music Book* 8 (Spring-Summer 1974): 27-35.
Summary in English.

2865. Rösing, Helmut. "RISM-Handschriftenkatalogisierung und elektronische Datenverarbeitung (EDV)." *Fontes Artis Musicae* 26 (1979): 107-09.

2866. ———. "Zur Planung und zum gegenwärtigen Stand des RISM- Handschriftenprojekts." *Fontes Artis Musicae* 23 (1976): 2-6.
RILM 76 12.

2867. Rowley, Gordon S. "CIPHOR: A Computer-Assisted Bibliography of Organ and Harpsichord Music." *Current Musicology* 19 (1975): 122-29.

2868. Rudén, Jan Olof. "Advantages and Disadvantages of Small Self-Made Computerized Cataloguing System for Music and Sound Recordings: Experiences after Five Years of Use." *Fontes Artis Musicae* 29 (1982): 34-35.

2869. Schiødt, Nanna. "Commissions de travail: Checklist for Cataloguing Music Manuscripts and Prints." *Fontes Artis Musicae* 19 (Sept./Dec. 1972/73): 171-74.

2870. ———. "Commissions de travail: katalog-kommission." *Fontes Artis Musicae* 19 (1972): 163-74.

2871. ———. "Danish Holdings of Music Manuscripts Written Before 1800. A Thematic Catalogue and A Cataloguing Method." *Musikforskning* 2 (1976): 103-15.
In English; summary in Danish.
RILM 76 66.

2872. ———. "MUSICAT. A Method of Cataloging Music Manuscripts by Computer, as Applied in the Danish RISM Manuscript Project." *Fontes Artis Musicae* 23 (1976): 158-66.
RILM 76 4553.

2873. ———. "Overvejelser vedrørende dataregistrering." [Considerations Concerning Data Registration] *Bogens verden* 50 (1968): 239-41.
In Danish.

2874. ———. "*RILM*: Répertoire International de Litterature Musicale." *Dansk musiktidsskrift* 45 (1970): 168-73.

2875. ———, and Bjarner Svejgaard. "A Method of Indexing Musical Incipits." In *IMS Report 1972,* ed. Henrk Glahn, Soren Sorensen, and Peter Ryom. Copenhagen: W. Hansen, 1974: 777.
RILM 76 13.

2876. Sieber, Wolfgang. "Automatisierte Literaturdokumentation als Hilfsmittel der regionalen Musikforschung. Anmerkung und Erläuterungen zur Literatur-dokumentation zur Oberpfälzer Musikgeschichte (LOM)." *Musik in Bayern* 16 (1978): 41-50.

2877. Sirovátka, Oldřich. "Tradiční způoby katalogizace písňových textů a per-spektivy zpracování písní na samočinnýcy počítačích." [Traditional Means of Cataloging Choral Texts and Perspectives of Choral Work in Data Processing] In *Lidová píseň a samočinný počítač I,* ed. Dušan Holý and Oldřich Sirovátka. Brno: Klub uživatelů MSP, 1972: 111-23. In Czech; summary in English.

2878. Smiley, Barbara. "The Canadian Music Centre." *Ontario Libraries Review* 58 (Mar. 1974): 24-27. *RILM* 75 15.

2879. Smiraglia, Richard P. "Names of Persons and Organizations Associated with Musical Creation." In *Retrospective Conversion of Music Materials,* ed. Dorothy Gregor. Washington, D.C.: Bibliographic Service Development Program, Council on Library Resources, 1984: 9-21.

2880. Smith, James A. "Be Wise—Computerize." *The Choral Journal* 20,3 (1979): 23.

2881. Snell, John. "Computer Music Bibliography." *Dr. Dobbs Journal of Computer Calisthenics and Orthodontia* 1,7 (1976): 223-25. Also in *Creative Computing* 3 (Mar.-Apr. 1977): 54-56. 1

2882. Šramkova, Marta. "Pokus o strojové zpracování baladického typu." [Experimental Cataloging of Ballads by Computers] *Slovenský národopis* 21 (1973): 217-26. In Slovak.

2883. Stein, Evan. *The Use of Computers in Folklore and Folk Music: A Preliminary Bibliography.* Washington: Archive of Folk Song, Library of Congress, 1979. 12 p. *ERIC*: ED 190 112.

2884. Steinbeck, Wolfram. "Die Liederbank Kiel." *Jahrbuch des Staatlichen Instituts für Musikforschung* 1976 (1977): 94-108. *RILM* 77 1228.

2885. Steinberger, Naomi. "Selected Problems in Searching the *RILM* Database." In *National Online Meeting, Proceedings of the Second National Online Meeting, March 24-26 1981.* Medford, N.J.: Learned Information Inc., 1981: 455-60. *C&CA* 17 (1982): 2219.

2886. Stiebritz, Martin. "Untersuchungen zur Informations-speicherung und -Verarbeitung im Musikunterricht: Ein Beitrag zur Rationalisierung der Lehrerbildung im Fach Musikerziehung." Ph.D. diss., University of Halle, 1975. 282 p. *RILM* 76 7284.

2887. Storey, Cheryl Ewing. *A Bibliography of Computer Music.* Denton, Tex.: North Texas State University Music Library, 1981. 41 p.

2888. Swanzy, David. "The Instant Library." *Music Educators Journal* 57 (Jan. 1971): 90–91, 141–43.

2889. Tanno, John W. "Automation and Music Cataloguing." *College Music Symposium* 8 (Fall 1968): 48–50.

2890. ———; Alfred G. Lynn; and Robert E. Roberson. "An Automated Music Library Catalog for Scores and Phonorecords." In *The Computer and Music,* ed. Harry B. Lincoln. Ithaca: Cornell University Press, 1970: 328–46.

2891. Tjepkema, Sandra. *A Bibliography of Computer Music: A Reference for Composers.* Iowa City: Iowa Press, 1981. 265 p.
Review by Ann P. Basart in *Notes* 38 (June 1982): 848–49.
Review by R. L. Blevins in *Computer Music Journal* 5,3 (Winter 1981): 76.

2892. Turriciano, Albert J. "Design and Development of a Computerized Music Library Inventory System as an Aspect of a Multi-Purpose Music Resource Report Generator." M.A. thesis, California State University, Long Beach, 1978. 58 p.
Masters Abstracts 17 (1979): 216.

2893. Uhlmann, Wolfram. "The Computerized Concert Index of the Swedish Archives of Music History: An Example for the Retrieval of Historical Data." Stockholm: The Swedish Research Institute for National Defense, Nov. 1967. 30 p. (Technical Report C 0616–10)

2894. Van Werkhoven, H. B. M. "The Automation Plans of the Music Library of the Nederlandse Omrope Stichting (Dutch Broadcasting Foundation)." *Fontes Artis Musicae* 24 (1977): 72–74.
Summaries in French and German.
RILM 77 14.

2895. Williams, David B., and Sue L. Beasley. "Computer Information Search and Retrieval: A Guide for the Music Educator." *Bulletin of the Council for Research in Music Education* 51 (Summer 1977): 23–40.
ERIC: ED 140 846.

2896. Wittlich, Gary E. "New Computer Tools for Music Research." *Indiana Theory Review* 1,2 (1978): 8–27.

2897. Zimmerman, Franklin B. "Music Indexing for General and Specialized Use." *Notes* 22 (1965–66): 1187–92.

SOUND GENERATION
FOR MUSIC—
HARDWARE

2898. Agnello, Anthony, and Stephen F. Hoge. "A Development System for Real-Time Digital Audio Signal Processing." *Computer Music Journal* 9,3 (Fall 1985): 24–38.

2899. Aikin, Jim. "Casio CZ-101 Mini-Keyboard." *Keyboard* 11 (Mar. 1985): 95–96.

2900. ———. "Digital Sampling Keyboards: What's Available, How They Work, Why They're Hot." *Keyboard* 11 (Dec. 1985): 32–41.

2901. ———. "First Steps in Programming: Everything You Need to Know to Get Your Feet Wet." *Keyboard* 11 (June 1985): 18–22.

2902. ———. "Keyboard Report: Akai S612 Rack-Mount Digital Sampler." *Keyboard* 11 (Nov. 1985): 107–8.

2903. ———. "Keyboard Report: Casio CZ-5000 Synthesizer." *Keyboard* 11 (Sept. 1985): 80–81.

2904. ———. "Keyboard Report: Korg SDD-2000 & Roland SDE-2500 Digital Delays." *Keyboard* 11 (Oct. 1985): 110–11.

2905. ———. "Keyboard Report: Moog Song Producer, Dr. T's Keyboard Controlled Sequencer & Musicdata Midi Sequencer for the Commodore 64." *Keyboard* 11 (1985): 82–91.

2906. ———. "Keyboard Report: Yamaha REV7 & Roland SRV-2000 Digital Reverbs & Lexicon PCM 70 Digital Effects Processor." *Keyboard* 12 (Feb. 1986): 122–27, 149.

2907. Alarcon-Gomez, J. R. "A Programmable Melody Generator." *Revista Española de electronica* 31 (Apr. 1984): 36–40. *E&EA* 87 (1984): 55112.

2908.   Allen, Jonathan. "Computer Architecture for Signal Processing." *Proceedings of the IEEE* 63 (1975): 624–33.

2909.   Alles, Harold G. "A 256-Channel Performer Input Device." *Computer Music Journal* 1,4 (Nov. 1977): 14–15.
Revised version in *Foundations of Computer Music,* ed. Curtis Roads and John Strawn. Cambridge, Mass.: MIT Press, 1985: 257–60.
RILM 77 6039.

2910.   ———. "A Hardware Digital Music Synthesizer." *IEEE Transactions on Aerospace and Electronic Systems,* Vol. AES-11 (1975): 980.

2911.   ———. "An Inexpensive Digital Sound Synthesizer." *Computer Music Journal* 3,3 (Sept. 1979): 28–37.
Also in *Proceedings of the 1978 International Computer Music Conference,* comp. Curtis Roads. Evanston, Ill.: Northwestern University Press, 1979: 5–25.
C&CA 15 (1980): 14090. *C&IS* 24 (1980): 238880C.

2912.   ———. "A Modular Approach to Building Large Digital Synthesis Systems." *Computer Music Journal* 1,4 (Nov. 1977): 10–13.

2913.   ———. "Music Synthesis Using Real-Time Digital Techniques." *Proceedings of the IEEE* 68 (1980): 436–49.
C&IS 25 (1980): 249935C.

2914.   ———. "A Portable Digital Sound Synthesis System." *Computer Music Journal* 1,4 (Nov. 1977): 5–6.
Revised and updated version in *Foundations of Computer Music,* ed. Curtis Roads and John Strawn. Cambridge, Mass.: MIT Press, 1980: 244–49.
RILM 77 6040.

2915.   ———. "A Real-Time All-Digital Music Synthesis System." Paper presented at the 58th Convention of the Audio Engineering Society, Nov. 4–7, 1977, New York.
Abstract in the *Journal of the Audio Engineering Society* 25 (1977): 1067.

2916.   ———. "The Teaching Laboratory General Purpose Digital Filter Music Box." In *Proceedings of the 8th IEEE International Symposium on Circuits and Systems, 21–23 April 1975, Newton, MA.* New York: IEEE, 1975: 387–89.

2917.   ———, and Giuseppe Di Giugno. "A One-Card 64-Channel Digital Synthesizer." *Computer Music Journal* 1,4 (Nov. 1977): 7–9.
Also, Paris: IRCAM, 1978. (Rapports IRCAM 4/78)
Revised version with title "The 4B: A One-Card 64-Channel Digital Synthesizer." In *Foundations of Computer Music,* ed. Curtis Roads and John Strawn. Cambridge, Mass.: MIT Press, 1985: 250–56.
RILM 77 6041.

2918.   Allouis, Jean-Francois. "A Compact Signal Processor for High-Quality Digital Audio." Paper presented at the 75th Convention of the Audio Engineering Society, Mar. 27–30, 1984, Paris.
Abstract in *Journal of the Audio Engineering Society* 32 (1984): 467.

2919.   ————. "Un système multiprocesseur de synthèse digitale temps reel: SYTER." *Cahiers récherche/musique* 3 (1976): 62–90.

2920.   ————, and Jean-Yves Bernier. "The Syter Project: Sound Processor Design and Software Overview." In *Proceedings of the Venice 1982 International Computer Music Conference,* comp. Thom Blum and John Strawn. San Francisco, Calif.: Computer Music Association, 1985: 232–40.

2921.   Alonso, Sydney; Jon H. Appleton; and Cameron Jones. "A Computer Music System for Every University: The Dartmouth College Example." *Creative Computing* 3 (Mar.-Apr. 1977): 57–60.
         C&CA 12 (1977): 23184.

2922.   Andersen, Kurt H. "A Digital Sound Generation Unit." *Electronic Music and Musical Acoustics* 2 (1976): 25–42.

2923.   ————. "Digital Sound Synthesizer Keyboard." *Electronic Music and Musical Acoustics* 2 (1976): 5–23.
         Revised version in: *Computer Music Journal* 2,3 (Dec. 1978): 16–23.
         C&IS 22 (1978): 214534C.

2924.   Anderton, Craig. "Build a Vocoder: Versatile Signal Processing for Keyboards and Drum Machines." *Keyboard* 11 (May 1985): 18–23.

2925.   ————. "Computer Literacy: How to Deal with Microprocessor-Based Keyboards." *Keyboard* 9 (June 1983): 48–54.
         Reprinted as "Computer Literacy for Musicians: Learn How to Deal with Microprocessor-Based Keyboards." In *Synthesizers and Computers.* Milwaukee, Wis.: H. Leonard Pub. Corp., 1985: 102–7.

2926.   ————. "Signal Processors." *Musicians Equipment Guide* 1 (Spring 1985): 46–51.

2927.   Appleton, Jon H. "The Synclavier: A Complex Tool for Performance, Teaching, and Composition." *Music Educators Journal* 69 (Jan. 1983): 67.

2928.   Arfib, Daniel. "The Architecture of a Digital Sound Synthesis System." In *Proceedings of ICASSP 82, IEEE International Conference on Acoustics, Speech, and Signal Processing, Paris, France, 3-5 May 1982.* New York: IEEE, 1982: vol. 3, 1466–68.
         C&CA 18 (1983): 7242. *E&EA* 86 (1983): 9599.

2929.   Armbruster, Greg. "Devo's Customized Digital Control System: An Inside Report from Technician Jim Mothersbaugh." *Keyboard* 10 (June 1984): 68–71.
         Reprinted in *Synthesizers and Computers.* Milwaukee, Wis.: H. Leonard Pub. Corp., 1985: 107–113.

2930.   ————. "Keyboard Report: Midibass Digital Audio Generator from 360 Systems." *Keyboard* 11 (Nov. 1985): 110.

2931.   "ARP Announces Plans for 'Chroma'." *The Music Trades* 128 (Dec. 1980): 80, 82.

2932. Arveiller, Jacques; Marc Battier; Christian Colere; Gilbert Dalmasso; Giuseppe G. Englert; Patrick Greussay; and Didier Roncin. "Le système portable de synthèse hybride de Vincennes." In *Informatique musicale 1977, Textes des conférences. Equipe ERATTO.* Paris: Centre de documentation sciences humaines, 1978: 191–204.
Abstracts in English, French, and German.

2933. Asta, Vito. "Un modèle de machine musicale interagissant avec l'homme: caractérisation théorique et problèmes de réalisation." In *Computer Music/ Composition musicale par ordinateur; Report on an International Project Including a Workshop at Aarhus, Denmark in 1978,* ed. Marc Battier and Barry Truax. Ottawa: Canadian Commission for Unesco, 1980: 29–45.

2934. ——. "Unità elettronica par la modifica in tempo reale du suoni strumentali in segnale vocale." [Electronic Unit for the Real-Time Transformation of Instrumental Sounds into Vocal Sounds] Paper presented at the A.I.A. Conference, Siena, Italy, Oct. 1979.

2935. ——; Alain Chauveau; Giuseppe Di Giugno; and Jean Kott. "The Real Time Digital Synthesis System 4x." In *Musica ed elaboratore elettronico.* Milan: FAST, 1980: 95–137.

2936. ——; Alain Chauveau; Giuseppe Di Giugno; and Jean Kott. "Il sistema di sintesi digitale in tempo reale 4x." [The Real Time Digital Synthesis System 4x] *Automazione e strumentazione* 28 (Feb. 1980): 119–33.
Abstract in English.
C&CA 15 (1980): 26296.

2937. ——, and Adrian Freed. "The DSY8201 Digital Music Synthesizer." In *Proceedings of the Venice 1982 International Computer Music Conference,* comp. Thom Blum and John Strawn. San Francisco, Calif.: Computer Music Association, 1985: 172–87.

2938. "Australian Fairlight Instrument Blends High Technology, Sound." *Billboard* 92 (June 7, 1980): 10.

2939. Balasubramanian, K. "On a Versatile Digital Music Synthesizer." *IETE Technical Review* [India] 1 (Apr. 1984): 51–52.
C&IS 33 (1985): 85–4005C. *E&EA* 87 (1984): 61136.

2940. ——. "Simple Digital Music Synthesizer." *Wireless World* 90 (May 1984): 54.

2941. Battier, Marc, and Thierry Lancino. "Simulation and Extrapolation of Instrumental Sounds Using Direct Synthesis at IRCAM." In *Proceedings of the Venice 1982 International Computer Music Conference,* comp. Thom Blum and John Strawn. San Francisco, Calif.: Computer Music Association, 1985: 375–85.
Also in *Contemporary Music Review* 1 (Oct. 1984): 77–81.
French version: "Simulation et extrapolation de sons instrumentaux par synthèse directe à l'IRCAM." *Musique de notre temps* 1 (Oct. 1984): 81–85.

2942.   Beauchamp, James W. "Electronic Music Equipment, 1950–70: A Technical Survey." Urbana: University of Illinois Experimental Music Studio, Feb. 1970. (Technical Report no. 21)

2943.   ———; Ken Pohlman; and Lee Chapman. "The TI 980A Computer-Controlled Music Synthesizer." In *Proceedings of the Second Annual Music Computation Conference, November 7–9, 1975 at the University of Illinois at Urbana-Champaign. Part 3, Hardware for Computer Controlled Sound Synthesis,* comp. James Beauchamp and John Melby. Urbana, Ill.: University of Illinois: 1–36.

2944.   Beigel, Michael L. "A Digital Phase Shifter for Musical Applications Using the Bell Labs (Alles-Fischer) Digital Filter Module." *Journal of the Audio Engineering Society* 27 (1979): 673–77.
E&EA 83 (1980): 6590.

2945.   Bernardini, Nicola. "La serie DX Yamaha." [The Yamaha DX Series] *AudioReview* 34 (1984): 102–06.

2946.   ———. "Il sistema 4X." [The 4X System] *AudioReview* 30 (1984): 78–83.

2947.   Bertini, Graziano; M. Chimenti; and F. Denoth. "TAU2: An Audio Terminal for Computer Music Experiments." In *Proceedings of the International Symposium on Technology for Selective Dissemination of Information, Republic of San Marino, Italy, 8–10 September 1976.* New York: IEEE, 1976: 143–49.
Italian version: "TAU2: un terminale audio per esperimenti di 'Computer Music'." *Alta Frequenza* 46 (1977): 600–09.
C&CA 12 (1977): 5021. *C&IS* 16: 168932C.

2948.   Bondy, Jon. "The Casheab Music Synthesizer." *Creative Computing* 7 (Jan. 1981): 30–35.
C&CA 16 (1981): 27618.

2949.   Boothman, A. "E&MM Digital Music: The Programmable Digital Sound Generator. Part I." *Electronics & Music Maker* 4 (May 1984)

2950.   ———. "E&MM Digital Music: The Programmable Digital Sound Generator. Part II, Applying the PDSG." *Electronics & Music Maker* 4 (June 1984): 86–88.
C&CA 19 (1984): 47423. *E&EA* 87 (1984): 48641.

2951.   ———. "E&MM Digital Music: The Programmable Digital Sound Generator. Part III, The Detailed Program Interface." *Electronics & Music Maker* 4 (July 1984): 88–89.
C&CA 19 (1984): 47432. *E&EA* 87 (1984): 55097.

2952.   ———. "E&MM Digital Music: The Programmable Digital Sound Generator. Part IV, Further Hardware Details." *Electronics & Music Maker* 4 (Oct. 1984): 80–81.
C&CA 20 (1985): 7984. *E&EA* 88 (1985): 8640.

2953. ———. "E&MM Digital Music: The Programmable Digital Sound Generator. Part V, Sound Systems Revisted." *Electronics & Music Maker* 4 (Nov. 1984): 80–82.
C&CA 20 (1985): 21599. E&EA 88 (1985): 26148.

2954. Brescia, M. "Il nuovo sistema XML20 suona la musica disegnata: sintesi in tempo reale pilotata da input grafico-ottico." [The New XML20 System Plays Drawn Music: Graphical-Optical Input Driven Real Time Synthesis] In *Atti del Quinto Colloquio di Informatica Musicale*. Ancona: Università di Ancona, 1983: 13–23.

2955. Bristow, David. "Voicing the DX7." Paper presented at the 1984 International Computer Music Conference, Oct. 19–23, Paris, France.

2956. Bromose, Ole. *Beskrivelse of programmet SIM*. [Description of the SIM Program] Aarhus: Institute of Musicology, Dept. of Musical Acoustics, 1975.

2957. ———. "SIM-projektets status pr 1/9 1974." [The SIM Project Status as of Jan. 9, 1974] Aarhus, 1974.
In Danish.

2958. ———. "Simulering af en 200 UT." [Simulation of 200 UT] Aarhus, n.d.
In Danish.

2959. Browen, Rodney. "1024 Note User-Programmable Music Synthesizer." *IEEE Student Papers* (1978): 87–92.

2960. Buchla, Don, and Richard Friedman. "A Computer Aided Analog Electronic Music System." Paper presented at the 42nd Convention of the Audio Engineering Society, May 2–5, 1972, Los Angeles.
Abstract in the *Journal of the Audio Engineering Society* 20 (1972): 422.

2961. Burhans, R. W. "Single-Bus Keyboard Control for Digital Musical Instruments." *Journal of the Audio Engineering Society* 19 (Nov. 1971): 865.

2962. Buxton, William; E. A. Fogels; Guy Fedorkow; Lawrence H. Sasaki; and Kenneth C. Smith. "An Introduction to the SSSP Digital Synthesizer." *Computer Music Journal* 2,4 (late Dec. 1978): 28–38.
Also in *Proceedings of the 1978 International Computer Music Conference*, comp. Curtis Roads. Evanston, Ill.: Northwestern University Press, 1979: 46–56.
Revised and updated version in *Foundations of Computer Music*, ed. Curtis Roads and John Strawn. Cambridge, Mass.: MIT Press, 1985: 206–24.
C&CA 14 (1979): 31239. C&IS 23 (1979): 219786C.

2963. ———; William Reeves; Guy Fedorkow; Kenneth C. Smith; and Ronald Baecker. "A Computer-Based System for the Performance of Electroacoustic Music." AES Preprint 1529 (J-1), 1979.

2964. Byrd, Donald, and Christopher Yavelow. "The Kurzweil 250 Digital Synthesizer." *Computer Music Journal* 10,1 (Spring 1986): 64–86.

2965.   Cadoz, Claude; Anasthasie Luciani; and Jean-Loup Florens. "Gesture, Instrument, and Musical Creation: The System ANIMA/CORDIS." Paper presented at the 75th Convention of the Audio Engineering Society, Mar. 27–30, 1984, Paris. Preprint no. 2086.
Abstract in the *Journal of the Audio Engineering Society* 32 (1984): 467.
C&CA 19 (1984): 36726. *E&EA* 87 (1984): 44349.

2966.   ———; Anasthasie Luciani; and Jean-Loup Florens. "Responsive Input Devices and Sound Synthesis by Simulation of Instrumental Mechanisms: The Cordis System." *Computer Music Journal* 8,3 (Fall 1984): 60–73.
Original title: Synthèse sonore par simulation des mechanismes instrumentaux: le système cordis.
C&CA 20 (1985): 17260. *E&EA* 88 (1985): 20425.

2967.   Capuzzo, G. "Consolle per l'ingresso gestuale al sistema 4i tramite otto potenziometri a cursore." [A Console for Analog Input to the 4i System Using Eight Slide Rheostats] *Bollettino LIMB* 4 (1984): 93–97.

2968.   Carlos, Michael, and Tom Stewart. *FAIRLIGHT Computer Musical Instrument: User Manual.* Sydney, Australia: Fairlight Instruments, 1984. 205 p.

2969.   Castro, Caesar. "A 32-Channel Digital Waveform Synthesizer." In *Microprocessor Applications Handbook,* ed. David F. Stout. New York: McGraw-Hill, 1982: 10/1–10/24.

2970.   ———. "The Casheab Synthesizer: How It Works." Paper presented at the 1981 International Computer Music Conference, Nov. 5–8, Denton, Tex.

2971.   Cavaliere, Sergio; Giuseppe Di Giugno; V. Fedullo; and Immacolata Ortosecco. "Un calcolatore veloce orientato per la sintesi di segnali acustici in tempo reale." [A Fast Computer Developed for Real Time Synthesis of Acoustic Signals] In *Aspetti teorici di Informatica Musicale.* Milan: CTU-Istituto di Cibernetica, Università di Milano, 1977: 115–23.

2972.   ———; Immacolata Ortosecco; Pasquale Parascandolo; and Aldo Piccialli. "An Efficient Method to Implement Amplitude Modulation: A Hardware Realization." In *Proceedings of the Venice 1982 International Computer Music Conference,* comp. Thom Blum and John Strawn. San Francisco, Calif.: Computer Music Association, 1985: 133–53.

2973.   ———; Immacolata Ortosecco; Pasquale Parascandolo; and Aldo Piccialli. "Un sistema hardware per la sintesi ed il trattamento di segnali acustici." [A Hardware System for Synthesizing and Processing Acoustic Signals] In *AICA, Associazione Italiana per il Calcolo Automatico: Atti del congresso annuale, Padova, 6–8 Ottobre 1982.* Padua: AICA, 1982: 407–14.

2974.   ———; Immacolata Ortosecco; Pasquale Parascandolo; Aldo Piccialli; and S. Vergara. "Un banco microprogrammato di oscillatori." [A Microprogrammed Oscillator Bank] In *Atti del Quarto Colloquio di Informatica Musicale.* Pisa: CNUCE-CNR, 1981: 86–103.

2975.   Ceely, Robert P. *Electronic Music Resource Book.* Boston: Multimedia NEV Publication, 1979.

2976. Cesari, Carol Andrea. "Application of Data Flow Architecture to Computer Music Synthesis." M.S. thesis, Dept. of Electrical Engineering and Computer Science, Massachusetts Institute of Technology, 1981. 129 p.

2977. Chadabe, Joel. "The CEMS System." Albany, N.Y.: State University of New York at Albany, Feb. 1970. (Technical Report)

2978. Chamberlain, Howard W. "Experimental Fourier Series Universal Tone Generator." *Journal of the Audio Engineering Society* 24 (1976): 271–76.

2979. Chamberlin, Hal. "Fourier Series Waveform Generator. Part 1." *Electronotes* 5 (May 1974): 2–5.

2980. Chapman, J. "Understanding the DX7. Part III." *Electronics & Music Maker* 4 (June 1984): 70–71.
E&EA 87 (1984): 48640.

2981. ———. "Understanding the DX7. Part IV." *Electronics & Music Maker* 4 (July 1984): 68–70.
E&EA 87 (1984): 55095.

2982. ———. "Understanding the DX7. Part V." *Electronics & Music Maker* 4 (Aug. 1984): 68–72.
E&EA 87 (1984): 61124.

2983. ———. "Understanding the DX7. Part VI." *Electronics & Music Maker* 4 (Sept. 1984): 70–72.
C&CA 20 (1985): 4080. *E&EA* 88 (1985): 3782.

2984. ———. "Understanding the DX7. Part VII." *Electronics & Music Maker* 4 (Oct. 1984): 70–72.
E&EA 88 (1985): 8639.

2985. Chouinard, L.; L. N. Bélanger; and H. T. Huynh. "A Computer-Based Harmonic Analysis/Additive Synthesis System." In *Proceedings of the International Computer Music Conference, 1985,* ed. Barry Truax. San Francisco, Calif.: Computer Music Association, 1985: 135–39.

2986. Christiansen, Steven. "A Microprocessor-Controlled Digital Waveform Generator." *Journal of the Audio Engineering Society* 25 (1977): 299–309.

2987. Cody, Daniel W. "The RTM5 Signal Processing Architecture." *Computer Music Journal* 6,2 (Summer 1982): 52–60.

2988. Conly, Paul, and Allen Razoow. "Digital Composition and Control of an Electronic Music Synthesizer." Paper presented at the 41st Convention of the Audio Engineering Society, Oct. 5–8, 1971, New York.

2989. Cooper, James. "A Hybrid Microcomputer Voice and Music Synthesis System." Paper presented at the 58th Convention of the Audio Engineering Society, Nov. 4–7, 1977, New York.

2990.   Coren, Daniel, and Harry Mendell. "A Mini-Computer-Based Sound Manip-
        ulation System." Paper presented at the 57th Convention of the Audio Engi-
        neering Society, May 10–13, 1977, Los Angeles.
        Abstract in *Journal of the Audio Engineering Society* 25 (1977): 514.

2991.   Darter, Tom. *The Whole Synthesizer Catalogue.* Milwaukee, Wis.: H. Leonard
        Pub. Corp., 1985. 158 p. (The Keyboard Synthesizer Library)

2992.   Davis, A. L., and J. A. Stanek. "A Computer Music Synthesis Study on a Tree
        Structured Data-Driven Machine." In *VLSI: New Architectural Horizons,
        COMPCON 80, Twentieth IEEE Computer Society International Conference,
        February 25–28.* Long Beach, Calif.: IEEE Computer Society, 1980: 188–201.

2993.   Dawson, Giles. "Machines Alive with the Sound of Music." *New Scientist* 99
        (Aug. 4, 1983): 333–35.

2994.   De Furia, Steve. "Systems & Applications: Creative Applications: After-
        Touch and Pitch-Bending." *Keyboard* 12 (Feb. 1986): 105.

2995.   ———. "Systems & Applications: Pushing the Envelope." *Keyboard* 12
        (Apr. 1986): 98.

2996.   ———. "Systems & Applications: Pushing the Envelope. Part II." *Keyboard*
        12 (May 1986): 94, 142.

2997.   Debiasi, Giovanni B. "M.I.N.I. (Musical Instruments Numerical Interface)."
        In *Proceedings of the International Computer Music Conference, 1985,* ed.
        Barry Truax. San Francisco, Calif.: Computer Music Association, 1985:
        331–35.

2998.   ———. "Sistema di comando gestuale per il processore 4i." [A System for
        Analog Control of the 4i Processor] *Bollettino LIMB* 4 (1984): 29–31.

2999.   ———, and Maurizio Rubbazzer. "Architecture of a Processor for the Digital
        Analysis/Synthesis of Sound." In *Proceedings of the Venice 1982 International
        Computer Music Conference,* comp. Thom Blum and John Strawn. San Fran-
        cisco, Calif.: Computer Music Association, 1985: 225–31.

3000.   Dermott, Jim. "For Today's Young Beethoven: A Computer that Com-
        poses." *Electronic Design* 19 (Jan. 7, 1971): 36–38.

3001.   Devarahi. *The Complete Guide to Synthesizers.* Englewood Cliffs, N.J.:
        Prentice-Hall, 1981. 214 p.

3002.   Di Giugno, Giuseppe. "Il processore di sintesi ed elaborazione numerica del
        suono in tempo reale 4i." [The 4i Real Time Sound Processor] *Bollettino LIMB*
        4 (1984): 25–27.

3003.   ———. "Il processore professionale per la sintesi digitale del suono 4X/02."
        [The 4X/02 Professional Digital Sound Synthesizer] Paper presented at the
        1982 International Computer Music Conference, Sept. 27-Oct. 1, Venice.

3004.   ———. "A Real-Time Computer Controlled Digital Oscillator Bank." Paper
        presented at the International Conference on Computer Music, October 28–31,
        1976, Massachusetts Institute of Technology.

3005. ————, and E. Guarino. "Un processore rapido floating-point." [A Fast Floating-Point Processor] In *Atti del Quinto Colloquio di Informatica Musicale.* Ancona: Università di Ancona, 1983: 36–42.

3006. ————, and Jean Kott. "The IRCAM Real-Time Digital Sound Processor." Paper presented at the 1980 International Computer Music Conference, November 13-15, 1980, Queens College of the City University of New York.

3007. ————, and Jean Kott. *Presentation du système 4X: processeur numerique de signal en temps réel.* Paris: IRCAM, 1981. (Rapports IRCAM 32/81)

3008. ————; Jean Kott; and Andrew Gerzso. "Progress Report on the 4X Machine and Its Use." Abstract in *Proceedings, 1981 International Computer Music Conference, November 5-8,* comp. Larry Austin and Thomas Clark. Denton, Tex.: North Texas State University, 1983: 281.

3009. "Dispositivi elettronici per l'elaborazione musicale." [Electronic Devices: For Computer Music] *Automazione e strumentazione* 28 (Feb. 1980): 154–56.

3010. Doerschuk, Bob. "Many Mountains, Many Peaks: Encounters with the Driving Forces in Japan's Synthesizer Industry." *Keyboard* 11 (Aug. 1985): 48–58.

3011. Drane, M. "Action Replay: Sound Sampler for Sinclair Spectrum." *Electronics & Music Maker* 4 (Nov. 1984): 30.
E&EA 88 (1985): 26143.

3012. Duesenberry, John. "The Yamaha CX5M Music Computer: An Evaluation." *Computer Music Journal* 9,3 (Fall 1985): 39–51.

3013. Dworak, Paul E., and Alice C. Parker. "Envelope Control with an Optical Keyboard." Paper presented at the 1977 International Computer Music Conference, University of California, San Diego, 26–30 October 1977.

3014. Ehle, Robert C. "A Computer Electronic Music System." *db, The Sound Engineering Magazine* 3 (Aug. 1969): 23–25.

3015. ————. "Survey of Digital Synthesizers." *Music Journal* 36 (Dec. 1978): 28–31.

3016. Ellis, David. "Kurzweil 250 Digital Keyboard." *Electronics & Music Maker* 4 (Dec. 1984): 12–16.
E&EA 88 (1985): 31252.

3017. ————. "The Syndrom. Part II, Getting It Together." *Electronics & Music Maker* 4 (June 1984): 90–91.

3018. ————; C. Buxton; and K. Pykett. "The Syndrom. Part IV, Walking the Dog." *Electronics & Music Maker* 4 (Dec. 1984): 78–80.
E&EA 88 (1985): 31262.

3019. Farber, Jim. "Computers that Make Waves: Digital Synthesizers Take to the Road." *Rolling Stone* n310 (Feb. 7, 1980): 64.

3020. Faulhaber, M. E. "Digital Control of a New Hybrid Electronic Music Synthesizer." In *Proceedings: Micro-Delcon '80.* New York: IEEE, 1980: 38–44. *C&CA* 15 (1980): 20923.

3021. Favreau, Emmanuel; Andrew Gerzso; and Patrick Potacsek. "Programmation du processeur numerique temps réel 4X." In *Proceedings of the International Computer Music Conference, 1984,* ed. William Buxton. San Francisco, Calif.: Computer Music Association, 1985: 127–29.

3022. Federer, Bob. "Synthesizers: Digital Synthesizers—the PPG Wave 2.2." *Canadian Musician* 5 (June 1983): 60.

3023. ———. "Synthesizers: The Synclavier II." *Canadian Musician* 5 (Oct. 1983): 66.

3024. Fedorkow, Guy. "Audio Network Control." M.Sc. thesis, University of Toronto, 1978.

3025. ———; William Buxton; Sanand Patel; and Kenneth C. Smith. "A Microprocessor Controlled Clavier." In *Proceedings of the 1980 International Computer Music Conference,* comp. Hubert S. Howe. San Francisco, Calif.: Computer Music Association, 1982: 96–99.

3026. Ferguson, Lee. "A Polyphonic Music Synthesizer Utilizing Master Programmed Electronic Synthesis Modules for Each Key." *Journal of the Audio Engineering Society* 25 (Sept. 1977): 592–95.

3027. Florens, Jean-Loup, and Claude Cadoz. "Instrumental Gesture, Computer, and Retroactive Gestic Transducers." Paper presented at the 1984 International Computer Music Conference, Oct. 19–23, Paris, France.

3028. Frederick, Dave. "Keyboard Report: Casio RZ-1 Sampling Drum Machine." *Keyboard* 12 (May 1986): 110.

3029. ———. "Keyboard Report: Korg DVP-1 Digital Voice Processor." *Keyboard* 12 (May 1986): 120.

3030. ———. "Keyboard Report: Yamaha SPX90 Digital Effects Processor." *Keyboard* 12 (May 1986): 122, 142.

3031. Freedman, M. David. "A Digital Computer for the Electronic Music Studio." *Journal of the Audio Engineering Society* 15 (1967): 43–50.

3032. Freeny, Stanley L. "Special-Purpose Hardware for Digital Filtering." *Proceedings of the IEEE* 63 (1975): 633–48.

3033. Friedman, Dean. *The Complete Guide to Synthesizers, Sequencers & Drum Machines.* New York: Amsco Publications, 1985. 111 p.

3034. Friend, David. "A Time-Shared Hybrid Sound Synthesizer." *Journal of the Audio Engineering Society* 19 (1971): 928–35.

3035. Fry, Christopher. "Audio Analysis II: Read-only Optical Disks." *Computer Music Journal* 9,2 (Summer 1985): 9–19.

3036. Fugazza, G. F. "Il computer dietro i tasti: concert, Uranus II, vocal, synth." [A Computer Behind the Keyboard: Concert, Uranus II, Vocal, Synth.] *Strumenti musicali* 1 (1979): 100–01.

3037. ———. "Il computer dietro i tasti: il Synclavier." [A Computer Behind the Keyboard: Synclavier] *Strumenti musicali* 4 (1980): 76–77.

3038. ———. "Yamaha CX5M: un computer per musica." [Yamaha CX5M: A Music-Oriented Computer] *Strumenti musicali* 60 (1984): 91–93.

3039. ———, and Sergio Menchinelli. "Dispositivo per la generazione di suoni mediante sintesi additiva armonica operante per mezzo di periferiche veloci controllate da un microcalcolatore." [A Sound Generator Using Harmonic Additive Synthesis Working by Microcomputer-Controlled Fast Peripherals] In *Aspetti teorici di Informatica Musicale*. Milan: CTU - Istituto di Cibernetica, Università di Milano, 1977: 109–14.

3040. Fullmer, Douglas E. "Sequencers and Programmable Controllers. Part I." *Electronotes* 7 (June 1975): 4–7.

3041. Gabel, Robert A. "A Parallel Arithmetic Hardware Structure for Recursive Digital Filtering." *IEEE Transactions on Acoustics, Speech, and Signal Processing* ASSP-22 (1974): 255–58.

3042. Gabura, A. James. "An Analogue/Hybrid Instrument for Electronic Music Synthesis." Ph.D. diss., University of Toronto, 1974. *C&CA* 11 (1976): 14779. *C&IS* 15: 137870C. *DA* 36:1313B.

3043. ———, and Gustav Ciamaga. "Computer Control of Sound Apparatus for Electronic Music." *Journal of the Audio Engineering Society* 16 (1968): 49–51.

3044. ———, and Gustav Ciamaga. "Digital Computer Control of Sound Engineering Apparatus for the Production of Electronic Music." *Electronic Music Review* 1 (Jan. 1967): 54–57.

3045. Genega, Thomas; Edward Goldberg; and Joshua Pines. "A Frequency Tracking Fourier-Based Musical Instrument." *IEEE Student Papers* (1978): 17–21.

3046. Ghent, Emmanuel. "Paper-Tape Control of Electronic Music Synthesis." *Proceedings of the American Society of University Composers* 4 (1969): 23–26.

3047. Goldstein, D. "D Drums-Electronic Percussion System." *Electronics & Music Maker* 4 (Oct. 1984): 12. *E&EA* 88 (1985): 8630.

3048. ———. "Roland TR707: Digital Rhythm Composer." *Electronics & Music Maker* 4 (Dec. 1984): 18–19. *E&EA* 88 (1985): 31253.

3049. ———. "Sequential MAX Preset Polysynth." *Electronics & Music Maker* 4 (Jan. 1985): 25–27. *E&EA* 88 (1985): 31269.

3050. Gooch, Sherwin. "Cybernetic Music System." *U.S. Patent Office Gazette* 995 (June 10, 1980): 450.
C&IS 26 (1981): 261711C.

3051. Gordon, John W. "Music Applications for the MSSP System." In *Proceedings of the International Computer Music Conference, 1985,* ed. Barry Truax. San Francisco, Calif.: Computer Music Association, 1985: 159–63.

3052. ———. "System Architectures for Computer Music." *ACM Computing Surveys* 17 (1985): 191–233.

3053. Grant, J. "The Fairlight Explained. Part II." *Electronics & Music Maker* 4 (Sept. 1984): 86–88.
C&CA 20 (1985): 4082. *E&EA* 88 (1985): 3784.

3054. ———. "The Fairlight Explained. Part III." *Electronics & Music Maker* 4 (Oct. 1984): 86–87.
C&CA 20 (1985): 7986. *E&EA* 88 (1985): 8642.

3055. ———. "The Fairlight Explained. Part IV." *Electronics & Music Maker* 4 (Nov. 1984): 94–95.
C&CA 20 (1985): 21602. *E&EA* 88 (1984): 26151.

3056. ———. "The Fairlight Explained." *Electronics & Music Maker* 5 (Mar. 1985): 86–87.
C&CA 20 (1985): 35107.

3057. Grappel, Robert. "Electronic Organ Chips for Use in Computer Music Synthesis." In *The BYTE Book of Computer Music,* ed. Christopher P. Morgan. Peterborough, N.H.: BYTE Books, 1979: 91–96.

3058. Greenwald, Ted. "Keyboard Report: E! Enhancement from Grey Matter for the DX7." *Keyboard* 12 (Apr. 1986): 116–19.

3059. ———. "Keyboard Report: Yamaha DX21 Synthesizer." *Keyboard* 11 (Dec. 1985): 110–11.

3060. ———. "The Synclavier Phenomenon." *Keyboard* 12 (Apr. 1986): 48–55.

3061. Grokett, Russell A. "PET-MUSE: Interfacing the Commodore PET to PAIA Synthesizers." *Polyphony* 4 (Sept./Oct. 1978): 40–41.

3062. Gross, Robert. "The CME Synthesizer." In *Proceedings of the Second Annual Music Computation Conference, November 7–9, 1975 at the University of Illinois at Urbana-Champaign. Part 3, Hardware for Computer-Controlled Sound Synthesis,* comp. James Beauchamp and John Melby. Urbana, Ill.: University of Illinois: 37–42.

3063. Grossman, Gary R., and James A. Cuomo. "Provisional Sound Generator." In "Four Sound Processing Programs for the Illiac II Computer and D/A Converter," ed. James W. Beauchamp. Urbana: University of Illinois Experimental Music Studio, Sept. 1968: 50–68. (Technical Report no. 14)

3064. "Guitars Imitate Church Organs." *New Scientist* 101 (Feb. 23, 1984): 27.

3065. Haflich, Steven M., and Mark A. Burns. "Following a Conductor: The Engineering of an Input Device." Paper presented at the 1983 International Computer Music Conference, Oct. 7–10, 1983, Rochester, N.Y.

3066. Hammond, Ray. "Fairlight Music Computer." *Practical Electronics* 19 (July 1983): 32–37.
C&CA 18 (1983): 34510. *E&EA* 86 (1983): 51508.

3067. Hansen, Finn E. "Sonic Demonstration of the EGG Synthesizer." *Electronic Music and Musical Acoustics* 3 (1977): 5–47.

3068. Harasek, Richard. "The Scalatron: A Digitally Programmable Keyboard Instrument." Paper presented at the Midwest Acoustics Conference, Apr. 5, 1975, Evanston, Ill.

3069. Hastings, Chuck. "A Recipe for Homebrew ECL." In *Proceedings of the Second West Coast Computer Faire,* ed. J.C. Warren. Palo Alto, Calif.: West Coast Computer Faire.
Rev. version in *Computer Music Journal* 2,1 (July 1978): 48–59.
Further rev. and updated in *Foundations of Computer Music,* ed. Curtis Roads and John Strawn. Cambridge, Mass.: MIT Press, 1985: 335–62.

3070. Haus, Goffredo. "Aggiornamento Synclavier." [Synclavier Update] *Strumenti musicali* 7/8 (1980): 104–05.

3071. ———. "Hardware per scopi musicali: linee di tendenza." [Hardware for Musical Purposes: Current Trends] In *Atti del Terzo Colloquio di Informatica Musicale,* ed. G. De Poli. Padua: Università di Padova, 1979: 258–59.

3072. ———. "Un sintetizzatore digitale a costi quasi accessibili: Alpha Syntauri." [An Almost Cheap Digital Synthesizer: Alpha Syntauri] *Strumenti musicali* 38 (1983): 82–85.

3073. ———. "Soundchaser: uno strumento digitale a basso costo." [Soundchaser: A Low-Cost Digital Instrument] *Strumenti musicali* 46 (1983): 75–77.

3074. ———. "Strumenti digitali e sistemi per l'elaborazione musicale." [Digital Instruments and Sound Processing Systems] *Strumenti musicali* 18/19 (1981): 60–65.

3075. ———. "Strumenti digitali (I): il GDS (General Development System)." [Digital Instruments (I): GDS—General Development System] *Strumenti musicali* 14 (1981): 108–10.

3076. ———. "Strumenti digitali (II): il CMI (Computer Musical Instrument)." [Digital Instruments (II): CMI—Computer Musical Instrument] *Strumenti musicali* 15 (1981): 98–101.

3077. ———. "Strumenti digitali (III): il Synclavier." [Digital Instruments (III): The Synclavier] *Strumenti musicali* 16 (1981): 104–7.

3078. ———. "Strumenti digitali (IV): il DMX-1000 Signal Processing Computer." [Digital Instruments (IV): The DMX-1000 Signal Processing Computer] *Strumenti musicali* 17 (1981): 48–52.

3079.   ———. "Strumenti digitali (V): il sistema 4X." [Digital Instruments (V): The 4X System] *Strumenti musicali* 18/19 (1981): 60–65.

3080.   ———. "Strumenti digitali (VI): l'ADS 200." [Digital Instruments (VI): The ADS 200] *Strumenti musicali* 20/21 (1981): 114–19.

3081.   ———, and Mario Malcangi. "A Portable "Walsh" Synthesizer." In *Proceedings of the Venice 1982 International Computer Music Conference,* comp. Thom Blum and John Strawn. San Francisco, Calif.: Computer Music Association, 1985: 116–32.

3082.   Hawkins, Cameron. "David McLey." *Canadian Musician* 4 (Apr. 1982): 38, 53–57.

3083.   Hayes, Alan B. "A Digital Musical Instrument." Ph.D. diss., University of Utah, 1972. 97 p.
          DA 30:3033B.

3084.   Haynes, Stanley. "Design Considerations for a Multiprocessor Digital Sound System." *Interface* 10 (1981): 221–44.

3085.   Heftman, Gene. "Software-Controlled LSI Sound Generator Makes Music While the μP Sits it Out." *Electronic Design* 27 (Feb. 15, 1979): 56–58.

3086.   Henke, W. L. "Musical Interactive Tone Synthesis System." Mimeographed. Cambridge: Massachusetts Institute of Technology, 1970.

3087.   Henry, Thomas. "Build a Digital-to-Analog Converter: Control Your Analog Synthesizer with a Home Computer." *Keyboard* 10 (June 1984): 64–67.
          Reprinted in *Synthesizers and Computers.* Milwaukee, Wis.: H. Leonard Pub. Corp., 1985: 45–51.

3088.   ———. "Low-Key Digital Keyboard." *Electronotes* 14 (June 1981): 2–10.

3089.   Hester, Allen. "Welcome to the 80's: Keyboards & Computers." *Creem Magazine* 14 (Jan. 1983): 41–44, 61–62.

3090.   Hibino, Masahiro, and Kenji Shima. "A 16-Channel Real-Time Music Synthesizer." Paper presented at the 61st Convention of the Audio Engineering Society, Nov. 3–6, 1978, New York.
          Abstract in the *Journal of the Audio Engineering Society* 26 (1978): 998.

3091.   Hillen, Peter. "Computer Controlled Triggers & Gates." *Synapse* 2 (Summer 1978): 48.

3092.   ———. "Digital Delay Lines." *Synapse* 2 (Mar./Apr. 1978): 41.

3093.   ———. "The Link between Computers & Synthesizers. Part 1." *Synapse* 1 (Jan./Feb. 1977): 4.

3094.   ———. "The Link between Computers & Synthesizers. Part 2." *Synapse* 1 (Mar./Apr. 1977): 32.

3095.   ———. "The Link between Computers & Synthesizers. Part 3." *Synapse* 2 (May/June 1977): 44–45.

3096.   ———. "A Microprocessor-Based Sequencer for Voltage-Controlled Electronic Music Synthesizers." Paper presented at the 57th Convention of the Audio Engineering Society, May 10–13, 1977, Los Angeles. Preprint no. 1229. Abstract in *Journal of the Audio Engineering Society* 25 (1977): 516.

3097.   Hiller, Lejaren A.; J. L. Divilbiss; David Barron; Herbert Brün; and Erh Lin. "Operator's Manual for the CSX-1 Music Machine." Urbana: University of Illinois Experimental Music Studio, Mar. 1966. 35 p. (Technical Report no. 12)

3098.   Hoge, Stephen F., and Anthony Agnello. "A Low-Cost Development System for Digital Audio Signal Processing." In *Proceedings of the International Computer Music Conference, 1985,* ed. Barry Truax. San Francisco, Calif.: Computer Music Association, 1985: 103–10.

3099.   Holtzman, Steven R. "An Automated Digital Sound Synthesis Instrument." *Computer Music Journal* 3,2 (June 1978): 53–61.

3100.   Hovey, Carl A., and David A. Seamans. "A Polyphonic Keyboard for a Voltage-Controlled Music Synthesizer." *Journal of the Audio Engineering Society* 23 (1975): 459.

3101.   Howell, S. "Nine Times Out of Ten: A User Report on the Yamaha DX9." *Electronics & Music Maker* 4 (July 1984): 12–14.
           E&EA 87 (1984): 55091.

3102.   Hudson, James M. "Equipping a Computer to Play a Recorder." B.S. thesis, Massachusetts Institute of Technology, Dept. of Electrical Engineering, 1974. 36 p.

3103.   Hutchins, Bernard A. "Application of a Real Time Hadamard Transform Network to Sound Synthesis." *Journal of the Audio Engineering Society* 23 (1975): 558–62.
           Reprinted in *Electronotes* 7 (Dec. 1975): 8–13.

3104.   ———. "Thoughts on Digital Keyboards." *Electronotes* 52 (1975): 7–10.

3105.   James, David V. "Real-Time Music Synthesis Using High Speed Signal Processing Computer Networks." Ph.D. diss., Massachusetts Institute of Technology, 1978.

3106.   ———. "Real-Time Tone Synthesis from White Noise Using High Speed Digital Speech Processors." Paper presented at the International Conference on Computer Music, October 28–31, 1976, Massachusetts Institute of Technology.

3107.   Johnson, Brian D. "Melodic and Rhythmic Ghosts in the Machine." *Macleans* 95 (Feb. 1, 1982): 62.

3108.   Johnstone, Eric. "The Rolky: A Poly-Touch Controller for Electronic Music." In *Proceedings of the International Computer Music Conference, 1985,* ed. Barry Truax. San Francisco, Calif.: Computer Music Association, 1985: 291–95.

3109.   Jones, M. "Chroma Polaris." *Electronics & Music Maker* 4 (Nov. 1984): 10–12.
E&EA 88 (1985): 26139.

3110.   Kaczmarek, T., and Steven W. Smoliar. "An Experiment in Interaction Between Independent Music and Graphics Processors." Paper presented at the ACM Computer Science Conference, Washington, D.C., 18–20 February 1975.
Also in *Proceedings of the 2nd Annual Conference on Computer Graphics and Interactive Techniques—SIGGRAPH '75, 25–27 June 1975, Bowling Green, Ohio,* ed. A. P. Lucido. New York: ACM, 1975: 208–11.
C&CA 11 (1976): 12108. *C&IS* 14: 133228C.

3111.   Kahrs, Mark. "Notes on Very-Large-Scale Integration and the Design of Real-Time Digital Sound Processors." *Computer Music Journal* 5,2 (Summer 1981): 20–28.
C&CA 17 (1982): 8910.

3112.   ———. "VLSI and Digital Sound Processors." Paper presented at the 1980 International Computer Music Conference, November 13–15, 1980, Queens College of the City University of New York.

3113.   Kaplan, S. Jerrold. "Developing a Commercial Digital Sound Synthesizer." *Computer Music Journal* 5,3 (Fall 1981): 62–73.
C&CA 17 (1982): 62–73.

3114.   Kinsel, Tracy S., and John H. Wuorinen. "A Digital Signal Generator." *IEEE Micro* 1 (Nov. 1981): 6–15.
Reprinted in *Selected Reprints on Microprocessors & Microcomputers,* ed. J. T. Cain. Silver Spring, Md.: IEEE Computer Society Press, 1984: 337–46.

3115.   Kitamura, John; William Buxton; Martin Snelgrove; and Kenneth C. Smith. "Music Synthesis by Simulation Using a General-Purpose Signal Processing System." In *Proceedings of the International Computer Music Conference, 1985,* ed. Barry Truax. San Francisco, Calif.: Computer Music Association, 1985: 155–58.

3116.   Knockaert, Yves. "Typeles: Synthesizer en Computer in de Muziek." [Typeles: Synthesizer and Computer In Music] *Adem* 19,1 (1983): 30–34.
In Dutch.

3117.   Körtge, Detlef. "Heute hau'n wir auf die Pauke: elektronisches Schlagzeug eröffnet neue Möglichkeiten." *Funkschau* 6 (Mar. 15, 1985): 78–81.
E&EA 88 (1985): 37379.

3118.   Kusek, David M. "A Microcomputer-Based Polyphonic Sequencer for Music Synthesizers." Paper presented at the Convention of the Audio Engineering Society, May 1979, Los Angeles. AES Preprint No. 1499.
Abstract in *Journal of the Audio Engineering Society* 27 (1979): 604.

3119. ———. "The Soundchaser Computer Music System." In *The Best of the Computer Faires. Volume VII, Conference Proceedings of the 7th West Coast Computer Faire,* ed. Jim C. Warren. Woodside, Calif.: Computer Faire, 1982: 148–52.

3120. Larsson, Bjorn. "Music and Singing Synthesis Equipment (MUSSE)." *Speech Transmission Laboratory Quarterly Progress and Status Report* 1 (1977): 38–40. *RILM* 77 1958.

3121. Leonard, Steve. "Computers for Keyboardists: Choosing a Computer, MIDI Interface Card, & Software Sequencer & Librarian." *Keyboard* 11 (Aug. 1985): 74–75.

3122. Lerner, Eric J. "Electronically Synthesized Music." *IEEE Spectrum* 20 (June 1983): 46–51.
C&IS 31 (1983): 83–12286C.

3123. Levine, Steven. "A Comparison of Digital Signal Processing Chips." In *Proceedings, Symposium on Small Computers in the Arts, November 20–22, 1981, Philadelphia, Pennsylvania.* New York, N.Y.: IEEE, 1981: 45–50.
C&CA 17 (1982): 18272.

3124. Liu, Bede, and Abraham Peled. "A New Hardware Realization of High Speed Fast Fourier Transformers." *IEEE Transactions on Acoustics, Speech, and Signal Processing,* Vol. ASSP-23 (1975): 543–47.

3125. Liu, Hsui-Lin; Carver Mead; John Wawrzynek; and Lounette M. Dyer. "Models for Real-Time Music Synthesis Using UPEs." Paper presented at the 1984 International Computer Music Conference, Oct. 19–23, Paris, France.

3126. Loy, D. Gareth. "Systems Concepts Digital Synthesizer Operations Manual and Tutorial." Stanford: CCRMA, 1980. (Report STAN-M-6)

3127. Loye, Martin de. "Real Time Control System for Digital Synthesizer." In *Proceedings of the Venice 1982 International Computer Music Conference,* comp. Thom Blum and John Strawn. San Francisco, Calif.: Computer Music Association, 1985: 241–44.

3128. Lutton, Mark. "Comments/Questions." *Polyphony* 2 (1976): 7.

3129. Manthey, Michael J. "The Egg: A Purely Digital Real-Time Sound Synthesizer." *Computers and the Humanities* 11 (1977): 353–65.
C&CA 14 (1979): 14053. *E&EA* 82 (1979): 19223. *RILM* 77 5650.

3130. ———. "The EGG Synthesizer, A Purely Digital, Real-Time Sound Synthesizer." *Electronic Music and Musical Acoustics* 1 (1975): 7–44.
Revised version: "The Egg: A Purely Digital Real-Time Polyphonic Sound Synthesizer." *Computer Music Journal* 2,2 (Sept. 1978): 32–37.

3131. ———. "A User Manual for the EGG Real-Time Digital Sound Synthesizer." Aarhus: Institute of Musicology, University of Aarhus, 1976.

3132. Massie, Dana C. "The Emulator II Computer Music Environment." In *Proceedings of the International Computer Music Conference, 1985,* ed. Barry Truax. San Francisco, Calif.: Computer Music Association, 1985: 111–18.

3133. Mathews, Max V. *The Sequential Drum.* Paris: IRCAM, 1980. 15 p. (Rapports IRCAM 27/80)

3134. ————, and Curtis Abbott. "The Sequential Drum." *Computer Music Journal* 4,4 (Winter 1980): 45–59.
C&IS 28 (1982): 81–16039C.

3135. Mauchly, J. William, and Steve Levine. "Fairlight CMI." Paper presented at the 1980 International Computer Music Conference, November 13–15, 1980, Queens College of the City University of New York.

3136. McDonough, J. "Syntauri's Innovations Continue." *Billboard* 94 (Oct. 23, 1982): 38.

3137. McGrath, T. "Korg DDM220 Programmable Percussion Machine." *Electronics & Music Maker* 4 (Oct. 1984): 34.
E&EA 88 (1985): 8635.

3138. ————. "Siel MK900 Personal Keyboard." *Electronics & Music Maker* 4 (Jan. 1985): 30–31.
E&EA 88 (1985): 31271.

3139. ————. "Technics Digital 10 PCM Digital Keyboard." *Electronics & Music Maker* 4 (Dec. 1984): 22–24.
E&EA 88 (1985): 31255.

3140. McKay, Blair D.; Barry L. Wills; and David W. Carr. "Polyphonic Velocity-Sensitive Keyboard Interface." In *Proceedings of the 1980 International Computer Music Conference,* comp. Hubert S. Howe. San Francisco, Calif.: Computer Music Association, 1982: 583–94.

3141. McLean, Barton. "The Fairlight CMI and Its Uses in Advanced Laser Graphics." Abstract in *Proceedings, 1981 International Computer Music Conference, November 5–8,* comp. Larry Austin and Thomas Clark. Denton, Tex.: North Texas State University, 1983: 283.

3142. Menchinelli, Sergio. "Jedem Finger seinen Synthesizer." *Funkschau* 51 (1979): 521–23.
C&CA 14 (1979): 28227. *E&EA* 82 (1979): 39938.

3143. Milani, Mario. *DCMP: versione per il display 2250 IBM.* Pisa: CNUCE, 1976. 17 p.

3144. Milano, Dominic. "Drum Machines." *Musicians Equipment Guide* 1 (Spring 1985): 57–59.

3145. ————. "Ensoniq Mirage Digital Sampling Keyboard." *Keyboard* 11 (June 1985): 93–96.

3146. ————. "Jan Hammer Scores Big with Miami Vice." *Keyboard* 11 (Sept. 1985): 38–54.

3147. ————. "Keyboard Report: Roland MSQ-100 MIDI Digital Keyboard Recorder." *Keyboard* 11 (July 1985): 97–98.

3148. ———. "Keyboard Report: Sequential Prophet 2000 Sampling Keyboard." *Keyboard* 11 (Dec. 1985): 108–9.

3149. ———. "Korg DW-6000 Polyphonic Synthesizer." *Keyboard* 11 (May 1985): 80–81.

3150. ———. "Oscar Programmable Monophonic Synthesizer." *Keyboard* 11 (Feb. 1985): 90–92.

3151. ———. "PPG Wave Synthesizer 2.2 to 2.3 Update." *Keyboard* 11 (May 1985): 82.

3152. ———. "Roland MKB-1000 MIDI Keyboard & MKS-80 Super Jupiter Synthesizer." *Keyboard* 11 (Feb. 1985): 97–98.

3153. ———. "The Soundchaser." *Keyboard* 7 (Dec. 1981): 72–73.

3154. ———. "Yamaha CX5M Music Computer." *Keyboard* 11 (Apr. 1985): 88–90.

3155. ———. "Yamaha RX11 Digital Drum Machine." *Keyboard* 11 (Mar. 1985): 98.

3156. "Monolithic Music Makers Croon Lullabyes, Sound Alarms." *EDN Magazine* 25 (Apr. 20, 1980): 241.

3157. Moog, Robert A. "The Alpha Syntauri." *Keyboard* 7 (Nov. 1981): 76–77.

3158. ———. "Computer-Synthesizer Interfaces." *Keyboard* 8 (Jan. 1982): 70, 72.

3159. ———. "Digital-Controlled Electronic Music Modules." Paper presented at the 37th Convention of the Audio Engineering Society, Oct. 13–16, 1969, New York.
Abstract in *Journal of the Audio Engineering Society* 17 (1969): 710.

3160. ———. "Experimental Computer-Synthesizer Interfaces: Design and Build Circuits for Nuance Control." In *Synthesizers and Computers.* Milwaukee, Wis.: H. Leonard Pub. Corp., 1985: 57–71.
From articles in *Keyboard,* Jan. 1982-June 1982, and Aug. 1982.

3161. ———. "Introducing Digital Synthesizers." *Down Beat* 47 (Feb. 1980): 72–74.

3162. ———. "Introduction to Programmed Control." *Electronic Music Review* 1 (Jan. 1967): 23–29, 32.

3163. ———. "The Keyboard Explosion: Ten Amazing Years in Music Technology." *Keyboard* 11 (Oct. 1985): 36–48.

3164. ———. "More on Computer-Based Sequencers." *Keyboard* 7 (July 1981): 72.

3165. ———. "A Multiply-Touch-Sensitive Clavier for Computer Music Systems." In *Proceedings of the Venice 1982 International Computer Music Conference,* comp. Thom Blum and John Strawn. San Francisco, Calif.: Computer Music Association, 1985: 601–5.

3166. ———. "On Synthesizers: More on Computer Interface." *Keyboard* 9 (Oct. 1982): 66, 82.

3167. ———. "On Synthesizers: Random Signals." *Keyboard* 8 (Aug. 1982): 60.

3168.   ———. "On Synthesizers: Sampling Instruments. Part 4, More Listening Tests for Digital Samplers." *Keyboard* 12 (Feb. 1986): 94.

3169.   ———. "On Synthesizers: Sound Sampling Machines. Part 2, Technical Specs & Sound Quality in Digital Sampling." *Keyboard* 11 (Oct. 1985): 97.

3170.   ———. "On Synthesizers: Sound Sampling Instruments. Part 3, Quick Listening Tests for Digital Samplers." *Keyboard* 11 (Nov. 1985): 84.

3171.   ———. "On Synthesizers: The Apple II/Rhodes Chroma Interface." *Keyboard* 8 (Sept. 1982): 58.

3172.   ———. "On Synthesizers: Unexplored Resources of the Casio CZ- 101." *Keyboard* 12 (Apr. 1986): 94.

3173.   ———. "Real-Sounds Sampling Instruments." *Keyboard* 10 (May 1984): 66. Reprinted as: "Approaches to Digital Synthesis: Real-Sounds Sampling Instruments." In *Synthesizers and Computers*. Milwaukee, Wis.: H. Leonard Pub. Corp., 1985: 34–35.

3174.   ———. "The Soundchaser Computer Music Systems." *BYTE* 7 (Dec. 1982): 260–77.
E&EA 86 (1983): 15069.

3175.   Moore, Bob. "A Hybrid Synthesizer." Paper presented at the 54th Convention of the Audio Engineering Society, May 4–7, 1976, Los Angeles. AES Preprint no. 1129.
Abstract in the *Journal of the Audio Engineering Society* 24 (1976): 487.

3176.   ———. "Hybrid Synthesizers." Paper presented at the 53rd Convention of the Audio Engineering Society, Mar. 2–5, 1976, Zurich.
Abstract in the *Journal of the Audio Engineering Society* 24 (1976): 306, 308.

3177.   Moore, F. Richard. "The CARL Computer Music Workstation: An Overview." In *Proceedings of the International Computer Music Conference, 1985,* ed. Barry Truax. San Francisco, Calif.: Computer Music Association, 1985: 5–8.

3178.   ———. "Computer Controlled Analog Synthesizers." Murray Hill, N.J.: Bell Telephone Laboratories, 1973. (Computer Science Technical Report 10)

3179.   ———. "The FRMbox: A Modular Digital Music Synthesizer." In *Digital Audio Engineering,* ed. John Strawn. Los Altos: W. Kaufmann, 1985: 95–107. (The Computer Music and Digital Audio Series)

3180.   ———. "Real-Time Interactive Computer Music Synthesis." Ph.D. diss., Stanford University, 1978. 118 p.
C&IS 19 (1978): 203623C. *DA* 38:6078B.

3181.   ———. "Signal Processing Requirements for Computer Music." In *Real-Time Signal Processing II, Washington, D.C., April 19–20, 1979.* Bellingham, Wash.: Society of Photo-Optical Instrumentation Engineers, 1979: 33–40. (Proceedings of the Society of Photo-Optical Instrumentation Engineers vol. 180)
C&CA 15 (1980): 19702. *C&IS* 24 (1970): 236718C. *E&EA* 83 (1980): 25121.

3182. ———. "Table Lookup Noise for Sinusoidal Digital Oscillators." *Computer Music Journal* 1,2 (Apr. 1977): 26–29.
Revised and updated version in *Foundations of Computer Music,* comp. Curtis Roads and John Strawn. Cambridge, Mass.: MIT Press, 1985: 326–34.
RILM 77 4019.

3183. Moorer, James A. "The Lucasfilm Audio Signal Processing Station."
Abstract in *Proceedings, 1981 International Computer Music Conference, November 5–8,* comp. Larry Austin and Thomas Clark. Denton, Tex.: North Texas State University, 1983: 245.

3184. ———. "The Lucasfilm Audio Signal Processor." *Computer Music Journal* 6,3 (Fall 1982): 22–32.
C&CA 18 (1983): 5435. *C&IS* 31 (1983): 83–1760C.

3185. ———. "The Lucasfilm Audio Signal Processor." In *ICASSP 82 Proceedings, IEEE International Conference on Acoustics, Speech, and Signal Processing, Paris, France, 3–5 May 1982.* New York: IEEE, 1982: vol. 1, 85–88.
E&EA 86 (1983): 3793.

3186. ———. "The Lucasfilm Audio Signal Processor: A Progress Report." Paper presented at the 1982 International Computer Music Conference, Sept. 27–Oct. 1, Venice.

3187. ———. "Synthesizers I Have Known and Loved." *Computer Music Journal* 5,1 (Spring 1981): 4–12.
C&CA 16 (1981): 36850 *C&IS* 29 (1982): 82–04146C.

3188. ———; Jeffrey Borish; and John Snell. "A Gate-Array Multiplier for Digital Audio Processing." Paper presented at the 78th Convention of the Audio Engineering Society, May 3–6, 1985, Anaheim. AES Preprint no. 2243.

3189. ———; Alain Chauveau; Curtis Abbott; Peter Eastty; and James R. Lawson. "The 4C Machine." *Computer Music Journal* 3,3 (Sept. 1979): 16–24.
Revised and updated version in *Foundations in Computer Music,* ed. Curtis Roads and John Strawn. Cambridge, Mass.: MIT Press 1985: 261–80.
C&CA 15 (1980): 14088. *C&IS* 24 (1979): 238878C.

3190. Munford, R. "Special Report." *Computing Today* 4 (Dec. 1982): 52–54.
C&CA 18 (1983): 11085. *E&EA* 86 (1983): 15078.

3191. Muro, Don. "Synthesizer Update." *Music Educators Journal* 69 (Jan. 1983): 63–65.
CIJE 15 (1983): EJ 275 329.

3192. "Music Board Works on 6800." *Computerworld* 13 (July 9, 1979): 44.
C&IS 24 (1979): 234501C.

3193. Nelson, Gary. "Real-Time Digital Sound Synthesizer." West Lafayette, Ind.: Dept. of Creative Arts, Purdue University.
C&IS 13: 107873C.

3194. ———, and John Talbert. "The Alles Machine Revisited." In *Proceedings of the Rochester 1983 International Computer Music Conference*, comp. Robert W. Gross. San Francisco, Calif.: Computer Music Association, 1984: 104–10.

3195. Neues, John, and Steve Kolupaev. "Construction: Digital Audio Delay Unit." *Polyphony* 6 (May/June 1980): 19–22.

3196. Neuhaus, Cable. "No One Laughs When David McLey Sits Down at the Keyboard: His Computer Knows How to Score." *People* 17 (May 10, 1982): 116.

3197. Nottoli, Giorgio. "L'unita per l'analisi, elaborazione e sintesi del suono SPU/ 01 (Sound Processing Unit/Versione 1)." [The SPU/01 Unit for Sound Analysis, Processing, and Synthesis] In *Atti del Quinto Colloquio di Informatica Musicale*. Ancona: Università di Ancona, 1983: 70–71.

3198. Olsen, Thomas E. "A Computer Controlled Audio Generator." In *First West Coast Computer Faire Conference Proceedings*, ed. Jim C. Warren, Jr. Palo Alto, Calif.: Computer Faire, 1977: 134–36.

3199. "Optical Electronics Provides Computer Music." *Electro-Optical Systems Design* 10 (Dec. 1978): 6–7.

3200. Orr, T. "Powertran MCS1. Part II, The Circuit." *Electronics & Music Maker* 4 (Nov. 1984): 57–62.
E&EA 88 (1985): 26145.

3201. ———. "Powertran MCS1. Part III, How It Works." *Electronics & Music Maker* 4 (Dec. 1984): 62–64.
E&EA 88 (1985): 31259.

3202. ———. "Powertran MCS1. Part IV, Testing, Testing." *Electronics & Music Maker* 4 (Jan. 1985): 57–62.
E&EA 88 (1985): 31272.

3203. ———; R. Monkhouse; and Pristen Bird. "Powertran MCS1. Part I, Playing with Time." *Electronics & Music Maker* 4 (Oct. 1984): 62–65.
E&EA 88 (1985): 8637.

3204. Otis, Alton B. "An Analog Input/Output System for the ILLIAC II." Mimeographed. Urbana: University of Illinois Experimental Music Studio, Sept. 1967. 72 p. (Technical Report no. 17)

3205. Parks, David. "Hardware Design of a Digital Synthesizer." *Computer Music Journal* 7,1 (Spring 1983): 44–65.
C&CA 18 (1983): 31053. *C&IS* 32 (1984): 84–13317C. *E&EA* 86 (1983): 45722.

3206. Pennycook, Bruce; Jeffrey Kulick; and Dave Dove. "The Image and Audio Systems Audio Workstation." In *Proceedings of the International Computer Music Conference, 1985*, ed. Barry Truax. San Francisco, Calif.: Computer Music Association, 1985: 145–51.

3207. Pfister, Henry L. "Computer Controlled Percussion Music." In *The Best of the Computer Faires. Volume 4, Conference Proceedings of the 4th West Coast Computer Faire*, ed. Jim C. Warren. Woodside, Calif.: Computer Faire, 1979: 284–86.

3208. Piggott, Thomas G. "A Computer Synthesizer for Real-Time Performance." Paper presented at the 66th Convention of the Audio Engineering Society, May 6–9, 1980, Los Angeles, California.
Abstract in *Journal of the Audio Engineering Society* 28 (1980): 542.

3209. ———. "Crumar General Development System." Paper presented at the 1980 International Computer Music Conference, November 13–15, 1980, Queens College of the City University of New York.

3210. Potard, Yves, and Jan Vandenheed. "Implantation d'un synthesiteur CHANT sur un processeur vectorel FPS100." Paris: IRCAM, 1984 (Internal Report)

3211. Powell, Roger. "Home Computer Sequencer. Part 1." *Contemporary Keyboard* 7 (Feb. 1981): 67.

3212. ———. "Practical Synthesis: A Quick Tour of Digital Synthesizers." *Keyboard* 8 (July 1982): 59.

3213. Prevot, P. "Controllo in tempo reale di un sistema di trattamento/sintesi del suono." [Real Time Control of a Sound Processing System] In *Atti del Quarto Colloquio di Informatica Musicale.* Pisa: CNUCE-CNR, 1981: 131–59.

3214. Puckette, Miller. "MUSIC-500: A New Real-Time Digital Synthesis System." Paper presented at the 1983 International Computer Music Conference, Oct. 7–10, 1983, Rochester, N.Y.

3215. "Rapporto del laboratorio 'Il sistema 4i ed il tempo reale'." [Report on the Laboratory 'The 4i System and Real Time'] *Bollettino LIMB* 4 (1984): 85–90.

3216. Risberg, Jeffrey S. "Evolution of Interactive Control and Real-Time Synthesis in a Digital Music System." Abstract in *Proceedings, 1981 International Computer Music Conference, November 5–8,* comp. Larry Austin and Thomas Clark. Denton, Tex.: North Texas State University, 1983: 285.

3217. "Roland Corp. Introduces Piano Plus." *Billboard* 95 (Oct. 8, 1983): 35.

3218. Rolnick, Neil B. "Idiomatic Instruments." Abstract in *Proceedings, 1981 International Computer Music Conference, November 5–8,* comp. Larry Austin and Thomas Clark. Denton, Tex.: North Texas State University, 1983: 284.

3219. Rosenboom, David. "The Touché." Paper presented at the 1980 International Computer Music Conference, November 13–15, 1980, Queens College of the City University of New York.

3220. Rossum, David P. "A Computer-Controlled Polyphonic Synthesizer." *Journal of the Audio Engineering Society* 29 (Dec. 1981): 895–901.
C&CA 17 (1982): 17973.

3221. ———. "Some Aspects of Sample Rate Conversion." In *Proceedings of the International Computer Music Conference, 1985,* ed. Barry Truax. San Francisco, Calif.: Computer Music Association, 1985: 119–24.

3222.   ———, and Scott Wedge. "A Microprocessor-Based Polyphonic Keyboard for Modular Electronic Music Systems." Paper presented at the 57th Convention of the Audio Engineering Society, May 10–13, 1977, Los Angeles. AES Preprint no. 1231.
Abstract in *Journal of the Audio Engineering Society* 25 (July 1977): 516.

3223.   Roy, John. "A Digital Sound Synthesizer." In *Proceedings of the Second Annual Music Computation Conference, November 7–9, 1975 at the University of Illinois at Urbana-Champaign. Part 3, Hardware for Computer-Controlled Sound Synthesis,* comp. James Beauchamp and John Melby. Urbana, Ill.: University of Illinois: 49–57.

3224.   Rozenberg, Maurice. *Constant High Q Bandpass Filters.* Paris: IRCAM, 1979. 8 p. (Rapports IRCAM 20/79)

3225.   ———. *A Digitally Programmable Filter.* Paris: IRCAM, 1978. (Rapports IRCAM 16/78)

3226.   Rubbazzer, Maurizio; Maurizio Santoiemma; and Gianantonio Patella. "A New Architecture for a Digital Sound Synthesizer." Abstract in *Proceedings of the International Computer Music Conference, 1985,* ed. Barry Truax. San Francisco, Calif.: Computer Music Association, 1985: 153.

3227.   Sacks, T. "Review: Yamaha CX-5M." *Your Computer* 4 (Dec. 1984): 72–74. *C&CA* 20 (1985): 31005.

3228.   Samson, Peter R. "Architectural Issues in the Design of the Systems Concepts Digital Synthesizer." In *Digital Audio Engineering,* ed. John Strawn. Los Altos: W. Kaufmann, 1985: 61–93. (The Computer Music and Digital Audio Series)

3229.   ———. "A General Purpose Digital Synthesizer." *Journal of the Audio Engineering Society* 28 (1980): 106–13.

3230.   ———. "The Systems Concepts Digital Synthesizer." Paper presented at the 1977 International Computer Music Conference, University of California, San Diego, 26–30 October 1977.

3231.   ———. "Systems Concepts Digital Synthesizer Specifications." San Francisco, Calif.: Systems Concepts, 1977.

3232.   ———, and R. Clements. "Music Systems for the PDP-10." *DECUS* 10 (Apr. 1973)

3233.   Sapir, Sylviane. "Il sistema 4i." [The 4i System] *Bollettino LIMB* 4 (1984): 15–24.

3234.   Sasaki, Lawrence H. "System Design Criteria for the Composition and Performance of Abstract Musics, with Case Study." Ph.D. diss., University of Toronto, 1980.
C&IS 27 (1981): 81–519C. *DA* 41:2274B.

3235. ———; Guy Fedorkow; William Buxton; C. Retterath; and Kenneth C. Smith. "A Touch-Sensitive Input Device." In *Proceedings, 1981 International Computer Music Conference, November 5-8,* comp. Larry Austin and Thomas Clark. Denton, Tex.: North Texas State University, 1983: 293-97.

3236. Schramke, R. W. "The Hills Are Alive . . . with the Synthesis of Music." *IEEE Potentials* 3 (May 1984): 12-17.
E&EA 87 (1984): 55103.

3237. Scott, David. "Music Computer: You Draw Sounds You Want to Hear." *Popular Science* 224 (May 1984): 154.

3238. Shearer, Hal P., and Alan C. Ashton. "Stylus and Tablet: A Convenient Method for Music Input." Paper presented at the International Conference on Computer Music, October 28-31, 1976, Massachusetts Institute of Technology.

3239. Shimony, Uri; Arnon Kanfi; and Itai Shelef. "A Real-Time Multiprocessor Musical Synthesizer." In *Electrotechnology for Development, Proceedings of MELECON '81, The First Mediterranean Electrotechnical Conference, Tel-Aviv, Israel, 24-28 May 1981.* New York: IEEE, 1981: 5.1.2/1-2.
C&CA 17 (1982): 24527.

3240. Simonton, John S. "Blessed Are the SEQUE." *Polyphony* 4 (Nov./Dec. 1978): 30-35.

3241. ———. "Controlling Exponential Systems." *Polyphony* 5 (May/June 1979): 39-41.

3242. ———. "Digitizers." *Polyphony* 5 (July/Aug. 1979): 32-37.

3243. ———. "Equally Tempered Digital to Analog Converter." *Polyphony* 2,4 (1976): 18-21.

3244. ———. "John Says." *Polyphony* 2,1 (1976): 19-22.

3245. ———. "Lab Notes." *Polyphony* 2,3 (1976): 37-42.

3246. ———. "MUS 1 with the New Miracle Ingredient—STG." *Polyphony* 3 (Apr./May 1978): 32-36.

3247. ———. "OG93: An Interpretive Arpeggiation Programmer & Editor." *Polyphony* 5 (Nov./Dec. 1979): 30-34.

3248. ———. "Poly-Split." *Polyphony* 5 (Sept./Oct. 1979): 18-19.

3249. ———. "The Polyphonic Synthesizer." *Polyphony* 3 (Feb. 1978): 28-33.

3250. ———. "Programmable Drum Set." *Polyphony* 2,4 (1976): 8-9, 31.

3251. Sims, Greg. "Applications of Air-Pressure Transducers in Digitally Synthesized Sound." Paper presented at the 60th Convention of the Audio Engineering Society, May 2-5, 1978, Los Angeles.
Abstract in the *Journal of the Audio Engineering Society* 26 (1978): 574.

3252. Small, G. W. "Rate-Feedback Binary Counters in Musical Scale Generation." *Journal of the Audio Engineering Society* 21 (1973): 702-05.

3253.   Smith, Dave. "A Microcomputer-Controlled Performance Synthesizer."
        Paper presented at the 60th Convention of the Audio Engineering Society, May
        2–5, 1978, Los Angeles.
        Abstract in the *Journal of the Audio Engineering Society* 26 (1978): 574.

3254.   Smith, Howard, and Lin Harris. "McMusic." *Village Voice* 26 (Oct. 28, 1981):
        28.

3255.   Smith, Stuart. "The Ultimate Music-Machine." *Computers and People* 26
        (Sept. 1977): 10–13.
        C&IS 17: 183305C.

3256.   Snell, John. "Design of a Digital Oscillator Which Will Generate up to 256
        Low-Distortion Sine Waves in Real Time." *Computer Music Journal* 1,2
        (Apr. 1977): 4–25.
        Revised and updated version in *Foundations of Computer Music,* ed. Curtis
        Roads and John Strawn. Cambridge Mass.: MIT Press, 1985: 289–325.
        RILM 77 4024.

3257.   ———. "Design of High Fidelity Real-Time Digital Hardware for Music
        Synthesis." In *First West Coast Computer Faire Conference Proceedings,* ed.
        Jim C. Warren, Jr. Palo Alto, Calif.: Computer Faire, 1977: 96–117.

3258.   ———. "Desirable Features of an Inexpensive Computer Used for Sound
        Synthesis." *Computer Music Journal* 1,2 (Apr. 1977): 36–38.
        RILM 77 3968.

3259.   ———. "A Gate-Array ASP Implementation." Paper presented at the 1984
        International Computer Music Conference, Oct. 19–23, Paris, France.

3260.   ———. "High Speed Multiplication." *Computer Music Journal* 1,1 (Feb.
        1977): 38–45.
        RILM 77 1961.

3261.   ———. "Lucasfilm Audio Signal Processor and Music Instrument." In
        *Micro/Mini West, 1983 Computer Conference and Exhibition, San Francisco,
        CA, 8–11 Nov. 1983.* Los Angeles, Calif.: Electron Conventions, 1983: 14/5/
        1–8.
        C&CA 20 (1985): 17275. *E&EA* 88 (1985): 20433.

3262.   ———. "Real-Time Console for Live Performance of Computer Music and
        for Recording Studios." In *Proceedings, 1981 International Computer Music
        Conference, November 5–8,* comp. Larry Austin and Thomas Clark. Denton,
        Tex.: North Texas State University, 1983: 246–63.
        Revised and updated version: "The Lucasfilm Real-Time Console for Record-
        ing Studios and Performance of Computer Music." *Computer Music Journal*
        6,3 (Fall 1982): 33–45.
        C&CA 18 (1983): 5436. *C&IS* 31 (1983): 83–1761C.

3263.   ———. "Sensors for Playing Computer Music with Expression." In *Proceed-
        ings of the Rochester 1983 International Computer Music Conference,* comp.
        Robert W. Gross. San Francisco, Calif.: Computer Music Association, 1984:
        114–27.

3264. "Soundless Instrument Synthesizes Real Music." *Piano Technicians Journal* 26 (Mar. 1983): 28.

3265. Spyker, Len. "Design of a Computer for Music Synthesis." In *Proceedings of the International Music and Technology Conference, August 24–28, 1981, University of Melbourne*. Parkville, Vic.: Computer Music Project, Dept. of Computer Science, University of Melbourne, 1981: 150–56.

3266. Steele, Douglas J., and Barry L. Wills. "A Microcomputer-Based Keyboard Music System." In *Proceedings of the 1980 International Computer Music Conference,* comp. Hubert S. Howe. San Francisco, Calif.: Computer Music Association, 1982: 595–606.

3267. Street, R. "Sounds Synthetic." *Systems International* 8 (June 1980): 45–46. *C&CA* 15 (1980): 30707.

3268. Suchoff, Michael. "A Microprocessor-Based Controller for a Live-Performance Music Synthesizer." Paper presented at the 61st Convention of the Audio Engineering Society, Nov. 3–6, 1978, New York. Abstract in the *Journal of the Audio Engineering Society* 26 (1978): 998.

3269. *Synthesizer Basics.* Milwaukee, Wis.: H. Leonard Pub. Corp., 1984. 111 p. (Keyboard Synthesizer Library v. 1)

3270. *Synthesizer Technique.* Milwaukee, Wis.: H. Leonard Pub. Corp., 1984. 113 p. (Keyboard Synthesizer Library v. 2)

3271. Tedde, G. "Un sistema per la computer music con generazione hardware di suoni e di timbri." [A Computer Music Oriented System Having a Hardware Generator for Sounds and Timbres] In *Atti del Quinto Colloquio di Informatica Musicali.* Ancona: Università di Ancona, 1983: 56–61.

3272. Teitelbaum, Richard. "The Digital Piano and the Patch Control Language System." In *Proceedings of the International Computer Music Conference, 1984,* ed. William Buxton. San Francisco, Calif.: Computer Music Association, 1985: 213–16.

3273. Tempelaars, Stan. "VOSIM Sound Synthesis." Paper presented at the International Conference on Computer Music, October 28–31, 1976, Massachusetts Institute of Technology.

3274. "Tom Swift and the Electronic Muse." *High Fidelity/Musical America* 21 (Mar. 1971): 34.

3275. Tomlyn, Bo. "How to Program the DX7: Understanding and Applying the Concepts of Digital FM Synthesis." *Keyboard* 11 (June 1985): 66–71.

3276. Torelli, Guido, and Giancarlo Caironi. "New Polyphonic Sound Generator Chip with Integrated Microprocessor—Programmable ADSR Envelope Shaper." *IEEE Transactions on Consumer Electronics* CE-29 (Aug. 1983): 203–12.

3277.   Towers, Thomas Dundas. *Master Electronics in Music.* London: Butterworth, 1976. 120 p. (Newnes Technical Books)
RILM 76 15154.

3278.   Tucker, Warren H.; R. H. T. Bates; Susan D. Frykberg; J. R. Howarth; W. K. Kennedy; Martin R. Lamb; and R. G. Vaughan. "An Interactive Aid for Musicians." *International Journal of Man-Machine Studies* 9 (1977): 635–51. *C&CA* 13 (1978): 18652. *C&IS* 19 (1978): 198819C. CR 19 (1978): 33,106.

3279.   Twigg, G. "Siel DK600 Programmable Polysynth." *Electronics & Music Maker* 4 (Dec. 1984): 20.
E&EA 88 (1985): 31254.

3280.   Vance, Scott. "Optrix: A New Method of Human Coupling with Electronic Media in Live Performance." Paper presented at the 1980 International Computer Music Conference, November 13–15, 1980, Queens College of the City University of New York.

3281.   Vercoe, Barry. "A 1972 Synthesizer Design and What We Can Learn from It Today." Paper presented at the 1983 International Computer Music Conference, Oct. 7–10, 1983, Rochester, N.Y.

3282.   Vidolin, Alvise. "Il progetto 4i." [The 4i Project] *Bollettino LIMB* 4 (1984): 9–13.

3283.   Vilardi, Frank, with Steve Tarshis. *Electronic Drums.* New York: Amsco Publications, 1985. 84 p.

3284.   Wallraff, Dean. "The DMX-1000 Signal Processing Computer." *Computer Music Journal* 3,4 (Dec. 1979): 44–49.
Also in *Proceedings of the 1978 International Computer Music Conference,* comp. Curtis Roads. Evanston, Ill.: Northwestern University Press, 1979: 57–69.
Revised and updated version in *Foundations of Computer Music,* ed. Curtis Roads and John Strawn. Cambridge Mass.: MIT Press, 1985: 225–43.
C&CA 15 (1980): 22351.

3285.   Walsh, John P. "Design Considerations for Computer Music Systems." Paper presented at the 1977 International Computer Music Conference, University of California, San Diego, 26–30 October 1977.

3286.   "Watch Chip Sings Four Tunes." *Electronics* 53 (Jan. 3, 1980): 196–98.

3287.   Wawrzynek, John; Carver Mead; Tzu-Mu Lin; Hsui-Lin Liu; and Lounette M. Dyer. "A VLSI Approach to Sound Synthesis." In *Proceedings of the International Computer Music Conference, 1984,* ed. William Buxton. San Francisco, Calif.: Computer Music Association, 1985: 53–64.

3288.   Weber, M. "Computer Sequencer PPG 350." *Instrumentenbau-Musik International* 33 (1979): 28.

3289.   West, Marcus. "An Interactive Hybrid Music System." In *Computer Music in Britain, 8th–11th April 1980.* London: Electro-Acoustic Music Association of Great Britain, 1980: 9–12.

3290. White, P. "360 Systems Digital Keyboard." *Electronics & Music Maker* 4 (Oct. 1984): 20.
E&EA 88 (1985): 8632.

3291. ———. "Akai AX80 Programmable Polysynth." *Electronics & Music Maker* 4 (Dec. 1984): 28–29.
E&EA 88 (1985): 31256.

3292. ———. "Casio CT6000, Electronic Keyboard." *Electronics & Music Maker* 4 (Nov. 1984); 26–27.
E&EA 88 (1985): 26142.

3293. ———. "Chase Bit One, Programmable Polysynth." *Electronics & Music Maker* 4 (Nov. 1984): 20–21.
E&EA 88 (1985): 26141.

3294. ———. "Korg DDM110 Programmable Drum Machine." *Electronics & Music Maker* 4 (Dec. 1984): 34–35.
E&EA 88 (1985): 31257.

3295. ———. "Korg PSS50 Programmable Super Section." *Electronics & Music Maker* 4 (July 1984): 10–11.
E&EA 87 (1984): 55090.

3296. ———. "MFP 512 Digital Drum Machine." *Electronics & Music Maker* 4 (June 1984): 24.
E&EA 87 (1984): 48632.

3297. ———. "MicroLink System ML10 for Casio MT200 and Sinclair Spectrum." *Electronics & Music Maker* 4 (Sept. 1984): 26–27.
C&CA 20 (1985): 4077. *E&EA* 88 (1985): 3778.

3298. ———. "MPC DSM8 Auto Tom." *Electronics & Music Maker* 4 (Dec. 1984): 40.
E&EA 88 (1985): 31258.

3299. ———. "Synclavier: A New Appraisal." *Electronics & Music Maker* 4 (Aug. 1984): 22–24.
E&EA 87 (1984): 61122.

3300. ———. "TED Digisound Revisited." *Electronics & Music Maker* 4 (Jan. 1985): 28.
E&EA 88 (1985): 31270.

3301. White, Stanley A. "On Mechanization of Vector Multiplication." *Proceedings of the IEEE* 63 (1975): 730–31.

3302. Wiffen, P. "Casio CZ101: Programmable Phase Distortion Polysynth." *Electronics & Music Maker* 4 (Jan. 1985): 10–12.
E&EA 88 (1985): 31265.

3303. Williams, David B., and Richard K. Hoskin. "A Programmable Tone Generator for Presenting Melodic and Harmonic Patterns in Music Research." *Behavior Research Methods and Instrumentation* 8 (Oct. 1976): 447–49.
C&CA 12 (1977): 19083. *RILM* 76 16757.

3304. Williams, N. "Australian Synthesizer Cracks the World Market." *Electronics Australia* 44 (Aug. 1982): 30–54.
C&CA 18 (1983): 8776. *E&EA* 86 (1983): 15079.

3305. Wood, K. "Computer-Controlled Synthesizer Keyboard." *Electronics Today International* 10 (Aug. 1981): 81.
C&CA 16 (1981): 36857.

3306. Wood, Thomas. "A High-Speed Digital-to-Analog Conversion System for Digital Music Synthesizers." Paper presented at the 54th Convention of the Audio Engineering Society, May 4–7, 1976, Los Angeles. AES Preprint no. 1121.
Abstract in the *Journal of the Audio Engineering Society* 24 (1976): 488.

3307. Wrightson, K. "Yamaha RX11 & RX15 Programmable Rhythm Machines." *Electronics & Music Maker* 4 (Oct. 1984): 16.
E&EA 88 (1985): 8631.

3308. *Yamaha Digital Programmable Algorithm Synthesizer Operating Manual.* Hamamatsu, Japan: Yamaha, 1984.

3309. *Yamaha DX9 Digital Programmable Algorithm Synthesizer.* Hamamatsu, Japan: Yamaha, 1984.

3310. Yantis, Michael A. "SBASS-1 Hybrid Synthesizer." Paper presented at the 1980 International Computer Music Conference, November 13–15, 1980, Queens College of the City University of New York.

3311. Yunik, M.; M. Borys; and G. W. Swift. "A Microprocessor Based Digital Flute." In *Proceedings of the Rochester 1983 International Computer Music Conference,* comp. Robert W. Gross. San Francisco, Calif.: Computer Music Association, 1984: 128–37.

3312. Zinovieff, Peter. "VOCOM: A Synthetical Engine." London: Electronic Music Studio London, Ltd., 1972. (Technical Report)

SOUND GENERATION FOR MUSIC— SOFTWARE

3313. Abbott, Curtis. "The 4CED Program." *Computer Music Journal* 5,1 (Spring 1981): 13–33.
C&CA 16 (1981): 36851 *C&IS* 29 (1982): 82–04145C.

3314. ———. "Automated Microprogramming for Signal Processing: A Tutorial." In *Foundations of Computer Music,* ed. Curtis Roads and John Strawn. Cambridge, Mass.: MIT Press, 1985: 491–511.

3315. ———. "Cleopatra: A Language for ASPs (and Other Snakes)." San Rafael, Calif.: Lucasfilm, 1983. (Technical Report 88)

3316. ———. "INV: A Language for Music Processing and Generation." Paper presented at the 1977 International Computer Music Conference, University of California, San Diego, 26–30 October 1977.

3317. ———. "Microprogramming a Generalized Signal Processor Architecture." Abstract in *Proceedings, 1981 International Computer Music Conference, November 5–8,* comp. Larry Austin and Thomas Clark. Denton, Tex.: North Texas State University, 1983: 264.

3318. ———. "A Software Approach to Interactive Processing of Musical Sound." *Computer Music Journal* 2,1 (July 1978): 19–23.
Reprinted in *Foundations of Computer Music,* ed. Curtis Roads and John Strawn. Cambridge, Mass.: MIT Press, 1985: 512–22.
C&IS 20 (1978): 207144C.

3319. ———. "Software for Distributed Real-Time Applications." Paper presented at the 1984 International Computer Music Conference, Oct. 19–23, Paris, France.

3320. ———. "System Level Software for the Lucasfilm ASP System." San Rafael, Calif.: Lucasfilm, 1982. (Technical Memo 58)

3321. ——, and Bernard Mont-Reynaud. "Scheduling Real-Time Sound I/O on Ordinary Disks." Paper presented at the 1984 International Computer Music Conference, Oct. 19–23, Paris, France.

3322. Ahl, David H. "Software Technology Music System." *Creative Computing* 3 (Sept.-Oct. 1977): 96–100.
C&IS 17: 181348C.

3323. Aikin, Jim. "Computer Software for Musicians." *Keyboard* 10 (June 1984): 34–35.

3324. ——. "Keyboard Report: Roland MPS Sequencing/Notation Software." *Keyboard* 12 (Apr. 1986): 124–29, 146.

3325. ——. "Keyboard Report: Sound Designer Editing Software for the Prophet 2000." *Keyboard* 12 (Apr. 1986): 110–12.

3326. *Algorithmic Music Language: An Interface Guide to AML-1.0.* Montrose, Calif.: Electronic Arts Research, 1981. 28 p.

3327. *Algorithmic Music Language: An Intrc ...ction and User's Guide to AML-1.0.* Montrose, Calif.: Electronic Arts Research, 1981. 55 p.

3328. Amuedo, John W. "SPIRAL: A Signal Processing Research Language." Paper presented at the International Conference on Computer Music, October 28–31, 1976, Massachusetts Institute of Technology.

3329. Appleton, Jon H. "Problems of Designing a Composer's Language for Digital Synthesis." Paper presented at the 57th Convention of the Audio Engineering Society, May 10–13, 1977, Los Angeles. Preprint no. 1230.
Abstract in *Journal of the Audio Engineering Society* 25 (1977): 516.

3330. Arfib, Daniel. "Is MUSIC V a Real Time Program? (Oldies but Goodies)." In *Proceedings of the Venice 1982 International Computer Music Conference,* comp. Thom Blum and John Strawn. San Francisco, Calif.: Computer Music Association, 1985: 341–49.

3331. ——. "Synthesis Methods for Musical Sounds and Digital Signal Processing (DSP) Software." Paper presented at the 75th Convention of the Audio Engineering Society, March 27–30, 1984, Paris.
Abstract in *Journal of the Audio Engineering Society* 32 (1984): 467–68.

3332. Askenfelt, Anders, and Kjell Elenius. "Editor and Search Programs for Music." *Speech Transmission Laboratory Quarterly Progress and Status Report* 4 (1977): 9–12.
RILM 77 3614.

3333. Attree, Richard. "Wee Also Have Sound-Houses." *Sound International* 1 (July 1978): 61.

3334. Austin, Larry. "Composing Hybrid Music with an Open, Interactive System." Paper presented at the International Conference on Computer Music, October 28–31, 1976, Massachusetts Institute of Technology.

3335. Avio, G.; P. Danti; and S. Gabrielli. "Il data base relazionale di suoni realizzato in ISELQUI." [The Relational Sounds Data Base at ISELQUI] In *Atti del Quinto Colloquio di Informatica Musicale.* Ancona: Università di Ancona, 1983: 89–91.

3336. Azzolini, Franco. "Un sistema per la gestione in tempo reale del processore di suoni 4i." [A System for the Management of the 4i Real Time Sound Processor] Tesi di laurea, Università degli Studi di Padova, Istituto di Elettrotecnica e di Elettronica, 1984.

3337. ———, and Sylviane Sapir. "Score and/or Gesture—The System RTI4I for Real Time Control of the Digital Processor 4i." In *Proceedings of the International Computer Music Conference, 1984,* ed. William Buxton. San Francisco, Calif.: Computer Music Association, 1985: 25–34.

3338. ———, and Sylviane Sapir. "Il sistema RTI4I par il controllo in tempo reale del processore 4i." [The RTI4I System for Real Time Control of the 4i Processor] *Bollettino LIMB* 4 (1984): 33–40.

3339. Baczewski, Philip, and Dan W. Scott. "An Intuitive Control Structure for the Generation of Computer-Synthesized Musical Sound." In *Proceedings, 1981 International Computer Music Conference, November 5–8,* comp. Larry Austin and Thomas Clark. Denton Tex.: North Texas State University, 1983: 172–77.

3340. Balleras, Jon. "An Expandable Control System for Computer Assisted Synthesizer: Chameleon 0.25." *Polyphony* 5 (Nov./Dec. 1979): 21–23.

3341. Banger, Colin, and Bruce Pennycook. "GCOMP: Graphic Control of Mixing and Processing." In *Proceedings, 1981 International Computer Music Conference, November 5–8,* comp. Larry Austin and Thomas Clark. Denton, Tex.: North Texas State University, 1983: 196–212.

3342. ———, and Bruce Pennycook. "Gcomp: Graphic Control of Mixing and Processing." *Computer Music Journal* 7,4 (Winter 1983): 33–39. *C&CA* 19 (1984): 19378. *C&IS* 32 (1984): 84–6919. *E&EA* 87 (1984): 21934.

3343. Banks, Rick, and David Theriault. "Preparation PILE2." Utrecht, Nov. 1978. 32 p.

3344. Battier, Marc. "A Composing Program for a Portable Sound Synthesis System." *Computer Music Journal* 3,3 (Sept. 1979): 50–53. *C&CA* 15 (1980): 14092. *C&IS* 24 (1980): 238883C.

3345. Bayer, Douglas. "Realtime Software for a Digital Music Synthesizer." *Computer Music Journal* 1,4 (Nov. 1977): 22–23. *C&IS* 18 (1978): 197089C; and 20 (1978): 207138C. *RILM* 77 6042.

3346. Beauchamp, James W., ed. "Four Sound Processing Programs for the Illiac II Computer and D/A Converter." Urbana: University of Illinois Experimental Music Studio, Sept. 1968. 68 p. (Technical Report no. 14) Contains items: 1147, 1148, 3036, 3827.

3347. ———, and Gary R. Grossman. "A Provisional Sound Generation Program for the Illiac II Computer and D/A Converter." Urbana: University of Illinois Experimental Music Studio, Sept. 1968. (Technical Report no. 14)

3348. ———; Ken Pohlmann; and Lee Chapman. "Modular Addressing of a Computer Controlled Synthesizer." Paper presented at the 54th Convention of the Audio Engineering Society, May 4–7, 1976, Los Angeles.

3349. Beeler, Michael D. *Peter Sampson's Music Processor, BIG.* Cambridge: MIT Artificial Intelligence Laboratory, 1970. 15 p. (Artificial Intelligence Memo no. 202)

3350. Bentley, Andrew. "The SYNTHEX Program." *Electro Acoustic Music* 1,2 (1985): 23–26.

3351. Berg, Paul. "ASP Report." Utrecht, May 1975. 7 p.

3352. ———. "PILE: A Description of the Compiler." Utrecht, Feb. 1977. 19 p.

3353. ———. "PILE: A Description of the Language." Utrecht, Dec. 1976.

3354. ———. "PILE: A Language for Sound Synthesis." *Computer Music Journal* 3,1 (Mar. 1979): 30–37.
Reprinted in *Foundations of Computer Music,* ed. Curtis Roads and John Strawn. Cambridge, Mass.: MIT Press, 1985: 160–87.
C&CA 14 (1979): 33898. *C&IS* 24 (1980): 230386C.

3355. ———. "PILE2: A Description of the Language." Utrecht, Jan. 1978. 11 p.

3356. ———. "A Procedural Control Language for a Digital Signal Processor." In *Proceedings of the International Computer Music Conference, 1984,* ed. William Buxton. San Francisco, Calif.: Computer Music Association, 1985: 1–3.

3357. Boudinot, Reginald D. "Development of INSGEN: An Orchestra Compiler for Computer-Generated Sound." Ph.D. diss., University of Miami, 1972. 268 p.
DA 34:6681A. *RILM* 76 1565.

3358. Bridwell, Nelson J. "Interactive Synthesis Without Obscure Diagnostics." In *Proceedings of the 1978 International Computer Music Conference,* comp. Curtis Roads. Evanston, Ill.: Northwestern University Press, 1979: 108–18.

3359. Brinkman, Alexander R. "Data Structures for a Music-11 Preprocessor." In *Proceedings, 1981 International Computer Music Conference, November 5–8,* comp. Larry Austin and Thomas Clark. Denton, Tex.: North Texas State University, 1983: 178–95.

3360. Bromose, Ole, and Finn E. Hansen. "A Survey of the SIM System, a Computer System for Performing Acoustical Analysis and Synthesis." *Electronic Music and Musical Acoustics* 1 (1975): 45–73.

3361. Buxton, William. *Manual for the POD Programs.* Utrecht: Institute of Sonology, University of Utrecht, 1975.

3362. ———. *Music Software User's Manual.* Toronto: University of Toronto Computer Systems Research Group, 1981. (Technical Note no. 22)

3363. ———. "A Practical Manual for POD6." Utrecht: Institute of Sonology, 1975.

3364. ———. "A Tutorial Introduction to *sced*." In *Music Software User's Manual*, ed. William Buxton. 2nd ed. Toronto: Computer Systems Research Group, University of Toronto, 1981.

3365. ———; William Reeves; Ronald Baecker; and Leslie Mezei. "The Use of Hierarchy and Instance in a Data Structure for Computer Music." *Computer Music Journal* 2,4 (late Dec. 1978): 10–20.
Also in *Proceedings of the 1978 International Computer Music Conference*, comp. Curtis Roads. Evanston, Ill.: Northwestern University Press, 1979: 119–29.
Revised and updated version in *Foundations of Computer Music*, ed. Curtis Roads and John Strawn. Cambridge, Mass.: MIT Press 1985: 443–66.
C&CA 14 (1979): 31237.

3366. ———; William Reeves; Sanand Patel; and T. O'Dell. "SSSP Programer's Manual." Toronto: unpublished manuscript, SSSP/CSRG, University of Toronto.

3367. Caselli, O., and G. Gobb. "Progettiamo in Basic un filtro attivo." [A Basic Program for an Active Filter] *Bit* [Milan] 19 (1981): 80–85.

3368. Casserley, Lawrence. "Series Phi." In *Computer Music in Britain, 8th–11th April 1980*. London: Electro-Acoustic Music Association of Great Britain, 1980: 21–25.

3369. Ceely, Robert P. "A Composer's View of MITSYN." Paper presented at the 41st Convention of the Audio Engineering Society, Oct. 5–8, 1971, New York. Preprint no. 811.

3370. Chadabe, Joel, and Roger Meyers. "An Introduction to the PLAY Program." *Computer Music Journal* 2,1 (July 1978): 12–18.
Revised and updated version in *Foundations of Computer Music*, ed. Curtis Roads and John Strawn. Cambridge, Mass.: MIT Press, 1985: 523–38.
C&IS 20 (1978): 207143C.

3371. Chafe, Chris. "Specifying Envelopes by Rule." Paper presented at the 1984 International Computer Music Conference, Oct. 19–23, Paris, France.

3372. Christopherson, Leo. "Celestial Music." *Creative Computing* 8 (Mar. 1982): 134–42.
C&CA 17 (1982): 28471.

3373. Clark, Robert K. "A Program for the Real-Time Generation of Musical Sounds." *Journal of the Audio Engineering Society* 14 (1966): 21–29.

3374. Clements, Peter J. "Musical Data Structures for a Multi-Use Environment." In *Proceedings of the 1980 International Computer Music Conference*, comp. Hubert S. Howe. San Francisco, Calif.: Computer Music Association, 1982: 231–44.

3375.   Clough, John. "TEMPO: A Composer's Programming Language." *Perspectives of New Music* 9 (Fall-Winter 1970): 113-25.

3376.   Cohen, David. "User's Manual for PERFORM." Arizona State University, 1968.

3377.   ———. "Yet Another Sound Generation Program." *Proceedings of the American Society of University Composers* 4 (1971): 20-22.

3378.   Cohn, George. "SOUND Language." Paper presented at the International Conference on Computer Music, October 28-31, 1976, Massachusetts Institute of Technology.

3379.   ———. "User's Manual for SOUND." Bloomington, Ind.: Wrubel Computer Center, Indiana University.

3380.   Collinge, D. J. "MOXIE: A Language for Computer Music Performance." In *Proceedings of the International Computer Music Conference, 1984,* ed. William Buxton. San Francisco, Calif.: Computer Music Association, 1985: 217-20.

3381.   Creutz, Tom. "An Interactive Graphical Interface for MIT's MUSIC 360 Language for Digital Sound Synthesis." Paper presented at the International Conference on Computer Music, October 28-31, 1976, Massachusetts Institute of Technology.

3382.   Cummings, Conrad. "Using the Program 'Chant'." Paris: IRCAM, Mar. 24, 1980. 17 p.

3383.   Dannenberg, Roger B., and Paul McAvinney. "A Functional Approach to Real-Time Control." In *Proceedings of the International Computer Music Conference, 1984,* ed. William Buxton. San Francisco, Calif: Computer Music Association, 1985: 5-15.

3384.   De Furia, Steve. "Software for Musicians: Language and Software Design." *Keyboard* 12 (Apr. 1986): 106-09.

3385.   ———. "Software for Musicians: Operations and Statements." *Keyboard* 12 (May 1986): 108, 117.

3386.   ———. "Software for Musicians: Program Your Own." *Keyboard* 12 (Feb. 1986): 92.

3387.   De Poli, Giovanni, and Ermanno Doardi. "Un sistema per l'interpretazione ed esecuzione di testi musicali mediante elaboratore." [A Computer-Based Interpreter of Musical Texts] In *Atti del Terzo Colloquio di Informatica Musicale,* ed. G. De Poli. Padua: Università di Padova, 1979: 90-106.

3388.   ———, and Goffredo Haus. "Ingegneria del software ed informatica musicale." [Engineering of Software and Computer Music] In *AICA, Associazione Italiana per il Calcolo Automatico: Atti del congresso annuale Padova, 6-8 Ottobre 1982.* Padua: AICA, 1982: 415-30.

3389. ———, and Sylviane Sapir. "Verso MUSIC V in tempo reale: un software per il processore numerico di suoni 4i." [Towards Real Time MUSIC V: Software for the Digital Sound Processor 4i] In *Atti del Quinto Colloquio di Informatica Musicale.* Ancona: Università di Ancona, 1983: 24–35.

3390. ———, and Alvise Vidolin. "EMUS: un programma per l'elaborazione di strutture musicali." [EMUS: A Processor of Musical Structures] In *Aspetti Teorici di Informatica Musicale.* Milan: CTU—Istituto di Cibernetica, Università di Milano, 1977: 26–37.
Also published: Padua: Università di Padova, 1981. (Rapporto UPee 81/06)

3391. ———, and Alvise Vidolin. *Manuale MUSIC V.* [MUSIC V Manual] Padua: Centro di Sonologia Computazionale, Università di Padova, 1983.

3392. ———, and Alvise Vidolin. *MUSIC 5: Manuale Operativo.* [MUSIC 5: Operators Manual] Padua: Centro di Sonologia Computazionale, Università di Padova, 1984. 94 p.

3393. Decker, Shawn L., and Gary S. Kendall. "A Modular Approach to Sound Synthesis Software." In *Proceedings of the International Computer Music Conference, 1984,* ed. William Buxton. San Francisco, Calif.: Computer Music Association, 1985: 243–50.

3394. ———, and Gary S. Kendall. "A Unified Approach to the Editing of Time-Ordered Events." In *Proceedings of the International Computer Music Conference, 1985,* ed. Barry Truax. San Francisco, Calif.: Computer Music Association, 1985: 69–77.

3395. Dyer, Lounette M. "Toward a Device Independent Representation of Music." In *Proceedings of the International Computer Music Conference, 1984,* ed. William Buxton. San Francisco, Calif.: Computer Music Association, 1985: 251–55.

3396. Eisenhardt, Lucie. "Le software musical." *Chroniques de l'art vivant* 3 (Juin/Juil. 1969): 30.

3397. Ellis, Bruce. "Music in C: A Digital Synthesis Program." In *Proceedings of the International Music and Technology Conference, August 24–28, 1981, University of Melbourne.* Parkville, Vic.: Computer Music Project, Dept. of Computer Science, University of Melbourne, 1981: 26–40.

3398. Espelien, Rune H. "Man/Machine Communications and Computer Music Synthesis." Paper presented at the 49th Convention of the Audio Engineering Society, Sept. 9–12, 1974, New York. Preprint no. 997.

3399. Fagarazzi, G. "Programma per il controllo di parametri timbrici mediante il volo di Levy applicato al MUSIC V." [A Monitor of Timbric Parameters Using Levy's Flight Applied to MUSIC V] In *Atti del Quinto Colloquio di Informatica Musicale.* Ancona: Università di Ancona, 1983: 137–45.

3400. Freed, Daniel J., and Shawn L. Decker. "Inslib: A Library of Routines for Building Sound Synthesis Instruments." Paper presented at the 1984 International Computer Music Conference, Oct. 19–23, Paris, France.

3401.   Gerzso, Andrew. "Trasformazioni strumentali e compositive in tempo reale." [Real-Time Instrumental and Compositional Transformations] Paper presented at the 1982 International Computer Music Conference, Sept. 27-Oct. 1, Venice.

3402.   Gino, Tocchetti. "MUSIC 6: un preprocessore per il compilatore MUSIC 5: implementazione del linguaggio MUSIC 6." [MUSIC 6: A Preprocessor for the MUSIC 5 Compiler: Implementation of the MUSIC 6 Language] Padua: Università di Padova, Centro di Sonologia Computazionale, 1984. 34 p.

3403.   Glassner, Andrew S. "Music Box in C: An Interactive, Graphic Digital Sound Editing System." Paper presented at the 1980 International Computer Music Conference, November 13–15, 1980, Queens College of the City University of New York.

3404.   Gonzato, G., and G. Parladori. "Manuale operativo e documentazione relativa al Programma MV4I." [Operators Manual and Documentation Relating to the Program MV4I] Padua: Università di Padova, 1983. (Rapporto interno C.S.C.)

3405.   ———, and G. Parladori. "Manuale operativo e guida per l'utente del programma MV4I." [Operator's Manual and Guide for Users of the MV4I Program] *Bollettino LIMB* 4 (1984): 137–39.

3406.   Greussay, Patrick; Jacques Arveiller; Marc Battier; Christian Colere; Gilbert Dalmasso; Giuseppe G. Englert; and Didier Roncin. "Software musical: descriptions et abstractions de générations et de mixage." In *Informatique musicale 1977, Textes des conférences. Equipe ERATTO*. Paris: Centre de documentation sciences humaines, 1978: 205–19.
English translation: "Musical Software: Descriptions and Abstractions of Sound Generation and Mixing." *Computer Music Journal* 4,3 (Fall 1980): 40–47.
C&CA 16 (1981): 21866. *C&IS* 26 (1981): 81–00517C.

3407.   Grogono, Peter. "MUSYS: Software for an Electronic Music Studio." *Software Practice and Experience* 3 (Oct.-Dec. 1973): 369–83.
Review by Richard Friedman in *Computing Reviews* 15 (May 1974): 26,810.
Review in *Page* 35 (1975)
Abstract in *Data Processing Digest* 20 (May 1974): 4.

3408.   Gross, Robert; Bruce Leibig; and J. Goldstein. *Timbre Tuning System (Version I), TTS Operating Manual*. La Jolla, Calif.: Center for Music Experiment, University of California at San Diego, 1975.

3409.   Grossi, Pietro. "L'automazione integrale: un approccio." [Integrated Automation: An Approach] In *Atti del Terzo Colloquio di Informatica Musicale*, ed. G. De Poli. Padua: Università di Padova, 1979: 41–43.

3410.   ———. *Musical Studies I—Instruction Manual of DCMP*. Pisa: University of Pisa, 1970. 20 p.
Abstract by Hubert S. Howe in *Computers and the Humanities* 7 (1972–73): 188–89.

3411. ———, and Tommaso Bolognesi. *Studi musicali: modalita operative del TAUMUS software di gestione del terminale audio TAU2.* Pisa: CNUCE, 1979. 119 p.

3412. Grossman, Gary R. "A Computer Sound-Generating Program Allowing User-Defined Signal Production Algorithms." Abstract in *Journal of the Audio Engineering Society* 15 (1967): 96.

3413. Hadley, May. "Twonky." *Electronics Today International* 8 (Feb. 1979): 79–84.
C&CA 14 (1979): 31240.

3414. Haflich, Steven. "Computer On-Line Music Editing in a Compositional Environment: Some Special Considerations." Paper presented at the International Conference on Computer Music, October 28–31, 1976, Massachusetts Institute of Technology.

3415. ———. "Representation of Musical Entities: LISP Active Objects and PROLOG." Paper presented at the 1984 International Computer Music Conference, Oct. 19–23, Paris, France.

3416. Harris, Kim R., and Jeff C. Morriss. "Computer Music Synthesis: A Real-Time Application in FORTH." In *1983 Rochester FORTH Applications Conference, June 7–11, 1983.* Rochester, N.Y.: Institute for Applied Forth Research, 1983: 43–66.
C&CA 19 (1984): 14749.

3417. Haynes, Stanley. "The Musician-Machine Interface in Digital Sound Synthesis." Ph.D. diss., Music Dept., Southampton University, 1980. 203 p.

3418. ———. "The Musician-Machine Interface in Digital Sound Synthesis." *Computer Music Journal* 4,4 (Winter 1980): 23–44.
C&CA 16 (1981): 36847. *C&IS* 28 (1982): 81–16040C.

3419. ———. "The Musician-Machine Interface in Digital Sound Synthesis." In *Computer Music in Britain, 8th-11th April 1980.* London: Electro-Acoustic Music Association of Great Britain, 1980: 27–63.

3420. Hicks, Bruce. "Dompier Plus: A 'Musical Keyboard'." *Dr. Dobbs Journal of Computer Calisthenics and Orthodontia* 2 (June-July 1977): 21.
C&IS 18 (1978): 189704C.

3421. Hiller, Lejaren A. "Instruction Manual for Sound Generation by Means of the CSX-1 Computer." Urbana: University of Illinois Experimental Music Studio, June 1965. (Technical Report no. 11)

3422. ———, and Antonio Leal. "Revised MUSICOMP Manual." Mimeographed. Urbana: University of Illinois Experimental Music Studio, May 1966. 89 p. (Technical Report no. 13)

3423. Hills, Arthur. "The Medieval Melody-Maker: A LISP Program." In *The Best of the Computer Faires. Volume VII, Conference Proceedings of the 7th West Coast Computer Faire,* ed. Jim C. Warren, Jr. Woodside, Calif.: Computer Faire, 1982: 140–47.

3424.   Howe, Hubert S. "MUSIC 4BF: A FORTRAN Version of MUSIC 4B." Princeton: Princeton University Music Dept., 1967.

3425.   ———. *MUSIC7 Reference Manual.* New York: Queens College Press, 1972. 109 p.

3426.   "An Introduction to SCOT." Cambridge, Mass.: MIT Experimental Music Studio, 1979.

3427.   "Introduktion till musikprogrammet EMS 1." [Introduction to the Music Program Language EMS 1] *EMS-Information* 5 (1972): 1-31.
In Swedish.
RILM 73 4540.

3428.   Jaffe, David A. "Ensemble Timing in Computer Music." In *Proceedings of the International Computer Music Conference, 1984,* ed. William Buxton. San Francisco, Calif.: Computer Music Association, 1985: 185-91.
Also in *Computer Music Journal* 9,4 (Winter 1985): 38-48.

3429.   ———. "A Synthesizer Debugger." In *Proceedings of the Rochester 1983 International Computer Music Conference,* comp. Robert W. Gross. San Francisco, Calif.: Computer Music Association, 1984: 111-13.

3430.   Jaffrennou, Pierre-Alain; Pierre Jaubert; and Ludovic Champenois. "SINFONIE: Numerical Process Command with Gestual Input Control." In *Proceedings of the International Computer Music Conference, 1984,* ed. William Buxton. San Francisco, Calif.: Computer Music Association, 1985: 201-2.

3431.   Jones, Cameron. "Input Language Bandwidth: A Statistical Study." Paper presented at the 60th Annual Convention of the Audio Engineering Society, May 2-5, 1978, Los Angeles.

3432.   Jurgens, Raymond F. "Algorithmic Music Language, A Music Emulator and Assembler-Compiler for Analog Synthesizers." Paper presented at the 1980 International Computer Music Conference, November 13-15, 1980, Queens College of the City University of New York.

3433.   Kahrs, Mark. "A Computer Language for Psychoacoustic Study and Musical Control of Timbre." Paper presented at the 1977 International Computer Music Conference, University of California, San Diego, 26-30 October 1977.

3434.   Kobrin, Edward G. "HYBRID IV Users' Manual." La Jolla, Calif.: Center for Music Experiment, 1975.
German version: "HYBRID IV: Ein Echtzeit-Computersynthese-System für Komposition und Affführung." Berlin: DAAD Berliner Künstlerprogramm, 1975.

3435.   ———, and Jeffrey Mack. "The HYBRID II: A Real-Time Composing/Performing Computer Synthesis System." La Jolla, Calif.: Center for Music Experiment, University of California at San Diego, Jan. 10, 1974. 14 p.

3436.   Krasner, Glenn. "Machine Tongues VIII: The Design of a Smalltalk Music System." *Computer Music Journal* 4,4 (Winter 1980): 4-14.
C&CA 16 (1981): 36846. *C&IS* 28 (1982): 81-16037C.

3437.   Krautzig, Walter. "Ein Musik-Programm für den Computer." *Funkschau* 51 (1979): 105–9.
C&CA 14 (1979): 25004.

3438.   Landrieu, Walter G., and L. Goethals. "Electronic Programming of Electro-Acoustical Music: Design and Application of an Electronic Device Cutting Down Realization Time of Electronic Music at the I.P.E.M. Studio at Ghent, Belgium." *Interface* 2 (1973): 71–99.

3439.   Laske, Otto E. "Considering Human Memory in Designing User Interfaces for Computer Music." *Computer Music Journal* 2,4 (late Dec. 1978): 39–45.
Also in *Music and Mind*. Boston, Mass.: O. Laske, 1981: 131–38.
Revised version in *Foundations of Computer Music,* ed. Curtis Roads and John Strawn. Cambridge, Mass.: MIT Press, 1985: 551–67.
C&IS 23 (1979): 219787C.

3440.   ———. "Subscore Manipulation as a Tool for Compositional and Sonic Design: An Experience with the Score Editor SED, of the SSSP, Toronto." Paper presented at the 1980 International Computer Music Conference, November 13–15, 1980, Queens College of the City University of New York. In *Music and Mind*. Boston, Mass.: O. Laske, 1981: 197–218.

3441.   Laursen, Thorkild, and Erik Bak Kristensen. "Brugermanual til 960A SAL-Cross-Assembler." Aarhus, Denmark: Dept. of Musical Acoustics, Institute of Musicology, University of Aarhus, Apr. 1974. (DAIMI MD-8)

3442.   Lawson, James R., and Max V. Mathews. "Computer Program to Control a Digital Real-Time Sound Synthesizer." *Computer Music Journal* 1,4 (Nov. 1977): 16–21.
C&IS 20 (1978): 207137C. *RILM* 77 5647.

3443.   Leibig, Bruce. "Scheduler for 4B Everyman Project." San Diego, Calif., 1978. 6 p.

3444.   Lentczner, Mark G. "EAMES: A Language and Environment for Computer Music." B.A. thesis, Harvard College, 1984. 105 p.

3445.   Lester, D., and Denis Jaeger. "Manual for Outperform." Unpublished manuscript. Toronto: University of Toronto, Dept. of Music.

3446.   Lifton, John. "Some Technical and Aesthetic Considerations in Software for Live Interactive Performance." In *Proceedings of the International Computer Music Conference, 1985,* ed. Barry Truax. San Francisco, Calif.: Computer Music Association, 1985: 303–6.

3447.   Lin, Erh. "Playing the Computer." *Gravesaner Blätter* 27–28 (Nov. 1965): 73–84.

3448.   Loy, D. Gareth. "An Experimental Music Composition Language with Realtime Capabilities." In *Proceedings of the Rochester 1983 International Computer Music Conference,* comp. Robert W. Gross. San Francisco, Calif.: Computer Music Association, 1984: 1–6.

3449. ———. "Introduction to the Csound File System." La Jolla: Computer Audio Research Laboratory, Center for Music Experiment and Related Research, University of California, San Diego, 1983.

3450. ———. "Notes on the Implementation of MUSBOX: A Compiler for the Systems Concepts Digital Synthesizer." *Computer Music Journal* 5,1 (Spring 1981): 34–50.
C&CA 17 (1982): 2728. *C&IS* 29 (1982): 82–4144C.

3451. ———. "A Sound File System for UNIX." In *Proceedings of the Venice 1982 International Computer Music Conference,* comp. Thom Blum and John Strawn. San Francisco, Calif.: Computer Music Association, 1985: 162–71.

3452. ———, and Curtis Abbott. "Programming Languages for Computer Music Synthesis, Performance, and Composition." *ACM Computing Surveys* 17 (1985): 235–265.

3453. Ludwig, D. "Exprsn Manual." Evanston: Northwestern University, Computer Music Studio, 1985.

3454. MacInnis, Donald. "Sound Synthesis by Computer: MUSIGOL, A Program Written Entirely in Extended ALGOL." *Perspectives of New Music* 7 (Fall-Winter 1968): 66–79.

3455. Mailliard, Bénédict. "Les distorsions de MUSIC V." *Les cahiers récherche/musique* 3 (1976): 207–46.

3456. ———. "Notes sans ourlet." *Cahiers récherche/musique* 3 (1976): 164–75.

3457. ———. "Souvenir d'un larson." *Cahiers récherche/musique* 3 (1976): 143–63.

3458. ———. "Surgeons." *Cahiers récherche/musique* 3 (1976): 250–78.

3459. Manthey, Michael J. "Real Time Sound Synthesis: A Software Microcosm." Ph.D. diss., State University of New York at Buffalo, 1980. 207 p.
C&IS 27 (1981): 81–3684C. *DA* 41:3102B.

3460. Marr, Alan, and Bruce Pennycook. "An Alternative Approach to Software for the DMX-1000." In *Proceedings of the Venice 1982 International Computer Music Conference,* comp. Thom Blum and John Strawn. San Francisco, Calif.: Computer Music Association, 1985: 100–115.

3461. Marti, Jed B. "ELMOL: A Language for the Real-Time Generation of Electronic Music." *SIGPLAN Notices* (July 1973): 23–20.

3462. Mathews, Max V. "An Acoustic Compiler for Music and Psychological Stimuli." *Bell System Technical Journal* 40 (1961): 677–94.

3463. ———. "The Computer as a Musical Instrument." *Computer Decisions* 4 (Feb. 1972): 22–25.

3464. ———. "Computer Program to Generate Acoustic Signals." Abstract in *Journal of the Acoustical Society of America* 32 (1960): 1493.

3465. ———. "The Conductor Program." Paper presented at the International Conference on Computer Music, October 28–31, 1976, Massachusetts Institute of Technology.

3466. ———. "A Graphical Language for Composing and Playing Sounds and Music." Abstract in *Journal of the Audio Engineering Society* 15 (1967): 96.

3467. ———. "Immediate Sound Generation." Abstract in *Journal of the Acoustical Society of America* 15 (1967): 1245.

3468. ———, and N. Guttman. "Generation of Music by a Digital Computer." In *Proceedings of the Third International Congress on Acoustics, Stuttgart, 1959,* ed. L. Cremer. Amsterdam: Elsevier, 1961: 253–54.

3469. ———, and Joan E. Miller. "Computer Program for Automatic Composition and Generation of Music." Abstract in *Journal of the Acoustical Society of America* 35 (1963): 1908.

3470. ———, and Joan E. Miller. "Music IV Programmer's Manual." Murray Hill: Bell Telephone Laboratories, 1965.

3471. *MAX Language Reference Manual.* White River Junction, Vt.: New England Digital Corporation, 1982. 25 p.

3472. *MAX Language User Guide.* White River Junction, Vt.: New England Digital Corporation, 1982.

3473. Menard, Philippe. "Présentation du programme AUTOMUSE." *Artinfomusinfo* 15 (1973): 19–37.

3474. Milano, Dominic. "Keyboard Report: Digidesign Sound Designer Emulator II Software." *Keyboard* 11 (Oct. 1985): 112–14.

3475. ———. "Keyboard Report: DX-Pro, DX Heaven & Data/7 DX7 Voicing Software." *Keyboard* 11 (Oct. 1985): 118–29.

3476. ———. "Music Software." *Musicians Equipment Guide* 1 (Spring 1985): 63–66.

3477. Milne, Steven H. "A Digital Sound Editor." B.S. thesis, Massachusetts Institute of Technology, 1980. 48 p.

3478. Moore, F. Richard. "Music Signal Processing in a UNIX Environment." In *Proceedings of the International Music and Technology Conference, August 24–28, 1981, University of Melbourne.* Parkville, Vic.: Computer Music Project, Dept. of Computer Science, University of Melbourne, 1981: 89–111.

3479. Murray, David J.; James W. Beauchamp; and Gary Loitz. "Using the Plato/ TI 980A Music Synthesis System: The PLACOMP Language." In *Proceedings of the 1978 International Computer Music Conference,* comp. Curtis Roads. Evanston, Ill.: Northwestern University Press, 1979: 151–66.

3480. Nelson, Gary. "Digital Sound Synthesis." West Lafayette, Ind.: Dept. of Creative Arts, Purdue University.
C&IS 13: (1974) 107880C.

3481. ———. "MPL: A Program Library for Musical Data Processing." *Creative Computing* 3 (Mar.-Apr. 1977): 76–81.
C&CA 12 (1977): 23188.

3482. O'Beirne, T. H. "Computer Programs Which Play Music with Microtones." *Computer Journal* 13 (1970): 344–49.

3483. Pennycook, Bruce. "A Critical Evaluation of the CARL Music Software." Paper presented at the 1983 International Computer Music Conference, Oct. 7–10, 1983, Rochester, N.Y.

3484. ———. "Music Languages and Preprocessors: A Tutorial." In *Proceedings of the Rochester 1983 International Computer Music Conference,* comp. Robert W. Gross. San Francisco, Calif.: Computer Music Association, 1984: 275–98.

3485. ——— and Colin Banger. "Soundfile Editing and Mixing System." Abstract in *Digest of Papers, Spring COMPCON 83: Intellectual Leverage for the Information Society, San Francisco, CA, 28 Feb.–3 March 1983.* New York: IEEE, 1983: 112.
C&CA 18 (1983): 28849.

3486. Pierce, John R.; Max V. Mathews; and Jean-Claude Risset. "Further Experiments on the Use of the Computer in Connection with Music." *Gravesaner Blätter* 27–28 (Nov. 1965): 85–97.
Parallel English and German texts.

3487. Pope, Stephen T. "Introduction to the Mshell." In *Proceedings of the Venice 1982 International Computer Music Conference,* comp. Thom Blum and John Strawn. San Francisco, Calif.: Computer Music Association, 1985: 194–201.

3488. Powell, Roger. "Home Computer Sequencer. Part II." *Contemporary Keyboard* 7 (June 1981): 65.

3489. ———, and Mark Styles. "ACT: An Automatic Composition Translator." *Polyphony* 5 (Mar./Apr. 1980): 14–17.

3490. Prooijen, Kees Van. "CYCLE: A Simple Sound Synthesis Program." Utrecht. 4 p.

3491. Puckette, Miller. "The M Orchestra Language." In *Proceedings of the International Computer Music Conference, 1984,* ed. William Buxton. San Francisco, Calif.: Computer Music Association, 1985: 17–19.

3492. ———; Barry Vercoe; and John P. Stautner. "A Real-Time Music 11 Emulator." Abstract in *Proceedings, 1981 International Computer Music Conference, November 5–8,* comp. Larry Austin and Thomas Clark. Denton, Tex.: North Texas State University, 1983: 292.

3493. Rader, Gary M. "A Music Composing Language." Paper presented at the ACM Computer Science Conference, Washington, D.C., 18–20 February 1975.
C&CA 11 (1976): 11386. *C&IS* 14: 133219C.

3494. Richer, Jean Louis. *Music V, manuel de référence.* Paris: IRCAM, 1979. 158 p.

3495. Roads, Curtis. "An Introduction to Computer Music and Applications of the Pascal Programming Language." Paper presented at the Fall U.S. DECUS Symposium, Nov. 28, 1978, San Francisco, Calif.

3496. Roberts, Arthur. "An ALL-FORTRAN Music-Generating Computer Program." *Journal of the Audio Engineering Society* 14 (1966): 17–20.

3497. ———. "Some New Developments in Computer-Generated Music." In *Music by Computers,* ed. Heinz von Foerster and James W. Beauchamp. New York: Wiley, 1969: 63–68.

3498. ———. "Some Notes on Computer-Generated Music." *Journal of the Acoustical Society of America* 39 (1966): 1245–46.

3499. Rodet, Xavier, and Pierre Cointe. "FORMES: Composition and Scheduling of Processes." *Computer Music Journal* 8,3 (Fall 1984): 32–50.
C&CA 20 (1985): 17259. *E&EA* 88 (1985): 20424.

3500. ———; Pierre Cointe; Jean-Baptiste Barrière; Yves Potard; Bernard Serpette; and Jean-Pierre Briot. "Applications and Developments of the FORMES Programming Environment." Paper presented at the 1983 International Computer Music Conference, Oct. 7–10, 1983, Rochester, N.Y.

3501. ———; Pierre Cointe; Jean-Baptiste Barrière; Yves Potard; Bernard Serpette; and Jean-Pierre Briot. "Demonstration of FORMES and Its Use for Driving Synthesizers in Music Research and Production." Paper presented at the 1984 International Computer Music Conference, Oct. 19–23, Paris, France.

3502. Rogers, Bruce. "A User's Manual for the Stochastic Music Program." Bloomington: Indiana University, 1972.

3503. Rogers, John E., and John Rockstroh. "Score-Time and Real-Time." In *Proceedings of the 1978 International Computer Music Conference,* comp. Curtis Roads. Evanston, Ill.: Northwestern University Press, 1979: 332–54.

3504. Rolnick, Neil B. "A Composer's Notes on the Development and Implementation of Software for a Digital Synthesizer." *Computer Music Journal* 2,2 (Sept. 1978): 13–22.
Also Paris: IRCAM, 1978. 10 p. (Rapports IRCAM 18/78)
Also in *Proceedings of the 1978 International Computer Music Conference,* comp. Curtis Roads. Evanston, Ill.: Northwestern University Press, 1979: 332–54.
Revised version in *Foundations of Computer Music,* ed. Curtis Roads and John Strawn. Cambridge, Mass.: MIT Press, 1985: 467–90.
C&IS 21 (1978): 210981C. *RILM* 78 3865.

3505. Rosenbloom, Michael H. "Computer Music." *Machine Design* 56 (Sept. 6, 1984): 152.

3506. Roth, James M.; Gary S. Kendall; and Shawn L. Decker. "A Network Sound System for UNIX." In *Proceedings of the International Computer Music Conference, 1985,* ed. Barry Truax. San Francisco, Calif.: Computer Music Association, 1985: 61–67.

3507. Rowe, Robert. "Recur: Composition and Synthesis." In *Proceedings of the International Computer Music Conference, 1984,* ed. William Buxton. San Francisco, Calif.: Computer Music Association, 1985: 21–24.

3508. Santoiemma, Maurizio. "Formal Representation of Basic Blocks for Sound Synthesis." In *Proceedings of the Venice 1982 International Computer Music Conference,* comp. Thom Blum and John Strawn. San Francisco, Calif.: Computer Music Association, 1985: 297–307.

3509. ———. "Rappresentazione formale delle strutture di base degli strumenti per la sintesi del suono." [A Formal Representation of Underlying Structures in Sound Synthesis Devices] *Bollettino LIMB* 2 (1982): 52–61.

3510. Sapir, Sylviane. "Descrizione del programma NOT4I." [A Description of Program NOT4I] *Bollettino LIMB* 4 (1984): 123–28.

3511. ———. "Descrizione dell'insieme dei programmi 4I." [A Description of the 4I Programs as a Whole] *Bollettino LIMB* 4 (1984): 115–22.

3512. ———. "Manuale dei comandi per la definizione degli algoritmi di sintesi." [Reference Manual for Synthesis Algorithms Definition] *Bollettino LIMB* 4 (1984): 99–102.

3513. ———. "Programmi applicativi didattici e di dimostrazione." [Educational and Demonstration Programs] *Bollettino LIMB* 4 (1984): 133–34.

3514. ———. "Programmi di utilita." [Utility Programs] *Bollettino LIMB* 4 (1984): 129–30.

3515. Sasaki, Lawrence H. "A Description Language Approach to Compositional System Design." Unpublished manuscript, Dept. of Electrical Engineering, University of Toronto, Toronto, 1978.

3516. ———. "Macro Music I User's Guide and Language Reference Manual." Toronto: Dept. of Electrical Engineering, University of Toronto, 1977.

3517. Scholz, Carter. "Do-It-Yourself Software: Any MIDI Keyboard Can Play in Just Intonation with Computerized Pitch-Bending." *Keyboard* 12 (Feb. 1986): 49–52, 142–43.

3518. Schottstaedt, Bill. "Pla: A Composer's Idea of a Language." *Computer Music Journal* 7,1 (Spring 1983): 11–20.
C&CA 18 (1983): 32101.

3519. *SCRIPT User Guide.* Norwich, Vt.: New England Digital Corporation, 1981. 59 p.

3520. Siegel, Dorothy. "Low-Cost Multi-Part Music Programmed in BASIC." In *The Best of the Computer Faires. Volume 3, Conference Proceedings of the 3rd West Coast Computer Faire,* ed. Jim C. Warren, Jr. Los Angeles: Computer Faire, 1978: 42–43.

3521. Simioni, E. "Analisi del filtro FB1 del MUSIC V." [An Analysis of the FB1 filter of MUSIC V] In *Atti del Quarto Colloquio di Informatica Musicale.* Pisa: CNUCE-CNR, 1981: 184–210.

3522. Simonton, John S. "SEQUE and Ye Shall Find." *Polyphony* 4 (Sept./Oct. 1978): 15–18.

3523. Slawson, A. Wayne. "Input Languages Affect System Design." Paper presented at the International Conference on Computer Music, October 28–31, 1976, Massachusetts Institute of Technology.

3524. ———. "MUSE: A Sound Synthesizer." In *Information Processing 1962: Proceedings of the IFIP Congress* 62, ed. Cicely M. Popplewell. Amsterdam: North Holland, 1963: 451–55.
Includes abstracts in five languages and a discussion.

3525. ———. "A Speech-Oriented Synthesizer of Computer Music." *Journal of Music Theory* 13 (1969): 94–127.

3526. Smith, Bennett K., and David E. Ehresman. "A Computer-Controlled Display-Oriented Digital Sound Editor." Paper presented at the 1978 International Computer Music Conference, November 1–5, Northwestern University, Evanston, Illinois.

3527. Smith, Leland. "SCORE: A Musician's Approach to Computer Music." *Journal of the Audio Engineering Society* 20 (1972): 7–14.
Also in *Numus-West* 4 (1973): 21–28.
RILM 74 1145.

3528. Smoliar, Stephen W. "A Data Structure for an Interactive Music System." *Interface* 2 (1973): 127–40.
Also issued as Israel Institute of Technology Department of Computer Science Technical Report No. 21, Haifa, Israel, Oct. 1972.
RILM 74 1146.

3529. ———. "EUTERPE: A Computer Language for the Expression of Musical Ideas." Mimeographed. Cambridge: Massachusetts Institute of Technology Project MAC, Apr. 1967. (Artificial Intelligence Memo no. 129)

3530. ———. "EUTERPE-8: A PDP-8-Based Music Processor." Paper presented at the ACM Computer Science Conference, Washington, D.C., 18–20 February 1975.
C&CA 11 (1976): 12102. *C&IS* 14: 133221C.

3531. ———. "EUTERPE-LISP: A LISP System with Music Output." Mimeographed. Cambridge, Mass.: Massachusetts Institute of Technology, Sept. 1967. 16 p. (Artificial Intelligence Memo no. 141)

3532. ———. "Music Programs and Their Syntactic Aspects; Semantic Aspects of Music Programs; Sonological Aspects of Music Programs; The Interaction of Syntax, Semantics, and Sonology." Philadelphia, Pa.: Dept. of Computer Science, University of Pennsylvania, 1974. 42 p. (CIS 580D Lecture Notes)

3533. ———. "A Parallel Processing Model of Musical Structures." Ph.D. diss., Massachusetts Institute of Technology, 1971. 2 v., 275 p.
Revised version published Cambridge: Massachusetts Institute of Technology Project MAC, Sept. 1971. 276 p. (Technical Report no. 91)
RILM 71 94.

3534. ————. "Using the EUTERPE Music System." Cambridge: Massachusetts Institute of Technology, Artificial Intelligence Laboratory, 1971. 15 p. (AI Memo no. 243)

3535. Sordillo, Donald. "Music Playing on the PDP-6." Cambridge: Massachusetts Institute of Technology, Project MAC, Aug. 1966. (Artificial Intelligence Project Memo no. 107)

3536. Steiger, Richard. "OEDIT—An Interactive Orchestra Editing System." Paper presented at the International Conference on Computer Music, October 28–31, 1976, Massachusetts Institute of Technology.

3537. Stenson, E. "Alternatives." *Electronics & Music Maker* 4 (Jan. 1985): 98–99. *E&EA* 88 (1985): 31277.

3538. Stickney, Kimball P. "MUSIC-11 and ST-10: Classic Stochastic Concepts Revisited." In *Proceedings of the 1980 International Computer Music Conference,* comp. Hubert S. Howe. San Francisco, Calif.: Computer Music Association, 1982: 607–13.

3539. Strawn, John. "Editing Time-Varying Spectra." Paper presented at the 78th Convention of the Audio Engineering Society, May 3–6, 1981, Anaheim. Preprint no. 2228 (A-10)

3540. ————. "eMerge: Toward a Knowledge-Based Spectral Editor." Abstract in *Proceedings of the Rochester 1983 International Computer Music Conference,* comp. Robert W. Gross. San Francisco, Calif.: Computer Music Association, 1984: 55–56.

3541. Tarabella, Leonello. "PRIMULA, un linguaggio interattivo di PRogrammazione MUsicale." [PRIMULA, an Interactive Musical Programming Language] In *Atti del Terzo Colloquio di Informatica Musicale,* ed. G. De Poli. Padua: Università di Padova, 1979: 194–210.

3542. ————. *PRIMULA: un linguaggio interattivo per la PRogrammazione MUsicale.* [PRIMULA, an Interactive Musical Programming Language] Pisa: CNUCE, 1979. 22 p.

3543. ————. "Una realizzazione del linguaggio PRIMULA." [A Realization of the Language PRIMULA] In *Atti del Quarto Colloquio di Informatica Musicale.* Pisa: CNUCE-CNR, 1981: 300–312.

3544. Taylor, Hal. "SCORTOS: Implementation of a Music Language." *BYTE* 2 (Sept. 1977): 12–28.
Also in *The BYTE Book of Computer Music,* ed. Christopher P. Morgan. Peterborough, N.H.: BYTE Books, 1979: 1–8.
Review by Michael Kassler in *Computing Reviews* 19 (1978): 32, 699.
C&CA 13 (1978): 2570. *C&IS* 17 181349C.

3545. Tisato, Graziano. "An Interactive Software System for Real-Time Sound Synthesis." Paper presented at the International Conference on Computer Music, October 28–31, 1976, Massachusetts Institute of Technology."

3546.   ———. "Un sistema interattivo di software per la sintesi del suono in tempo reale." [An Interactive Software System for Real Time Sound Synthesis] In *Aspetti Teorici in Informatica Musicale.* Milan: CTU—Istituto di Cibernetica, Università di Milano, 1977: 96–108.

3547.   ———. *Sistema musica: manuale operativo.* [Music System: Operator's Manual] Padua: Centro di Sonologia Computazionale, Università di Padova, 1983. 162 p.

3548.   Tovar. "Music Manual." Unpublished user's manual. Stanford: Center for Computer Research in Music and Acoustics, 1977.

3549.   ———, and Leland Smith. "MUS10 User Manual." Unpublished user's manual. Stanford: Center for Computer Research in Music and Acoustics, 1977.

3550.   Truax, Barry D. "The Computer Composition-Sound Synthesis Programs POD4, POD5, and POD6." *Sonological Reports 2.* Utrecht: Institute of Sonology, State University of Utrecht, 1973.

3551.   ———. "Computer Music Composition: The Polyphonic POD System." *Computer* 11 (Aug. 1978): 40–50.
C&CA 13 (1978): 32031. *C&IS* 20 (1978): 207148C.

3552.   ———. "General Techniques of Computer Composition Programming." *Numus-West* 4 (1973): 17–20.

3553.   ———. "The POD Programs at Simon Fraser University." Unpublished manuscript, Vancouver, Aug., 1975.

3554.   ———. "The POD Programs for Sound Synthesis at Simon Fraser University." Mimeographed. Vancouver, Dec. 1974. 23 p.

3555.   ———. "The POD System of Interactive Composition Programs." *Computer Music Journal* 1,3 (June 1977): 30–39.
Excerpt from "A Communicational Approach to Computer Sound Programs." *Journal of Music Theory* 20 (1976): 227–300.
C&IS 18 (1978): 189688C. RILM 77 3751.

3556.   ———. "The PODX System: Interactive Compositional Software for the DMX-1000." *Computer Music Journal* 9,1 (Spring 1985): 29.

3557.   ———. "The Polyphonic POD System and Its Use in Timbral Construction." In *Computer Music/Composition musicale par ordinateur; Report on an International Project Including a Workshop at Aarhus, Denmark in 1978,* ed. Marc Battier and Barry Truax. Ottawa: Canadian Commission for Unesco, 1980: 169–89.

3558.   ———. "Some Programs for Real-Time Computer Synthesis and Composition." *Interface* 2 (1973): 159–63.

3559.   Ungvary, Tamas. "Sound Image Synthesis." In *Proceedings of the 1980 International Computer Music Conference,* comp. Hubert S. Howe. San Francisco, Calif.: Computer Music Association, 1982: 484–97.

3560. Vercoe, Barry. "Composing with Music-11." Paper presented at the 1978 International Computer Music Conference, November 1–5, Northwestern University, Evanston, Illinois.

3561. ———. "Computer Generated Sound Programs." *Proceedings of the American Society of University Composers* 4 (1969): 36–37.

3562. ———. "Man-Computer Interaction as a Creative Aid in the Formulation of Digital Sound Structures." Paper presented at the 52nd Convention of the Audio Engineering Society, Oct. 31–Nov. 3, 1975, New York. Abstract in *Journal of the Audio Engineering Society* 23 (1975): 833.

3563. ———. "The Music 360 Language for Sound Synthesis." *Proceedings of the American Society of University Composers* 6 (1973): 16–20.

3564. ———. "Reference Manual for the Music 360 Language for Digital Sound Synthesis." Mimeographed. Cambridge: Massachusetts Institute of Technology, Studio for Experimental Music, 1973.

3565. Wallraff, Dean. "Implementation of the MUSIC-1000 Language." Paper presented at the 1982 International Computer Music Conference, Sept. 27–Oct. 1, Venice.

3566. ———. "MUSIC-1000: Real-Time Synthesis Software for the DMX-1000 Signal Processing Computer." Paper presented at the 1980 International Computer Music Conference, November 13–15, 1980, Queens College of the City University of New York.

3567. Warfield, Gerald. "Beginner's Manual of MUSIC 4B." Mimeographed. Princeton: Princeton University Music Dept.

3568. Willson, M. Joseph. "A Computational Model of Music Synthesis." Ph.D. diss., University of Pennsylvania, 1978. 234 p. *C&IS* 23 (1979): 219782C. *DA* 39:3419B.

3569. Winham, Godfrey. "How MUSIC 4B Generates Formants and Non-Harmonic Partials, and Improves Loudness Control and 'Quality'." *Proceedings of the American Society of University Composers* 1 (1968): 42–46.

3570. ———. "The Reference Manual of MUSIC 4B." Mimeographed. Princeton: Princeton University Music Dept. 1966. 74 p.

3571. Winkleman, Jim. *Introduction to Music 11.* Tri-College Group for Electronic Music, 1980. 53 p.

3572. Yannes, Bob. "Letters: Computer Aided Music." *Polyphony* 4 (July/Aug. 1978): 5, 27–28.

3573. ———. "Shazam, or, Maestro, a Little Software, Please." *Polyphony* 4 (Nov./Dec. 1978): 13–17.

3574. Youngblood, Joseph. "Computer Music." *Computers and the Humanities* 7 (1972): 28.

3575. Zinovieff, Peter. "Problems in Programming a Complex Computer Controlled Electronic Music Studio." Paper presented at the 1978 International Computer Music Conference, November 1-5, Northwestern University, Evanson, Ill.

3576. Zuckerman, Faye. "Computer Software Starts Singing: Leading Firms Marketing Low-Cost Music Programs." *Billboard* 95 (Oct. 22, 1983): 4, 70.

SOUND GENERATION
FOR MUSIC—
SYNTHESIS
TECHNIQUES

3577.   Arfib, Daniel. "Digital Synthesis of Complex Spectra by Means of Multiplica-
        tion of Non-linear Distorted Sine Waves." In *Proceedings of the 1978 Interna-
        tional Computer Music Conference,* comp. Curtis Roads. Evanston, Ill.:
        Northwestern University Press, 1979: 70–84.
        Also in *Journal of the Audio Engineering Society* 27 (1979): 757–68.
        Also, paper presented at the 59th convention of the Audio Engineering Society,
        Hamburg, February 28-March 3, 1978. Preprint no. 1319.
        E&EA 83 (1980): 10746.

3578.   ———. "Digital Synthesis of Complex Spectra by Means of Non-linear Dis-
        tortion of Sine Waves and Amplitude Modulation." Paper presented at the
        1977 International Computer Music Conference, University of California, San
        Diego, 26–30 October 1977.

3579.   ———. "The Musical Use of NonLinear Distortion (Waveshaping)." In *Pro-
        ceedings of the 1980 International Computer Music Conference,* comp. Hubert
        S. Howe. San Francisco, Calif.: Computer Music Association, 1982: 498–511.

3580.   ———. "La synthèse des sons par ordinateur par distorsion non lineaire et
        modulation d'amplitude." In *Computer Music/Composition musicale par
        ordinateur; Report on an International Project Including a Workshop at Aarhus,
        Denmark in 1978,* ed. Marc Battier and Barry Truax. Ottawa: Canadian Com-
        mission for Unesco, 1980: 1–14.

3581.   Ashcraft, Cliff; Frank Covitz; and K. A. Sproul. "Noise in Real Time Digital
        Sound Generation." In *Proceedings, 2nd Symposium on Small Computers in
        the Arts, October 15–17, 1982, Philadelphia, Pa.* Los Angeles, Calif.: IEEE
        Computer Society, 1982: 5–14.
        C&CA 18 (1983): 28832. *E&EA* 86 (1983): 40735.

3582. Asuar, José V. "Programmed Control of Analog Sound Generators." Buffalo: National Science Foundation Project No. GK-14191, Jan. 1973. 46 p. (Technical Report no. 5)

3583. Bader, Karl Otto, and Barry A. Blesser. "Klangumformung durch Computer." In *Tonmeistertagung (10.) 19.–22. November 1975, Köln Bericht.* Cologne: Welzel and Hardt, 1976.

3584. Barrière, Jean-Baptiste; J. Holleville; Yves Potard; and Xavier Rodet. "Musical Synthesis: Evolution of the 'Chant' Project." Abstract in *Proceedings, 1981 International Computer Music Conference, November 5–8,* comp. Larry Austin and Thomas Clark. Denton, Tex.: North Texas State University, 1983: 282.

3585. Bass, Steven C. "A Technique for the Generation of Harmonically-Rich Waveforms." In *Proceedings, IEEE International Conference on Circuits and Computers, ICCC 80,* ed. N.B. Guy Rabbat. New York: IEEE, 1980: vol. 2, 1063–66.

3586. Beauchamp, James W. "A Computer Orchestra." In *Proceedings of the Venice 1982 International Computer Music Conference,* comp. Thom Blum and John Strawn. San Francisco, Calif.: Computer Music Association, 1985: 354–57.

3587. ———. "Data Reduction and Resynthesis of Connected Solo Passages Using Frequency, Amplitude, and 'Brightness' Detection and the Nonlinear Synthesis Technique." In *Proceedings, 1981 International Computer Music Conference, November 5–8,* comp. Larry Austin and Thomas Clark. Denton, Tex.: North Texas State University, 1983: 316–23.

3588. ———. "Practical Sound Synthesis Using a Non-linear Processor (Waveshaper) and a High-pass Filter." *Computer Music Journal* 3,3 (Sept. 1979): 42–49.
C&CA 15 (1980): 14091. *C&IS* 24 (1980): 238882C.

3589. ———. "Synthesis by Amplitude and Spectral Center Matching of Analyzed Musical Instrument Tones." Paper presented at the 1980 International Computer Music Conference, November 13–15, 1980, Queens College of the City University of New York.

3590. ———. "Synthesis by Spectral Amplitude and 'Brightness' Matching of Analyzed Musical Instrument Tones." *Journal of the Audio Engineering Society* 30 (1982): 396–406.

3591. ———. "Time-Variant Spectrum Analysis-Synthesis." Paper presented at the 1983 International Computer Music Conference, Oct. 7–10, 1983, Rochester, N.Y.

3592. Bennett, Gerald, and Xavier Rodet. "Research in Music Synthesis Using a Model of Vocal Production." Paper presented at the 1980 International Computer Music Conference, November 13–15, 1980, Queens College of the City University of New York.

3593.   Berg, Paul; Robert Rowe; and David Theriault. "SSP and Sound Description." *Computer Music Journal* 4,1 (Spring 1980): 25–35.
Review by Michael Kassler in *Computing Reviews* 22 (1981): 37,869.
C&CA 16 (1981): 18376. *C&IS* 26 (1981): 265455C.

3594.   Bernardini, Nicola. "Tecniche di sintesi (I): la sintesi additiva." [Synthesis Techniques (I): Additive Synthesis] *AudioReview* 25 (1984): 96–100.

3595.   ———. "Tecniche di sintesi (II): la sintesi per funzioni di Walsh." [Synthesis Techniques (II): Synthesis by Walsh Functions] *AudioReview* 26 (1984): 96–101.

3596.   ———. "Tecniche di sintesi (III): la sintesi sottrattiva." [Synthesis Techniques (III): Subtractive Synthesis] *AudioReview* 27 (1984): 109.

3597.   ———. "Tecniche di sintesi (IV): la sintesi per predizione lineare." [Synthesis Techniques (IV): Synthesis by Linear Prediction] *AudioReview* 28 (1984): 118–21.

3598.   ———. "Tecniche di sintesi (V): la modulazione di frequenza (I)." [Synthesis Techniques (V): Frequency Modulation (I)] *AudioReview* 32 (1984): 120–23.

3599.   ———. "Tecniche di sintesi (V): la modulazione di frequenza (II)." [Synthesis Techniques (V): Frequency Modulation (II)] *AudioReview* 33 (1984): 109–11.

3600.   ———. "Tempo reali: sintesi digitale verso sintesi analogica." [Real Time: Digital Versus Analog Synthesis] *AudioReview* 23 (1983): 49–52.

3601.   Bernstein, Alan D., and Ellis D. Cooper. "The Piecewise Linear Technique of Electronic Music Synthesis." *Journal of the Audio Engineering Society* 24 (1976): 446–54.

3602.   Bolognesi, Tommaso; A. Casini; and G. Castellini. "Sintesi dei suoni ed elaborazione di strutture musicali." [Sound Synthesis and Computation of Musical Structures] *Informatica Oggi* n2 (1981): 60–65.

3603.   Borgonovo, Aldo, and Goffredo Haus. "Musical Sound Synthesis by Means of Two-Variable Functions: Experimental Criteria and Results." In *Proceedings of the International Computer Music Conference, 1984,* ed. William Buxton. San Francisco, Calif.: Computer Music Association, 1985: 35–42.

3604.   ———; Goffredo Haus; and C. Trogu Roehrich. "Esperienze sulla sintesi di segnali audio mediante funzioni di due variabili." [An Experience on Synthesis of Audio Signals Using Two-Variable Functions] In *Atti del Quinto Colloquio di Informatica Musicale.* Ancona: Università di Ancona, 1983: 92–98.

3605.   Boudinot, Reginald D. "Development of a Standard Orchestra for Computer-Generated Sound." *Computers and the Humanities* 6 (Nov. 1971): 123.

3606.   Boulanger, Richard. "The Transformation of Speech into Music: A Musical Interpretation of Two Recent Digital Filtering Techniques." Ph.D. diss., University of California, San Diego, 1985.

3607. Bowler, Ian. "The Synthesis of Complex Audio Spectra by Cheating Quite a Lot." In *Proceedings of the International Computer Music Conference, 1985,* ed. Barry Truax. San Francisco, Calif.: Computer Music Association, 1985: 79–84.

3608. Brown, Frank. "Synthèse totale de musique." D.E.A., Faculté des Sciences du Mans, Laboratoire d'Acoustique, Dec. 1974.

3609. Burhans, R. W. "Digital Tone Synthesis." *Journal of the Audio Engineering Society* 19 (1971): 660–663.

3610. Buxton, William; S. Hull; and A. Fournier. "On Contextually Adaptive Timbres." Abstract in *Proceedings, 1981 International Computer Music Conference, November 5–8,* comp. Larry Austin and Thomas Clark. Denton, Tex.: North Texas State University, 1983: 414–16.

3611. ———; Sanand Patel; William Reeves; and Ronald Baecker. "Objed and the Design of Timbral Resources." *Computer Music Journal* 6,2 (Summer 1982): 32–44.
C&IS 29 (1982): 82–13613C.

3612. Cann, Richard. "An Analysis/Synthesis Tutorial." In *Foundations of Computer Music,* ed. Curtis Roads and John Strawn. Cambridge, Mass.: MIT Press, 1985: 114–44.
Reprinted from *Computer Music Journal* 3,3 (Sept. 1979): 6–11; 3,4 (Dec. 1979): 9–13; and 4,1 (Spring 1980): 36–42.

3613. ———. "An Analysis/Synthesis Tutorial. Part 1." *Computer Music Journal* 3,3 (Sept. 1979): 6–11.
C&CA 15 (1980): 14086. *C&IS* 24 (1980): 238884C.

3614. ———. "An Analysis/Synthesis Tutorial. Part 2." *Computer Music Journal* 3,4 (Dec. 1979): 9–13.
C&CA 15 (1980): 22348. *C&IS* 25 (1980): 243463C.

3615. ———. "An Analysis/Synthesis Tutorial. Part 3." *Computer Music Journal* 4,1 (Spring 1980): 36–42.
C&IS 26 (1981): 265456C.

3616. ———. "A Musical View of Analysis-Synthesis." In *Proceedings of the 1978 International Computer Music Conference,* comp. Curtis Roads. Evanston, Ill.: Northwestern University Press, 1979: 130–41.

3617. ———. "Speech Analysis/Synthesis for Electronic Vocal Music." Ph.D. diss., Princeton University, 1978. 191 p.
DA 39:3205A. *RILM* 78 4010.

3618. ———; Paul Lansky; Kenneth Stieglitz; and Mark Zuckerman. "Practical Considerations in the Application of Linear Prediction to Music Synthesis." Paper presented at the International Conference on Computer Music, October 28–31, 1976, Massachusetts Institute of Technology.

3619.   ———, and Kenneth Stieglitz. "Toward Improved Analysis-Synthesis Using Cepstral and Pole-Zero Techniques." Paper presented at the 1977 International Computer Music Conference, University of California, San Diego, 26–30 October 1977.

3620.   Carlos, Wendy. "Wendy Carlos on Additive Synthesis: Tearing Apart Acoustic Sounds and Putting Them Back Together." *Keyboard* 11 (June 1985): 46–54.

3621.   Castro, Caesar. "FM Synthesis and the Casheab 32 Channel Synthesizer." In *The Best of the Computer Faires: Conference Proceedings of the 6th West Coast Computer Faire,* ed. Jim C. Warren. Woodside, Calif.: Computer Faires, 1981: 91–95.

3622.   Cerruti, Roberto, and Giorgio Rodeghiero. "Comments on 'Musical Sound Synthesis by Forward Differences'." *Journal of the Audio Engineering Society* 31 (1983): 446.

3623.   Chowning, John M. "FM Synthesis: Its Evolution." Paper presented at the 1983 International Computer Music Conference, Oct. 7–10, 1983, Rochester, N.Y.

3624.   ———. "Naturalness and Synthesis: Tending to Detail." Abstract in *Proceedings of the International Music and Technology Conference, August 24–28, 1981, University of Melbourne.* Parkville, Vic.: Computer Music Project, Dept. of Computer Science, University of Melbourne, 1981: 13.

3625.   ———. "The Synthesis of Complex Audio Spectra by Means of Frequency Modulation." *Journal of the Audio Engineering Society* 21 (Sept. 1973): 526–34.
Reprinted in the *Computer Music Journal* 1,2 (Apr. 1977): 46–54.
Reprinted in *Musical Aspects of the Electronic Medium, Report on Electronic Music,* ed. F. Weiland. Utrecht: Institute of Sonology, 1975.
Reprinted in *Foundations of Computer Music,* ed. Curtis Roads and John Strawn. Cambridge, Mass.: MIT Press, 1985: 6–29.
RILM 77 1956.

3626.   Cohen, Howard. "MX-2, A Real Time Frequency Modulation Sound Synthesis System." La Jolla, Calif.: Center for Music Experiment, University of California at San Diego, 1977. 7 p.

3627.   Conyngham, Barry E., and Andrew Mander-Jones. "Direct Computer Synthesis of Music." *Australian Computer Conference* 7 (Aug. 1976): 947–59.
RILM 76 15621.

3628.   Corinaldesi, M. "Sintesi ottimizzata di filtri attivi." [Optimized Synthesis by Active Filters] *Bit* [Milan] 20 (1981): 108–18.

3629.   Cotton, Robert B. "Tempered Scale Generation from a Single Frequency Source." *Journal of the Audio Engineering Society* 20 (1972): 376–82.

3630. Covitz, Frank, and Cliff Ashcraft. "Analysis & Generation of Complex Sounds Using Small Computers." In *Proceedings, Symposium on Small Computers in the Arts, November 20–22, 1981, Philadelphia, Pennsylvania.* New York, N.Y.: IEEE, 1981: 33–43.
C&CA 17 (1982): 19788.

3631. Dashow, James. "Spectra as Chords." In A*tti del Terzo Colloquio di Informatica Musicale,* ed. G. De Poli. Padua: Università di Padova, 1979: 78–89.
Also in *Computer Music Journal* 4,1 (Spring 1980): 43–52.
Review by E. Gagliardo in *Computing Reviews* 22 (Mar. 1981): 37, 589.
C&CA 16 (1981): 15681. *C&IS* 26 (1981): 263661C.

3632. ———. "Three Methods for the Digital Synthesis of Chordal Structures with Non-Harmonic Partials." *Interface* 7 (1978): 69–94.
E&EA 82 (1979): 18586.

3633. De Poli, Eva, and Giovanni De Poli. "Determinazione dei parametri VOSIM di un suono quasi periodico." [Determination of the Parameters of a Quasi Periodic Sound in VOSIM] In *Atti del Congresso dell'Associazione Italiana di Acustica '79.* ESA, 1979: 41–43.

3634. ———, and Giovanni De Poli. "Identificazione dei parametri di un oscillatore VOSIM a partire da una descrizione spettrale." [Identification of VOSIM Oscillator Parameters Based on a Spectral Description] In *Atti del Terzo Colloquio di Informatica Musicale,* ed. G. De Poli. Padua: Università di Padova, 1979: 151–67.

3635. De Poli, Giovanni. "Frequency Dependent Waveshaping." In *Proceedings of the International Computer Music Conference, 1984,* ed. William Buxton. San Francisco, Calif.: Computer Music Association, 1985: 91–101.

3636. ———. "Sintesi dei suoni FM con modulante modulata." [Synthesis of FM Sounds Using a Modulated Modulator] In *Atti del Quinto Colloquio di Informatica Musicale.* Ancona: Università di Ancona, 1983: 99–105.

3637. ———. "Sintesi dei suoni mediante funzione distorcente con poli complessi coniugati." [Sound Synthesis Using a Distortion Function with Complex Conjugate Poles] In *Atti del Quarto Colloquio di Informatica Musicale.* Pisa: CNUCE-CNR, 1981: 103–30.

3638. ———. "Sound Synthesis by Fractional Waveshaping." *Journal of the Audio Engineering Society* 32 (1984): 849–61.

3639. ———. "Tecniche numeriche di sintesi della musica." [Numerical Techniques for Music Synthesis] *Bollettino LIMB* 1 (1981): 12–44.

3640. ———. "A Tutorial on Digital Sound Synthesis Techniques." *Computer Music Journal* 7,4 (Winter 1983): 8–26.

3641. De Santis, Antonio. "A Microprocessor Oriented Toward the Frequency Synthesis." In *Proceedings of the Venice 1982 International Computer Music Conference,* comp. Thom Blum and John Strawn. San Francisco, Calif.: Computer Music Association, 1985: 367–74.

3642.   ———. "L'uso dei microprocessori nella sintesi di frequenze." [Using Micro-processors for Frequencies Synthesis] In *Musica ed elaboratore - Atti del convegno.* Milan: FAST, 1980: 143–57.

3643.   Dierback, Charles. "Some Initial Ideas on the Control of Digital Sound Synthesis Through AI Techniques." In *Proceedings of the Rochester 1983 International Computer Music Conference,* comp. Robert W. Gross. San Francisco, Calif.: Computer Music Association, 1984: 236–52.

3644.   Doati, R. "Riduzione di dati per la costruzione di spazi timbrici e loro utilizzazione nella composizione musicale: una pulce da sabbia (1981–82)." [Reducing Data to Build Timbral Spaces and Using Them in Musical Composition] In *Atti del Quinto Colloquio di Informatica Musicale.* Ancona: Università di Ancona, 1983: 131–36.

3645.   Dunn, John. "A Hybrid Approach in the Esthetic Use of Computer Tools." Paper presented at the 57th Convention of the Audio Engineering Society, May 10–13, 1977, Los Angeles.
          Abstract in *Journal of the Audio Engineering Society* 25 (1977): 516.

3646.   Durr, Bernard. "Utilisation par John Chowning de la modulation de fréquence des timbres." *Programme-bulletin GRM* 6 (Fev. 1974): 36–40.

3647.   Ernst, David. "QUA4: An Advanced STG Control System." *Polyphony* 5 (Mar./Apr. 1980): 24–27.

3648.   Ferretti, Ercolino. "Sound Synthesis by Rule." In *Proceedings of the Second Annual Music Computation Conference, November 7–9, 1975 at the University of Illinois Urbana-Champaign. Part 1, Software Synthesis Techniques,* comp. James Beauchamp and John Melby. Urbana, Ill.: University of Illinois: 1–21.

3649.   Forin, A. "Spettri dinamici prodotti mediante distorsione con polinomi equivalenti in un punto." [Dynamic Spectra Generated by Distortion Using One-Point Equivalent Polynomials] *Bollettino LIMB* 2 (1982): 62–76.

3650.   Freed, Daniel J. "Waveshaping Analysis and Implementation: A Generalized Approach Using Complex Arithmetic." In *Proceedings of the Rochester 1983 International Computer Music Conference,* comp. Robert W. Gross. San Francisco, Calif.: Computer Music Association, 1984: 194–235.

3651.   Freedman, M. David. "On-Line Generation of Sound." In *Music by Computers,* ed. Heinz von Foerster and James W. Beauchamp. New York: J. Wiley, 1969: 13–18.

3652.   Frydén, Lars, and Johan Sundberg. "Performance Rules for Melodies: Origin, Functions, Purposes." In *Proceedings of the International Computer Music Conference, 1984,* ed. William Buxton. San Francisco, Calif.: Computer Music Association, 1985: 221–24.

3653.   ———, and Johan Sundberg. "Teaching a Computer to Play Melodies Musically." Paper presented at the Annual Conference on Postgraduate Psychology, St. Andrews University, 6–8 Apr. 1983.
          Abstract in *Bulletin of the British Psychological Society* 36 (Nov. 1983): A122.

3654. Fryer, Terry. "Digital Sampling: How to Control Aliasing by Filtering and Half-Speed-Mastering Your Sampling." *Keyboard* 12 (Apr. 1986): 102.

3655. ———. "Digital Sampling: More Distortion Solutions." *Keyboard* 12 (May 1986): 106–7.

3656. ———. "Digital Sampling: Sampling Resolution Bit by Bit." *Keyboard* 12 (Feb. 1986): 99, 148.

3657. Gerzso, Andrew. *Density of Spectral Components: Preliminary Experiments.* Paris: IRCAM, 1980. (Rapports IRCAM 31/80)

3658. Goeddel, Thomas W. "Technique for Real-Time Digital Synthesis of Complex Audio Spectra." Ph.D. diss., Purdue University, 1982. 176 p. *C&IS* 31 (1983): 83–14488. *DA* 43:4088B.

3659. ———, and Steven C. Bass. "Some Examples of Discrete-Time Musical Sound Synthesis Using Window Function Waveforms." In *IEEE 1983 International Symposium on Circuits and Systems.* New York: IEEE, 1983: 1087–89.

3660. Gordon, John W., and Julius O. Smith. "A Sine Generation Algorithm for VLSI Applications." In *Proceedings of the International Computer Music Conference, 1985,* ed. Barry Truax. San Francisco, Calif.: Computer Music Association, 1985: 165–68.

3661. Graziani, Mauro. "Il trattamento dei suoni naturali mediante elaboratore elettronico." [Natural Sound Processing Using a Computer] *Strumenti musicali* 26 (1982): 76–83.

3662. Gressel, Joel W. "Variable Amplitude Modulation by BUZZ." Paper presented at the International Conference on Computer Music, Oct. 28–31, 1976, Massachusetts Institute of Technology.

3663. Griese, J., and E. Werner. "Vocoder Techniques for Synthetic and Voice Controlled Sound Generation." Paper presented at the 56th Convention of the Audio Engineering Society, Mar. 1–4, 1977, Paris.

3664. Gross, Robert. "Generating Pitch Deviation Functions for a Sound Synthesis System." La Jolla, Calif.: Center for Music Experiment, University of California at San Diego, 1978. 9 p.

3665. Hamilton, Richard L. "A Study of Timbre Modulation Using a Digital Computer, with Applications to Composition." M.M. thesis, North Texas State University, 1977. 101 p. *Masters Abstracts* 16 (1978): 111.

3666. Haynes, Stanley. "New Developments in Computer Music Synthesis." *Music and Musicians* 28 (Apr. 1980): 20–22.

3667.   Howe, Hubert S. *Electronic Music Synthesis: Concepts, Facilities, Techniques.*
New York: Norton, 1975. 271 p.
Review by Fredrick Geissler in *Notes* 32 (Sept. 1975): 55–57.
Review by John Lansdown in *Page* 36 (July 1975): 4.
Review by Emerson Meyers in *American Music Teacher* 25 (Sept.-Oct. 1975):
45.
RILM 76 1567.

3668.   Hunt, Jerry. "Audio/Video Synthesis." *Synapse* 1 (Mar./Apr. 1977): 26–29.

3669.   Hutchins, Bernard A. "A Proposed FIR Digital Filter Approach to Variable-
Slope Filtering." *Electronotes* 14, special issue B (Mar. 1983): 29–32.

3670.   ———. "A Review of Fourier Methods in Signal Processing and Musical
Engineering." *Electronotes* 15, special issue D (Nov. 1983): 3–52.

3671.   Jacoby, Benjamin. "Walsh Functions: A Digital Fourier Series." *BYTE* 2
(Sept. 1977): 190–98.
Also in *The BYTE Book of Computer Music,* ed. Christopher P. Morgan.
Peterborough, N.H.: BYTE Books, 1979: 65–74.

3672.   Jaffe, David A., and Julius O. Smith. "Extensions of the Karplus-Strong
Plucked-String Algorithm." *Computer Music Journal* 7,2 (Summer 1983):
56–69.
C&IS 32 (1984): 84–537C.

3673.   Jaffrennou, Pierre-Alain. "Une évolution de MUSIC V vers la synthèse de
sons à caractère concrèt." *Les cahiers recherche/musique* 3 (1976): 93–116.

3674.   Kaegi, Werner. "The MIDIM System." In *Proceedings of the Rochester 1983
International Computer Music Conference,* comp. Robert W. Gross. San Francisco, Calif.: Computer Music Association, 1984: 253–61.

3675.   ———. "A New Approach to a Theory of Sound Classification." *Interface* 1
(Nov. 1972): 93–109.

3676.   ———. "Il sistema MIDIM." [The MIDIM System] Paper presented at the
1982 International Computer Music Conference, Sept. 27-Oct. 1, Venice.

3677.   ———, and Stan Tempelaars. "VOSIM—A New Sound Synthesis System."
Journal of the Audio Engineering Society 26 (1978): 418–24.

3678.   Karplus, Kevin, and Alex Strong. "Digital Synthesis of Plucked-String and
Drum Timbres." *Computer Music Journal* 7,2 (Summer 1983): 43–55.
C&CA 18 (1983): 40674. *C&IS* 32 (1984): 84–538C.

3679.   Lake, Robin B., and Ralph Cherubimi. "Orthogonal Transforms for Sound
Synthesis." In *Proceedings of the Second Annual Music Computation Con-
ference, November 7–9, 1975 at the University of Illinois at Urbana-Champaign.
Part 1, Software Synthesis Techniques,* comp. James Beauchamp and John
Melby. Urbana, Ill.: University of Illinois: 77–79.

3680.   Lansky, Paul. "Imagination and Linear Prediction." In *Proceedings of the
1980 International Computer Music Conference,* comp. Hubert S. Howe. San
Francisco, Calif.: Computer Music Association, 1982: 374–81.

3681. ———. "Linear Prediction." Paper presented at the 1983 International Computer Music Conference, Oct. 7–10, 1983, Rochester, N.Y.

3682. ———, and Kenneth Stieglitz. "Synthesis of Timbral Families by Warped Linear Prediction." *Computer Music Journal* 5,3 (Fall 1981): 45–49.
Also in *ICASSP 81, Proceedings, March 30–31, April 1, Atlanta, Georgia: IEEE International Conference on Acoustics, Speech, and Signal Processing.* New York: IEEE, 1981: 576–78.
Review by R. M. Mason in *Computing Reviews* 23 (June 1982): 39,471.
C&CA 17 (1982): 24518. *C&IS* 29 (1982): 82–1626C.

3683. Lay, J. E. "Walsh Functions in Audio Education and Electronic Music." Paper presented at the 50th Convention of the Audio Engineering Society, Mar. 4–7, 1975, London.
Published in *Collected Preprints of the 50th AES Convention.* London: Audio Engineering Society, 1975.
Abstract in the *Journal of the Audio Engineering Society* 23 (1975): 408.

3684. LeBrun, Marc. "A Derivation of the Spectrum of FM with a Complex Modulating Wave." *Computer Music Journal* 1,4 (Nov. 1977): 51–52.
Reprinted in *Foundations of Computer Music,* ed. Curtis Roads and John Strawn. Cambridge, Mass.: MIT Press, 1985: 65–67.

3685. ———. "Digital Waveshaping Synthesis." *Journal of the Audio Engineering Society* 27 (1979): 250–66.

3686. Lehmann, R., and Frank Brown. "Synthèse rapide des sons musicaux." *Revue d'acoustique* 38 (1976): 211–15.

3687. Logemann, George W. "Techniques for Programmed Electronic Music Synthesis." *Electronic Music Review* 1 (Jan. 1967): 44–53.

3688. Mailliard, Bénédict. "Petite pedagogie de la modulation de frequence." *Les cahiers recherche/musique* 3 (1976): 199–204.

3689. ———. "Sur la modulation de fréquence." *Les cahiers recherche/musique* 3 (1976): 179–198.

3690. ———; Jean-Francois Allouis; and Yves Geslin. "Trasformazione di suoni naturali due esempi di metodi: filtre risonanti e manipolazione nel dominio temporale." [Transformation of Natural Sounds, Two Examples of Methods: Resonating Filters and Time Domain Manipulation] Paper presented at the 1982 International Computer Music Conference, Sept. 27-Oct. 1, Venice.

3691. Martin, Steven L. "Creating Complex Timbre Through the Use of Amplitude Modulation in the Audio Band." Paper presented at the 42nd Convention of the Audio Engineering Society, May 2–5, 1972, Los Angeles.
Abstract in the *Journal of the Audio Engineering Society* 20 (1972): 422.

3692. Mattox, Janis R. "Synthesis for a Shaman." Paper presented at the 1982 International Computer Music Conference, Sept. 27-Oct. 1, Venice.

3693.   McGill, James F. "Music Synthesis by Optimal Filtering." Paper presented at the International Conference on Computer Music, October 28-31, 1976, Massachusetts Institute of Technology.

3694.   Mian, Gianantonio. "Sound Structuring Techniques Utilizing Parameters Derived from a Voice Analysis/Synthesis System." In *Proceedings of the International Computer Music Conference, 1984,* ed. William Buxton. San Francisco, Calif.: Computer Music Association, 1985: 67-81.

3695.   Milani, Mario, and Mirto Busico. *Forme d'onda e timbri: distinguibilità e criteri di scelta.* [Waveform and Timbre: Discriminability and Criteria for Selection] Pisa: CNUCE, 1976. 23 p.

3696.   Mitsuhashi, Yasuhiro. "Audio Signal Synthesis by Functions of Two Variables." *Journal of the Audio Engineering Society* 30 (1982): 701-06.

3697.   ———. "Musical Sound Synthesis by Forward Differences." *Journal of the Audio Engineering Society* 30 (1982): 2-9.
          C&CA 17 (1982): 17378.

3698.   ———. "Piecewise Interpolation Technique for Audio Signal Synthesis." *Journal of the Audio Engineering Society* 30 (1982): 192-202.

3699.   ———. "Waveshape Parameter Modulation in Producing Complex Audio Spectra." *Journal of the Audio Engineering Society* 28 (1980): 879-95.
          Correction in *Journal of the Audio Engineering Society* 29 (1981): 265.

3700.   Moog, Robert A. "On Synthesizers: Digital Synthesis. Part I." *Keyboard* 9 (Sept. 1983): 68-69.
          Reprinted as:"Approaches to Digital Synthesis: An Overview." In *Synthesizers and Computers.* Milwaukee, Wis.: H. Leonard Pub. Corp., 1985: 19-21.

3701.   ———. "On Synthesizers: Digital Synthesis. Part II." *Keyboard* 9 (Oct. 1983): 73, 82.
          Reprinted as: "Approaches to Digital Synthesis: Waveform Generation, Wave Tables, and Encoding." In *Synthesizers and Computers.* Milwaukee, Wis.: H. Leonard Pub. Corp., 1985: 22-24.

3702.   ———. "On Synthesizers: Digital Synthesis. Part III, Fourier Synthesis." *Keyboard* 9 (Nov. 1983): 70, 96.
          Reprinted as: "Approaches to Digital Synthesis: Fourier Synthesis." In *Synthesizers and Computers.* Milwaukee, Wis.: H. Leonard Pub. Corp., 1985: 25-27.

3703.   ———. "On Synthesizers: Digital Synthesis. Part IV." *Keyboard* 9 (Dec. 1983): 72, 85.
          Reprinted as: "Approaches to Digital Synthesis: Digital FM Synthesis." In *Synthesizers and Computers.* Milwaukee, Wis.: H. Leonard Pub. Corp., 1985: 28-30.

3704. ———. "On Synthesizers: Digital Synthesis. Part V, Some Alternatives." *Keyboard* 10 (Jan. 1984): 72–73.
Reprinted as: "Approaches to Digital Synthesis: Alternative Techniques for Digital Synthesis." In *Synthesizers and Computers.* Milwaukee, Wis.: H. Leonard Pub. Corp., 1985: 31–33.

3705. Moorer, James A. "The Synthesis of Complex Audio Spectra by Means of Discrete Summation Formulae." *Journal of the Audio Engineering Society* 24 (1976): 717–27.
Reprinted as the Stanford University, Dept. of Music, Report No. STAN- M-5, 1975.

3706. ———. "The Use of Linear Prediction of Speech in Computer Music Applications." *Journal of the Audio Engineering Society* 27 (1979): 134–40.
Also Paris: IRCAM, 1978. 27 p. (Rapports IRCAM 6/78)
C&CA 14 (1979): 19614. *E&EA* 82 (1979): 28123. *RILM* 78 4328.

3707. Nottoli, Giorgio. "Sintesi additiva: teoria e realizzazione mediante elaboratore elettronico." [Additive Synthesis: Theory and Realization through Electronic Computers] *Prospettive musicali* 1 (1982): 29–34.

3708. Parodi, Alexandre. "Low Cost Sound Analysis/Synthesis Technique." Abstract in *Proceedings, 1981 International Computer Music Conference, November 5–8,* comp. Larry Austin and Thomas Clark. Denton, Tex.: North Texas State University, 1983: 280.

3709. Paseman, William G. "Some New Methods of Music Synthesis." M.S. thesis, Dept. of Electrical Engineering and Computer Science, Massachusetts Institute of Technology, 1980. 107 p.
Also issued by: Cambridge: Massachusetts Institute of Technology, Laboratory for Computer Science, 1980. 72 p.

3710. Petersen, Tracy L. "Analysis-Synthesis as a Tool for Creating New Families of Sound." Paper presented at the 54th Convention of the Audio Engineering Society, May 4–7, 1976, Los Angeles. Preprint No. 1104.
Abstract in the *Journal of the Audio Engineering Society* 24 (1976): 488.

3711. ———. "Composing with Cross-Synthesis." Paper presented at the International Conference on Computer Music, Oct. 28–31, 1976, Massachusetts Institute of Technology.

3712. ———. "Dynamic Sound Processing." In *Proceedings of the 1976 ACM Computer Science Conference, Feb. 10–12, 1976, Anaheim, Calif.*

3713. ———. "Spiral Synthesis." In *Digital Audio Signal Processing: An Anthology,* ed. John Strawn. Los Altos, Calif.: W. Kaufmann, 1985: 137–47. (The Computer Music and Digital Audio Series)

3714. ———. "Vocal Tract Modulation of Instrumental Sounds by Digital Filtering." In *Proceedings of the Second Annual Music Computation Conference, November 7–9, 1975 at the University of Illinois at Urbana-Champaign. Part 1, Software Synthesis Techniques,* comp. James Beauchamp and John Melby. Urbana, Ill.: University of Illinois: 33–41.

3715.   Powner, E. T.; D. H. Green; and G. T. Taylor. "Digital Waveform Synthesis." *Electronic Engineering* 41 (Aug. 1969): 50–54.

3716.   Puckette, Miller. "Control of Real-Time Synthesis." Paper presented at the 1982 International Computer Music Conference, Sept. 17-Oct. 1, Venice.

3717.   Reinhard, P. "Algoritmi non lineari per la sintesi di segnali audio." [Nonlinear Algorithms for the Synthesis of Audio Signals] Tesi di laurea, Istituto di Elettrotecnica e di Elettronica, Università di Padova, 1982.

3718.   Riotte, André. "Un modèle informatique pour la transformation continue de sons inharmoniques." In *Proceedings of the International Computer Music Conference, 1984,* ed. William Buxton. San Francisco, Calif.: Computer Music Association, 1985: 43–51.

3719.   Risberg, Jeffrey S., and Gerald M. Shapiro. "Digital Additive Synthesis for Computer Music." *Journal of the Audio Engineering Society* 29 (1981): 902–5. *C&CA* 17 (1982): 17974.

3720.   Risset, Jean-Claude. "Concerning the Synthesis of Musical Sounds by Computer." *Faire* 4/5 (1977): 49–50.
        French and English texts.

3721.   ———. "Digital Sound Techniques: Their Impact and Their Promises in Music." In *Proceedings of the International Music and Technology Conference, August 24–28, 198., University of Melbourne.* Parkville, Vic.: Computer Music Project, Dept. of Computer Science, University of Melbourne, 1981: 237–243.

3722.   ———. *An Introductory Catalogue of Computer-Synthesized Sounds.* Murray Hill: Bell Telephone Laboratories.
        Review by James W. Beauchamp in *Perspectives of New Music* 9/10 (Fall-Winter 1971): 348–50.
        Also published: Cambridge, Mass.: Massachusetts Institute of Technology, 1971.
        RILM 71 4440.

3723.   ———. "The Musical Development of Digital Sound Techniques." In *Computer Music/Composition musicale par ordinateur; Report on an International Project Including a Workshop at Aarhus, Denmark in 1978,* ed. Marc Battier and Barry Truax. Ottawa: Canadian Commission for Unesco, 1980: 127–58.

3724.   ———. "Synthèse des sons à l'aide d'ordinateurs." *La revue musicale* 268–69 (1971): 113–23.
        English version: "Synthesis of Sounds by Computer and Problems Concerning Timbre." In *Music and Technology.* Paris: La revue musicale, 1971: 117–28.

3725.   ———; Gerard Charbonneau; and P. Karantchentzeff. "Un système de synthèse directe des sons à l'aide d'ordinateurs." *Revue d'acoustique* 21 (1972): 289–96.

3726. Roads, Curtis. "Automated Granular Synthesis of Sound." *Computer Music Journal* 2,2 (Sept. 1978): 61–62.
Revised and updated version with title: "Granular Synthesis of Sound." In *Foundations of Computer Music,* ed. Curtis Roads and John Strawn. Cambridge, Mass.: MIT Press, 1985: 145–59.
C&IS 21 (1978): 210983C.

3727. ———. "A Tutorial on Non-Linear Distortion or Waveshaping Synthesis." *Computer Music Journal* 3,2 (June 1979): 29–34.
Revised and updated version in *Foundations of Computer Music,* ed. Curtis Roads and John Strawn. Cambridge, Mass.: MIT Press, 1985: 83–94.

3728. Rodet, Xavier. "Time-Domain Formant-Wave Function Synthesis." In *Spoken Language Generation and Understanding: Proceedings of the NATO Advanced Study Institute held at Bonas, France, June 26-July 7, 1979,* ed. J. C. Simon. Dordrecht; Boston: D. Reidel Pub. Co., 1980: 429–41.
Reprinted in *Computer Music Journal* 8,3 (Fall 1984): 9–14.

3729. ———; Jean-Baptiste Barrière; Pierre Cointe; and Yves Potard. "The CHANT Project: Modelization and Production, an Environment for Composers, Including the FORMES Language for Describing and Controlling Sound and Musical Processes." In *Proceedings of the Venice 1982 International Computer Music Conference,* comp. Thom Blum and John Strawn. San Francisco, Calif.: Computer Music Association, 1985: 398–408.

3730. ———; Yves Potard; and Jean-Baptiste Barrière. "The CHANT Project: From the Synthesis of the Singing Voice to Synthesis in General." *Computer Music Journal* 8,3 (Fall 1984): 15–31. With soundsheet.

3731. Rozenberg, Maurice. "Applications of Digital Signal Processing to Musical Composition/Algorithms and Realisation on the UPIC." Paper presented at the 1984 International Computer Music Conference, Oct. 19–23, Paris, France.

3732. ———. "Linear Sweep Synthesis." *Computer Music Journal* 6,3 (Fall 1982): 65–71.
C&CA 18 (1983): 7235. *C&IS* 31 (1983): 83–423C.

3733. ———. "Music and Informatics: From Linear Sweep to Stochastic Methods." *Micro systeme* 21 (Jan.-Feb. 1982): 107–18.
In French.
C&CA 17 (1982): 28467.

3734. Sasaki, Lawrence H., and Kenneth C. Smith. "Music Synthesis." Toronto, Ont.: Dept. of Electrical Engineering, University of Toronto, 1978.

3735. ———, and Kenneth C. Smith. "A Simple Data Reduction Scheme for Additive Synthesis." *Computer Music Journal* 4,1 (Spring 1980): 22–24.
C&IS 26 (1980): 263660C.

3736.   Saunders, Steve. "Improved FM Audio Synthesis Methods for Real-Time Digital Music Generation." *Computer Music Journal* 1,1 (Feb. 1977): 53–55.
Revised version in *Foundations of Computer Music,* ed. Curtis Roads and John Strawn. Cambridge, Mass.: MIT Press, 1985: 45–53.
C&CA 11 (1976): 12103. *C&IS* 14: 133217C; and 18 (1978): 189689C. *RILM* 77 3643.

3737.   ———. "Real-Time Digital FM Audio Synthesis." In *Proceedings of the Second Annual Music Computation Conference, November 7–9, 1975 at the University of Illinois at Urbana-Champaign. Part 1, Software Synthesis Techniques,* comp. James Beauchamp and John Melby. Urbana, Ill.: University of Illinois: 42–52.

3738.   Schaefer, Richard A. "Control and Synthesis of Cyclic Waveforms for Music." In *Proceedings of the 1979 National Computer Conference on Personal Computing: New York, June 4–7, 1979,* ed. J. P. Lucas and R. E. Adams. Arlington, Va.: AFIPS Press, 1979: 113–22.

3739.   Schindler, Keith W. "Dynamic Timbre Control for Real-Time Digital Synthesis." *Computer Music Journal* 8,1 (Spring 1984): 28–42.
C&CA 19 (1984): 36713. *C&IS* 32 (1984): 84–13316C. *E&EA* 87 (1984): 44311.

3740.   Schneider, Thomas G. "Simple Approaches to Computer Music Synthesis." *BYTE* 2 (Oct. 1977): 140–44.
Also in *The BYTE Book of Computer Music,* ed. Christopher P. Morgan. Peterborough, N.H.: BYTE Books, 1979: 75–80.
C&CA 13 (1978): 13015.

3741.   Schottstaedt, Bill. "The Simulation of Natural Instrument Tones Using Frequency Modulation with a Complex Modulating Wave." *Computer Music Journal* 1,4 (Nov. 1977): 46–50.
Reprinted in *Foundations of Computer Music,* ed. Curtis Roads and John Strawn. Cambridge, Mass.: MIT Press, 1985: 54–64.
C&IS 18 (1978): 197088C; and 20 (1978): 207141C.

3742.   Schwartz, Gary. "Sound Synthesis by Hierarchic Sampling." In *Proceedings of the International Computer Music Conference, 1985,* ed. Barry Truax. San Francisco, Calif.: Computer Music Association, 1985: 33–38.

3743.   Sims, Greg. "Enhancement of Synthetic Sounds by Dynamic Parameter Reverberation." Paper presented at the 60th Convention of the Audio Engineering Society, May 2–5, 1978, Los Angeles.
Abstract in the *Journal of the Audio Engineering Society* 26 (1978): 573–74.

3744.   Slaymaker, Frank H. "Synthesizing Musical Tones from an Impulse Response Stored in a Digital Memory." *Journal of the Acoustical Society of America* 67 (1980): 713–15.
C&CA 15 (1980): 19701.

3745.   Stapelfeldt, Roelif. "Approximating the Frequencies of the Musical Scale with Digital Counter Circuits." *Journal of the Acoustical Society of America* 46 (1969): 478–79.

3746. Strawn, John. "Approximation and Syntactic Analysis of Amplitude and Frequency Functions for Digital Sound Synthesis." *Computer Music Journal* 4,3 (Fall 1980): 3–24.
Also in *Proceedings of the 1980 International Computer Music Conference,* comp. Hubert S. Howe. San Francisco, Calif.: Computer Music Association, 1982: 116–37.
C&CA 16 (1981): 21865. *C&IS* 27 (1981): 81–00516C.

3747. Tempelaars, Stan. "The VOSIM Signal Spectrum." *Interface* 6 (1977): 81–96.

3748. ———. "The VOSIM Sound Synthesis System." In *Computer Music/ Composition musicale par ordinateur; Report on an International Project Including a Workshop at Aarhus, Denmark in 1978,* ed. Marc Battier and Barry Truax. Ottawa: Canadian Commission for Unesco, 1980: 159–68.

3749. Terry, Kenneth. "Synthesized Speech Researcher: Charles Dodge." *Down Beat* 45 (Jan. 12, 1978): 23.

3750. Thomas, A. A. "Sound Synthesis Using Walsh Functions." *Wireless World* 87 (July 1981): 60–64.

3751. Truax, Barry D. "Organizational Techniques for c:m Ratios in Frequency Modulation." *Computer Music Journal* 1,4 (Nov. 1977): 39–45.
Reprinted in *Foundations of Computer Music,* ed. Curtis Roads and John Strawn. Cambridge, Mass.: MIT Press, 1985: 68–82.
RILM 77 5782.

3752. ———. "Timbral Construction as a Stochastic Process." In *Proceedings of the 1980 International Computer Music Conference,* comp. Hubert S. Howe. San Francisco, Calif.: Computer Music Association, 1982: 43–60.
Also in *Proceedings of the International Music and Technology Conference, August 24–28, 1981, University of Melbourne.* Parkville, Vic.: Computer Music Project, Dept. of Computer Science, University of Melbourne, 1981: 157–74.
Italian version: "Costruzione del timbro come processo stocastico." In *Musica e elaboratore.* Venice: Biennale di Venezla, 1980: 129–37.

3753. Vandenheede, Jan, and Jonathan Harvey. "Identity and Ambiguity: The Construction and Use of Timbral Transitions and Hybrids." In *Proceedings of the International Computer Music Conference, 1985,* ed. Barry Truax. San Francisco, Calif.: Computer Music Association, 1985: 97–102.

3754. Voss, Richard F., and John Clarke. "'1/f Noise' in Music: Music from 1/f Noise." *Journal of the Acoustical Society of America* 63 (1978): 258–63.
C&CA 13 (1978): 13019.

3755. Wessel, David L. "Perceptually Based Controls for Additive Synthesis." Paper presented at the International Conference on Computer Music, October 28–31, 1976, Massachusetts Institute of Technology.

3756. Wilson, Timothy A. "Data Reduction of Musical Signals." In *Proceedings of the International Computer Music Conference, 1985,* ed. Barry Truax. San Francisco, Calif.: Computer Music Association, 1985: 25–31.
Abridged version of the author's thesis.

3757.   Winham, Godfrey, and Kenneth Stieglitz. "Input Generators for Digital Sound Synthesis." *Journal of the Acoustical Society of America* 47 (1970): 665–66.

3758.   Wold, Erling Henry, and Mark A. Z. Dippé. "Alias-Free Sound Synthesis by Stochastic Sampling." In *Proceedings of the International Computer Music Conference, 1985,* ed. Barry Truax. San Francisco, Calif.: Computer Music Association, 1985: 39–46.

3759.   Youngblood, Joseph E. "Ongaku Hassei Yō 'MUSIC V Program'." [Music Synthesis Using the MUSIC V Program] Tokyo: University of Tokyo Computer Centre News, 1972.
        In Japanese.

3760.   Zuckerman, Mark, and Kenneth Stieglitz. "Using Circulant Markov Chains to Generate Waveforms for Music." In *Proceedings of the Second Annual Music Computation Conference, November 7–9, 1975 at the University of Illinois at Urbana-Champaign. Part 1, Software Synthesis Techniques,* comp. James Beauchamp and John Melby. Urbana, Ill.: University of Illinois: 58–76.

SOUND GENERATION WITH REAL-TIME APPLICATIONS

3761. Abbott, Curtis. "Remembering Performance Gestures." In *Proceedings of the Venice 1982 International Computer Music Conference,* comp. Thom Blum and John Strawn. San Francisco, Calif.: Computer Music Association, 1985: 188–93.

3762. Appleton, Jon H. "Live and In Concert: Composer/Performer Views of Real-Time Performance Systems." *Computer Music Journal* 8,1 (Spring 1984): 48–51.

3763. Bartlett, Martin. "The Development of a Practical Live-Performance Music Language." In *Proceedings of the International Computer Music Conference, 1985,* ed. Barry Truax. San Francisco, Calif.: Computer Music Association, 1985: 297–302.

3764. Behrman, David. "Cello with Melody Driven Electronics for David Gibson." In *Pieces 3,* ed. Michael Byron. Downview, Ont.: York University, 1977.

3765. Bertini, Graziano; Tommaso Bolognesi; and Pietro Grossi. "Computer Music in tempo reale: l'esperienza di Pisa (I)." [Real Time Computer Music: The Experience at Pisa(I)] *Strumenti musicali* 5 (1980): 69–75.

3766. ———; Tommaso Bolognesi; and Pietro Grossi. "Computer Music in tempo reale: l'esperienza di Pisa (II)." [Real Time Computer Music: The Experience at Pisa (II)] *Strumenti musicali* 5 (1980): 78–80.

3767. ———; Tommaso Bolognesi; and Pietro Grossi. "TAU2-TAUMUS: Il sistema di computer music in tempo reale realizzato a Pisa, descrizione ed esperienze." [TAU2-TAUMUS: The Real-Time System for Computer Music Developed at Pisa, Description and Experiences] *Automazione e strumentazione* 28 (Feb. 1980): 134–43.
Abstract in English.
C&CA 15 (1980): 27743.

3768. Bischoff, John; Richard Gold; and Jim Horton. "Music for an Interactive Network of Microcomputers." *Computer Music Journal* 2,3 (Dec. 1978): 24–29.
Reprinted in *Foundations of Computer Music,* ed. Curtis Roads and John Strawn. Cambridge Mass.: MIT Press, 1985: 588–600.
C&IS 22 (1978): 214535C.

3769. Bloch, Joshua J., and Roger B. Dannenberg. "Real-Time Computer Accompaniment of Keyboard Performances." In *Proceedings of the International Computer Music Conference, 1985,* ed. Barry Truax. San Francisco, Calif.: Computer Music Association, 1985: 279–89.

3770. Bozzola, P. "Musica elettronica e microcomputer: una proposta di applicazione real-time con il SYM–11 (I)." [Electronic Music and Microcomputers: A Proposal for Real-Time Applications with the SYM–11. Part 1] *Bit* [Milan] 8/9 (1980): 83–89.

3771. ———. "Musica elettronica e microcomputer: una proposta di applicazione real-time con il SYM–11 (II)." [Electronic Music and Microcomputers: A Proposal for Real-Time Applications with the SYM–11. Part 2] *Bit* [Milan] 10 (1980): 80–85.

3772. ———. "Musica elettronica e microcomputer: una proposta di applicazione real-time con il SYM–11 (III)." [Electronic Music and Microcomputers: A Proposal for Real-Time Applications with the SYM–11. Part 3] *Bit* [Milan] 12 (1980): 62–71.

3773. ———. "Musica elettronica e microcomputer: una proposta di applicazione real-time con il SYM–11 (IV)." [Electronic Music and Microcomputers: A Proposal for Real-Time Applications with the SYM–11. Part 4] *Bit* [Milan] 18 (1981): 75–80.

3774. ———. "Musica elettronica e microcomputer: una proposta di applicazione real-time con il SYM–11 (V)." [Electronic Music and Microcomputers: A Proposal for Real-Time Applications with the SYM–11. Part 5] *Bit* [Milan] 20 (1981): 79–97.

3775. ———. "Musica elettronica e microcomputer: una proposta di applicazione real-time con il SYM–11 (VI)." [Electronic Music and Microcomputers: A Proposal for Real-Time Applications with the SYM–11. Part 6] *Bit* [Milan] 21 (1980): 97–106.

3776. Buxton, William, and Paul Pignon. "Systèmes en temps réel et interaction homme-machine." *Faire* 2–3 (1975): 185–86.

3777. Cadoz, Claude; Anasthasie Luciani; Jean-Loup Florens; and Talin Dars-Berberyan. "The Control Channels of Instrumental Playing in Computer Music: Real Time in Computer Music, Incidence on the Basic Models." In *Proceedings of the Venice 1982 International Computer Music Conference,* comp. Thom Blum and John Strawn. San Francisco, Calif.: Computer Music Association, 1985: 73–91.

3778. Caussé, René. *Unité électronique destinée à la transformation du son en temps reel, programmable et controlable par l'instrumentiste.* Paris: IRCAM, 1978. (Rapports IRCAM 2/78)

3779. Chabot, Xavier. "User Software for Realtime Input by a Musical Instrument." In *Proceedings of the International Computer Music Conference, 1985,* ed. Barry Truax. San Francisco, Calif: Computer Music Association, 1985: 19–23.

3780. ———, and L. Beauregard. "Control of a Real-Time Sound Processor by a Traditional Instrument." Paper presented at the 1984 International Computer Music Conference, Oct. 19–23, Paris, France.

3781. Chadabe, Joel. "'Solo': A Specific Example of Realtime Performance." In *Computer Music/Composition musicale par ordinateur; Report on an International Project Including a Workshop at Aarhus, Denmark in 1978,* ed. Marc Battier and Barry Truax. Ottawa: Canadian Commission for Unesco, 1980: 87–94.

3782. Clough, John. "IRMA: An Interactive, Real-Time, Digital System for Electronic Music." In *1971 IEEE International Convention Digest: Synopses of Papers Presented at the 1971 IEEE International Convention, March 22–25, 1971, New York, N.Y.* New York, N.Y.: IEEE, 1971: 40–41.

3783. Dannenberg, Roger B. "An On-Line Algorithm for Real-Time Accompaniment." In *Proceedings of the International Computer Music Conference, 1984,* ed. William Buxton. San Francisco, Calif.: Computer Music Association, 1985: 193–98.

3784. Dworak, Paul E., and Alice C. Parker. "An Input Interface for a Real-Time Digital Sound Generation System." *Proceedings of the 3rd Symposium on Computer Architecture, 19–21 January 1976, Clearwater, Florida.* New York: IEEE, 1976: 68–73.

3785. ———, and Alice C. Parker. "An Input Interface for the Real-Time Control of Musical Parameters." Paper presented at the International Conference on Computer Music, October 28–31, 1976, Massachusetts Institute of Technology.

3786. ———; Alice C. Parker; and Richard D. Blum. "The Design and Implementation of a Real-Time Sound Generation System." In *Proceedings of the Fourth Annual Symposium on Computer Architecture, 23–25 March 1977, Silver Spring, Md.* New York: IEEE; New York: ACM, 1977: 153–58.

3787. Franco, Sergio. "Hardware Design of a Real-Time Musical System." Ph.D. diss., University of Illinois, Urbana, 1974. 96 p.
Also issued as University of Illinois Dept. of Computer Science Technical Report No. R-74-677.
C&CA 11 (1976): 2045. *DA* 35:5378B.

3788. Gillett, Ross; Kenneth C. Smith; and Bob Pritchard. "MADDM—Dance-Directed Music." In *Proceedings of the International Computer Music Conference, 1985,* ed. Barry Truax. San Francisco, Calif.: Computer Music Association, 1985: 329–30.

3789. Gresham-Lancaster, Scot. "Macintosh as a Live Performance Tool." In *Proceedings of the International Computer Music Conference, 1985,* ed. Barry Truax. San Francisco, Calif.: Computer Music Association, 1985: 307–12.

3790. Haynes, Stanley. "Live Electronic Music with Digital Synthesizers." Paper presented at the 1984 International Computer Music Conference, Oct. 19–23, Paris, France.

3791. Kobrin, Edward G. *KOBRIN: Computer in Performance.* West Berlin: Berliner Künstler-Programm des Deutschen Akademischen Austauschdienstes; La Jolla, Calif.: Lingua Press [distributor], 1977. 24 p.
Review by John Strawn in *Computer Music Journal* 2,4 (late Dec. 1978): 8–9.

3792. Lesle, Lutz. "Der Computer als Musizierpartner—neue Musik im Lüneburger Glockenhaus." *Neue Musikzeitung* 27 (1978): 4.

3793. Mathews, Max V. "A Facility and Program for Generating and Editing Functions of Time." Mimeographed. Murray Hill, N.J.: Bell Telephone Laboratories, Aug. 23, 1968. 6 p.

3794. ———, and F. Richard Moore. "GROOVE—A Computer Program for Real Time Music and Sound Synthesis." Abstract in *Journal of the Acoustical Society of America* 47 (1970): 132.

3795. ———, and F. Richard Moore. "GROOVE, A Program for Real Time Control of a Sound Synthesizer by Computer." *Proceedings of the American Society of University Composers* 4 (1971): 27–31.

3796. ———, and F. Richard Moore. "GROOVE—A Program to Compose, Store, and Edit Functions of Time." *Communications of the Association for Computing Machinery* 13 (1970): 715–21.

3797. ———, and Joseph C. Pasquale. "RTSKED, A Scheduled Performance Language for the Crumar General Development System." Abstract in *Proceedings, 1981 International Computer Music Conference, November 5–8,* comp. Larry Austin and Thomas Clark. Denton, Tex.: North Texas State University, 1983: 286.

3798. Moore, F. Richard. "GROOVE—A Program for Composing and Editing Functions of Time in Real-Time." Murray Hill, N.J.: Bell Telephone Laboratories Report, Mar. 1969.

3799. Morrill, Dexter G. "Loudspeakers and Performers: Some Problems and Proposals." *Computer Music Journal* 5,4 (Winter 1981): 25–29.
C&CA 17 (1982): 32045. *C&IS* 29 (1982): 82–1631C.

3800. Muggler, Fritz. "Live-Computermusik mit dem GAIV." *Schweizerische Musikzeitung* 117 (1977): 166–67.

3801. Mumma, Gordon, and Stephen W. Smoliar. *The Computer as a Performing Instrument.* Cambridge: MIT Artificial Intelligence Laboratory, 1971. 11 p. (AI Memo no. 213)

3802. Rasch, Rudi. "Synchronisatie bij ensemblespel." [Synchronization with Ensemble Playing] *Mens en melodie* 33 (1978): 41–47.

3803. Sapir, Sylviane. "Computer Music in tempo reale." [Computer Music in Real Time] *Strumenti musicali* (1985)

3804. Sigurbjornson, Thörkel. "Introduction to the HYBRID IV Working." *Faire* 4/5 (May 1978): 10.

3805. "Le système portable de synthèse hybride de Vincennes." In *Informatique musicale 1977. Textes des conférences. Equipe Eratto,* ed. Henri Ducasse. Paris: Centre de documentation sciences humaines, 1978: 193–219. *RILM* 78 3864.

3806. Truax, Barry D. "Real-Time Interactive Computer Music Systems." Unpublished paper, 1976.

3807. Vercoe, Barry. "Look-ahead and Performance Interpretation Strategies for Real-Time Control." Paper presented at the 1983 International Computer Music Conference, Oct. 7–10, 1983, Rochester, N.Y.

3808. ————. "The Synthetic Performer in the Context of Live Performance." In *Proceedings of the International Computer Music Conference, 1984,* ed. William Buxton. San Francisco, Calif.: Computer Music Association, 1985: 199–200.

3809. ————, and Miller Puckette. "Synthetic Rehearsal: Training the Synthetic Performer." In *Proceedings of the International Computer Music Conference, 1985,* ed. Barry Truax. San Francisco, Calif.: Computer Music Association, 1985: 275–78.

3810. Vidolin, Alvise. "Sistemi in tempo reale." [Real Time Systems] In *La scelta trasgressiva.* Venice: Biennale di Venezia, 1983: 24–33.

3811. Young, Gayle. "Hugh Le Caine's 1948 Sackbut Synthesizer: Performance Mode of Electronic Instruments." In *Proceedings of the International Computer Music Conference, 1984,* ed. William Buxton. San Francisco, Calif.: Computer Music Association, 1985: 203–12.

SPATIAL SIMULATION AND ROOM ACOUSTICS

3812. Beauchamp, James W. "Acoustics of Musical Instruments and Rooms." Paper presented at the 1978 International Computer Music Conference, November 1–5, Northwestern University, Evanston, Ill.

3813. Bernfeld, Benjamin, and Bennett K. Smith. *Computer-Aided Model of Stereophonic Systems.* Paris: IRCAM, 1978. 24 p. (Rapports IRCAM 15/78) *RILM* 78 4323.

3814. Chowning, John M. "The Simulation of Moving Sound Sources." *Journal of the Audio Engineering Society* 19 (1971): 2–6.
Reprinted in *Computer Music Journal* 1,3 (June 1977): 48–52.
Reprinted, in part, in *Sound Sculpture: A Collection of Essays by Artists Surveying the Techniques, Applications; and Future Directions of Sound Sculpture,* ed. John Grayson. Vancouver: Aesthetic Research Centre of Canada, 1975: 142–47.
C&IS 18 (1978): 189697C. *RILM* 77 3639.

3815. Easton, Robert. "Synthesis of Moving Sound Sources." Paper presented at the 40th Convention of the Audio Engineering Society, Apr. 27–30, 1971, Los Angeles.
Abstract in *Journal of the Audio Engineering Society* 19 (1971): 443.

3816. Eysholdt, Ulrich. "Subjektive Untersuchungen an digitalen Nachbildungen von Schallfeldern aus Konzertsälen." Ph.D. diss., University of Göttingen, 1976. 65 p.
RILM 76 16896.

3817. Fedorkow, Guy; William Buxton; and Kenneth C. Smith. "Computer-Controlled Sound Distribution System for the Performance of Electroacoustic Music." *Computer Music Journal* 2,3 (Dec. 1978): 33–42.
C&IS 22 (1978): 214536C.

3818. Graziani, Mauro. "Riverbero e spazializzazione nel processore 4i." [Reverberation and Spatialization in the 4i] *Bollettino LIMB* 4 (1984): 41–48.

3819.　———, and Gianantonio Patella. "Alcune macro in M360 per la elaborazione, la riverberazione e la spazializzazione stereofonica di segnali precedente-
mente memorizzati su nastro o su disco." [Some Music 360 Macros for
Elaborating, Reverberation, and Stereo Spatialization of Signals Previously
Stored on Tape or Disk] In *Atti del Terzo Colloquio di Informatica Musicale,*
ed. G. De Poli. Padua: Università di Padova, 1979: 248–57.

3820.　Kendall, Gary S., and William L. Martens. "Simulating the Cues of Spatial
Hearing in Natural Environments." In *Proceedings of the International Com-
puter Music Conference, 1984,* ed. William Buxton. San Francisco, Calif.:
Computer Music Association, 1985: 111–25.

3821.　———, and C. A. Puddie Rodgers. "The Simulation of Three-Dimensional
Localization Cues for Headphone Listening." In *Proceedings, 1981 Interna-
tional Computer Music Conference, November 5–8,* comp. Larry Austin and
Thomas Clark. Denton, Tex.: North Texas State University, 1983: 225–43.

3822.　Marsh, Theodore A. "Considerations of a Low-Cost Sound Image Location
Synthesis Device on an Interactive Computer Music System." Paper presented
at the 66th Convention of the Audio Engineering Society, May 6–9, 1980, Los
Angeles, Calif.
Abstract in *Journal of the Audio Engineering Society* 28 (1980): 540.

3823.　Moore, F. Richard. "A General Model for Spatial Processing of Sounds."
Computer Music Journal 7,3 (Fall 1983): 6–15.
C&CA 19 (1984): 6764. *C&IS* 32 (1984): 84–2130C.

3824.　———. "A General Model for Spatial Processing of Sounds." Paper presented at the 1982 International Computer Music Conference, Sept. 27-Oct. 1,
Venice.

3825.　Moorer, James A. "About this Reverberation Business." *Computer Music
Journal* 3,2 (June 1979): 13–28.
Reprinted in *Foundations of Computer Music,* ed. Curtis Roads and John
Strawn. Cambridge, Mass.: MIT Press, 1985: 605–39.
Also, Paris: IRCAM, 1978. 69 p. (Reports IRCAM 17/78)
RILM 78 4349.

3826.　———. "Digital Simulation of Concert-Hall Reverberation." Paper presented at the 66th Convention of the Audio Engineering Society, May 6–9,
1980, Los Angeles, Calif.
Abstract in Journal of the Audio Engineering Society 28 (1980): 538.

3827.　Otis, Alton B. "Artificial Reverberation." In "Four Sound Processing Programs for the Illiac II Computer and D/A Converter," ed. James W. Beauchamp. Urbana: University of Illinois Experimental Music Studio, Sept. 1968:
16–37. (Technical Report no. 14)

3828.　Schroeder, M. R. "Computer Models for Concert Hall Acoustics." *American
Journal of Physics* 41 (1973): 461–71.

3829.   Sheeline, Christopher W. "An Investigation of the Effects of Direct and Reverberant Signal Interaction on Auditory Distance Perception." Ph.D. diss., Stanford University, Nov. 1982. 81 p. (Report no. STAN-M-13)

3830.   Sheeline, Kip. "Reverberation Modelling and Spatial Cues for Computer Music." Paper presented at the 1982 International Computer Music Conference, Sept. 27-Oct. 1, Venice.

3831.   Smith, Julius O. "A New Approach to Digital Reverberation Using Closed Waveguide Networks." In *Proceedings of the International Computer Music Conference, 1985,* ed. Barry Truax. San Francisco, Calif.: Computer Music Association, 1985: 47-53.

3832.   Stautner, John P. "A Flexible Acoustic Ambience Simulator." In *Proceedings of the Venice 1982 International Computer Music Conference,* comp. Thom Blum and John Strawn. San Francisco, Calif.: Computer Music Association, 1985: 386-97.

3833.   ———, and Miller Puckette. "Designing Multi-Channel Reverberators." *Computer Music Journal* 6,1 (Spring 1982): 52-65.
Review by N. Chapin in *Computing Reviews* 24 (1983): 40,019.
C&IS 29 (1982): 82-6393C.

3834.   ———; Barry Vercoe; and Miller Puckette. "A Four-Channel Reverberation Network." In *Proceedings, 1981 International Computer Music Conference, November 5-8,* comp. Larry Austin and Thomas Clark. Denton, Tex.: North Texas State University, 1983: 265-79.

SPEECH

3835.   Benbassat, Gérard, and Daniel Serain. "Vocal Editor." *IEEE Transactions on Consumer Electronics* CE-29 (Aug. 1983): 226–232. *C&IS* 32 (1984): 84–4077C.

3836.   Bennett, Gerald. "Singing Synthesis in Electronic Music." In *Research Aspects on Singing*, ed. Johan Sundberg. Stockholm, Sweden: Royal Academy of Music, 1981: 34–50. (Publication no. 33)

3837.   Chowning, John M. "Computer Synthesis of the Singing Voice." In *Sound Generation in Winds, Strings, and Computers*, ed. J. Sundberg and E. Jansson. Stockholm: Kungl. Musikaliska Akademien, 1980: 4–14. (Publications Issued by the Royal Swedish Academy of Music no. 29)

3838.   ———. "The Synthesis of Sung Vowel Tones." Paper presented at the 1982 International Computer Music Conference, Sept. 27-Oct. 1, Venice.

3839.   David, E. E.; Max V. Mathews; and H. S. McDonald. "A High-Speed Data Translator for Computer Simulation of Speech and Television Devices." Bell Telephone System Technical Monograph No. 3405 (Mar. 1959): 169–72.

3840.   Denes, F. B., and Max V. Mathews. "Computer Models for Speech and Music Appreciation." *AFIPS Conference Proceedings, Fall Joint Computer Conference* 33 (1968): 319–27.

3841.   Dodge, Charles M. "Computer Generation of Human Vocal Sound." *Proceedings of the American Society of University Composers* 6 (1971): 40–45.

3842.   ———. "Synthesizing Speech." *Music Journal* 34 (Feb. 1976): 14, 44.

3843.   Frigo, Luciano; Sylviane Sapir; and Tiziano Sinigaglia. "Sintesi della voce con il processore digitale 4i." [Voice Synthesis Using the 4i Digital Processor] In *Atti del Quinto Colloquio di Informatica Musicale*. Ancona: Università di Ancona, 1983: 106–13.

3844.   Goeddel, Thomas W., and Steven C. Bass. "High Quality Synthesis of Musical Voices in Discrete Time." *IEEE Transactions on Acoustics, Speech, and Signal Processing* ASSP-32 (June 1984): 623–33. *C&IS* 32 (1984): 84–14951C.

3845.   Mathews, Max V. "External Coding for Speech Transmission." *IRE Transactions on Information Theory* Vol. IT-5 (Sept. 1959): 129–36.

3846.   Mian, Gianantonio, and Graziano Tisato. "Sintesi del canto mediante predizione lineare." [Synthesis of the Singing Voice by Means of Linear Prediction] In *Atti del Terzo Colloquio di Informatica Musicale,* ed. G. De Poli. Padua: Università di Padova, 1979: 260.

3847.   Roads, Curtis. "A Report on SPIRE: An Interactive Audio Processing Environment." *Computer Music Journal* 7,2 (Summer 1983): 70–74. *C&IS* 32 (1984): 84–215C.

3848.   Rodet, Xavier, and Gerald Bennett. "Synthèse de la voix chantee par ordinateur." In *Conférence des Journées d'études. Festival international du son haute fidelite sterephonie-Paris,* 1980: 73–91.

3849.   ———, and Philippe Depalle. "High Quality Synthesis-by-Rule of Consonants." In *Proceedings of the International Computer Music Conference, 1985,* ed. Barry Truax. San Francisco, Calif.: Computer Music Association, 1985: 91–96.

3850.   Sundberg, Johan. "Synthesis of Singing." *Svensk tidskrift för musikforskning* 60,1 (1978): 107–12.

3851.   Vandegrift, Jeffrey M. "Speech Synthesis by Linear Prediction for Computer Music Applications." B.S. thesis, Dept. of Electrical Engineering and Computer Science, Massachusetts Institute of Technology, 1978. 30 p.

3852.   Walcott, Ronald. "The *Chöömij* of Mongolia: A Spectral Analysis of Overtone Singing." In *Selected Reports in Ethnomusicology,* Volume II, No. 1, ed. Mantle Hood. Los Angeles: University of California, 1974: 54–60.

3853.   Zera, Jan; Jan Gauffin; and Johan Sundberg. "Synthesis of Selected VCV-Syllables in Singing." In *Proceedings of the International Computer Music Conference, 1984,* ed. William Buxton. San Francisco, Calif.: Computer Music Association, 1985: 83–86.

STUDIOS

3854. Abbott, Curtis; James R. Lawson; Alan Marr; James A. Moorer; and John Snell. "The Lucasfilm Digital Audio Studio." Videotape presented at the 1983 International Computer Music Conference, Oct. 7–10, 1983, Rochester, N.Y.

3855. ———; Alan Marr; and James A. Moorer. "Lucasfilm Report." Videotape presented at the 1984 International Computer Music Conference, Oct. 19–23, Paris, France.

3856. Albers, Bradley. "Designing an Integrated Environment for the Composer and Teacher." Abstract in *Proceedings, 1981 International Computer Music Conference, November 5–8,* comp. Larry Austin and Thomas Clark. Denton, Tex.: North Texas State University, 1983: 73.

3857. ———. "SYCOM's Studio A, an Integrated Environment for Electronic and Computer Music Composition." In *Proceedings of the 1980 International Computer Music Conference,* comp. Hubert S. Howe. San Francisco, Calif.: Computer Music Association, 1982: 145–158.

3858. Alewine, Murray L. "The Establishment and Utilization of an Electronic Music Studio in Small Colleges and Universities." Ph.D. diss., University of Miami, 1973. 136 p.
DA 34:5224A.

3859. Arfib, Daniel, and Michel Redolfi. "Computer Music in Marseille, at Group de musique experimentale de Marseille, and at Centre national pour la recherche scientifique." Paper presented at the 1978 International Computer Music Conference, November 1–5, Northwestern University, Evanston, Illinois.

3860. Austin, Larry. "SYCOM—Systems Complex for the Studio and Performing Arts." *Numus West* 5 (1974): 57–60.

3861.   ———, and Larry Bryant. "A Computer-Synchronized, Multi-Track Recording System." In *Proceedings of the Second Annual Music Computation Conference, November 7–9, 1975 at the University of Illinois at Urbana-Champaign. Part 4, Information Processing Systems,* comp. James Beauchamp and John Melby. Urbana, Ill.: University of Illinois: 1–12.

3862.   Bales, W. Kenton; Richard L. Hamilton; and Dan W. Scott. "Computer-Aided Composition and Performance with AMUS." In *Proceedings of the 1978 International Computer Music Conference,* comp. Curtis Roads. Evanston, Ill.: Northwestern University Press, 1979: 450–70.

3863.   Balibar, Francoise. "Musique pour ordinateur à Beaubourg." *Recherche* 6 (1975): 565–68.

3864.   Baruzzi, G.; Pietro Grossi; and Mario Milani. *Musical Studies: Summary of the Activity from 1969–1975.* Pisa: CNUCE, 1975. 49 p.

3865.   Beauchamp, James W. "A Report on the Magnavox Sponsored Research Investigation, 'The Development of New Electronic Systems for Generating Musical Sound'." Urbana: University of Illinois Experimental Music Studio, Aug. 1964. 49 p. (Technical Report no. 10)

3866.   ———. "A Statement of Progress on the Research Investigation, Generation and Creation of New Electronic Sounds." Urbana: University of Illinois Experimental Music Studio, Aug. 1963. 37 p. (Technical Report no. 7)

3867.   ———, and Scot Aurenz. "New Computer Music Facilities at the University of Illinois at Urbana-Champaign." In *Proceedings of the International Computer Music Conference, 1985,* ed. Barry Truax. San Francisco, Calif.: Computer Music Association, 1985: 407–14.

3868.   Beckwith, Sterling. *The Interactive Music Project at York University.* Toronto: Ontario Ministry of Education, 1975.

3869.   Bennett, Gerald. *Research at IRCAM in 1977.* Paris: IRCAM, 1978. 12 p. (Rapports IRCAM 1/78)
         In English or French.

3870.   ———. *Research at IRCAM in 1978.* Paris: IRCAM, 1979. 27 p. (Rapports IRCAM 19/79)

3871.   ———; R. Boesch; A. Greco; and Bruno Spoerri. "The Swiss Center for Computer Music." Paper presented at the 1984 International Computer Music Conference, Oct. 19–23, Paris, France.

3872.   Bernardini, Nicola. "Il Centro di sonologia computazionale dell'Università di Padova." [The Centre of Computational Sonology at Padua University] *AudioReview* 28 (1984): 114–17.

3873.   ———. "L'IRCAM di Parigi." [IRCAM in Paris] *AudioReview* 29 (1984): 96–100.

3874.   ———. "Lo Studio per l'Informatica Musicale (S.I.M.) di Roma." [The Studio for Computer Music at Rome] *AudioReview* 31 (1984): 128–32.

3875. Bernfeld, Benjamin. "IRCAM, or, Music and Technology." Paper presented at the convention of the Audio Engineering Society, May 1979, Los Angeles. Abstract in *Journal of the Audio Engineering Society* 27 (1979): 608.

3876. Bodin, Lars-Gunnar. "Två studior för Elektronisk Music." [Tva Studio for Electronic Music] *Nutida musik* 17,3 (1973/1974): 31–32.

3877. Bosetto, A., and A. Pezzani. "L'attività di informatica musicale all'ISELQUI." [Activity in Computer Music at ISELQUI] In *Atti del Quinto Colloquio di Informatica Musicale.* Ancona: Università di Ancona, 1983: 75–77.

3878. Buxton, William, ed. *Computer Music 1976/77: A Directory to Current Work.* Ottawa, Ont.: Canadian Commission for UNESCO, 1977. 239 p.

3879. ———. "Recherches effectivées à Utrecht." *Faire* 2–3 (1975): 101–02.

3880. ———, and Guy Fedorkow. *The Structured Sound Synthesis Project (SSSP): An Introduction.* Toronto: University of Toronto, 1978. (Technical Report CSRG-92)

3881. ———; Guy Fedorkow; Ronald Baecker; Gustav Ciamaga; Leslie Mezei; and Kenneth C. Smith. "An Overview of the Structured Sound Synthesis Project." In *Proceedings of the 1978 International Computer Music Conference,* comp. Curtis Roads. Evanston, Ill.: Northwestern University Press, 1979: 471–85.

3882. Cappielo, C. "Aspetti della ricerca al CEMAMU." [Aspects of Research at CEMAMU] In *Atti del Quinto Colloquio di Informatica Musicale.* Ancona: Università di Ancona, 1983: 78–83.

3883. Cary, Tristram. "Quarts in Pint Pots." In *Proceedings of the International Computer Music Conference, 1984,* ed. William Buxton. San Francisco, Calif.: Computer Music Association, 1985: 311–15.

3884. Celona, John A., and Michael Longton. "Real Time Synthesis at the University of Victoria." In *Proceedings of the Venice 1982 International Computer Music Conference,* comp. Thom Blum and John Strawn. San Francisco, Calif.: Computer Music Association, 1985: 26–32.

3885. Chadabe, Joel. "Das elektronische Studio von Albany." *Melos* 33 (May 1971): 188–90.

3886. ———. "Studio Report: State University of New York at Albany." Paper presented at the 1977 International Computer Music Conference, University of California, San Diego, 26–30 October 1977.

3887. Chong, John. "The Studio in London." In *Musical Aspects of the Electronic Medium, Report on Electronic Music,* ed. Frits Weiland. Utrecht: Institute of Sonology, 1975.

3888. Chowning, John M. "Stanford Computer Music Project." *Numus West* 1 (1972): 12–14.

3889. ———; Chris Chafe; John W. Gordon; and Patte Wood. "The Stanford Center for Computer Research in Music and Acoustics." Paper presented at the 1982 International Computer Music Conference, Sept. 27-Oct. 1, Venice.

3890. ———; John W. Gordon; Julius O. Smith; and Patte Wood. "The Stanford Center for Computer Research in Music and Acoustics." Paper presented at the 1983 International Computer Music Conference, Oct. 7-10, 1983, Rochester, N.Y.

3891. ———; David A. Jaffe; Julius O. Smith; and Patte Wood. "The Stanford Center for Computer Research in Music and Acoustics." Paper presented at the 1984 International Computer Music Conference, Oct. 19-23, Paris, France.

3892. ———, and James A. Moorer. "The Stanford Computer Music Project." In *First West Coast Computer Faire Conference Proceedings,* ed. Jim C. Warren, Jr. Palo Alto, Calif.: Computer Faire, 1977: 91-95.

3893. Christensen, Louis. "Interview." *Numus-West* 4 (1973): 29-30.

3894. Ciamaga, Gustav. "Kennwort UTEMS." *Melos* 38 (1971): 517-19.

3895. ———, and William Buxton. "Current Facilities at University of Toronto for Computer Music." Toronto: SSSP, 1976.

3896. Clark, H. D. "New Electronic Music Studio in Norway." Paper presented at the 50th Convention of the Audio Engineering Society, Mar. 4-7, 1975, London.
Included in *Collected Preprints of the 50th Audio Engineering Society Convention.* London: Audio Engineering Society, 1975.
Abstract in the *Journal of the Audio Engineering Society* 23 (1975): 408.

3897. Clough, John. "Computer Sound Generation: An Educational Resource at Oberlin College." In *Proceedings of a Conference on Computers in the Undergraduate Curricula: June 16, 17, 18 1970.* University of Iowa, Center for Conferences and Institutes, Sept. 1970: 1.18-1.19.
RILM 71 3104.

3898. ———. "An Interactive System for Computer Sound Generation." *Proceedings of the American Society of University Composers* 6 (1973): 22-26.

3899. ———. "A Report from Oberlin." *Computer Music Newsletter* 1 (Feb. 1971): 2-5.

3900. "Computer Music at U. of Indiana." *Variety* 233 (Nov. 9, 1966): 61.

3901. "Computer Research Center." *Music Educators Journal* 62 (Nov. 1975): 118.

3902. Cott, Jonathan. "Paris' Sci-fi Music Center." *Rolling Stone* 242 (June 30, 1977): 40-43.

3903. Cummings, Conrad. "An American at IRCAM." *High Fidelity/Musical America* 30 (Sept. 1980): MA37-MA38.

3904. Dannenberg, Roger B.; Paul McAvinney; and Marilyn Taft Thomas. "Carnegie-Mellon University Studio Report." In *Proceedings of the International Computer Music Conference, 1984,* ed. William Buxton. San Francisco, Calif.: Computer Music Association, 1985: 281–86.

3905. Dashow, James; Giovanni De Poli; Graziano Tisato; and Alvise Vidolin. "Computer Music at the University of Padova." In *Proceedings of the 1978 International Computer Music Conference,* comp. Curtis Roads. Evanston, Ill.: Northwestern University Press, 1979: 486–93.

3906. De Poli, Giovanni. "Il Centro di Sonologia Computazionale dell'Università di Padova." [The Centre of Computational Sonology at the University of Padova] In *Musica ed elaboratore elettronico—Atti del convegno.* Milan: FAST, 1980: 27–42.

3907. Debiasi, Giovanni B.; Giovanni De Poli; Graziano Tisato; and Alvise Vidolin. "Centro di Sonologia Computazionale C.S.C., University of Padova." In *Proceedings of the International Computer Music Conference, 1984,* ed. William Buxton. San Francisco, Calif.: Computer Music Association, 1985: 287–97.

3908. Del Duca, Lindoro; Francesco Galante; Michelangelo Lupone; Giorgio Nottoli; and Nicola Sani. "Societa di Informatica Musicale: Studio Report." In *Proceedings of the International Computer Music Conference, 1984,* ed. William Buxton. San Francisco, Calif.: Computer Music Association, 1985: 299–302.

3909. Diemer, Emma Lou. "Electronic Music at UCSB." *Numus West* 8 (Spring 1975): 56–58.

3910. Divilbiss, J. L. "The Real-Time Generation of Music with a Digital Computer." *Journal of Music Theory* 8 (1964): 99–111.

3911. Dolson, Mark B.; D. Gareth Loy; and F. Richard Moore. "Computer Audio Research Laboratory Studio Report." Paper presented at the 1984 International Computer Music Conference, Oct. 19–23, Paris, France.

3912. Dupuy, Robert, and Denis Lorrain. "L.E.N.A.: Laboratoire d'electroacoustique numerique-analogique." Université de Montréal, Mars 1972. 10 p.

3913. "E.m.a.mu., Equipe de mathématique et d'automatique musicales." *La revue musicale* 265–266 (1969): 53–59.

3914. Emmerson, Simon. "Electronic Studios in Britain." *Music and Musicians* 23 (July 1975): 24–26.

3915. "The Experimental Music Studio, University of Illinois." *Page* 22 (Apr. 1972): 3–4.

3916. Fredlund, Lorne D. "A Computer-Aided Music Facility." M.Sc. thesis, University of Alberta, 1973.

3917. Fugazza, G. F. "Un incontro tra stampa e computer all'IRCAM di Parigi." [A Meeting of Press and Computers at IRCAM in Paris] *Strumenti musicali* 14 (1981): 100–101.

3918.   Fuller, Wesley. "Computer Studio Report, Tri-College Group for Electronic and Related Research, Worcester, Massachusetts." In *Proceedings of the 1980 International Computer Music Conference,* comp. Hubert S. Howe. San Francisco, Calif.: Computer Music Association, 1982: 211–25.

3919.   Galante, Francesco, and Nicola Sani. "Computer Music a Roma: lo Studio per l'Informatica Musicale." [Computer Music at Rome: The Studio for Computer Music] *Strumenti musicali* 40 (1983): 72–79.

3920.   Gardner, John K. *Computer Facilities for Music at IRCAM, as of October 1977.* Paris: IRCAM, 1978. 6 p. (Rapports IRCAM 3/78)

3921.   Graebner, E. H. "Southampton Studio Report." In *Computer Music in Britain, 8th–11th April 1980.* London: Electro-Acoustic Music Association of Great Britain, 1980: 3–4.

3922.   Greenhough, Michael; Ian Bowler; and Stephen Morris. "The Electronic Music Studio at University College, Cardiff." In *Proceedings of the International Computer Music Conference, 1985,* ed. Barry Truax. San Francisco, Calif.: Computer Music Association, 1985: 415–18.

3923.   Grippe, Ragnar. "La musique experimentale en Suede." *Faire* 2–3 (1975): 113–17.

3924.   Gross, Robert. "The Center for Music Experiment, UCSD." Paper presented at the 1978 International Computer Music Conference, November 1–5, Northwestern University, Evanston, Illinois.

3925.   Grossi, Pietro. "Computer Music al Conservatorio di musica di Firenze." [Computer Music at the Conservatory of Music at Florence] In *Musica ed elaboratore—Atti del Convegno.* Milan: FAST, 1980: 139–41.

3926.   ———. "Outline of the Research at the CNUCE-CNR of Pisa, Italy." Paper presented at the International Conference on Computer Music, October 28–31, 1976, Massachusetts Institute of Technology.

3927.   ———. "Studies and Research at CNUCE." Paper presented at the 1977 International Computer Music Conference, University of California, San Diego, 26–30 Oct. 1977.

3928.   Harris, R. P., and Barry E. Conyngham. "An Integrated Software System for Computer Music Synthesis." Paper presented at the 1980 International Computer Music Conference, November 13–15, 1980, Queens College of the City University of New York.

3929.   Haus, Goffredo. "Computer music a Milano." [Computer Music in Milan] *Strumenti musicali* 50 (1984): 75–79.

3930.   ———. "Computer Music at the Institute of Cybernetics of the University of Milan." In *Proceedings of the 1980 International Computer Music Conference,* comp. Hubert S. Howe. San Francisco, Calif.: Computer Music Association, 1982: 178–201.

3931. ———. "Informatica musicale all'Istituto di Cibernetica dell'Università di Milano." [Computer Music at the Istituto di Cibernetica of the University of Milan] In *Musica ed elaboratore—Atti del convegno*. Milan: FAST, 1980: 61–80.
Also published: *Informatica oggi* 9 (1981): 131–39.

3932. ———. "Informatica musicale alla Biennale di Venezia." [Computer Music at the Biennale di Venezia] *Strumenti musicali* 11 (1980): 68–72.

3933. Hawthorne, David. "Droids Shoot the Works to Post Electronically." *Millimeter* 13 (Apr. 1985): 87–94.

3934. Haynes, Stanley. "Software Sound Synthesis in the United Kingdom." Paper presented at the International Conference on Computer Music, October 28–31, 1976, Massachusetts Institute of Technology.

3935. Hiller, Lejaren A. "Report on Contemporary Experimental Music, 1961." Urbana: University of Illinois Experimental Music Studio, June 1962. 92 p. (Technical Report no. 4)

3936. ———. "Z prac studia muzyki eksperymentalnej University of Illinois." [From the Works of the Experimental Music Studio at the University of Illinois] *Horyzonty muzyki* 38 (Mar. 26, 1964): 1–5.
In Polish.

3937. Hinton, Michael; Erik Nyberg; and Göran Svensson. "WSP—'The Missing Link' Computer Music System for Realtime Interactive Composition." Paper presented at the 1984 International Computer Music Conference, Oct. 19–23, Paris, France.

3938. Howe, Hubert S. "Toronto's Structured Sound Synthesis Project." *Computers and the Humanities* 14 (1980): 65–66.

3939. "Hum a Few Bars, CARL Can Sing It." *Quarterly, Alumni & Friends* 4 (Winter 1981): 1, 5.

3940. Jaffrennou, Pierre-Alain. "L'informatique au G.R.M." *Programme-Bulletin GRM* 6 (Fev. 1974): 20–35.

3941. Kaehler, Ted. "Some Music at Xerox PARC." In *Proceedings of the Second Annual Music Computation Conference, November 7–9, 1975 at the University of Illinois at Urbana-Champaign. Part 1, Software Synthesis Techniques,* comp. James Beauchamp and John Melby. Urbana, Ill.: University of Illinois: 53–57.

3942. Kendall, Gary S. "The Computer Music Studio at Northwestern University." Paper presented at the 1980 International Computer Music Conference, November 13–15, 1980, Queens College of the City University of New York.

3943. Kirchberg, Klaus. "Ein Laboratorium für die Musik von Morgen." *Musikhandel* 30 (1979): 333–35.

3944.   Knapp, K. H. "From the Massachusetts Institute of Technology: Digital Orchestra—Computer Music Comes of Age." *Funkschau* 20 (Sept. 30, 1983): 56–58.
In German.
E&EA 87 (1984): 6975.

3945.   Koenig, Gottfried Michael. "Construction and Working Methods of the Utrecht University Studio." *Electronic Music Reports* 1 (1969): 61–67.

3946.   Lederer, Jeffrey H. "Performance System User's Manual." Pittsburgh: Dept. of Computer Science, University of Pittsburgh, 1976.

3947.   Lehrman, Paul D. "Inside IRCAM: A Guided Tour of Europe's Leading Electronic Music Facility." *Keyboard* 11 (July 1985): 12, 118.

3948.   Lonchampt, Jacques. "L'IRCAM, département ordinateurs avec Jean-Claude Risset." *Le monde* (Oct. 23, 1974): 15.

3949.   Loy, D. Gareth. "System Design for Computer Music at the Computer Audio Research Laboratory, UCSD." In *Proceedings, IEEE 1982 Region 6 Conference.* New York: IEEE, 1982: 152–57.
C&CA 17 (1982): 24529.

3950.   Lupone, Michelangelo. "Lo Studio per l'Informatica Musicale di Roma: il sistema per la sintesi in tempo reale." [The Studio for Computer Music in Rome: A Real Time Synthesis System] In *Atti del Quinto Colloquio di Informatica Musicale.* Ancona: Università di Ancona, 1983: 62–69.

3951.   Lynner, Doug, and Virginia Quesada. "Jean-Claude Risset—IRCAM from the Inside Out." *Synapse* 2 (Mar.-Apr. 1978): 41.

3952.   Machover, Tod, ed. *Musical Thought at IRCAM.* London: Harwood, 1984. (Contemporary Music Review v. 1, pt. 1)

3953.   ———. "A View of Music at IRCAM." *Contemporary Music Review* 1 (Oct. 1984): 1–10.
French version: "Un apercu de la musique à l'IRCAM." *Musique de notre temps* 1 (Oct. 1984) 1–11.

3954.   Mailliard, Bénédict, and Yves Geslin. "Research and Musical Tools: Experience in a Non-Real Time Studio at INA-GRM." Paper presented at the 1984 International Computer Music Conference, Oct. 19-23, Paris, France.

3955.   ———; Yann Geslin; and Jean-Francois Allouis. "The GRM Digital Studio for Treating Natural Sounds." In *Proceedings of the Venice 1982 International Computer Music Conference,* comp. Thom Blum and John Strawn. San Francisco, Calif.: Computer Music Association, 1985: 20–25.

3956.   Manning, Peter D. "Electronic and Computer Music at Durham University." *Page* 23 (May 1972): 2.

3957.   Marr, Alan. "Acoustical Laboratory Report, Computer Music Conference." In *Proceedings, 1981 International Computer Music Conference, November 5-8,* comp. Larry Austin and Thomas Clark. Denton, Tex.: North Texas State University, 1983: 89–93.

3958. McBride, Stewart. "IRCAM in Paris, Where Composers Go to Play with Sound." *Christian Science Monitor* (Feb. 11, 1982): sec. B, p. B2-B3, B5, B10, B12.

3959. Mechtler, Peter. "Ein universeller Musikcomputer in Wien." *Österreichische Musikzeitschrift* 34 (1979): 157–58.

3960. Mendel, Arthur, and Thomas B. Hall. "Princeton Computer Tools for Musical Research." *Informatique et sciences humaines* 19 (Dec. 1973): 41–65. French summary: p. 61–65.

3961. Mintner, Thomas. "Art and Technology at the University of Iowa (Iowa City)." *Numus West* 7 (Winter 1975): 29–32.

3962. "M.I.T. Music Project Uses DEC Computer." *Computers and Automation* 22 (Nov. 1973): 43–44.

3963. Moore, F. Richard. "The Computer Audio Research Laboratory at UCSD." *Computer Music Journal* 6,1 (Spring 1982): 18–29. *C&IS* 29 (1982): 82–6395C.

3964. ———. "Computer Audio Research Laboratory Report." In *Proceedings of the 1980 International Computer Music Conference,* comp. Hubert S. Howe. San Francisco, Calif.: Computer Music Association, 1982: 159–77.

3965. ———, and D. Gareth Loy. "Computer Audio Research Laboratory Studio Report." In *Proceedings of the Venice 1982 International Computer Music Conference,* comp. Thom Blum and John Strawn. San Francisco, Calif.: Computer Music Association, 1985: 16–19.

3966. Moore, Robert. "New Music at Oberlin in the 70's." *Numus West* 5 (1974): 53–55.

3967. Moorer, James A. "The Lucasfilm Digital Audio Facility." In *Digital Audio Engineering,* ed. John Strawn. Los Altos: W. Kaufmann, 1985: 109–135. (The Computer Music and Digital Audio Series)

3968. "Music System in Pisa." *Page* 36 (July 1975): 3.

3969. Nelson, Gary. "Computer Music at the Oberlin Conservatory of Music." Paper presented at the 1980 International Computer Music Conference, November 13–15, 1980, Queens College of the City University of New York.

3970. Oppenheimer, Larry. "CCRMA: Computer Music at Stanford." *Mix* 8 (June 1984): 14–26.

3971. Parker, Alice C.; Richard D. Blum; and Paul E. Dworak. "The Carnegie-Mellon Computer Music System Digital Hardware." Paper presented at the 1977 International Computer Music Conference, University of California, San Diego, 26–30 October 1977.

3972. Pennycook, Bruce. "The Audio Composition System at the Defense and Civil Institute for Environmental Medicine." In *Proceedings of the Venice 1982 International Computer Music Conference,* comp. Thom Blum and John Strawn. San Francisco, Calif.: Computer Music Association, 1985: 202–16.

3973. ————. "Computer Music at Queen's University." In *Proceedings, 1981 International Computer Music Conference, November 5–8,* comp. Larry Austin and Thomas Clark. Denton, Tex.: North Texas State University, 1983: 75–88.

3974. Petrarca, Stefano, and Nicola Sani. "Lo Studio per l'Informatica Musicale di Roma: uso di tecnologie digitali avanzate per scopi musicali." [Studio Report S.I.M./Rome: Use of Advanced Digital Technology for Musical Purposes] In *Proceedings of the Venice 1982 International Computer Music Conference,* comp. Thom Blum and John Strawn. San Francisco, Calif.: Computer Music Association, 1985: 33–39.

3975. Peyser, Joan. "American Technology Thrives in Paris." *New York Times* (May 6, 1984): sec. 2, H25.

3976. Pohlmann, Ken. "Theory & Practice: Waiting for Godot." *DB, Sound Engineering Magazine* 17 (July-Aug. 1983): 24–27.
E&EA 87 (1984): 11418.

3977. Randall, J. K. "A Report from Princeton." *Perspectives of New Music* 3 (Spring-Summer 1965): 84–92.

3978. Razzi, Fausto. "Progetto per la costruzione di un centro di informatica musicale da localizzare nella zona di Napoli." [Project for the Construction of a Center for Computer Music to Be Located near Naples] *Quaderni di Informatica Musicale* 2 (1983): 4–9.

3979. *Research at IRCAM in 1979.* Paris: IRCAM, 1980. (Rapports IRCAM 29/80)

3980. Rogers, Bruce. "The Center for Studies in Mathematical and Automated Music, Paris." *Numus West* 4 (1973): 6–10.

3981. Rosenboom, David, and Larry Polansky. "Studio Report: Recent Developments at the Center for Contemporary Music, 1981–, Mills College." In *Proceedings of the International Computer Music Conference, 1985,* ed. Barry Truax. San Francisco, Calif.: Computer Music Association, 1985: 419–23.

3982. Scaletti, Carla. "The CERL Music Project at the University of Illinois." *Computer Music Journal* 9,1 (Spring 1985): 45–58.

3983. Schindler, Allan; Robert W. Gross; and Alexander R. Brinkman. "The Eastman School of Music Computer Music Studio." Abstract in *Proceedings, 1981 International Computer Music Conference, November 5–8,* comp. Larry Austin and Thomas Clark. Denton, Tex.: North Texas State University, 1983: 74.

3984. Silverston, Stefan M.; Terry A. Smay; and Gary C. White. "ISMUS, Iowa State Computerized System." *Page* 35 (1975): 4–5.

3985. ————, and Gary C. White. "Report on the Iowa State Computerized Music System." *Numus-West* 7 (1975): 32–37.

3986. Slawson, A. Wayne. "Composer-Centered Development: A Studio Report from Pittsburgh." In *Proceedings of the 1980 International Computer Music Conference,* comp. Hubert S. Howe. San Francisco, Calif.: Computer Music Association, 1982: 202–210.

3987. ———. "Computer Music at the University of Pittsburgh." In *Proceedings of the 1978 International Computer Music Conference,* comp. Curtis Roads. Evanston, Ill.: Northwestern University Press, 1979: 494–500.

3988. ———. "Sound Color and Filters: The Hybrid Studio Revisited." In *Proceedings, 1981 International Computer Music Conference, November 5–8,* comp. Larry Austin and Thomas Clark. Denton, Tex.: North Texas State University, 1983: 94–100.

3989. Smith, Brian R. "Bracknell Computer Arts Centre." *Studio International* 189 (May-June 1975): 244.

3990. Smith, Julius O.; John W. Gordon; David A. Jaffe; Bernard Mont-Reynaud; W. Andrew Schloss; Bill Schottstaedt; and Paul Wieneke. "Recent Research in Computer Music at CCRMA." In *High Technology in the Information Industry: COMPCON '82; Digest of Papers.* Los Alamitos, Calif.: Computer Society Press, 1982: 35–39.
C&CA 17 (1982): 28476.

3991. Smoliar, Stephen W., and M. Joseph Willson. "Proposal for an Interactive Computer-Music Facility." *Numus-West* 5 (1974): 39–43.
RILM 76 3944.

3992. Souster, Tim. "Keele Computer Music Project." In *Computer Music in Britain, 8th–11th April 1980.* London: Electro-Acoustic Music Association of Great Britain, 1980: 4.

3993. Sundberg, Johan. "Institut de Recherche et Coordination Acoustique/ Musique (IRCAM): ett nytt centrum för musikforskning." [IRCAM: A New Center for Music and Music Research] *Svensk tidskrift för musikforskning* 60,1 (1978): 113–14.

3994. Sylvander, Stefan. "Electronic Musical Composition in Sweden, 1952–1970." Ph.D. diss., University of Wisconsin, 1974. 258 p.
DA 36:21A. *RILM* 75 1647.

3995. Tempelaars, Stan. "Voltage Control in the Utrecht University Studio." *Electronic Music Reports* 1 (Sept. 1969): 68–77.

3996. ———, and Gottfried Michael Koenig. "The Computer at the Institute of Sonology, Utrecht." *Interface* 1 (1972): 167–74.

3997. Tisato, Graziano. "Computer music a Padova: Centro di Sonologia Computazionale (I)." [Computer Music at Padova: The Centre of Computational Sonology (I)] *Strumenti musicali* 22 (1981): 104–12.

3998. ———. "Computer music a Padova: Centro di Sonologia Computazionale (II)." [Computer Music at Padua: The Centre of Computational Sonology (II)] *Strumenti musicali* 23 (1981): 86–96.

3999. Truax, Barry D. "The New Electronic and Computer Music Facility at Simon Fraser University." In *Proceedings of the Venice 1982 International Computer Music Conference,* comp. Thom Blum and John Strawn. San Francisco, Calif.: Computer Music Association, 1985: 1–15.

4000. Turco, Carlo. "Un progetto dello IASM per la costituzione di un 'Centro di Informatica Musicale' nel napoletano." [Studio Report ISAM Napoli] In *Proceedings of the Venice 1982 International Computer Music Conference,* comp. Thom Blum and John Strawn. San Francisco, Calif.: Computer Music Association, 1985: 40–53.

4001. Valentin, Karl-Otto. "Om operaarbetet i EMS." [About the Opera Work at the Stockholm Electronic Music Studio] *Nutida musik* 12,1 (1968–69): 19–20. In Swedish.

4002. Vercoe, Barry. "MIT Experimental Music Studio." Paper presented at the 1983 International Computer Music Conference, Oct. 7–10, 1983, Rochester, N.Y.

4003. ————. "The MIT Music-11 System." Paper presented at the 1978 International Computer Music Conference, November 1–5, Northwestern University, Evanston, Ill.

4004. Vidolin, Alvise. "La Biennale di Venezie—Settore Musica." [Biennale di Venezia—Music Department] In *Musica ed elaboratore elettronico. Verso il laboratorio musicale personale.* Milan: FAST, 1980: 159–62.

4005. ————. "Due anni di attività del LIMB." [Two Years of Activity at LIMB] In *Informatica: Musica/Industria.* Milan: Unicopli, 1983.

4006. ————. "Laboratorio permanente per l'informatica musicale." [A Permanent Laboratory for Computer Music] In *Musica nella secessione.* Venice: Biennale di Venezia, 1980: 155–56.

4007. Weiland, Frits C. "Electronic Music in the Netherlands." *Sonorum Speculum* 33 (Winter 1967–68): 1–20.
Parallel English and Dutch texts.

4008. ————. "The Institute of Sonology at Utrecht State University." *Sonorum Speculum* 52 (1973): 12–27.
Parallel text in English and German.
Reprinted in *Musical Aspects of the Electronic Medium, Report on Electronic Music.* Utrecht: Institute of Sonology, 1975.

4009. Wein, M., and N. Burtnyk. "A Computer Facility for Film Animation and Music." In *Proceedings of the Canadian Computer Conference Session, Montreal, June 1–3, 1972:* 21201–5.

4010. Wessel, David L. "A Studio Report from IRCAM." Paper presented at the 1980 International Computer Music Conference, November 13–15, 1980, Queens College of the City University of New York.

4011. White, Brian. "Computer Arts." *Studio International* 188 (Nov. 1974): 196.

4012. White, Gary C. "Iowa State Computerized Music System: MUS." Ames, Iowa, Apr. 4, 1973. (Bulletin no. 1)

4013. ————; Terry A. Smay; and Stefan M. Silverston. "Iowa State Computer Music System (ISMUS)." *Page* 35.

4014. Wiggen, Knut. "The Electronic Music Studio at Stockholm: Its Development and Construction." *Interface* 1 (Nov. 1972): 127–65.
Reprinted in *Musical Aspects of the Electronic Medium, Report on Electronic Music,* ed. Frits Weiland. Utrecht: Institute of Sonology, 1971.

4015. ———. "An Overview of Systems for Programming Music at the EMS Stockholm." *Page* 32 (1974)

4016. Willson, M. Joseph. "A Computer-Assisted Music Facility." Paper presented at the 46th Convention of the Audio Engineering Society, New York, Sept. 10–13, 1973.
Abstract in *Journal of the Audio Engineering Society* 21 (1973): 759.

4017. ———, and Tom H. Johnson. "A Computer Assisted Music Facility at the Moore School of Electrical Engineering." *Proceedings, DECUS Symposium* (1973): 175–79.

4018. Witts, Dick. "IRCAM: Le marteau sans matière?" *Contact* 18 (Winter 1977–78): 16–19.

4019. Wolterink, Charles P. "Stanford University: The Center for Computer Research in Music and Acoustics." *Current Musicology* 21 (1976): 7–8.

4020. Wright, Geoffrey. "Electronic and Computer Music at the Peabody Conservatory." In *Proceedings of the International Computer Music Conference, 1985,* ed. Barry Truax. San Francisco, Calif.: Computer Music Association, 1985: 425–28.

4021. Wuellner, Guy. "IRCAM: An Update." *American Music Teacher* 31,2 (1981): 43–44.

4022. Xenakis, Iannis. "Le dossier de l'Equipe de mathematique et automatique musicales, (E.M.A.Mu.)." *Coloquio artes* 13 (Dec. 1971): 40–48.
RILM 72 873.

4023. Yates, Peter. "Musical Computers at Urbana." *Arts and Architecture* 82 (June 1965): 8, 34–35.

4024. Yehuda, Yair, and Uri Shimony. "A Fast Digital Real-Time Sound Processor—AMOS: Studio Report." Paper presented at the 1984 International Computer Music Conference, Oct. 19–23, Paris, France.

4025. Zinovieff, Peter. "A Computerized Electronic Music Studio." *Electronic Music Reports* 1 (Sept. 1969): 5–22.

4026. ———. "Two Electronic Music Projects in Britain." In *Cybernetic Serendipity,* ed. Jasia Reichardt. New York: Praeger, 1969: 28–29.

GENERAL

4027.   Aaronson, Steve. "With a Song in His Digital Computer." *The Sciences* 14 (May 1974): 13–16.

4028.   Ager, Klaus. "Computermusik—Ende der Euphorie?" *Österreichische Musikzeitschrift* 37 (1982): 432–33.

4029.   Aharonian, Croiun; Jon H. Appleton; Pierre Boeswillwald; William Buxton; Wlodizimierz Kotonski; Leo Kupper; and Philippe Menard. "L'ordinateur—pour quoi faire?" *Faire* 2–3 (1975): 187–93.

4030.   Ahl, David H. "Digital Audio." *Creative Computing* 6 (June 1980): 38–50.

4031.   Aikin, Jim. "Digital Synthesis: Introducing the Technology of Tomorrow." *Contemporary Keyboard* 4 (Sept. 1978): 11–13.
        Reprinted in *Synthesizers and Computers*. Milwaukee, Wis.: H. Leonard Publishing Corp. 1985: 1–7.

4032.   ———. "John Chowning: Computer Synthesis Expert at Stanford." *Contemporary Keyboard* 4 (Sept. 1978): 14, 50–51.
        Reprinted in *Synthesizers and Computers*. Milwaukee, Wis.: H. Leonard Pub. Corp., 1985: 10–14.

4033.   ———. "Max Mathews: Digital Systems Innovator with Bell Labs." *Contemporary Keyboard* 4 (Sept. 1978): 14, 48.
        Reprinted in *Synthesizers and Computers*. Milwaukee, Wis.: H. Leonard, 1985: 8–9.

4034.   Albrecht, Gustav. "Letter." *Scientific American* 194 (Apr. 1956): 18–19.

4035.   Alston, E.; B. Griffin; and D. Seegars. "Chord Spelling and Melody Translation." *IBM Technical Disclosure Bulletin* 24 (July 1981): 960–61.
        C&CA 17 (1982): 5231.

4036.   Aperghis-Tramoni, Christian. "Un instrument de musique concu autour d'un ordinateur." In *Informatique et musique, Second Symposium International,* ed. Hélène Charnassé. Ivry: ELMERATTO, CNRS, 1983: 115–25.

4037.   ———. "Système d'acquisition et de restitution de musique." Thèse de troisième cycle, Institut de Programmation, Paris, 1977.

4038. Appleton, Jon H. "Electronic Music: Questions of Style and Compositional Technique." *Musical Quarterly* 65 (1979): 103–10.

4039. ———. "Not Healthy." *Computer Music Journal* 7,1 (Spring 1983): 7–8. Reply by C. Roads, p. 8.

4040. ———. "The State of Electronic Music: 1972." *College Music Symposium* 12 (Fall 1972): 7–10.

4041. Armbruster, Greg. "The Information Source of the Future in On-line Now: Electronic Bulletin Boards." *Keyboard* 11 (Dec. 1985): 12, 103.

4042. "Art et informatique à l'heure musicale." *Courrier de l'ouest* 31 (Avr. 23, 1974): 6.

4043. Arveiller, Jacques. "Apropos de l'enseignement de l'informatique musicale à l'université." In *Computer Music/Composition musicale par ordinateur; Report on an International Project Including a Workshop at Aarhus, Denmark in 1978,* ed. Marc Battier and Barry Truax. Ottawa: Canadian Commission for Unesco, 1980: 15–28.

4044. ———. "L'informatique musicale, qu'est-ce que c'est?" In *Art et ordinateur:* [exposition, Forest-National, 18 Avril-18 Mai 1974]. Brussels: Institut supérieur pour l'etude du langage plastique, 1974: 29–31.

4045. ———; Marc Battier; and Giuseppe G. Englert. *Un repertoire d'informatique musicale.* Paris: Groupe art et informatique de Vincennes, Université de Paris VIII, 1976. 127 p. (Artinfo/musinfo 23–25)

4046. Ashton, Alan C. "Electronics, Music, and Computers." Ph.D. diss., University of Utah, 1970. 183 p. *DA* 31:4627B.

4047. *Aspetti teorici di informatica musicale.* [Theoretical Features in Computer Music] Milan: CTU - Istituto di Cibernetica, Università di Milano, 1977. 123 p.

4048. Asta, Vito. "Poesia, algebra lineare e musica: un'esperienza." [Poetry, Linear Algebra, and Music: An Experience] In *Atti del Quarto Colloquio di Informatica Musicale.* Pisa: CNUCE-CNR, 1981: 1–25.

4049. Asuar, Jose V. "Haciendo musica con un computador." [Making Music with a Computer] *Revista musical Chilena* 27 (July-Dec. 1973): 81–83.

4050. ———. "Musica con computadores: como hacerlo?" [Music with Computers: How Is It Done?] *Revista musical Chilena* 26 (Apr.-June 1972): 36–66. *RILM* 74 3953.

4051. ———. "La segunda generacion de musica electronica." [The Second Generation of Electronic Music] *Revista musical Chilena* 30 (Apr.-Sept. 1976): 75–110.

4052. "Austrian Technicians Develop New Computer." *Billboard* 94 (Feb. 6, 1982): 55.

4053. Bachmann, Claus-Henning. "Bonn: Kybernetisches Projekt, Computer-Planspiele und Klangautomaten." *Melos/Neue Zeitschrift für Musik* 2 (1976): 131–32.

4054. ———. "Musik und Computer in den U.S.A." *Melos/Neue Zeitschrift für Musik* 1 (1975): 467–68.
Also in *Schweizerische Musikzeitung* 116 (1976): 30–32.

4055. ———. "Ein neues Musikinstrument: Der Computer; 'Musik und Computer in den USA'—eine Veranstaltung in Berlin." *Neue Musikzeitung* 24,5 (1975): 4.

4056. ———. "Vergügungen mit Computern—Josef Anton Riedls Tage neuer Musik in München." *Musikalischer Jugend* 17,6 (1968–1969): 2.

4057. Baggiani, Guido. "Il pensiero musicale nel mezzo elettronico ed il passaggio fra tecnica analogica e tecnica digitale." [On Musical Thought in Electronic Media: Passing from Analog to Digital Technology] In *Atti del Terzo Colloquio di Informatica Musicale,* ed. G. De Poli. Padua: Università di Padova, 1979: 1–14.

4058. Barbaud, Pierre. "Avenement de la musique cybernétique." *Les lettres nouvelles* 7 (Apr. 22, 1959): 28.

4059. ———. "Les informaticiens et la musique—'Ingenieurs en emotions musicales' ou 'Musiciens en emotions ingenieuses'?" *0-1 Informatique* 4 (Oct. 1960): 15–17.

4060. ———, and Robert Philippe. "L'ordinateur et la musique." *Communication et langages* 3 (Sept. 1969): 17–25.

4061. Barenholtz, Jerry; Z. Wolofsky; I. Ganapathy; Thomas W. Calvert; and D. O'Hara. "Computer Interpretation of Dance Notation." In *Computing in the Humanities: Proceedings of the Third International Conference on Computing in the Humanities,* ed. Serge Lusignan and John S. North. Waterloo, Ont.: The University of Waterloo Press, 1977: 235–40.
C&CA 13 (1978): 13040.

4062. Baroni, Mario. "Problemi di un compositore: conversazione con Iannis Xenakis." [Problems of a Composer: Interview with Iannis Xenakis] *Musica/Realtà* 3 (1980): 127–43.

4063. Barta, Janusz. "Autorskoprawne problemy muzyki nowoczesnej." [Copyright Problems of New Music] *Nowe prawe* 34 (1978): 1286–1300.
RILM 78 2152.

4064. Bartlett, Martin. "Computer-Controlled Electronic Accompaniment Systems." Paper presented at the 1980 International Computer Music Conference, November 13–15, 1980, Queens College of the City University of New York.

4065. Bateman, Wayne. *Introduction to Computer Music.* New York: J. Wiley, 1980. 314 p.
Review by John Strawn in *Computer Music Journal* 5,1 (Spring 1981): 65–73.
Rebuttal by Wayne Bateman in *Computer Music Journal* 5,2 (Summer 1981): 7–8.
Reply by John Strawn in *Computer Music Journal* 5,2 (Summer 1981): 8–9.
Review by Stan Tempelaars in *Interface* 10 (1981): 147–48.

4066. Battier, Marc. "Quelques remarques sur l'activité electroacoustique et la syn-·thèse de sons." In *Computer Music/Composition musicale par ordinateur; Report on an International Project Including a Workshop at Aarhus, Denmark in 1978,* ed. Marc Battier and Barry Truax. Ottawa: Canadian Commission for Unesco, 1980: 63–72.

4067. ———. "Quelques tendances récentes de la production musicale par ordinateur." *Informatique et sciences humaines* 45 (Juin 1980): 13–24.

4068. ———. "Les tendances recentes des musiques electroacoustiques et l'environnement informatique." Thèse, Docteur de 3ème cycle, Université Paris X, 1981.

4069. Bauer-Mengelberg, Stefan. "The Truth, the Whole Truth, and Nothing but the Truth." *Computer Studies in the Humanities and Verbal Behavior* 1 (1968): 52–54.

4070. Baxter, M. A. "High-Performance Digital Music Synthesis." In *Northcon/83, Electronics Show & Convention, Portland, OR, USA, 10–12 May 1983.* El Segundo, Calif.: Electronics Conventions, 1983: 24/1/1–12.
E&EA 86 (1983): 45749.
Also in *Mini/Micro West, 1983 Computer Conference and Exhibition, San Francisco, CA, USA, 8–11 Nov. 1983.* Los Angeles, Calif.: Electronics Conventions, 1983: 14/1/1–21.
C&CA 20 (1985): 17274. *E&EA* 88 (1985): 20432.

4071. Bearson, James. "Music by Computer—The Sound of the Future?" *Random Bits* 4 (Nov. 1968): 3–4, 6.

4072. Beckwith, Sterling. "The Altar, Music ROM Pack." Paper presented at the Music Symposium, Sheridan College, June 1980, Oakville, Ont.

4073. ———. "The Human Interface to Computer Music." Paper presented at the Music Symposium, Sheridan College, June 1980, Oakville, Ont.

4074. Bernardini, Nicola. "Authors of *Computer Music Journal,* Volumes 1–9, 1977–1985." *Computer Music Journal* 10,1 (Spring 1986): 37–39.

4075. ———. "Computer Music." *Scienza2000* 8 (1984): 48–52.

4076. ———. "Il computer parla in padovano." [Computers Speak Padovano] *Il messaggero* (Feb. 25, 1984): 21.

4077. ———. "Contents of *Computer Music Journal,* Volumes 1–9, 1977–1985." *Computer Music Journal* 10,1 (Spring 1986): 17–36.

4078. ———. "Un'intera orchestra con il computer." [A Whole Orchestra Inside the Computer] *Il messaggero* (Oct. 1, 1983): 23.

4079. ———. "La musica per calcolatore: studi ricerca e sperimentazione." [Computer Music: Theoretical and Practical Research] *AudioReview* 23 (1983): 44–47.

4080. ———. "Strumenti analogici e strumenti digitali nella musica elettronica: principi di funzionamento." [Analog and Digital Instruments in Electronic Music: Working Principles] *AudioReview* 24 (1984): 78–83.

4081. Bied, Alphonse. "Robots compositeurs de musique." *Technica* (Nov. 1955)

4082. Binurkar, M. G., and Padma Rangachari. "Generating Instrumental Music by the Computer." *Journal of the National Centre for the Performing Arts* [India] 1 (Dec. 1972): 55–64.

4083. Bird, Pristen; Bill Dempsey; Ted Detjen; LeRoy Finkel; and Stanley Pogrow. "Tracking Down the 'Right' Computer: How to Choose the One That's Best for You." *Electronic Learning* 3 (Jan. 1984): 39–49.
   CIJE 16 (1984): EJ 291 956.

4084. Bodin, Lars-Gunnar. "Mobilis in Mobile." *Nutida musik* 16,2 (1972–73): 29–30.
   In Swedish.

4085. ———. "Om analog och digital produktion av elektronisk musik." [On Analog and Digital Production of Electronic Music] *Nutida musik* 24,1 (1980–81): 12–14.
   In Swedish.

4086. ———. "Samtal med Alan Sutcliffe och Jonathan Harvey." [A Conversation with Alan Sutcliffe and Jonathan Harvey] *Nutida musik* 16,2 (1972–73): 33–36.
   In Swedish.
   RILM 73 4269.

4087. Bonnycastle, Michael. "A Canadian Music System." Paper presented at the Music Symposium, Sheridan College, June 1980, Oakville, Ont.

4088. Borruso, P.; P. Giua; Giorgo Nottoli; and S. Santoboni. "Il sistema per la sintesi del suono in corso di realizzazione presso l'Istituto di Acustica 'O.M. Cordino'—C.N.R. Roma." [The Sound Synthesis System in Preparation at the Istituto di Acustica 'O.M. Corbino' — C.N.R. Rome (National Research Council)] In *Atti del Terzo Colloquio di Informatica Musicale,* ed. G. De Poli. Padua: Università di Padova, 1979: 225–36.

4089. Borry, Linda. "Computers and Music?" *AEDS Monitor* 19 (July-Sept. 1980): 17.
   C&CA 16 (1981): 3163.

4090. ———. "M.E.C.C. Music." Paper presented at the Music Symposium, Sheridan College, June 1980, Oakville, Ont.

4091. Boulez, Pierre. "Maestro Computer: Exploring the New Frontiers of Sound." *Unesco Courier* (Apr. 1980): 28.

4092. Bourdain, G. S. "The Electronic World of Pierre Boulez." *Saturday Review* 9 (Feb. 1982): 43–45.

4093. "Brain Computes New Tunes for TV." *New York Times* 105 (July 3, 1956): 51: 5.

4094. Branchi, Walter. "The State of Anxiety." *Computer Music Journal* 7,1 (Spring 1983): 8–10.

4095. Brincker, Jens. "Den store spilledåse." [The Great Music Box] *Dansk musiktidsskrift* 45 (1970): 89–90. In Danish.

4096. Brower, Brock. "Why 'Thinking Machines' Cannot Think." *The New York Times* CX (Feb. 19, 1961) magazine section: 19, 24–26.

4097. Brown, Frank. "Computer Music Produced with the Aid of a Digital-to-Analog Converter." *Leonardo* 11 (1978): 39–40.

4098. Brown, L. C. "Introduction to Music." In *Indiana University Computing Network 8th Annual Conference on Academic Computing Applications,* ed. B. Boggs. Indianapolis, Ind.: Indiana University, Purdue University at Indianapolis Computing Service, 1981: 145–47.

4099. Browne, Richmond. "Computers and Music." *Keyboard* (May 1967): 4.

4100. Bruderer, Herbert. *Nichtnumerische Informationsverarbeitung.* Rorschach: Verlag Lingustik, 1980. 190 p.
Review by John Strawn in *Computer Music Journal* 5,1 (Spring 1981): 78–79.

4101. Brün, Herbert. "Computer-Plotted Graphics." *Computer Music Journal* 5,2 (Summer 1981): 29–35.
C&CA 17 (1982): 8911.

4102. ———. "The Premise Is That There Be Music." In *Proceedings of the International Computer Music Conference, 1985,* ed. Barry Truax. San Francisco, Calif.: Computer Music Association, 1985: 1–4.

4103. ———. *Über Musik und zum Computer.* Karlsruhe: G. Braun, 1971. 121 p. With sound recording.
Review by Carl Dahlhaus in *Musik und Bildung* 3 (1971): 503.
Review by Erhard Karkoschka in *Melos* 39 (1972): 285–88.
Review by Hermann Matzke in *Instrumentenbau-Zeitschrift* 25 (1971): 560.
Review by Wolfgang Seifert in *Neue Zeitschrift für Musik* 133 (1972): 104–6.

4104. Brush, Leif. "Terrain Instrument/Riverharps Affiliate." *Numus-West* 7 (Winter 1975): 47–50.
RILM 76 3283.

4105. Bruskin, Sam. "Music: The Arts." *Omni* 2 (May 1980): 26–30.

4106. Budzyński, Gustaw, and Marianna Sankiewicz. "Komputer analogowy w muzyce eksperymentalnej." [The Analog Computer in Experimental Music] *Zeszyty naukowe państwowa wyzsza szkota muzyczna* 12 (1973): 107–20. In Polish. *RILM* 74 3955.

4107. Bulkeley, William M. "These Avant-Garde Musical Scores May Stimulate Both Eyes and Ears." *Wall Street Journal* (Dec. 14, 1984): 27(W), p. 29 (E) col. 1.

4108. Bushert, Al. "The Dawn of the Future Computer." *Electronotes* 7 (Dec. 1975): 14–16.

4109. Butterfield, Jim. "First Steps in Making Music." Paper presented at the Music Symposium, Sheridan College, June 1980, Oakville, Ont.

4110. Buxton, William. "A Composer's Introduction to Computer Music." *Interface 6* (1977): 57–71. *C&CA* 13 (1978): 4387. *RILM* 77 3742.

4111. ———. "Introduzione alla computer music." [An Introduction to Computer Music] In *Musica e elaboratore*. Venice: Biennale di Venezia, 1980: 25–36.

4112. ———. "Les ordinateurs et le compositeur: une introduction generale." *Faire* 4/5 (1978): 15–20.

4113. ———. "Towards a Computer Based System for Music Composition and Performance." Paper presented at the ACM/SIGLASH Meeting, New York University, October 1977.

4114. "By the Numbers." *Music America* 76 (Sept. 1956): 13.

4115. Byrd, Donald. "Humanities Programming for Creative Work." *Random Bits* 6 (Jan. 1971): 8–12.

4116. ———. "They Laughed When I Sat Down at the Computer." *Random Bits* 10 (Nov. 1974): 2–3, 7.

4117. Cadoz, Claude, and Anasthasie Luciani. "Processes, Sound Synthesis Models, and the Computer Designed for Musical Creation." Paper presented at the 1984 International Computer Music Conference, Oct. 19–23, Paris, France.

4118. Cage, John. "Choosing Abundance." *The North American Review* 6 (Fall 1969): 9–17.

4119. ———. "Things to Do." *The North American Review* 6 (Winter 1969): 12–16.

4120. *Les cahiers recherche musique, 3 (1976). Synthetiseur, ordinateur.* Paris: Groupe de recherche musicale, 1976. *RILM* 76 4772.

4121. Cahill, P. "ILLIAC, Mechanical Brain, Takes Up Composing Music." *Champaign-Urbana News Gazette* (Jul. 8, 1956)

4122. ———. "ILLIAC Proves Musical Skills." *Champaign-Urbana News Gazette* (Aug. 10, 1956)

4123. Canby, Edward Tatnall. "Audio, etc." *Audio* 65 (Feb. 1981): 8–12.

4124. ———. "Audio, etc." *Audio* 66 (Mar. 1982): 87–88.

4125. ———. "Silva-Tongued Computer." *Audio* 67 (Dec. 1983): 21–25.

4126. Carpenter, Allan. "Amazing New Uses for Robot Brains." *Science Digest* 41 (Feb. 1957): 1–5.

4127. Cary, Tristram. "The Composer and the Machine: A 30 Year Overview." In *Proceedings of the International Music and Technology Conference, August 24– 28, 1981, University of Melbourne*. Parkville, Vic.: Computer Music Project, Dept. of Computer Science, University of Melbourne, 1981: 219–35.

4128. Castman, Bernt. "Musik och computer." [Music and Computer] *Svensk tidskrift för musikforskning* 52 (1970): 46–50.

4129. Cavaliere, Sergio, and Loreto Papadia. "Informatica, musica, teatro— Progetto di teatro cibernetico." [Computer Science, Music, Theater—A Project of the Cybernetic Theater] In *Atti del Quarto Colloquio di Informatica Musicale*. Pisa: CNUCE-CNR, 1981: 323–36.

4130. ———; Loreto Papadia; and Pasquale Parascandolo. "From Computer Music to the Theater: The Realization of a Theatrical Automaton." *Computer Music Journal* 6,4 (Winter 1982): 22–35.
C&CA 18 (1983): 19320.
Review by Harry B. Lincoln in *Computing Reviews* 24 (Nov. 1983): 40,854.

4131. Ceccato, Silvio. "Art, nombre, machine." In *Actes du Colloque international 'Art, technologie et communication', Lausanne, Oct. 1971*. Lausanne: Dossier I.E.R.I.V., 1972: 9–13.

4132. Chabrel, Stephane. "Le debut d'un son." *Quebec science* 13 (Juin 1975): 20–24.

4133. Chadabe, Joel. "Some Reflections of the Nature of the Landscape within which Computer Music Systems Are Designed." *Computer Music Journal* 1,3 (June 1977): 5–11.
C&IS 18 (1978): 189686C. *RILM* 77 3638.

4134. Charbonneau, Gerard. "L'ordinateur, instrument de musique: synthèse directe des sons." In *Conférences des journées d'études festival international du son*. Paris: Ed. Radio, 1973.

4135. Charnassé, Hélène. "L'informatique musicale en 1974." *Journal de la Societé de statistique de Paris* 115 (1974): 210–15.

4136. ———, and Henri Ducasse. "Avant-propos." In *Informatique musicale, journées d'études 1973. Textes des conférences, E.R.A.T.T.O.* Paris: C.N.R.S., 1973: ii.

4137. Chion, Michel, and Guy Reibel. *Les musiques electroacoustiques*. Aix-en-Provence: Edisud, 1976. 339 p.
RILM 76 1566.

4138. Choate, Robert A. "Impact and Potential of Technology." In *Documentary Report of the Tanglewood Symposium*. Washington: Music Educators' National Conference, 1968: 123–26.

4139. Chong, John A. *Computer and Electronic Music in Europe, 1973*. Ottawa, Ont.: National Research Council, 1974. 48 p.

4140. Chopin, Henri. "Electronics and the Computer." *Page* 13 (Jan. 1971): 4.

4141. Chowning, John M. "La nouvelle musique et la science: interdependance des concepts." In *Le compositeur et l'ordinateur*. Paris: IRCAM, 1981: 34–37.

4142. Christensen, Louis. "Conversation with Ligeti at Stanford." *Numus West* 2 (1972): 17–20.

4143. "Ciani Explores New Sound Frontiers." *Backstage* 25 (Apr. 20, 1984): 20B.

4144. Ciarcia, Steve. "Control the World." *BYTE* 2 (Sept. 1977): 30–43, 156–61.

4145. Civan, David. "The Coming of Computer Audio." *Rolling Stone* n346 (June 25, 1981): 78.

4146. Cohen, David. "Computer-Generated Music." *Composer* 26 (Winter 1967/1968): 29–30.

4147. ———. "Computer Performance as Model and Challenge." *Proceedings of the American Society of University Composers* 7/8 (1972/1973): 22–24.

4148. Colbert, Paul. "Computing into the Future." *Melody Maker* 57 (Oct. 23, 1982): 35.

4149. Collins, G. "Canada, Computers & Music." *CIPS Computer Magazine* (June 1973)

4150. Comerford, P. J. "Musical Instruments from Numbers." *Computer Bulletin* ser. 3, no. 1 (Mar. 1985): 26–30.
C&CA 20 (1985): 30997. *E&EA* 88 (1985): 37374.

4151. "Composer—The 'Brain'." *Melody Maker* 31 (July 21, 1956): 2.

4152. *Le compositeur et l'ordinateur*. Paris: IRCAM, 1981. 113 p.

4153. "Computer and Laser." *Chip* 5 (May 1981): 30–34.
In German.
C&CA 16 (1981): 36853.

4154. "The Computer Copyright Controversy." *Computers and the Humanities* 9 (1975): 151.

4155. "Computer Errechnet Stimmung der Metallblasinstrumente." *Instrumentenbau-Zeitschrift* 27 (1973): 702–03.

4156. "The Computer is a Music Maker." *Infosystems* 23 (May 1976): 27.

4157. "Computer Magic." *The Diapason* 58 (May 1967): 24.

4158. "Computer Music Association Update." *Computer Music Journal* 4,1 (Spring 1980): 4.

4159. "Computer Software Starts Singing: Leading Firms Marketing Low-Cost Music Programs." *Billboard* 95 (Oct. 22, 1983): 4.

4160. "Computer Sounds: Electronic Art." *Chip* 11 (Nov. 184): 50–52. In German.
C&CA 20 (1985): 12317.

4161. "Computers & Music." *Music Trades* 130 (Dec. 1982): 94–101, 103.

4162. Cony, Ed. "Canny Computers—Machines Write Music, Play Checkers, Tackle New Tasks in Industry." *Wall Street Journal* 148 (Sept. 19, 1956): 1, 12.

4163. Cope, David H. *New Directions in Music.* 4th ed. Dubuque, Iowa: Wm. C. Brown, 1984: 182–206.

4164. Covitz, Frank, and Cliff Ashcraft. "Advanced Examples in Making Music." Paper presented at the Music Symposium, Sheridan College, June 1980, Oakville, Ont.

4165. Cowen, Mary S. "Computers and the Arts." *Christian Science Monitor* (Feb. 24, 1981): sec. B, p. 6–7.

4166. Cross, Lowell M. *A Bibliography of Electronic Music.* Toronto: University of Toronto Press, 1967. 126 p.

4167. ———. "Electronic Music, 1948–1953." *Perspectives of New Music* 7 (Fall-Winter 1968): 32–65.
Reprinted in *Musical Aspects of the Electronic Medium, Report on Electronic Music,* ed. Frits Weiland. Utrecht: Institute of Sonology, 1975.

4168. Crowhurst, Norman H. *Electronic Musical Instruments.* Blue Ridge Summit, Pa.: Tab Books, 1971. 188 p.

4169. "La cybernetique et la musique." *Musica disques* 101 (Aug. 1962): 58.

4170. Dalmasso, Gilbert. "Réseaux d'improvisation." *Informatique et sciences humaines* 45 (Juin 1980): 77–90.

4171. Dashow, James. "Far musica con un grande computer (Il S/370 ed io)." [Making Music with a Great Computer—S/370 and I] In *Musica ed elaboratore elettronico—Atti del convegno.* Milan: FAST, 1980: 43–60.

4172. De Panafieu, Jacques. "L'ordinateur et l'art." *Communication et langages* 2 (Juin 1969): 29–36.

4173. De Poli, Giovanni. "Informatica musicale in Italia: inquadramento e prospettive." [Computer Music in Italy: Organization and Perspectives] In *Atti del Congresso AICA '81.* Pavia: AICA, 1981: 441–47.

4174. ———. "La ricerca di informatica musicale in Italia." [Research on Computer Music in Italy] In *Musica e elaboratore.* Venice: Biennale di Venezia, 1980: 171–80.

4175. Debelius, Ulrich. "Szene und Technik. Zwei Aspekte einer Entwicklung." In *Die Musik der Sechziger Jahre.* Regensburg: G. Bosse, 1973: 53–64.

4176.   "Le DEC system 10 connait la musique." *01-Informatique Hebdo* 340 (Juin 23, 1975)

4177.   DeCampo, Leila. "Introducing the Computer at a Small Liberal Arts College." *ACM/SIGLASH Newsletter* 5 (Dec. 1970)

4178.   Delâtre, Jean-Luc. *Le systeme de traitement de signaux digitaux 'junior'.* Paris: IRCAM, 1980. 13 p. (Rapports IRCAM 28/80)

4179.   Demarne, Pierre. "La création par ordinateur: principe général." *Communication et langages* 7 (Sept. 1970): 15–23.

4180.   Deutsch, Herbert A. *Synthesis: An Introduction to the History, Theory & Practice of Electronic Music.* Sherman Oaks, Calif.: Alfred Pub. Co., 1985. 120 p.

4181.   Deihl, Ned C.; Darhyl S. Ramsey; and Stephen E. Stern. "Using the Computer for Charting Halftime Shows." *The Instrumentalist* 33 (July 1979): 92–93.

4182.   "Digital Synths Key to New World of Musical Potential; Wow Artists." *Variety* 311 (July 6, 1983): 67.

4183.   "Digitale Tonerzeugung." *Instrumentenbau-Zeitschrift* 26 (May 1972): 332–333.

4184.   Douglas, Alan. "Electrical Synthesis of Music." *Electronics and Power* 10 (1964): 83–86.

4185.   Dumm, Robert. "Running the Gamut." *The Piano Quarterly* 57 (Fall 1966): 22–23.

4186.   Eckert, Thor. "Long a Composer, Now a Performer: The Computer." *Christian Science Monitor* 71 (Sept. 5, 1979): 18.

4187.   "Electronic and Computer Music." *Creative Computing* 3 (Mar.-Apr. 1977): 67.

4188.   Ellis, David. "Common Chords." *Computer Answers* (July-Aug. 1984): 29–30.

4189.   ———. "Digital Synthesis." *Windfall* 1,4 (1981): 36–39.

4190.   Emerson, Paul. "Computer Music Requires New Way of Thinking." *Palo Alto Times* (Nov. 10, 1978): Sec. III, p. 15.

4191.   Erickson, Raymond F. "Music and the Computer in the Sixties." *AFIPS Conference Proceedings* 36 (1970): 281–85.

4192.   Everett, Tom. "10 Questions: 270 Answers." *The Composer* 10–11 (1980): 70–74.

4193.   Fatus, Claude. "La musique 'télématique'." *Interface* 12 (1983): 557–72. *C&CA* 19 (1984): 23724. *E&EA* 87 (1984): 27172.

4194.   Ferretti, Ercolino. "The Computer as a Tool for the Creative Musician." In *Computers for the Humanities?* New Haven: Yale University Press, 1965: 107–12.

4195. ———. "Exploration and Organization of Sound with the Computer." Abstract in *Journal of the Acoustical Society of America* 39 (1966): 1245.

4196. Ferretti, Marc. "L'intelligence artificielle: l'ordinateur artiste." *Le haut parleur* 1396 (1973): 128–30.

4197. Foerster, Heinz von, and James W. Beauchamp, eds. *Music by Computers*. London: Wiley, 1969. 139 p.
Review by Stephen Arnold in *Tempo* 90 (Autumn 1969): 39–40.
Review by Norbert Böker-Heil in *Die Musikforschung* 25 (1972): 571–72.
Review by Jens Brincker in *Dansk Musiktidsskrift* 45,4 (1970): 89–90.
Review by Helmuth Horvath in *Österreichische Musikzeitschrift* 27 (1972): 573–75.
Review by Hubert S. Howe in *Computers and the Humanities* 4 (1969–70): 277–83; and in *Perspectives of New Music* 8 (Spring-Summer 1970): 151–57.
Review by Alvin Lucier in *Music Educators Journal* 56 (Dec. 1969): 60–62.
Review by Fred K. Prieberg in *Melos* 37 (1970): 238–39.
Review in *Page* 3 (June 1969): 4.
Review in *Recorded Sound* 37 (Jan. 1970): 593.
Contains items: 18, 363, 486, 519, 1087, 1892, 2693, 3497, 3651, 4521.

4198. Forte, Allen. "Music and Computing: The Present Situation." *Computers and the Humanities* 2 (1967–68): 32–35.
Expanded version in *AFIPS Conference Proceedings* 31 (1967): 327–29.

4199. Fox, Barry. "The Man Who Switched on Bach." *New Scientist* 96 (Dec. 16, 1982): 753.

4200. ———. "Moog on Music." *Studio Sound* (Jan. 1983): 32–33.

4201. Franke, Herbert W. *Computergraphik—Computerkunst*. München: Bruckmann, 1971. 136 p.
Review by Erhard Karkoschka in *Melos* 39 (1972): 285–88.
RILM 73 1305.

4202. ———, and G. Jäger. *Apparative Kunst vom Kaleidoskop zum Computer*. Cologne: Dumont Schauberg, 1973. 288 p.

4203. Frankel, Robert E.; Stanley J. Rosenschein; and Stephen W. Smoliar. *The Modeling of Musical Perception on a Digital Computer via Schenkerian Theory*. Philadelphia: Moore School of Electrical Engineering, University of Pennsylvania, 1975. (Music Report no. 4, Apr. 1975)

4204. French, R. J. "Computer Music." *Computer Education* 23 (June 1976): 3–4. *C&CA* 11 (1976): 27925.

4205. Froehlich, Leopold. "Give Tchaikovsky the News." *Datamation* 27 (Oct. 1981): 130–40. *C&CA* 17 (1982): 2729.

4206. Fry, Christopher. "Dancing Musicians." *Perspectives of New Music* 21 (Fall/Winter 1982-Spring/Summer 1983): 585–89.

4207. Fugazza, G. F. "Computer music e diritto d'autore." [Computer Music and Copyright] *Strumenti musicali* 40 (1983): 114.

4208. Genovese, C. "Suono—colore." [Sound—Color] In *Atti del Quarto Colloquio di Informatica Musicale.* Pisa: CNUCE-CNR, 1981: 317–22.

4209. Genuys, Francois. "L'informatique musicale." *L'arc* 51 (1972): 41–46.

4210. ———. "Ordinateur et musique." *IBM-informatique* 3 (1971): 3–9.

4211. ———; Francois-Bernard Mache; Oliver Revault-D'Allones; and Iannis Xenakis. "Du bon usage de l'ordinateur." *L'arc* 51 (1972): 47–49.

4212. "Get Close to Computers . . . Hands-on Games, Music, and Art Display." *Sunset* 167 (Nov. 1981): 5–6.

4213. Gilbert, J. V. "The Well Tempered McLeyvier: Music Marries the New Technolgy." *Symphony Magazine* 33,3 (1982): 50–54.

4214. "Glossary of Computer Terms." *Music Educators Journal* 69 (Jan. 1983): 79–81.
    CIJE 15 (1983): EJ 275 332.

4215. Goebel, Johannes. "Zu den Zielsetzungen der deutschen Gesellschaft für Computermusik." *Feedback Papers* 27–28 (März 1982): 2–7.

4216. Goldberg, Theo, and Guenther F. Schrack. "Computer-Aided Correlation of Music and Graphic Image." *Computers & Graphics* 8,1 (1984): 109.

4217. Golden, Richard. "The Economies of Proper Data Tagging." *Institute for Computer Research in the Humanities* 4 (Nov. 1968): 1–2, 7–8.

4218. Gould, Murray. "Computer Synthesis of Music in the New York Area: A Report." *Contemporary Music Newsletter* 2 (Jan. 1968): 2–5.

4219. "Grand Finale." *Home Computer Advanced Course* 30 (1980): 581–84.
    C&CA 20 (1985): 4087. *E&EA* 88 (1985): 3819.

4220. Graziani, Mauro. "The Silent God." *Bollettino LIMB* 1 (1981): 68–72.

4221. Greco, A. "Computer Music." *Output* 12 (May 10, 1983): 33–35.
    In German.

4222. Green, Bert F. "Non-Computational Uses of Digital Computers." *Behavioral Science* 4 (1959): 164–67.

4223. Greussay, Patrick, and Jacques Arveiller. "Vive l'informatique musicale." *Informatique et sciences humaines* 45 (Juin 1980): 9–12.

4224. Grossi, Pietro; Graziano Bertini; and R. Andreoni. "Computer Music as a Permanent Service Towards Musical Telematics." In *Proceedings of the Venice 1982 International Computer Music Conference,* comp. Thom Blum and John Strawn. San Francisco, Calif.: Computer Music Association, 1985: 409–25.

4225. Gunn, David. "Electronic Music." *Microcomputing* 47 (Dec. 1980): 29.

4226. Halacy, Daniel Stephen. *Computers—The Machines We Think With.* New York: Harper and Row, 1962. 279 p.

4227. Hansen, William D. "This is Music?" *Chicago Sunday Tribune* 118, 15 (Apr. 12, 1959): magazine, 43.

4228. Harrison, Mike. "The American Invasion." *Billboard* 94 (Jan. 16, 1982): 21.

4229. Hasselbring, Ted S., and Nancy A. Duffus. "Using Microcomputer Technology in Music Therapy for Analyzing Therapist and Client Behavior." *Journal of Music Therapy* 18 (1981): 156–65.

4230. Hatano, Giyō. "Onagaku-e-no Jōhōron-Teki Sekkin." [An Informational Approach to Music] *Ongaku Gaku* 14 (1968): 54–64.
In Japanese, summary in English.
RILM 73 4337.

4231. Haus, Goffredo. "Anche il calcolatore vuole la sua partitura." [Computers Need a Score as Well] *Strumenti musicali* 2 (1979): 117–22.

4232. ———. "Cibernetica musicale." [Cybernetic Music] In *Annuario 1983 della Enciclopedia Scientifica Tecnica Mondadori*. Milan: Mondadori, 1983.

4233. ———. "L'evoluzione della musica elettronica." [The Evolution of Electronic Music] *Strumenti musicali* 54/55 (1984): 89–91.

4234. ———. "Informatica musicale." [Computer Music] *Le Science* 156 (1981): 7.

4235. ———. "Informatica musicale in fermento." [Computer Music in Ferment] *Strumenti musicali* 24 (1981): 114–19.

4236. ———. "L'informatica puo aiutare l'industria degli strumenti musicali." [Computer Science Can Help the Musical Instrument Industry] *Strumenti musicali* 12 (1980): 112–14.

4237. ———. "La matematica nella musica (I)." [Mathematics in Music (I)] *Strumenti musicali* 7/8 (1980): 36–39.

4238. ———. "La matematica nella musica (II)." [Mathematics in Music (II)] *Strumenti musicali* 9 (1980): 50–54.

4239. ———. "Il punto sulla computer music in Italia al convegno di Milano." [The State of Computer Music in Italy] *Strumenti musicali* 6 (1980): 90–92.

4240. ———. "Strumenti digitali e sistemi per l'elaborazione musicale: introduzione." [Digital Instruments and Sound Processing Systems: An Introduction] *Strumenti musicali* 13 (1981): 62–65.

4241. Haynes, Stanley. *The Computer as a Sound Processor*. Paris: IRCAM, 1980. 25 p. (Rapports IRCAM 25/80)

4242. ———. "The Computer as a Sound Processor: A Tutorial." *Computer Music Journal* 6,1 (Spring 1982): 7–17.
Review by P. J. Drummond in *Computing Reviews* 25 (Nov. 1984): 8411–0966.
C&IS 29 (1982): 82–6398C.

4243. ———. "Computers and Synthesizers." *Music and Musicians* 26 (Feb. 1978): 28–29.

4244. Hellström, Gunnar. "Datamaskinmusik i Sverige—läget 1965." [Computer Music in Sweden—the Situation in 1965] *Nutida musik* 9,3 (1965-66): 28-29.

4245. Helmers, Carl. "Interfacing Pneumatic Player Pianos." *BYTE* 2 (Sept. 1977): 112-20, 168.
Also in *The BYTE Book of Computer Music,* ed. Christopher P. Morgan. Peterborough, N.H.: BYTE Books, 1979: 85-90.
C&CA 13 (1978): 2573. *C&IS* 17: 181345C.

4246. Heppenheimer, T. A. "Chipmaster." *Omni* 7 (Feb. 1985): 86.

4247. Hillen, Peter. "How Computers Store Numbers." *Synapse* 1 (Nov.-Dec. 1976): 4.

4248. ———. "How Computers Talk to Synthesizers." *Synapse* 1 (Sept.-Oct. 1976): 3.

4249. Hiller, Lejaren A. "Acoustics and Electronic Music in the University Curriculum." *American Music Teacher* 12 (Mar.-Apr. 1963): 24-25, 37.

4250. ———. "Computer Music." In *Cybernetic Serendipity,* ed. Jasia Reichardt. New York: Praeger, 1969: 21-23.

4251. ———. "Computer Music." *Scientific American* 201:6 (Dec. 1959): 109-20.

4252. ———. "Electronic Synthesis of Microtonal Music." *Proceedings of the American Society of University Composers* 2 (1969): 99-106.

4253. ———. "The Generation of Music by High-Speed Digital Computers." *Scanfax* 10 (1956): 7.

4254. ———. "Music Composed with Computer: An Historical Survey." Mimeographed. Urbana: University of Illinois Experimental Music Studio, Feb. 1968. 98 p. (Technical Report no. 18)
Also in *The Computer and Music,* ed. Harry B. Lincoln. Ithaca: Cornell University Press, 1970: 42-96.

4255. ———. "Musical Applications of Electronic Digital Computers." *Gravesaner Blätter 27-28 (Nov. 1965): 46-72.*
Parallel English and German texts.

4256. ———. "Some Comments on Computer Sound Synthesis." *Proceedings of the American Society of University Composers* 1 (1968): 47-49.

4257. ———. "These Electrons Go Round and Round and Come Out Music." *IRE Student Quarterly* 8 (Sept. 1961): 36-45.

4258. ———, and James W. Beauchamp. "Research in Music with Electronics." *Science* 150 (1965): 161-69.

4259. ———, and Leonard M. Isaacson. "Experimental Music." In *The Modeling of Mind: Computers and Intelligence,* ed. Kenneth M. Sayre and Frederick J. Crosson. Notre Dame, Ind.: University of Notre Dame Press, 1963: 43-71.

4260. Holmes, Thomas B. *Electronic and Experimental Music.* New York: Scribner, 1985. 278 p.

4261. Holmes, W. H., and A. E. Karbowiak. "Modern Approaches to Electronic Music Synthesis." In *IREECON International Digest of Papers, Melbourne, 1977.* Victoria, Australia: IREE, 1977: 349–51.
C&IS 18 (1978): 191699C.

4262. Holtzman, Steven R. *Music as System.* Edinburgh: Dept. of Artificial Intelligence, Apr. 1978. (DAI Working Paper 26)

4263. Holynski, Marek. *Sztuka i komputery.* [Art and Computers] Warsaw: Wiedza powszechna, 1976. 196 p.
Review by Mieczyslaw Kominek in *Ruch Muzyczny* 21,15 (1977): 4–5.

4264. Hoon, Stephen R., and Brian K. Tanner. "The Physics of Music." *Physics Education* 16 (1981): 300–311.
CIJE 14 (1982): EJ 252 851.

4265. Howe, Hubert S. "Computer Music and Technology." In *Proceedings of the Second Annual Music Computation Conference, November 7-9, 1975 at the University of Illinois at Urbana-Champaign. Part 2, Composition with Computers,* comp. James Beauchamp and John Melby. Urbana, Ill.: University of Illinois: 31–36.

4266. ———. "Concetti base di computer music (I)." [Basic Principles of Computer Music. Part 1] *Quaderni di Informatica Musicale* 4 (1984): 46–52.

4267. ———. "Panel Discussion: Computer Synthesis of Sound; New Ideas." *Proceedings of the American Society of University Composers* 6 (1973): 13–48.

4268. Howe, S. F. "Computers in Art and Music." *Media Methods* 20 (Mar. 1984): 24–25.

4269. Huggins, Phyllis. "Three-Part Music with a Computer as One Part." *Computers and Automation* 7 (Mar. 1958): 8.

4270. Hutchins, Bernard A. "Choices between Analog and Digital Synthesis." *Electronotes* 14 (Oct. 1982): 1–3.

4271. ———. "Redundancy in Music as a Reason for Parametric Music Synthesis." *Electronotes* 13 (June 1981): 10–12.

4272. "The Idea Behind the Creation of DR's Television Interval Signal." *Numus-West* 4 (1973): 42–44.

4273. "Impact and Potentials of Technology." In *Documentary Report of the Tanglewood Symposium,* ed. Robert A. Choate. Washington: Music Educators National Conference, 1968: 123–26.

4274. "Industry Resources Directory." *Music Educators Journal* 69 (Jan. 1983): 75–77.
CIJE 15 (1983): EJ 275 331.

4275. "Informatique-musique." *Opus international* 35 (Mai 1972): 36.

4276. "Interactive Woman-Machine Improvisations, or, Live Computer-Music, Performed by Dance." *Creative Computing* 3 (Mar.-Apr. 1977): 66.

4277. "It Had to Come." *Musical Opinion* 90 (Apr. 1967): 374.

4278. Jaffrennou, Pierre-Alain. "Du synthètiseur électronique à l'ordinateur." *Les cahiers recherche/musique* 3 (1976): 29–61.

4279. ———. "Histoires d'energie." *Les cahiers recherche/musique* 3 (1976): 120–42.

4280. Jameux, Dominique. "Boulez and the 'Machine': Some Thoughts on the Composer's Use of Various Electro-Acoustic Media." *Contemporary Music Review* 1 (Oct. 1984): 11–22.
French version: "Boulez et la 'Machine': esquisse d'une reflexion sur l'utilisation par le compositeur de divers dispositifs electro-acoustiques." *Musique de notre temps* 1 (Oct. 1984): 13–24.

4281. Jarrett, Alfred. "New Music in the U.S.A., 1960–1966." M.M. diss., Howard University, 1967. 86 p.

4282. Johnson, Tom H. "Digital Music." *Village Voice* 27 (Feb. 23, 1982): 76.

4283. Johnston, Ben, and Edward G. Kobrin. "Phase la." *Source* 7 (Jan. 1970): 27–45.

4284. Johnston, J. D., and D. J. Goodman. "Digital Transmission of Commentary-Grade (7 kHz) Audio at 56 or 64 kb/s." In *ICASSP 79, 1979 IEEE International Conference on Acoustics, Speech & Signal Processing, Held at the International Inn, Washington, D.C., April 2–4, 1979: Record.* Piscataway, N.J.: IEEE Acoustics, Speech, and Signal Processing Society, 1979: 442–44.

4285. Jones, Kevin J. "Computer Music in Great Britain." In *Atti del Quarto Colloquio di Informatica Musicale.* Pisa: CNUCE-CNR, 1981: 346–52.

4286. ———. "Computers and Musicians in Concert." *New Scientist* 91 (Aug. 1981): 544–546.

4287. ———. "Music is Food for Thought in Computers." *New Scientist* 89 (Mar. 5, 1981): 605.

4288. Jones, Marvin. "Early Experiments with Computer Music." *Polyphony* 3 (Feb. 1978): 6.

4289. Jones, Peter. "Computer-Game Single Is Released by EMI U.K." *Billboard* 95 (June 11, 1983): 9.

4290. "Junge Musik für junge Hörer." *Saarbrücker Zeitung* (Nov. 11, 1979): 8.

4291. Justice, James H. "Synthesis and Harmony in Computer Music." In *Sixth International Conference on Computers and the Humanities,* ed. S. K. Burton and D. D. Short. Rockville, Md.: Computer Science Press, 1983: 318–22.
Review by E. Gagliardo in *Computing Reviews* 25 (Aug. 1984): 8408–0682. *C&CA* 19 (1984): 52031.

4292. Kaegi, Werner. "Musik und Computer." *Schweizerische Muskizeitung* 123 (Jan.-Feb. 1983): 3–8.

4293. ———. "Musique et technologie dans l'Europe de 1970." *La revue musicale* 268–69 (1971): 9–30.
English version: "Music and Technology in the Europe of 1970." In *Music and Technology*. Paris: La revue musicale, 1971: 110–31.

4294. ———. *Was ist elektronische Musik.* Zurich: Orell Füssli Verlag, 1967. 254 p.

4295. Kaptainis, Arthur. "The Realistic Bill Buxton." *Canadian Composer* n179 (Mar. 1983): 16–21.
Also in French.

4296. Karkoschka, Erhard. "Letzter Schreck: Der Computer." *Melos* 39 (1972): 285–88.

4297. Kassler, Michael, and Hubert S. Howe. "Computers and Music." In *The New Grove Dictionary of Music and Musicians,* ed. Stanley Sadie. London: Macmillan, 1980: v. 4, 603–15.

4298. Keith, Michael. "Data Compression of Computer Music." In *Proceedings, 4th Symposium on Small Computers in the Arts, October 25–28, 1984, Philadelphia, Pennsylvania.* Silver Spring, Md.: IEEE Computer Society Press, 1984: 98–102.
C&CA 20 (1985): 17290.

4299. Kelley, Linda. "Making Music with Machines." *Canadian Composer* n195 (Nov. 1984): 16–23.
Also in French.

4300. Kitsz, Dennis B. "A Short History of Computer Music." *Kilobaud Microcomputing* no. 12 (Dec. 1980): 27–28, 30.
C&CA 16 (1981): 15683.

4301. Kleen, Leslie D. "Two Research Projects in Musical Applications of Electronic Digital Computers." Mimeographed. Buffalo: National Science Foundation Project No. GK-14191, June 1972. 133 p. (Technical Report no. 3)

4302. Klein, Martin L. "Uncommon Uses for Common Digital Computers." *Instruments and Automation* 30 (Feb. 1957): 251–53.

4303. Klotman, Robert H., ed. *Scheduling Music Classes.* Washington, D.C.: Music Educators National Conference, 1968.
ERIC: ED 034 309.

4304. Knopoff, Leon. "Progress Report on an Experiment in Musical Synthesis." *Selected Reports* 1,1 (1966): 49–60.

4305. "Knut Wiggen, Ideas Machine Which Never Stops." *Page* 34 (Feb. 1975): 6.

4306. Kominek, Mieczysław. "Muzyka i komputery." [Music and Computers] *Ruch muzyczny* 21,15 (July 1977): 3–5.
In Polish.
RILM 77 4938.

4307. Kottwitz, R. L. "From Whence We Came: Music from the Machine." *Soft-Side* 6 (Oct. 1982): 19-21.
C&CA 18 (1983): 11077.

4308. Lachartre, Nicole. "Les musiques artificielles." *Diagrammes du monde* 146 (Apr. 1969): 1-96.

4309. Lake, Larry. "Electronic Music: A Canadian Art." *Musicanada* 40 (Sept. 1979): 18-19.
Also in French.

4310. Lansdown, John. "An Introduction to the Use of Computers in Music." In *Computers in the Creative Arts (A Studyguide)*, ed. J. D. Lomax. Manchester: National Computing Centre, 1973: 31-35.

4311. Lansky, Paul. "Musikmaschinen." *Österreichische Musikzeitschrift* 31 (1976): 497-500.

4312. Laske, Otto E. "An Acoulogical Performance Model for Music." *Electronic Music Reports* 4 (1971): 31-64.

4313. ———. "Computer Musik und programmierte Wissenserzeugung." Boston, Mass: O. Laske, 1981. 10 p.

4314. ———. *Music and Mind: An Artificial Intelligence Perspective*. Boston, Mass.: O. Laske, 1981. 497 p.
Also published: San Francisco, Calif.: Computer Music Association, 1981. (Computer Music Association Reports).
Contains items: 281, 283, 788, 2350, 2658, 2659, 2663, 2666, 2667, 3439, 3440, 4317, 4318.

4315. ———. "Observations on the Computer Music Scene in West Germany." *Computer Music Journal* 7,1 (Spring 1983): 6-7.

4316. ———. "Requirements Analysis and Specification for a Computerized Music System." Boston, Mass.: O. Laske, 1980. 36 p.

4317. ———. "Toward a Center for Studies in Musical Intelligence." *Numus-West* 5 (1974): 44-46.
Also in *Music and Mind*. Boston, Mass.: O. Laske, 1981: 53-55.

4318. ———. "Toward a Musical Intelligence System: OBSERVER." *Numus West* 4 (1973): 11-16.
Also in *Music and Mind*. Boston, Mass.: O. Laske, 1981: 47-52.
RILM 74 1113.

4319. Lavallard, Jean-Louis. "Les mathématiques aujourd'hui—art et logique." *Le monde* (Juin 23, 1972): 9.

4320. Layzer, Arthur. "Some Idiosyncratic Aspects of Computer Synthesized Sound." *Proceedings of the American Society of University Composers* 6 (1973): 27-39.

4321. Lederer, Jeffrey H. "An Inexpensive Computer-Music System." Ph.D. diss. University of Pittsburgh, 1977.

4322. Leipp, Emile. *Acoustique et musique.* Paris: Barcelone, 1976. 344 p.

4323. Leise, Fred. "The Computer and the Symphony Orchestra: A New Tune in Programming." *Symphony News* 27 (Apr. 1976): 10–12.

4324. Leonard, Steve. "Computers for Keyboardists: Glossary of Computer Terms for Keyboardists." *Keyboard* 11 (Nov. 1985): 88–89.

4325. Lesle, Lutz, and György Ligeti. "Computer-Musik als Kreativer Dialog zwischen Musiker und Maschine? Gespräch mit dem Komponisten György Ligeti." *Musik und Medizin* 2/5 (1976): 43–45.

4326. Levy, S. "Bliss, Microchips, and Rock & Roll: The Inside Data on the US Festival." *Rolling Stone* n380 (Oct. 14, 1982): 14–16.

4327. Lewis, Flora. "Boulez, Computers, and Music." *New York Times* (Jan. 7, 1980): C16.

4328. Lewis, Gainer. "Hardware: The Sound of Things to Come." *Rolling Stone* 263 (Apr. 20, 1978): 79.

4329. Lohner, Henning. "Interview with Robert Moog." *Computer Music Journal* 9,4 (Winter 1985): 62–65.

4330. Loy, D. Gareth. "Designing an Operating Environment for a Realtime Performance Processing System." In *Proceedings of the International Computer Music Conference, 1985,* ed. Barry Truax. San Francisco, Calif.: Computer Music Association, 1985: 9–13.

4331. ———. "PROCOM: Interprocess Sample Data Communication Facility for UNIX." La Jolla: Computer Audio Research Laboratory, Center for Music Experiment and Related Research, University of California, San Diego, 1984.

4332. Lueck, B. "Synthesizing a Symphony." *Illinois Technograph* 79 (May 1964): 6.

4333. "The Machine Closes In." *Time* 79 (Feb. 16, 1962): 65.

4334. "Magnetic Tape Moves the Piano Keys." *Musik International-Instrumentenbau Zeitschrift* 35 (July 1981): 539.

4335. Malcangi, Mario. "Design and Development of Systems for Musical Processing." *Elettronica oggi* 6 (June 1982): 185–90.
In Italian.
C&CA 17 (1982): 44185.

4336. ———. "DMX-TSL: un sistema interattivo per l'elaborazione del segnale in tempo reale." [DMX-TSL: An Interactive System for Real Time Signal Processing] In *Atti del Quinto Colloquio di Informatica Musicale.* Ancona: Università di Ancona, 1983: 43–48.

4337. ———. "Esperienze di progettazione e sviluppo di sistemi efficienti per l'elaborazione musicale." [Experiences of Design and Development of Efficient Systems for Music Processing] In *Atti del Quarto Colloquio di Informatica Musicale.* Pisa: CNUCE-CNR, 1981: 277–99.

4338. ———. "Electronic Music and the Composer." Ph.D. diss., University of Durham, England, 1977. 658 p.
C&IS 13:107879C. *RILM* 77 1468.

4339. Manning, Peter D. *Electronic and Computer Music.* Oxford: Clarendon Press; New York: Oxford University Press, 1985. 291 p.

4340. Mansfield, R. "Music in the Computer Age." *Compute! The Journal for Progressive Computing* 7 (Jan. 1985): 31–39.
C&CA 20 (1985): 17261.

4341. Manuel, Bruce A. "Anyone Can Make Music—Computer Uses Space-Age Parts to Invent and Perform Tunes." *Christian Science Monitor* 63 (Nov. 8, 1971): 13.

4342. Martin, Charles, and Anthony A. Debruyn. "Computer Illustrated Display for Marching Bands." *Journal of Band Research* 8 (Spring 1972): 44–48.

4343. Mathews, Max V. "The Digital Computer as a Musical Instrument." *Science* 142 (1963): 553–57.

4344. ———. "Lektrowsky's Will." *Creative Computing* 3 (Mar.-Apr 1977): 82–87.

4345. ———. "L'ordinateur en tant qu'instrument de musique." In *La musique en projet.* Paris: Gallimard, 1975: 69–79.

4346. ———. "Le studio de sons électroniques des années 70." *La revue musicale* 268–69 (1971): 125–37.
English version: "The Electronic Sound Studio of the 1970s." In *Music and Technology.* Paris: La revue musicale, 1971: 129–41.

4347. ———, and Gerald Bennett. *Real-Time Synthesizer Control.* Paris: IRCAM, 1978. 7 p. (Rapports IRCAM 5/78)

4348. ———; Joan E. Miller; F. Richard Moore; John R. Pierce; and Jean-Claude Risset. *The Technology of Computer Music.* Cambridge: MIT Press, 1969. 188 p.
Review by Stephen Arnold in *Tempo* 92 (Spring 1970): 41–43.
Review by Alan C. Ashton in *Page* 22 (Apr. 1972): 3.
Review by Gilbert Chase in *Inter-American Institute for Musical Research Yearbook* 5 (1969): 106–7.
Review by Lejaren Hiller in *Notes* 26 (1970): 764–65.
Review by Robert M. Mason in *Music Educators Journal* 57 (May 1971): 66–68.
Review by Fred K. Prieberg in *Melos* 37 (1970): 238.
Review by A. Wayne Slawson in *Journal of Music Theory* 13 (1969): 148–51.
Review by Stephen W. Smoliar in *Technology Review* 72 (Oct./Nov. 1969): 19–21.
Review by Franklin B. Zimmerman in *Computers and the Humanities* 6 (1971–72): 293–94. Letter to the editor by Joseph E. Youngblood, 7 (1972–73): 28. Letter to the editor by Hubert S. Howe, 7 (1972–73): 97–98. Review in *Numus West* 3 (1973): 57.

4349. ———; F. Richard Moore; and Jean-Claude Risset. "Computers and Future Music." *Science* 183 (Jan. 25, 1974): 263–68.
Also in *Numus-West* 6 (1974): 40–47.
Rebuttal by Allen D. Allen in *Science* 185 (July, 26 1974): 304.
Rebuttal by A. Wayne Slawson in *Science* 185 (July 26, 1974): 304–06.
Reply by Max V. Matthews in *Science* 185 (July 26, 1974): 306.
RILM 75 2542.

4350. ———; John R. Pierce; and N. Guttman. "Musical Sounds from Digital Computers." *Gravesaner Blätter* 23–24 (1962): 109–25.
Parallel English and German texts.
English version in *IEEE Student Journal* 1 (Sept. 1963): 25–31.

4351. Matsuyama, Tatsuro; Tsuneo Imai; and Akiko Yukimoto. "Real Time Automatic Music Composition and Playing." In *Proceedings of the First USA-Japan Computer Conference.* Montvale, N.J.: American Federation of Information Processing Societies; Tokoyo: Information Processing Societies, Inc., 1972: 116–23.

4352. Mazzola, G. "Beethoven in the Computer." *Chip* 5 (May 1983): 40–45.
In German.
C&CA 18 (1983): 32105.

4353. McCarthy, Frank L. "Electronic Music Systems: Structure, Control, Product." *Perspectives of New Music* 13 (Spring-Summer 1975): 98–125.

4354. McKay, Andy. *Electronic Music.* Minneapolis, Minn.: Control Data Pub., 1981. 124 p.

4355. Mechtler, Peter. "Einige Anmerkungen zum Verhältnis Mensch und Computer." *Österreichische Musikzeitschrift* 37 (1982): 348–49.

4356. Melby, John. "Some Recent Developments in Computer-Synthesized Music." *Proceedings of the American Society of University Composers* 5 (1972): 111–21.

4357. "A Microcomputer for Helping to Tune Musical Instruments." *Elettronica Oggi* 10 (Oct. 1981): 342–44.
In Italian.
C&CA 17 (1982): 16864.

4358. Mikulska, Małgorzata. "Autor: Komputer?" [The Composer: A Computer?] *Ruch muzyczny* 24,7 (1980): 5–6.
In Polish.

4359. ———. "Dźwiek z komputera." [Sound and Computers] *Ruch muzyczny* 24,8 (1980): 12–13.
In Polish.

4360. Milano, Dominic. "Roger Powell." *Contemporary Keyboard* 6 (July 1980): 44–53.

4361. Mitchell, Peter W. "Loudspeakers and Computers: The Quiet Revolution." *High Fidelity/Musical America* 33 (Nov. 1983): 41–44.

4362.   Mitroo, J. B.; Nancy Herman; and Norman I. Badler. "Movies from Music: Visualising Musical Compositions." *Computer Graphics* 13 (Aug. 1979): 218–25.
Abstract in *Computing Reviews* 20 (1979): 35,201.

4363.   Moles, Abraham A. "Des machines a creer de la musique." *Atomes* 14,159 (1959): 307.

4364.   ———. *Les musiques expérimentales.* Paris: Editions du cercle d'art contemporain, 1960. 166 p.

4365.   ———. "Perspectives de l'instrumentation électronique." *Revue Belge de musicologie* 13 (1959): 11–25.

4366.   Moog, Robert A. "A Brief Introduction to Electronic Music Synthesizers." *BYTE* 7 (Dec. 1982): 278–86.
E&EA 86 (1983): 15070.

4367.   ———. "Future Trends in Sound Modification." Paper presented at the Midwest Acoustics Conference, Illinois Institute of Technology, Chicago, Ill., Apr. 25, 1981.
Abstract in *Journal of the Audio Engineering Society* 29 (1981): 458.

4368.   ———. "An Objective Look at Electronic Music Equipment." *Proceedings of the American Society of University Composers* 4 (1971): 32–35.

4369.   ———. "On Synthesizers: Pack Up Your Computer in Your Ol' Gig Bag." *Contemporary Keyboard* 7 (May 1981): 58.

4370.   ———. "Pitch, Intonation & Tone Color." *Keyboard* 10 (Sept. 1984):

4371.   Moore, F. Richard. "Musica ed elaboratori elettronici." *Encyclopedia della scienza e della tecnica* (1971): 490–98.

4372.   ———, and D. Gareth Loy. "Essays About Computer Music." La Jolla, Calif.: Computer Audio Research Laboratory, Center for Music Experiment, University of California, San Diego, 1982. 34 p.

4373.   Moorer, James A. "How Does a Computer Make Music?" *Computer Music Journal* 2,1 (July 1978): 32–37.
C&IS 20 (1978): 207146C.

4374.   ———. "Keynote Address." Paper presented at the 1983 International Computer Music Conference, Oct. 7–10, 1983, Rochester, N.Y.

4375.   Morgan, Christopher P., ed. *The BYTE Book of Computer Music.* Peterborough, N.H.: BYTE Books, 1979. 144 p.
Review by Bob Doerschuk in *Contemporary Keyboard* 5 (Sept. 1979): 6.
Review by P. Drummond in *Computing Reviews* 21 (1979): 36,045.
Review by Michael J. Manthey in *Computers and the Humanities* 14 (1980): 72–73.
Review by Robert Poor in *Computer Music Journal* 4,1 (Spring 1980): 82–84.
Review in *Polyphony* 5 (July/Aug. 1979): 14.

Abstract in *Music Educators Journal* 66 (Jan. 1980): 177.
Contains items: 381, 1233, 1300, 1381, 1467, 1487, 1554, 1619, 1631, 1634, 1669, 2014, 3057, 3544, 4245.

4376. Motz, Wolfgang. "Sotto pressione." [Under Pressure] *Bollettino LIMB* 4 (1984): 71–84.

4377. Muro, Don. "The Contemporary Musician and the Electronic Medium: Digital Synthesizers." *International Musician* 82 (Oct. 1983): 1, 22.

4378. Murray, Fran. "Computer Plays Jazz, Rock and Roll, or Classical Music." *Computers and People* 23 (Aug. 1974): 38.

4379. *Music and Technology.* Paris: La revue musicale, 1971. 208 p.
Contains items: 34, 54, 59, 122, 261, 643, 969, 3724, 4293, 4346, 4496, 4533.

4380. "Music, Computers, and Moods; Earthly Noise—Computer Acoustic Music." *Chip* 7 (July 1984): 272–73.
In German.
C&CA 19 (1984): 47411. *E&EA* 87 (1984): 55085.

4381. *Musica e elaboratore. Orientamenti e prospettive.* [Music and Computers: Trends and Perspectives] Venice: Biennale di Venezia, 1980. 200 p.
Contains items: 264, 441, 1141, 1840, 2484, 2634, 2734, 3752, 4111, 4174, 4441.

4382. "Musicians Play on Computer Power." *New Scientist* 88 (Dec. 18–25, 1981): 783.

4383. "Musique et machines." *Faire* 2/3 (1975): 183–206.

4384. Nagosky, John P. "Opera Workshop Codex." Mimeographed. Tampa: University of South Florida, Dept. of Music, 1969.

4385. Nawrocki, Bolesaw. "Creation musical et societe de consommation (quelques reflexions) = Musical Creation and Consumer Society (Some Reflections) = Creacion musical y sociedad de consuma (algunas reflexiones)." *Revue internationale du droit d'auteur* 83 (Jan. 1975): 56–105; 84 (Apr. 1975): 3–39.
RILM 76 2005.

4386. Nelson, Gary. "Pattern Recognition in Musical Score." West Lafayette, Ind.: Dept. of Creative Arts, Purdue University.
C&IS 13: 107422C.

4387. ———; Willard Bellman; and Jonell Polansky. "Computer Technology for the Performing Arts: Education is the Key." In *Computer Technology to Reach the People. Digest of Papers from the 10th IEEE Computer Society International Conference, 25-27 February 1975, San Francisco, CA.* New York: IEEE, 1975: 291–93.

4388. Niedzielski, Rudi H. "Electronics Ring in the Future: The New Sound of Music." *Music Journal* 37 (Nov./Dec. 1979): 12–14.

4389. Norbeck, E. "Computer-Assisted Woodwinds." *Woodwind World* 12,5 (1973): 8–9.

4390. Nosselt, Volker. "Die programmierte elektroakustische Musikrealisation mittels elektronischer Digital-Datenverarbeitungsanlage. Die Programmierung—ein musikalisches Steuerungsproblem." *IPEM-Yearbook* 2 (1967)

4391. O'Beirne, T. H. "Music from Paper Tape." *Bulletin of the Institute of Mathematics and Its Applications* 6 (Apr. 1970): 68–69.
Also in *Cybernetic Serendipity,* ed. Jasia Reichardt. New York: Praeger, 1969: 29–30.

4392. ———. "Music, Numbers, and Computers." *Bulletin of the Institute of Mathematics and Its Applications* 3 (July 1967): 57–66.

4393. O'Keeffe, Vincent. "Computerized Band Uniform Assignment." *The Instrumentalist* 26 (Aug. 1971): 26–27.

4394. Oehlschlagel, Reinhard. "Neue Musik von A–Z." *Opern Welt* (July 1970): 43.

4395. Okal, E. A. "Listening to Earth's Music." *IBM Perspectives on Computing* 2 (May 1982): 28–39.

4396. Olive, Joseph P. "The Use of the Digital Computer in the Generation of Music." Paper presented at the Midwest Acoustics Conference, Apr. 5, 1975, Evanston, Ill.

4397. Olson, Harry F. "Electronic Music Synthesis for Recordings." *IEEE Spectrum* 8 (Apr. 1971): 18–30.

4398. Oppenheimer, Larry. "Music from Mathematics: The Contributions of Bell Labs' Max Mathews." *Mix* 8 (Dec. 1984): 16–28.

4399. Oram, Daphne. *An Individual Note: Of Music, Sound, and Electronics.* London: Galliard Ltd.; New York: Galaxy Music Corp., 1972. 145 p.

4400. ———. "Oramics." *Musical Events* 23 (Nov. 1968): 6–7.

4401. "PDP-8 Plays Stereo Music." *Computers and Automation* 19 (Aug. 1970): 60.

4402. Pennycook, Bruce. "Electro-Acoustic Music in the University: A New Paradox." *ElectroAcoustic Music* 1,2 (1985): 18–22.

4403. Pepper, Charles E. "The Computer, Big Machine on Campus." *University, A Princeton Quarterly* 29 (Summer 1966): 6–9, 29–34.

4404. Perrot, Michel. "Entretien avec Iannis Xenakis." *La revue musicale* 265–66 (1969): 61–76.

4405. "Peter Nero at the Computer Keyboard." *Computers and Electronics* 21 (Nov. 1983): 62–66.

4406. Peyser, Joan. "Pierre Boulez—From Wagner's 'Ring' to Computer Practice." *New York Times* (Dec. 7, 1980): sec. 2, D21.

4407. Philippot, Michel P. "La musique et les machines." *Situation de la recherche, cahiers d'etudes de radio-television* 27–28 (1960): 274–92.

4408. Pierce, John R. "The Computer as a Musical Instrument." *Journal of the Audio Engineering Society* 8 (1960): 139–40.

4409. ———. "Computers and Music." *New Scientist* 25 (1965): 423–24. Reprinted in *Cybernetic Serendipity,* ed. Jasia Reichardt. New York: Praeger, 1969: 18–19.

4410. ———. "Some Thoughts on Computers and Music." In *The Liberation of Sound,* ed. Herbert Russcol. Englewood Cliffs: Prentice- Hall, 1972: 269–75.

4411. ———. "Technologie et musique au XXe siècle." In *Passage du XXe siècle.* Ire partie. Paris: IRCAM, Centre Georges Pompidou, 1977: 65–78.

4412. Pinzarrone, Joseph. "Interactive Woman-Machine Improvisations or Live Computer-Music Performed by Dance." *Creative Computing* 3 (Feb. 1977): 66.

4413. Piotrowski, Zbigniew. "Muzyka na tasme." [Music on Tape] *Muzyka* 20,4 (1975): 28–48. In Polish.

4414. Polansky, Larry. "Interview with David Rosenboom." *Computer Music Journal* 7,4 (Winter 1983): 40–44.

4415. Pollack, Andrew. "Computers Turn Artistic and the Artists Like It." *New York Times* (May 31, 1981): sec. 4, E20.

4416. Pope, Stephen T. "Types of Digital Synthesis Systems." Paper presented at the 1983 International Computer Music Conference, Oct. 7–10, 1983, Rochester, N.Y.

4417. Porter, Andrew. "Sound Houses." *New Yorker* 60 (July 9, 1984): 80–83.

4418. Powell, Roger. "Synthesizer Technique: Computer-Synthesizer Hybrids." *Contemporary Keyboard* 3 (Oct. 1977): 60.

4419. ———. "Synthesizer Technique: Computers and Synthesis." *Contemporary Keyboard* 3 (Sept. 1977): 54.

4420. Pressing, Jeff. "Towards an Understanding of Scales in Jazz." *Jazz Forum* 9 (1977): 25–35. Summary in German. *RILM* 77 3457.

4421. Prieberg, Fred K. *Musica ex Machina.* Berlin: Ullstein, 1960. 300 p.

4422. Pujolle, J. "L'apport de l'informatique à l'acoustique." In *Conférences des journées d'études du Festival international du son.* Paris: Edition Chiron, 1971: 5–14.

4423. Pulkert, Oldřich. "Hudba, samočinné počítače a jiné novinky." [Music, Data Processing, and Other News] *Hudební věda* 4 (1967): 479–84. In Czech.

4424. Quijano, Jean-Pierre. "Musique et ordinateurs electroniques." *Vie musicale* 16 (June 1970): 21–25.

4425. Rainbow, Edward. "Instrumental Music: Recent Research and Considerations for Future Investigations." *Bulletin of the Council for Research in Music Education* 33 (Summer 1973): 8–17.

4426. Rapoport, Paul. "Sorabji and the Computer." *Tempo* 117 (June 1976): 23–26.

4427. Raskin, Jef. "A Hardware Independent Computer Graphics System." M.S. thesis, Pennsylvania State University, 1967.

4428. Razzi, Fausto. "A voi che lavorate sulla terra." [To You, This Work on This Earth] *Bollettino LIMB* 3 (1983): 57–66.

4429. ———. "Relazione costante tra 'produttori' (musicisti e scienziate) e pubblico." [The Steady Relationship Between 'Producers' (Musicians and Scientists) and the Public] In *Aspetti teorici di Informatica Musicale*. Milan: CTU—Istituto di Cibernetica, Università di Milano, 1977: 68–71.

4430. "Recherche musique et informatique." *Systèmes d'informatique magazine—Honeywell Bull* 13 (Winter 1971/1972): insert between p. 16 & 17.

4431. Reckziegel, Walter. "Musik im Datenspeicher." *Die Musikforschung* 21 (1968): 427–38.

4432. Reichardt, Jasia, ed. *Cybernetic Serendipity*. New York: Praeger, 1969. 101 p. Contains items: 119, 409, 581, 4026, 4250, 4391, 4409.

4433. Rey, Anne. "Le compositeur Jean-Claude Risset et les ordinateurs de l'IRCAM." *Le monde* (Oct. 17, 1974): 17.

4434. Rhea, Thomas. "Electronic Perspectives: Music & the Computer." *Contemporary Keyboard* 7 (June 1981): 73.

4435. ———. "Music & the Computer." *Contemporary Keyboard* 7 (June 1981): 73.

4436. Rich, Alan. "Machine as Maestro." *House and Garden* 153 (Sept. 1981): 20, 24.

4437. Riotte, André. "Computer Music: New Meeting-Point of Art and Science." *Euro-Spectra* 13 (Mar. 1974): 2–15.

4438. ———. "Il nanosecondo ben temperator." [The Well-Tempered Nanosecond] *Rivista IBM* 5,2 (1969)

4439. Risset, Jean-Claude. *Archivage numérique des sons: rapport final*. Paris: IRCAM, 1979. 23 p. (Rapports IRCAM 23/79)

4440. ———. "Computer Music Experiments 1964. . ." *Computer Music Journal* 9,1 (Spring 1985): 11–18. With soundsheet.

4441. ———. "Musica, calcolo segreto?" [Music, A Secret Computation?] In *Musica e elaboratore*. Venice: Biennale di Venezia, 1980: 15–24.

4442. ———. "Musique, électronique et théorie de l'information." *L'onde electrique* 451 (1964): 1055–63.

4443. ———. "Musique et informatique." In *La musique en projet*. Paris: Gallimard, 1975: 48–68.

4444. ———. "Musique et ordinateur." *Cahier musique* 3 (1983): 2–9.

4445. ———. "L'ordinateur comme instrument de musique." *GAM* 45 (Dec. 1969): 1–10.

4446. ———. "Ordinateur et création musicale." In *Art et science: de la créativité, Actes du Congrès "La créativité artistique et scientifique", Cerisy-la-Salle,* 1970. Paris: Union Générale d'Editions, 10/18, 1972: 269–88.

4447. ———. "Ordinateur et création musicale." *Bulletin de l'Institut de recherche en informatique et automatique* (1979)

4448. ———. "L'ordinateur et la musique." *La presse informatique* 26 (Dec. 18, 1972)

4449. ———. "L'ordinateur et la synthèse des sons musicaux." *Science, progrès, découverte* (Juin 1970): 8–16.

4450. ———. "L'ordinateur, instrument de musique." *Conférences des Journées d'études du festival international du son haute fidelité sterephonie.* Paris: Editions Chiron, 1970: 150–59.
Reprinted in *Revue d'acoustique* 16 (1971): 286–90.

4451. ———. "Problèmes de droit d'auteur découlant de l'utilisation d'ordinateurs pour la création d'oeuvres." In *Le droit d'auteur.* Geneva: Unesco, 1979: 244–254.
English version: p. 232–242.

4452. ———. "Quelques remarques sur les musiques pour ordinateur et l'interpreta-tion." *Musique en jeu* 3 (1971): 5–11.

4453. ———. "La situation de l'acoustique musicale aux U.S.A." *GAM* 14 (Sept. 1965): 4–11.

4454. ———. "Tecniche digitali del suono: influenza attuale e prospettive future in campo musicale." [Digital Techniques of Sound: The Present Influence and Future Perspectives in the Musical Context] *Bollettino LIMB* 2 (1982): 8–11.

4455. ———. "Utvecklingen inom digitaltekniken: en vändpunkt för elektronmu-siken?" [The Development of Digital Techniques: A Turning Point in Elec-tronic Music?] *Nutida musik* 22,1 (1978–1979): 56–66.
Also published as: *The Development of Digital Techniques: A Turning Point for Electronic Music?* Paris: IRCAM 1978. (Rapports IRCAM 9/78)

4456. Rittenbach, Bruce E. "Aspects of Computer Music System Design." Paper presented at the International Conference on Computer Music, October 28–31, 1976, Massachusetts Institute of Technology.

4457. Roads, Curtis. "Advanced Directions for Computer Music." Toronto, Ont.: SSSP, Computer Systems Research Group, University of Toronto, 1979. 17 p.

4458. ———. "Artificial Intelligence and Music." *Computer Music Journal* 4,2 (Summer 1980): 13–25.
C&CA 16 (1981): 21868. *C&IS* 29 (1982): 82–489C.

4459. ———. "A Conversation with James A. Moorer." *Computer Music Journal* 6,4 (Winter 1982): 10–21.

4460.   ———. "An Interview with Gottfried Michael Koenig." *Computer Music Journal* 2,3 (Dec. 1978): 11–15.
Reprinted in *Foundations of Computer Music,* ed. Curtis Roads and John Strawn. Cambridge, Mass.: MIT Press, 1985: 568–80.

4461.   ———. "An Interview with Harold Cohen." *Computer Music Journal* 3,4 (Dec. 1979): 50–57.
C&IS 25 (1980): 243457C.

4462.   ———. "Interview with Marvin Minsky." *Computer Music Journal* 4,3 (Fall 1980): 25–39.
Revised version: "Music and the Levels of Thought." *Oak Music Report* (Fall 1981): 20–21.

4463.   ———. "Interview with Max Mathews." *Computer Music Journal* 4,4 (Winter 1980): 15–22.

4464.   ———. "Interview with Paul Lansky." *Computer Music Journal* 7,3 (Fall 1983): 16–24.

4465.   ———. "Introduction to Computer Music History." Paper presented at the 1983 International Computer Music Conference, Oct. 7–10, 1983, Rochester, N.Y.

4466.   ———. "An Introduction to Computer Music History and Fundamentals." *Recreational Computing* 8 (May-June 1980): 4–7, 38–45.
C&CA 15 (1980): 33886.

4467.   ———. "Look at Computer Music." *Dr. Dobb's Journal of Computer Calisthenics and Orthodontia* 4 (June-July 1979): 33–36.
C&IS 23 (1979): 228074C.

4468.   ———. "Magazine Review: *Faire.*" *Computer Music Journal* 2,3 (Dec. 1978): 10.

4469.   ———. "Music and Artificial Intelligence: A Research Overview." In *AICA, Associazione Italiana per il Calcolo Automatica: Atti del congresso annuale, Padova, 6–8 Ottobre 1982.* Padua: AICA, 1982: 401–06.
German translation: "Musik und Künstliche Intelligenz: Ein Forschungsüberblick" *Feedback Papers* 30,2 (1983): 4–36.

4470.   ———. "Research in Music and Artificial Intelligence." *ACM Computing Surveys* 17 (1985): 163–90.

4471.   ———, and John Snell, with Curtis Abbott, and John Strawn. "A History of *Computer Music Journal*." *Computer Music Journal* 10,1 (Spring 1986): 13–16.

4472.   ———, and John Strawn, eds. *Foundations of Computer Music.* Cambridge, Mass.: MIT Press, 1985. 712 p.
Review by D. Gareth Loy in *Computer Music Journal* 9,3 (Fall 1985): 80–81.
Contains items: 334, 478, 1251, 1261, 1818, 1985, 2017, 2484, 2681, 2735, 2909, 2914, 2917, 2962, 3069, 3182, 3189, 3256, 3284, 3314, 3318, 3354, 3365, 3370, 3439, 3504, 3612, 3625, 3684, 3726, 3727, 3736, 3741, 3751, 3768, 3825, 4460.

4473. Rockwell, John. "Music: Third in Series of Computer Works." *New York Times* (June 6, 1984): C24(L).

4474. ———. "What's New?" *High Fidelity/Musical America* 23 (July 1973): MA9–MA10.

4475. Rogers, John E. "The Uses of Digital Computers in Electronic Music Generation." In *The Development and Practice of Electronic Music,* ed. Jon H. Appleton and Ronald C. Perera. Englewood Cliffs, N.J.: Prentice-Hall, 1975: 189–285.

4476. Rogers, Michael. "Programming the Sound of One Hand Clapping." *Rolling Stone* 206 (Feb. 12, 1976): 46–47, 50.

4477. Rosenbloom, Michael. "On the State of Computer Music." *Computer* 16 (Apr. 1983): 98.

4478. Rosenboom, David. "In Support of a Systems Theoretical Approach to Art Media." *Proceedings of the American Society of University Composers* 5 (1972): 56–68.

4479. Rosenfeld, P. L. "Home (Computer) Terminal Musical Program Selection." *IBM Technical Disclosure Bulletin* 23 (Dec. 1980): 3440–41.
C&CA 16 (1981): 21875.

4480. Rossing, Thomas D. *The Science of Sound: Musical, Electronic, and Environmental.* Reading, Mass.: Addison-Wesley, 1980.

4481. Rowe, P. "Compuers Find a Role in Films, Music, and Art." *Computer Weekly* 30 (Jan. 29, 1981): 11.
C&CA 16 (1981): 15679.

4482. Ruiz, E. V. "Performance of Music by Means of an Information System." *Mundo electronico* 52 (May 1976): 61–74.
In Spanish.
C&CA 11 (1976): 22473.

4483. Rundel, T. "I Took My Computer to a Party. . ." *Computer Systems* 3 (June 1983): 44–45.
C&CA 18 (1983): 36170.

4484. Schaeffer, Pierre. "Musique, linguistique, informatique." *La revue musicale* 274–275 (1971): 67–78.

4485. ———. "A quel titre employer l'ordinateur en musique." *Programme-bulletin GRM* 6 (Fev. 1974): 40–49.

4486. Scherpenisse, J. "Digital Control in Electronic Music Studios." *Interface* 6 (Sept. 1977): 73–80.
Also presented at the 56th Convention of the Audio Engineering Society, Mar. 1–4, 1977, Paris. Preprint no. 1195.
RILM 77 5947.

4487. Schloss, W. Andrew. "Computer Music: Past and Future Directions." In *Western Educational Computing Conference, 1983, San Francisco, CA.* North Hollywood, Calif.: Western Periodicals, 1983: 142.
C&CA 19 (1984): 36727.

4488. Schmidt, Brian L., and James M. Roth. "The Synchronization of Audio Production in Computer Music." In *Proceedings of the International Computer Music Conference, 1985,* ed. Barry Truax. San Francisco, Calif.: Computer Music Association, 1985: 341–45.

4489. Schrader, Barry. *Introduction to Electro-Acoustic Music.* Englewood Cliffs, N.J.: Prentice-Hall, 1982. 223 p.
Review by Paul Griffiths in *The Musical Times* 124 (1983): 302–03.
Review by Curtis Roads in *Computer Music Journal* 6,4 (Winter 1982): 41–42.
Review by Peter Zinovieff in *Composer* n76–77 (1982): 35–36.

4490. Schrage, M. "Video News & Notes: FM Can Program Your Computer." *Rolling Stone* n384 (Dec. 9, 1982): 72.

4491. Schultz, Brad. "Grateful Dead's Bass Player Finds DP Indispensable." *Computerworld* 13 (Nov. 5, 1979): 11.

4492. ———. "Music Pioneer of '60s Ready to Take on '80s." *Computerworld* 13 (Nov. 5, 1979): 11.
C&IS 24 (1980): 238886C.

4493. Schwede, Gary W. "A Fuzzy Hierarchical System Model for Real-Time Visual Interpretation in Musical Experiences." Paper presented at the 1977 International Computer Music Conference, University of California, San Diego, 26–30 October 1977.

4494. Sedelow, Sally Y. "The Computer in the Humanities and Fine Arts." *Computing Surveys* 2 (1970): 89–110.

4495. Shaffer, Richard A. "Magic Flutes: Instruments Powered by Computers Invade the World of Music." *Wall Street Journal* 61 (July 24, 1981): 1, 17.

4496. Shibata, Minao. "Musique et technologie au Japon." *La revue musicale* 268–69 (1971): 173–80.
English version: "Music and Technology in Japan." In *Music and Technology.* Paris: La revue musicale, 1971: 173–80.

4497. Simonton, John S. "A Time Trip—Ready." *Polyphony* 2,3 (1976): 9–11.

4498. Sittner, Hans. "Technische Medien im Dienst der Musik." *Österreichische Musikzeitschrift* 23 (1968): 121–22.

4499. "Situation de la musique électroacoustique en 5 themes: musique et machines." *Faire* 2/3 (1974): 183–206.

4500. Skołyszewski, Franciszek. "Dotychczasowe proby zastosowan cybernetyki do muzyki." [Hitherto Existing Tests for the Application of Cybernetics in Music] *Muzyka* 11,3–4 (1966): 36–63.

4501. Skyvington, William. "Aperçu sur l'informatique musicale." *Information et gestion* 23 (Dec. 1970): 25–27.
Service de la recherche de l'ORTF, Congres de l'AFCET, Paris, 25 Sept. 1970, brochure no. 10. A3.2.-164—A3.2.-175.

4502. ———. "Musique et intelligence artificielle." *Communication et langages* 10 (Juin 1971): 31–42.

4503. ———. "Un nouvel instrument de musique: l'ordinateur." *Communication et langages* 8 (Dec. 1980): 43–54.

4504. ———. "Préambule à un propos en suède." *La revue musicale* 274–275 (1971): 51–53.

4505. Smith, Irwin S. "Communications." *Perspectives of New Music* 11 (Spring–Summer 1973): 269–77.
RILM 73 4344.

4506. Smith, Leland. "Computer Generation of Music." Paper presented at the 40th Convention of the Audio Engineering Society, Apr. 27–30, 1971, Los Angeles. Abstract in *Journal of the Audio Engineering Society* 19 (1971): 443.

4507. ———. "Humanization of Computer Music." Abstract in *Journal of the Acoustical Society of America* 48 (1970): 88.

4508. Smith, Patricia. "Computers Make Music." *Creative Computing* 9 (July 1983): 111–15.
C&CA 18 (1983): 40669.

4509. Smith, Stuart. "Communications." *Perspectives of New Music* 11 (Spring–Summer 1973): 269–77.

4510. ———. "The Computer May Turn Us All into Artists." *Computers and People* 23 (Aug. 1974): 29–30.

4511. ———. "Computer Music in 1972." *Computers and Automation* 21 (Oct. 1972): 16–17, 42.

4512. Smoliar, Stephen W. "Basic Research in Computer-Music Studies." *Interface* 2 (1973): 121–25.
Originally published as Israel Institute of Technology, Dept. of Computer Science, Haifa, Israel, October 1972. (Technical Report no. 20)

4513. ———. "Emotional Content Considered Dangerous." *Communications of the Association for Computing Machinery* 17 (Mar. 1974): 164–65.

4514. Snell, John, ed. *Computer Music Journal.* Abstract and review in *Computing Reviews* 18 (1977): 32,037.

4515. Spoerri, Bruno. "Computer und Musik." *Electronic Sound + RTE* 5 (Dec. 1982): 30–32.
C&CA 19 (1984): 36716. *E&EA* 87 (1984): 44317.

4516. ———. "Musik aus der Retorte." *RTE* 7 (1980): 38–43.

4517. Starr, R. "ILLIAC Tackles the Arts." *Champaign-Urbana Courier* (Aug. 10, 1956)

4518.   Staton, Ted. "Computer Tools for Tuners." *Piano Technicians Journal* 26 (Jan. 1983): 18–19.

4519.   Strang, Gerald. "Computer Music: Analysis, Synthesis, and Composition." Abstract in *Journal of the Acoustical Society of America* 39 (1966): 1245.

4520.   ———. "Music and Computers." In *The Man-Computer Team.* Los Angeles: American Federation of Information Processing Societies, 1967.

4521.   ———. "The Problem of Imperfection in Computer Music." In *Music by Computers,* ed. Heinz von Foerster and James W. Beauchamp. New York: J. Wiley, 1969: 133–39.

4522.   Strange, Allen. *Electronic Music: Systems Techniques and Controls.* 2nd ed. Dubuque, Iowa: Wm. C. Brown, 1983. 274 p.

4523.   Strasser, Bruce E., and Max V. Mathews. "Music from Mathematics." Murray Hill: Bell Telephone Laboratories, 1961. 24 p.

4524.   Strawn, John. "How Computer Systems Make Music." Paper presented at the 1983 International Computer Music Conference, Oct. 7–10, 1983, Rochester, N.Y.

4525.   Suchoff, Benjamin. "Compute Program News." *Spectra* 2 (Apr. 1975): 2.

4526.   "Sur deux notes les mathematiciens de l'avenir composent une symphonie complete." *Courrier Bull* 49 (Oct. 1961)

4527.   Sutcliffe, Alan. "Computers for Music—An Introduction." In *Computers in the Creative Arts.* Manchester: National Computing Centre, 1970: 2–11.

4528.   ———. "Xenakis on Computers." *Page* 34 (Feb. 1975): 2.

4529.   Swanzy, David. "Setting the Marching Band to Computer." *The Instrumentalist* 26 (June 1972): 28–30.

4530.   Sychra, Antonin. "Hudba a kybernetika." [Music and Cybernetics] *Nove cesty hudby* 1 (1964): 234–67.
            In Czech; summary in German, p. 278–79.

4531.   "Symphonic Sound Creation—'Earth Sound', Computer Orchestra." *Chip* 5 (May 1982): 29–30.
            C&CA 17 (1982): 36185.

4532.   *Synthesizers and Computers.* Milwaukee, Wis.: H. Leonard Pub. Corp., 1985. 129 p.
            Contains items: 1034, 1521, 1587, 1588, 1589, 1732, 1733, 1742, 1743, 2612, 2925, 2929, 3087, 3160, 3173, 3700, 3701, 3702, 3703, 3704, 4031, 4032, 4033.

4533.   Szlifirski, Krzysztof. "Technologie nouvelle et initiation des compositeurs à la musique experimentale." *La revue musicale* 268–69 (1971): 149–55.
            English version: "New Technology and the Training of Composers in Experimental Music." In *Music and Technology.* Paris: La revue musicale, 1971: 151–56.

4534. Tamburini, Alessandro. "Computer music in concerto. 1 parte." [Computer Music in Concert (I)] *Strumenti musicali* 41 (1983): 68–75.

4535. ————. "Computer music in concerto. 2 parte." [Computer Music in Concert (II)] *Strumenti musicali* 42/43 (1983): 102–12.

4536. ————. "Computer music, tra utopia e realtà." [Computer Music, between Utopia and Reality] *Quaderni di Informatica Musicale* 2 (1983): 36–40.

4537. ————. "Incontro con Fausto Razzi e Guido Baggiani." [Interview with Fausto Razzi and Guido Baggiani] *Strumenti musicali* 53 (1984): 89–93.

4538. ————. "Incontro con Giorgio Nottoli e James Dashow." [Interview with Giorgio Nottoli and James Dashow] *Strumenti musicali* 51 (1984): 79–84.

4539. ————. "Incontro con Graziano Tisato e Alvise Vidolin." [Interview with Graziano Tisato and Alvise Vidolin] *Strumenti musicali* 59 (1984): 102–07.

4540. ————. "Incontro con Luigi Nono." [Interview with Luigi Nono] *Strumenti musicali* 60 (1984): 96–99.

4541. ————. "Incontro con Mauro Graziani e Marco Stroppa." [Interview with Mauro Graziani and Marco Stroppa] *Strumenti musicali* 58 (1984): 93–101.

4542. ————. "Musica colta ed extracolta: il computer come media linguistico." [Cultured and Extra-Cultured Music: Computers as Linguistic Media] *Strumenti musicali* 47 (1983): 113–19.

4543. Tänzer, Peter. "Musik und Kybernetik." *Neue Zeitschrift für Musik* 134 (1973): 483–92.

4544. Tempelaars, Stan. "Computer Music: Utopian Fantasy?" *Keynotes* 8,2 (1978): 13–16.

4545. Tenney, James. "Sound-Generation by Means of a Digital Computer." *Journal of Music Theory* 7 (1963): 24–70.

4546. Terhardt, Ernest. "Impact of Computers on Music: An Outline." In *Music, Mind, and the Brain,* ed. Manfred Clynes. New York: Plenum Press, 1982: 353–369.

4547. Terry, Kenneth. "Charles Dodge: Synthesized Speech Researcher." *Downbeat* 45 (Jan. 12, 1978): 23.
Also in *Page* 41 (Nov. 1978): 10–11.

4548. Thie, Joseph A. "Computers in the Arts." *Computers and Automation* 10 (Sept. 1961): 23–24, 28.

4549. Truax, Barry D. "A Communicational Approach to Computer Sound Programs." *Journal of Music Theory* 20 (1976): 227–300.
RILM 76 15155.

4550. ————. "Computer Music in Canada." *Numus-West* 8 (1975): 17–26.

4551. ————. "The Inverse Relation Between Generality and Strength in Computer Music Programs." *Interface* 9 (1980): 49–57.
C&CA 16 (1981): 3175.

4552. Ungvary, Tamas. "The Performance Situation of Electroacoustic Music." In *Computer Music/Composition musicale par ordinateur; Report on an International Project Including a Workshop at Aarhus, Denmark in 1978,* ed. Marc Battier and Barry Truax, eds. Ottawa: Canadian Commission for Unesco, 1980: 191–202.

4553. ———. "Tonsättaren—en datadirgent." [The Composer—A Computer Director?] *Nutida musik* 17,4 (1973–1974): 29–32.

4554. Ussachevsky, Vladimir. "Applications of Modern Technology in Musicology, Music Theory, and Composition in the U.S." In *Papers of the Yugoslav-American Seminar on Music,* ed. Malcom Brown. Bloomington: Indiana University Press, 1970: 123–42.

4555. ———. "Primena moderne tehnologije u muzikologiji i muzičkoj teoriji u sad." [Applications of Modern Technology in Musicology and Music Theory] *Zvuk* 87–88 (1968): 457–63.
Summary in English.

4556. Van Sickel, Pete. "Computer Sounds Now Make 'Music to the Ears'." *The Stanford Daily* (Nov. 10, 1978): 6.

4557. Vasilenko, Vladimir. *Ispolnenie muzykal nykh proizvedenii na EVM.* [The Performance of Musical Works by Means of Electronic Devices] Moscow: Sovetskoje Radio, 1973. 51 p.
In Russian.
RILM 73 4270.

4558. Vercoe, Barry. "Man-Computer Interaction in Creative Applications." Cambridge: Studio for Experimental Music, M.I.T., Nov. 1975.

4559. ———. "New Dimensions in Computer Music." *Trends & Perspectives in Signal Processing* 2 (Apr. 1982): 15–23.
C&CA 18 (1983): 7228. *E&EA* 86 (1983): 9587.

4560. Victor, Michèle. "L'informatique musicale." *Musique en jeu* 18 (Apr. 1975): 45–62.
RILM 75 4421.

4561. Vidolin, Alvise. "Informatica musicale." [Computer Music] *Laboratorio musica* 28 (1981): 28–30.

4562. ———. "Il tecnico del conservatorio." [The Technician of the Conservatory] *Laboratorio musica* 20 (1981): 36–37.

4563. Wallraff, Dean, and Pamela Marshall. *Computer Music Catalog.* Boston, Mass.: Digital Music Systems, 1983. 75 p.

4564. Weiland, Frits C. "Relationships Between Sound and Image." *Electronic Music Reports* 4 (Sept. 1971): 66–91.

4565. Wexelblat, R. L. "Another Comment on Computer Music." *Communications of the Association for Computing Machinery* 16 (May 1973): 313–14.

4566. Wiggen, Knut. "Datamaskinsmusikens historia." [The History of Computer Music] *Dansk musiktidsskrift* 41 (1966): 182–84.
In Danish.

4567. ———. "Fondement de la musique par ordinateur." *Bulletin de fylkingen* (1969).

4568. Winckel, Fritz. "Berliner Elektronik." *Melos* 30 (1963): 279–83.

4569. ———. "Computermusik." *Musica, Zweimonatsschrift für alle Gebiete des Musiklebens* 19,1 (1965): 45.

4570. ———, ed. *Experimentelle Musik. Raum-Musik, Visuelle Musik, Medien Musik, Wort Musik, Elektronik Musik, Computer Musik. Internationale Wocke für experimentelle Musik 1968.* Berlin: Mann, 1970. 101 p. (Schriftenreihe der Akademie der Künste Berlin 7)
Review in *Neue Zeitschrift für Musik* 133 (1972): 228–29.
Review by Rudolf Stephan in *Österreichische Musikzeitschrift* 26 (1971): 522.
RILM 73 1605.

4571. Wittlich, Gary E. "Music as Information." *Your Musical Cue* 8 (Dec./Jan. 1970/1971): 3–9.

4572. Wright, Maurice. "Plucking." In *Proceedings of the 1978 International Computer Music Conference,* comp. Curtis Roads. Evanston, Ill.: Northwestern University Press, 1979: 378–91.

4573. "Xenakis at the Mount Orford Arts Centre." *The Canadian Composer* 123 (Sept. 1977): 14.

4574. Xenakis, Iannis. "New Proposals and Realizations in Computer Sound Synthesis: Probabilities into Microstructures; UPIC, a Graphic System for Sound Generation." Paper presented at the 1978 International Computer Music Conference, November 1–5, Northwestern University, Evanston, Illinois.

4575. ———, and Mario Bois. "L'entretien du 4 mars 1966." *Bulletin d'information, Boosey and Hawkes* 23 (Sept. 1966): 2–22.

4576. ———, and Daniel Caux. "Dominer la technologie de notre epoque." *Chroniques de l'art vivant* 34 (Nov. 1972): 28–29.

4577. Yates, Peter. *Twentieth Century Music: Its Evolution from the End of the Harmonic Era into the Present Era of Sound.* New York: Pantheon Books, 1967. 367 p.
Reprint. Westport, Conn.: Greenwood Press, 1980.

4578. Young, Gayle. "Hugh Le Caine, Canada's Pioneer of Electronic Music." *Keyboard* 11 (1985): 32–37.

4579. Zaffiri, Enore. *La musica elettronica al di là del laboratorio.* Padua: G. Zanibon, 1976. 36 p. (Collana di studi musicali 12)
RILM 76 15163.

4580. Zaripov, Rudolf K. *Kibernetika i muzyka.* [Cybernetics and Music] Moscow: Nauka, 1971. 235 p.
In Russian.
English abstract in *Soviet Cybernetics Review* 1 (Nov. 1971): 64.

4581. Zemanek, Heinz H. "Automaten und Denkprozesse." In *Digital Information Processors,* ed. Walter Hoffman. New York: Interscience, 1962: 1–66.

4582. Zielinski, Gerard. *Zastowania Komputerow w Sztuce.* [Computer Applications in the Arts] Warsaw: Centrum Obliczeniowe Polskiej Akademii Nauk, 1972. 16 p. (Prace Centrum Obliczeniowego Pan81)
In Polish; summaries in English and Russian.
RILM 73 1387.

4583. Zijlstra, Miep. "Computer-Pöezie." [Computer Poetry] *Mens en melodie* 29 (1974): 120–22.
In Dutch.

4584. Zingheim, T. Joseph. "Introduction to Computer Music Techniques." *Electronotes* 6 (Aug. 1974): 1–5.

4585. Zinovieff, Peter. "The Special Case of Computer Intuitive Music Scores." *Composer* 66 (Spring 1979): 21–26.

INDEX

A Software Approach to Interactive Processing of Musical Sound, **3318**
Software for Distributed Real-Time Applications, **3319**
System Level Software for the Lucasfilm ASP System, **3320**
Abeles, Harold F.
Using an EXPER SIM (Experimental Simulation) Model in Teaching, **594**
Able, John F.
Computer Composition of Melodic Deep Structures, **72**
Abram, Michae
A Minicomputer-Controlled Music Synthesizer, **1243**
Abstracts from the Third Colloquium on Musical Informatics, Padua, **919**
Actor, L.
Advanced Music System, **1244**
Adamo, Giorgio
Towards a Grammar of Musical Performance: A Study of a Vocal Style, **2043**
Adams, G. J.
Measuring Speaker Motion with a Laser, **1085**
Adams, R. M.
Development of a Concept-Centered Ear-Training CAI System, **817**
Addison, Don
Elements of Style in Performing the Chinese P' i-p' a, **2044**
Adelson, R. M.
Music Keys for the BBC Microcomputer, **1245**
Music Keys for the BBC Microcomputer. Part II, **1246**
Adrien, Jean-Marie
Physical Models of Instruments: A Modular Approach, Applications to, **1982**
Ager, Klaus
Computermusik—Ende der Euphorie?, **4028**
2. Internationale Computermusik-Konferenz, **920**
Agnello, Anthony
A Development System for Real-Time Digital Audio Signal Processing, **2898**
A Low-Cost Development System for Digital Audio Signal Processing, **3098**
Aharonian, Croiun
L'ordinateur—pour quoi faire?, **4029**
Ahl, David H.
Digital Audio, **4030**
Micro Composer from Micro Music, Inc., **1247**
Software Technology Music System, **3322**
Ahn, Young Kyung
A Music Information Processing System, **2549**
Aho, Alan C.
MUSIM: Simulation of Music Composition Using GASP, **73**
Aikin, Jim
Casio CZ-101 Mini-Keyboard, **2899**
Computer Software for Musicians, **3323**
Digital Sampling Keyboards: What's Available, How They Work, Why, **2900**
Digital Synthesis: Introducing the Technology of Tomorrow, **4031**
Educational Software, 1984: An Overview, **595**
First Steps in Programming: Everything You Need to Know to Get Your Feet, **2901**
John Chowning: Computer Synthesis Expert at Stanford, **4032**
Keyboard Report: Akai S612 Rack-Mount Digital Sampler, **2902**
Keyboard Report: Casio CZ-5000 Synthesizer, **2903**

Report on the 1982 International Computer Music Conference, **935**
SYCOM—Systems Complex for the Studio and Performing Arts, **3860**
Australian Fairlight Instrument Blends High Technology, Sound, 2938
Austrian Technicians Develop New Computer, 4052
Avio, G
   Il data base relazionale di suoni realizzato in ISELQUI, **3335**
Avram, Henriette D.
   Commissions de travail: Cataloguing and the Computer, **2831**
Azzolini, Franco
   Score and/or Gesture—The System RTI4I for Real Time Control of the Digital, **3337**
   Un sistema per la gestione in tempo reale del processore di suoni 4i, **3336**
   Il sistema RTI4I par il controllo in tempo reale del processore 4i, **3338**

B

Babb, Larry R.
   Microcomputers and Music, **1678**
Babbitt, Milton
   The Use of Computers in Musicological Research, **2052**
Bachmann, Claus-Henning
   Bonn: Kybernetisches Projekt, Computer-Planspiele und Klangautomaten, **4053**
   Musik und Computer in den U.S.A., **4054**
   Ein neues Musikinstrument: Der Computer; 'Musik und Computer in den USA', **4055**
   Verguegnungen mit Computern—Josef Anton Riedls Tage neuer Musik in München, **4056**
Baczewski, Philip
   Computer-Assisted Instruction in Music, **755**
   An Intuitive Control Structure for the Generation of Computer-Synthesized, **3339**
   Report on the 1981 International Computer Music Conference, **1020**
   Research Applications in Music CAI, **754**
   A Vector Field Model of Compositional Creativity, **161**
Bader, Karl Otto
   Klangumformung durch Computer, **3583**
Badler, Norman I.
   Movies from Music: Visualising Musical Compositions, **4362**
Baecker, Ronald
   A Computer-Based System for the Performance of Electroacoustic Music, **2963**
   The Evolution of the SSSP Score Editing Tools, **1818**
   Ludwig: An Example of Interactive Computer Graphics in a Score Editor, **1935**
   A Microcomputer-Based Conducting System, **1283**
   Objed and the Design of Timbral Resources, **3611**
   On the Specification of Scope in Interactive Score Editors, **127**
   An Overview of the Structured Sound Synthesis Project, **3881**
   Scope in Interactive Score Editors, **128**
   Towards an Effective Characterization of Graphical Interaction, **87**
   Towards Facilitating Graphical Interaction: Some Examples from Computer, **88**
   The Use of Hierarchy and Instance in a Data Structure for Computer Music, **3365**
Baeder, Karlo
   A Real-Time Digital Computer for Simulating Audio Systems, **1039**
Baffioni, Claudio
   The Theory of Stochastic Processes and Dynamical Systems as a Basis for, **89**

Borys, M.
  A Digital Flute, **2042**
  A Microprocessor Based Digital Flute, **3311**
Bosetto, A.
  L'attività di informatica musicale all'ISELQUI, **3877**
Bossemeyer, Robert W.
  Performed Music: Analysis, Synthesis, and Display by Computer, **1926**
Bouchard, Richard
  You Can Have Sound on Your Computer!!!, **1275**
Boudinot, Reginald D.
  Development of a Standard Orchestra for Computer-Generated Sound, **3605**
  Development of INSGEN: An Orchestra Compiler for Computer-Generated Sound, **3357**
Boulanger, Richard
  Interview with Roger Reynolds, Joji Yuasa, and Charles Wuorinen, **484**
  The Transformation of Speech into Music: A Musical Interpretation of Two, **3606**
Boulez, Pierre
  L'in(dé)fini et l'instant, **113**
  Maestro Computer: Exploring the New Frontiers of Sound, **4091**
Bourdain, G. S.
  The Electronic World of Pierre Boulez, **4092**
Bowen, J.
  Professional Music Perspectives, **1276**
Bowers, Phillip
  Musical Notes for the Apple, **1277**
Bowler, Ian
  The Electronic Music Studio at University College, Cardiff, **3922**
  The Synthesis of Complex Audio Spectra by Cheating Quite a Lot, **3607**
Bowles, Edmund A.
  Computerized Research in the Humanities: A Survey, **2749**
  Computers in Musicology, **2104**
  Musicke's Handmaiden: Or Technology in the Service of the Arts, **2105**
  Musicology and the Computer: Discussion, **2106**
Bowles, Garrett H.
  Automated Bibliographic Control of Music, **2750**
  Computer-Produced Thematic Catalog: An Index to the *Pièces de violes* of, **2751**
  A Computer-Produced Thematic Catalog: The 'Pièces de violes' of Marin, **2752**
  Directory of Music Library Automation Projects, **2753**
Bowsher, J. M.
  Calculator Program for Musical Notes, **114**
  The Measurement of the Acoustic Impedance of Brass Instruments, **2022**
Boyde-Shaw B.
  Speech and Music, **1278**
Bozzola, P.
  Musica elettronica e microcomputer: una proposta di applicazione real-time, **3770**
  Musica elettronica e microcomputer: una proposta di applicazione real-time, **3771**
  Musica elettronica e microcomputer: una proposta di applicazione real-time, **3772**
  Musica elettronica e microcomputer: una proposta di applicazione real-time, **3773**
  Musica elettronica e microcomputer: una proposta di applicazione real-time, **3774**
  Musica elettronica e microcomputer: una proposta di applicazione real-time, **3775**
Bradley, J.
  The Computer as Interdisciplinary Catalist: Music and Psychology, **2636**

Brinkman, Alexander R.
Another Look at the Melodic Process in Johann Sebastian Bach's 'Orgelbüchlein', **2110**
A Binomial Representation of the Pitch Parameter for Computer Processing of, **2111**
A Computer-Assisted Analysis of Melodic Borrowing from the Cantus Firmus in, **2112**
A Data Structure for Computer Analysis of Musical Scores, **2113**
Data Structures for a Music-11 Preprocessor, **3359**
A Design for a Single Pass Scanner for the DARMS Music Coding Language, **2114**
The Eastman School of Music Computer Music Studio, **3983**
Johann Sebastian Bach's 'Orgelbüchlein': A Computer-Assisted Analysis , **2115**
The Melodic Process in Johann Sebastian Bach's 'Orgelbüchlein', **2116**
Toward a Library of Utility Computer Programs for the Music Theorist, **2117**

Briot, Jean-Pierre
Applications and Developments of the FORMES Programming Environment, **3500**
Demonstration of FORMES and Its Use for Driving Synthesizers in Music Research, **3501**

Bristow, David
Sounds Inviting, **1581**
Voicing the DX7, **2955**

Brody, Martin
Report on the National Meeting of the Society for Music Theory, **933**

Broeckx, Jan L.
Comparative Computer Study of Style, Based on Five Liedmelodies, **2118**

Bromose, Ole
Beskrivelse of programmet SIM, **2956**
SIM-projektets status pr 1/9 1974, **2957**
Simulering af en 200 UT, **2958**
A Survey of the SIM System, a Computer System for Performing Acoustical, **3360**

Bronson, Bertrand H.
Mechanical Help in the Study of Folk Song, **2119**
Toward the Comparative Analysis of British-American Folk Tunes, **2120**

Brook, Barry S.
Music Bibliography and the Computer, **2754**
Music Documentation of the Future, **2755**
Music Literature and Modern Communication: Revolutionary Potentials of the, **2756**
Musicology and the Computer. Musicology 1966-2000: A Practical Program. Three, **2121**
Notating Music with Ordinary Typewriter Characters (A Plaine and Easie Code), **2125**
The Plaine and Easie Code, **2122**
Repertoire international de litterature musicale (RILM) Report No. 5:, **2757**
The Research Center for Musical Iconography of the City University of New York, **2767**
RILM, **2758**
RILM—ein neuartige internationale Fachbibliographie der Musikwissenschaft, **2759**
RILM Inaugural Report: January 1967, **2760**
RILM Report No. 2: September 1967, **2761**
RILM Report No. 3: September 1968, **2770**
RILM Report No. 6: St. Gall, August 1971, **2771**
RILM: Report No. 7: Bologna and Copenhagen, September-August 1972, **2772**
RILM: Report No. 8: London, August 26-31, 1973, **2773**
RILM: Report No. 9: Jerusalem, August 18-24, 1974, **2768**
RILM: Report No. 10: Montreal, August 1975, **2762**
RILM: Report No. 11: Bergen, August 1976, **2774**
RILM: Report No. 12: Mainz, September 11-16, 1977, **2775**

Bryant, Larry
A Computer-Synchronized, Multi-Track Recording System, **3861**

Bryden, John R.
Chant Index—Incipit Title, Thematic, and Selected Melodic Pattern Index of, **2126**

Buchla, Don
A Computer Aided Analog Electronic Music System, **2960**

Buckley, V.
A User-Interface for Teaching Piano Keyboard Techniques, **786**

Buda, Patrick
Jig, **123**

Budzyński, Gustaw
Komputer analogowy w muzyce eksperymentalnej, **4106**

Buehning, Walt
Simulation Can Teach Teachers, **638**

Bukharaev, R. G.
Simulating a Probabilistic Process Connected with Composing a Melody, **129**

Bukspan, Y.
MUSIMPLE: Computer-Based Learning of 7-Sign Music Notation System, **639**

Bulkeley, William M.
These Avant-Garde Musical Scores May Stimulate Both Eyes and Ears, **4107**

Burden, D.
Electronic Drum Sequencer: Software for BBC Micro, **1280**
OMDAC Update. Part I, **1384**
OMDAC Update. Part II, **1385**

Burhans, R. W.
Digital Tone Synthesis, **3609**
Single-Bus Keyboard Control for Digital Musical Instruments, **2961**

Burkhart, Charles
Schoenberg's *Farben:* An Analysis of Op. 16, No. 3, **2127**

Burlingame, M.
Concert Production's New Ally: A Computer Learns the Score, **1761**

Burns, Betty Berly Remy
An Electronic Data Processing System for the Organization and Documentation of, **2128**

Burns, Mark A.
Following a Conductor: The Engineering of an Input Device, **3065**

Burrowes, Sharon
Improving CAI in BASIC, **640**

Burrowes, Ted
Improving CAI in BASIC, **640**

Burtnyk, N.
A Computer Facility for Film Animation and Music, **4009**

Bushert, Al
The Dawn of the Future Computer, **4108**

Busico, Mirto
Forme d'onda e timbri: distinguibilità e criteri di scelta, **3695**

Butterfield, Jim
Commodore 64 Music, **1281**
Commodore 64 Music: Happy Birthday, **1282**
First Steps in Making Music, **4109**

C

Cadoz, Claude
The Control Channels of Instrumental Playing in Computer Music: Real Time in, **3777**
Gesture, Instrument, and Musical Creation: The System ANIMA/CORDIS, **2965**
An Instrument-Simulation Based System for Sound Synthesis in Real Time, **2005**
Instrumental Gesture, Computer, and Retroactive Gestic Transducers, **3027**
Processes, Sound Synthesis Models, and the Computer Designed for Musical, **4117**
Responsive Input Devices and Sound Synthesis by Simulation of Instrumental, **2966**
Synthèse sonore par simulation des mechanismes instrumentaux: le système, **2966**

Cage, Gary
Melody Dice, **1284**

Cage, John
Choosing Abundance, **4118**
Things to Do, **4119**

Les cahiers recherche musique, 3 (1976). Synthetiseur, ordinateur, 4120

Cahill, P.
ILLIAC, Mechanical Brain, Takes Up Composing Music, **4121**
ILLIAC Proves Musical Skills, **4122**

Cahn, Frederick
Pitch Translation of Trumpet Tones, **1090**

Cain, Charles
Anglican Chants by Computer, **148**

Caine, Hugh Le
A Preliminary Report on the Serial Sound Structure Generator, **129**

Caironi, Giancarlo
New Polyphonic Sound Generator Chip with Integrated Microprocessor, **3276**

The Calcomp Plotter, 1823

Callegari, Laura
A Grammar for Melody: Relationships Between Melody and Harmony, **2069**
Musical Grammars and Computer Analysis: Atti del Convegno (Modena, 4–6, **927**

Callery, Michael
Commodore Magic: Create Astonishing Graphics and Sound Effects for Your, **1285**

Calvert, Thomas W.
Computer Interpretation of Dance Notation, **4061**

CAM Computer Given Complete Musical Access, 1762

Camilleri, L.
Aspetti di grammaticalità a musicalità nella melodia, **2129**

Campbell, T.
Musicalc, **1286**

Campbell, Warren C.
Computer Analysis of Musical Performance, **1824**
Computer Analysis of the Auditory Characteristics of Musical Performance, **2653**
A Computer Simulation of Musical Performance Adjudication, **2631**
Music Performance Analysis, **1867**

Camus, Elizabeth
Two-Voice Music Programming System: The PDP-9 as an Automatic Electronic, **1216**

Canadian Computer Disk Catalog Given a New Synthesized Voice, 1763

A Sampling of Techniques for Computer Performance of Music, **1300**
Simulation of Musical Instruments. Part 1, **1301**
Simulation of Musical Instruments. Part 2, **1302**
Software Techniques of Digital Music Synthesis. Part 1, **1303**
Techniques for the Computer Performance of Music, **1304**

Champenois, Ludovic
SINFONIE: Numerical Process Command with Gestual Input Control, **3430**

Champernowne, D. G.
Music from EDSAC, **1828**

Chang, Jih-Jie
Program for Automatically Plotting the Scores of Computer Sound Sequences, **1829**
Score-Drawing Program, **1830**

Chapman, J.
BeeBMIDI. Part I, **1305**
BeeBMIDI. Part II, **1311**
BeeBMIDI. Part III, **1306**
BeeBMIDI. Part IV, **1307**
BeeBMIDI. Part V, **1308**
BeeBMIDI. Part VI, **1309**
BeeBMIDI. Part VII, **1310**
Understanding the DX7. Part III, **2980**
Understanding the DX7. Part IV, **2981**
Understanding the DX7. Part V, **2982**
Understanding the DX7. Part VI, **2983**
Understanding the DX7. Part VII, **2984**

Chapman, Lee
Modular Addressing of a Computer Controlled Synthesizer, **3348**
The TI 980A Computer-Controlled Music Synthesizer, **2943**

Charbonneau, Gérard
Acoustique: circularité de jugements de hauteur sonore, **2633**
L'ordinateur, instrument de musique: synthèse directe des sons, **4134**
Sound Analysis by Mini-Computer in Conversational Mode, **1091**
Un système de synthèse directe des sons à l'aide d'ordinateurs, **3725**
Timbre and the Perceptual Effects of Three Types of Data Reduction, **2632**

Charles, Daniel
L'eterno ritorno del timbro, **2634**

Charnassé, Hélène
Automatic Transcription of German Lute Tablatures: From Abstract to Polyphonic, **1831**
Avant-propos, **4136**
Data Processing Makes Old Instrumental Music Accessible, **2143**
De l'emploi de l'ordinateur pour la transcription des tablatures, **1836**
Des presses de Pierre Ballard à l'ordinateur, **1837**
A French Experience in the Field of Music Information: The ERATTO System, **1832**
Informatique et musicologie en 1981—Musicology and Data Processing in 1981, **2137**
Informatique et musique, Second Symposium International: Organisé par, **942**
L'informatique musicale en 1974, **4135**
Les instruments a cordes pincées (luth, vihuela, cistre, guitare) et la, **1833**
Musicologie et informatique: les grands axes de recherche, **2138**
Ein newes sehr Künstlichs Lautenbuch, Hans Gerle, (1552), Books I, II, **2145**
Une nouvelle application de l'informatique aux sciences humaines: la, **2144**

Goodman, D. J.
Digital Transmission of Commentary-Grade (7 kHz) Audio at 56 or 64 kb/s, **4284**
Gordon, John W.
A Different Drummer, **502**
An Introduction to the Phase Vocoder, **1111**
Music Applications for the MSSP System, **3051**
Perception of Attack Transients in Musical Tones, **2645**
Perception of Spectral Modifications on Orchestral Instrument Timbres, **2651**
Perception of Spectral Modifications on Orchestral Instrument Tones, **2647**
Perceptual Attack Time of Orchestral Instrument Tones, **2646**
Recent Research in Computer Music at CCRMA, **3990**
A Sine Generation Algorithm for VLSI Applications, **3660**
The Stanford Center for Computer Research in Music and Acoustics, **3889, 3890**
System Architectures for Computer Music, **3052**
Gorgens, A.
Formula 1, **1383**
Gosovskij, Vladimir, look under Hosovsky, Vladimir
Gotlieb, C. C.
A System for Keypunching Music, **2220**
Goudy, Allie Wise
Music Coverage in Online Databases, **2793**
Gould, Murray
ALMA: Alphanumeric Language for Music Analysis, **2231**
Computer Synthesis of Music in the New York Area: A Report, **4218**
A Keypunchable Notation for the Liber Usualis, **2230**
Notating Music with Ordinary Typewriter Characters (A Plaine and Easie Code, **2125**
Die Notierung thematischer Incipits auf 'Mark-Sense-Cards', **2183**
Graebner, E. H.
Southampton Studio Report, **3921**
Graham, Richard M.
An Information Retrieval System for Music Therapy, **2846**
Grand Finale, 4219
Grant, J.
The Fairlight Explained, **3056**
The Fairlight Explained. Part II, **3053**
The Fairlight Explained. Part III, **3054**
The Fairlight Explained. Part IV, **3055**
OMDAC Update. Part I, **1384**
OMDAC Update. Part II, **1385**
Spectrum MIDI, **1722**
Grappel, Robert
Electronic Organ Chips for Use in Computer Music Synthesis, **3057**
Grauer, Victor A.
Some Song-Style Clusters—A Preliminary Study, **2232**
Gray, Stephen B.
Electronic Music in Small Packages, **1386**
TRS-80 Strings, **1387, 1388, 1389**
Graziani, Mauro
Alcune macro in M360 per la elaborazione, la riverberazione e la, **3819**
Esecuzione all'elaboratore di *Parafrasi*, **503**
Report from the 1984 International Computer Music Conference, **967**

Hart, Glenn
The Musicraft Development System, **1398**

Harvey, Jonathan
Identity and Ambiguity: The Construction and Use of Timbral Transitions and, **3753**
Mortuos Plango, Vivos Voco; a Realization at IRCAM, **508**
Notes on the Realization of *Bhakti,* **509**

Hassan Ben Mohammed, Mohammed El-, look under El-Hassan Ben Mohammed

Hasselbring, Ted S.
Using Microcomputer Technology in Music Therapy for Analyzing Therapist and, **4229**

Hastings, Chuck
A Recipe for Homebrew ECL, **3069**

Hatamian, Mehdi
Performed Music: Analysis, Synthesis, and Display by Computer, **1926**

Hatano, Giyō
Onagaku-e-no Jōhōron-Teki Sekkin, **4230**

Hatley, H. Jerome
Eclipse for Orchestra and Microcomputer Synthesized Tape, **510**

Hatzis, Christos
Towards an Endogenous Automated Music, **211**

Haus, Goffredo
Aggiornamento Synclavier, **3070**
Analysis and Compacting of Musical Texts, **2093**
Anche il calcolatore vuole la sua partitura, **4231**
L'automazione electronica applicata alla elaborazione musicale, **212**
Cibernetica musicale, **4232**
Computer music a Milano, **3929**
Computer Music at the Institute of Cybernetics of the University of Milan, **3930**
Descrizione di processi musicali per mezzo di operatori geometrici: un esempio, **2167**
Digital audio alla AES Convention, **961**
EMPS: A System for Graphic Transcription of Electronic Music Scores, **1865**
EMPS: un sistema per la trascrizione grafica di partiture elettroniche, **1866**
Esperienze sulla sintesi di segnali audio mediante funzioni di due variabili, **3604**
L'evoluzione della musica elettronica, **4233**
The Fourth Colloquium on Musical Informatics, **937**
Hardware per scopi musicali: linee di tendenza, **3071**
Informatica musicale, **4234**
Informatica musicale all'Istituto di Cibernetica dell'Università di Milano, **3931**
Informatica musicale alla Biennale di Venezia, **3932**
Informatica musicale in fermento, **4235**
L'informatica puo aiutare l'industria degli strumenti musicali, **4236**
Ingegneria del software ed informatica musicale, **3588**
JEN Music Computer: un personal musicale italiano, **1399**
Matematica e musica (Cronaca di una ricerca: i Colloqui di Informatica Musicale), **962**
La matematica nella musica (I), **4237**
La matematica nella musica (II), **4238**
Music and Causality, **17**
Musica e causalità, **17**
Musical Sound Synthesis by Means of Two-Variable Functions: Experimental, **3603**
Numero e Suono: International Computer Music Conference 1982 (I), **963**
Numero e Suono: International Computer Music Conference 1982 (II), **964**

Composing by Computer, **238**
Compositional Technique in Computer Sound Synthesis, **239**
Computer Music and Technology, **4265**
Computers and Music, **4297**
Concetti base di computer music (I), **4266**
Creativity in Computer Music, **26**
Electronic Music and Microcomputers, **1423**
Electronic Music Synthesis: Concepts, Facilites, Techniques, **3667**
A General View of Compositional Procedure in Computer Sound Synthesis, **240**
IML, An Intermediary Musical Language, **2303**
Multi-Dimensional Arrays, **528**
MUSIC 4BF: A FORTRAN Version of MUSIC 4B, **3424**
Music and Electronics: A Report, **973**
MUSIC7 Reference Manual, **3425**
Panel Discussion: Computer Synthesis of Sound; New Ideas, **4267**
Report on the International Music and Technology Conference, **974**
Some Applications of Microcomputers in Electronic Music Synthesis, **1424**
Some Combinatorial Properties of Pitch Structures, **2288**
Timbral Structures for Computer Music, **2655**
Toronto's Structured Sound Synthesis Project, **3938**

Howe, S. F.
Computers in Art and Music, **4268**

Howell, S.
Nine Times Out of Ten: A User Report on the Yamaha DX9, **3101**
Siel 16-Track Live Sequencer, **1425**

Hudson, Barton
Toward a Comprehensive French Chanson Catalog, **2289**

Hudson, James M.
Equipping a Computer to Play a Recorder, **3102**

Huggins, Phyllis
Three-Part Music with a Computer as One Part, **4269**

Hughes, C. E.
Imagination: Music, **1548**

Huglo, Michel
Le classement par ordinateur des listes de repons liturgiques: les problèmes, **2290**
Musicologie medievale et informatique, **2291**

Hull, S.
On Contextually Adaptive Timbres, **3610**

Hullfish, William R.
A Comparison of Response-Sensitive and Response-Insensitive Decision Rules in, **735**
A Comparison of Two Computer-Assisted Instructional Programs in Music Theory, **736**
Take on a Digital Assistant: The Computer as a Teaching Aid, **737**

Hultberg, Mary Lou
CAI in Music Theory! Paradigms: Potential: Problems, **739**
Computer-Assisted Instructional Programs in Music Theory. Parts I and II, **740**
Project CLEF: CAI in Music Theory, **738**

Hultberg, Warren E.
CAI in Music Theory! Paradigms: Potential: Problems, **739**
Computer-Assisted Instructional Programs in Music Theory. Parts I and II, **740**

I

L

Levitt, David A.
Machine Tongues X. Constraint Languages, **2610**
A Melody Description System for Jazz Improvisation, **291**
Levy, Burt
General System Theory as Applied to Music Analysis. Part 1, **2274**
Levy, S.
Bliss, Microchips, and Rock & Roll: The Inside Data on the US Festival, **4326**
Lewin, David
An Interesting Global Rule for Species Counterpoint, **292**
Lewis, David S.
Two Parameters of Melodic Line as Stylistic Discriminants, **2359**
Lewis, Flora
Boulez, Computers, and Music, **4327**
Lewis, Gainer
Hardware: The Sound of Things to Come, **4328**
Lewis, Tony
Build a Digital VCO!, **1480**
Microcomputers in Real Time Audio. Part 1, Hardware, **1481**
Microcomputers in Real Time Audio. Part 2, Software, **1482**
Libbey, Robert L.
The Ideal Combo—A Microprocessor and a Music Synthesizer, **1483**
Library of Congress Has Received a $25,000 Grant From the Kulas, 1973
Library of Congress to Translate Music into Braille, 1974
Libretti, Andrea
Report from the 1984 International Computer Music Conference, **967**
Lichtman, Irv
PolyGram Develops Royalty, Copyright Computer System, **1779**
Lidov, David
A Melody Writing Algorithm Using a Formal Language Model, **293**
Lieberman, Frederic
The Chinese Long Zither Ch'in: A Study Based on the *Mei-an Ch'in-p'u*, **2360**
Computer-Aided Analysis of Javanese Music, **2361**
Lieberman, Henry
Machine Tongues IX: Object-Oriented Programming, **2611**
Lifton, John
Some Technical and Aesthetic Considerations in Software for Live Interactive, **3446**
Ligeti, György
Computer-Musik als Kreativer Dialog zwischen Musiker und Machine?, **4325**
Lillehaug, Leland A.
The Computer, a New Assistant in Your Music Library, **2819**
Lima, Cândido
Réflexions sur l'intuition et la rationalité en composition musicale:, **294**
Limmer, W. Schroder-, look under Schroder-Limmer, W.
Lin, Erh
Operator's Manual for the CSX-1 Music Machine, **3097**
Playing the Computer, **3447**
Lin, Tzu-Mu
A VLSI Approach to Sound Synthesis, **3287**
Lincoln, Harry B.
The Computer and Music, **2362**
The Computer and Music Research: Prospects and Problems, **2820**

The EGG Synthesizer, A Purely Digital, Real-Time Sound Synthesizer, **3130**
Real Time Sound Synthesis: A Software Microcosm, **3459**
A User Manual for the EGG Real-Time Digital Sound Synthesizer, **3131**
Manuel, Bruce A.
Anyone Can Make Music—Computer Uses Space-Age Parts to Invent and Perform, **4341**
Marc, Joseph
Computer Music Language Aids Interaction Between Composer and Choreographer, **548**
Report on the 1982 International Computer Music Conference, **935**
Margolin, Jed
A Musical Synthesizer for the KIM-1, **1495**
Marillier, Cecil G.
Computer Assisted Analysis of Tonal Structure in the Classical Symphony, **2386**
Tonal Structure in the Symphonies of F.J. Haydn, **2387**
Marmet, Jean
Un périphérique d'ordinateur à l'usage des musiciens: composants, **1855**
Marquis, Dave
Machine Language Programming of Computer Music, **1496**
Marr, Alan
Acoustical Laboratory Report, Computer Music Conference, **3957**
An Alternative Approach to Software for the DMX-1000, **3460**
The Lucasfilm Digital Audio Studio, **3854**
Lucasfilm Report, **3855**
Report on the 1982 International Computer Music Conference, **935**
Mars, P.
Automatic Transcription of Keyboard Music, **1890**
Keyboard Music Transcription by Computer, **1891**
Marsh, Theodore A.
Considerations of a Low-Cost Sound Image Location Synthesis Device on an, **3822**
Marshall, D. B.
Development of a Concept-Centered Ear-Training CAI System, **817**
Marshall, Pamela
Computer Music Catalog, **4563**
Marshall, Tom
Atari Music Player, **1497**
Martens, William L.
Palette: An Environment for Developing an Individualized Set of, **2673**
Psychophysical Scaling of Synthetic Timbres: An Essential Step in Interfacing, **2674**
Simulating the Cues of Spatial Hearing in Natural Environments, **3820**
Marti, Jed B.
ELMOL: A Language for the Real-Time Generation of Electronic Music, **3461**
Martin, Charles
Computer Illustrated Display for Marching Bands, **4342**
Martin, Steven L.
Creating Complex Timbre Through the Use of Amplitude Modulation in the Audio, **3691**
Micro Mixdown: There's a 65K Helper in the Recording Studio, **1498**
Martinet, Richard Kronland-, look under Kronland-Martinet, Richard
Martinez, J.
Alcuni aspetti del rapporto composizione/modalità di fruizione dell'opera, **132**
Martissa, E.
Estratto dalla tesi di laurea: 'Analisi e sintesi di processi pseudo- musicali', **1134**

McKay, Andy
Electronic Music, **4354**
McKay, Blair D.
Microcomputers and Music: Lowcost Systems with Multiple Applications, **1671**
Microprocessor-Supervised Digital Synthesizers, **1506**
Polyphonic Velocity-Sensitive Keyboard Interface, **3140**
McLean, Barton
The Fairlight CMI and Its Uses in Advanced Laser Graphics, **3141**
McLean, Bruce
Current Problems in Score Input Methods, **2392**
The Design of a Portable Translator for DARMS, **2393**
Translating DARMS into Musical Braille, **1975**
McLean, Priscilla
At North Texas State: Computer Music, **989**
McLuen, Roy E.
A Comprehensive Performance Project in Saxophone Literature with an Essay, **1976**
McMahan, Mike
Graphics and Sound for Your Personal Computer, **1507**
McMorrow, Clyde H.
Concerning Music and Computer Composition in Computational Linguistics, **316**
McNabb, Michael
Dreamsong: The Composition, **552**
McRae, Lynn T.
Computer Catalog of Ninteenth-Century American-Imprint Sheet Music, **2834**
Mead, Carver
Models for Real-Time Music Synthesis Using UPEs, **3125**
A VLSI Approach to Sound Synthesis, **3287**
Mecchia, W.
PET pratico: sintesi sonora, **1508**
Mechtler, Peter
Einige Anmerkungen zum Verhaeltnis Mensch und Computer, **4355**
Der Heimcomputer als neues Musikinstrument?, **1509**
Ein universeller Musikcomputer in Wien, **3959**
Medsker, Larry
A Course in Computers and Music, **805**
Meehan, James R.
An Artificial Intelligence Approach to Tonal Music Theory, **2394**
Meertens, Lambert
Componist en Computer, **78**
Megill, D.
Combined Art and Music Performances on Microcomputers, **1510**
Meinecke, Jon
Stochastic Melody Writing Procedures: An Analysis Based Approach, **317**
Melanson, Jim
Computers Vital Link to Publishing Future, **1897**
Melby, Carol
Computer Music Compositions of the United States 1976, **2835**
Melby, John
Composition with Computers: Proceedings of the Second Annual Music, **929**
Compositional Approaches to the Combination of Live Performers with, **318**
Hardware for Computer-Controlled Sound Synthesis: Proceedings of the Second, **930**

Musique et informatique, **4443**
Musique et ordinateur, **4444**
L'ordinateur comme instrument de musique, **4445**
Ordinateur et création musicale, **4446, 4447**
L'ordinateur et la musique, **4448**
L'ordinateur et la synthèse des sons musicaux, **4449**
L'ordinateur, instrument de musique, **4450**
Ordinateurs et graphisme musical, **1939**
Paradoxes de hauteur, **2703**
Paradoxes de hauteur: le concept de hauteur n'est pas le meme pour tout le, **2704**
Passages per flauto e nastro magnetico, sintetizzato mediante elaboratore, **566**
Pitch Control and Pitch Paradoxes Demonstrated with Computer-Synthesized, **2705**
Pitch Paradoxes Demonstrated with Computer-Synthesized Sounds, **2706**
Problèmes de droit d'auteur découlant de l'utilisation d'ordinateurs pour, **4451**
Quelques remarques sur les musiques pour ordinateur et l'interpretation, **4452**
La situation de l'acoustique musicale aux U.S.A., **4453**
Some Recent Developments in Computer-Generated Tone Qualities, **2707**
Stochastic Processes in Music and Art, **369**
Sur l'analyse, la synthèse, et la perception des sons etudiées à l'aide, **2708**
Synthèse de sons à l'aide de calculateurs électroniques appliquée à, **2026**
Synthèse des sons à l'aide d'ordinateurs, **3724**
Synthesis of Sounds by Computer and Problems Concerning Timbre, **3724**
Un système de synthèse directe des sons à l'aide d'ordinateurs, **3725**
The Technology of Computer Music, **4348**
Tecniche digitali del suono: influenza attuale e prospettive future in campo, **4454**
Utvecklingen inom digitaltekniken: en vändpunkt för elektronmusiken?, **4455**

Rittenbach, Bruce E.
Aspects of Computer Music System Design, **4456**

Roads, Curtis
Advanced Directions for Computer Music, **4457**
An Analysis of the Composition *ST/10* and the Computer Program *Free*, **567**
Artificial Intelligence and Music, **4458**
Automated Granular Synthesis of Sound, **3726**
Composers and the Computer, **370**
Composing Grammars, **371**
A Conversation with James A. Moorer, **4459**
Foundations of Computer Music, **4472**
Grammars as Representations for Music, **2484**
A History of *Computer Music Journal*, **4471**
Improvisation with George Lewis, **372**
Interactive Orchestration Based on Score Analysis, **373**
An Interview with Gottfried Michael Koenig, **4460**
An Interview with Harold Cohen, **4461**
Interview with Herbert Brün, **208**
Interview with James Dashow, **374**
Interview with Marvin Minsky, **4462**
Interview with Max Mathews, **4463**
Interview with Paul Lansky, **4464**
An Introduction to Computer Music and Applications of the Pascal Programming, **3495**
Introduction to Computer Music History, **4465**
An Introduction to Computer Music History and Fundamentals, **4466**